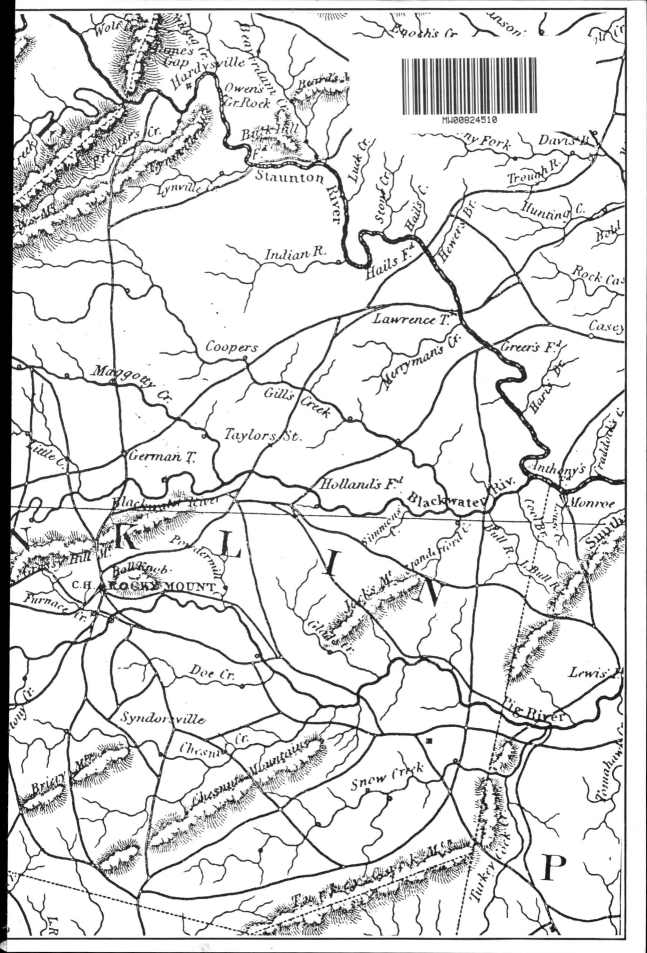

FRANKLIN COUNTY VIRGINIA 1786–1986

A BICENTENNIAL HISTORY

JOHN S. SALMON AND EMILY J. SALMON

FRANKLIN COUNTY BICENTENNIAL COMMISSION
ROCKY MOUNT, VIRGINIA • 1993

Jacket photographs: (front) *"Emblem of Justice"* (Jim Young Photography, Rocky Mount, Va.), *Booker T. Washington* and *Jubal A. Early* (Leib Photo Archives, York, Pa.); (back) *Great Wagon Road at Carolina Bottoms* (Virginia Department of Historic Resources.)

To the people of Franklin County,
and to the memories of Helen H. Amos, Jesse S. Amos,
Ruby H. Amos, and Neville L. Ramsey

Library of Congress Cataloging-in-Publication Data

Salmon, John S., 1948–
Franklin County, Virginia, 1786–1986: a bicentennial history /
    John S. Salmon and Emily J. Salmon.

Includes bibliographical references (p.) and index.
1. Franklin County (Va.)—History. I. Salmon, Emily J.
II. Title.
F232.F7S25   1993   975.5′68—dc20   93–20392
ISBN 0–9635730–0–4   (hard cover: acid-free paper)

The following publisher has generously given permission to use extended quotations from copyrighted works: The Virginia State Library and Archives, Richmond, for John S. Salmon, "Ironworks on the Frontier: Virginia's Iron Industry, 1607–1783," *Virginia Cavalcade 35* (1986): 184–191; Salmon, *The Washington Iron Works of Franklin County, Virginia, 1773–1850* (1986); and Emily J. Salmon, "Thicker'in Huckleberries: Franklin County, 1900–1930," *Virginia Cavalcade* 41 (1992): 132–143.

CONTENTS

FOREWORD: BICENTENNIAL REFLECTIONS

In September 1984 representatives of the Franklin County Bicentennial Commission appeared before the Franklin County Board of Supervisors to request the Board's funding and sponsorship of a bicentennial history of Franklin County. The Board unanimously approved our request for a "well written, easily readable, well documented and historically accurate history of Franklin County." It funded the project in the amount of $50,000, to include the costs of research, writing, and publication. This book is the result.

To this Board of Supervisors we are indebted for much of the success of the Franklin County Bicentennial Celebration during 1986 as well as for this book. Individually and collectively the Board members gave their full support to the efforts to collect and preserve our local heritage and enthusiastically participated in the activities celebrating our two-hundredth anniversary. Attired in eighteenth-century costume for Board meetings as well as for bicentennial activities during the commemorative year, both the supervisors and the Bicentennial Commission members exemplified the spirit of participation that spread throughout the county. Subsequent boards likewise have generously supported this publication.

The centerpiece of the Bicentennial Celebration is this history of Franklin County, the only complete history ever attempted. The first published history of the county appeared in 1926, when the *County News* printed a supplement, "Franklin County, Virginia: Historical and Industrial—Past, Present and Future." In 1964 Dr. Marshall Wingfield, a county native, published *Franklin County, Virginia: A History*. This was a compilation of miscellaneous historical notes compiled by Wingfield and Walter Hopkins, as well as Wingfield's personal reminiscences of turn-of-the-century life in the county. Wingfield's *Pioneer Families of Franklin County, Virginia* (1964) and *Marriage Bonds of Franklin County, 1786–1858* ([1939]) added to the body of genealogical knowledge about Franklin County families. Under the direction of Anne Carter Lee Gravely and in conjunction with our 1976 National Bicentennial, several historical monographs on county history were published, as well as a two-volume abstract of *Eighteenth-Century Franklin County Deeds*.

An annual photodocumentary, *Franklin County, Virginia: Yesterday and Today*, published by the Franklin County Retail Merchants Association under the direction of Mrs. Dorothy Cundiff, has contributed significantly to preserving the images of yesterday and documenting current county history. This photodocumentary was further enhanced during the Bicentennial by a program coordinated with the Blue Ridge Institute of Ferrum College to collect and preserve photographs of early Franklin County. The institute's project resulted in the publication *Franklin County Life and Culture: A Pictorial Record*. In 1986 the Bicentennial Commission published *Bicentennial Reflections*, a booklet that featured many articles and photos pertinent to Franklin County history. A special Bicentennial Edition of the *Franklin News-Post* likewise focused on local history and documenting the present state of the county. In 1986 the Virginia State Library published *The Washington Iron Works of Franklin County, Virginia, 1773–1850*, by John S. Salmon. This study of Franklin County's first industry was an important contribution to our understanding of a heretofore poorly understood aspect of our history. During the same year the Franklin County Historical Society published a volume of *Cemetery Records of Franklin County*. This completed a project initiated years ago by Mrs. Gertrude Mann to record the inscriptions found on headstones in Franklin County's cemeteries.

One of the local contributors to the written history of Franklin County is T. Keister Greer, a member of the Bicentennial Commission. While a student at the University of Virginia, he wrote "Genesis of a Virginia Frontier: The Origins of Franklin County, Virginia, 1740–1785" for his senior honors thesis. In 1976 another student, Glenna Donelle Hawkins, wrote "Free Black Persons of Color in Franklin County, Virginia, 1786–1865" for her master's thesis at Virginia Polytechnic Institute and State University. Dr. Frank Benjamin Hurt published *A History of Ferrum College: An Uncommon Challenge, 1914–1974* in 1977, and *The Heritage of the German Pioneers in Franklin County, Virginia* in 1982. Other chroniclers of western Franklin County lore include Raymond Sloan and Mrs. Mabel France.

Two other important researchers and writers have left voluminous records as evidence of their many years of inquiry, although neither formally published her compilations. Mrs. Essie W. Smith compiled an unfinished manuscript and notes in 1963 for her proposed history of Franklin County. More recently Mrs. Gertrude Mann, the quintessential researcher and preserver of local history, left to the people of Franklin County her voluminous records, including genealogical and historical data and correspondence that she had collected over many years of dedicated service to this county. These records along with her personal library are housed in a special Gertrude Mann Room for research at the Franklin County Public Library.

Henry Hopkins is currently active in extensive countywide research. The depth of his investigation of such topics as the Civil War, agriculture, industry, and railroads has far exceeded any earlier efforts in these fields. In addition to his work, a limited number of privately researched and printed family histories continue to become available and are a source of enlightenment for discovering who we the people of Franklin County really are.

The Blue Ridge Institute of Ferrum College is dedicated to the ongoing investigation, documentation, and preservation of the folkways of our area. Under the direction of J. Roderick Moore, the establishment of a living farm museum, as well as a permanent curatorial facility with expansive record and artifact archives and the annual nationally recognized Blue Ridge Folklife Festival, have done much to focus attention and interest on the history of our area. This continuing academic research and documentation as a part of Ferrum College are a source of pride for all Franklin County.

Despite this voluminous research and these varied publications, the majority of the people of Franklin County have little actual knowledge of their heritage. To date there has been no single work that provides a comprehensive historical overview of the county's history. Such a source has been badly needed by our citizens and by our school system in order to inculcate and perpetuate in today's youth a greater local pride. With the influx to the lake area of so many new citizens with both ancestry and past life-experiences in such marked contrast to that of natives of this county, it is important that such a history be available for all to understand better the cultural, ethnic, and sociological background of the area. It is hoped that this publication will also create an even more widespread appreciation and interest in the preservation of this heritage. It is our desire, likewise, that through this publication a better understanding of our history will foster a continued harmonious relationship on behalf of all the peoples of Franklin County.

The Bicentennial Commission was most fortunate to find qualified authors for this history of Franklin County. The commission agreed to engage a professional historian for the Bicentennial History Project and contracted with John S. Salmon, of Richmond, who holds a bachelor of arts degree in history from the University of Virginia and a master's degree in history from the College of William and Mary. At the beginning of this project, John was employed as an archivist at the Virginia State Library in Richmond. Two years later he became the staff historian at the Virginia Department of Historic Resources where he is presently employed. Among his other duties, he manages the state highway marker program.

In the late 1960s John and I became friends while at the University of Virginia, and his interest in Franklin County began with visits to my parents' farm. In 1971 my wife and I purchased the ironmaster's house of the Washington Iron Works and after visiting here John was struck by the importance of the Washington Iron Works to the county's development and how little was actually known of its history. On his own time he delved into the State Archives for years, piecing together bit by bit the history of Franklin County's first industry from obscure correspondence and official records. In 1986 the State Library published *The Washington Iron Works of Franklin County, Virginia, 1773–1850* as part of its mission to publish works derived from original records in the State Archives. Through this effort and his years of research John became very familiar with Franklin County, its peculiarities, its industry, its agriculture, its scandals, and its achievements. Through his numerous visits here he also became familiar with its topography, its people, and its surviving historical structures.

Fortune, indeed, smiled upon us even more when John's wife, Emily J. Salmon, likewise a former archivist at the Virginia State Library, agreed to co-author our history. Emily holds a bachelor of science degree in psychology from Virginia Commonwealth University and a master's degree in history from North Carolina State University at Raleigh. For the past fifteen years she has been a historian and editor at the Virginia State Library and Archives in the Division of Publications and Cultural Affairs, which publishes the state history magazine *Virginia Cavalcade*. As picture editor and now as copy editor, Emily has made numerous contributions to that magazine. In 1983 Emily edited the third edition of *A Hornbook of Virginia History*, and will soon bring out the fourth edition.

Together John and Emily had written several *Virginia Cavalcade* articles and collaborated on photographic research for a pictorial history of Richmond. To the Bicentennial Commission they had all the credentials we were looking for. We were thrilled to be able to contract with such respected professionals for writing our Bicentennial History. Their broad knowledge and understanding of history are much in evidence throughout this publication as they skillfully weave our county's history into the greater fabric of national and state history.

The Book Committee of the Bicentennial Commission has worked tirelessly over the years with the authors to provide support, assistance, input, and local direction to this project. The original committee with myself as chairman consisted of Mrs. Gertrude Mann, Mr. T. Keister Greer, Mrs. Mary Hopkins, Mr. Morris Law, and Mr. John Lester, Franklin County administrator. We suffered an irreplaceable loss in the death of Mrs. Gertrude Mann, Franklin County's preeminent historian, before the completion of this work. We were fortunate to name as her replacement Mrs. Ginnie Greer Williams, also an accomplished local researcher. It has been a great privilege to work with these dedicated committee members and we are indebted to them for their many contributions to this book.

* * *

As impressive as this volume is in its comprehensiveness, it is not the last word on Franklin County history. Unfortunately not everything about the county could be included in one volume. In order to cover more than two hundred years of history, the narrative has had to be somewhat cursory even on subjects about which much more is known than herein recorded. This book, however, will serve as a stimulus for further investigation and documentation into specific areas where a more detailed study is justified and sources are available. We look forward to that eventuality. The story here presented is an overview of this county's history, a well-documented narrative that sticks to the facts but uses limited anecdotal, genealogical, and oral history as primary sources that complement the overall picture. Indeed these sources many times provide color for an otherwise mundane subject. This is a narrative history, not a compilation of facts and figures, tables and dry data, but an interesting readable account of how people lived and of what happened locally, along with an interpretative account of what was taking place simultaneously in the state and the nation. This is an attempt to bring history home to the people of Franklin County and to the millions of their descendants who for generations will cherish a record of their ancestors' contributions to this commonwealth and this nation.

Diversity has epitomized Franklin County from its beginning. Among the original settlers were English, Scots, Germans, Scotch-Irish, and Africans. To that mixture is now added an even more heterogeneous blend of "lake people" from all parts of the country who have settled around Smith Mountain Lake. Their arrival has introduced a leisure class of retired persons, which is something of a novelty for the agricultural and light-industrial workers who have constituted much of the population of Franklin County for years.

The small, full-time family farm has largely disappeared as economic factors have forced the small farmer to supplement his income with industrial employment. Today the rule is to "farm big" or not farm at all. The once-thriving tobacco industry is dwindling as farmers abandon it in favor of raising cattle, becoming more diversified, or leaving the farm altogether.

The rural landscape reflects these changes. Abandoned fields sprout cedars and weeds, while old family woodlots fall to clear-cutting machinery. Traditional wooden barns are disappearing in favor of sheet-metal alternatives. The log tobacco barns that once dotted the countryside are vanishing as less tobacco is grown and as tobacco harvesting and processing methods change. Log houses are no longer built except from kits, and the old I-house is being replaced by the new vernacular dwelling: the mobile home. Concrete animals and other forms of "yard art" rise and fall in popularity. The shade trees in front of the farmhouse are no longer whitewashed at the base as grandmother would have done. Many now feel the need to improve on nature by regularly topping their trees—a practice that baffles many newcomers to the area. Who knows what the rural Franklin County landscape will look like fifty years from now?

Sadly, there has been a widespread lack of appreciation for our history. Our oral and cultural traditions, as well as our visible heritage, are rapidly disappearing. Many people who were attracted to this rural area by its beauty and historic old structures despair at the "modernizations" and irreversible changes to the land. Every day, it seems, some part of what makes Franklin County a special place vanishes forever. Old homes that our ancestors cherished for generations are bulldozed to make way for new ranch-style dwellings that could have been built anywhere in the country. Other old properties are sadly neglected until they collapse; only after they are lost are they appreciated for what they were.

Over the years our natural heritage has been violated with polluted water, polluted air, acid rain, and chemicals on every hand. Forests and woodland have been harvested without adequate attention to reforestation. Wetlands have been drained and hillsides leveled. Our land has changed before our eyes. It is becoming more and more difficult to imagine how this country looked to William Byrd and William Bartram, much less Batts and Fallam, when they visited the region more than two hundred and fifty years ago.

Modern conservation practices and a trend toward an increasing awareness of our environment are healthy signs for the future, however. Already we are encouraged by the return of some of our native wildlife, including deer, bear, and turkeys, that even our most recent forefathers did not enjoy in such abundance. Our historic resources are the subjects of renewed interest from concerned citizens and property owners. During the last few years, the Roanoke Regional Preservation Office of the Virginia Department of Historic Resources has conducted surveys of the county to identify more of our architectural and archaeological treasures.

As we enter the twenty-first century, we are certain of our ability to change to meet those challenges ahead of us. We place our faith in God and face the future with confidence just as our ancestors did on arriving here more than two centuries ago. We are today presented with challenges and opportunities never afforded our ancestors. We hope that their efforts and achievements as described in this book will engender a continuing devotion to our homeland as we strive to make Franklin County an even better place to live, work, and enjoy. May God bless us all in this endeavor.

Rocky Mount   J. FRANCIS AMOS, M.D.

Franklin County Bicentennial Commission, 1986. Standing, left to right: *Edith Sigmon; J. Roderick Moore; McKinley Hamilton; Frank Hurt; Jeanne Bernard; Paige Robertson; Macie Woods; Marion Ellis; Anne Carter Lee; Nancy Pinkard; Cyrus Dillon, Jr.* Seated, left to right: *Virginia Crook, secretary; Mary Hopkins, vice-chairman; J. Francis Amos, chairman; Mike Meeks, treasurer; Gertrude Mann.* Not pictured: *Geraldine Bell; Jerryanne Bier; Dorothy Cundiff; Willard Finney; Marshall Flora; Virgil Goode; T. Keister Greer; Joyce Jamison; Homer Murray; Roscoe Powell; Kathryn Shay; Maxine Simms; Elizabeth Webster.*

PREFACE

This work is not "The History" of Franklin County, but rather "A History." Although we have spent the better part of seven years researching and writing this book, it is only one of several that could have been written. There is a wealth of data and documentary resources still available to be interpreted and reinterpreted. Other writers might have approached the data differently or emphasized different aspects of the county's history. They might even have chosen other sources for this story.

We chose, for example, to explore the rich vein of county records—deeds, wills, court orders, suit papers—that exist for the period before the end of the Civil War. We also hunted through the many state records with which we are familiar: land and personal property tax books, records concerning slaves convicted of crimes, internal improvement records, and school superintendents' reports. We examined census records, family papers, and military service records, as well as Freedman's Bureau papers, business directories, and federal records concerning prisoner-of-war camps in Virginia during World War II. We read newspapers, journal articles, theses and dissertations, and books.

In the course of our research we learned anew the extent to which the interpretation of history depends not only on the records that have survived, but on the contents of those records. Some of the early court records mentioned in this book give tantalizing glimpses of human relations, then end abruptly before any resolution is reached. The records of suits from the 1780s through the 1830s especially provide a wealth of detail. For human interest during the antebellum period we quoted extensively from the great collection of Saunders letters at the University of Virginia, not because we thought this family was the most important in the county, but because this marvelous wealth of material existed. From the 1880s on, we made extensive use of newspapers because the official records became relatively uninformative. The late-nineteenth-century press was notorious for its sensationalism, however, so avoiding a skewed interpretation of the local history was difficult.

Although we used family genealogies to identify the relationships between some of the people in the county, we did not linger over them. Nor did we wish to write the sort of county history that contains only stories about the wealthy or the politically powerful; we chose to include the other 97 percent of society too.

We sought to write a county history that, first, got the facts and dates straight and, second, separated fact from legend or tradition. We wanted to discuss some of the slowly disappearing historical resources of the county that residents can still see, before they are swept away by the tide of development surging southward from Smith Mountain Lake. We wanted to apply recent historical scholarship to certain topics, such as Franklin County native Jubal Early's "loss" of the Valley in 1864.

As we worked—on nights and weekends—our ambition was tempered by the realization that it would take seventy years rather than seven to accomplish all we hoped to do. The antebellum political power structure of the county, and the roles that such families as the Saunderses, Greers, Hales, Hairstons, and others played, is worth a book itself. Similarly, the story of the slaves and free blacks, and their lives both before and after the Civil War, can hardly be told in a couple of chapters. Moreover, the history of religious denominations such as the Dunkards and the story of women on the frontier and in antebellum and postwar society remain for others to explore more thoroughly. Our goals changed, then, from trying to be all-inclusive to attempting to lay a solid groundwork for the historians who come after us.

We decided to allow the long-gone inhabitants of Franklin County to speak for themselves as much as possible, hence the relatively large number of direct quotations. Editing was kept to a minimum, except when words were so poorly spelled that some editorial explanation had to be offered [in square brackets]. Until the mid-nineteenth century at least, most nonprofessional writers spelled phonetically. Read their words aloud, and you will almost hear these people speak.

We found it necessary to make some difficult decisions concerning place-names. Because the names of watercourses, land forms, and other places often have changed over the years, we decided to adopt a convention for the sake of consistency. At first we thought we might use the original spellings and give modern names in parentheses. We found, however, that there was no standard eighteenth-century spelling for many place-names. Reluctantly we decided to use the names that appear on modern topographic maps and road signs; earlier versions are mentioned parenthetically. Maggodee Creek is therefore rendered in its modern spelling, rather than the eighteenth-century version, Maggotty Creek. Although we much prefer the old spellings, Maggodee is what a driver will see on the bridge sign as he crosses the creek on Route 122. The modern spelling also appears on the various topographic quadrangles compiled by the United States Geological Survey and in the book we used as our authority for spelling such names: Thomas H. Biggs, *Geographic and Cultural Names in Virginia* (Charlottesville: Virginia Division of Mineral Resources, 1974). Place-names in quotes and road names and numbers form the major exceptions to this rule. In most cases we used the older road names that apply to the topic under discussion and mentioned the modern names or numbers parenthetically.

Since modern history cannot be treated with any degree of judgment until enough time has passed to allow some perspective, the history of Franklin County in the post–World War II era has been introduced but not analyzed in depth. This task awaits the future historian of the Eisenhower years of the 1950s, the civil rights movement of the 1960s, the Vietnam experience of the late 1960s and 1970s, and the Reagan era of the 1980s.

As we said above, we have not written "the" history of Franklin County, nor have we written a monograph on any particular aspect of Franklin County life. Rather we have introduced as much of its history and people as possible and tried to shed some light on areas that until recent years have been left in darkness.

No one writes a book like this without help from many quarters. We have been aided in our work by a host of friends and colleagues who read and critiqued various chapters. No historian knows everything; if one is lucky one knows the historians and others who are authorities in their fields of study. We have been especially fortunate in that regard. We wish especially to thank William C. Luebke, who reviewed the discussion of geology; Keith T. Egloff and Dr. E. Randolph Turner, archaeologists at the Virginia Department of Historic Resources, and the late Richard P. Gravely, Jr., of Martinsville, for comments on Native American prehistory; David A. Edwards, architectural historian at the Department of Historic Resources, who reviewed the descriptions of houses in the county; Dr. John Kneebone and J. Brent Tarter, historians and editors in the Division of Publications and Cultural Affairs of the Virginia State Library and Archives, who gave us the benefit of their knowledge of black history and of the events and people of the colonial and revolutionary periods. Daphne Gentry, also an editor in the State Library's Publications Division, meticulously proofread the notes. Patricia Nelson edited the typescript, and Sara Bearss indexed the page proofs. Both of these careful workers are employed at the Virginia Historical Society, where the eminent *Virginia Magazine of History and Biography* benefits from their attention. We also wish to thank Louise G. Jones, Emily's sister, for her assistance with the research and her other contributions to the project.

Many institutions and individuals provided us with illustrations or guided us to new sources. We are grateful to J. Roderick Moore and his staff at the Blue Ridge Institute; Corrine P. Hudgins, at The Museum of the Confederacy; Carolyn Parsons, at the Virginia State Library and Archives; Virginia Department of Historic Resources; Virginia Department of Transportation; National Park Service; U.S. Army Military History Institute; Jim Young Photography; J. Francis Amos; Sue Parcell Bindewald; Elizabeth Cooper; Loretta Cooper; Dorothy Cundiff; Keith Egloff; Kathleen R. Georg; John Booth Joplin; Frank Lynch; Michele Moldenhauer; John M. Murphy; Don Troiani; and Marie Willis.

Neither of us is a native of Franklin County. While that may give us a certain objectivity concerning people and events, it also means that we can never fully appreciate all the nuances of life and history that make Franklin County a special place. It was our good fortune and pleasure to work with a book committee that offered many useful insights into the county's history. The members of the book committee—especially T. Keister Greer, Mary G. Hopkins, Morris Law, and Virginia Lee Williams—were generous with their time and comments, and we wish to acknowledge our appreciation. Committee chairman Dr. J. Francis Amos, a walking encyclopedia of information and local lore (perhaps second only to the late Gertrude C. Mann) as well as our friend, gave generously of his knowledge and hospitality. Deborah Trail and Sarah Spitzer, medical transcriptionists at Family Physicians in Rocky Mount, adeptly handled the letters, minutes, and other paperwork necessary for the smooth running of the Bicentennial Commission and the completion of this project. To all who spent their time helping us go our heartfelt thanks.

Richmond   JOHN S. SALMON
                                                                    EMILY J. SALMON

FRANKLIN COUNTY
VIRGINIA
1786–1986

A BICENTENNIAL HISTORY

ONE

Prehistory and European Exploration

Virginia can be divided into five geographical and three cultural regions. The geographical regions include the Tidewater, the coastal plain between the ocean and the upper reaches of navigation (the fall line) on the rivers that flow to the sea; the Piedmont, the rolling country between the fall line and the Blue Ridge; the Blue Ridge, the eastern wall of the Allegheny Mountains; the Valley of Virginia, which runs northeast-to-southwest between the two mountain ranges; and the Allegheny Mountains, which now form the boundary between Virginia and West Virginia. The state's cultural regions are Northern Virginia, which is composed largely of those counties and cities that are virtually suburbs of Washington, D.C.; Southwest Virginia, which is all that area to the west of the Blue Ridge and south of Roanoke; and Southside Virginia, which in its broadest sense encompasses all of Virginia that lies to the east of the Blue Ridge and to the south of the James River.[1]

Franklin County is located in what might be called, to mix cultural and geographical terms, the Southside Piedmont. It abuts the eastern slope of the Blue Ridge and is separated from the James River by Bedford County to the north. The county line is also just south of Roanoke, a city that marks both the southern terminus of the Valley of Virginia and the northern extremity of Southwest Virginia. Culturally, geographically, and historically, therefore, Franklin County is a crossroads, and that fact has affected its development.

Franklin County's diversity is reflected in its geological history. Two hundred miles to the east of Franklin County is the ocean. The land in Tidewater Virginia, close to sea level, is flat; to the west, the land first ripples, then rises and falls in ever more frequent waves through the Piedmont, until at last it breaks against the wall of the Blue Ridge. The land appears to carry the memory of the rolling sea that covered much of the state long before there was a Virginia.

In reality, the waves of land were formed by the many faultings and foldings of

3

rock that took place over millions of years of slow geological time. That part of the history of Franklin County is difficult to interpret because the rock record is incomplete and fossils are virtually unknown. Sediments and fossil assemblages representing the different geological periods may not have been deposited or preserved, or if they were they may have been highly altered or eroded away.

The rock formations called the Ashe and Alligator Back gneisses, which underlie most of Franklin County and some of the Southside Piedmont area, originated more than six hundred million years ago, in the late Precambrian time. Geologists believe that at this time a landmass known as the Grenville Continent split asunder just to the east of the present-day Blue Ridge. As the rift widened, the Iapetus Ocean was formed. The wind and rain washed gravel and silt from the western edge of the rifted continent; this deposit eventually became the Ashe formation. Farther offshore in the Iapetus Ocean sediments settled to the bottom to form the future Alligator Back formation.[2]

About 280 million years ago a new supercontinent, Pangaea, began to assemble itself. Crustal movements closed the Iapetus Ocean and docked the landmasses that were to be Europe and Africa onto the proto–North American continent. It was probably at this time that the Precambrian deposits, which in the intervening geological periods had been lithified into sedimentary rocks, metamorphosed (if they had not earlier) into the present-day gneisses. Magnetite, an iron oxide mineral mined as an iron ore in Franklin County in the eighteenth and nineteenth centuries, may also have been formed at this time. The metamorphism resulted from the intense heat and pressure caused by the formation of the new continent. The tectonic forces of the colliding landmasses folded, faulted, and uplifted the Blue Ridge Mountains and the Piedmont areas, exposing their surfaces to weathering and erosion. This mountain-building episode put the finishing touches on most of the geological structures that are evident today.

The supercontinent Pangaea did not stay welded together for long (in geological terms). About fifty million years after the continent was formed it began to rift apart just east of the Blue Ridge and created the Atlantic Ocean. The landmasses that were to be Europe and Africa began the slow movement to their present positions on the earth's surface. The pulling-apart processes created rift basins and stretched and down-warped the crust, causing the eastward river drainages of today. These series of basins, called Triassic basins after the period in which they were formed, paralleled the Blue Ridge to the east. From the creation of the Appalachian Mountains to the present, the principal geological activity has been erosion. Weathering attacked the uplifted Blue Ridge and Piedmont, including the Franklin County area, wearing away the mountains and overlying rock deposits, creating the topography evident today. Erosional debris filled the Triassic basins and spread beyond, forming the coastal plain. In the Triassic basins fossil evidence of dinosaurs has been found. Dinosaurs can be imagined roaming an ancient Franklin County landscape as erosional material from the area helped fill the Danville Triassic basin.

The pushing back of the Atlantic Ocean by the growing North American continent was a slow process. By about one hundred million years ago most of present-day Tidewater Virginia was still part of the ocean floor.[3] The eventual victory of the land over the sea was a sometime thing, however; during the last 1.8 million years alone, the ocean recovered much of its old territory on six occasions. During part of the last Ice Age (about 12,000 to 35,000 years ago) the Atlantic shore was about fifty miles farther out to sea than it is now.[4]

Thus the good earth of Virginia, which now seems so tranquil, fairly seethed with activity—geologically speaking—during its long history. Mountains arose and eroded, oceans filled and then drained, and the earth's mantle was folded, crushed, and refolded many times. The result was a geological puzzle that, although it may not be intelligible to laymen, nonetheless had clear implications for the future of Franklin County.

Most of Franklin County lies between two geological faults or fractures in the earth's surface: the Fries fault to the northwest and the Bowens Creek fault to the southeast. Franklin County—the land between the faults—is composed of certain minerals and types of rock that are buried deep underground or found close to the surface, depending upon how the land was folded and eroded. The most common rock present near the surface (and therefore easily accessible) in the formations is granite and its variants. Other mineral deposits that were found in Franklin County and mined there include iron ore (high grade magnetite), copper, gold, titanium, asbestos, mica, talc, vermiculite, and soapstone. There is also an isolated occurrence of limestone in the county.[5]

All of the geological activity produced a county that, like a plate broken over a rock, slopes slightly in two directions. Most of the county tilts to the east and north, while the southwestern part of it slopes primarily to the south. This means that the creeks and rivers in Franklin County drain in either of two directions: most of them empty into the Staunton River (which forms the northeastern boundary of the county) and the others drain into the Smith River (which forms a small part of the county's southern boundary). The Staunton River flows generally southeastward, while the Smith River merges with other streams to form the Dan River in North Carolina. The Dan flows northeastward, back into Virginia, where it joins the Staunton to become the Roanoke River, and plunges once more into North Carolina and then to the sea. Like its watercourses, Franklin County and its inhabitants historically have faced in two directions: to the northeast toward most of the rest of Virginia, and to the south toward North Carolina.[6]

The county's watercourses flow among mountains, hills, and rolling terrain. On the west Franklin County is bounded by the ancient wall of the Blue Ridge, which is pierced by several gaps. The ridge runs diagonally from southwest to northeast and is paralleled to the east by clumps of hills that decrease in size to a rolling, typically Piedmont terrain that bulges with occasional knobs and ridges. Some of these features, such as Chestnut Mountain and Turkeycock Mountain in the southeastern corner of the county, are quite large. Between those mountains and present-day Smith Mountain Lake to the north, however, the terrain is flatter.

A late-nineteenth-century geologist attributed the fertility of Franklin County's soil to its topography:

> The Blue Ridge lying on the southeast side of the [Floyd] plateau, rises and expands as it goes southwest, sending off spurs into the Piedmont country of Franklin and Patrick counties. It forms a broad swell of land containing several ridges. All these are comparatively gently undulating in contour. The easy decay of the component strata has prevented the formation of

precipitous slopes, and gives to many of the ridges wide and nearly level tops. This topography, combined with the deep light soil formed out of the hornblendic mica schists, greatly favors the agricultural character of the region.[7]

At about the same time that the Grenville Continent rifted apart (some six hundred million years ago), the first vertebrate life-forms appeared in Virginia, which at that time was close to the Equator. The hot climate supported rain forests, conifers, ferns, ginkgoes, and other plant life. Dinosaurs roamed the Piedmont, as well as the ancestors of such mammals as horses, cattle, elephants, and rats.[8] Over the next several hundred million years the part of the Grenville Continent that contained Virginia drifted northward.

About twenty-five thousand years ago the warm climate of Virginia changed dramatically when the last Ice Age occurred. The height of the glacial march southward took place from about 21,000 to 14,500 B.C., when the climate of the southeastern part of the continent was similar to that of present-day northern Minnesota or central Maine.[9] Jack pine, shrubs, and herbs dominated other flora in Virginia, and alpine tundra was present in the upper elevations. After the peak of the glacial advance, as temperatures slowly moderated, spruce and fir began to replace jack pine. Hardwoods such as oak and birch appeared for the first time. Modern environmental conditions in terms of moisture and temperature were not reached until several thousand years ago; eventually the northern conifers disappeared and oak and hemlock rose to dominance.

Human beings first appeared in Virginia, according to the best information available to archaeologists, about twelve thousand years ago. What is known of the subsequent history of these so-called Native Americans is derived largely from the remains of their material culture: projectile points, tools, pottery, grave sites, and animal bones. Over the years enough evidence has been gathered and analyzed by archaeologists to permit a few generalizations about the first Virginians.[10]

The history of Native Americans in Virginia is divided into several periods. The earliest (10,000 B.C.–8000 B.C.) is called the Paleoindian Period. Typically, the Paleoindians used wooden spears tipped with stone projectile points to kill game. During the Archaic Period (8000 B.C.–1000 B.C.), which is subdivided into Early, Middle, and Late periods, the Native Americans appear to have developed a greater variety of specialized stone tools than their antecedents. Some of the stone tools that have been found, for instance, are related to the preparation of plant foods. By the Late Archaic Period (3000 B.C.–1000 B.C.), Native Americans produced durable vessels prepared from soapstone to supplement such containers as woven baskets and carved wooden bowls. During the Woodland Period (1000 B.C.–A.D. 1600), two inventions were produced by—and in turn influenced the development of—the Native American society encountered by European settlers. They were ceramic pottery and the bow and arrow. Differences in pottery styles over time may reflect the strengthening of group identities among the residents of various regions. The bow and arrow enabled a community's hunters to kill game from a relatively safer distance than did the spear or the *atlatl* (a weighted wooden shaft with a hook on the end to hold a spear in place). By 1607, the beginning of the Contact Period, when the first European settlers arrived in Virginia, the Native American community consisted largely of distinguishable tribes that occupied winter and summer villages as well as smaller hunting camps or hamlets. In addition, several groups in Tidewater Virginia had united into a highly formalized sociopolitical system under a chief known as Powhatan.

Relatively little is known of specific Native American life-styles during the various periods. The American climate of 10,000 B.C. (Paleoindian Period) was somewhat cooler than today's, and such animals as mammoth, mastodon, moose, and caribou wandered through the grasslands and forests of eastern North America. The humans hunted the large animals, which congregated in herds, as well as smaller game. Gradually, as the temperature continued to rise over the next few thousand years, the large mammals became extinct and were supplanted in human diets by such smaller mammals as deer and elk. By about 1500 B.C., the forest encountered by the first European settlers in Franklin County had come into being. It consisted largely of oak and chestnut with stands of beech, hemlock, yellow poplar, red maple, sugar maple, basswood, hickory, black gum, and black walnut.[11]

Perhaps three to five thousand years ago (Late Archaic Period) early Virginians began to cultivate crops as well as to hunt and fish for their food, and to establish villages near their fields. By A.D. 1000 they raised pumpkins, beans, maize, and sunflowers. They caught fish in rivers and streams with fish traps and nets, and hunted deer, bear, squirrel, and rabbit—game that usually was available near their villages.

Many Woodland Period villages contained substantial structures, not just a few huts. The buildings were clustered together and sometimes surrounded by a wooden palisade.

> Houses were framed of flexible wooden posts thrust into the ground, bent toward the middle, and lashed together. This skeleton was then covered with bark, thatch, or mats. House shapes were primarily circular, although rectangular long-houses are also known to have existed. The interior of the house was probably very crowded: benches for sleeping might have lined the walls; storage space could have been supplied by ceiling platforms; and storage pits may have been dug into the floor. Hearths were located in the center of the house as well as outside.[12]

Some of the village structures may have had specialized uses, as for religious or political functions.

As the time of initial European contact drew near, then, these first Virginians had developed a complex and sophisticated society composed of tribes and clans that were mostly settled in villages and survived both by hunting and by cultivating crops. Linguistically, the Native Americans in central Piedmont Virginia were Siouan. Other groups in or near Virginia included the Cherokee of the southwest (Iroquian), the Susquehanna of the northwest (also Iroquian), and what by 1607 was the most powerful group, the Powhatan Chiefdom of Tidewater (Algonkin).

Although a good deal is known about the Tidewater tribes, just the opposite is

Projectile Points of Virginia

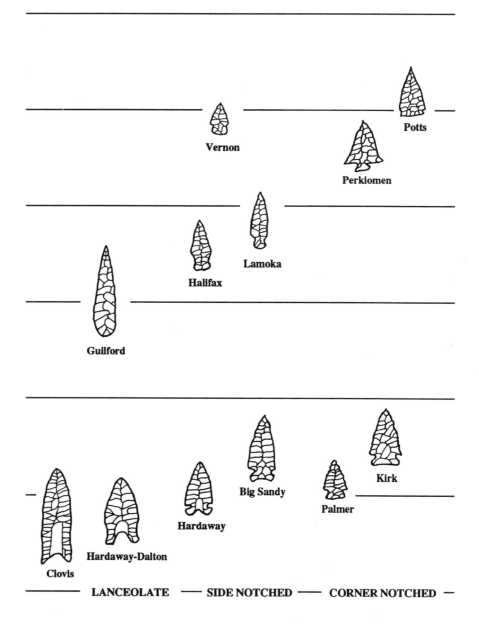

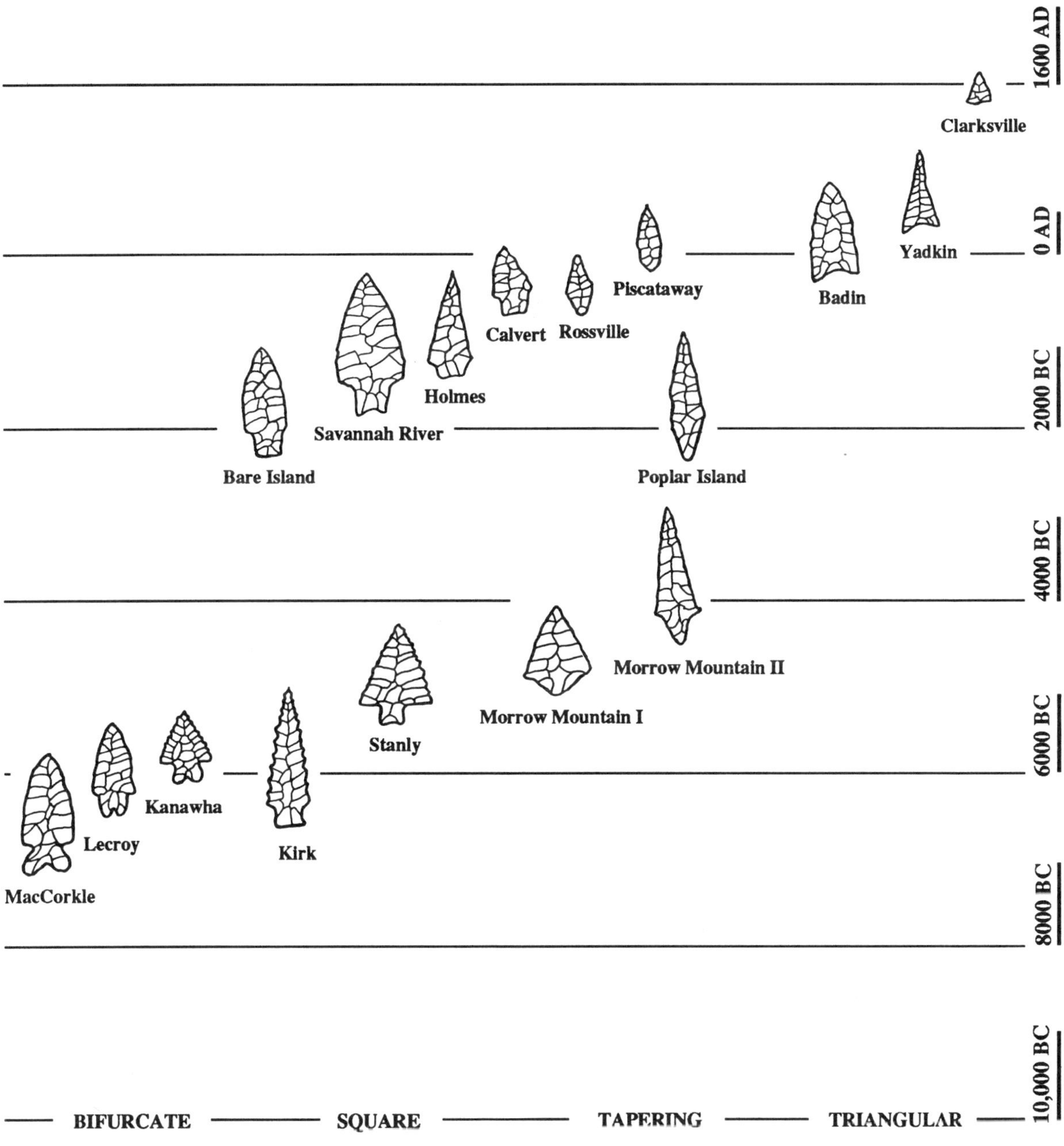

1600 AD

Clarksville

0 AD

Yadkin

Piscataway

Badin

Calvert Rossville

2000 BC

Holmes

Savannah River

Bare Island

Poplar Island

4000 BC

Morrow Mountain II

Stanly

Morrow Mountain I

6000 BC

Kanawha

Lecroy

Kirk

MacCorkle

8000 BC

10,000 BC

BIFURCATE ——— SQUARE ——— TAPERING ——— TRIANGULAR

the case with those of the Piedmont. There was relatively little contact between the new settlers and the Piedmont tribes, hence few records were written concerning them. By the time white Virginians moved west of the fall line, most of the Native Americans had abandoned the region. What little is known about the Piedmont tribes, therefore, is largely the result of archaeological investigation, not documentary evidence.

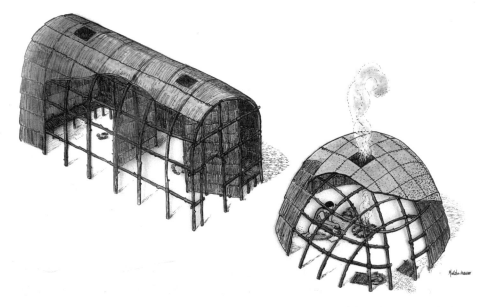

Two types of Native American dwellings found in the Franklin County vicinity: a longhouse shared by up to twenty family members (left) *and a domed house for a smaller family group* (right). (Michele Moldenhauer, Archeological Society of Virginia.)

Several tribes were active in the Piedmont region of Virginia and North Carolina; although they may not have been resident in Franklin County, they probably hunted there or passed through the county in times of war. These tribes include the Monacan, who lived on the James River between the falls and the mouth of the Rivanna River; the Occaneechee, whose village was on Long Island in the Roanoke River near Clarksville;[13] and the Sara or Saura, whose village called Upper Sauratown was located in North Carolina near present-day Madison.[14]

In southern Piedmont and Blue Ridge Virginia two tribes—the Saponi and the Tutelo—predominated. The Saponi lived in what is now Halifax County on the lower waters of Staunton River near the Roanoke (which white men first called the Saponi), while the Tutelo occupied much of present-day Montgomery County, near the headwaters of the Staunton. The Saponi and the Tutelo competed for game in some of the same Piedmont territory, particularly in what is now Franklin County.[15]

The names of the tribes that preceded the Saponi and the Tutelo into the

Franklin County area are not known. The first signs of human occupation—a few spear points of the type called Clovis—date to the Paleoindian Period, about 10,000 B.C. By the beginning of the Early Archaic Period (8000 B.C.), the extinction of mammoths and giant bison meant that Native Americans subsisted primarily on smaller mammals such as bear, deer, squirrel, and rabbit. Evidence that these hunters used an important invention, the *atlatl,* has been verified in Franklin County by the excavation of *atlatl* weights. The device extended the effective length of the user's arm and enabled him to throw the spear with greater force and for a longer distance. With this increased accuracy came a better food supply and a corresponding increase in the human population.[16]

The artifacts left by Native Americans and found at the sites of their camps and villages in Franklin County shed some light on the life-styles of the inhabitants. Hunting camps often were used by successive groups over several centuries; one example, known as the Patterson Site and located near Sydnorsville, was used by several generations of Native Americans between roughly 3000 B.C. and A.D. 1000 (*atlatl* weights were found there).[17] Small groups occupied a similar camp—the Brubaker Site—sporadically between about 3000 B.C. and A.D. 1600.[18] Both sites date to the Late Archaic Period.

Several village sites have been located in or near Franklin County. One of the largest, Bone Bottom—also known as Gobbling Town or Goblintown—stood on the Smith River near the mouth of Nicholas Creek; it is now under the waters of Philpott Reservoir.[19] The Turners Creek Indian Town is located on Pigg River at the mouth of Turners Creek; another town is believed to be on Otter Creek at

3 IN.

8 CM.

Dan River Ware ceramics, Otter Creek Site. 1984 photo. (Virginia Department of Historic Resources.)

the mouth of either Tharp Creek or Shively Branch.[20] South of Franklin County in what is now Henry County stood Buttrum Town (also called Buttramstown) on the north bank of Smith River near the mouth of Town Creek. According to the archaeological site report, the village stood "at the western terminus of an 18th century 'Traders Path'/'Indian Path'/'Hickeys Road.' . . . Charred wood from a refuse-filled pit was radiocarbon dated to A.D. 1745. This date was considered questionable until European trade goods were found in burials exposed in 1985."[21] The accuracy range of carbon dating for this sample is considered to be plus or minus fifty-five years on either side of 1690; 1745 is therefore at the most recent extreme of that range. If the 1745 date is accurate, however, it may mean that Native Americans were still in the area, or recently had left it, when the first permanent white settlers arrived.[22]

In 1984 archaeologists excavated a small Late Woodland settlement on Otter Creek instead of an expected hunting camp. They discovered a "hamlet perhaps occupied throughout the year."[23] Among the faunal remains found at the site were turtles, deer and other small mammals, shells of freshwater mussels and snails, and fish. (The last three do not live in Otter Creek near the site today.) The archaeologists also excavated the remains of seeds and nuts, as well as a multitude of pipe and pottery fragments, including "fired lumps of pottery clay and coil fragments, which suggest on-site manufacture of vessels and pipes."[24] The potsherds suggest a period of occupation ranging from A.D. 1500 to 1650; radiocarbon analysis of charred wood found on the site points to a date of A.D. 1320 (plus or minus fifty years).[25]

Evidence of only one posthole was found by the archaeologists, but the time available for excavations was limited. If there was a village on Otter Creek at this location, then it is

> the only known site in the region . . . that has been identified as a hamlet located on a remote upland spur of the Blue Ridge escarpment. . . . The people hunted deer and small game, [as well as] turtles, and gathered from Otter Creek snails, mussels, and fish. They harvested nuts and perhaps cultivated crops, made pottery, and buried their dead [there]. . . . Apparently the area was a sheltered and productive place to live, and if so, then there are many such locations along the Blue Ridge.[26]

Despite the seemingly remote location of the Otter Creek site, it probably was "strategically situated near or along a trail that crossed the Blue Ridge escarpment, connecting groups that lived along the Smith River with those living along the Little and New River drainages."[27] If the hamlet or village at Otter Creek was at all typical of Native American villages of the last three centuries or so before European contact, then it may have been fortified with a palisade. Occasionally warfare between tribes resulted in the burning of a village and the deaths of its warriors. The dead were buried in oval graves, dressed for the afterlife, and placed in a fetal position facing the rising sun. Scalping was sometimes practiced.[28]

Much of the warfare among the Indian tribes occurred as a result of changes in territories and populations brought about by the arrival of the English colonists in 1607. As the Virginia colony grew, and as other colonies were founded, more and more tribes were displaced from their traditional lands. Up and down the eastern seaboard, tribes jostled each other as they competed for land and game. Some tribes ranged far from their homes; the Iroquois, of New York, for example, raided other tribes that lived even farther south than Virginia. The route they took— later called by the whites the Warriors' Path or Great Warrior Trace, and later still the Great Wagon Road—led up the Valley of Virginia past present-day Roanoke and entered the northern end of Franklin County through Windy Gap. The path swerved to the west of Rocky Mount, then east again and south to the Carolinas.

Otter Creek Site. A 1748 deed mentioned an "Indian town" on the south branch of the creek. 1984 photo. (Virginia Department of Historic Resources.)

As the contestants warred up and down the path, the smaller tribes in the Valley and the Southside Piedmont hid, fled, or were destroyed. By the time the first white men passed through Franklin County in 1671, the Native Americans were either so dispersed or so well hidden that the English did not encounter or report them.

The names of these English discoverers of Franklin County were Thomas Batts and Robert Fallam; they were the leaders of the expedition to which historians have assigned their names. As in most such enterprises, however, there were others involved who have received less credit; Batts and Fallam were accompanied by Thomas Wood, Jack Weston (formerly one of Wood's indentured servants), and Perecute, an Appomattox Indian.

These five explorers were but the most recent of many such adventurers who had probed the interior of Virginia, beginning even before the settlement at Jamestown was fairly established. The first, of course, was the intrepid Captain John Smith, who in 1607 explored the James River as far west as the falls (Richmond). Not until 1650 was the next expedition, led by Edward Bland, sent from a settlement (Fort Henry at present-day Petersburg) to explore the backcountry. The backcountry that Bland explored, however, lay not to the west but to the south—probably almost due south of Petersburg toward Weldon, North Carolina. In 1669 and 1670 John Lederer, a young German physician, made three journeys into the Piedmont; during his second visit he explored the country to the west of Richmond, then turned south in Buckingham County and visited the Native American village of Sapon in Charlotte County before heading into North Carolina.

The expedition led by Batts and Fallam in 1671 was the most ambitious yet attempted. The two leaders had a commission from Abraham Wood, a wealthy planter and trader, "for the finding out the ebbing and flowing of the Waters on the other side of the Mountaines in order to [accomplish] the discovery of the South Sea."[29] Their party left Fort Henry on horseback on 1 September 1671; only four days later, when the group reached the town of the Occaneechee tribe, Thomas Wood was so ill he had to be left behind (he soon died there). The remaining members of the expedition pressed on despite an inauspicious beginning that must have increased their apprehensions about what lay ahead. In many ways Batts, Fallam, and Weston were typical colonists in their attitudes toward the wilderness:

> Quite the opposite of being heroic, they stood in dread of the unknown, savage-inhabited wilderness beyond the fall line. Its vastness and the cruelty of its inhabitants, man and animal, were so feared that almost no one ventured into the interior.[30]

Despite their fears, however, they went so far west into the unknown that not only did they eventually enter the Appalachian Mountains, but they "emerged on their western slope. Batts and Fallam crossed the southern tip of present-day West Virginia and gazed westward into Kentucky."[31] Of course they failed to accomplish the "discovery of the South Sea," but they were the first white men known to have passed through Franklin County and written about it.

After leaving Thomas Wood at the Occaneechee village, Batts and Fallam rode west to the junction of the Staunton and Pigg rivers in Pittsylvania County and camped nearby on the evening of 6 September. The next day they rode into Franklin County and, wrote Fallam, "about three of the clock we had sight of the mountains, we travelled twenty-five miles over very hilly and stony Ground our course westerly."[32] Fallam's diary entry for 8 September, when the men completed their journey across Franklin County, noted evidence that another white explorer had been there before them:

> We set out by sunrise and Travelled all day a west and by north course. About one of the clock we came to a Tree mark'd in the past with a coal M. A N I. About four of the clock we came to the foot of the first mountain went to the top and then came to a small descent, and so did rise again and then till we came almost to the bottom was a very steep descent. We travelled all day over very stony, rocky ground and after thirty miles travill this day we came to our quarters at the foot of the mountains due west.[33]

Recently the historian Alan V. Briceland used the series of 7.5-minute topographical maps produced by the United States Geological Survey to retrace the route of the Batts and Fallam expedition. Although earlier historians placed the explorers' route just to the north of Franklin County, Briceland maintained—by identifying topographic features described by Batts and Fallam—that the route actually passed through the middle of the county. Briceland noted, for instance, that according to Fallam's diary entry for 7 September, the group traveled west and

> covered twenty-five miles that day. Twenty-three miles west of Pigg River [at its junction with Staunton River] is present-day Rocky Mount. The Blue Ridge can be seen in the distance from east of Rocky Mount. The explorers probably skirted Rocky Mount to the north and camped in its vicinity.[34]

On 8 September, according to Briceland, Batts and Fallam trekked northwest-ward through Franklin County; they crossed the Blue Ridge on the same day, probably at Adney Gap near the present intersection of Route 602 and the Blue Ridge Parkway. They were led there by a Saponi whom they had hired, wrote Fallam, "to be our guide towards the Teteras, a nearer way than usual."[35] The explorers reached the Tetera or Tutelo town, which stood in Montgomery County on the site of what is now the United States Army Radford Arsenal, on 9 September.[36]

After resting for two days at the town, Batts and Fallam proceeded on foot to the northwest, crossing one mountain range after another as they hiked through the Alleghenies in what is now southern West Virginia. On 16 September they reached the westernmost point of their explorations and stood on the bank of the Tug River at present-day Matewan, West Virginia; across the river lay Kentucky. Out of provisions, the explorers marked trees to claim the land for king and country, then tried to convince themselves that the river actually ebbed and flowed from the tidal currents caused by the ocean that they hoped lay just on the other side of the mountains to the west.[37]

Batts and Fallam were most of a continent away from the western ocean, but they must have been close enough to the enemies of the Tutelo to make their Saponi guide nervous. After studying the Tug River for evidence of tidal motions, Batts and Fallam turned away because the

> Indians kept such a hollowing that we durst not stay any longer to make further tryal. Immediately upon coming to our quarters we returned homewards and when we were on the top of a Hill we turned about and saw over against us, westerly, over a certain delightful hill a fog arise and a glimmering light as from water. We supposed there to be a great Bay.[38]

The explorers retraced their path and arrived at the Tutelo village in Montgomery County on 19 September. There they heard that William Byrd I and his group of adventurers had been seen "three miles from the Tetera's [Tutelo] Town."[39] No doubt marveling at how quickly others had followed in their wake, Batts and Fallam mounted their horses once again and rode eastward, arriving at Fort Henry on 1 October 1671. Despite their failure to find the South Sea or the bay of their imagining, Batts and Fallam had traversed a greater distance west of the frontier than any other colonists. And on their way they had twice traversed what is now

Franklin County, the first colonists—other than whoever wrote the mysterious "M. A N I" on a tree—to do so.

After this first invasion, no white man recorded a visit there for more than half a century. When the colonists next appeared in Franklin County, they came not only to explore but to settle.

TWO

Southside Frontier

The country that Batts and Fallam explored was rich in game and useful flora. William Byrd II reported its abundance half a century later when he surveyed the dividing line between Virginia and North Carolina in 1728, and again in 1733 on a visit to his lands in North Carolina. Besides deer, bears, raccoons, squirrels, opossums, and rabbits, Byrd encountered buffaloes and evidence of elks in the Southside Piedmont. He saw wild geese, ducks, turkeys, and passenger pigeons, and observed that wolves, wildcats, and cougars roamed the area to prey on smaller game. Byrd and his companions found themselves plagued by mosquitoes, ticks, and horseflies, and saw but were not threatened by a few large rattlesnakes.[1]

The rivers and streams of the Southside contained many varieties of fish. The eminent naturalist John Banister described a type of trap made by Native Americans of the region in the late 1600s to catch large numbers of fish:

> [They] make a Dam of loose stones (where there is plenty at hand) across the river, & in it, one, two, or more pipes or tunnels for the water to pass; at the mouth of which is set a pot of reeds, wove in form of a Cone, whose base is about three feet & altitude ten into which the Swiftness of the current carries the fish, & wedges them so fast that they cannot possibly return.[2]

The stone remnants of these ancient fish traps still exist; one stands in Blackwater River about fifty yards above the present-day Route 220 bridge.

The earliest government documents relating to the Southside Piedmont—the land entry books kept by county surveyors—describe the kinds of trees that forested the area in the second and third quarters of the eighteenth century. Often the trees that designated boundary corners were marked and recorded by the surveyors. Also, watercourses were named for the trees that grew along their banks. The local trees included red oaks, white oaks, poplars, pines, ashes, beeches, blackjacks, cherries, crab apples, "sugar trees" (sugar maples), maples, sycamores, chestnuts, birches, laurels, mulberries, black walnuts, white walnuts,

17

willows, and hickories. Other vegetation included canes, cattails, reeds, brush, ivy, clover, blackberries, strawberries, and briars.[3]

No settlers moved into the Franklin County area for many years after the Batts and Fallam expedition. The Native American uprisings of 1622 and 1644, as well as the other Indian wars of the seventeenth century, were still fresh in the minds of white colonial officials; the risks inherent in settling the Southside Piedmont outweighed the possible benefits. The government made a few grudging exceptions but generally restricted settlement to avoid conflicts between Europeans and Native Americans and because of a boundary dispute with North Carolina. Until 1714 the Nottoway River formed the western boundary of the Southside, which served as a useful buffer between the English settlements in Tidewater and the Native American warriors who used the path called the Great Warrior Trace to raid up and down the Valley. Individuals and small groups, however, infiltrated the Southside Piedmont to trade with peaceful Indians—a practice that the colonial government regulated.[4]

By the late seventeenth century both whites and Indians had grown dependent on trade with each other. It was a mixed blessing. John Banister wrote that

> the Indian trade (tho it be esteem'd the great cause of all our troubles by many of the inland inhabitants that look with an evil eye on the advantages some men towards the heads of the rivers make thereof) is, if rightly weighed & considered our vinculum pacis [bond of peace], & the only means we have to live in quiet with them, for since there has been any way laid open for the preservation of their lives which they wanted not before, because they never had them; if obstruction be made, so that they cannot supply their wants by barter no marvel if they do it by force. Not to mention venison, Deer-suit [suet], & feathers, baskets, &c. which the English buy of the neighbor Indians; the trade consists of the furrs of Beaver, Otter, Mynk, Musk-quash, or Musk-rat (as we call them here), ffox, cat, Racoon, bear, wolf & Deer skins, which they exchange for guns, gun-locks, powder, shot, cut flints, small hoes & hatchets, felling axes, scissors, knives, tobacco-tongues, beads (great blew & red to the westward, & small black & white to the southward), Jews-harps, tinshears, Redlead, Duffields, Cotton & plains [plaids?] red & blew.[5]

The swift disappearance of the Indian tribes that roamed the Franklin County area, as well as the long distances covered by the Iroquois in their raids against them, were linked to the power of trade. Although Native American tribes long had jostled and fought each other over access to hunting grounds among other reasons, the opportunity for trade with the Europeans made a dramatic difference in the technological and economic bases of the Indian way of life.

In other parts of the world, whenever one country invaded another, there usually was some commonality of culture that allowed the invader and the invaded at least to understand each other. In addition, each country was roughly equal in terms of technology. In North America, on the other hand, a sophisticated European civilization "met the Stone Age face to face," as one writer has stated.[6] By 1607, when the first English settlers arrived at what was to become Jamestown, Native Americans throughout North and Central America already had encountered Spanish, French, Dutch, and other English invaders, each of whom employed advanced trading techniques to obtain whatever they wanted—gold, silver, pelts, or land—from the Indians. When those techniques failed, the Europeans casually employed gunpowder and bullets to achieve the same ends. Disease, too, became an ally of the invaders, wiping out entire villages or tribes.

Before the end of the seventeenth century virtually the entire Atlantic seaboard was occupied by Europeans, most of them eager to trade with Native Americans. By then probably most eastern North American Indians had encountered or heard of the foreigners and the useful or desirable things they had to trade. (Such items included a "French Scalping Knife" that was recovered in Franklin County after a raid in 1757.)[7] For their part, the Indians usually were "frantically eager" to trade; desire became necessity, and the result was a fundamental change in the political and economic conditions of the Native Americans. If the white man's weapons, gunpowder, and metal products granted one tribe technological superiority over another, it also made that tribe dependent on continued access to the source of that technology. The colonists granted access only to those Indians who brought to the trade those goods the white settlers wanted, mostly pelts and skins.[8]

As each tribe depleted or outgrew its own hunting or trading territory, it looked longingly upon its neighbor's. With advanced weaponry it could browbeat, shove, or, if need be, exterminate that neighbor. Even such a large and powerful group as the Iroquois found the necessity to range hundreds of miles to wage war and conquer new hunting grounds. The prize—a near monopoly on trade with the white man—was worth any trouble. Eventually, the constant frontier warfare became too great an annoyance for the colonists to allow to continue; then even the mighty Iroquois were brought low. Until the early eighteenth century, however, they ranged unchecked through the southern backcountry, and such lesser tribes as the Tutelo and Saponi found life in their former territories not worth living.

In 1728 William Byrd II observed what he believed were the distant effects of raids by the northern Indians. He and his companions, who were surveying the dividing line between Virginia and North Carolina, were in the vicinity of present-day Henry County when Byrd reported that

> the atmosphere was so smoky all round us that the mountains were again grown invisible. This happened not from the haziness of the sky but from the firing of the woods by the Indians, for we were now near the route the northern savages take when they go out to war against the Catawbas and other southern nations. On their way, the fires they make in their camps are left burning, which, catching the dry leaves that lie near, soon put the adjacent woods into a flame. Some of the men in search of their horses discovered one of those Indian camps, where not long before they had been a-furring and dressing their skins.[9]

The route mentioned by Byrd was the Warriors' Path or Great Warrior Trace. In more peaceable times, a few decades later in the century, it became the Great Wagon Road from Philadelphia to the Carolina backcountry, and it led white settlers—as it had Native Americans—southward through Franklin County.

By 1701, before Byrd's journey, many of the Tutelo and Saponi were gone. Some joined the Occaneechee, who lived along the Staunton River near present-day Clarksville, while others moved from the Franklin County area into North Carolina, where they settled with the Saura near the Catawba River. John Lawson, the surveyor general of North Carolina, encountered a palisaded settlement of Saponi on the Yadkin River near modern Salisbury while on a visit to the Carolina backcountry in 1701.[10] The palisade may have reflected the Saponi fear of attack by other tribes. By 1712 the Tutelo and the Saponi had moved east to Fort Christanna, in Brunswick County, at the instigation of Lieutenant Governor Alexander Spotswood. About 1742 the Saponi, the Tutelo, and the Occaneechee moved north and joined their old enemies the Iroquois. The last full-blooded Tutelo died near Buffalo, New York, in 1871, and the last man who could speak the language fluently died in 1898. By the time the first white settlers came to the Franklin County area to stay, the Indian inhabitants of that region largely had vanished, not only from the county but from the colony as well.[11]

The Native Americans did not vanish without a trace, however. They survived not only in the collective imagination of white settlers who tended their farms with an occasional nervous glance toward the dark forest, but also in the place-names that the frontiersmen used in their patents and deeds. There are found references to "Indian Towns," "Indian Fields," and even an "Indian Fort," and a stream in northeastern Franklin County is still called Indian Creek.[12]

With the Southside Piedmont virtually emptied of Indians, the colonial government changed its attitude toward white settlement. The House of Burgesses encouraged settlement in 1738 when it passed an act that exempted settlers within the region before 1740 from payment of all public, county, and parish levies for the next ten years. The royal governors granted great tracts of land to such men as William Byrd II, of Westover, who accumulated more than one hundred thousand acres with which to speculate. One of the largest landowners in what became Franklin County was Richard Randolph, of Henrico County, and his heirs. In 1755 alone patents were issued to Randolph's heirs for more than ten thousand acres, most of which lay in Franklin County. Byrd and Randolph stood in a long line of wealthy speculators who helped settle the frontier in the 1740s by establishing such "colonies" of pioneers as the Mayo Settlement in present-day Patrick County and the New River settlements in Montgomery County. Indeed, the lone settler in the woods is a mythical figure. The pioneers knew there was safety, as well as help, to be found in numbers, and that was how they chose to move to the frontier.[13]

Several ethnic groups settled the Franklin County area. From Tidewater and Piedmont Virginia came pioneers of English stock and their Negro slaves. Up the Valley from Pennsylvania migrated German families with such names as Barnhart, Boon, Cundiff, Darst, Flora, Gearheart, Harkrider, Huffman, Miller, Noftsinger, Pickleshimer, Prillaman, and Spangler. The Scotch-Irish, many of whom settled in southwestern Franklin County, included such names as Burnet, Ferguson, Ross, Scott, Sloan, Thompson, Wade, Webster, and Whitlowe.

Much of the settling of the Southside Piedmont was accomplished by the thousands of families who followed the government's rules for obtaining inexpensive land in the backcountry, rather than purchasing tracts from the speculators. First, of course, it was necessary to find vacant land that no one else had claimed. To learn where the good farmland lay, the prospective settler listened to travelers, interviewed surveyors, and awaited letters from relatives and friends who had gone before him, or—most likely—he went exploring himself. He followed watercourses, roads and trails, and trading paths. After he found a promising tract, he notified the county surveyor, who either went himself or sent a deputy to survey the property. One copy of the survey was entered in the county plat book and another copy was sent to the secretary of the colony in Williamsburg, along with a fee of five shillings for every fifty acres claimed. If, after an interval that may have lasted as long as ten years, no one filed a caveat (a warning that an earlier claim had been filed), the settler received his patent, which was issued in the name of the Crown and signed by the governor. He then had three years in which to "seat and plant" (settle on and cultivate) three acres in every fifty. In addition, the colony required the settler to pay a quitrent of two shillings per hundred acres every year to keep alive his title to the land. Failure to comply with either provision might result in the forfeiture of the land if another settler filed a claim that was upheld by the General Court.[14]

Much of the land was settled, at least temporarily, by impoverished but imaginative people who practiced the ancient custom of squatting. Even a settler who eventually obtained a patent probably lived for a while as a squatter between the time he filed his claim and the time the patent was issued. There were many others, however, who could not or would not file for patents and were content to farm unclaimed land for a few years and then move on. And there were those who neither sowed nor reaped but used the land only for its animal bounty—the so-called long hunters.

The long hunters, to a degree, followed such traders as Abraham Wood and William Byrd I into the frontier, and preceded the permanent settlers. They traded with the Native Americans too, but on a smaller scale as the Indians were forced ever farther from the white settlements. The long hunters used Indian hunting grounds for their own and hunted and trapped bear, beaver, and other animals for their pelts. According to John Redd, himself a long hunter, the typical group set out on a hunt

> about the first of October, and each man carried two horses, traps, a large supply of powder, led and a small hand vise and bellows, files and screw plates for the purpose of fixing the guns if any of them should get out of fix, they returned about the last of March or the first of April. . . . In their hunts there rarely ever went more than two or three in a company, their reason for this was very obvious, they hunted in the western part of Virginia and Kentucky. The country they hunted in was roamed over by the Indians and if they happened to be discovered by the Indians two or three would not be so apt to excite their fears about having their game killed up, besides this small parties were mutch more sucksesful in taking game than large ones.[15]

Many of the long hunters passed through Franklin County from the east on their way to Kentucky and Tennessee, and crossed over the Blue Ridge at several gaps: Adney, Buffalo, Choat's, and Flowers. Long hunters who lived in or near the county in the mid-eighteenth century included John Redd, Elisha Walden (who lived in present-day Henry County about two miles west of Martinsville), William Pittman, Henry Skags (and his brothers Charles and Richard), and William

Blevin.[16] Others, such as Mark Cole, of Augusta County, entered the county from the Valley. A survey of land on Blackwater River above the mouth of Gills Creek in April 1747 referred to "Coles Camping Place." Two April 1748 surveys for Mark Cole on Chestnut Creek and at the head of Town Creek (Buttram Town Creek) mentioned his hunting activities, in one instance noting "a Poplar that was fell'd for a Bear," and in the other referring to another of his camps.[17]

It was but a short step from pitching a winter hunting camp to staying for a year to plant and harvest a crop. Those who did so, using land that belonged to the colony or to someone else, were called squatters. Because squatting was a widespread but extralegal practice it is impossible to determine the name of the first white settler or squatter in present-day Franklin County. Such a person— who obtained no patent, purchased no land, and paid no taxes—tended to remain nameless, insofar as the few extant records from the colonial period showed.

The first recorded, legal white settler in the area is also difficult to identify. The descriptions of land entered in the county surveyor's books often are so vague as to defy precise location; gaps in the records during the frontier period also confuse the issue. In addition, although a prospective settler may have filed half a dozen claims with the county surveyor, only one may have resulted in the issuance of a patent. An entry for land, in other words, is no proof of actual residence.

John Pigg, one of the first men to enter a claim for land that was situated at least partially in present-day Franklin County, probably came to the area from King and Queen County.[18] On 21 May 1741 Pigg claimed four hundred acres "on the N[or]th Side of the S[ou]th fork of Stant[on] River beginning opposite to the Mouth of Snow Cr. thence up and down," as well as another four hundred acres "on the Sth Side of the sd fork beginning at the Mouth of Snow Cr thence down."[19] (At that time the south fork of Staunton River had no name—within two years it was named for John Pigg—but Snow Creek had already been named.)

Two months later, on 12 July, Thomas Caldwell claimed four hundred acres in the fork of Snow Creek and Turkeycock Creek; on the same date David Caldwell filed an entry for four hundred acres "on both sides of the Nth Fork of Snow Cr [the main branch of the creek]."[20] William Gray and Ashford Hughes filed a joint claim—almost certainly as a speculative venture—for ten thousand acres on "Pig River" on 9 January 1743.[21]

But who was the first settler? John Pigg probably never lived in present-day Franklin County, if the patents are any indication; he never received a patent for the land he entered in 1741, or for any land that now lies in Franklin County. Later records showed him to have settled no farther west than Pittsylvania County.[22] Thomas Caldwell's claim in the fork of Snow Creek and Turkeycock Creek actually lies in present-day Pittsylvania County. David Caldwell received a patent for land on Snow Creek on 5 September 1749,[23] more than eight years after he made his first entry. The patent, however, was for land lying on both Snow Creek and Crabtree Branch, which may have been farther west in present-day Franklin County than Caldwell's 1741 entry.

Although several claims were entered on Pigg River between 1743 and 1745, most of them were voided and it is virtually impossible to locate the remainder with accuracy. Israel Pickens entered the first claim that was clearly within the present bounds of Franklin County on 26 September 1745. He claimed four hundred acres "on both sides Chesnut Cr. beginning at a Beech mark'd D.S. thence up."[24] (The initials probably stood for Drury Stith, surveyor of Brunswick County.) Pickens appeared not to have received a patent for this claim, however. His only patent was for three hundred acres of land on Chestnut Creek that he entered on 24 March 1747. On 5 September 1749, a mere two years after filing his entry, he secured a patent.[25]

Pickens sought to add to his holdings by acquiring adjacent land on Chestnut Creek. Robert Hodges, for instance, transferred to Pickens his claim for two hundred acres on Chestnut Creek, beginning "at his [Hodges's] Cabbin," that he entered on 20 March 1746.[26] The fact that Pickens wanted to enlarge and improve his original tract might indicate that he actually was resident on the property. Pickens, therefore, may have been the first landowner of record to live in present-day Franklin County. Other evidence casts doubt on this theory, however. The Lunenburg County tax lists for 1748 and 1749 list Israel Pickens in the district of William Caldwell, and Caldwell's district encompassed parts of the present-day counties of Appomattox, Campbell, and Charlotte—not Franklin.[27]

If Pickens was not the first landowning resident of Franklin County, perhaps it was Robert Hodges. After all, when he transferred his claim to Pickens in 1746, Hodges already had a "Cabbin" on the property. Also, in 1748 he was recorded in the tax district of John Phelps and in 1749 in the district of Nicholas Haile or Hale; both districts include that portion of Bedford County north of Blackwater River and south of Staunton River that became part of Franklin County in 1786.[28] Unfortunately, the cabin on Chestnut Creek lay far south of Blackwater River, in Cornelius Cargill's tax district. Presumably it was a temporary shelter, perhaps for hunting expeditions, and Hodges's permanent residence was north of Blackwater River in either present-day Bedford County or in Franklin County. Or perhaps Hodges used the cabin for periodic trips to his Chestnut Creek property to clear land there while continuing to reside north of Blackwater River. In any case, a Robert Hodges eventually became a resident of Franklin County; he was issued two patents on Chestnut Creek before the county was formed (one for 388 acres on 17 September 1755 and another for 193 acres on 20 July 1781).[29]

Many settlers, in fact, may have made the move from old to new homesites by slow degrees rather than all at once. On 22 April 1748, for instance, Walter Matthews, Roger Turner, Thomas Jones, John Hilton, and George Griffith each filed an entry for land "including his Cabin," and Joseph Morton claimed three hundred acres "including David Griffith's Cabin."[30] If a new homesite was only a journey of a week or less from the old place, then a prospective pioneer may have built a cabin, cleared some land, and even planted some crops before bringing his family to the new home.

Tax and voting lists drawn up between 1748 and 1750 indicated that most early settlers of the area moved in gradually. Few of the pioneers came to what was then Lunenburg County from the Northern Neck, the Eastern Shore, or the lower Chesapeake Bay region. Most of them emigrated from the central Virginia counties of Goochland, Hanover, and Henrico—"the counties closest to the Southside itself."[31] Surprisingly, the Southside Tidewater counties from Isle of Wight to the east provided relatively few settlers; the general movement into the area was from the northeast.

A great many of the eighteenth-century immigrants passed from north to south, from Pennsylvania through the Valley of Virginia by way of the Great Wagon Road and on to the backcountry of the Carolinas. Some of the migration even occurred against the tide, from south to north along the road. This important migratory path passed through present-day Franklin County; traces of it can still be seen in the western part of the county.[32] The Great Wagon Road, according to one local historian, saw "the face of America" pass by:

> the Cherokee, Count Casimir Pulaski and his revolutionary soldiers, Bishop Francis Asbury, Lorenzo Dow and other noted and unknown ministers, Daniel Boone, Andrew Jackson, frontiersmen, settlers, large transport wagons, droves of cattle and hogs, [and] armies of blue and gray.[33]

The heyday of the road began in the 1740s. It started on Market Street in Philadelphia and passed westward through Lancaster to the Alleghenies. As the ridges swung to the south, so did the road, traversing western Maryland and entering the Shenandoah Valley at the lower end of the Valley of Virginia. It followed the Valley south to present-day Roanoke, then broke through the Blue Ridge to its eastern slope at Maggotty Gap near Boones Mill, in Franklin County. The road went south across the Blackwater River at a place still called Carolina Bottoms, near Dugwell, then by the Carolina Springs Church to the west of Grassy Hill. It crossed the Pigg River near Waidsboro, went over Thornton Mountain, and then passed into Henry County near Oak Level. The road—particularly in hilly Franklin County—was no highway; it followed ancient animal trails and the old Iroquois warpath; sometimes the road was clearly marked and sometimes it disappeared altogether; often it was full of fallen trees and mudholes.

Great Wagon Road at Carolina Bottoms. 1988 photo. (Virginia Department of Historic Resources.)

Several other roads traversed Franklin County in the mid-eighteenth century. The Morgan Bryan Road, cleared by a Pennsylvanian of that name who lived for a while in Virginia, closely followed the route of the Wagon Road southward through the county, but veered farther to the west after it crossed Blackwater River. Three important roads ran from east to west and served emigrants from eastern Virginia. One was the Warwick Road, which was a local branch of the main Warwick Road from Richmond to Roanoke; it left the main road at New London, in Bedford County, and followed generally present-day Route 122 to the vicinity of Burnt Chimney, where it swung westward toward Callaway, crossed the Blue Ridge, and led eventually to the New River. The other early roads were the Pigg River Road and the Chiswell Road, with the latter being essentially an extension of the former. Entering the southeastern part of the county from Pittsylvania County, the Pigg River Road followed approximately the course of present-day Routes 809, 890, 715, and 718 from Snow Creek to the Sontag area. The Chiswell Road connected the Pigg River Road to the Warwick Road near Callaway.[34]

One early settler within the present bounds of Franklin County was closely associated with the Great Wagon Road: Benjamin Ray (also spelled Rae, Reh, and Wray). Apparently he was a squatter, for he never owned any land; almost nothing is known of him except that he lived on the upper waters of Maggodee Creek, probably just east of present-day Boones Mill. There his dwelling, a simple cabin, became something of a landmark. He was first mentioned in a surveyor's book in

Great Wagon Road ford at Blackwater River. 1988 photo. (Virginia Department of Historic Resources.)

relation to an entry made on 8 April 1747 for Colonel Richard Randolph for four hundred acres beginning "at Benja. Ray's on Maggot Cr."[35] He also appeared on the tax list of John Phelps in 1748, and Phelps's district included Maggodee Creek.[36] And on 4 November 1753 a traveler reported a firsthand encounter with Benjamin Ray.

The traveler was a Moravian diarist, probably the Reverend B. A. Grube, who was on a journey with other Moravians from Pennsylvania to North Carolina by way of the Great Wagon Road. Even after an exhausting struggle up and over the Blue Ridge (a hill near Boones Mill was called Moravian Ridge) the band found the going still rough, instead of better:

> On November 4, we found an almost impassable way and were compelled to remove many trees. Our wagon stuck fast in a mud hole and it took two hours before we could get it out. (The pulley was of much service to us.) After a mile we found water again, after four miles we came to a little creek, where we ate our dinner. We had a good road thus far. In the afternoon we crossed "Maggedi Creek." Nearby dwells *Benjamin Reh*, an old man of some ninety years, and his wife who is about a hundred years old. They are both active and cheerful people, who gave us milk to drink and were very friendly. Close to this house is a deep mud hole, then follows a steep hill almost immediately.[37]

Grube then cast an aspersion on the early inhabitants of Franklin County when he wrote, "We had to watch our horses closely in this place, for we had heard that there were people in this neighborhood who steal horses." Just past Benjamin Ray's house the Moravians encountered the Warwick Road, which Grube rated "pretty good."[38]

The Moravians camped for the night about five miles south of the Warwick Road, then arose early in the morning of 5 November 1753 and proceeded through the county. "For several miles," Grube wrote,

> we had a good road, running along on the mountains. After having driven five miles we came to Mr. *Robert Kohl's* [perhaps Mark Cole], a justice of the peace, from whom we bought some corn. He is a very modest man. He regretted very much that he had not known of our coming or he would have gone to meet us and shown us a better and nearer way, so that we could have avoided the high mountains and many hills. The way had not been cut out completely, but as we had so many hands, we could easily have done it. He would see to it that this way would soon be made. Some of the brethren stayed here and helped to husk several bushels of corn, which we had bought. We had to drive again on a pretty steep road, after half a mile we came to a little creek, and again half a mile farther to the "Black Water," a large creek with steep banks. After another mile we came again to a creek; and two miles farther to another, where we ate our dinner. There were several mud holes here, but we passed them safely. Then the road branched to the left up the mountain. We missed it, by turning to the right and coming to an old mill race at *Ringfros* [Rentfro's] Mill. We then stayed on the left and turned up again to the mountain, where we came to the right way. Going a mile we came to a little creek and a mud hole. Half a mile beyond we came to another creek, a mile farther to the left was a new plantation, and half a

mile from it we had to pass through a bad swamp and creek. A mile farther we came to *Robert Johnsen*, from whom we bought some hay. He accompanied us half a mile to show us the way across the creek and a comfortable place, where we could pitch our tent. Our course today was west and southwest. We had gone sixteen miles. The road was pretty good, except some mud holes and steep banks along the creeks.[39]

The Moravians reached the Smith River, in present-day Henry County, late in the afternoon of 7 November. Part of Grube's diary entry for that day gives an idea of the difficulties the party faced:

On November 7, we started at daybreak and got out of the swamp [where they had camped]. We had to climb a mountain, which was very precipitous on the other side. Having crossed we forded a pretty large creek. Then the way was up hill again, and we had much trouble before we reached the top, because the ground was slippery so that the horses could not step firmly. Then we had a good road for a mile, whereupon it turned again into a swamp and crossed a creek several times. Our wagon was somewhat damaged, because the banks of a creek were so steep and the wagon went down so deep that the rear part struck the ground, and one of the boards of the wagon bed was broken. We repaired this very quickly and then ate dinner at the creek.[40]

Other settlers by the thousands repeated the experiences of the Moravians.

These immigrants did not come steadily, but in waves. A Lunenburg County surveyor's entry book indicated that the first great wave of settlement in the Franklin County area may have occurred in the period 1747–1749, judging from the large number of entries made in those years. Among the settlers in that first wave were John, Mark, and Stephen Cole (along Blackwater River); Peter Elliot (on Maggodee Creek); Thomas Gill (for whom Gills Creek is named); Benjamin and John Greer (Blackwater River); David Griffith (Pigg River); Nicholas Hale (Staunton River); Thomas Hall (Maggodee Creek); Robert Hill (at present-day Rocky Mount); Robert Hooker (Pigg River); Patrick Johnson (Maggodee Creek); Robert and Thomas Jones (Turners Creek); John Lynas (at Rocky Mount); Robert Pusey (Otter Creek); Benjamin, Joseph, and Moses Ray (near Boones Mill); James and Joseph Rentfro (near Callaway); James Standifer (Staunton River); Roger Turner (for whom Turners Creek was named); and Obadiah Woodson (Snow Creek).[41] Some of these men have been mentioned before and may in fact have settled in the area before 1747.

The flood of pioneers ebbed significantly during the years of the French and Indian War (1754–1763) but soon quickened after hostilities ended. This second wave continued at least until the beginning of the revolutionary war. Among the settlers in the second wave were Tully Choice (Snow Creek); John Donelson (who lived in Pittsylvania County but owned land in Franklin County); Peter Finney (Pigg River); Archibald Gordon (Snow Creek); Robert Hairston (Pigg River); Stephen Heard (Blackwater River); Hugh Innes (Snow Creek); Josiah Morton (Blackwater River); Anthony Pate (Gills Creek); Samuel Patterson (Chestnut Creek); John Ramsey (near Sydnorsville); Amos Richardson (Snow Creek); Peter Saunders (near Endicott); and John Smith (Gills Creek).[42] Several of them were among the first of Franklin County's officeholders and may properly be said to be the founders of the county.

From among the earliest settlers perhaps the life of Robert Hill, who is well known in local lore, might be taken as representative of them all. According to family tradition, he came to Virginia from Dublin, Ireland, "sometime prior to 1740, and secured possession of a large tract of land in the wilderness, where he built his home [and] spent the remainder of his life."[43] His name first occurred in area records on Nicholas Hale's 1749 tax list for Lunenburg County,[44] which indicates Hill probably was in present-day Franklin County by that date. He definitely was in residence by 14 February 1753 when the "Robt. Hill Mill Road where it Crosses the Grassey Hill" north of Rocky Mount was mentioned in a land entry.[45]

Hill married Violet Lynas, daughter of fellow pioneer John Lynas, and together they reared a family of at least five sons and four daughters, of whom two sons and all four daughters survived him.[46] The other three sons allegedly met various untimely ends during the early settlement period. According to local tradition, "two were killed by Indians, one tomahawked and scalped near Bald Knob, the other shot by an arrow in the very door of the blockhouse. Still a third son was killed by a panther."[47] Another historian attributed the third son's death to a fall from a colt.[48]

Robert Hill's "blockhouse," or at least the remnants of its stone walls, still stands to the southwest of Rocky Mount. This structure is an enigma—the only known dwelling like it in the county (Thomas Ramsey built a similar one in

Robert Hill's stone "fort." 1980s photo. (J. Francis Amos, Rocky Mount, Va.)

Pittsylvania County). Whether in fact Hill constructed the building, and whether it ever really functioned as a blockhouse or fort, or was merely a stone dwelling, is as uncertain as the stories about the deaths of Hill's three unnamed sons. If indeed they were killed by Indians, the attackers most likely were Shawnee from the Ohio River valley who infiltrated the area about 1757 or 1758 rather than any lingering Saponi or Tutelo. The fact that Hill's name does not occur in other firsthand accounts of Indian-white encounters in the area appears to contradict the local traditions.

There were several recorded instances in present-day Franklin County of white settlers being killed or carried into captivity by Indian allies of the French during what was known in America as the French and Indian War. This conflict began over competing claims to the Ohio territory between the British and the French. In December 1753 George Washington delivered an ultimatum from Virginia's lieutenant governor Robert Dinwiddie to the French commander at Fort le Boeuf that the French withdraw from the Ohio River valley. The French not only refused to leave but also drove the English settlers from the valley, thereby commencing hostilities.

By 1755 the conflict had spread eastward to the Valley and Blue Ridge provinces of Virginia, and many of the settlers there fled to the relative safety of the Carolinas, or eastward into Tidewater Virginia. A Louisa County minister wrote in 1756 that "by Bedford Courthouse in one week, 'tis said, and I believe truly said, near 300 Persons, Inhabitants of this Colony, past, on their way to Carolina."[49] When the threat passed, many settlers returned to their homes only to flee again when circumstances changed. A writer in 1760 noted that "several families that had since the former troubles returned to their settlements on the frontiers, are again frightened and have left them—so that Halifax is much confused and as unfit for my business [surveying] as when I left it."[50] Those settlers who lingered too long sometimes became the victims of the frontier warfare waged by bands of Cherokee or Shawnee. When attacks were imminent, settlers often sought refuge at a nearby fort.

At the beginning of the war, the colonial government took steps to protect the frontier and its settlers by constructing a chain of forts along the eastern front of the Blue Ridge and in the Valley. In September and October 1756 George Washington again prowled the frontier on behalf of Governor Dinwiddie; he inspected the forts and in so doing passed through present-day Franklin County on 12 October,[51] traveling along the Great Wagon Road.

Three of the frontier forts were built in the Southside Piedmont. They included Fort Mayo, built on the North Mayo River in present-day Patrick County; Fort Trial or Hickey's Fort, near the junction of Reed Creek and Smith River, in Henry County; and Fort Blackwater, on the Blackwater River in Franklin County near a gap in the Blue Ridge through which the Indians were expected to attack. The exact location of Fort Blackwater is unknown. (In 1970 archaeologists investigated a promising site near the junction of the north and south forks of the Blackwater River and adjacent to a trace of the Warwick Road, but found no material evidence of the fort.)[52]

Fort Blackwater probably was small, about eighty feet on a side. It may have been constructed on a plan similar to Fort Trial, which was described in 1774 as a

quadrangular polygon, inclosed with large timbers and cuts of trees split
into, about twelve or sixteen feet above the ground, standing erect, about
three or four feet in the earth and quite close together, with loopholes cut
through about four or five feet from the ground for small arms. There was
something like a bastian at each angle . . . and a log house, musket proof, on
each side of the gate. Within the area, nearly in the center, were two
common framed houses and boarded, filled in to the height of five feet with
stone and clay on the inside as a defense against small arms.[53]

The frontier forts were not designed for permanent habitation. When no danger
threatened, they were not garrisoned. In times of war, however, civilians as well
as soldiers crowded inside for protection. A twenty-man company of western
Halifax County militia commanded by Captain Nathaniel Terry guarded Fort
Blackwater, but at the time of Washington's tour it may not have been occupied.
In November 1756, after Washington reported his findings to Governor Robert
Dinwiddie, the governor ordered Forts Blackwater and Trial to be abandoned in
favor of Fort Mayo, which was to be garrisoned with a captain, a lieutenant, an
ensign, two sergeants, two corporals, and about forty men. By February 1757,
when the orders still had not been carried out, Dinwiddie repeated them.[54]

Ironically, Fort Blackwater was abandoned just a year before the French and
Indian War reached Franklin County. An engagement between militiamen and
Indians occurred in the spring of 1758 and resulted in a small battle on the banks
of the Blackwater River, not far from the fort. A Halifax County militia unit on its
march to Bedford County came to the house of a settler named Standiford near
Blackwater River. One of the militiamen, Pinkethman Hawkins,

found the house of Standiford strip of everything, the Bed Ticks ripped open
and carryed away, and the feathers scattered all over the House, and the
Family gone, whilst there he heard a hollowing and a noise of Indians.
Ordered his men then with him fifteen in Number to go with twenty five of
the Inhabitants, who had collected themselves and way lay the Indians at a
pass he was advised by his Guide, they must go through. . . . [Meanwhile] he
himself and another, namely one Tarbro, would go to the Indians (who by
the noise he imagined was over the River not far of[f]) and treat with them in
a Friendly manner about the Prisoners and Plunder they had gott. . . . When
they came to the River Eight or Ten Indians came over the River to them, that
he endeavoured to come to terms with them, proposed peace and Friendship, and called them Brothers, they surlily answered, no, no, no Brothers,
English damned Rogues, and clapping their Hands, on their Brea[s]ts called
themselves, and making signs signifyed to them, there was a great many
Shawanees all about them, that the wood and Mountains were full of them,
that he still mentioned peace and told them that he and Tarbro were
unarmed and came as Brothers, but the Indians not withstanding his
mentions for peace, Striped him of his Coat, Waiscoat, Shirt, Shoes,
Stockings, and Hatt, and gave him several Blows with their Tomhawks and
ordered him away, he remembering that in his Breeches (which was all the
C[l]oaths they had left him) he had about five shillings in Cash, gave it to one
of the Indians, who thereupon returned him his Coat, upon which . . .
Hawkins thinking they were in a better humour, again proposed to treat with
them, upon which they beat him and Tarbro very severely, and Cut him thro'

the upper Lip with a Blow of a Scalping knife, led them both by the Hands up the River Banck and ordered them to run away or they would kill them, which Order they readily Obeyed, and being at two great a distance, and as they were bare footed did not come up with the men till the Battle with the Indians was over.[55]

As Hawkins and Tarbro attempted to negotiate, the rest of the militiamen and civilians climbed a ridge overlooking Blackwater River in order to ambush the Indians. One of the civilians named Byrd watched Hawkins and Tarbro being beaten, then informed the others, and, as William Morgan reported,

directed them to be ready prepaired for the Enemy was approaching, in a very little time after they heard the Indian War Whoop and a Gun fired upon which a running fi[gh]t began, that the Indians tryed to get them into a half moon three times which at last they effected and that in the Engagement he saw two Indians fall, that at last the Enemys half moon being broken, both parties fled from each other. . . . [The next day several settlers] came to View the Field where the Engagement happened, where they found one Indian dead which was scalped, Nineteen fine horses, and much plunder, and among the plunder a French Scalping Knife.[56]

This was the only recorded battle with Native Americans to occur within the boundaries of present-day Franklin County.

In March 1758 Indians attacked the home of Robert Pusey, who had settled on Otter Creek in western Franklin County during the first wave of immigration. Pusey,

with his Wife and Child, was taken Prisoner by the Shawanese Indians, and carried to their Country [Ohio], where he remained a long time until he redeemed his liberty; and . . . returning home he could not find any of his effects, by which he might have subsisted himself and his family, some of them having been destroyed by the enemy, and the residue lost during his captivity.[57]

Pusey remained a prisoner until at least November 1764, when colonial officials listed him and seventy-six other whites in captivity at the "Lower Sawana Towns."[58]

In June 1758 another Franklin County settler, Patrick Johnson, who lived on Maggodee Creek, reported that "a parcel of Indians of what Nation he knew not, came to his House [and] shot a Bull in his yard. Robbed him of eight Horses and all he had in the world."[59]

The Franklin County area was spared the worst effects of the war that took place largely on the other side of the Blue Ridge, so neither Fort Blackwater nor Robert Hill's "blockhouse" was severely tested. Many of the other structures built during the early years of settlement hardly survived a few hard winters, much less an assault by Indians. Frontier housing generally was meant to be temporary; it was put up quickly to shelter a family for a few seasons until the land yielded enough crops to make a more permanent structure worthwhile. Although the idea of the log cabin has become a hoary cliché in the American mind, it was the reality in frontier-era Franklin County. A log cabin was easy to construct and timber was abundant. Sawmills, on the other hand, were virtually nonexistent at first. Frame dwellings were only built when a settler used the tedious process of pit sawing to produce lumber. Brickmaking took too much time. This is not to say that the "log cabin myth"—that most settlers aspired only to a simple cabin in a clearing in the woods—is an accurate depiction of what people wanted. Rather, pioneers settled for log cabins until they prospered enough to build something better.

In 1785 Robert Woods, who became the first sheriff of Franklin County in 1786, compiled "A List of Whit pepol & Buildings in the Bounds of Capt. [Owen] Rubles Company." He recorded seventy-eight households in present-day south-western Franklin County and northwestern Henry County. For each one Woods listed the name of the head of the household, the number in the family, the material of which the dwelling was constructed (in one case he omitted this information), and any outbuildings. In seventy-six instances the family's house was a "Log Dewling [dwelling] Hous"; only one—the property of Peter Saunders, Sr.—was of frame construction. Thirty households occupied only a single dwelling, while the remainder (more than half) had at least one outbuilding. The most common outbuilding was a "Chicken [kitchen]" (thirty-two), followed by "Barons [barns]" (seventeen), dairies (five), six shops (for a hatter, a turner, a smith, and three of unspecified purpose), four "quarters," stables and smoke-houses (two of each), and one mill. The number of family members ranged from two to fourteen, with the average being just under six. If Woods counted only white people, then the households with slaves were even larger. If only four households had slave "quarters," then the other slaveholding families likely

Nineteenth-century cabin typical of a dwelling of a century earlier, located in Henry County near North Fork Church. 1974 photo. (Virginia Department of Historic Resources.)

shared their log dwellings with their servants (unless the slaves slept in the kitchens, barns, or other outbuildings).[60]

Assuming that Woods's list is representative, then, it presents a vivid image of the typical pioneer farmstead, at least in western Franklin County. (Residents in the eastern part may have had earlier access to sawmills and built more frame dwellings.) The log dwelling constituted the dominant building type in western Virginia, even fairly late in the eighteenth century. The logs that formed its walls usually were hewn, but sometimes were left round; they measured twelve to sixteen feet in length. Gaps between the logs were stuffed with scraps of wood or rock and daubed with clay or mud. A chimney made of sticks and mud, or rocks and mud, was constructed at one end of the dwelling. Windows often consisted of holes in the walls covered with shutters. Glass windows were rare, unless the old homestead had been dismantled and the windows brought to the new site. There was a batten door or two of hewn or sawed boards. Overhead the roof was covered with split shingles or poles, and underfoot the floor was hard-packed clay. Such dwellings were cold and drafty in winter, hot and stuffy in summer, and all of them have vanished—some of them burned down, many were abandoned to decay, and others were incorporated into later, weatherboarded structures.

Into this temporary shelter the settler wedged himself, his wife, four or five children, and perhaps even a slave or two (privacy as it is known today did not then exist). Although the dwelling was uncomfortable and bug-ridden, it provided basic shelter while the family carved a farmstead out of the forest. Unless the farmer built a barn for his animals, his cattle and hogs roamed the woods. To help identify them when they strayed he cut marks of ownership into their ears and registered the marks at the county courthouse.

Frontier farmers did not rely only on produce and livestock for their livelihoods. As Woods's list indicates, they practiced trades as well. William Griffith, for example, made hats, while his next-door neighbor, Owen Ruble, had both a smith's shop and a turner's shop. The next man on the list, Bailey Carter, owned a shop for which the purpose was not stated. Perhaps the three farms, which were located on Turners Creek near the intersection of present-day Routes 748 and 752, formed a community of home industries that attracted purchasers from the general neighborhood. A couple of miles to the east lived Samuel Darst, a German potter who had moved to the area from Shenandoah County about 1780. Darst, who owned about 220 acres on Story Creek near the future site of the Carron Iron Works, died in 1791. His land was located on a vein of excellent potter's clay. The inventory of his estate listed potter's tools and earthen plates and dishes that he probably made himself.[61]

The Franklin County area did contain one true industry at an early date: John Donelson's bloomery forge for the manufacture of iron. It was located close by Pigg River near the center of the present-day county, about where the Washington Iron Works furnace stack still stands. Established by 1773, the forge employed ten white men and slaves and soon became a local landmark. By 1779 the enterprise was purchased and enlarged by James Callaway and Jeremiah Early, of Bedford County, and during the revolutionary war under the name of the Washington Iron Works it served as a point of rendezvous for militiamen. The ironworks was unique in its importance to the community: an industrial complex in a region occupied primarily by first-generation settlers who barely scratched out a living.

If a settler's farm was a failure despite all his efforts, he could move to a new tract without having invested a great deal of time and energy in home building. If he succeeded, however, perhaps in a few years he could build another dwelling and turn the old one into a kitchen or slave quarters. Assuming there were no sawmills in the neighborhood, the new house might be another log structure, but larger, with glass windows, a wooden floor, and a stone or brick chimney. Perhaps it was a story and a half or a full two stories high with a room on each floor. Perhaps it had two rooms on the first floor in what is called a hall-parlor plan: the front door opened into a large room (the hall) and a door in a partition (interior wall) led into a smaller room (the parlor) to one side. Each room usually had its own exterior chimney. As soon as the settler could afford to do so, he covered the exposed log walls with plaster on the inside and weatherboarding on the outside to provide additional insulation and a more sophisticated appearance. (Exposed, "rustic" log walls are largely a twentieth-century affectation.)

Several examples of this type of structure still survive in Franklin County. One of the most notable is off present-day Route 748 on the land occupied by William Griffith in 1785. Two log outbuildings, one of which is reputed to be the remnant of Griffith's hat factory, stand near a simple log dwelling covered with weatherboards. The house consists of two parts, a one-room main section called a single pen, and a smaller one-room addition. The main section is a story and a half (with a loft) and has an exterior stone chimney on one end. The rear ell also has an exterior stone chimney. The front elevation of the main section has only two bays, a door (the original batten door with strap hinges was removed by August 1988) and a window to the right. On the chimney end are one window to the right of the stack and two on either side in the loft. There is also a window in the loft on the opposite end. The roof is standing-seam metal and has no dormers. The house probably dates to the mid-nineteenth century, although it could be earlier.[62]

Nearby stands another—perhaps earlier—example that consists of two parts (double pen) of almost equal size, separated by an open breezeway called a dogtrot. This story-and-a-half dwelling has four bays (two doors and two windows across the front), a front porch supported by seven posts, two exterior end chimneys of stone, and a standing-seam-metal roof. Unlike the first house, this one has exposed logs. It is a rare survival, because most dogtrot cabins have long since been enclosed.[63]

Double-pen log dwelling with dogtrot, located near Truevine. 1972 photo. (Virginia Department of Historic Resources.)

Some settlers who lived near sawmills built their houses of framing and weatherboarding rather than of logs, or replaced their initial log structures with frame dwellings, as had Peter Saunders, Sr., by 1785. The familiar hall-parlor floor plan probably predominated, but the interior walls and partition were plastered above a simple chair rail, with wainscoting (usually plain board paneling) below. Most of these dwellings were a story and a half in height, often with dormer windows in the roof. In building this house style, the settler followed tradition and familiar patterns, for the story-and-a-half hall-parlor-plan house was the most common building type in eighteenth-century Tidewater and Piedmont Virginia.

The Frederick Rives house, which stands on the Pigg River about four miles southeast of Glade Hill, is a typical but rare surviving example of the hall-parlor plan. It probably dates to the late eighteenth century and may be as early as 1779. The house, which is attached to a kitchen of slightly later construction by a narrow breezeway, is of one story with a garret reached by an enclosed stair. The interior of the house may be unique to the county. Instead of the usual plaster

Above: *Frederick Rives House exterior, with the dwelling to the right and a later kitchen to the left.*

Left: *Rives House interior, showing exposed framing members and mud-and-rock infill. 1991 photos.* (Virginia Department of Historic Resources.)

walls, the framing members of the walls were left exposed, and mud and rocks were used as infill; this rough interior was then whitewashed. The Rives house may be one of the oldest structures in the county; it is certainly one of the most unusual. In its general form and simplicity, however, it is typical of the houses in which most middle-class farmers resided during the late eighteenth and early nineteenth centuries.[64]

In contrast to the Rives house, Liberty Hall, a large, elaborate example of a hall-parlor-plan dwelling, was built for John S. Hale about 1800. A two-story, three-bay, gable-roofed dwelling of frame-and-weatherboard construction, Liberty Hall has two exterior end chimneys of brick laid in Flemish bond. The foundation is stone. At one time the front entrance was sheltered by a plain, one-story porch with four square wooden columns. Inside, both the hall and the parlor have plain plaster walls above simple chair rails and paneled wainscoting. At the ceiling is a cornice molding that is unusually elaborate for the place and time. Each room has its own stair leading to corresponding rooms on the second floor. The stair in the parlor is fully enclosed, while that in the hall is open, with a square newel, turned balusters, and closed stringers. The upstairs rooms have simple chair rails with plain wainscoting beneath. Throughout the house, most of the doors are painted to resemble wood graining. All but one of the surviving mantels are Greek Revival in style and probably replaced Federal-style mantels (of which one is left) in the mid-nineteenth century. Although Liberty Hall followed a traditional plan, the elaborate woodwork made the house one of the finest of its period in Franklin County.[65]

Most pioneers wanted to feel "at home" as soon as circumstances permitted. They accomplished this both by building in traditional styles and by otherwise replicating as soon as possible the material and social structures they had left behind. As early as January 1755, for example, a survey mentioned a "School

Above left: *Liberty Hall, facade.* Above right: *Liberty Hall, closed-stringer stair in hall. 1970 photos.* (Virginia Department of Historic Resources.)

House on Fox Run a Branch of Black Water River."[66] Another survey, made in February 1763, referred to "Race paths" near Chestnut Creek,[67] while a 1774 Pittsylvania County road order mentioned "Standefer's Track" near Blackwater River (presumably the Standifer of Indian battle fame).[68] James Rentfro's mill near the Great Wagon Road was considered "old" by the Moravian diarist in 1753. In present-day Patrick County, John Hickey's store served travelers as well as local residents; he probably opened it about 1746 and Moravians bought salt there in 1753. Hickey's store stood at the end of a road that linked the Staunton River in northern Halifax County with the frontier community known as the Mayo Settlement. Hickey's Road, which stretched about 120 miles and became a well-known route to the West, was constructed beginning in 1749, passed to the south of Franklin County, and crossed the Great Wagon Road near Hickey's store on Smith River.[69]

Frontier inhabitants often went for long periods of time without satisfying their religious needs. The Moravian diarist, the Reverend B. A. Grube, reported in 1753 that Robert Johnson, who lived south of Blackwater River in Franklin County, "had not heard a sermon for nine years."[70] Whether this was because ministers did not come that far west or because Johnson was a dissenter who refused to attend Anglican services when they were available is not known. There is little doubt, however, that such settlers lived so far from churches that to attend regularly was virtually impossible. Gradually, however, the established church brought its services to the frontier. When Antrim Parish and Halifax County were organized in 1752, the parish vestry ordered the construction of six new churches, one of them on Pigg River, and that a chapel be built at Snow Creek. In 1769, two years after the formation of Camden Parish and Pittsylvania County, the new vestry ordered the construction of a new church on Snow Creek near the chapel,

> the size to be 24 by 32 feet. A framed house with clap board roof, a plank floor with a pulpit and desk two doors, five windows in it 12 feet in the Pitch [of the roof], with a Small Table and Benches in it.[71]

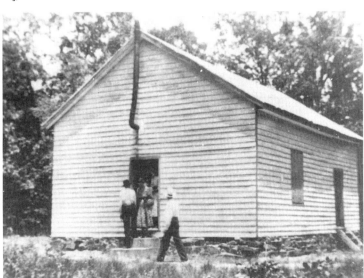

Old Chapel, before alterations. 1950s photo. (Blue Ridge Institute, Ferrum, Va.)

The old Snow Creek Church may still exist today as a Primitive Baptist church.

The Baptists, who dissented from the Church of England, established four meetinghouses in Franklin County before the Revolution. The first was built about 1761 on Blackwater River, the second on Snow Creek in 1771, the third on Pigg River two years later, and the fourth on Gills Creek about 1774.[72] Because of their aggressive proselytizing the Baptists met with greater success in organizing active congregations than did the established church. This was particularly true in the backcountry, where settlers were eager to band together and listen to words of comfort and consolation.

In addition to their dwellings and churches, early settlers found that their familiar possessions helped them feel at home. Some belongings were brought from the old place and others were made or purchased after the new homesite was found. Fashions and styles changed slowly, especially under frontier conditions; items generally were discarded only after they had worn out or were no longer needed. To be a pioneer was to be a member of a highly mobile society, even if the distances traveled were relatively short. Of necessity, each family's possessions were limited to what would fit in a wagon or two. And to acquire new things required an exchange of money or—more likely in what was a barter economy—an exchange of goods or services. The result often was that the sum total of a lifetime of acquiring and discarding household property could be listed on a page or two of the inventory and appraisal required by law at one's death.

In the case of Robert Hill, an inventory and appraisal of his personal property was made after his death on 19 August 1777.[73] The inventory listed all the property found in and around his home except land; it did not record the property he may have used that was owned by his wife or children, nor did it record the property he may have given away during his lifetime. The inventory described the possessions of a modestly prosperous pioneer at the end of his life. Hill owned twelve head of cattle, twelve sheep, three hogs, a white horse, a roan (red-coated) filly, and two mares, one of them a roan that wore a bell. He had a man's and a woman's saddle, and one bridle, as well as two other bells for his livestock. His farming equipment included a set of harrow teeth, three hoes, a mattock, a shovel, a set of plow irons, plowshares, and a quantity of bar iron to make repairs and replace worn-out tools. A pair of steelyards was used to weigh produce, and containers and measures included two pails, two bottles, and a half bushel.

Like many eighteenth-century farmers, Hill owned enough carpenter's and farrier's tools to make necessary repairs to his house—perhaps even to build one—and to care for his horses. Among the carpenter's tools were an iron wedge for splitting logs, two mauls for driving the wedge, and a "Variety of Carpenters and Joiners Tools" (probably saws, planes, and augers). He also owned a shoe hammer, pincers, and nippers for working with horseshoes.

The remainder of Hill's property reflected the routine of his domestic life. Violet Hill used two "old" flax wheels to spin flax into thread and a loom to weave it into linen cloth. The kitchenware consisted of a sifter, two pots, a potrack, a pan, two chains (presumably for suspending cooking utensils over a fire), an "old" skimmer, a flesh fork, a gridiron, five basins, three dishes, eleven plates, three tinned cups, and an uncounted assortment of knives, forks, and pewter spoons. The household furniture included only six chairs, a table, a chest, a looking glass, and two "beds, bedsteads, and furniture." The last reference is to the mattress or ticking (bed), the wooden bed frame (bedstead), and the sheets, blankets, and pillows (furniture) for each bed. Robert Hill, at least, was literate; after his day's work he had his choice of "a law Book and Bible" from which to read. When he finished his reading and the Hills retired for the evening, he put out his candle with a pair of snuffers.

The inventory is interesting not only for what, and how little, is listed, but also for what is absent. Hill owned no slaves, no gun, and no still. Such clothing, foodstuffs, and crops that he possessed at his death were not considered worth valuing. Yet Robert Hill was a fairly prosperous man. Although he had little in the way of furniture—about what would fit into a one-room house—he had more livestock than many other settlers.

In his will, Robert Hill distributed the remainder of his property.[74] His house and the surrounding land went to Violet Hill for her use during her lifetime; after her death the property was to be sold and the income divided among their six children. He left his daughter Ruth a gray horse (so he died owning a total of five horses). He directed that the rest of his lands be sold to pay his debts and that any money left over be divided equally among his children. Swinfield and Thomas Hill, his sons, were appointed executors.

Hill's situation compares favorably to that of another early settler, Robert Hodges, who may represent those pioneers who fared less well than their neighbors. The fortunes of Hodges, who was one of present-day Franklin County's first settlers,[75] declined as he grew older. On 24 June 1779 the Henry County court appointed Robert Woods "to furnish Robert Hodges with such necessities as he needs to support him and his wife."[76] The court clarified this appointment on 28 October 1779 when it ordered that "Robert Holliday be allowed the sum of 13 pounds for necessities for Robert Hodges, whose sons are in the Continental Service of the United States."[77] Evidently Hodges had grown so feeble and poor that he would have been supported by his sons had they not been in the army; because of their absence he was forced to rely upon the charity of the county.

The fate of Robert Hodges illustrates the risks associated with life in a frontier economy where merely to subsist was a goal beyond the reach of some settlers. Many of them moved on, hoping for a better crop on some new land over the next ridge. Others, who were too old or worn out to work any longer, relied upon their children, their neighbors, or the county for their survival. When or where Robert Hodges died is not known; no will or inventory of his estate has been found in the counties of Henry or Franklin. Presumably, this means he died owning nothing of value, nothing to appraise or distribute to his sons. The life of Robert Hodges was worth something, however, for he had played a part in subduing the wilderness that was to become Franklin County, and he had fathered sons who played a role in defeating the greatest empire on the globe, thus establishing a new country. He gave his sons a home to defend and they successfully defended it during what is known as the American Revolution.

THREE

Revolution in the Backcountry

ometimes even seemingly simple historical questions are nearly impossible to answer. During what period, for example, did the American
Revolution occur? John Adams, who helped it to happen, declared that
"The Revolution was . . . effected in the period from 1761 to 1775. I mean a
complete revolution in the minds of the people . . . [in other words a] change
of the opinions and affections of the people and a full confidence in the
practicability of a union of the colonies."[1]

Adams may have been correct in dividing the Revolution into intellectual and
military phases, but he oversimplified matters when he wrote of "the people."
The inhabitants of British North America were far from unified as a people, even
by 1775; some supported independence, others strongly opposed it, and many
straddled the fence or fled the settled parts of the country for the wilds of
Kentucky to avoid the issue. Nevertheless, the view offered by Adams is the one
most commonly held today by Americans: that right-thinking men joined in
opposing the tyranny of the king and his ministers, abandoned their fields to form
a ragtag army, vanquished both the British army and those scoundrels known as
tories, and established a new nation with relatively little dissension. The issues,
seen in hindsight, seem clear, and the proper course obvious.

In reality, the era of the Revolution—from roughly the end of the French and
Indian War until the treaty of peace was signed in 1783—was a period of turmoil
and uncertainty. The revolutionary war was in many ways a civil war that split
communities and families and caused hard feelings that lasted for years. Neither
side had a monopoly on virtue or on dastardliness; heroism and villainy existed
on both sides. Some called themselves patriots and labeled their opponents
tories; others called themselves loyalists and accused their opponents of being
rebels. Both sides occasionally used the conflict as an excuse to settle personal
scores, or to escape debt, or to gain political advantage.

41

It is arguable that in a military sense the war was not so much won by the rebellious Americans as it was lost by the British. Inadequate sources of supply, poor morale in the army, political meddling by civilians in military activities, corruption and looting by officers and soldiers, incompetent commanders, and a growing army of surly taxpayers—these things afflicted both the Americans and the British but proved devastating to the British war effort. The Americans, after all, fought in their native land, occasionally used guerrilla tactics to good effect, and often were motivated by a desire to defend home and hearth. American soldiers, in other words, may have had a better sense of why they were fighting than did their British counterparts.

But what had brought the colonists to a state of rebellion, which all agreed was a desperate act? At the end of the French and Indian War in 1763 the inhabitants of the British colonies considered themselves to be British, not American, and subjects of the greatest and freest empire on the globe. A decade later many of these same people were convinced they were the victims of a dark plot to enslave them—a plot that they believed had been hatched by those whom they formerly considered to be their fellow countrymen.

The dark plot, insofar as one existed, revolved around taxes. The French and Indian War had cost the British empire dearly, and some English ministers thought that because the war had benefited the colonists most directly, the colonists should bear more of the burden for paying off the war debt. Most colonists, however, believed that it was the duty of the empire to defend them, that they had nevertheless fought well in their own defense, and that, because hard currency was in such short supply in the colonies, they ought not to have their tax burdens increased. Furthermore, the colonists complained, they elected no members to Parliament; therefore, they were not represented in that body and should not be taxed without their consent. Those in England who believed the colonists should pay their fair share replied that although they were not *actually* represented in Parliament, each member also had the duty to consider the interests of the colonists as well as his constituents in England; therefore, the colonists were *virtually* represented. The response to such hairsplitting was the colonial equivalent of a loud raspberry.

Matters soon deteriorated even further. In 1764 First Lord of the Treasury George Grenville proposed that the colonists pay stamp duties on legal documents in order to help defray the costs of the war. The Virginia House of Burgesses complained loudly, but to no avail; King George III approved the Stamp Act of 1765. This resulted in a firestorm of remonstrances, resignations, and riots among the colonial assemblies, elected officials, and citizens respectively. In 1766 the gentlemen justices of Northampton County, Virginia, took it upon themselves to declare the Stamp Act invalid. Soon thereafter the Stamp Act was repealed by a pouting Parliament, which issued the Declaratory Act reaffirming its right to legislate for the colonies.

No sooner had the celebrations in the colonies died down, however, than Charles Townshend, chancellor of the exchequer, introduced to the House of Commons a tax program directed at the colonies. The Townshend Duties, as they became known, aroused even greater opposition than had the Stamp Act. Furthermore, colonial leaders—who had gained valuable experience during the Stamp Act furor—were willing to press their demands against the actions of

Parliament. In 1769 the House of Burgesses censured Parliament and on 17 May was dissolved as a result. The next day the former burgesses met at the Raleigh Tavern in Williamsburg and formed a nonimportation association to protest the Townshend Duties. Many Virginians who were about to begin their careers as revolutionaries were among those who signed the agreement; they included Patrick Henry, George Washington, and Thomas Jefferson. These luminaries were joined by most of the former burgesses present, including Charles Lynch and John Talbot, of Bedford County, and John Donelson and Hugh Innes, of Pittsylvania County.[2] Together, these last four men represented the area of present-day Franklin County.

In 1770 three events occurred that further divided England and the colonies: Frederick Lord North became the king's first minister, the Boston Massacre took place, and the Townshend Duties were repealed—except for a tax on tea. Most Virginians were saddened in October by the death of Norborne Berkeley, third baron de Botetourt, who, although the royal governor of the colony, was popular because of his moderate approach to controversy and his engaging personality. His replacement, John Murray, fourth earl of Dunmore, in time proved far less appealing.

The more Lord North and his adherents attempted to force the tax on tea down the throats of the colonists, the greater grew the opposition on the western shore of the Atlantic. A second nonimportation association was formed by burgesses and merchants in Williamsburg on 22 June 1770. This time, of the burgesses from Bedford and Pittsylvania counties, only John Talbot and John Donelson signed the agreement (Lynch and Innes probably were absent from the colonial capital).[3] The first agreement had been voluntary, but the second one provided for the appointment of a committee of five in each county to supervise the citizenry and persuade them to comply. The introduction of coercion implied that the first agreement had not been universally observed. Eventually some of the hotter heads in Boston decided that what could not be obtained voluntarily or through intimidation might be achieved through more violent means. On 16 December 1773 they held a "tea party" in Boston harbor and destroyed a small fortune in tea owned by the East India Company.

The British ministers and Parliament were outraged. The Port Act, which closed Boston harbor effective 1 June 1774, was followed by other so-called coercive acts directed against Massachusetts. All of this led to a general boycott of British goods in the colonies and, in Virginia on 27 May 1774, to yet another nonimportation association. Once again, John Donelson, Hugh Innes, Charles Lynch, and John Talbot signed the agreement for Pittsylvania and Bedford counties.[4] Innes, Lynch, and Talbot quickly departed for their homes, but Donelson tarried in Williamsburg for a few days. He was still there when the news arrived on Sunday morning, 29 May, that a meeting in Boston on 13 May had resolved not only to boycott British goods but also to refuse to sell American goods to the mother country. At 10·00 A.M. on Monday, the twenty-five former burgesses still in Williamsburg hastily reassembled and drafted a circular letter to all their colleagues. The letter, of which Donelson was a joint signer, called on the burgesses to return to Williamsburg on 1 August to discuss the Boston proposal and decide on a course of action. "Things seems to be hurrying to an alarming Crisis," the letter concluded, "and demand the speedy, united Councils of all those who have a Regard for the common Cause."[5] The gathering of the former burgesses, which met 1–6 August 1774 and is known as the first revolutionary convention (there were five in Virginia), formed yet another nonimportation-nonexportation association. More important, it elected seven of its number delegates to a general congress of the colonies (the first Continental Congress) in Philadelphia, thereby helping to unify the colonies as war approached.

As the crisis deepened, local revolutionaries became more active. On 28 January 1775 many of the voters in Pittsylvania County assembled at the courthouse and elected a committee to enforce the most recent association. Among those elected to the committee was Peter Saunders. One of the first citizens reprimanded by the committee was the early settler John Pigg; his confrontation with the committee on 22 February 1775 was reported in the *Virginia Gazette* as the "Case of a Tea-Drinking Pigg." When accused of drinking the "detestable" East India Company tea, Pigg not only admitted that he and his family did so, but he also retorted "that his intention was to do as he pleased." The committee recommended that all Pittsylvanians snub Pigg until he changed his ways.[6] The outcome of this case is not recorded.

Each county in Virginia elected a committee such as Pittsylvania's to oversee the behavior of its citizens. After the fighting began at Lexington and Concord in Massachusetts in April 1775, a revolutionary army surrounded Boston and like-minded Virginians marched north to join it. In Virginia that same month Governor Dunmore seized the colony's gunpowder and later fled to a British warship near Norfolk. Some colonists marched against him while others, led by Daniel Morgan, followed Benedict Arnold on his ill-fated campaign from Maine against Quebec the next winter. Virginia's first battle of the Revolution took place at Great Bridge on 9 December 1775, when the colonists defeated British troops. On 1 January 1776 drunken Virginia and North Carolina troops burned most of Norfolk to the ground and blamed Dunmore. The fourth revolutionary convention of Virginia proclaimed a constitution on 29 June 1776 and elected Patrick Henry governor. On 2 July 1776 Congress adopted the resolution offered by Virginia's representatives calling for independence.

The Declaration of Independence was also a declaration of war, and the revolutionary war that followed was waged on two levels, the national and the local. Each colony contributed men and supplies to the national, or Continental, army authorized by Congress, but each also undertook its own defense. At the local level that defense was coordinated by the committees of safety and the county courts that the revolutionaries quickly took over. The military defense of the Revolution rested primarily upon the local militia, which was a frail reed indeed. Although much scorned by the regular army, and not without good reason, the often poorly trained and equipped militia did serve several important functions: it enforced the revolutionary laws and policies adopted by state and local governing bodies; it provided a first line of defense when a locality was threatened; and it released Continental and state army troops for battle when it was used in the rear echelon to guard supplies, prisoners, and the like.

The militia system was virtually as old as the colony itself. Each county's militia was under the overall command of a county lieutenant, who served as the local commander in chief and held the rank of senior colonel. The militia was organized into one or two battalions, depending upon the size of the eligible population of the county, and each battalion was commanded by either a colonel or a lieutenant colonel. A major served as adjutant for the battalion, which was divided into several companies, each of which was led by a captain. Under the captain usually were four lieutenants, one for each platoon in the company. Each company also had at least one ensign, the lowest-ranking commissioned officer, whose duties included bearing the company standard or flag. Forty or so enlisted men—white males between the ages of sixteen and fifty—held the ranks of sergeants, corporals, and privates.

It was one thing to organize a militia unit and quite another to prepare it for combat. Those factors that ordinarily build esprit de corps and some sense of security, such as uniform dress, weaponry, and training, largely were absent. There were laws on the books, to be sure, that prescribed dress and equipment, but the realities of life in the backcountry probably meant that they were honored more in the breach than in the observance. The Pittsylvania County militia company that served in the 6th Battalion in early 1776, for example, was to carry powder horns, shot bags, and cartouche boxes (leather pouches to hold paper cartridges). The officers and men were to wear fringed, linen hunting shirts all dyed the same color,

> the men's shirts to be short and plain, the sergeants' shirts to have a small white cuff and plain; the Drummers shirts to be with dark cuffs: both officers and soldiers to have hatts cut round and bound with black; the Brims of their Hatts to be 2 inches deep, and cocked on one side with a button and Loup and Cockades, which is to be worn on the left. Neither men nor officers to do duty in any other uniform. The officers and men are to wear their Hair short and as near alike as possible.[7]

The men generally wore britches of rough oznaburg (the denim of its day), and the hats and shoes typical of farmers. Weapons consisted of muskets, squirrel guns, and rifles of every description and bore, as well as knives and tomahawks. In even shorter supply than uniform clothing and weapons was uniform training, which consisted typically of a few musters each year, perhaps some tactical exercises left over from the last war, a bit of marching around the local parade, and a quick and welcome adjournment to the nearest tavern before the men got testy. Not surprisingly, the militia was scarcely fit for combat against the British army, which was widely regarded as the finest fighting machine on earth.

On the other hand, nothing else should have been expected. These militiamen were farmers, not warriors, and their lack of discipline and suspicion of authority were typical of the colonial population generally. Indeed, it was at least partly because of this independent attitude that there was a revolution in the first place. The commanders who were the most successful understood the shortcomings of the militia and overcame the natural contrariness of the men. Eventually the state government shortened the tours of active duty and rotated militia units in the field (one company was discharged when another arrived to take its place).

Before the militia faced British troops in Virginia, however, it had to deal with two other adversaries, Indians and loyalists. The backcountry of Virginia and the Carolinas was open to attack from the west by the British and their Native American allies. In the summer and fall of 1776 the colonists mounted an expedition to the Cherokee towns of eastern Tennessee, hoping either to defeat the Indians in battle or to persuade them to sign treaties of nonaggression. Part of the expeditionary force comprised several militia companies from Pittsylvania County and the newly formed Henry County. Some of the companies, such as those commanded by Captains Jesse Heard and Peter Perkins, passed through Franklin County and Maggotty Gap on their way west. At least one company, Captain James Lyon's, rendezvoused at a present-day Franklin County landmark, the Washington Iron Works, before joining the others at Long Island in the Tennessee River (now Knoxville). Throughout the war soldiers marched through the county on the Warwick Road and the Great Wagon Road on their way to suppress Indians and loyalists in the backcountry. In April 1779, for example, Alexander Brownlee caught a stray horse belonging to Count Casimir Pulaski's Legion "on their march to Georgia," no doubt by way of the Wagon Road. The horse was found "Two Miles from Joseph Earleys [Washington] Iron works."[8]

Earlier in the summer of 1776 other troops had constructed a fort on Long Island that they named in honor of Patrick Henry, the first governor of Virginia under the commonwealth. From Fort Patrick Henry the expeditionary force marched more than a hundred miles through the wilderness to the Cherokee towns. Rather than fight, the Indians fled into the hills and the frustrated militiamen burned and looted several of their towns, then marched back to Long Island and eventually home. A similar force followed the same route to the Tennessee in April 1777; this time a treaty resulted. Although the expeditions did not produce any combat, they made the Virginia backcountry relatively safe from attack. Most of the border warfare that occurred, particularly later in the conflict, took place in present-day Kentucky and even farther west.

To protect the backcountry settlers from the Indians, however, some revolutionary troops remained in present-day West Virginia for much of the war. Jacob McNiel, Sr., served on the Greenbrier River in 1776, and in 1777 at Fort Randolph (present-day Point Pleasant, West Virginia). His duties at Fort Randolph included guarding the Shawnee Indians captured after the Battle of Point Pleasant on 10 October 1774. This battle constituted the culminating event in the last colonial campaign against the Indians, which was known as Dunmore's War. The Indians, led by their chief Cornstalk, were defeated by Virginians commanded by Colonel Andrew Lewis. Cornstalk and some of his tribe were imprisoned at Fort Randolph when McNiel arrived there in November 1777. Soon after, a white mob broke into the fort and murdered Cornstalk, who had been much admired by the soldiers. McNiel was

> one of the guards over the celebrated Indian chief Corn Stock—that when he was murdered he this affiant did all he could to prevent—but that it was all in vain the americans exasperated at the depredations of the Indians broke through the guards and killed the said prisoner Corn Stock—to the very great regret of this affiant.[9]

McNiel underscored the atmosphere of fear that prevailed on the frontier when he testified that he "was frequently out against the Indians obeying every call made with alacrity. . . . He worked in the field with his gun close to him and was constantly in readiness to act at a moments notice." After the war McNiel settled in Franklin County, where he died in 1844.[10]

A more immediate threat than the Native Americans to the Revolution in the backcountry were the loyalists who lived in southwestern Virginia, including Henry and Bedford counties (especially on Blackwater River in the latter) as well as the country across the Blue Ridge. Whereas in the northern colonies, such as Pennsylvania and New York, many loyalists lived in urban areas, in the South they were concentrated in the backcountry. Some people remained loyal to the king for economic reasons, some from philosophical motives, and some because they opposed the politics of the revolutionaries. Loyalists were found at every social and economic level, and in every ethnic group, as were their rebellious opponents. Local revolutionary leaders, aided by the militia, rooted out the loyalists wherever they found them.

The most famous, or infamous, loyalist later associated with Franklin County was John Hook, whose career in some ways typified what now would be called an American success story. Hook was a Scottish merchant who lived in Bedford County at New London until 1784, when he moved himself and his store to a plantation just south of Halesford on the Staunton River in present-day Franklin County. Born in Glasgow, Scotland, in 1745, Hook arrived in Richmond, Virginia, in 1758 as an indentured apprentice clerk. He worked for several years at the port of Warwick, in Chesterfield County, just downriver from Richmond. In 1766, when he was preparing to abandon Virginia and return to Scotland, Hook was persuaded to open a store in Bedford County for the Scottish firm of Donald and Company. He moved to New London and ran the store until 1771, when he quit the firm to form a partnership with David Ross, a Petersburg merchant who was probably the wealthiest man in Virginia. Hook built a new store in New London; on 29 February 1772 he married Elizabeth Smith.[11]

Hook's store must have been one of the best-stocked in the area, judging from a list of goods sent to him from England in 1772. He received fourteen muskets ranging in length from four feet to four feet four inches and in bore from .50 caliber to .81 caliber, as well as a thousand "Neat french Gun Flints" and gunpowder. Among the fabrics his store carried were calicoes, muslins, cambrics, and chintzes. He also stocked dutch ovens, skillets, iron pots, teapots, blue and white butter pots, nails, grindstones, paints, tobacco pipes, and shirt-button molds.[12]

When the Revolution became a reality, those very qualities that had enabled John Hook to become a prosperous, self-made man—aggressiveness, stubbornness, self-confidence, ruthlessness, and a prickly personality—made him a thorn in the side of the revolutionaries. The Revolution, Hook probably believed, was a nuisance that threatened commerce and moneymaking; the quicker it was suppressed, the sooner trade would resume its tranquil ways. No doubt Hook was not alone in his views, but he was the sort of man who could not keep them to himself. On 23 May 1775, about a month after the Bedford County revolutionaries formed a committee of safety, its members ordered Hook to appear before them and respond to charges made against him by Charles Lynch. Hook fired back a demand that the charges be presented to him in writing and refused to appear before the committee until it complied.[13]

The committee meekly obliged. It wrote that Charles Lynch had reported a conversation with Hook concerning the protest of a Botetourt County militia company that had been ordered to serve outside the boundaries of Virginia. The two men agreed that there were enough troops in the army already, but John Hook meant that there were more than enough:

> Hook then expressed himself in the warmest manner, & swore by God, there never will be peace till the Americans get well Floged, the sd. Lynch then reproached the sd. Hook with being an unworthy member of Society, & accused him with dispersing a number of Pamphlets wrote against the American cause with an intention of raising divitions among the People, which he did not deny but; endeavoured to justify, by saying that a majority of the Country was of his Opinion, at least he was certai[n] a majority of the People of Bedford were.[14]

Hook appeared before the committee on 27 June and read his response to the charges. "If I said there never would be Peace 'till the Americans get well flog'd, I meant to say the Bostonians," he began. He explained that his opinion about this "unhappy dispute" was that the Bostonians had been wrong to destroy the tea in 1773 and it was also wrong to take their side. As far as the pamphlets were concerned, he admitted that he had acquired pamphlets both for and against the American cause "to inform my Self both sides of the question." Although he had shown some of them around, he did not "recollect of there ever being dispersed by me to any one, except two or three of the inhabitants of this Town and one of lending them to Mr. Robt. Cowan" at Cowan's request. Hook said it had only been his belief that a majority of the people of Bedford County were against "the Present violent Measures"; given his recent experiences, however, he had changed his mind. Hook concluded on a defiant note:

> Since I find my Political sentiments disagreeable to this Committee which I wish ever to live in Friendship with, I assure them that in time to come I will conceil them, and as to the Pamphlets I will deliver them up to the committee to be delt with as they please.
> When I Assure this Committee that I wish the Liberty and Prosperity of this Countrey as sincerely as any of them possibly can do, I hope a difference in oppinion as to the mode of Attaining the same, will not be judged sufficient grounds for declaring one of such Sentiments an enemy to American Liberty.[15]

Privately, Hook seethed. In 1776 he scribbled in a memorandum to himself his thoughts concerning some action the committee had taken that he considered unfair. Had the committee listened to reason, he wrote, it "would have avoided great injustice & been deservedly esteemed, but allas they Have branded themselves for prejudiced Stupid Villans. I am sorry for them."[16]

Although Hook escaped the wrath of the revolutionaries initially, his views were too well known and his temper was too short for him to stay out of trouble for long. On 27 January 1777 he came to court accused of the "Ill Treatment" of Robert Irvine, an officer of the guard. Hook was ordered to post a £100 bond for his good behavior; Robert Cowan (by 1786 a Franklin County resident) and Robert Alexander served as his securities. As Hook left the courtroom, William

Ray assaulted him. Ray not only had to post a £20 bond but was fined fifty shillings for contempt of court as well.[17] One assumes Hook allowed himself a small private smile as he went on his way.

Hook's next encounter with revolutionary hotheads occurred about 18 June 1777, when he was dragged from his house by a mob that threatened to destroy it over his head if he did not come out, then tar and feather him (if he was still alive). Upon promising to go quietly with the mob to the house of one of its members, Hook was assured he would not be harmed. The ringleaders apparently thought he was selling illegal goods at his store. "I was charged," wrote Hook, by William Mead, the mob's leader and a county court justice, "in behalf of the mob at my parell not to carry on any kind of Trade in this County until after Court. . . . I am informed Meads orders was to bring my body dead or alive." Hook either was "persuaded" by this affair, or decided on his own, to improve his standing in the community by taking the oaths of allegiance to the commonwealth and to the United States on 10 October 1777.[18]

Hook stayed out of trouble until 25 July 1780 when he was fined £5 for his "Contempt in Refusing to serve on the Guard over the Prisoners now in Gaol."[19] The prisoners, of course, were other loyalists.

On 28 June 1779 James Ayres, Azariah Doss, and Joseph Greer (a Franklin County resident in 1786) were brought before the Bedford County Court and charged with violating the act of the General Assembly entitled "An Act for the Punishment of Certain Offences" that smacked of loyalism. All three were found guilty. Ayres was fined £100, Doss was fined £50 and sentenced to jail for three months, and Greer was fined £20. Robert Mead faced the same charge on 26 June 1780 and was ordered to pay a £90 fine and spend one hour in jail. Owen Owens was less fortunate; on 24 July 1780 he was fined £50 and sentenced to five years' imprisonment. The next day John Craighead (who lived in present-day Franklin County) was ordered to prison for six months and fined £1,000.[20]

Some of those accused of loyalism were openly defiant. On 29 August 1780 William Cheek, Jacob Feazle, Anthony Epperson, and James Ayres—obviously unrepentant after his earlier sentence—were brought before the Bedford County Court accused of treason. All pleaded guilty and were remanded to jail pending a trial before the General Court in Richmond.[21]

Perhaps to deter other loyalists, the Bedford County Court levied heavy fines on those found guilty. On 25 September 1780 Robert Cowan was fined £20,000; the next day John Murphy was fined £5,000. The court sentenced each man to a year in jail. Although the sentence was carried out immediately, the court did show some leniency toward the pair. It allowed them to

> associate together as also the wives & Children & Relations of the said Cowan and Murphey may have access to them as often as they shall think fit . . . [and] leave is granted them to Walk out once a Day or oftener if it should appear necessary for their Health under a Strong Guard not to Exceed 800 Yds. from the Ct. House.[22]

During the court meeting of 27 September Robert Mead came forward to post bond for his appearance at the next court. Once again he had said or done something that resulted in a charge of loyalism. He posted a £20,000 bond with Archelaus Moon, William Moon, and John Hook as securities.[23]

Mead was lost in the shuffle, however, when the court next convened on 30 September and 2 October. Eleven men, including John Bradshaw, Richard Bundy, Bernard Feazle, Edward Hore, Daniel Huddleston, Thomas Hunt, Josiah Meadors, Randolph Richeson, Thomas Watts, Rowland Wheeler, and Joseph Wilson pleaded guilty to taking an oath of loyalty to the king and administering it to others. All were remanded to jail pending their trial before the General Court. Robert Mead's case did not come before the court. By 1786 Bundy, Hunt, Richeson, and Watts were living in present-day Franklin County. Perhaps they were part of the nest of loyalists reported living on Blackwater River during the war.[24]

If the court had difficulty keeping track of all the cases before it, John Mead (the county jailer) clearly was confused by all the activity at his jail. On 23 October the Bedford County Court sympathetically acknowledged his problems:

> John Mead Gaoler having been at considerable expence in Maintaining a Number of Disaffected Persons confined in the Gaol of this County. The Court are of Opinion that his acco[unt] here produced for the same is Reasonable and Do Recommend it to the Assembly of Virginia to make him such allowance as the Uncertainty of the Number of Persons to be Confined & the time of their Continuance in custody rendered it too uncertain for the appointment of a Commissary for that Business.[25]

Mead earlier had forwarded his accounts to the state auditors of public accounts for payment, but they refused to give him "a warrant for anything more than the Common fees allowed for Criminals."[26] The General Assembly agreed on 5 December to pay him £3.12 (three pounds, twelve shillings) per day per prisoner. Evidently this did not satisfy Mead, as he resubmitted his request and was allowed £4.10 per day on 19 December.

After the frenzy of accusations and trials near the end of 1780, the loyalist threat in Bedford County appears to have subsided. If the harsh response of the county court toward its "disaffected" citizens had not conciliated them, it had at least elicited their surly silence.

Henry County, to judge from the court records, either never had as much trouble with loyalists as Bedford County, or dealt with them outside the court system. All was quiet until 21 January 1777, when four reputed British subjects (Archibald Gordon, Arthur Robinson, George Elliot, and Walter Lamb) were ordered to appear before the Henry County Court to show cause why they should not be considered enemy aliens and be made to leave the country. On 30 January Gordon and Robinson appeared before justices John Salmon, Edmund Lyne, Abraham Penn, and Peter Saunders. The court found that an act of the General Assembly concerning enemy aliens did not apply to Gordon, who became a resident of Franklin County in 1786; because Robinson "has shewn a Friendly disposition to America," he was "acquitted." Elliot and Lamb, however, were found subject to the act and were reported to the governor.[27]

Between 1779 and 1781 seven other Henry County residents appeared in court to answer charges ranging from treason to conspiracy to "being inimical to the Common Cause" or to the "rights & Libertys of America." Three of the men—

Robert Bowman, John Graham, and Sams (first name not given)—were acquitted. The others—James Bennett, Robert Holliday, William Greer, and Abraham Cristman—either confessed or were found guilty. They were fined £1,000, £100, £500, and £2,000 respectively. In addition, Greer posted a £10,000 bond for his good behavior and Cristman was sentenced to four months' imprisonment.[28] Two of the men (Greer and Holliday) were Franklin County residents in 1786.

The center of loyalist activity in Henry County appears to have been in present-day Patrick County. According to Major John Redd, a Henry County militia officer, "The people on the headwaters of Dan and Ararat Rivers were mostly Tory, they had no regular organized parties among them, they generally met in small parties, robbed and murdered and then cleared out."[29] The story of this war within a war may never be fully told because of the lack of supporting records.

During its session begun in October 1780, the General Assembly passed an act offering pardons to those in Bedford, Botetourt, Henry, Montgomery, Pittsylvania, and Washington counties who may have taken oaths of fidelity to the Crown or enlisted in its service but who had not committed any overt acts harmful to the revolutionary cause. The act mentioned by name fourteen prisoners in the Henrico County jail who had been transferred there from Bedford County to await their trials before the General Court: James Ayres, Richard Bundy, William Cheek, Anthony Epperson, Bernard Feazle, Joseph Greer, Edward Hore, Daniel Huddleston, Thomas Hunt, Josiah Meadors, Randolph Richeson, Thomas Watts, Rowland Wheeler, and Joseph Wilson. The act provided that the prisoners, most of whom had been remanded to jail in September and October 1780,

> may take and subscribe the oath of allegiance in the presence of some justice of the peace of the said county of Henrico; and upon certificate to the governour from the justice administering the same, and notification thereof from the governour to the keeper of the public jail, shall be by him discharged . . . [and] fully and absolutely pardoned, exempted, cleared, and exonerated from all and every punishment, pains, and penalties whatsoever for the said offences.[30]

The offer of pardon was only partially successful in conciliating the disaffected of Bedford County. On 23 March 1781 James Callaway, the county lieutenant, wrote to Governor Thomas Jefferson that

> a considerable part of the late Conspirators in this County have Refused to accept the Benefit of the Act of Pardon intended for them, and that the Conduct of a part of those who have complyed with the Law, together with the others, Discover a Disposition to become Hostile, whenever it may be in their Powers, Several Informations having been Lodged with me to this purpose already, Threats have been giving out. I understand they never were oblig'd to their Country for this Act of Pardon, as they were taught by their Attorneys that they had done nothing Capitol for which they could be Punished, and that they were not in need of such a Law.[31]

Jefferson replied on 5 April that it was his opinion that

such of the Conspirators as knew of the Act of pardon and failed to comply with the Condition of it by taking the Oath of fidelity before the last Day of February, and those who did not know of it and on being informed shall refuse to take the Oath ought to be put into a due Course of prosecution.[32]

Even so, no other loyalist prosecutions were recorded in the court minute books of Bedford or Henry counties.

Many of the alleged loyalist plots existed only in the minds of suspicious revolutionaries who took angry threats seriously. Sometimes, however, such plots really did exist. Just across the Blue Ridge from Bedford and Henry counties in Montgomery and Washington counties, for instance, loyalists planned to kill Colonel William Campbell (commander of the Washington County militia), capture the state lead mines near modern Wytheville, and raise a fighting force to join the British army. Colonel William Preston, the head of the Montgomery County militia, complained in July 1780 "that Tory leaders in his neighborhood had promised to divide his land among their followers, even blazing trees to mark the planned boundaries."[33]

In the face of such plots—or with even less provocation—it was little wonder that the supporters of the Revolution reacted swiftly and often violently. When William Campbell and Walter Crockett, commanding militia from Washington and Montgomery counties, captured a group of loyalists in the summer of 1779, they "shot one, Hanged one and whipt several."[34] In Bedford County James Callaway joined with Charles Lynch and others in suppressing loyalists and their plots (real or imagined) with such vigor that he was among the creators of what became known as Lynch Law. After the war the General Assembly passed an act to protect Callaway, Lynch, and their followers from any prosecutions arising from their quasi-legal activities.

The actual threat to the Revolution from loyalists was directly related to the proximity of the British army. Except for flurries of combat in Virginia early in the conflict, most of the actual fighting before 1780 took place in New England, New York, New Jersey, and Pennsylvania. The focus of the war suddenly shifted in February 1780, however, when most of the British army landed near Charleston, South Carolina, after a voyage from New York. During the next year and a half the theater of war moved to the southern states between Charleston and Yorktown. Loyalist activity increased significantly, and local revolutionary leaders relied on the militia to suppress their opponents as well as defend against the British army.

The militia was more effective in doing the former than the latter. Generally the militia served in and around their home counties when called to active duty, except for special expeditions such as those to discourage loyalists in Southwest Virginia and the Carolinas in 1779 and 1780, to join Major General Horatio Gates's ill-fated march to Camden in 1780, to face the British with General Nathanael Greene at Guilford Courthouse in 1781, or to march against General Charles, second earl Cornwallis, at Yorktown. The militia's terms of active service usually ranged from a few days to a few months. In contrast, Virginia's Continental soldiers served from Canada to Georgia and their terms of enlistment usually lasted two years or more. In March 1781 Thomas Jefferson estimated the number of militiamen in Bedford County as 1,535 and in Henry County as 1,004.[35] Not all of the service-age men went into the militia, of course. Some were exempted for disabilities and others enlisted in the Continental army.

Two Franklin County soldiers among the many who saw service against the loyalists were Walter Bernard and John Law, Sr. In the summer of 1778 they joined a company of cavalry in the Henry County militia under Captain Jesse Heard, and from then until the spring of 1781 were "engaged in suppressing Tories."[36] In 1780 the company marched with others to North Carolina and then to South Carolina to serve with the militias of those states against loyalists in the backcountry.

For some soldiers from present-day Franklin County the great adventure of the war was the disastrous Battle of Camden, South Carolina. Led by Brigadier General Edward Stevens, about seven hundred Virginia militiamen (including men from Bedford and Henry counties) marched in the summer of 1780 to join the army of Major General Baron de Kalb in the South Carolina backcountry. By the time they arrived on 14 August General Horatio Gates, a former British officer who had settled in Virginia, had assumed command of de Kalb's army. Usually cautious and plodding, Gates decided to attack the army of Cornwallis near Camden. Gates ordered a complicated night march on 15 August that resulted in a collision with Cornwallis's army near dawn on 16 August. The two forces were nearly equal in number (about three thousand each), but with a huge advantage to the British. Nearly half of Gates's army was composed of untried militia, whereas the British force comprised hardened veterans. After the initial skirmish in the dark Gates set up a battle line with the Virginia militia on his left flank, the North Carolina militia toward the center, and the Delaware and Maryland Continentals on the right. At the first British charge the Virginia militia broke and ran, and the rest of Gates's army soon followed. De Kalb's Continentals held out bravely until their general was mortally wounded, then joined the rout. Gates, widely believed to have been one of the first to flee, did not stop until he reached Charlotte, North Carolina, some sixty miles away. The Battle of Camden was regarded at the time as the most total American defeat of the war.[37]

John Boon, a Pennsylvanian and nephew of Daniel Boone serving in the Delaware regiment, later recalled that

> the army suffered much fatigue & hardship marching toward where the enemy were encamped. They had to cut a road fourteen miles from Santee river toward Camden Called Gates Folly. the army while on the march toward Camden at night encountered a party of the British and halted. the next morning the two armys met & fought but the enemy prevailed & Genl. Gates & his army was [outmaneuvered] and dispersed. He [Boon] served in the battle and was among the last to retreat. He saved himself from the previous enemy by fleeing through an unknown Country as well as his fatigue & previous hardships would allow. at length he arrived at the Washington Ironworks in Henry County where he remained some years. . . . After that dreadful defeat the Officers and soldiers with whom he served had all fled in different directions. He knew not where to find them so as to get a discharge consequently he did not get a discharge.[38]

Boon apparently discharged himself from further service.

At the Battle of Guilford Courthouse the Virginia militia made up in part for its sorry performance at Camden. Militiamen from Bedford County commanded by Colonel Charles Lynch and their neighbors from Henry County under Colonel

Abram Penn played essential roles in the battle on 15 March 1781. General Nathanael Greene, the American commander, drew up three battle lines at Guilford Courthouse to defend against an attack by Cornwallis. Lynch's riflemen were in the first line, which was composed largely of Continentals. Greene placed most of the Virginia militia in the second line under Brigadier Generals Edward Stevens and Robert Lawson. The third and principal line stood in the rear of the American force on the crest of the courthouse hill; it was composed almost entirely of Continental soldiers from Virginia and Maryland. Most of the militiamen were protected by woods, which may have helped them steady their nerves as they watched the red British ranks coming forward. The militia fought well, delivering one volley after another with good effect before retiring. When the British finally struck the third American line the fighting grew intense and bloody. At last Greene withdrew his army and left the field to Cornwallis. Although technically a British victory, the Battle of Guilford Courthouse proved so costly to Cornwallis that he soon abandoned the Carolinas and began his ill-fated Virginia campaign. The American militia gained confidence (this time it was the Maryland Continentals who broke and ran) and experience, and because Greene had removed his army from the field on his own terms the affair was seen as a moral victory for the revolutionaries. It was a major step toward Yorktown.[39]

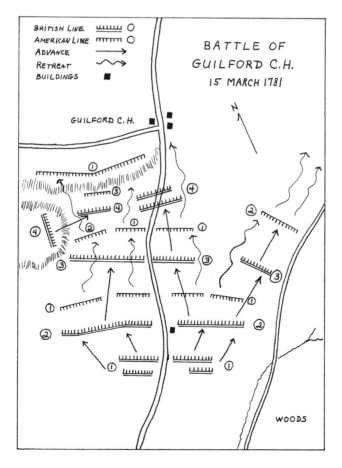

(John S. Salmon)

John Vest, who settled in Franklin County after the war, was present at Guilford Courthouse although he scarcely mentioned it when he applied for a pension years later. He enlisted in Buckingham County for a two-year stint in the southern theater in 1780 and 1781. He "joined General [Nathanael] Green[e] at Hanging Rock on the Yadkin River in North Carolina, marched from there to Booker's Ferry in Virginia thence to Guilford, and was in that battle[,] also in the battle of Ninety-Six and marched from there to Congaree Fort."[40]

Some soldiers of the Revolution served long tours, while the careers of others ended quickly. Thomas Booth, for instance, who was a resident of Bedford County at the time of his enlistment, joined the company of Captain Gross Scruggs in the 5th Virginia Regiment of the Continental Line on 15 February 1776. Just five months later, in July, he was discharged because of a wound to his right hand. As a result of the wound, Booth lost the middle finger and much of the use of his forefinger, which limited the amount of labor he could perform. On 28 October 1786 Governor Patrick Henry ordered Booth placed on the state pension roll; he received £6 a year thereafter.[41]

A comrade of Booth, George Asbury, fared much better. Born in 1756, Asbury also joined Captain Scruggs's company in February 1776, but instead of being wounded he served out his full two-year enlistment. He was discharged at Valley Forge, Pennsylvania, in February 1778, having fought in the Battles of Brandywine and Germantown. Asbury married Mary Hatcher on 27 May 1785 and died in Franklin County on 12 November 1834.[42]

Abraham Abshire served his tour of duty within the state of Virginia. Born in 1763, Abshire was sixteen years old when he was called into Captain Moses Greer's company of Bedford County militia in 1779 and marched to protect the state's lead mines in present-day Wythe County. Even before that tour, he had served at least one other against the loyalists in the nearby mountains; Abshire went on several similar expeditions while in service. In 1780 or 1781 he marched with Greer's company to Petersburg, probably to guard military supplies there. He was pensioned in 1832 and died on 28 July 1842.[43]

John Campbell was born in Halifax County in 1760 and was living in Pittsylvania County when he enlisted in 1777 in Captain John Donelson's company of militia. The company left Pittsylvania County and marched to Long Island on the Holston River on 1 March 1777. Campbell returned home on 17 July. Later he moved to Bedford County and marched under Captain Charles Callaway and Lieutenant Jacobus Early to Yorktown, where he witnessed the surrender of Cornwallis on 19 October 1781 and was discharged by Early the next day. Campbell resided in Franklin County after the war.[44]

Eiles Cooper, who was born in 1746, served two tours of duty from Bedford County early in the war. About 1775 he went to the lead mines in present-day Wythe County to guard them against a possible Indian attack. According to his recollection, he marched with the militia company of Captain Henry Buford to the Holston River against the Cherokee in 1776. He died in Franklin County on 4 December 1843, at the age of ninety-seven.[45]

Richard Dale moved from Richmond County to Bedford County about 1768, when he was nine years old. In February 1780 he was called out for six months' service in the militia; he marched to Richmond, then across the river to Manchester to guard the magazine there. When Richmond was threatened by the

British, the magazine was moved to New London, and Dale went with it. He was called out again in 1781 to march to Yorktown, but because he found it "inconvenient" to leave home at that time he hired a man to serve as his substitute and remained in Bedford County. He died in Franklin County in February 1841.[46]

One soldier who lived in Franklin County after the war served twice as a substitute for other men. Sterling Cooper was born on 20 June 1760 in Amelia County. As an adventuresome teenager, he enlisted as a substitute in Lunenburg County for Lowry Booker and marched to Valley Forge, Pennsylvania, where he was attached to the 14th Virginia Regiment of the Continental Line. Cooper fought in the Battle of Monmouth; he was discharged soon afterward and returned home. He served several three-month tours with the Lunenburg County militia— one of them as a substitute—and was drafted near the end of the war. On his last tour he marched to Yorktown and was present at the surrender. After the war he moved to Franklin County, where he died on 9 January 1836.[47]

During the war soldiers usually enlisted or assembled for duty at courthouse towns. In the backcountry that later became Franklin County, however, the Washington Iron Works became the landmark where the militia came together. Lewis Davis, for instance, mustered there in 1776 as a resident of Henry County and marched under Captain James Lyon to the Holston River. He served several three-month tours with the Henry County militia and was at the Battle of Guilford Courthouse and the surrender at Yorktown. He even served a tour after the surrender to help transport supplies to the American army on the Potomac River. He died in Franklin County on 8 December 1841, aged eighty-seven.[48]

William Wade served in both the northern and the southern theaters of war. He enlisted in the 5th Virginia Regiment of the Continental Line in 1776, he later testified, and soon thereafter he and his comrades

> were marched to Williamsburg, thence to Suffolk, thence to Norfolk, thence to Portsmouth, thence back to Williamsburg, thence to Little York from thence took shipping and went around the head of Elk [the head of Chesapeake Bay in Maryland], thence marched and joined General Washington's army at White Plains [New York]. That he was in the battles of Germantown and Brandywine and remained in General Washington's army until he was discharged by General [Peter] Muhlenburg at the Valley Forge, after serving two years. . . . he was enlisted again [by the summer of 1779] for eighteen months under Captain William Norvell, in Hanover County, Virginia, in the First Virginia Regiment, commanded by Colonel William Parker, and joined the Bragade at Petersburg under Capt. Thomas Parker and marched to Georgia where the Brigade was commanded by General [Charles] Scott, thence to Savannah in Georgia, where on the siege of that place [in the fall of 1779] he was wounded in the leg. Thence he marched to Charleston, South Carolina, where the said Colonel Richard Parker was killed and where he was taken prisoner when the place was surrendered [on 12 May 1780] to Clinton and Cornwallis. That he made his escape from the British Barracks on the day on, or thereabouts on which the said last term of service expired, by which means he did not obtain a discharge for the last term of service.[49]

Most of the accounts left by veterans of the revolutionary war are so brief that it is difficult to get a sense of just what the men experienced or witnessed. When a soldier wrote that he fought in a certain battle, it is possible to learn in general terms what he may have done, but the specifics are seldom revealed. The account left by Thomas Craig is an exception to the rule. Craig was born in 1751 in Albemarle County and in 1776 enlisted there in a company commanded by Captain John Marks and attached to the 2d Virginia Regiment. He took part in the Battles of Germantown, Brandywine, and Monmouth, and—most notably—at the capture of Stony Point, in New York.

Stony Point was a fortified position on the Hudson River about twenty-five miles north of New York City. The British had captured it in June 1779 but were slow about strengthening the fortifications. Washington ordered General Anthony Wayne to capture the post in a surprise attack, which took place on the night of 15–16 July. Before the attack Wayne offered a reward of $500 to the first man to enter the enemy works. Thomas Craig was not that man, but he was not far behind. The honor went to François Louis Teissedre de Fleury, a French aristocrat who had joined the American army as a volunteer and distinguished himself in several battles. Craig later reported that he saw Fleury "enter the fort and heard him exclaim he would not take, naming some sum [probably $500], for the enemy's flag when he took possession of it."[50] During the war Congress ordered the striking of only eight medals, and three of them were for gallantry at Stony Point; one went to Fleury.[51] The fighting at Stony Point was vicious, hand-to-hand combat, and many of the troops involved were Virginians. Indeed, of the first five men into the fort, two were from Virginia.

Another postwar resident of Franklin County took part in a near-legendary event of the Revolution, Washington's crossing of the Delaware River at Trenton, New Jersey, on Christmas Day 1776. Thomas Dunn, who was born in October 1750 in Ireland, immigrated to Pennsylvania in 1771 and enlisted in a Pennsylvania regiment in August 1776. He later testified that he

> was marched from Philadelphia to Trent-Town, New Jersey, from thence to Prince Town in New Jersey under the Command of Genl. George Washington and was in the Battle at Trent-Town, new Jersey, and assisted in Killing and Taking about 1500 Hessions whose Cammanders names was, Ralph, Kniphousen, [and] Losburg.[52]

Dunn was discharged after the Battle of Princeton but later served another tour. After the war he moved to Campbell County, Virginia, then to Franklin County in 1800. He died there on 18 February 1838.

At least two free blacks who later resided in Franklin County served in the revolutionary army. William Cuff, who was born about 1760, served in the Continental Line under Captain Samuel Wilson "and was afterwards attached to Capt. Stribling's Company in Colonel Campbell's Regiment . . . [and] was discharged from the service in the County of Rowan, North Carolina."[53]

Sylvester Beverley enlisted early in the war for three years from Buckingham County. Later he testified that he served

> under Captain John Nicholas and was soon afterwards attached to the 1st Virginia Regiment on Continental Establishment, commanded by Colonel

George Gibson. That he served the time for which he was enlisted and at the expiration thereof received a discharge from his commanding officer at Lancaster, Pennsylvania. That he marched to Williamsburg [after he first enlisted], from thence to Alexandria where he with other troops was innoculated for small pox. After his recovery he marched to Valley Forge and remained there during the winter thence marched northward and remained there another winter.[54]

Although Continental soldiers generally served for longer periods of time than did their counterparts in the militia, an active militiaman could spend much of the war in the field in short tours. Such was the case of Moses Greer, Sr., one of the founding justices of Franklin County. Born in Maryland on 2 June 1744, Greer settled in Bedford County, Virginia, before the war. Years afterward, as an old man of eighty-eight, Greer remembered his role in the creation of the United States. Referring to himself in the third person, Greer testified that he

commanded a company of militia in actual service in the year 1779—two full terms of service to-wit, six months, that during the said six months his company and others were stationed at the lead mines in Grayson County, Va., not far from the Carolina line, the object to protect said mines from the Indians and Tories, that he repaired to and remained at said mines above by the orders of Col. James Callaway. That he marched from his then and now place of residence to the mines, to-wit from Bedford—now Franklin County. After the service above in which he gave entire satisfaction, [he] received from Gov. Jefferson a special commission as Lieutenant in a company of volunteers to serve under General [Robert] Lawson. . . . [He] being devoted to the cause of independence tho' a captain [in the militia] accepted this appointment and repaired with his company to Petersburg where he joined the army under General Lawson—that the captain being absent, he filled his place, that he served about three months in the service at this time, when not being wanted longer his company was honorably discharged—that his company were what was called minute men under an obligation to march when ordered—that while at Petersburg and vicinity Baron Steuban was attached to the army—and Major Tucker also—that he frequently during the war acted under the orders of those patriotic and gallant officers Col. Charles Lynch, Col. William Leftwich and Col. James Callaway. That he marched with his company at another time into North Carolina, the object was to attack the Tories at Kings Mountain. That from the circumstance of the greater distance he and his company had to march, he did not arrive till the battle was over, but by forced marches he got there in a very short time after the battle. That at this time he was out at least three months. That he was out on various tours besides those enumerated after the Tories on the North Carolina line and in the mountains to which they had repaired in great numbers—that he was on the march to York Town when the British surrendered. That his zeal in the cause of American independence is well remembered by many old persons yet living and has been rewarded by honorable promotion in civil life since the war. He was after the war elected to the state legislature from Franklin County nine years. He was made a member of the County Court and is now the presiding judge of that court. That from age and bodily infirmity he can no longer attend court, being nearly blind and unable to ride or walk about with being in danger of falling. . . . [He] verily believes he was in actual service more than two years that he considered himself a volunteer thro' all his service—that he obeyed every order to enter the service and never quit till discharged—he has lost or mislaid all his discharges and . . . he is now old and poor—and infirm, and dependent in great measure on his children for support.[55]

From the defense of the lead mines to the assault on Stony Point to the victory at Yorktown, soldiers from the vicinity of present-day Franklin County played essential roles. No one could be considered typical because of the variety of service each man saw. The assertion could be made, however, that Moses Greer, Sr., exemplified the spirit of those who fought for independence. Other area residents supported the Revolution politically or financially; a few, such as the pacifist German Baptists known as Dunkards, refused to participate. No one knows what the black slaves in the neighborhood thought about the war. And a small but vocal minority called loyalists actively opposed the Revolution in the face of community censure, fines, and imprisonment. Once the war was over, all these groups had to put it behind them and get on with life. Most succeeded but some did not.

No one clung to a grudge more tenaciously than John Hook. Still stinging from the humiliations he had suffered during the war, Hook attempted in September 1789 to pay back his enemies. He sued John Venable, an army commissary who, in 1781, had impressed two of Hook's steers for the use of the troops. Venable was acting under the authority of several acts that had been passed by the General Assembly late in the war to authorize the taking—rather than the purchasing—of goods needed by the military authorities. This was in response to the problems created by the worthless currency issued by Virginia and the United States: inflation was rampant, paper money was so depreciated that the saying "not worth a Continental" meant that something had no value, and people tired of several years of war were unwilling to sell supplies to the army.

Impressment was not popular, but the government tried to administer the program fairly. Commissioners of the provision law were appointed in each county. In exchange for goods or services the commissioner issued certificates on which were noted the date, the name of the person from whom the property was impressed, a description of the property, its value, the number of the certificate, and the signature of the commissioner or his deputy. The certificates were transferable, which meant that they could be sold or exchanged. In 1782 and 1783 special courts were held in each county to examine and verify all the certificates that citizens cared to submit. Those certificates authenticated by the courts were sent to Richmond, where several commissioners issued warrants to the bearers.

Hundreds of residents of Bedford and Henry counties, as elsewhere in the state, had goods and services impressed. Typically, corn, wheat, whiskey, guns, horses, and cattle were subject to seizure. Sometimes the commissioners issued certificates for such services as shoeing horses, repairing gear, fixing weapons, ferrying troops, and providing meals or "diets." It is impossible to know how much was given willingly and how much was seized while an armed, glaring militiaman intimidated the property owner.[56]

Whether there was some irregularity in the procedure that caused John Hook to feel cheated, or whether he was merely being vindictive is impossible to determine. But one wonders whether, when he met John Venable in the district court at New London in September 1789, his heart sank when he saw who was to represent the commonwealth on Venable's behalf—none other than that preeminent orator Patrick Henry himself.

Hook should have dropped his suit at that point. Instead, he allowed the court and the citizens in attendance to be treated to one of Henry's stellar oratorical performances; Hook emerged a laughingstock. Henry contrasted the sacrifices of the American army with the meanspiritedness of Hook:

> He painted the distresses of the American army, exposed almost naked to the rigour of a winter's sky, and marking the frozen ground over which they marched, with the blood of their unshod feet—"where was the man," he said, "who had an American heart in his bosom, who would not have thrown open his fields, his barns, his cellars, the doors of his house, the portals of his breast, to have received with open arms, the meanest soldier in that little band of famished patriots? Where is the man?—*There* he stands—but whether the heart of an American beats in his bosom, you, gentlemen, are to judge." He then carried the jury, by the powers of his imagination, to the plains around York, the surrender of which had followed shortly after the act complained of: he depicted the surrender in the most glowing and noble colours of his eloquence—the audience saw before their eyes the humiliation and dejection of the British, as they marched out of their trenches—they saw the triumph which lighted up every patriot face, and heard the shouts of victory, and the cry of Washington and liberty, as it rung and echoed through the American ranks, and was reverberated from the hills and shores of the neighbouring river—"but hark! what notes of discord are these which disturb the general joy, and silence the acclamations of victory—they are the notes of *John Hook*, hoarsely bawling through the American camp, *beef! beef! beef!*"[57]

The audience was convulsed with laughter. James Steptoe, the clerk of the court, restrained himself until a brief recess was ordered, whereupon he

> rushed out of the court-house, and threw himself on the grass, in the most violent paroxysm of laughter, where he was rolling, when Hook, with very different feelings, came out for relief into the yard also. "Jemmy Steptoe," said he to the clerk, "what the devil ails ye, mon?" Mr. Steptoe was only able to say, that *he could not help it.* "Never mind ye," said Hook, "wait till Billy Cowan gets up: *he'll show* him the la'." Mr. Cowan [William Cowan, Hook's attorney], however, was so completely overwhelmed by the torrent which bore upon his client, that when he rose to reply to Mr. Henry, he was scarcely able to make an intelligible or audible remark.[58]

Despite Henry's oratorical flair and Cowan's lack of it, the latter evidently succeeded in showing the jury the law, for Hook actually won the case. It was a Pyrrhic victory, however; the jury awarded Hook one penny in damages and another penny in court costs.[59]

Although he must have been bitter, Hook was honest enough to acknowledge Patrick Henry's talents. This unabashed loyalist hired the revolutionary Henry as his attorney in several cases and even wrote him in one instance, "If you will only manage this case for me with the same energy and ability, as you did against me when you defeated the ends of Justice in Venable's case, we shall be sure to win."[60] For sheer brass, John Hook had few equals. When he died in 1808, Hook's estate inventory revealed that he owned two engravings of King George III and his queen, and that they were hanging proudly in his house.

The case of *Hook* v. *Venable*—or at least the account of Henry's oratory—illustrates how quickly the Revolution and its participants passed into the realm of myth and legend. Both Henry and his listeners conveniently forgot, for instance, that there were many who called themselves Americans who would not throw open their fields, their barns, or their cellars, much less the doors of their houses, to the "famished patriots." That failure underlay the very reason for the passage of the provision law that Hook challenged. But Henry's side, not Hook's, had won the war; to the victor went the right to create myths.

Before the turmoil caused by the war was settled, however, area residents had yet another dispute to resolve. It began, in fact, in the midst of the war and dragged on for six years. It was the struggle to create Franklin County.

FOUR

"Called and known by the name of Franklin"

The evolution of the counties from which Franklin was formed reflects the westward march of settlement across the Southside Piedmont of Virginia. Lunenburg County was carved out of Brunswick County in 1745 and encompassed the present-day counties of Lunenburg, Mecklenburg, Charlotte, Halifax, Campbell, Pittsylvania, Bedford, Franklin, Henry, Patrick, and the southern third of Appomattox. Halifax County, which included Pittsylvania, Henry, Patrick, and Franklin south of Blackwater River, was established in 1752. Bedford County was formed in 1753 and included Campbell and that part of Franklin lying north of Blackwater River. In 1766 Pittsylvania County was formed from Halifax, and Henry County was created from Pittsylvania in 1776. Bedford County was divided in 1781 to form Campbell County, and Henry County was divided in 1790 to form Patrick County. Meanwhile, in 1785, Franklin County was created from the northern half of Henry County and that part of Bedford County lying south of Staunton River and north of Blackwater River.

Few subjects stirred up as much local controversy in eighteenth-century Virginia as a proposal to divide an old county and form a new one. The enabling legislation for a new county usually required its justices to determine its geographical center and construct the county offices there. Generally the area of a new county was large but sparsely settled. As time went on and the settlements grew thicker some residents found themselves separated from the courthouse by such physical barriers as mountains and watercourses. Bad roads and weather and swollen streams sometimes barred them from the legal and social amenities of the court village. Eventually the distant settlers grew numerous enough to demand their own county and facilities in a more convenient location. Yet the residents near the existing courthouse often objected, citing the loss of tax revenues that would accompany the removal of land and population from the now-old county. They also pointed out that a division of the county would require that the

63

courthouse, which probably was not yet paid for, be moved as the geographical center of the old county changed. Sometimes there was little opposition but often the arguments dragged on for years.

In May 1779, barely three years after Henry County had been formed from Pittsylvania, petitions for and against the creation of another county from parts of Henry and Bedford counties were sent to the General Assembly, accompanied by the usual arguments. Those Henry County residents in favor of the plan wanted a new line to be run from the head of Shooting Creek east to the head of Turkeycock Creek to form the northern boundary of Henry and the southern boundary of the proposed new county. Residents of Bedford County living between the south bank of Staunton River and the north bank of Blackwater River (then the northern boundary of Henry County) wanted their area added to the new county. Those in favor of the division complained about the long distances to their respective courthouses and the problem of crossing rivers at times of high water. Those who were opposed belittled the others' complaints and warned of the financial hardships that would result if almost half the tax base was lost. The General Assembly sided with the opposition and rejected the petition for a new county.[1]

The supporters of division continued to present other schemes, which were also rejected. Some residents of Bedford County wanted the county split by a line drawn down the middle from north to south; others opposed this plan.[2] (Eventually the prodivision forces won and Campbell County was formed in 1781.) In Henry County, some residents wanted an area in the western part of the county known as the Hollow to be separated from the rest of the county and joined to Montgomery County.[3] This plan was defeated.

During the next six years the battles for and against the formation of Franklin County were fought with more than two dozen petitions presented to the General Assembly. The arguments varied little. Those in favor of division cited the large size of each county, the bad roads, the many rivers to cross, and the long distance to the courthouse. Those in opposition voiced their opinion that the already high taxes levied upon them would rise even higher if they had to pay for a new courthouse and other buildings.

As time went by, both sides became more imaginative. The advocates for division asserted in 1782 that if the new county was formed and the courthouse fixed near its center, "the Inhabitants in the Extreme Corners of the same, will not have more than 20 Miles to Court a convenience rarely to be met with in the back Country, and [furthermore] only a few Interested Individuals are the Opposers, who Encourage others to the same."[4] To illustrate their point they submitted a sketch map of the proposed county that showed the prominent position of the Washington Iron Works near its center. In 1783 the opponents noted wearily that soon another petition for a division would be presented to the General Assembly, "at which they are Justly alarmed and at the same time concerned to see so many repeated applications to the same purpose shewing a spirit of Obstinacy no less Tiresome to your Petitioners than to this Honourable House."[5] The petitioners preferred to see their taxes spent to secure the freedom of the commonwealth "and not be spent in projects Calculated for the Benefit of a few Individuals. For your petitioners cannot account for the perseverance of some who are Continually stirring up this Matter no otherwise." In 1785 the opponents elaborated on the issue of taxes, maintaining that to escape the already heavy taxes "Very Many of the People from their County are gone & are going to Reside in Georgia & other Distant Places," thereby increasing the tax burden of those who remained behind.[6]

The prodivision forces countered these assertions with numbers that indicated the population of Bedford and Henry counties was growing, not shrinking, and that the number of taxpayers in the proposed new county was remaining stable. In May 1779 residents of Henry County thought the new county would contain about one thousand tithables, or white males above the age of sixteen.[7] Another petition from the proponents of division, filed in November of the same year, estimated that the portion of Henry County to be deleted contained about four hundred tithables and that the new county would have between one thousand and twelve hundred.[8] In 1782 petitioners in Bedford and Henry counties offered firmer numbers: Bedford had 1,576 tithables, Henry 1,500, and the proposed new county 1,000, with 400 coming from Bedford and 600 from Henry.[9] These figures were repeated in several more petitions submitted between 1782 and 1785.

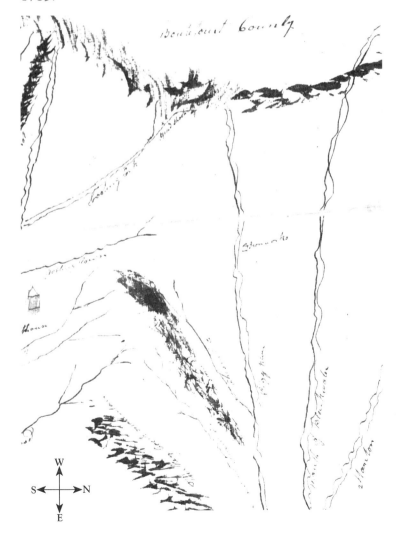

Map of proposed new county, 1782, with Washington Iron Works at center. (Virginia State Library and Archives.)

Finally the legislature yielded to the proponents of division. During the October 1785 session the General Assembly passed an act to create a new county "from and after the first day of January next . . . [to be] called and known by the name of Franklin," and specified that the first meeting of the new county court would take place "at the house of James Callaway, at his iron works in the said county."[10] On 12 December 1785 Governor Patrick Henry issued a commission appointing the justices of the new county.

The court met as directed on 2 January 1786 at Callaway's house at the Washington Iron Works. James Callaway actually owned four "dwelling houses" at the ironworks, besides one cabin and ten "Out Houses."[11] Presumably one of the houses, a bit finer and larger than the others, was reserved for the use of Colonel Callaway when he visited his ironworks. It probably was a one-story frame dwelling that consisted of three rooms of roughly equal size, with exterior brick chimneys that stood at either end of the structure. The two-story house currently owned by Dr. and Mrs. J. Francis Amos is regarded by local tradition to incorporate this structure, a tradition that is not contradicted by the architectural evidence. The court probably met in the first-floor room to the right of the

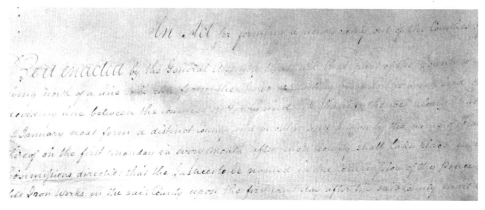

Part of the engrossed bill creating Franklin County, 1785. (Virginia State Library and Archives.)

present central stair hall.[12] The court continued to meet in this building until April, when a "courthouse" was mentioned in the minutes for the first time.[13] This courthouse, a log structure hastily erected near the intersection of Court and Main streets, stood until a brick building was constructed in 1831.[14]

During the period when the new county's leaders met at Callaway's house, they organized the government of Franklin County. At the first meeting, on 2 January 1786, the court and other officers were sworn in: Thomas Arthur, John Gipson, Moses Greer, Sr., Robert Hairston, Swinfield Hill, Jonathan Richeson, Peter Saunders, Sr., and John Smith as justices; Robert Woods as sheriff; William Ryan as deputy sheriff; and Stephen Smith as clerk. The court adjourned until 6 February, when Spencer Clack, Hugh Innes, and John Rentfro took the oath as justices; Robert Williams as commonwealth's attorney; and William Cannady, James Prunty, John Smith, Edward Stewart, John Stewart, John Terry, and George Wright as constables. In addition, John Booth, Sr., Thomas Charter, Joel Cheatwood, Asa Holland, Will Martin, Tobias Miller, Shores Price, William Rentfro, George

Turnbull, William Walton, and Peter Wood were each appointed road surveyor—a thankless job that required each surveyor periodically to call out gangs of his neighbors to repair the county's dusty ruts and mudholes. Having attended to law, order, and transportation, the justices next appointed themselves the personal property tax collectors.[15]

The court largely completed the organization of the county government during its March meetings. The justices recommended Hugh Innes to Governor Patrick Henry for appointment as coroner and John Dickenson as county surveyor. They appointed Moses Greer, Sr., and Robert Hairston as commissioners of the land tax and selected Obadiah Richardson to be a deputy sheriff. They also appointed additional road surveyors: Thomas Arthur, James Beaver, John Divers, Isaac Rentfro, Daniel Richardson, and Samuel Webb.[16]

Relatively little is known of the lives of the first justices of Franklin County. Hugh Innes probably was the court's most eminent member, having served successively on the courts of Pittsylvania, Henry, and Franklin counties. He also represented Pittsylvania and Henry counties first in the House of Burgesses (1769–1774), then in the first revolutionary convention (1774), and finally in the House of Delegates (1783). He lived in southeastern Franklin County near Snow Creek and the Pittsylvania County line, close to Old Chapel Church.[17]

Robert Hairston also served as a justice in the three counties of Pittsylvania, Henry, and Franklin, as well as a militia captain during the revolutionary war. He represented Henry County in the House of Delegates during its sessions of 1777 and 1778. Hairston lived near the Henry County line; when he died in 1791 he was one of the wealthiest men in the county. He also was the great-grandfather of Jubal A. Early.[18]

Thomas Arthur lived on the north side of Blackwater River on Maggodee Creek not far from Boones Mill. He proved to be one of the most contentious members of

The Farm, site of the first meeting of the Franklin County Court, 1786. 1988 photo. (Virginia Department of Historic Resources.)

the new court, although he had served on the Bedford County Court. He not only represented Franklin County in the House of Delegates during its 1787–1788 session, but also served in the Convention of 1788 that ratified the new Constitution of the United States.[19]

Moses Greer, Sr., had the longest career on the bench of all of the county's first justices. Forty-one years old when the new court convened, Greer had served on the Bedford County Court and, as his pension affidavit stated, as a militia captain for most of the revolutionary war. He represented the county in the House of Delegates during its sessions of 1793 and 1794, again from 1798 through 1804, and once more in the session of 1806–1807. Greer lived on the north side of Blackwater River near present-day Gogginsville. He died at the age of eighty-nine in 1834.[20]

Peter Saunders, Sr., resided in the western part of Franklin County, near the headwaters of Pigg River, at his plantation called Bleak Hill, in one of the few frame dwellings in the county. A former justice on the Henry County Court, Saunders also represented that county in the House of Delegates during its sessions from 1778 to 1785. His colleague in the chamber from Henry County for most of that period was none other than Patrick Henry.[21]

Swinfield Hill was the only justice who actually lived at the courthouse village. A son of one of the area's early settlers, Hill had been a member of the Henry County Court and commanded a militia company at the Battle of Guilford Courthouse. He represented Franklin County in the House of Delegates in 1792, 1794, and 1795.[22]

John Rentfro had served as a Henry County justice and, like Hill, had led a company at Guilford Courthouse. He represented Henry County in the House of Delegates in the session of 1785–1786, at which time Franklin County was created, and returned for the new county in 1786–1787.[23]

Robert Woods served as a Henry County justice and as a militia captain. He must have been highly regarded by his fellow justices on the new court for he became the first sheriff of Franklin County in 1786, a high honor. He lived in the southern part of the county near the present-day community of Henry.[24]

Jonathan Richeson lived on Gills Creek in the northeastern section of Franklin County. He had been a Bedford County justice but little else is known about him. The same is true of fellow justice John Smith, who lived on the north side of Blackwater River, near present-day Smith Mountain Lake. After 1796 Smith moved to Montgomery County, where he died in 1820.[25]

Virtually nothing is known of the other two justices, Spencer Clack (formerly of the Henry County Court) and John Gipson (who had served on the Bedford County bench). Gipson either never lived in the county at all or else left immediately after its formation. Clack apparently sold his land in the southern part of the county to Hugh Innes and moved away in 1788.[26]

The new justices found that organizing a county was hard and thirsty work. Fortunately for them and the other officers, their temporary courthouse also was an ordinary—a place where lodging, food, and ardent spirits could be bought at set prices. James Callaway had first been licensed to keep an ordinary at his ironworks by the Henry County Court on 24 September 1784.[27] The justices of Franklin County meeting there on 9 March 1786 likewise granted him a license "for Keeping an Ordinary at this Place."[28] Callaway had anticipated the justices' action and their needs when on 2 February he wrote to his friend Ralph Smith, of Pocket Plantation in Pittsylvania County, to ask him for a cask of brandy. "Unless I get this brandy," stated Callaway, "I am to be without any thing to Drink at our Franklin Court Monday next [6 February]. . . . P.S. Let the Cask be full if Possible."[29]

On 6 March—a month after Callaway's cask no doubt was emptied—the justices set the rates that ordinary keepers such as Callaway could charge. The goods and services controlled by the court included "Good West India Rum," "Continent Rum," peach brandy, whiskey, wine, strong beer, cider, breakfast and dinner "If hott," lodging, pasturage, and feed for horses.[30]

After the county was organized, the principal officers appointed, and the tavern rates set, the court soon settled into a familiar routine. The justices heard disputes, rendered judgments, ordered the clerk to record wills and deeds, and supervised the collection of taxes. All these activities resulted in the creation of records that reveal much about the lives of county residents.

The land and personal property tax books for 1786, for example, present a profile of the social and economic structure of Franklin County during its first year with regard to slaveholding, landownership, and the distribution of horses and cattle among the population. Few residents of Franklin County owned many taxable slaves (twelve years of age or older). Only 24 percent of the inhabitants were slave owners; just over 76 percent of Franklin County residents owned no slaves at all. Of the population that owned slaves, almost 25 percent of them paid taxes on one slave; about three-quarters of the slave owners had five or fewer taxable slaves; only 10 percent of slave owners paid taxes on ten or more slaves. The vast majority of Franklin County's citizens—almost 95 percent—either owned no slaves or owned only five or fewer taxable slaves. Theodrick Webb, who probably was the wealthiest man in the county, owned the largest number of taxable slaves, thirty-seven.[31]

It was possible, indeed common, to operate a farm or plantation without owning slaves, but it was nearly impossible to do so without horses. Less than 10 percent of Franklin County's population owned no horses. Half the population owned one or two horses; only 2 percent owned nine or more. David Ross, whose taxes were the fifth highest in the county, owned the most horses, twenty-five.

Cattle were somewhat less common. Almost 20 percent of the county's residents owned none at all. Three-quarters of the resident taxpayers owned fewer than twenty cattle, with half of the total owning between one and six; less than 5 percent of the population owned twenty or more. Robert Hairston, one of the founding justices and the third-wealthiest man in the new county, owned a herd of sixty.

The rarest of all possessions was land. More than half the resident taxpayers in 1786 owned none. No doubt many of these landless taxpayers were young people farming land actually owned by their parents or other relatives; others were renters or squatters; a few were overseers hired by nonresident landlords or landowners who had several scattered tracts to farm. The sizes of single tracts ranged from ten to twenty-two hundred acres, but the average farm contained about two hundred eighty acres.[32] Almost 60 percent of the landowning taxpayers farmed at least one tract of between one hundred and three hundred acres. Only 10 percent of the landowners had tracts of fewer than one hundred acres and only 11 percent owned tracts of more than five hundred acres. The largest landowners—those who owned at least one tract of nine hundred acres or more—constituted less than 2 percent of all landowners.

America in 1786 was a country of much economic promise but almost no real security for the workingman and his family. In an age when there were no pensions, unemployment insurance, banks, paid vacations, health insurance, and little in the way of public assistance, an individual had to create his own security. He thus acquired and kept the resources that enabled him to support himself and his family: land, slaves, horses, and cattle. Owning a large quantity of land did not automatically make a person wealthy or secure. Owning no land at all did not necessarily mean that a person was poor or insecure. It is difficult to measure relative wealth or poverty as it existed in 1786 using the available documentation; it is possible, however, to describe generally what made some persons better off than others.

No one resource was enough to provide the secure source of income that a farmer sought. Land was useful but not absolutely necessary; slaves were even less essential. Both land and slaves could be rented as necessary and paid for in produce or in labor.

Horses and cattle, in contrast, contributed far more to economic well-being. About 90 percent of taxpayers owned at least one horse and 80 percent owned at least one cow. Horses provided transportation and strength for plowing and hauling; cattle provided milk, meat, and—in the case of oxen—muscle power. A person who had neither horse nor cow was at a disadvantage in producing income for himself and his family.

A resident who lacked land, slaves, horses, and cattle was certainly less prosperous than one who had them all. It is easy, then, to distinguish between the poorest and the most affluent members of Franklin County society in 1786, or between those with the lowest and the highest degrees of wealth. It is less easy to distinguish among what would today be called the lower-middle, middle, and upper-middle classes. A person who owned slaves, horses, and cattle but no land probably would be in the middle category somewhere; so would a person who owned horses, cattle, and land but no slaves. Combinations of resources, therefore, are important measures of relative wealth, but so are quantities, to a certain extent. A farmer with four horses and twenty cattle certainly was better off than one with two horses and ten cattle, but was he twice as well off?

The most reliable and universal measuring devices for determining relative wealth are the personal property and land tax lists, which first were recorded for every county in the state in 1782. Even the tax lists, however, measured only quantities of certain articles, not their quality. In 1786 a horse was taxed at two shillings (twenty-four pence), for example, whether it was in its prime or a broken-down old nag. A milk cow was worth three pence in taxes, as was a work ox. A twenty-one-year-old male slave was taxed at ten shillings—the same as a sixty-year-old slave woman. Tracts of land varied in their value per acre, but the lists did not show how many acres were under cultivation, what kinds of crops were grown and their worth, or whether the property contained a house.

There is no accurate way, in short, of measuring the fine distinctions of wealth among individuals. Modern society provides a host of such measures: gross, net, and disposable income; investments; number, age, and type of automobiles;

house value and location; number of television sets; educational level; number of dependents; occupation; number of wage earners; and many others. All that is known of the economic status of Peter Saunders, Sr., in 1786, for example, is that he paid £2.13 (two pounds, thirteen shillings) in personal property taxes for three slaves, four horses, twenty cattle, and himself (each taxable white male paid a ten-shilling tax on himself). He also paid £1.18.2 (one pound, eighteen shillings, and twopence) on two tracts of land, one of 351 acres and the other of 280 acres. His total tax burden of £4.11.2 gave him a ranking of 74 out of 342 different total amounts of taxes paid; this placed him in the upper 22 percent of county residents in terms of relative prosperity as measured by taxes paid. The tax lists, on the other hand, reveal nothing of his income, the condition of his horses and cattle, the size and quality of his house, the number of dependents in his household, whether his children provided him with free labor, how much of his land was in cultivation, or how much income he derived from the county offices he held. Any of these factors might have shown that Saunders probably was more prosperous than mere numbers indicated.

It is difficult to distinguish among social or even economic classes in America. Most distinctions are based on measures—such as income—that have little to do with traditional class distinctions. In Europe, for example, membership in the aristocracy is based on birth and inheritance more than wealth or income; the United States is too young and rootless to permit the growth of a similar class. Here the definition of what constitutes a particular social class varies from one locality to another, but relative wealth usually is the accepted measure, with some attention shown to family prominence. Given the limited types of measures available for late-eighteenth-century Virginia, relative prosperity must be based on known values: horses, cattle, land, and slaves. Perhaps the best measure of prosperity was land. In the least prosperous group were nonlandowners—363 out of 689 taxpayers owned no land, and 338 of the nonlandowners (93 percent) fell below the median land and personal property tax sum of £2.1.7.

At the very bottom of the economic ladder were those who lacked horses, cattle, land, and slaves. Forty-two taxpayers—about 6 percent of all taxpayers—belong to this category; one of them (a woman) paid no tax, while the rest paid ten shillings apiece on themselves. They probably lived a mean existence laboring for others or surviving on what little charity the county offered.

Just above them were persons who possessed one or two horses and perhaps two to six cattle; they had a slight measure of security but were likely to tumble toward the bottom category if only a few of their animals sickened or died.[33] Of 202 taxpayers in this group (29 percent of the total), only half a dozen owned any land. The members of these two categories constituted the poor of Franklin County, who eked out a marginal living.

The next-higher category was composed of residents who generally owned at least three horses, several cattle, and some land; their total tax burden fell below the average, ranging from sixteen shillings to £2.1.3. These farmers could afford to lose a few animals and still maintain their status because of the extra security landowning provided. Almost without exception the landowners possessed at least one horse or one cow; a few owned between one and three slaves. Most of the landowners in this group, which consisted of 266 taxpayers (about 39 percent of the total), owned fewer than the median of 280 acres: 38 percent owned no land, 50 percent owned fewer than 280 acres, and 12 percent owned more.[34] The lower-middle class of Franklin County, therefore, were the subsistence farmers who had some reasonable chance of improving their lot and acquiring more property if their animals remained healthy and their crops were good.

Almost in a class by themselves in this group were thirteen women, six of whom were landowners. Their total tax burdens ranged from only one shilling to nine shillings, eight pence (partly because women were not subject to the ten-shilling tithe, or tax on individuals, that men had to pay). All of them owned either land or animals, or both; none owned slaves. Probably they were widows who had been left some property by their husbands. Those with no land most likely owned a few animals and lived with their children. Their economic status probably was lower-middle class because they were dependent to some extent on their children.

The next most prosperous group was distinguished by the fact that its members were largely slave owners, almost all of them owned land, and most owned horses or cattle or both. Their tax burden was above average and ranged from £2.1.1 to £6.12.6. There were 142 taxpayers—just over 20 percent of the total—in this category. This group constituted the upper-middle class of Franklin County.

The most prosperous of all residents were those who owned the largest amounts of land and slaves. These, the wealthy taxpayers of Franklin County, numbered only thirty-seven or just over 5 percent of the total. All the residents who owned more than ten slaves were in this group; the wealthy owned an average of about eight horses and twenty-one cattle each. Most of them owned several tracts of valuable land and their taxes ranged between £6.15.6 and £32.8.6. The one woman in this group owned no land, but she did own twelve taxable slaves, five horses, and a herd of twenty-two cattle.

It is possible, theoretically, to use the foregoing statistics to concoct some sort of "average" Franklin County resident for 1786; it would also be meaningless because there are several possible "averages." At the bottom of the economic ladder, for instance, the poorest residents constituted about one-third (35 percent) of the population and the degrees of poverty ranged from what is called "grinding" to just below the subsistence level. The middling class—lower and upper—was composed of just under three-fifths of the taxpayers (59 percent). The upper economic class amounted to hardly more than 5 percent of the total. Such classifications do little by themselves to describe the actual conditions under which Franklin County's citizens lived. They do at least provide a means of measuring relative prosperity.

James Akin was an example of a poor man who improved his condition between 1786 and his death by 2 March 1789.[35] He clearly ranked in the lower economic class in 1786: he owned no land and no slaves and was taxed only for one horse and one cow. At the time of his death in 1789, however, he owned a "Dark Bay horse & Bell," a "Sorrel Mare," and a man's riding saddle, as well as eight cattle and one sow and eight shoats. (Clearly, the tax records alone provide an incomplete picture of relative wealth.) Akin was literate, with a library of five books. His household furniture amounted to four chairs, a table, a chest, and two beds. There were two flax wheels, a reel, and two hackles for the use of Jane Akin. They shared a variety of cooking and eating utensils: two pots, a skillet, a small oven, nine pewter plates, one other plate (probably earthenware), three basins, a dish, four knives, four forks, seven spoons and a pair of spoon molds, a cream pot, two mugs, a milk pan, and a bowl. The Akins probably lived in a one-room log dwelling with a single fireplace, for they owned only one shovel and a pair of fire tongs. Their farming equipment consisted of two hoes, an ax, and a wedge; they also had three rawhides.[36] Akin and his wife probably were elderly,[37] and they may have worked as laborers for a more prosperous farmer.

Jacob Hickman, a German settler who was a joiner or carpenter, ranked in the lower-middle class in 1786. He owned two horses, five cattle, and no slaves. He was a landowner, however, with 178 acres valued at seven shillings an acre. When Hickman died in the spring of 1789 his estate, much as James Akin's, had improved. He owned three horses, eleven cattle, a small bull, a sow, a boar, eleven small hogs, and five sheep that provided him with wool. A religious man, Hickman possessed a library consisting of a large Bible, four testaments, and seven hymnbooks. Among his household furniture were four beds, two chests, a small box, and a table, as well as unspecified kitchen furniture and a pepper mill. Hickman owned a man's saddle, three bridles, and a gun. Four small spinning wheels were in the house, as well as a reel and two pairs of cards. He had harvested and stored fifty-seven bushels of wheat using such equipment as four scythes, seven sickles, a pitchfork, and an "Iron Tooth Rake." He also owned a spade, a broadax, five other axes, and two mattocks, in addition to plows, harnesses, and other farm equipment.[38]

Hickman wrote his will on 19 February 1789. In it he left his joiner's tools, as well as his coat, jacket, and hat, to his eldest son, Jacob, who was not yet twenty-one. With regard to his wife Hickman gave unusually detailed instructions. If she remarried she was to leave his land, but she could take with her two cows, her chest and spinning wheel, a bed, and what Hickman called *"housenfernsh"*: "Basons and Plates and Spoons Knives & forks and Such Like." The rest of the property was to be sold and the proceeds "Divided Amongst them All." If she remained a widow, however,

Mid-18th-century books owned by Coles and Doughton families. Clockwise from upper left: To the Pious Country Parishioner; A Pious Companion for Youth; The Book of Common Prayer; The Pilgrim's Progress. (J. Francis Amos, Rocky Mount, Va.)

she is to keep the Land until the Youngest Child is of Age and then She may Turn the Land over to which of her children she Pleases but the Child she turns the Land over too is to Build her a house of hued logs Eighteen and fifteen feet and a shingle Ruff and Laied above and Below with Sawed Plank and Two windows Eight Lights in Each and a Stone Chimney Built in the Middle of the house[, which] is to be Bilt where ever She Chose it to be Built.

She also was to receive an acre of meadowland and an acre of "Good Tendable Ground." Her children were to dung or fertilize the land every other year and provide her with two cows, all the grass and produce she needed, and twenty bushels of "Good Clean Wheat" and fifty pounds of beef annually. She also was to be provided annually with flax, hemp, and wool, and "one pear of Good Shoes."[39]

Henry Guthrey was a member of the upper-middle class in terms of total land and personal property tax paid. After he died in the summer of 1786 his property was inventoried and appraised. According to the personal property tax list he owned five taxable slaves, two horses, and ten cattle. His inventory, which was taken on 29 September 1786, revealed that he owned six slaves (one of them a child); a horse, a mare, and a colt; ten cattle; and nineteen hogs. He also owned two beds and furniture, three "Bed Steads and Cord," five chairs, two tables, a chest, a loom, a flax wheel, one "Silver Spoon & [a] Candle Stick," earthenware,

Household articles used by Franklin County residents. Back row: *wall sconce; candle mold; locally made redware covered jar; dunbull or bullroarer; pierced tin lantern.* Middle row: *egg basket; cow horn used for calling; pewter plate; iron spice mortar and pestle; burl wood chopping bowl.* Front row: *fat-burning lamp; flesh fork; iron dinner plate; skimmer; iron beaten-biscuit beater.* (J. Francis Amos, Rocky Mount, Va.)

knives and forks, "Potts & ovens," and the usual assortment of farming equipment.[40] Guthrey also owned two tracts of land, one of two hundred acres valued at thirteen shillings, eightpence per acre, and the other of one hundred acres valued at only two shillings, sixpence per acre. In his will, which he wrote on 20 October 1785, Guthrey left all his property to his wife, Penelope. He directed that at her death his estate was to be sold and the proceeds divided equally among their twelve children, after deducting the amounts he had given several of the children during his lifetime.[41]

Richard Edmondson was one of the wealthiest men in the county in 1786, according to the tax lists. He owned twelve taxable slaves, three horses, and eleven cattle, as well as two hundred acres of land valued at five shillings, twopence per acre. On 3 December 1788, when his estate was appraised, the inventory revealed that at his death he owned thirteen slaves, two mares, nine cattle, three beds "and Furniture," one cart, two old saddles, a rifle, two chests, seven chairs, and some old casks, as well as unspecified kitchen and household furniture and plantation tools.[42] Edmondson directed the distribution of his estate in his will: his land was to be sold and the proceeds divided equally among his heirs (except for his son Richard, who already had received his share); his daughter Cochran was left a slave and a bed and furniture; his son James was left a slave; his daughter Polly Smith was left a bed and furniture; his grandsons Thomas Edmondson and Samuel Edmondson each were left "one Childs part" of his estate; and his daughter Elizabeth Craighead was to receive only one shilling. This division was not to take place until after the death of his wife, Priscilla Edmondson, who would have the use of the estate for the rest of her life. After her death the estate was to be divided equally, except his daughters Cochran and Craighead and his son James were to receive no other slaves. Edmondson appointed his wife and his sons Humphrey, Richard, and James as executors of his will.[43]

Clearly, it is difficult to describe a "typical" Franklin County resident of 1786. It is possible, however, to describe a statistically "average" household, based on the land and personal property tax books and Robert Woods's "List of Whit pepol & Buildings" in 1785. From these sources the average household or farmstead appears to have contained about six people, including father, mother, children, and perhaps a brother or sister of one of the parents. The neighbors on the next farm were liable to be relatives, either by blood or by marriage. The family probably lived in a one-room log dwelling with a mud-and-stick or stone chimney; if there was any other structure on the farmstead it likely was a log kitchen. Despite the traditional notion that the backcountry contained abundant cheap land available to all, the odds were about even that the family rented its farm rather than owned it. The farmstead comprised about three hundred acres, most of them unimproved. The average family owned no slaves but relied on its own labor to tend the crops and livestock. Tobacco, corn, and garden crops were grown, and the family owned a couple of horses, half a dozen head of cattle, and ten or twelve hogs. The household furniture was sparse: a few beds, a table, four or five chairs, a chest or two, and odds and ends of cooking and eating utensils were jammed into the small dwelling. It was a difficult, hand-to-mouth existence for most such families, barely above the subsistence level. If the crops were good, the nonlandowning family might purchase some real estate eventually, while landowners might acquire more acreage or livestock or slaves. If the crops were poor, the family packed up and either moved in with relatives or headed westward for a new start.

Such was the social and economic structure of Franklin County in 1786, the year of its founding. Before a century had passed, that structure underwent profound changes, as did the political power, the business community, home and family life, the role of women, the diversity of religious faith, crime and punishment, internal improvements, public charity, and the lives of slaves and free blacks.

FIVE

Founding Fathers and County Politics

I n the eighteenth and early nineteenth centuries the powers and duties of the county court were wide ranging, and included judicial, record-keeping, and executive functions. The court usually divided its judicial role into two parts or sides: law and chancery. On the law side, the court rendered decisions on matters of law, particularly criminal law. If Smith was accused of stealing from Jones, the county justices sat as a court of law to hear the case. The chancery side pertained to matters of fairness in civil cases. If an heir disputed the provisions of a will or some disagreement arose between family members, the court sat in chancery to decide the issue. Many times the court sought to avoid a trial or protracted arguments by appointing referees or arbiters to settle the disagreement between the parties out of court, if possible. Often, however, the court ordered the sheriff to summon a jury and proceed to trial.

The county court served as a court of record. It examined documents, such as deeds and wills, to determine their authenticity. It appointed citizens to prepare inventories and appraisals of estates and recorded them so that heirs would receive their lawful shares.

The power to appoint many local officers, or to recommend individuals for appointment, rested with the county court in its role as an executive body. The court appointed, without review by any other authority, the court clerk and his deputies, deputy sheriffs, constables, commissioners of the revenue, surveyors of roads, and overseers of the poor. Subject to a commission from the governor, but selected or recommended by the county court, were the sheriff, the coroner, all militia officers, and the justices themselves.

Rank and seniority were of paramount importance, particularly among the justices. The date of the commission, and the order in which the justices were named if they were commissioned on the same date, determined their rank and seniority. The position of senior justice was one of high status; in addition, he issued the opinions of the court and signed the court minutes to attest to their accuracy. He also was first in line for other offices, such as that of sheriff.[1]

In the often-futile hope of avoiding jealousies and ensuring the smooth transfer of power, the court followed certain traditions and rules in making its recommendations to the governor. The sheriff, for example, was chosen by the justices from among their number. Because the office provided lucrative fees and emoluments, the sheriff was restricted to two one-year terms before another was chosen; his length of service on the bench was the deciding factor in his selection, because the office was considered the highest honor the court could bestow. Three candidates were recommended to the governor, who knew the rules: the first-named candidate was to be appointed and, unless he died or committed some malfeasance while in office, was to be reappointed when his initial term expired; the second-named candidate became the sheriff-in-waiting to be named first when the current sheriff's two terms were over; the third candidate might or might not move up to second place on the next recommendation—the third spot was largely honorary.

With regard to the appointment of militia officers, custom also held sway. Militia officers took themselves seriously, especially in counties such as Franklin where the frontier spirit lingered into the nineteenth century, and guarded their traditions jealously. Two traditions were particularly cherished: seniority of rank and promotion from within the regiment. Careful attention was given to seniority among officers of the same rank, and only in exceptional circumstances was a vacancy filled from another unit. Not every officer, no matter how long he served, could attain the command of a regiment, but each officer could expect that his opportunity would not be usurped by an interloper from outside the regiment. Any deviations from these customs were greeted with howls of outrage, for honor was at stake.

The first justices of Franklin County were especially sensitive to matters concerning their own dignity and honor. Most of them were unschooled in the law, but they were far from inexperienced in its practice. All of the new county's leaders also had been leaders in Bedford and Henry counties. Of the judges first appointed to the Franklin County Court, Thomas Arthur, John Gipson, Moses Greer, Sr., Jonathan Richeson, and John Smith had been justices in Bedford County;[2] Spencer Clack, Robert Hairston, Swinfield Hill, Hugh Innes, John Rentfro, and Peter Saunders, Sr., had been members of the Henry County Court.[3] Robert Woods, the first sheriff of Franklin County, had been a Henry County justice, and John Dickenson, the county surveyor, had been surveyor of Henry County.[4] Stephen Smith, the first clerk of the Franklin County Court (and of unknown kinship to John Smith), appears to have resided in Bedford County prior to the new county's formation, but he was not an officeholder.[5]

As Franklin County was founded shortly after the Revolution, it is worth considering whether the makeup of the first court was especially revolutionary. In other words, before the war county justices typically were among the economic elite of their communities. Did this trend change after the war, particularly in a backcountry (presumably more "democratic") county such as Franklin? Or did the old pattern by and large continue, with the majority of officeholders being the most prosperous men in the county?

In fact, the fourteen earliest high county officials were among the wealthiest of

Franklin County's citizens. Of the ten justices who lived in the county—John Gipson apparently never was a resident—seven of them (Hairston, Innes, Arthur, Smith, Rentfro, Hill, and Richeson) were in the upper 10 percent of taxpayers, as were the sheriff (Woods) and the surveyor (Dickenson). Peter Saunders, Sr., was only twenty-five pence short of the upper 10 percent; justice Spencer Clack and clerk Stephen Smith were in the upper 18 percent of taxpayers. Only Moses Greer, Sr., could be considered less wealthy by comparison: his taxes placed him in the thirty-ninth percentile. Two factors probably accounted for Greer's position: his many episodes of service in the Revolution and his relative youth (forty-one in 1786) may have prevented him from accumulating as much property as his fellow officials.[6]

Three of the men who took office in 1786 died within a dozen years of the county's formation: justice Robert Hairston (1791), surveyor John Dickenson (1791), and justice Hugh Innes (1797). Hairston and Innes were the third- and eighth-wealthiest residents of the county, respectively, in terms of taxes paid in 1786; Dickenson was within the upper 9 percent of county taxpayers.[7] In Franklin County alone Innes owned 2,924 acres in 1797 (he also owned land in other counties and in Kentucky). Robert Hairston owned 1,684 acres in 1791 and John Dickenson owned 364 acres in 1792. Most of the remainder of the justices' wealth was in slaves and livestock.

Hairston owned twenty-two slaves when he died in 1791, according to his will and the inventory of his estate.[8] He also owned eight horses and three colts, forty-one head of cattle, sixty-three hogs, and seventeen sheep. Besides the usual plantation equipment (plows, hoes, axes, and the like) he owned a wagon and a still. His household furniture consisted of eight feather beds, a "Chest with Drawers," another chest, a desk, four trunks, two looking glasses, two candlesticks, three tables, sixteen chairs, and a corner cupboard. In the kitchen, among the pots, pans, and skillets, were pewter and earthenware plates, dishes, and bowls; a coffee mill; a "Sett tea ware"; and two "Sets knives and forks." Hairston's personal possessions included a silver watch, an "Old Smoothe Bore Gun," and a "Parcell Books old."

Virginia-made Conestoga wagon. (Blue Ridge Institute, Ferrum, Va.)

Hairston divided his property among his wife, children, and grandchildren. Two of his sons, George and Samuel, were given five shillings each; they probably had received most of their inheritance in the form of gifts during their father's lifetime. His third son, Peter Hairston, was left a slave boy, Will, after Peter's mother's death. Hairston endowed each of his daughters—as did most fathers who were able to do so—with her own estate to control independently of her present or future husband. He gave Elizabeth Rowland a slave girl, Cintha, who was to be placed in the custody of George Hairston and hired out, with the income from her hire to be used for the benefit of Elizabeth. To his daughter Mary Smith he gave another slave girl, Delph, as well as a mare, a colt, and a feather bed. Ruth Hairston received two slave girls, Cate and Darkiz, as well as a bay mare and colt, seven head of cattle, a feather bed, a chest, and a trunk. To Agnes Hairston he gave two girls, Rose and Alice, a mare, seven head of cattle, a feather bed, a desk, and a trunk. He left his granddaughters Elizabeth and Martha (the children of his daughter Elizabeth Rowland) a slave woman, her child, and a feather bed, all of which were somehow to be divided equally between the two girls when they came of age. Hairston gave the remainder of his estate, which included his lands, the remaining slaves and livestock, and the residue of the household furniture and farm equipment, to his wife Ruth Hairston. He directed that after her death the property was "to be Equally divided between her Six Daughters viz. Martha Hunter, Elizabeth Rowland, Mary Smith, Ruth Hairston, Jenny Rentfro, and Agnes Hairston." Perhaps Martha Hunter and Jenny Rentfro were her daughters from a previous marriage, because they were not named with the others in Robert Hairston's will. The total value of Hairston's personal property listed in his inventory (which excluded the possessions he had disposed of in his will) was £499.1.6.

John Dickenson, the county surveyor, died in 1791 without a will and left a slightly smaller personal estate than did Hairston. The inventory and appraisement taken on 11 June 1792 valued Dickenson's property at £479.17.6. Among his effects were three male and five female slaves, a horse, a mare, thirty-two head of cattle, forty-one hogs, and twenty-five sheep. The household furniture consisted of four "flock" beds, a desk, a chest, a trunk, and a "meel Chest, Cubert, and table"; interestingly enough, no chairs were listed. Dickenson owned a "rifle Gun barrell and smoothe bore Gun," a "Grammer," and a set of surveyor's instruments, besides the usual farm equipment and kitchen utensils.[9]

To Elizabeth Dickenson, John Dickenson's widow, his estate was not enough for the comfortable support of their children. In 1793 she petitioned the General Assembly for permission to sell part of the land he had owned—land that, according to law, was supposed to be kept intact for later division among his heirs. Elizabeth Dickenson argued that the needs of the present outweighed those of the future for her "Several Small Children the Burthen of which together with the Tax of the land, She your petitioner find two heavy to Bear and raise her Children in Deacency." She asked that she be allowed to sell part of the land and "apply the Money arising From the Sale of Said land to the use and Benefit of the Children." The legislature, reluctant as always to make exceptions to the laws, rejected her petition and left her to struggle along as best she could.[10]

Hugh Innes, the wealthiest (and probably the eldest) of the three county officers, died in 1797. In his will he divided his extensive landholdings in

Franklin, Montgomery, and Patrick counties and Kentucky among his four sons, Harry, Hugh, James, and Robert, and his daughters, Margaret M. Patterson and Elizabeth Eggleston Innes. He also distributed to them money, slaves, horses, and household furniture, and provided for the education and upkeep of his younger sons, Harry, Hugh, and James. Innes also left to Sarah Turley, who was perhaps his housekeeper, the use of a slave girl; also she was to receive "a Cow and Calf, a Sow & Pigs, a Horse worth fifteen pounds and Provision to last for one year after she leaves this house."[11]

Innes's estate was inventoried early in 1798. His slaves numbered twenty-four, including five men, nine women, six boys, and four girls. His livestock included five horses, twenty-nine head of cattle, thirty-six hogs, and seven sheep. Among his farm equipment were a wagon, a riding chair, and a still (which was legal although the liquor was subject to a federal excise tax). Innes's household furniture included three beds, two children's beds, two desks, a bookcase, a "Library of Books," two cupboards, a "Fallen Leaf Table," a "Square Table," nine chairs, and two candlestands. His estate was valued at £1,721.7.0.[12]

That Hairston, Dickenson, and Innes were well-to-do or wealthy men is borne out by the county tax books. Most of their wealth, however, lay in land, slaves, and livestock, not in possessions conspicuously consumed. Except for Robert Hairston's silver watch, no silver or gold formed part of their estates; they owned no silver plate or flatware. There were no paintings or billiard tables or carriages listed (only Hugh Innes's riding chair). None of their houses have survived, but they probably were modest structures of three or four rooms. Most likely Hugh Innes owned the best house, and if it was typical of the finest lower Piedmont dwellings of the late eighteenth century, it could have been a two-story, frame, center-passage-plan house with two rooms on each floor, judging from the number of beds and types of other furniture he possessed. Alternatively, Innes might have owned a large hall-parlor-plan house on the order of Liberty Hall, which was built about 1800 for John S. Hale. No doubt Innes and his fellow officials built well but not too grandly.

The similar backgrounds and experiences of the Franklin County justices, however, did not meld them into a close-knit team. Perhaps their personalities clashed, or perhaps submerged rivalries rose to the surface as these men who had been leaders in their old counties assumed leadership roles in the new county. Whatever the reasons, tensions and animosities shook the court soon after it was formed.

The first justice to come under attack was Hugh Innes, who was accused by his colleague Thomas Arthur of inactivity bordering on loyalism during the Revolution. On 2 May 1786 Innes was recommended by the court to the governor as a proper person to be commissioned the colonel of the county militia. Arthur wrote to Governor Patrick Henry on 20 May, objecting to the appointment and claiming that Innes was

a man Very little Short of Sixty Years of Age, unactive and never Shew'd his Friend Ship to the Common Wealth, in our last War, and have jenerally been Suspected to disaffection, and certainly Not without a Very Just Cause. When a man Wou'd not assist his County, in So Gloomy an Aspect, an So just a Cause

as we were Ingaged in, and Now Cou'd Worthy Citizens bear to be
Commanded by Such an Officer[?]][13]

Arthur was joined in his complaint by another justice, John Rentfro, who was
more explicit concerning what he considered to be Innes's attitude toward the
Revolution: "he utterly Refused to Serve in any Commition & was Ruther
Conceivd by many to be on the contrayry part."[14] Arthur's and Rentfro's
complaints notwithstanding, Henry issued the commission, and Innes took his
oath of office on 3 July 1786. No doubt Henry was familiar with Innes's record as a
member from Pittsylvania County of the House of Burgesses and the first
revolutionary convention, as they had served together, and relied more on his
own knowledge than on anything Arthur and Rentfro had to say.

The next justice to find himself in trouble was Jonathan Richeson, who on 2
July 1787 was accused of declaring "himself Against the Payment of the Publick
Taxes. . . . [The court decided] that the said Richardson was rather Intoxicated and
Expressed great Concern for what he had Said" and therefore acquitted him.[15]
The court probably realized that Richeson's sentiments were shared by most of
the population; the years between the end of the revolutionary war and the
adoption of the Constitution were years of inflation, high taxes, and a shortage of
cash. These problems affected everyone, including the justices. The very next
month, in fact, Thomas Arthur was charged with having "Refused the Payment of
taxes and resisted Government and Endeavored to Excite the People Against the
Same," but he too was acquitted.[16]

If a county officer—justice, militia officer, or other official—moved out of the
county in which he was commissioned, he was supposed to resign his commission or at least cease to act on it. One of the first Franklin County justices, John
Gipson, moved to another county and not only failed to resign his commission
but also performed the duties of a justice whenever he passed through Franklin
County. On 4 February 1788 his former colleagues on the Franklin bench decided
that because of "the Illegal Practices of the said Gipson, he should be Expelled
from his Office and that the Clerk Certify the same to the Executive."[17] Gipson's
name was dropped from the list of county justices maintained by the governor's
secretary.

For about three years the justices of Franklin County appeared to get along.
Behind the scenes, however, another crisis was brewing. On 25 February 1791
Peter Saunders, Sr., the county lieutenant, suspended Thomas Arthur from his
duties as a colonel in the militia because of various charges against him,
including four instances of forgery beginning in 1788, one of perjury, and one of
"Bearing false Witness. . . . Also a Charge of Drawing a larger Sum of Money out of
the Treasury when on the Assembly than you was Entitled to, and for lying and not
Conducting your Self as an Officer of the Militia."[18] One of Arthur's alleged
forgery victims, Thomas Prunty, a former deputy sheriff, swore on 8 December
1789 that he feared death at Arthur's hands. Early in January 1790 Arthur was
forced to take out a bond to keep the peace, but soon he violated the bond when
he "did in a hostile manner with firearms, swords, and other offensive weapons
insult several good Citizens of this Commonwealth."[19]

Arthur's problems may have ended a budding career in the House of Delegates—he represented the county in the sessions of 1787 and 1788 as well as in

the Convention of 1788 (which ratified the Constitution)—but his behavior thereafter made him an anathema to his fellow justices. On 3 March 1791 attorney Richard N. Venable, who was representing a client before the Franklin County Court, reported in his diary that when "Thomas Arthur came on the bench, the rest of the court immediately ran off, and left Arthur sitting like an owl on a chicken roost. Arthur left the bench and we proceeded to business."[20] Five days later the court notified the governor of the charges against Arthur, "from which Charges this Court Conceive his Character to be Infamous, and refuseth to Sit on the Bench of Justice with him"; the justices also complained "that he frequently Interrupts the Court in the Progress of the Business of the County by Taking a Seat on the Bench."[21] The governor—who hesitated to interfere in local matters—initiated no action, but Thomas Arthur took the hint from his fellow justices and "absconded" from the county by August 1791.[22] Apparently Arthur immigrated to Knox County, Kentucky, where he was more successful in his public career, and where he died on 8 September 1833 "full of years and honors."[23]

The county's first surveyor, John Dickenson, died in 1791. In November and December 1792 Hugh Innes was ordered by the Franklin County Court to examine Dickenson's office and deliver all his record books and other papers to Stephen Smith, the county clerk.[24] The reason for the order (other than for good records management) became clear a year later when in November 1793 several county residents, including Moses Greer, Sr., one of the justices, petitioned the General Assembly. They alleged that when they examined Dickenson's records

it appeared that his book of Entries had been very incorrectly kept, and it also further appeared that after his death several persons had access to his said book of Entries, by some of whom there is good reason to believe two pages of the said book of Entries were torn out & secreted or destroyed, on which pages many Entries of land had been made by the sd. Jo. Dickerson in his lifetime on land warrants which have since been found among the papers in his Office. That some of the persons who had access as aforesaid to office of sd. Dickerson have since procured Entries to be made for the same land which in the life time of the sd. Dickerson had been entered in the names of your Petitioners on the warrants above mentioned to have been found in the Office of the Dickerson since his death. That your Petitioners are in possession of testimony from which they think this statement of their case may be substanciated, and which if substantiated will shew a palpable fraud & imposition to have been practiced on them to the annihilation of their most just Rights.[25]

Apparently the General Assembly regarded the petitioners' charges as too vague and impossible to prove, for the petition was rejected.

Even Franklin County's representatives in the House of Delegates were not exempt from accusations and controversies. John Early, one of Franklin County's delegates when the new county was created, almost immediately became the target of a whispering campaign concerning his religious beliefs—or the lack thereof. He defended himself by recording the articles of his faith in the county deed book on 6 March 1786: "Whereas I have been by Some persons Accused with DEASAM [deism] But I Believe the Scriptures of the Old and New Testament to be True and I put my faith and Confidence therein."[26]

Five years later charges of unfair campaign tactics and other irregularities were leveled against attorney Ashford Napier, the successful candidate for the House of Delegates from Franklin County in an election held on 6 April 1791. A number of citizens accused him of causing a witness to fail to testify in a case heard before the Franklin County Court in 1788, of advising a client who was charged with a felony in 1790 to flee the county, and—most seriously—of improperly "treating," or bribing, voters with liquor in return for their votes.

Napier denied the charges and several of his friends offered testimony in his behalf. Stephen Smith, the court clerk, swore that Napier had advised the witness, Mrs. Mary Lyon, not to testify against her son, Edward Lyon, who was accused of stealing a slave from his deceased father's estate, because he thought "it was wrong in Mrs. Lyon to bring her husband's son to Shame."[27] As for the accused felon, James Mason, who absconded before he could be tried for forgery, Guy Smith swore that Napier was convinced he would be acquitted and allowed to remain in the county. Napier had an ulterior motive in advising him to abscond, "as he looked upon the Said Mason in the Light of a Vagrant, and a pest to the County."[28] Alexander Ferguson offered as his opinion "that said Mason being a worthless person, he is glad that he run away & believes the County is fortunate that he is drove from amongst us."[29]

The principal charge against Napier, however, was that of "treating before the Ellection."[30] Joshua Rentfro said that "an agreement existed between the Candidites that no advantage should be taken for any treating before the day of the Ellection."[31] Thomas Charter testified that on 5 March 1791 he was

at the House of James Richardson where a Treat was given that Mr. Ashford Napper was presant, that the treat was said to be given by Mr. Napper who did not gainsay it, that some short time after at Capt. John Early's Muster where a treat was again given, Mr. Napper presant, who there declared himself a Candidate.[32]

James Richardson admitted that he sold to Napier "six or seven bottles of whiskey which he dealt out amongst his friends the freeholders & others in the Neighbourhood who were assembled there that day it being Capt. Skelton Taylor's muster day and his muster ground."[33] Anthony Pate swore that he had sold Napier the "four or five Gallons of Whiskey" with which he treated the crowd at Early's muster.[34] Amos Richardson said he attended a treat supposedly provided by Napier at a meetinghouse on Snow Creek.[35] Napier had a politician's concern with gaining support across ethnic lines, according to Jacob Boon, who

was desired by Ashford Napper to give notice to his Neighbours that on a certain day before the ellection, he the said Ashford Napper would meet at or neir the said Boons to get acquainted with the Dutch [Dunkards] and to drink with them and had Spirits and dealt the same amongst the people at the meeting appointed, that he does not know whos Spirits it was that was drunk.[36]

Hugh Innes knew whose spirits he was drinking, or claimed he did. He swore that about eight days before the late Ellection of delegates for the County of ffranklin he was presant at a treat given by the Candidates, that Ashford Napper was one of the Candadites presant, that Sd. Ashford Napper treated this Deponant to some Rum that he brought there in his Saddlebaggs & that the same was handed about to the rest of the Company, and that it was the constant custom of Mr. Napper when he came to the Store of the deponant to treat freely for some years past.[37]

Daniel Brown, who operated the tavern and store near the courthouse for James Callaway, said that he had been present at most of the treats the others had described and had witnessed Napier disbursing liquor. Furthermore, he alleged,

at some of those places he the said Napier Requested the People to Vote for him, and told them he had a quantity of Rum with which he Intended to Treat them as Soon as the Election was over, and that Agreeable to his Promise he brought a Quantity of Rum to the Courthouse & Distributed [it] amongst the People Immediately after Closing of the pools [polls].[38]

Brown added that during the campaign "it was agreed between the Candadites not to take Advantage of each other with respect to Treating the People."

Actually, such treats were a long-standing and familiar part of Virginia politics. If the candidates gave them, they did so largely because the electorate expected them. Not every treat was as genteel as Napier's, however, and not everyone thought they were a good thing, particularly if one's candidate had been out-treated by the opposition and lost. A traveling minister, the Reverend William Hill, observed a treat that was held at the Franklin County courthouse on 6 September 1790—a court day that also was election day—just a few months before Napier's own election:

I attended the Court of Franklin County to despatch some worldly business, and look after some property which I hold in that County. It was election day. I saw much wickedness this day, and felt much concerned to see my poor fellow mortals drinking and degrading themselves below the brutes that perish, and to hear them cursing and swearing, and using the very language of hell. Some were stripping and fighting, and tearing each other to pieces like incarnate devils. I saw one of the candidates walk through the court-yard with a large wooden can of stiff grog, and inviting the voters to come and drink with him; and what made the matter worse, this candidate had been an Episcopal clergyman before the Revolution. I was so disgusted at this sight, that I determined to go in and vote against him, and did so, though it was the first vote I ever gave, and I had no intention whatever of voting when I came to the place, although the property I had in the County entitled me to a vote.[39]

Despite the challenge to his election, Napier took his seat in the House of Delegates. He only served one term, however—the session held between 17 October and 20 December 1791—perhaps because he had violated the gentleman's agreement not to treat. Napier's life thereafter was not a happy one. In April 1800 he transferred all his property to several trustees in order that it be protected and his business transacted, perhaps because he had suffered a mental breakdown. On 7 September 1801 Benjamin Cook, Josiah Woods, and John Burwell informed the Franklin County Court "that Ashford Napier is in a State of Lunacy, that he Ought to be sent to the Hospital [present-day Eastern State Hospital] in the City of Williamsburg."[40]

This episode signaled the end of major controversies and disputes among the original members of the Franklin County Court and its other early officers. Even the appointment of the old loyalist John Hook, first as a justice in 1790 and then as sheriff in 1806, failed to cause a stir great enough to result in letters or petitions. It was as though the county's founders and their contemporaries had finally exhausted their capacity for outrage toward each other.

Ironically, soon after the county was founded John Hook had been one of the chief patrons—rather than a victim, which might have seemed more likely—of outrage. The target of his spleen was James Callaway, one of his old adversaries from the revolutionary war days. As a Bedford County justice and militia officer, Callaway had been especially vigilant in his pursuit of those whose loyalties lay with England; he joined with Charles Lynch and others to hold the extralegal proceedings, sometimes involving whippings, that became known as Lynch's Law. Although there is no evidence that Hook himself was ever "lynched," he no doubt continued to resent those who had opposed him. He also resented Callaway's status as the great "absentee landlord" of Franklin County who owned the courthouse lot, the surrounding village, and the county's major industry, the Washington Iron Works.

In several ways, James Callaway was the most important and powerful man who never lived in Franklin County during its formative years, or indeed at any period of his life. Born in Caroline County in 1736, Callaway had moved to Bedford County with his parents in the 1750s. His father soon was well established in the political and social hierarchy of the county; James Callaway himself served as a burgess in the legislative sessions held between 1766 and 1768. In 1770 Callaway became a business partner with Alexander and Peterfield Trent, of Rocky Ridge, in Chesterfield County. He built a store in Bedford County, shipped local and Pittsylvania County tobacco to the Trent brothers, and imported English dry goods from Liverpool.[41] Callaway and his partners bragged that the Bedford County store was located in "a large extent of Country, the lands fresh and good for Tobacco, the planters clear of Debt, and no store to interfere with us."[42] The political events of the 1770s soon interrupted the flow of trade, but despite the adverse effect on his pocketbook Callaway became an early and ardent revolutionary. At the beginning of the war he directed the state lead mines in present-day Wythe County. Soon he found that despite the loss of his store, the war presented other opportunities for enrichment. By 1779 he and his father-in-law, Jeremiah Early, purchased a bloomery forge from John Donelson in present-day Franklin County, built a blast furnace, and patriotically named the enterprise the Washington Iron Works. Soon thereafter Callaway joined with Charles Lynch and others in vigorously suppressing loyalists and their plots (real or imagined).

When Callaway and Early (who soon died) purchased and developed the Washington Iron Works in 1779, they created the largest industry in what would soon become the new county. One of Callaway's sons, James Callaway, Jr., was appointed clerk of the Franklin County Court in 1791, a position of power that he held for twenty-two years. Through his intermarriage with the Early family, the elder Callaway was allied with one of the most influential clans to inhabit the county during the first few decades of its existence. For instance, John Early, a son of Jeremiah Early, was commissioned a Franklin County justice in 1789 and served until his death in 1804, when he was holding the office of sheriff. He also represented the county in the House of Delegates in 1787 and 1788, in the ratification convention of 1788, and in the House again in 1790 and 1791.

Callaway's son-in-law, Daniel Brown, operated a tavern and store for him next to the courthouse once it was moved from the ironworks up the hill to what is now Rocky Mount. Callaway, with the heirs of Robert Hill, owned the very lot on which the courthouse sat. He therefore dominated the new county as an absentee landlord who controlled—or was thought by John Hook to control—much of its wealth and political power.

On 8 October 1787 Hook wrote a petition to the House of Delegates in which he charged that Callaway had influenced the selection of the site of the Franklin County courthouse for his own profit.[43] The boundary line of the new county, according to Hook, had not been run in compliance with the act creating the county, but "four or five Miles farther to the South West than was Intended." This had resulted in the "Manifest Injury and Inconvenience of a great Proportion of the Citizens of Said County . . . for the Immoluent of an Individual." The courthouse not only adjoined the Washington Iron Works property, but it also was

> very inconvenient to Water entirely without Pasture and very Scarce of Timber. There is only one Spring and that a considerable distance from the Seat laid off for the Court house and down a very long Steep Hill and no Wells. The Scarcity of Timber Joining Iron Works Lands is too obvious to be pointed at.

Hook lamented that the nearby countryside could not support the needs of the ironworks for grain and provisions, much less the demands of a courthouse village, and that the lack of foodstuffs had caused the shutdown of the furnace in 1787. Then Hook presented the heart of his complaint:

> The fact is that Immediately before the Court house was fix'd on to be on the Lands of Col. James Callaway Joining the Iron Works Land the Members Comprising the said Court before they convened in the business of fixing the Court house appeared to be unanimous in fixing on the Centre of the County by an Actual Survey . . . but to our great Surprise and disappointment on Col. Callaway Petitioning to them for the Court house on his Rocky-mount Land where they were then setting (no doubt with great Eloquence from the Effect) their Worships in Compliance Acquiessed in fixing on the same for a Centre.

Hook urged the House of Delegates to pass an act requiring that a new boundary survey be made to determine the true center of the county and to order that "the Court house shall be removed and fix'd as near the Centre of the County as Convenience Admit."

Either Hook did not submit his petition or he withdrew it before the legislature took any action. Perhaps he was merely venting his spleen against Callaway, whom he described as "very rich and Powerful," because the first courthouse had been built by the time he wrote his plea. He probably realized that no one would want to move the court now that it had settled into the courthouse; furthermore, as a glance at a map shows, Rocky Mount was not so far from the geographical center of the county as to be a great inconvenience to anyone. Hook's opinions, at any rate, did not prevent his being appointed to the court in 1790; he served peacefully enough with his revolutionary colleagues on the bench.

Hook had pointed out the irony that the county did not even own the land on which its courthouse had been constructed; instead it was owned by an absentee landlord, James Callaway. In actuality the courthouse lot and many of the acres that surrounded it were owned jointly by Callaway and Thomas Hill, the heir of Robert Hill. Most courthouse sites in Virginia soon developed into villages or towns. Besides the courthouse, jail, and clerk's office, such villages usually had a tavern, a store, a few tradesmen's workshops, and a small cluster of houses. These buildings required land, however, and all the land around the Franklin County courthouse was controlled by James Callaway, who refused to subdivide his property. Instead he constructed a tavern-store building, an office, a dairy, and two dwellings that he probably rented out.[44] Callaway in effect created his own town and enjoyed the rents and income it provided him.

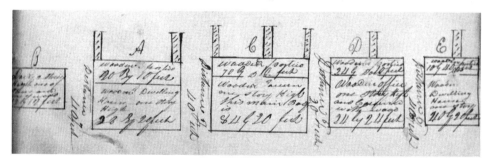

Insurance policy on James Callaway's buildings at Rocky Mount, 1803. Left to right: *dairy, dwelling, tavern, office, dwelling.* (Virginia State Library and Archives.)

Others were not pleased, however. Perhaps taking their cue from John Hook's petition of more than fifteen years earlier, several residents of the county filed a petition of their own with the General Assembly on 14 December 1803.[45] They wrote that they wished to establish a town around the public buildings of the county, "which cannot be the case while the Court House remains on the lands of two Individuals [James Callaway and Thomas Hill] determined not to Sell lots." The petitioners wished to move the court nearer to the center of the county and build a town there. They asserted that

the Court House that was built when this County was first laid off is in a state of decay and will soon require considerable repair [and] the Clerk's office which the Law directs shall be built is untouched upon the Ground as the Court in a late order asserts; that the Tennure by which the land is held is insufficient and that it is inexpedient to expend more money for publick purposes.

For these reasons, they concluded, the expense of moving the court would be less burdensome than if the public buildings were in good condition.

This was a mere ploy, of course, to prompt the General Assembly to compel Callaway and Hill to sell lots. The tactic worked. On 3 January 1804 the legislature passed an act authorizing the justices of Franklin County to determine the center of the county, purchase land, lay off half-acre lots, and establish a town to be called Mount Pleasant. Property owners would be required to build houses at least sixteen feet square with brick or stone chimneys. The General Assembly appointed trustees to supervise the establishment of the town: William A. Burwell, John Noftsinger, Benjamin Cook, William H. Shelton, William Greer, Josiah Woods, Skelton Taylor, Robert Innes, and Moses Greer, Sr. The justices were given until 7 May 1804 to locate the site of the new town, unless

> James Calloway and Thomas Hill the present proprietors of the land adjoining that on which the present public buildings stand, shall, on or before the seventh day of April next, consent that the said trustees or a majority of them shall lay off twenty-five acres of their said land into half acre lots with convenient streets, and to dispose of and convey the same to the purchaser or purchasers thereof.[46]

Callaway and Hill bowed to the inevitable and agreed to sell lots, thereby contributing to the establishment of the town of Mount Pleasant as the county's courthouse village.

The county built its first permanent courthouse by April 1786. The log structure probably was covered in weatherboards soon after. In 1790 contractors set the courthouse upon an underpinning of stone, cut two windows behind the justices' bench, and constructed a chimney of stone or brick. A year later workmen coated the courthouse roof with pitch and Spanish brown, a water-proofing material, and also painted the building inside and out. In 1809 the windows were glassed, and a decade later steps were added to the south entrance to the courthouse.[47]

By the late 1820s the county justices had decided, with no recorded strife, that the courthouse needed replacement. They adopted a plan for a new courthouse and appointed commissioners to oversee its construction, but for some unknown reason the project was delayed. On 8 June 1830 the court appointed as new commissioners its clerk, James Callaway, Jr., and two of its members, Peter Saunders, Jr., and Dr. Richard M. Taliaferro. The court instructed the three men

> to contract & to build the new Courthouse about to be erected for this County which is to be located on the public Lot on which the old Courthouse now stands, and to be built according to the plan or model heretofore adopted by the Court, with the exception of the door and window frames which are to be of wood except the cills [sills] which are to be of stone, and the said Commissioners last named are authorized to make any small or immaterial alteration in the plan so as not to change the figure of the building, or the dimentions, or arrangements of the several rooms & apartments, and to have the said building covered with tin or good chestnut shingles, as to them shall seem most expedient.[48]

To finance the new building the court levied a tax of fifty cents upon each tithable in the county and raised $2,319.[49]

The county advertised for bids in the newspaper and Silas Heston won the contract to build the courthouse; Abram Paul was the brickmason. Construction went relatively swiftly and on 7 November 1831 the court minutes noted: "The Courthouse Commissioners this day made their report that the said Courthouse is completed, upon Consideration whereof the Court being satisfied with the building, doth receive the same."[50]

Franklin County Courthouse, 1831. Ca. 1907 photo. (Blue Ridge Institute, Ferrum, Va.)

The court went on to appoint Dr. Richard M. Taliaferro keeper of the new courthouse and ordered him to

> contract for, and have the rubbish [remaining from construction] removed from the Public Lot, and also to procure four Setts of And Irons for the use of the Courthouse, and exhibit to the Court his bill for the same, and also to have a temporary enclosure erected around the new Courthouse, for its preservation, and also to procure water vessels for the use of the Court-house. . . . Whereupon the Court took possession of the new Courthouse and proceeded to do business therein.[51]

On the same day the court also decided that it was

> highly important, that some regulation should be adopted, for the preserva-tion of the public buildings in the County of Franklin. Be it resolved by the County Court that any person who shall deface any part of the new Courthouse, by setting up advertisements on the Door or Wall, or on the Columns, or by cutting the bar or bench, or in any other wise injuring the appearance of the building aforesaid, shall forfeit and pay the sum of five

dollars for every such offence to be appropriated to the lessening of the County levy. Resolved that it shall be the duty of the keeper of the Courthouse to preserve the Keys of the same, keep the doors and Windows closed except on Court days, keep the floors, etc., clean, provide water and fuel, for the use of the Court, and that he shall be paid annually for his services the sum of forty dollars. Ordered that Doctr. Richard M. Taliaferro cause to be erected a post, or some other convenience for advertisements in front of the Courthouse. Ordered that the Clerk of this Court do set up a copy of the foregoing resolutions in front of the Courthouse door.[52]

The next day, 8 November, the court approved the payment of $2,838 to Silas Heston for building the courthouse. Later he received another $212.[53]

The new courthouse was a handsome, if small, Classical Revival–style structure. Built of brick laid in Flemish bond (at least on the front elevation), it consisted of a high-ceilinged central section flanked by smaller one-story brick wings with exterior end chimneys. The central section was three bays wide and distinctly Jeffersonian in ambience, with a portico supported by four simple Doric columns. A half-round window, or oculus, adorned the gable end of the portico, and the wings each had one window. The commissioners had opted for a progressive roof of "tin" or standing-seam metal, which had gained popularity in the 1820s and lasted longer than wooden shingles. Although the arrangement of the interior is not known, presumably the court met in the central section while the flanking wings were used as a jury room and a chamber for the justices. Here the court met for almost eighty years, until the present courthouse was built during 1909 and 1910.[54]

Despite the impressiveness of the antebellum courthouse, it did not appear to influence the behavior of the citizens on court day. In April 1851 a Pennsylvania ironworker wrote to his brother,

> You wanted to [k]now the state of society hear. I will give you a little of the knolledge of it that I have sean at the time of court hear. The people turn out in a croud I suppose as large as ever you sean at a Big muster. The hoal town is filled with men and horses and it is nothing ottall to sea a half a dozen of ticklors or pint flasks turned up while you are passing up or down the streats and verry seldom it sow[?] that thear is now nockdowns before the court is over. But this place is like every place elce wher ther is large crowds collected there is allways some dissapated persons that attend large crowds. The society in the town is verry good and appear verry sociably. But not withstanding the place make a bad appearance on coart day.[55]

Little had changed since William Hill witnessed an election day in 1790.

By the early nineteenth century, as the founding members of the county court died off, the next generation began to assume positions of power and, as its members rose to prominence, they became as contentious as their elders. On 5 September 1808, for instance, when the Franklin County Court convened for business, Colonel Samuel Hairston entered the courtroom and announced his resignation as commanding officer of the 110th Regiment of militia. Major Shores Price, of the same regiment, also resigned. (As senior major in the regiment he would have been appointed to succeed Hairston.) Major Robert Innes, also of the

110th Regiment, arrived in the courthouse yard and was told of the resignations. Because Price's resignation left Innes the senior major, he walked into the courtroom and declared his candidacy for the rank of colonel. "When to his astonishment," Innes wrote in his petition to the governor, "Peter Saunders, Jr., Esq., was named and recommended in preferrence to your memorialist by a majority of one."[56]

The reaction to the election of Peter Saunders—one of three sons of Peter Saunders, Sr., an original county justice—was immediate and one of outrage. The other officers of the 110th Regiment had fully expected Innes to be recommended and they were furious at the usurper. "Captain Jacob Webb informed me," wrote Captain Joseph Hale, "if Saunders was elected he would give up his Commission in said Regiment, and after the baloting was over he did throw up said Commission."[57] Captain Joseph Webb reported that he "heard the Officers and Soldiers Express great dissatisfaction at the Recommendation of Peter Saunders, Jr., as their Commander."[58]

The other officers quickly rallied to Innes's support. In a two-page petition to the governor signed by fifteen officers in the 110th Regiment, they stated that

> our Major Robert Innes is a man of Great military turn of mind fully acquainted with the duties of a Colonel, and we do believe there is not an officer belonging to our Regiment more capable of discharging the duties of a Colonel than himself. A man of undaunted Courage, attended with prudence and Judgment, has always been attentive in discharge of his duties as an officer with that feeling pride that animates the breast of an Officer and Soldier in the Service of his Country. A man in high Standing in Society (believed by all those acquainted with him), one of our representatives to the General Assembly.[59]

Innes was only slightly more modest in his address to the governor. "Your memorialist," he wrote,

> has the benefit of some little experience. He has met all the expense incident to his rank with great pleasure, has diligently done his duty, never absenting himself from drill parades, and so constant in his attendance at the muster where by law he was compelled or required to attend, that he believes it to be proverbially remarkable. With respect to his capability to command a regiment your memorialist chooses to be silent, but in point of patriotism and zeal for the defence of his country he will acknowledge no superiority.[60]

No one, in contrast, came to the support of Peter Saunders, Jr., who had been appointed to the county's bench in 1803. He had been commissioned a lieutenant in a county artillery company in August 1796 but the company soon was disbanded for the lack of a cannon with which to train.[61] In 1799 Saunders and James Callaway, Jr., had been declared supernumerary or extra officers;[62] as such, they were first in line to fill vacancies in their rank in the county militia. Callaway soon became an infantry officer but, as several of his comrades explained to the governor,

Mr. Saunders has never attended a training of officers since the disolution of said company of artillery, nor paid any respect to [his] Commission [as lieutenant], and your honours knows if any officer cease to perform the duties of his office for eight months he shall be considered as resigned his Office and [the] vacancy thereby occasioned shall be filled as in other cases.[63]

Robert Innes concluded his statement to the governor with a couple of oblique swipes at Saunders's character and manhood, suggesting that:

however reputable Mr. Saunders may be in private life . . . his appointment will be a direct slur on all the officers of the militia in said Regiment, for surely of them many are to be found whose bravery will not be questioned and whose talents will put them on a footing with that Gentleman.[64]

(That Peter Saunders, Jr., had fathered a daughter out of wedlock about 1800 probably was well known and may explain Innes's sarcastic reference to Saunders's "reputable . . . private life.") Innes prevailed and was promoted in 1808. Peter Saunders, Jr., continued to serve as a county justice; he became a prosperous merchant and eventually co-owner—with his brothers—and iron-master of the Washington Iron Works. Between 1810 and 1815 he served as postmaster of Rocky Mount.

Public service and financial success, however, were not enough to satisfy Saunders. Doubtless he wished to equal or surpass his father, who not only had been one of the original county justices, the commander of the militia, and a wealthy merchant, but who had also attained the position of sheriff, the highest honor the county could bestow. The son's ambition embroiled him in one of the bitterest controversies that ever shook the political leadership of the county in the nineteenth century.

On 1 November 1830, the fifteen justices who sat on the bench in the county court balloted for a sheriff. Those voting were Benjamin Booth, John S. Burwell, Henry Carper, George W. Clements, Pleasant Dickenson, Joab Early, Robert Hairston, Patrick Hix, John M. Holland, Shores Price, Samuel Saunders, George Turner, John H. Wade, William B. Williams, and Stephen Wood; Peter Saunders, Jr., and Anthony Street were absent. The court recommended

to the Governor and Council Peter Saunders, Anthony Street and Patrick Hix, three of the acting Justices of the peace in the County as fit persons from whom to select and Commission a Sheriff for this County for the ensuing year.[65]

Anthony Street was furious, convinced that he should have been named first in the recommendation, thereby virtually guaranteeing his appointment. He rose in court and moved that he be permitted to submit evidence that Peter Saunders, Jr., had held the office of postmaster—a federal appointment—and had thereby vacated his position on the bench, which should have made him ineligible for selection as sheriff. The court overruled Street's motion and refused to hear his testimony. Later that same day Street wrote an angry letter to Governor John Floyd describing what had occurred and asking that he delay issuing the sheriff's commission until all the facts were presented to him.[66]

Among the statements sent to the governor by Anthony Street was that of Cassimer Cabiness, who had been a lieutenant in a company of Franklin County militia during the War of 1812. In 1814, wrote Cabiness, some of the militia were ordered to active duty, and

> Peter Saunders having came within the bounds of the Company to which I was attached I gave him notices to attend a call muster in order to fill up the quota from the Company and received from him a note informing me that he was Exempt from millitary duty on accoumpt of his being post master at Rockmont [Rocky Mount]. I Reported him to the Court marshall but he did not attend. The Court marshall Judged him Exempt for som of the members said they of their own knowledge knew him to be postmaster.[67]

Anthony Street, in his formal petition to the governor, pointed out that Saunders could not hold both a federal and a state office at the same time. If, as the evidence showed, he had accepted the federal office of postmaster, then he automatically vacated the state office of justice of the peace. By continuing to act as a justice, as Saunders had done, he violated the Constitution of the United States and the laws of Virginia. "It appears to me," wrote Street,

> their is an awful Squinting at purgery to Sware to Support a Constitution which forbids holding an office under any state government, and then directly in the face of that oath claim an office under the state government.[68]

Street also objected to the clannishness of those who held office in Franklin County, particularly that of the Saunders family. "There is such a train of Family Connection to Combat with," he complained. "I Stand alone in the County. There is not one drop of my blood that Circulates through the Veins of any magistrate in the County except my own."[69] Street contended that there was

> but verry little Chance for him or any other person to obtain the recommendation of Franklin County Court unless he be a favoured connection or Friend of the Saunders party. I will say without fear of Contradiction that we have four Colonels in our County, three of them are Nephews of Peter Saunders. The Commissioners of the revenue are each of them his Nephews and there is not a youth of the Harston, Saunders or Hale family that has arived to the age of 20 that is not an officer. The deputy Sheriffs, one of them [Samuel Hale] is said Saunders Nephew and the other his brother-in-law, and the Judge of the Superior Court of Law is his brother [Fleming Saunders], and I do assure your Honorable body we are too much under their goverment.[70]

Street pointed out other advantages enjoyed by Peter Saunders, Jr. Whereas Street himself lived

> say 16 or 18 miles from our Courthouse and have done he believes more of the drudgery of the office of Justice of the peace than any man in the County. My opponent lives in 5 or 6 hundred yards of the Courthouse. . . . He is a wealthy man and one of wealthy Connection and many of them in this

County and some in other Countys. Those things are advantages I possess none of. I have no connection in this County, only my own family.[71]

As though his charges that Saunders held office illegally and controlled the county through family influence were not enough, Street also alleged that Saunders had attempted to discredit him before the court balloted for a new sheriff. At the July 1830 session of the Superior Court of Law, a grand jury heard deputy sheriff Samuel Hale, a nephew of Peter Saunders, accuse Anthony Street of being drunk on the bench at the June session of the county court. Hale refused to say how he obtained this information. The witnesses who were to testify against Street soon changed their minds. One of them, Ransom Sutherlin, stated that

he was at the June Court and see Said Street on the bench. When he, said Sutherlin, first entered the Court house he thought Captain Street was intoxicated but on paying particular attention he found he was under a mistake, and he stated to the Jury that said Street was not drunk nor Intoxicated.[72]

Although the grand jury made no presentment against Street, he believed that the irregular and secretive manner in which the affair had been conducted proved that it was a plot hatched by Saunders and his supporters in order to deny Street the office of sheriff.[73]

After reading the letters and petitions of Street and the others, Governor John Floyd commissioned Anthony Street, "the second in nomination,"[74] on 18 December 1830 as the new sheriff of Franklin County. Among all the records of this contest there were found no letters or affidavits in behalf of Peter Saunders, Jr. Perhaps he refused to believe that the governor would dare to violate tradition by commissioning anyone but the first man named in the recommendation regardless of the circumstances.

When he discovered that he had misjudged the governor, Saunders wrote a blistering four-page petition to the House of Delegates in which he protested the governor's "high handed exercise of prerogative" and demanded that "the Executive be required to show why they refused to commission your memorialist."[75] The House of Delegates referred the petition to its Committee on Courts of Justice; on 22 January 1831 the committee summarily rejected it.[76]

Saunders's petition was a mixture of self-righteousness, outraged virtue, and arrogance. He wrote that being the first named in the recommendation, he fully expected to receive the commission in accordance with the unwritten "law of the land," but "to his supprize" Anthony Street was commissioned instead. This was almost the same, he wrote, as if the governor had "gone out of the nomination" entirely. Saunders ignored Street's charges of undue family influence and rumormongering, and he denied the accusation that he held the post of justice illegally. Then, in a fascinating piece of reasoning, Saunders suggested that even if the accusation was true, that would be no excuse to appoint another as sheriff:

Although your memorialist was not apprized of an objection that was made to commissioning him, as he conceives ought in justice to have been done, yet he has incidentally been informed that it was represented to the Executive that your memorialist had been a post master. Supposing for the sake of the argument that it was true, yet as your memorialist conceives under the laws of the land the Executive could not for that refuse to consider him as in the commission of the peace, and to issue the commission to him.

Peter Saunders reluctantly acknowledged that he had acted as postmaster, but "only for the accomodation of the neighbourhood and from no hopes of reward." For this selfless act of public service, he complained, he arbitrarily had been deprived by the governor of the office of sheriff. "He cannot imagine," wrote Saunders,

why he was selected as the subject of Executive proscription as unexpected as it is unjust? Why he has been stripped of his rights and deprived of the pitiful reward held out for years of public service? Why he has been tried, condemned and punished, without being informed that he was accused, of the names of his accusers, or his judges, and without having extended to him the sacred right of self defence and justification?

After the General Assembly had ignored Peter Saunders's pleas and rejected his petition, Anthony Street and his supporters thought they had no further cause for worry. Street later wrote, however, that when he appeared before the Franklin County Court in March 1831 to take the oath of office as sheriff,

Peter Saunders and his party . . . mounted the bench, Imployed council, and objected to my qualifying, charging the executive with doing what they had no right to do and objected to every deputy I offered for qualification. However in this there was a majority in favour of me and my deputies and we were after long discussion permited to qualify. . . . I only state these things to show how far the tide of opposition runs against me on the part of that family.[77]

Street's difficulties at the March 1831 court meeting were only a hint of things to come, for on 7 November 1831 (the day the court moved into the new courthouse), when the annual ballot for sheriff was taken, Peter Saunders again was named first in the recommendation, followed by Anthony Street. Another custom—that a sheriff who had conducted his office properly during his first term would be appointed to a second—had been violated.

Wearily, Anthony Street took up his pen and wrote to Governor John Floyd, "I am again reduced to the necessity of appealing to the Executive for the Commission of Sheriff of the County of Franklin." After describing the current controversy, Street added, "Peter Saunders informed me yesterday he Expected I would git the Commission but he intended to plague me."[78]

Anthony Street received his commission, but not before both sides presented statements to the governor. That there was a long-standing hatred between the two men was obvious from the vicious accusations that were made. Dr. Richard M. Taliaferro, a respected local physician, virtually charged Peter Saunders with cowardice. "In the early part of the year 1813," wrote Taliaferro,

I took charge of the Post office at Franklin Court House, Virginia, at the request of Mr. Peter Saunders (who was then Postmaster at said place). Mr. Saunders expressed an unwillingness to resign, and stated as a principal reason for it, that war was then going on in our country, and the Commission of Post Master which he held would exempt him from doing military duty. I was then Surgeon to one of the [militia] Regiments of this county, of course could not be compelled to do duty as a private, consequently agreed to do the business in the Post Office as Assistant to Mr. Saunders, and let him hold the Commission, by which he was relieved from serving a tour of duty.[79]

Several of Peter Saunders's friends rallied to his defense, one of whom was James Callaway, Jr., who had served as clerk of the county court for many years. To refute Dr. Taliaferro's suggestion of cowardice, Callaway wrote that he and Saunders were commissioned officers in a company of artillery in 1796, but that the unit was disbanded shortly thereafter and both men became supernumerary officers awaiting vacancies in the regular militia regiment. Callaway became the commander of the regiment, but Peter Saunders, Callaway asserted, "still stood as a Supernumerary Officer always ready to be promoted as I believe."[80]

Jubal Early, grandfather of the Confederate general, muddied the waters by alleging that Peter Saunders had never really been a postmaster during the War of 1812 at all:

At the time which it is said he [Peter Saunders] was Post Master at Rocky Mount a Mr. Edmund Saunders then lived with him and was the acting Post Master. Having had some transactions in the office with Mr. Edmund Saunders as such, that in fact I never new untill lately that any other Person but said Edmund was Post Master at that time.[81]

Because Dr. Taliaferro had delivered a personal attack on Peter Saunders for the benefit of Anthony Street, one of Saunders's defenders launched a similar attack on the character of Street, although the charge, as in Saunders's case, was hardly a new one. Tarleton Brown wrote that he had seen

Street at times in the discharge of his official Duties as a Magistrate under the influence of ardent Spirits. So much So, that he would [have] Considered his rights in Jeopardy had they been Submitted to the said Street's Discissions.[82]

Once again Governor Floyd decided the issue in favor of Anthony Street, to whom he issued a sheriff's commission on 18 November 1831.[83] Street had little time left to enjoy his victory, however, for he died in January 1832.[84] On 6 February 1832 the Franklin County Court met to nominate three justices to fill the vacancy caused by Street's death. Weary of controversy and recriminations, the court decided to record the vote of each justice, at least for the man to be named first in the recommendation. Peter Saunders and Patrick Hix were proposed to stand first and the justices voted ten to eight in favor of Hix.

For the next few years the county court continued the practice of recording its votes for sheriff, and although the office was denied Peter Saunders, he never protested. At the balloting for sheriff held on 5 November 1832, there were eight votes for Patrick Hix and five for Saunders;[85] on 2 December 1833 Peter Saunders received nine votes and Henry Carper five. The court, however, informed the governor

> that it was admitted by the said Peter Saunders . . . that he was appointed and Commissioned as Post Master at Rocky Mount in the year 1812, which said appointment he held until sometime in the year 1814, and . . . that the said Peter Saunders Continued to act as a Justice of the peace during his appointment as Post Master, and has Continued to act as such until this time.[86]

Perhaps one of the justices told Peter Saunders privately that he would never be commissioned sheriff until he admitted that he had been postmaster, or perhaps Saunders acted on his own in an effort to conciliate his enemies on the court. Although his name was listed first in the nomination, Saunders did not object when Henry Carper was commissioned instead.

When the court voted the next year, on 1 December 1834, Saunders's name again led Carper's, eight to seven.[87] This time Henry Carper protested, although mildly compared to Anthony Street. Carper merely pointed out that he was "the present Sheriff and wish to be continued in office one year after the Expiration of my present Commission."[88] His new commission was issued on 18 December 1834.[89]

At last, on 2 November 1835, Peter Saunders was nominated for sheriff without opposition and stood first in the court's recommendation. His commission was issued on 10 December 1835.[90] A friend of the family wrote to Fleming Saunders on 20 May 1836, "I was very glad to hear that Colonel Peter was Commissioned Sheriff. I have no doubt it was gratifying to him on many accounts."[91] Peter Saunders was recommended for a second term on 7 November 1836 and again was appointed without opposition.[92]

Peter Saunders's success in business as partner and ironmaster of the Washington Iron Works—the county's major antebellum industry—finally was matched by his success in attaining the high county office he desired. In this he may have been more of a model for others of his generation and social group than he was a typical example. In some ways he was a throwback to the rough-and-tumble personalities of the early period of the county's history. He was stubborn and belligerent, a gambler, and the father of a child born out of wedlock.

Most of the other county officials were nothing like Saunders, but instead were prosperous farmers or lawyers who carried out their public duties quietly and with little fanfare. Certain families besides the Saunderses, Hairstons, and Hales proved just as committed to public service but aroused little controversy. The public career of Moses Greer, Sr., for example, lasted nearly sixty years and included service in the Revolution, on the bench of Bedford and Franklin counties, and in the House of Delegates. His son Moses Greer, Jr., served in the militia of the new county and also as a Franklin County justice; he received his commission on 14 April 1803 and remained an active jurist until his death on 30 September 1848. He was also a Primitive Baptist minister of considerable reputation. Thomas Bailey Greer, another of the sons of Moses Greer, Sr., also served in the House of Delegates (1819–1820, 1824–1825, and 1825–1826), as did one of his grandsons, George H. T. Greer (1869–1871), and one of his great-grandsons, Moses Theodrick Greer (1875–1877). Thomas Bailey Greer, Jr., became a noted local physician and one of the first members of the State Board of Medical Examiners. Several of the male descendants of Moses Greer, Sr., served with distinction in the Confederate army, in particular Dr. John Henry Greer.[93]

Franklin County sent two of its citizens to the United States House of Representatives during the first half of the nineteenth century. The first, William Armistead Burwell, was born on 15 March 1780 in Mecklenburg County, the son of Thacker and Mary Armistead Burwell. Educated at the College of William and Mary, William A. Burwell moved to Franklin County in 1802. Two years later he became the private secretary to a family friend, President Thomas Jefferson. Burwell spent most of 1804 serving as an aide-de-camp to Jefferson (who wrote his own letters) in Washington, D.C., or at Monticello. Elected to the House of Delegates from Franklin County for the session beginning in December 1804, Burwell left what he called the most pleasurable employment of his life in January 1805 after he realized he did not have the time to be both secretary and delegate. He was reelected to the legislature for the sessions in December 1805 and December 1806, and he accepted a militia commission as a first lieutenant in a troop of Franklin County cavalry in 1805. In late 1806 the voters chose him to be their representative in the United States Congress, so Burwell resigned from the House of Delegates and journeyed to Washington, where he became one of Jefferson's staunchest congressional allies. John Quincy Adams, a Federalist and heartfelt opponent of the Jeffersonians, wrote a damned-with-faint-praise description of Burwell that reflected the political animosities of the day:

William Armistead Burwell (1780–1821). (Virginia State Library and Archives.)

He was a man of moderate talents and respectable private character, full of Virginian principles and prejudices, a mixture of wisdom and Quixotism, which has done some good and much mischief to the Union. Burwell took no lead in anything. He scarcely ever spoke; never originated a measure of any public utility, but fancied himself a guardian of the liberties of the people against Executive encroachments. His delight was the consciousness of his own independence, and he thought it a heroic virtue to ask no favors. He therefore never associated with any members of the Executive, and would have shuddered at the thought of going into the drawing-room. Jealousy of State rights and jealousy of the Executive were the two pillars of Burwell's political fabric, because they are the prevailing popular doctrines in Virginia. He floated down the stream of time with the current, and always had the satisfaction of being in his own eyes a pure and incorruptible patriot. Virginia teems with this brood more than any other State in the Union, and they are far from being the worst men among us. Such men occasionally render service to the nation by preventing harm; but they are quite as apt to prevent good, and they never do any.[94]

As Adams admitted, however, Burwell's politics exactly suited his constituents, who reelected him at every opportunity until his sudden death on 16 February 1821, following a brief illness.

His obituary characterized him as

a man of sterling integrity, which passed untouched, even by the breath of slander, the ordeal of this life. As a politician, he was virtuous, and he was consistent: as a friend he was beloved and admired. To his late wife, by whose side he is about to be laid, he was an exemplary consort, and to his only son a most affectionate father. He retained his senses to the end, and almost his last words were, that he had no reason to fear the approach of death.[95]

As a sign of respect, the House of Representatives met at 10:00 A.M. on Saturday, 17 February, to conduct a memorial ceremony:

The corpse of the deceased was brought into the Hall, and rested in front of the Speaker's Chair. The SENATE, preceded by its President and Secretary, having come into the Hall, and the President of the Senate being seated at the right hand of the Speaker of the House, an appropriate exhortation was delivered by the Rev. Mr. *Campbell*, and a prayer by the Rev. Dr. *Ryland*, the Chaplains to Congress; when the corpse was taken from the Hall, attended by the pall bearers, and by the Representatives from the State of Virginia as mourners. Next followed the Sergeant at Arms of the House; then the House of Representatives, preceded by its Speaker and Clerk; next, the Sergeant at Arms of the Senate, followed by the Senate.

The pall bearers were Messrs. Parker, of Mass.; Wood, of N.Y.; Bateman, of N.J.; Baldwin, of Pa.; Smith, of N.C.; and Robertson, of Kentucky.

The procession attended the hearse some distance on the road to Baltimore, and then returned, leaving the remains of the deceased in the hands of his friends, to be conveyed to that city [the home of his late wife, Letitia McCreery].[96]

Burwell was later interred in Washington in the Congressional Cemetery.[97]

Burwell's will was probated in Franklin County on 2 April 1821. He appointed the eminent lawyer Peachy R. Gilmer as guardian for his only child, William

McCreery Burwell. In case the boy died before reaching adulthood, however, Burwell's will included several unusual provisions. One was that his slaves be hired out for two or three years to provide them with a nest egg, then emancipated and removed from Virginia within five years. Part of his estate was to be sold and the money used to buy or rent land for his slaves in the western United States. In a clause that had a Jeffersonian ring to it, he also bequeathed to

> the County of Franklin . . . (in case of my sons death as before mentioned) a suitable piece of Land for a poor house, & my Library of Books & Maps provided they shall think proper to Accept them; but in the case of my Library, I hope they will take proper measures to have it preserved & enlarged for the use of the Inhabitants, as it may prove essentially service-able in promoting the morals & information of the people.[98]

Unfortunately for Burwell's slaves and "the people" of Franklin County, his son lived to adulthood and came into his inheritance.

Nathaniel Herbert Claiborne was the second congressman to serve from Franklin County. He was born in Sussex County on 14 November 1777 and, like Burwell, moved to Franklin County shortly after 1800. By 1803 he was a captain in the county's 43d Regiment of Virginia Militia, and before 1810 he became commonwealth's attorney for the county.[99] He represented Franklin County in both houses of the General Assembly: House of Delegates (1810–1812) and Senate (1821–1825). During the War of 1812 he served on the Council of Virginia, which shared executive powers with the governor. In 1818 he sat on the state commission that established the University of Virginia. In 1825 he was elected to the United States House of Representatives, where he remained until 1837. Throughout his legislative career he insisted on fiscal conservatism and gained a reputation as a "watchdog of the treasury," first in state government and then in national office. While a congressman, he opposed internal improvements at national expense, increased protective tariffs, and pension or relief bills. At the conclusion of his congressional career he returned to Franklin County and devoted himself to agricultural pursuits at his farm, Claybrook. He died there on 15 August 1859.[100]

Claiborne's first election to Congress in 1825 was not his first campaign for that seat. He had stood for the office in 1823 but lost to Jabez Leftwich, of Bedford County, in a technically illegal election that typified the political tactics of the day. Each county within a congressional district set its own dates for the vote, and usually the running tally was public knowledge before the election ended. In 1823 Leftwich lagged Claiborne by 814 votes after each county in the district had conducted its poll except for Bedford, Leftwich's home base. Sure enough, after the Bedford County election officials had kept the voting precincts open for several days longer than was legal, Leftwich outpolled Claiborne 1,180 to 47. In the 1825 election, however, Claiborne's lead—1,003—was too large for Leftwich to overcome, although he used the same methods as in 1823, and Claiborne won the election. Presumably, Claiborne utilized the same tactics to keep his seat until 1837.[101]

Another eminent and powerful local figure of the early nineteenth century was Caleb Tate, who served as the clerk of several courts for an unusually long period of time. He was clerk of the district court from 1797 to 1805, of the Franklin County Court from 1813 to 1838, and of the Superior Courts of Law and Chancery from 1809 to 1845. Renowned for his gracious manners and dignified bearing, Tate, appropriately enough, occupied a grand Greek Revival–style dwelling on a lofty height that overlooked the courthouse. The house, in which Tate died on 1 December 1857, still stands in its commanding position. Tate's reputation for stability gave birth to the local saying, "Things certainly have changed since Mr. Tate died."[102]

The death of the gentlemanly Caleb Tate occurred not long after a significant political change that affected the state as a whole, as well as the less prosperous and powerful of Franklin County's citizens. If the earlier complaints of Anthony Street were any indication, the people had grown weary of the perceived domination of the county's high offices by the Hairston, Hale, and Saunders families and were waiting for a chance to alter the composition of the court. They were given their chance in 1851.

In 1850 a convention of delegates assembled in Richmond to draft a new constitution for the state—its third such document. The convention adjourned on 1 August 1851 after adopting a constitution that not only provided for the popular election of the governor, but also the popular election of county justices as well. This provision gave the voters in each county the opportunity to elect a local governing body in their own image. In Franklin County, by and large, that is exactly what happened.

The county was divided into nine districts and four justices were elected in each district during 27–29 May 1852. The thirty-six justices were commissioned a month later, on 28 June. Only six of them were already on the bench: John S. Brown, Robert Bush, Joseph Dickenson, Jahn Griffith, Thomas S. Keen, and Richard M. Taliaferro. No members of the Hairston, Hale, or Saunders families— or Greer or Tate, for that matter—were elected. The old families had been unseated.[103]

The period between the creation of Franklin County and the mid-nineteenth century, then, saw the custody of the county offices change from the founding fathers to their sons to justices elected by the people. The Constitution of 1851 enabled the voting public to choose its own local leaders for the first time in the history of the commonwealth. Most white male citizens finally gained a voice in managing public affairs.

Minding the public business did not put food on the table, however. County officeholding never had been a particularly lucrative occupation, except perhaps in the case of the sheriff, nor was it a full-time career. The early officeholders, at least, tended to be wealthy before they occupied high office, not afterwards. Throughout the antebellum period local officials earned their livelihoods from the earth, from business, or from industry. Literally minding one's own business was the principal occupation of every breadwinner.

SIX

Minding the Business

The popular image of a pioneer family usually involves a small cabin in a clearing, a cornfield, grazing cattle and horses, and the doughty family engaged in a variety of activities—gardening, sewing, tending animals—all to achieve independence. Missing from this picture, however, are the shop-keepers, gunsmiths, lawyers, and other harbingers of civilization who followed hard on the heels of the pioneers.

John Hickey, one of the first businessmen in the Franklin County area, established his trading post and store about 1746 in present-day Henry County a few miles south of Smith River. Hickey located his store on a road that stretched about a hundred and twenty miles from the Staunton River in northern Halifax County to a frontier community known as the Mayo Settlement. The store also stood near the Great Wagon Road, along which a band of Moravians traveled to North Carolina from Pennsylvania in 1753. On 11 November the wagons of the Moravians became stuck in a mudhole in the road; they had just pulled them out when John Hickey,

> who lives half a mile from here and keeps a store (which is the nearest house, at which we can buy salt), came to us and showed himself very friendly. We had a miserable road to his house. Here we bought some provisions.[1]

The Moravian diarist did not name the provisions they bought from Hickey besides salt. No doubt he stocked cloth, ironware, and foodstuffs. In 1756 George Washington spent a night at Hickey's ordinary and bought supplies at his store during his inspection of Virginia's western forts at the beginning of the French and Indian War. During his lifetime, Hickey acquired large tracts of land and died in Henry County in 1784.[2]

James Callaway established another early store in the region in present-day Bedford County in 1770. He and his partners sent hogsheads of Bedford County and Pittsylvania County tobacco to the Liverpool firm of Dodson, Daltera, and

Company. The tobacco was traded for dry goods, which were shipped back to Callaway. Such goods in demand in the backcountry included cloths of oznaburg, Irish linen, cambric, flannel, duffle, "printed handk[erchief]s," and "Small fine Lin[en] hand[kerchief]s." The firm also sold teapots, teacups and saucers, coffee cups, "Blue & white Chamberpotts," "painted Looking Glasses," a "Nest [of] Gilt Trunks," women's scissors, needles, and ivory combs. These items were in addition to such mundane articles as hilling hoes, grubbing hoes, and grindstones.[3] The store prospered until 1775, when the impending hostilities with Great Britain forced it to close.

Each year county courts issued licenses for businessmen to keep stores, as well as ordinaries and mills. In 1787 alone, the court of Franklin County issued eight licenses for storekeepers: Daniel Brown and Company; Thomas Hill; William Kerby; Samuel Hairston; Peter Saunders, Sr.; Hugh Innes; John Martin; and John Hook. Some of these entrepreneurs had operated stores prior to the Revolution.[4]

One such colonial store owner, the loyalist John Hook, moved after the revolutionary war to Halesford in present–day Franklin County. There still stands a house alleged to have been constructed by him (although it appears to be a mid-nineteenth-century Greek Revival I-style dwelling), as does a small building thought to have been part of his store, which he continued to operate until his death in 1808. Hook was as feisty and independent—perhaps even unprincipled—after the war as he was during it. When Thomas Osbourne came to Hook to settle his accounts with the store owner, Hook took advantage of him. Osbourne had regular dealings with Hook on six months' credit, and he always settled them without looking over his accounts. That was a major error, as Osbourne revealed when he defended himself against Hook in a petition to the Franklin County Court in 1800:

John Hook's store. 1973 photo. (Virginia Department of Historic Resources.)

That your Orator [Osbourne] being a man subject to drink, and the said Hook keeping spirits for sale at his said Store, most of your Orators Settlements with the said Hook were entered into while in the habit of Drinking. . . . he is induced to believe that the said Hook in whom your Orator placed the most implicit confidence has over reached him by taking advantage of his situation.[5]

On 2 January 1810 the court recorded an inventory and appraisal of Hook's personal property. Hook owned 110 slaves; eleven families of slaves were identified by the persons who compiled the inventory.[6] The inventory suggests that Hook's house was a story-and-a-half, hall-parlor-plan structure; it described his household furniture in a hall, a "Chamber," and a "Garret" above each room.[7] The list also mentioned two objects that must have irritated all of Hook's adversaries who were compelled to do business with him: "2 Pictures, George the third & his Queen."[8] Near the house were the store, with a "Counting Room" probably attached to it, and a "Still house."[9] Apparently Hook devoted a good deal of his energies to the distilling business. In 1796 he wrote to one of his suppliers complaining about the quality of the still parts he had received. He thought a couple of the still bases he had purchased were cut off old West Indian stills, and noted that he had used a British-made still for nine years without encountering similar problems of quality.[10]

The remainder of John Hook's inventory reveals the variety of goods carried by a large store at the turn of the nineteenth century. Among the liquors in stock were whiskey, wine, and apple and peach brandy. Paints included yellow ocher, Spanish brown, and white lead. He carried bolts of cloth, thread, needles, thimbles, buttons, stockings, handkerchiefs, cravats, pantaloons, shoes, hats, and other articles of clothing. Foods included chocolate, coffee, tea, sugar, salt, and a variety of spices: black and white ginger, allspice, and pepper. Hook sold medical supplies, including magnesia, castor oil, chamomile flowers, Peruvian bark, and one of the most common sedatives of the time, laudanum. Customers could purchase a large variety of tableware: knives, forks, spoons, pitchers, mugs, cups, saucers, bowls, dishes, plates, platters, tureens, pots, and boats. Farm equipment was available, as well as bar iron and steel.[11]

Stills such as those owned—and sold—by Hook were perfectly legal at the time. The federal government occasionally levied excise taxes on liquor, but only as an attempt to raise revenue, not as a means of limiting or discouraging production. Although stills were common, not every family owned one. Those who did probably supplied their neighbors, but liquor was fairly inexpensive and readily available in such stores as Hook's.

Washington Dickinson, the proprietor of Dickinson's store, one of the county's most-noted landmarks, was another early shopkeeper. His store stood near the southeastern intersection of present-day Routes 715 and 646, on the early Pigg River Road. Some of these rural stores, such as Booth's store, Brown's store, Calhoun's store, Dickinson's store, Taylor's store, and Young's store, served as post offices as well.[12] Most stores also functioned as election precincts.

Close on the heels of shopkeepers, anxious for customers among the pioneers, were the industrial entrepreneurs. Some would-be manufacturers in the eighteenth century were especially attracted to the iron industry; consequently, the competition for ore-bearing land was intense in newly settled areas. The lure of profits even attracted "foreign" entrepreneurs.

The first ironworks in the Southside Piedmont was the Oxford bloomery forge in Bedford County, begun perhaps as early as 1768 by Pennsylvania investors. The Oxford was in operation when they sold it in 1773. By 1776 it was owned by David Ross, a Petersburg merchant and probably the wealthiest man in Virginia. He soon replaced the bloomery with a blast furnace and forge.

The second ironworks in the area was constructed by a true frontiersman, John Donelson, a Maryland native who had settled in the Southside wilderness of Brunswick County in the 1740s. He was a man of many talents and rose quickly to prominence in frontier society, becoming a vestryman, surveyor, justice, and militia colonel. In the late 1760s he decided to become an industrialist as well, and succeeded with a bit of deception.

The western reaches of the area in which Donelson had settled were thick with iron ore deposits. A settler named David Wilson entered a claim with the surveyor of Lunenburg County on 14 December 1750 for 400 acres of land near Jacks Mountain in what is now Franklin County. The claim included "several small Draughts of Pig River enter'd on account of a Suppos'd Mine."

Iron ore actually was found, not just "Suppos'd," by 3 May 1753, when John Wilcox, a Pennsylvanian who had moved to North Carolina, had 400 acres surveyed "on Iron Mine Branch of Pigg River." A year later Wilcox had an adjoining tract of 403 acres surveyed. On 10 June 1760 he patented 400 acres on lower Iron Mine Branch and Pigg River adjoining the other two tracts, thereby gaining control of 1,203 acres of iron ore deposits.

Wilcox eventually built a blast furnace and forge in North Carolina, but, inadvertently, he left the development of the Virginia property to John Donelson. In 1768 Wilcox agreed to sell the land to Donelson, but the deal was never consummated. Wilcox left for North Carolina, depositing money with Donelson for the annual payment of the quitrents due the colony (if they were not paid, the title to the property would lapse and be anyone's claim). In 1769 a settler named John Cox filed such a claim for the land with the General Court, asserting that the quitrents had not been paid. Donelson testified that he had in fact paid the quitrents, but his testimony was disallowed because a few days before the trial he had purchased Cox's right to the land if he was upheld, thereby becoming an interested witness. Since Wilcox had thought Donelson was looking out for his welfare, he did not attend the trial. Cox won by default, and title to the land passed to Donelson in 1772.

It is difficult to believe that Donelson, a county court justice and surveyor who must have been familiar with land laws and court procedures, did not deliberately bilk Wilcox out of his land. Many years later the Supreme Court of Virginia refused to impugn Donelson's motives, but upheld Wilcox when he cried "Foul!" By then Wilcox had no hope of recovering the land, although he did receive some compensation for his loss.

Donelson acted quickly to take advantage of his windfall and meet the demand for iron generated by the area's new settlers. In 1773 he hired four men—John Hollaway, Charles Hollaway, Amos Span, and Thomas Bolton—to construct and operate a bloomery forge. He also provided six slaves—Dick, Harry, James, Judith, Moody, and Nell—to mine and cart the ore and grow food for the workers.

John Donelson began his ironworks with a bloomery—a good choice because Donelson had no experience as an ironmaster. The bloomery resembled a blacksmith's forge, and consisted of a hearth and a brick fireplace and chimney. The fireplace was built atop the hearth and was constructed like a barbecue pit, about two feet square and twenty inches deep. An opening in the back wall of the fireplace, called a tuyere, tapered funnel-like from the outside in. A blast of air was injected into the fireplace through the tuyere by a water- or hand-operated bellows behind the bloomery. Although the tuyere had to be of a proper size and angle relative to the fireplace floor, the rest of the bloomery forge was not beyond the capabilities of a skilled chimney builder.

While Donelson worried over the bloomery, his colliers stacked their billets of oak and hickory in heaps to make charcoal. Covering each heap with twigs, leaves, and earth, the colliers started a fire in its center. After smoldering for three or four days the wood had been reduced to charcoal.

When the ore, bloomery, and charcoal were ready, Donelson gave the order to start making iron. Workers heated the bloomery fireplace slowly, then added layers of ore and charcoal and increased the blast. The molten iron settled to the bottom of the fireplace, and as it cooled workers pushed and stirred it with iron rods until it formed a dense, semisolid mass known as a bloom, about five inches in diameter and weighing almost a hundred pounds. The bloom was lifted from the fireplace with crowbars and tongs and carried to an anvil to be hammered into bar iron.

Hammering or refining the bloom probably was done by hand at first, but soon Donelson built a water-powered forge with a tilt hammer to ease the task. As flowing water turned a waterwheel, wipers on the wheel struck the tail of a hammer helve balanced on a fulcrum, causing the hammer to tilt and fall on the iron and anvil. This pounding by the tilt hammer drove impurities from the iron and flattened it into a bar for easier transportation.

In addition to the bloomery and forge, Donelson's ironworks probably contained a storage shed for the charcoal, another shed for extra iron ore, and a small warehouse for the bar iron. Slaves built dwellings for themselves and the white workmen. In 1773 a small industrial village was constructed where there had been only wilderness the year before.

The enterprise was not without risk, however. To finance the undertaking Donelson on 22 July 1773 mortgaged his home plantation, consisting of eighteen slaves and 1,019 acres on Banister River in Pittsylvania County, to his friend Hugh Innes in return for a loan of £1,000. The loan was to be repaid over two years in bar iron valued at £25 per ton, in eight equal payments of five tons each, due every three months. Since Donelson kept possession of his home, he evidently was able to meet the terms of the loan.

Despite his investment in the bloomery's success, Donelson soon was ready to follow the frontier westward into Tennessee. A biographer of Andrew Jackson asserted that the enterprise had failed—"a speculation in an iron-works in Pittsylvania County swept away the accumulations of thirty prosperous years"[13]—and the failure prompted Donelson's decision. Apparently regardless of his personal financial situation, two of Donelson's adult children were moving over the mountains, and Donelson himself agreed to lead a party of settlers to French Lick, the future site of Nashville. After he decided to sell the ironworks,

Donelson quickly found buyers who had both the money and the experience to enlarge and operate the business on a scale grand enough to compete with any ironworks in the state.

James Callaway and his father-in-law, Jeremiah Early, both of Bedford County, were acquaintances of Donelson. Both men were prominent leaders of their county during the years of the revolutionary war, serving as justices and as militia colonels. Callaway also managed the state lead mines in Montgomery County from early 1776 to late 1777, superintending the operation of the blast furnace as well as the mines themselves. He may have been associated with David Ross in the operation of the Oxford Iron Works in Bedford County, and together with Jeremiah Early he may have leased Donelson's bloomery prior to 1779. In April 1779 a stray horse belonging to Count Casimir Pulaski's Legion was found "Two Miles from Joseph Earleys [Washington] Iron works,"[14] indicating that Jeremiah Early's son was managing the works for him and Callaway. Donelson sold his bloomery to Callaway and Early on 17 June 1779 and headed west to Tennessee.

James Callaway and Jeremiah Early took what John Donelson had built and, with a large infusion of capital and technology, made what had been a primitive, backwoods ironworks into a state-of-the-art manufacturing complex. To accomplish this required the demolition of the bloomery and tilt hammer and the construction of a blast furnace and refinery forge. The new works may have been built while the partners were leasing the bloomery from Donelson prior to the sale.

Laborers quarried granite from Scuffling Hill across Furnace Creek from the furnace site, and dug a foundation about twenty-eight feet square for the furnace. The granite blocks were worried into place, and slowly the furnace rose tapering to a height of about thirty feet. A wooden bridge led from the top of the furnace to the low hill behind it, and between the furnace and the hill a wheel pit was dug

Washington Iron Works furnace; work arch to left and tuyere arch to right. 1990 photo. (Virginia Department of Historic Resources.)

and a waterwheel erected to power the bellows. Upstream, Furnace Creek was dammed and workers built a wooden trough from the top of the dam to the waterwheel.

The construction of the interior, or bosh, of the furnace was crucial to its efficient operation. This central cavity widened like a flask from a diameter of about three feet at the top of the furnace to about eight feet near its base, and was lined with firebrick. At the bottom of the furnace the bosh narrowed to two feet in diameter to form the crucible, into which the molten iron settled. On the east side of the crucible was a tuyere opening for the blast, and on the south side were two openings: a small one blocked by a clay plug and a larger one blocked with a dam stone. The clay plug filled the taphole through which molten iron could flow out to the casting–floor, and the dam stone was removed when it was necessary to clean out the crucible.

Two arches were recessed into the outside of the furnace. The tuyere arch on the east allowed insertion of the bellows into the tuyere. On the south, a large work arch permitted access to the taphole and dam stone. In front of the work arch was the sand casting-floor, into which channels and side grooves were dug so the iron could flow from the taphole. The long channels were called sows and the side grooves were called pigs, from their resemblance to sows nursing their young. The sand bed also was used for casting large flat pieces of ironware such as stove plates and firebacks.

Making iron in a blast furnace required some of the same procedures used with a bloomery: heating the furnace, alternating layers of charcoal and ore—and limestone flux to burn off impurities—and gradually increasing the blast. The quantities of materials and fuel used were enormous, and when the furnace was in blast it demanded round-the-clock attention. The furnace alone could consume the equivalent in charcoal of an acre of hardwood a day.

Instead of carrying the pigs and sows to a single trip-hammer, workers had to use several such hammers because of the greater volume of iron produced. For this reason Callaway and Early built a two-hammer refinery forge about a mile down Pigg River from the furnace, at the site of the present-day Rocky Mount sewage treatment plant. The forge had four fireplaces for heating the pigs, and the trip-hammers and bellows were all powered by waterwheels. Since the forge was walled and roofed over, the din inside must scarcely have been bearable.

Within a month of their purchase of Donelson's bloomery, Callaway and Early named their new enterprise for their fellow Virginian and patriotic leader, George Washington, and took out an advertisement in the *Gazette of the State of South-Carolina*. The advertisement was datelined "Washington Furnace, Henry County, in Virginia, July 21, 1779," and announced:

Notice is hereby Given, THAT the said FURNACE entered into Blast the 1st of the present month, and it is expected will continue until Christmas next: where may be had, by wholesale or retail, the following assortment of castings, to wit, POTS, KETTLES, CAMP-KETTLES, OVENS, SKELLETS, FLATIRONS, SPICE MORTARS, FIRE DOGS, SMITHS ANVILS, FORGE ANVILS, FORGE HAMMERS, WAGGON BOXES, STOVES, or any other kind of Castings that may be wanted.

It is significant that at such an early date, and in the midst of a war, this backcountry ironworks could trade with a state hundreds of miles away. The influence of Callaway's enterprise stretched far beyond Henry County to include the southern states as a whole. According to local tradition, after the war, iron was transported regularly to Georgia.

Jeremiah Early died in the summer of 1779, and his share of the partnership with Callaway fell to Early's three sons, Joseph, John, and Jubal Early. Joseph died a year later and John sold part of his inheritance to Callaway; as a result, by 1781 James Callaway owned two-thirds of the ironworks, while John and Jubal Early owned one-third.

As the revolutionary war came to an end in the fall of 1781, then, the Washington Iron Works had grown substantially. The extent of this change was indicated by the deed from John Early to James Callaway, wherein Early listed property belonging to the ironworks in which he had a share by inheritance from his father: "Slaves, Stocks of Horses, Hoggs and Cattle, Waggons and Gears, Plantation Utensils, Black Smith and Carpenters Tools, and all kind of Apparatus necessary for Carrying on and Erecting a Sett of Iron Works."

The Washington Iron Works was not alone on the frontier, of course. Other ironworks had grown similarly during the war, although they were scattered around Virginia such an extent that direct competition was avoided. This state of affairs soon would come to an end, however, as the conclusion of the war and increased settlement in the western parts of Virginia brought additional demand for iron products. Competition would strengthen the industry; demand would outstrip supply, bringing growth and prosperity to Virginia's iron manufacturers until the panic of 1837 and northern technology rendered the southern works obsolete.

In 1782, however, the future was bright for Virginia's ironworks. Thomas Jefferson, in his *Notes on the State of Virginia,* commented on the condition of the industry: "Callaway's, Ross's, Millar's, and Zane's, make about 150 tons of bar iron each, in the year. Ross's makes also about 1600 tons of pig iron annually; Ballendine's 1000; Callaway's, Millar's, and Zane's, about 600 each." According to Jefferson's figures, the Washington Iron Works forge produced about 25 percent of the bar iron, and the furnace about 14 percent of the pig iron, manufactured in Virginia.

By the end of the revolutionary war, the Washington Iron Works had grown in size and complexity well beyond the scope of John Donelson's backwoods bloomery. In addition to the furnace and forge, Callaway built a sawmill and gristmill, as well as a tavern and store. To house the increased number of slaves he constructed new quarters on Scuffling Hill (so called because there was a long scuffle up the hill to bed after a tiring day at the furnace), as well as stables for the horses, sheds for storing ore, charcoal, and iron, a blacksmith's shop to shoe the horses and repair tools, and an office for conducting the business of the ironworks. By the mid-nineteenth century the land associated with the works amounted to almost eighteen thousand acres, necessary because of the insatiable demand of the furnace for wood. From its unsophisticated beginning as a small bloomery forge, the Washington Iron Works had developed into a major frontier industry in less than a decade. It had indeed become an "iron plantation"—almost a feudal village—and would remain Franklin County's principal industry until the decade before the Civil War.[15]

The Washington Iron Works was not the only such industry in the county, however; James Callaway faced competition from time to time. In the early 1790s Swinfield Hill, Walter Bernard, and William Armstrong built a forge on Blackwater River and a furnace on Story Creek. Collectively the forge and furnace were known as the Carron Iron Works. By 1795 John Miller, of Botetourt County, had built his Elk Forge about eight miles upstream from the Carron Forge. In 1803 Robert Harvey, also of Botetourt County, was constructing a forge about the same

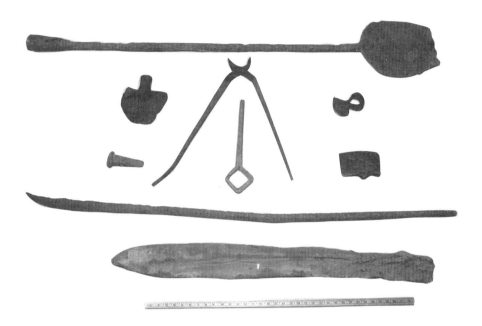

Ironworkers' tools. Top to bottom: *slag skimmer (missing wooden handle); shovel; tongs for handling hot castings; hoe head; wedge; wagon hub wrench; ax head; crowbar; pig iron from casting floor.* (J. Francis Amos, Rocky Mount, Va.)

Stoveplate cast at Washington Iron Works in 1786. (J. Francis Amos, Rocky Mount, Va.)

distance down Pigg River from the Washington Iron Works. Callaway responded to the threat of competition by purchasing the Carron Iron Works between 1801 and 1802. With the control of both of the county's furnaces and two of its four forges in his hands, Callaway secured domination of the local iron industry.[16]

After the death of James Callaway in 1809 his heirs operated the Washington Iron Works. In 1812 the heirs hired Peter Saunders, Jr., who was eager to learn all he could about the ironmaster's craft, and by 1815 he had become a partner. Two years later he and his two brothers, Fleming and Samuel Saunders, began to purchase shares in the ironworks from the heirs of Callaway and Early. By 1823 the three brothers owned the company, which continued to prosper until the panic of 1837. Peter Saunders retired from the business in 1846 and moved to a plantation in Pittsylvania County, where he died on 25 May 1847.

Although most of the ironworkers were slaves, the works also hired specialized free labor. In February 1851, for example, a white Pennsylvanian, William Sours, settled temporarily in Rocky Mount after having lived in the Valley of Virginia for almost a decade. Sours, who held a patent for an improved iron cooking stove, was joined by his brother Jacob in March. Together they purchased a house and lot in town while they worked at the Washington Iron Works. In letters to a third brother they wrote that they were "making Flasks and Fallow Board and other necessarys for making castings. . . . we expect to get to making casting now in about too weekes." They noted that the "Rocky Mount Furnace is about half mile from the Court house directly out the main street."[17]

The Washington Iron Works continued in operation until 22 August 1851, when a flash flood swept away Franklin County's oldest industry. Captain Peter Saunders, the son of Fleming Saunders, described the event in a letter to his mother on 1 September 1851:

> I found upon reaching this place [Rocky Mount] that they had been great sufferers from high water in this neighborhood. I Suppose you have heard of the damage done to the furnace. About half of the dam is washed away. The potting house & forge house are carried entirely away, Nobody knows where to. The Bellows house & the machinery in it are I believe uninjured. The water was up in the [furnace] stack. The generation of steam when the water entered the stack was so great as to produce a considerable explosion & the large portion of the contents of the stack were thrown some distance up into the air. The hearth I suppose is ruined. The stack is supposed to be otherwise uninjured. . . . The rain that produced the rise that carried away the furnace dam was said to be the hardest ever known about here. The stream rose so rapidly that the hands in the furnace had to make rather a precipitate retreat. The creek was so high that the houses I understand were started [washing away] before the dam gave away.[18]

William Sours also described the disaster in a letter to his brother John. After a dry summer the rain fell in gusts before dawn on 22 August, then

> in the afternoon of the same day there was another gust. The rain came down in torrents and the watter came down the Branch which drives the furnace in a wave as it ware about three ft. deep and drove through the furnace Casting [*illegible*] and through our casting house carrying all before it. It has entirely

broken us up here, carried of[f] all we had in the Foundry. What Patterns was in the ware House is still there but so racked as to be nearly distroyed excepting what was Iron. The water was some eight or nine inches over top of the doore of the house. The Furnace dam is also swept off but the Houses was gone first so we can do nothing here for a long time.[19]

The ironworks never recovered from the flood. The Franklin County iron industry, despite efforts to revive it, steadily declined until it virtually disappeared after the Civil War.

It was the location of the Washington Iron Works, in large measure, that first had determined the site of the county court complex. A village grew up around the courthouse square, although it was not immediately sanctioned by law. Despite the fact that Franklin County was a rural community, as was all America until the twentieth century, many of its citizens were anxious that towns be created.

An act of the General Assembly in 1792 established Wisenburgh and Germantown as the first towns in Franklin County, in response to petitions submitted to the legislature by interested citizens. Many of the petitioners had German surnames—including Gearhart, Muller, Prilliman, Nave, Gungnuiry [Kingery], Brubarger, and Pickleshimer—that no doubt suggested the names given the towns by the legislature. Wisenburgh was established on forty acres of land owned by Moses Greer, Sr., between modern-day Dugwell and Gogginsville, and Germantown was created on thirty-two acres owned by Daniel Layman and Stephen Peters, on Route 697 to the southeast of present-day Wirtz. Greer's land was vested in John Early, Jacob Boon, John Noftsinger, Daniel Barnhart, Samuel Thompson, William Wright, Jr., William Turnbull, and Swinfield Hill, as trustees for the sale of lots. Germantown already had been laid out into half-acre lots; Swinfield Hill, George Turnbull, Jacob Harkrider, Daniel Perry, Jubal Early, John Ferguson, and Tobias Miller were appointed trustees for their sale. The lots were to be sold at auction "subject to the condition of building on each a dwelling-house sixteen feet square at least, with a brick or stone chimney, to be finished fit for habitation within five years from the day of sale."[20]

The reasons given by the petitioners for wanting the towns established were centered around business. "They Conceive it useful," wrote the petitioners for Wisenburgh,

in all Countries to encourage by every Justifiable means the establishment of inland Manufacturing Towns, which they conceive, the more necessary in the parts of the State so remote from Navigation, as where your petitioners reside, inasmuch as thereby numbers of Artizans are Concenter'd to One Spot and a Lawdable Spirit of emulation in each to excell is excited, as well as a Certainty of reducing the Price of manufactured Necessaries to something like their real Value.[21]

Layman and Peters, who already had surveyed their land for Germantown, informed the General Assembly that they were acting "at the request of divers Inhabitants, Artizans & others."[22]

Ordinarily the major town in a county contained the seat of government. With James Callaway and Thomas Hill refusing to sell lots near the courthouse, however, it was possible that Wisenburgh or Germantown might surpass the courthouse village as business centers. This threat, together with personal antipathies and political conflicts, probably motivated the signers of the 1803 petition to establish a town at the courthouse and force the sale of lots. "A Town would form a rallying point," they wrote,

> to Merchants, Artisans, and Professional Characters, whose Settlement would prove an incalculable Source of convenience and wealth to the Industrious Farmer; it would banish those ruinous (Tho' legal) Traders [itinerant peddlers], who furnish us with goods & Receive money which is sent off, Scarcely leaving enough for the Ordinary purposes of Intercourse; it would Suppress those petty Stores whose Capitals are small & profits enormous, by giving Assylum to the true Merchants, whose connexions being coextensive with the County would employ large Capitals, sell cheap, and instead of draining the people of their Specie for the purpose of transportation, would furnish goods and receive produce of every description for which liberal and Sufficient prices would be given; Not only Tobacco, but that Superabundance of every kind, which Farmers can Spare (at present lost for want of a Market) would be Sold, & when collected in this place of general deposit would form an aggregate of Sufficient consequence to be exported. The Situation of those who have flourishing towns, will account for our anxiety upon this subject, & suggest to your honourable body the propriety of Granting what we ask.[23]

A town, the petitioners were convinced, would bring together craftsmen who were scattered around the countryside. Working and competing in close proximity, their skills would improve and their business increase, and they no longer would find it necessary to be part-time farmers.

Although the town of Mount Pleasant soon was established, the number of itinerant peddlers declined only briefly, for their goods remained in demand in the countryside where travel was difficult. These drummers and hawkers—clock salesmen, scissors grinders, and patent-medicine men—infested the countryside and yet brought their customers what they wanted. Some were the proverbial "Yankee traders," who peddled their goods, especially clocks, manufactured in New England, and gave local shopkeepers a taste of competition. In 1803 the Franklin County Court licensed nineteen peddlers, hawkers, and retailers of "goods of foreign manufacture" to practice their trade in Franklin County; in 1804 it issued thirteen such licenses and in 1805 the number rose to fourteen.[24] In 1806 the court once again licensed nineteen peddlers.[25]

The peddlers were a rough, crude, and independent lot. One of them left a diary of his journeys in 1807; although the author remains anonymous, he traveled in the company of Edward Downing, of Buckingham County. The two of them arrived in Liberty, the Bedford County seat, late in November, and found

> a very Poor Court no fighting or Gouging very few Drunken people [therefore few sales]. Left thence on Tuesday [24 November] about 2 OClock proceeding towards Henry C.H. Crossed Goose Creek forming a Conjunction with Wolf Fork another little Creek. Came that Night to a farmers House of the Name of John Hampton. . . . Next day traveled only about 8 or Nine miles. Hard fare, coarse and about double to pay that we Had the Night

before. Next Night came to my Old friend John Samples it Being late in the Evening rather night receive with the open Arms of Hospitality which indeed belongs to the real Hibernian. Remained there the next day to rest our Weary Bones. Departed from thence on Saturday [28 November] came to Franklin Court House where I met with one of the faculty [another peddler] who had settled himself with a handsome Store Of the name of [William] Culhoon from the old sod. Crossed Pig River and went right to an Entertainment kept by a Man of the Name of [Thomas] Whitworth who had two very Handsome Daughters.[26]

After becoming lost the next night on the road to Henry Court House, the diarist and Downing came to a millpond. Their subsequent experience illustrates the complete lack of privacy afforded by the typical dwelling of the time.

A Cabbin appearing in view upon the other side, we after Hallowing for Hearing and finding no relief determined to Cross the Stream to the Hutt; after Assending the Hill towards the house Mr. Downing Wrapt, no Answer. from my entreaties he Wrapped again, an Answer was made, and a female Voice I could distinguish. he requested admittance when she replyed that it was Cold and that he might push too the Door as she was unwilling to leave her nest. Downing Accordingly Opened the Door. She requested him to stir up the fire which he accordingly done, then turning Around and addressing himself to Her requested to Know if she Could give him a little Corn and admit him to rest by the fire. She refused replying that she Acted for Another and that she had never done so. all the entreaties that him or myself could make use of Could not persuade her to Comply. at Said Mr. Downing observing that she had No Companion in Bed with Her, and had a Couple of Children, My dear Madam said he where is your Husband. perhaps he may relieve us by Granting Our Request. She made reply that he was not at Home. Well My sweet Madam Said he do you not lay very Cold Without the Company of your Good man. his presence ought to be agreeable on Such a Night. I am Sorry both for your Sake and for my Own that he is not here. Downing Swaggered, Giving three or four turns round the little hutt, eying her and a Hoe Cake by turns that lay on a Shelf near the Bed. I viewed him, and Could not tell Whether of the two he wished for, but Concluding that she was not Handsome and his being within my Knowledge Hungry Guessed the Cake would be his Choice.

Finally the woman, no doubt terrified by the teasing of the two strangers, persuaded them to ride a mile down the road to the house of Major John Redd.

We proceeded and came to the House. the Family Being aBed, except a few Servants, it was with Great Entreaties that we prevailed upon one to let her Master know that we were there, and requesting him to admit us some relief and particularly some Corn for our Horses. He with a Great degree of Hospitality ordered some of the servants to assist us with our trunks and also sent us a Bottle of Good Whiskey and some Water a drink of which Greatly revived us. a Bed was also prepared which we enjoyed all of which was truly Grateful After our fatigue. he next Morning treated [us] kindly, and would receive no payment.

Eventually, as the number and quality of local stores improved, the hordes of peddlers swarming over the countryside declined. By 1829–1830, for example, the Franklin County Court licensed only six peddlers: Thomas Best, Dennis Boyton, Herman Crowl, Daniel Easton, Tracy G. Todd, and Yale and Dunley. Only three made their rounds in 1838–1839: John Gray, John W. O. Haynes, and John L. Sandefur.[27]

Although many peddlers were from other states, some were from nearby counties. One was Jonathan Cundiff, of Bedford County, who lived near Staunton River. Cundiff was a gunsmith who farmed, kept bees, made flaxseed oil, owned property on Blackwater River in Franklin County that he leased to Isham Cundiff, and manufactured gunpowder in his powder mill. He not only made rifles and shotguns but repaired them and made parts that he sold to other gunsmiths. He also kept a diary between 1820 and 1824, in which he mentioned riding to the Franklin County courthouse on court days to sell gunpowder and trade with such local gunsmiths as John Beheler. When Cundiff traveled to and from the courthouse he stayed with several friends or business acquaintances, including William Smith, Peter Holland, John Meador Holland, Michael Johnson, Peter Booth, George Beheler, and Thomas Hill.[28]

The hospitality of John Redd and other householders toward the peddlers was typical of the era—fortunately for the peddlers—at a time when taverns and ordinaries were scarce and the fare poor. The best inns were in the towns and county seats; in rural areas travelers usually had to rely upon the goodwill of men such as Redd. Towns, with their superior accommodations and services, were as great a boon to weary travelers as they were to their inhabitants.

Franklin County did not lack for ordinaries and houses of private entertainment, as they were called. An ordinary (also known as a house of *public* entertainment) was used as a hotel, primarily by travelers. A house of *private* entertainment was similar to a short-term boardinghouse, in that its lodgers usually stayed for brief periods—less than a month in a city or town, less than a week in the country. Food and drink were also provided.

The county court licensed ordinaries and houses of private entertainment, taking care that their proprietors ran sober, peaceful establishments and revoking their licenses if they did not. In 1829–1830, for example, the Franklin County Court licensed six ordinaries, the proprietors of which were John D. and Abram Booth, William Chitwood, Dickinson and Nowlin, Thomas Hale, Richard M. Taliaferro, and Skelton Taylor. During the same period it licensed fourteen houses of private entertainment: Isaac Boon, Andrew S. Brooks, Henry T. Callaway, James Callaway, David Cannaday, Aaron Feagle, William Greenwood, Chisholm Griffith, Samuel Hale, Thomas Helm, Peter Kesler, Benjamin Smith, William Williams, and James W. Williamson. By 1838–1839 the holders of ordinary licenses included John and Moses Booth, George A. Brown, Pleasant Dickinson, Henry Dillard, William G. Heptinstall, Heptinstall and Allen, Holland and Street, Moorman and Arnold, Littlebury Moon, Hopkins Nowlin, William L. Stockton and Company, Richard M. Taliaferro, and Luke Wade and Company. The houses of private entertainment were operated by John Boon, Andrew S. Brooks, Joseph Flora, Jr., David Goode, Chisholm Griffith, Thomas Helms, Miram Hill, Isaac Huff, Henry L. Muse, John Nafe, and Sterling Thornton. Some of the properties may have changed hands between licensing periods.[29]

A few of the old places still stand. One is the Brooks-Brown House in southeastern Franklin County near the intersection of present-day Routes 715 and 646, across the road from the site of Dickinson's store. Livestock drovers stopped at the house on their way to Pittsylvania County from the Valley. Another is Renfroes, the dwelling of Henry T. Callaway, who operated a house of private entertainment there in 1829–1830. It stands on Route 641 near the community of Callaway in the western part of the county.

Some of the ordinaries became famous or well known regionally. One that is indeed legendary is the Ashpone Tavern, said to have stood about five miles southeast of Rocky Mount on present-day Route 619 near the community of Sontag. Also known as Webb's Old Tavern, the inn—according to local tradition—lodged such notables as Patrick Henry and Andrew Jackson. Unfortunately for local tradition, however, the Franklin County Court apparently never issued an ordinary license to anyone surnamed Webb prior to Patrick Henry's death in 1799. The only official mention of such a tavern is in a court order issued in August 1863. Because the Pittsylvania, Franklin, and Botetourt Turnpike needed to be repaired, the Franklin County Court divided that part of the turnpike that ran through the county into sections and assigned work crews to each section. The fifth section extended from "Rocky Mount to the Ash Pone Tavern."[30] The mystery surrounding the tavern is deepened by the fact that it does not appear on either the field notes or the map drawn in 1838 when surveyors laid out the route of the turnpike.

Another ordinary, White's, which stood in southern Franklin County, was the site of an incident involving the itinerant Methodist preacher Lorenzo Dow. According to the story Dow, a colorful, intelligent man whom imaginative countrymen sometimes mistook for the devil because of his wild, dark hair and unkempt beard, slept upstairs while various revelers passed the evening in the barroom below.

Brooks-Brown House. 1989 photo. (Virginia Department of Historic Resources.)

At a late hour in the night, the alarm was given that one of the company had lost his pocket book, and a search proposed. Whereupon the landlord remarked, that Lorenzo Dow was in the house, and that if the money were there, he knew that Lorenzo could find it. . . . [He awakened Dow, who determined that no one had left the barroom.] "Then," said Lorenzo, turning to the landlady, "go and bring me your large dinner pot. . . . [Next] go and bring the old chicken-cock from the roost." This was also done, and at Lorenzo's directions, the cock placed in the pot, and covered over with a board, or lid. "Let the doors now be fastened, and the lights extinguished," said Mr. Dow, which was also done. "Now," said he, "every person in the room must rub his hands hard against the pot, and when the guilty hand touches, the cock will crow." Accordingly, all came forward, and rubbed . . . against the pot. But no cock crew. "Let the candles now be lighted," said Lorenzo . . . "[and] let us now examine the hands." This was the important part of his arrangement. For on examination, it was found that one man had not rubbed against the pot. The others' hands being black with the soot of the pot, was a proof of their innocence. "There," said Lorenzo, pointing to the man with *clean hands*, "there is the man who picked your pocket." The culprit seeing his detection, at once acknowledged his guilt, and gave up the money.[31]

This story was printed in small type at the end of one chapter in a book of Dow's writings published in 1855. The publisher also printed the following disclaimer in his introduction to the book:

It is due the reader, that he be informed that the *anecdotes, &c.,* found in *small type,* at the end of the several chapters, were added by the publishers, to give interest to the work, and are in substance believed to be genuine.[32]

The ordinaries were essential to travelers in the late eighteenth and early nineteenth centuries, when most journeys were largely a torturous struggle from one such accommodation to another over bad roads and steep hills. John Brown, a traveler in late December 1794, recorded such a trip in his journal as he passed from Botetourt County (present-day Roanoke County) through Franklin County and beyond by way of the Great Wagon Road. On 26 December he and his companions

came to Roownoak Rover & stade at a certain Tohrns [?] in the Morning on the 27th we Rode [over] the River Near 50 Yards Broad then we got out of the limestone in a Verry hilly Country But has some old livers [aged inhabitants] perhaps from Forty to fifty years we Rode 12 Miles to a Mr. Northsingers [John Nofsinger] on the watters of Black[water] River it emptys Rown oack River from there we Roade 9 Miles to [*blank*] where I got my hoarse shod from thence we Rode 8 Miles to a Widow Forgesons [probably Elizabeth Ferguson, widow of John Ferguson, who died in 1789 or 1790] where we met with about 30 Negroes at a Ball in what they Call a Negro house this was in Franklin County in the morning we Cros'd Pig River & Rode 4 Miles this was on Sunday the 28th and Breckfasted a Mr. Standford [perhaps Luke Standifer] from there ar Mountains for 18 Miles we Put 6 quarts oats in one of our Blankets & Came about 9 Miles and Seen a small Kind of a hous where we Lade our Blankets on the Ground & feed our hoarses & in the (Pen for that is

Name it shou'd have) an old Woman Lived in the Most desolate maner that I
had ever seen any of the Human Race we Rode 9 Miles to an old Gentleman
of the Name of Basdell [probably John Barksdale] who yused [treated] us well
we Drank some of his Jimmey that was the Peatch Brandy where we Staid all
Night and Crossed Smith River [into Henry County] in the morning.[33]

Brown stayed most nights with farmers and their families, as did many travelers.
Neither Nofsinger, Ferguson, Standifer, nor Barksdale had been licensed by the
Franklin County Court to operate an ordinary.

By the mid-1830s the amenities offered by Mount Pleasant—known popularly
as Rocky Mount—no doubt looked better to the traveler than what he could find
in the country. It may even have resembled the town its founders envisioned in
1803. A gazetteer published in 1836 reported that the community contained

> besides the usual county buildings, about 30 dwelling houses, 3 general
> stores, and 2 taverns. The mechanics are 2 tailors, a saddler, cabinet maker, 2
> blacksmiths, a boot and shoe manufacturer, a printing office, which issues a
> weekly paper, and a tanyard. In the vicinity there is an iron furnace and
> forge, which give employment to 100 operatives, and manufacture about
> 160 tons of bar iron and castings annually. Population (exclusive of the
> persons employed in the iron manufactory) 175 persons; of whom 3 are
> attorneys, and 1 a physician.[34]

The same gazetteer noted eleven post offices besides the one at Rocky Mount:
Boones Mill, Callaway's Mill, Cooper's, Dickinson, Halesford, Helm's, Hunter's
Hall, Shady Grove, Taylor's Store, Union Hall, and "Woodpecker's Level," present-
day Peckerwood Level. Union Hall was the only village except Rocky Mount that
was large enough to be described (no construction ever took place in Wisenburgh, and Germantown virtually had disappeared):

*Ferguson's (Waid's) stage stop
at Pigg River on the Great Wagon Road* (foreground). (Blue
Ridge Institute, Ferrum, Va.)

It contains 15 dwelling houses, 1 Methodist house of worship, at which an English school is kept, and one well organised temperance society. The mechanics are a tanner, tailor, blacksmith, and tobacco manufacturer. In the vicinity on Pig river is an extensive manufacturing flour mill, and a wool and cotton manufactory. Population 25 persons; of whom one is a physician.[35]

The gazetteer did not mention the town of Lawrence, although it had been created in 1818—as Halesborough—and still existed in 1832 when the gazetteer was compiled.[36] The county land tax books for that year reveal that forty-three of the town's two hundred half-acre lots had been sold.[37] The site of the town, which stood on the Staunton River between Halesford and Merriman Run, was submerged when Smith Mountain Lake was created in the 1960s. Lawrence's promoters, Philip Thurmond and Anslem Clarkson, waxed lyrical about the advantages of the location:

This situation has been for years marked by the judicious and enterprising as eligible for a town. . . . It commands a general and delightful view of the River, abounds with refreshing springs of the purest water, convenient to all parts of the town, and susceptible of being conveyed to every door. The adjacent country will supply any quantity of the best building timber of different growths, and excellent rock for the same purpose, to almost any extent may be obtained, within the limits of the town.[38]

Thurmond and Clarkson also planned to petition the General Assembly "for an inspection of Flour and Tobacco at this place, and also for permission to connect the counties of Bedford and Franklin by a Free Bridge." Another advertisement reported that a petition would be "offered to the next legislature for an act to divide the Counties of Franklin, Bedford and Pittsylvania, and form a new one, and this town will be the seat of justice for that County."[39] Apparently the promoters never carried out their intentions, however.

Despite the competition from other villages, the courthouse town of Mount Pleasant remained the political and economic center of Franklin County. By midcentury it was small but substantial, according to a Pennsylvanian who lived there briefly. He described the town and its inhabitants in a letter to his brother in March 1851:

The men here are most of them dark complected with tremendous large Whiskers. The Women are Generally fair and some of them pretty good looking. This but a small Town, probably some Hundred and fifty or 200 inhabitants. About one Half of the Buildings are of Brick. The Town lies on top of a hill and derives it name from a hill called Bald nob some 3/4 mile distant, the top of which is a mass of solid Rock and when on top of said hill can overlook the surrounding neighbourhood. I with some half dozen young Gentlemen & Ladies was on top of it the other day had a spy glass with us and had a fine View of the country. The Peaks of Otter can be seen very plain with the naked eye, which are some forty or fifty miles distant.[40]

In 1850, according to the United States census, the town boasted a hotel (operated by Robert Sutfin), a tavern (Creed G. Adams), four attorneys (Jubal A.

Early, Edmond Irvin, William Wingfield, and Robert G. Woods), three physicians (Robert Baldwin, William Hopkins, and Richard M. Taliaferro), a postmistress (Ann J. Greer), three schoolteachers (Letitia J. Baldwin, Charlotte Grimes, and James Milano), three carpenters (Middleton Davis, James C. Harper, and William Rout), a constable (Thomas F. Forbes), a tanner (Esome Sink), a saddler (Samuel Bright), a tailor (William M. Featherton), a blacksmith (Otey Hambrick), and four merchants (Peter Davis, Addison Lavinder, David Nininger, and Moses Greer).[41]

Chronicle Building (formerly Creed Adams's Rocky Mount tavern, then Early House hotel). Ca. 1909 photo. (Dorothy Cundiff, Franklin County, Virginia, Yesterday & Today, 1976. Reprinted with permission.)

In 1850 and 1860 census takers recorded information about local "industries"

Angle Mill. 1970 photo. (Virginia Department of Historic Resources.)

on both the general population schedules and on special schedules.[42] A comparison of the schedules reveals the apparent growth of Franklin County industries during the decade preceding the Civil War (because of occasional omissions by the census takers the growth may have been more apparent than real). In 1850 there were nine "manufacturing mills" in the county that ground corn and wheat into meal and flour; in 1860 there were thirteen. The county's fifteen tobacco factories increased to seventeen in the same period. There were only four gristmills to grind corn in 1850 (owned by Samuel Gilbert, Robert Pinkard, Robert Powell, and Fleming and Samuel Saunders), but by 1860 there were sixteen. Michael Zeigler owned the only sawmill in the county in 1850, if the census report was accurate; by 1860 there were fifteen others. Zeigler also owned a "wool machine" and a cotton gin in 1850, but in 1860 he faced competition from John Montgomery, C. and J. Musgrove, and the firm of Wray and Boon. In 1850 there were three tanneries, operated by Creed Bernard, Christopher Cundiff, and Daniel S. Simpson. Ten years later there were eleven: Creed and W. E. Bernard, Zadock Bernard, Christopher Cundiff, Joseph C. McGuffin, Lewis G. Mason, Samuel G. Mason, Joseph D. Meade, Owen Price, James L. Rice, Michael Scott, and Daniel S. Simpson. The Washington Iron Works, owned by Fleming and Samuel Saunders, still operated its furnace and forge in 1850, as did the Valley Forge, which was owned by two of Fleming Saunders's sons, Peter and Robert Saunders. By 1860 only the Valley Forge remained in operation, however, and the Saunders brothers had constructed a new Carron Furnace as well. One founder, Jacob Kirch, probably worked for the Saunders brothers in 1860. The 1860 census also listed two miners, G. S. Grasty and John H. Grasty. Two colliers (charcoal makers) were listed in 1850: Joseph Harrison and Peter Harrison; the latter was still working in 1860. Marion Hix worked as a "moulder" in 1860, while a blind, illiterate potter, Abner Beard, also was in business; perhaps Hix made casting molds for the ironworks and Beard produced storage containers for

Creed Bernard's tanyard stood across Tanyard Road from present-day National Guard Armory. (Dorothy Cundiff, *Franklin County, Virginia, Yesterday & Today, 1785–1978.* Reprinted with permission.)

domestic use. The 1860 census recorded a single plow maker, Crockett I. Saunders. John A. Smith operated a distillery in 1850; he also owned one of the "manufacturing mills" and a tobacco factory. In 1860 eleven men were listed as "manufacturers" in the census of inhabitants: Lewis Becker, William A. Burwell, Alexander Ferguson, J. H. Ferguson, T. B. Ferguson, B. N. Hatcher, A. T. Holland, Smithson G. Holley, Benjamin F. Preston, James C. Smith, and John A. Street.

Reuben Flora was recorded as a "maker of thrashers" in 1860, John H. Kinsey called himself a mechanic, and Eli W. Akers and Nicholas Cassell said they were machinists. Read Peasley was the county's sole reported distiller in 1860.

Blacksmithing had twenty-eight practitioners listed in 1850, and in 1860 there were fifty-one. Several men worked in the transportation industry. The 1850 census listed four wagonmakers and five wheelwrights, while the 1860 census reported one "waggoner," two coachmakers, and seventeen wheelwrights. Eight saddlers were listed in 1850, and the same number in 1860.

The traditional trades also were represented in the census records. There was one silversmith in 1860 (Philip L. Forbes) and one watchmaker (Paschal B. Peterman). In 1850 sixteen shoemakers were recorded; their number had increased to thirty in 1860. Seven tailors were working in 1850. Ten years later there were three tailors, one tailoress, and two seamstresses. Six men were listed as cabinetmakers in 1850, and a decade later there were eleven. One chair maker, Thomas Robinson, was recorded in 1850. There was one cooper, Joel Leftwich, in 1850; ten years later there were eight. John Beheler, a local gunsmith who was working in the county as early as 1820, was still active in 1850. Although he was not recorded as a gunsmith in 1860 (Thomas V. Bernard was), Beheler no doubt kept working; when he died in 1881 he still owned a workbench and "Riflings rods."[43]

Rifle made by John Beheler ca. 1840, with bullet mold, powder horn, pouch, and worm. (J. Francis Amos, Rocky Mount, Va.)

The building trades were well represented in both censuses. Twenty-two men worked as carpenters in 1850, and ten years later there were sixty-six, including one woman. There was one bricklayer (Micajah Saunders) in 1850, and three in 1860 (Daniel Ferguson, Andrew I. Hodges, and Charles T. McBride). Two men in 1860 called themselves stonemasons (John Bradner and John McLaughlin), while two others were recorded only as "masons" (Solomon G. Hensely and Thomas Quintrell).[44]

By 1860 two noteworthy examples of sophistication had come to the county. First, it had its own mail carrier, Thomas Mattox. Second, more surprisingly, there were three artists. One was R. H. W. Dillard, son of Dr. Henry Dillard. The other two were H. R. Phillips, of Maryland, and E. A. Haynes, of New York. Whether these artists were painters or "daguerrean artists," as photographers sometimes were known, is not clear.

The changes in the ownership of industries and the disappearance of several craftsmen in the course of a decade serve to illustrate the riskiness of private enterprise in the nineteenth century. During this age there was very little business insurance available, no paid vacations or sick leave, no workman's compensation or unemployment insurance or social security. Wage earners were paid at subsistence levels: in 1850 the average monthly wage a farmhand received (aside from his board) was $5; by 1860 the wage had doubled to $10. A common laborer in 1850 received $0.50 a day if boarded and $0.75 if not. Ten years later these figures had not changed. A carpenter earned $1.25 a day in 1850 without board and $1.50 in 1860.[45]

Each person was responsible for his or her own work and for accumulating the wealth to last through illnesses and old age. The failure to provide adequately could mean dependence upon the charity of friends, parents, children, or other relatives. At worst it led to a poverty-ridden old age or the poorhouse. Bankruptcies were common and the words "failure" and "ruin" were all too accurately applied to them.

Businessmen and entrepreneurs were distinctly in the minority in Franklin County as well as throughout the United States. The capital required to start a business or industry was inaccessible to many; the risk was too great for most. The residents of Franklin County, generally, were content to do as their fathers and grandfathers had done, and farm the land. Farming was no less dependent on weather and the markets then as now, but it was the way of life—as well as a business—enjoyed by most citizens for almost two hundred years of the county's history.

SEVEN

Agriculture and Transportation

J ust as there were successful and unsuccessful businessmen in nineteenth-
century Franklin County, so too some farmers were more successful than
others. But rural Franklin County was composed of more than only the rich
and the poor; there was a large, middling class that lived in a range of relative
prosperity from just above subsistence to very comfortable.

Each farm, whether large or small, underwent similar processes. Land had to be
cleared, using free labor, slave labor, and animal power. Farmers girdled trees,
felled them, and broke the land around the stumps. They used plows when they
had them, mattocks, shovels, spades, and hoes when they did not. Tobacco was
the principal money crop, but farmers also raised corn, wheat, oats, rye, flax,
hemp, and some cotton. Sometimes, however, the crop was not harvested. In the
late eighteenth or early nineteenth century the overseer for General Joseph
Martin, of Henry County,

> put in a field of wheat on Pig River . . . but [was] too indolent to fence it;
> there was something of a crop, friends and neighbors were invited to the
> reaping, a fiddler and whisky were also provided, most of the reapers got
> drunk, and the crop was never harvested.[1]

Usually, of course, crops were considered too precious to waste because for most
farmers the margin between subsistence and failure was very small. The large
families of the eighteenth and nineteenth centuries often resulted in reduced
economic opportunities for the children and other heirs. To divide the family
farm among several sons might create portions so small that they could not
support each family, much less produce the surplus crop that could mean
increased prosperity. Some sons went into a trade, moved to a city or another
county, or left Virginia with their eyes fixed on the western horizon. Before and
during the Revolution some adventurous souls emigrated from Franklin County
to the new frontier of Tennessee and Kentucky. Perhaps they had heard the tales of
Daniel Boone and his fellow explorers. The emigrants included William Cook,

125

who had lived on Hatchet Creek, a branch of Pigg River, not far from Peter Saunders, Sr. Cook settled in Kentucky about 1780 with Jesse Cook, Hosea Cook, Lewis Mastin, and Walter Dunn, at a colony on the Elkhorn River established by Hugh Innes. Although settlers in the area had had no conflicts with the Indians, the Native Americans soon attacked the colony and killed Jesse Cook, Lewis Mastin, and one of Innes's slaves. Another significant emigration occurred just after the revolutionary war, when many Virginians moved to Georgia. Emigrants who moved to Wilkes County, Georgia, by the early 1790s included members of the Heard family; John Starkey, of Gills Creek; George Griffith, of Little Creek; Daniel Richardson, of Snow Creek; and Parmenas and George Haynes, also of Snow Creek. William Swanson went to Oglethorpe County. About 1800 some of the Dunkards, under the leadership of Jacob Miller, left Franklin County for the Miami Valley in Ohio. A few young men joined the stampede to California after gold was discovered in 1848.[2]

A decade earlier, in 1838, a wagon train left Franklin County for the Missouri territory. Among the hundred or so emigrants, which included members of the Beard, Burwell, Carter, Harper, Maddox, Noble, Overfelt, Pollard, Webb, and Wright families, were Samuel Wood Greer and his family. Greer kept a diary of the two-month journey and recorded that the trip was relatively uneventful except for a frustrating experience with the nuts that held the wagon wheels on their axles. Apparently the axles were of a new type, and some of them were bent going over the mountains. The train stopped at a blacksmith's shop and the axles were disassembled and repaired, then reassembled. The blacksmith, however, was unfamiliar with the new axles and put them together incorrectly, causing the nuts to unscrew themselves as the wheels turned. For miles the men walked beside the wagons and resecured the nuts until they reached another blacksmith who reassembled the axles correctly, much to everyone's relief.[3]

Many of those who left Franklin County were adventurous or dissatisfied with their lives in Virginia. Others were impelled by economic motives, such as the rising price of available land, or the prospect of greater rewards elsewhere. Some, particularly, in the early years of the county's existence, may never have intended to remain. Most of the first dwellings built in the county, largely log buildings, have disappeared because—particularly in rural areas—they were not constructed for permanence. The farmer replaced his hastily erected house with a better structure if he prospered, and soon abandoned it if he did not.

Just as those who left had reasons for going, those who remained had reasons for staying. Some were well off and had no reason to leave. Perhaps they had inherited farms or were able to purchase and improve them. Other residents were committed to supporting elderly relatives, or were too attached to family and friends, or simply were overcome by inertia.

Regardless of one's economic status, however, every citizen had to cope with a complex economic system that often involved the exchange of labor and goods rather than money. Until at least the mid-nineteenth century many of the everyday transactions of American life were conducted by barter rather than by the exchange of cash. Hard currency was scarce, banks were few, and the more sophisticated aspects of the economic system were beyond the reach of many country people. Cash was reserved for the payment of taxes and to purchase goods that could not be obtained through barter. Credit was available, but only for the short term. Even farms frequently were purchased through deeds of mortgage that expired in just two or three years.

Landless farmers who rented others' farms (no doubt hoping to buy their own someday) often buried themselves in such debt that they were never able to extract themselves. Baxter Sympson, for instance, rented the Franklin County plantation of Harmon Cook, a Pittsylvania County resident, in December 1786. He began by owing Cook £8.0.0 in rent, "to be paid in Iron Tobacco or Corn." On 7 February 1787 Sympson purchased a gallon of brandy from Cook for eight shillings; he bought another pint of brandy for one shilling and a currycomb for three shillings on 29 April. By then he also owed Cook another £2 for "Services Done for plowing of Corn," bringing the total debt to £10.12.0. In four months of renting the farm Sympson only paid Cook the equivalent of £2.15 in corn and flax, to reduce his debt to £7.17.0. In desperation Sympson signed a promissory note for "one Tun and half of Iron by the Long hundred to be paid on or before The first Day of august next Ensuing," but failed to deliver on that promise as well.[4]

The economic system in use in the countryside in the late eighteenth and early nineteenth centuries was a complicated one in which debt itself was a commodity. Everyone was personally liable to everyone else, or so it seemed. Debts were bought, sold, and traded in a web of transactions and obligations that occasionally collapsed of its own weight into a confused tangle that only a court could unravel.

The saga of William Mavity and a host of his fellow citizens illustrates the bewildering dilemma of debt. The convoluted story is best told in Mavity's own words, in a letter he wrote to his attorney in 1786:

> I sold a Wagon to Joseph Jones Deceased on the following Conditions—I had sold her to Mr. Perkins for £23/0/0, and had gave an order to Peter Saunders to Receive the Money, the Bargain with Jones was if Saunders got the Money the Wagon was Perkins's and Jones was to pay the Hire, if Saunders did not get the Money Jones was to have the Wagon for £23/0/0 and his Contract of payment Run thus: he was to pay Peter Saunders £2/0/0 or there abouts that I owed him, he was to pay Thos Roberts Some Money I owed him, he was to pay Isaiah Willis Some Money I owed him, and to pay the Sherif My Taxes and to pay Moses Greer £5/0/0 Worth of Bar Iron which I owed Mr. Greer for the Sd Wagon, but he only paid Capt. Saml Hairston £2/3/0 for Thos Roberts though he was to pay all these Sums Emediately at Richmond and the Ballance at his Return of his Wagons and if I sustained any Damage through his failiour of paying the sums aforesaid he was to make it good. However he [Joseph Jones] died before he Returned and I wanted to get my Wagon again as he had not complyed with his contract, Neither could I see any way to make myself whole for the Imense damage I Sustained thereby. At lenght I was Informed by Capt. Hill that I could not get her, therefore I wrote to Mr. Thos Jones that I would Concern no more about it but give it up to god and his own Conscience. Some time after old Mr. Jones told me that Elijah Jones was Indebted to the Estate and if he would pay me, he would be glad. After Some time he Saw Elijah Jones and told him if he would pay me it would be good to him and satisfy him. Sir, this is near the Case and I have brought Suit against Thomas Jones and Wm Standifer Administrators of [Joseph Jones, for] Trespass on the Case and I hope you will undertake for me and Prosecute the Suit. It is Returnable next Court and if the Writt is Rong please to order one

Right and push for a tryal as soon as possable as I Suffer Exceedingly for the want of it this hard year being already forced to sell a cow that would give milk to my Children for Iron to pay Mr. Greer for the wagon. Your care herein shall be Rewarded besides your fee by your Humble Servant William Mavity.[5]

Unfortunately for Mavity, even the Franklin County Court could not unravel this skein. It dismissed the suit at the plaintiff's cost.

Sometimes a plaintiff asked an officer of the court to act on his behalf. In 1791 Samuel Henderson wrote to Stephen Smith, the clerk of the Franklin County Court, about his suit against Joseph Ritter. Henderson hoped to save himself some time and trouble at the expense of the clerk:

Sir, As my wife and my Selfe is so unwell that we are not able to attend Court and as Joseph Ritter has not paid the money I desair that the Sute may go on, and Sir if you think there is a Caishon for an atorney Pleas to imploy one for me and I will pay him and you to inform him the Nature of it, and if no attorney I hope you will moshan it to the Courte—and you will much Obledge your well wisher.[6]

In addition to a person's time, his labor—or the labor of his servants—was considered a valuable commodity. In January 1789 John Hook engaged Stephen Wood to "frame and build a barn for him." To assist Wood, Hook hired George, a slave owned by Henry Loving (no doubt at a cheap rate). Evidently Loving reneged on his promise, however, and when Wood went to Hook's to work he found that instead of George, "Hook was obliged to hyre Philip Railey to assist me" at the rate of £3.10 per month. Wood complained that "George could execuit the work about the Barn after the same was laid off for him neirly or quite as well as Mr. Railey, likewise a deal of work that said Hook had to do such as paleing [fencing] in a Yard and Garden." Hook sued Loving for breach of contract, but whatever excuse Loving offered for failing to supply George for the work satisfied the court and jury, which ruled in the defendant's favor.[7]

Thomas Arthur, the most controversial justice on the county court, found himself before the bench instead of behind it when his plan to pay off a large debt with slave labor failed in its execution. Arthur borrowed £98.14.0 in gold and silver from Nicholas Alley on 5 December 1785 and gave him a promissory note obliging Arthur

To Furnish a good Negro or sum other hand in sd Negros place To Work for sd Nickles alley untill he sd Arthur shude repay the mony Borrod of sd alley or Sell unto him sd alley a good Negro to his sattisfactson for Wich I Bind my self my Heirs & So forth. . . . NB the Negro or sd Hand is to Begind his Worke the first Day of Janny 86 or at Crismoss Day Next.[8]

Arthur planned to hire a slave or two belonging to his mother-in-law to work for Alley, but unexpected problems arose that stymied him. He wrote to Alley to explain the situation:

Whare as I Heird Two good Negros of my Mother in law Sum Desputs have since a Resin a monkst the Children it Semes I am Not lickley to have them in time But to pervent you Being Disappinted I Now Tell you that in or a Boute 5 or 6 Days I shall Come up With a young man a Son of Capt. Doggetts Wife that I have Heird for that Bessness To Worke for you one year if not Relest Be Fore[.] if He Dont Come then With me I must Bring up one of my Negros With me all tho thare are Verey unwillin To leve me on any oceason. But you may Relie on it I Will Behave To you like a Gentleman all tho I am informd that Sum people has mead them Selves Verey Besey in telling you I Want a man of my Word[.] I say thare are a lier that says so on any accompt What Ever.

Despite Arthur's defense of his honor he was unable to fulfill his agreement because the worker he had hired for Alley fell ill. On 10 May 1786 Arthur wrote Alley that

this Morning Thomas Sullers appuird at my House Wich I am Verey sorro to hear of his Being un Well But he says he Can go to Worke Tomorro morring a Gain[.] You may Depent if I have any onner in me for so Grate a Faver as you have Dun me I Will so you shall Be yoused [treated] licke a Prince all tho I am Suffering[.] the money you lent me I Wase a Bledge To Pay other mens Dets With[.] I Can onley say Harde Wase my Fourthan & it is Two late To Call yester Day Back But I Trust & hope I shall live To Se my [se]lf in C[lea]r in spite of that Harde luck [ye]t[.] I am Verey un Well at this Time & my Wife licke Wise[.] I hope yours is all Well at this Time. if I Dont Get Desappinted I think to oppen a Verey Fine store at the Cross Roads Verey sune as Capt Thorp is a Blidge a Way[.] if it shud Be the Case I Can sell goods as Cheep as any man this Sid of Richmond[.] I shud Be glad To se you thare then if so[.]

Although Arthur was able to repay part of his debt, Alley sued and was awarded £78.8.4 in damages.

Few farmers tended their farms unassisted. At a time when cheap land always was available just over the western horizon, the pool of labor was small outside the family. Slave ownership was not financially possible for many farmers; although slaves often were leased, the example of Thomas Arthur showed that leasing was not always an expedient option either. Property owners sometimes ranged far afield in search of laborers or renters. Owner dissatisfaction with their renters and workers, and the transient nature of those occupations, meant that turnover was frequent.

The rent usually was small and was paid either in produce or in labor. In 1785, for example, Obediah Ferguson rented Lucy Richardson's plantation in Bedford County for three barrels of corn.[9] Moses Hudgins, who served as trustee for the guardian of a minor's estate—which consisted of two Franklin County plantations on Linville Creek—rented the property to William King for a year beginning on 12 March 1788. In lieu of cash alone for the rent the two men agreed that King "is to Build two good good [sic] Cabins and as Much Ground as he tends he is to Put it Under a Lawful fence or 8 New Rails and is to give forty shillings Payable New years Day [1789]."[10]

If a tenant failed to keep his side of the bargain, he could expect to be sued by his landlord. If the jury or judge was more sympathetic to the landowner, the renter could lose what little personal property he possessed, as well as his lease.

When William King constructed only one cabin instead of the two he had agreed to, Moses Hudgins, who suspected that King was going to abscond from the county before the rent came due, took him to court. The jury decided the case in Hudgins's favor, and to satisfy the verdict King had to give up "a parcel of Corn & foder and a Mare and Colt."[11]

Parker Gee was more fortunate. On 21 April 1789 Gee leased from Thomas Livesay

> for one Yeare a plantation where his Son John Livesay lived the last year for the Consideracion of Eight barrels of corn to be paid at crismus or when Gedered as the said Livesay Pleases and the said Livesay Binds himself to Warrant and Defend the Said Gee from all persons what so ever in Desterbing or mollesting of him and the said gee Binds himself his heirs Excutors to pay unto Thos Livesay his heirs or assings eight barrels of corn as a bove menchand and keep possesion for the Saide Livesay and in his name the said gee is not to cut or destroy any timber but what he burns for fier wood in the house and the said gee binds his selfe his heirs Excutors and Assings to give up poss[ess]ion to the said Thos Livesay or his order at or upon the first day of march 1790.[12]

Apparently Gee did not live up to his agreement. Fearing that his tenant might flee the county, on 10 March 1790 Livesay persuaded constable John Coop to seize "two horses thirteen head of hogs & some household forniture" belonging to Gee. Livesay sued Gee in the Franklin County Court, but the jury rendered a verdict in Gee's favor. Presumably his property was returned.

In the late eighteenth century the overseer often worked for a share of the crops in addition to money. In return the landowner lent him the land and labor necessary to make a crop. Often the contract between landowner and overseer ran for a year at a time, usually from one Christmas to the next.

On 8 November 1785, for instance, Ralph Dangger and Archibald Graham signed articles of agreement that Dangger would serve as Graham's overseer. The articles stipulated that Graham had

> given into the Cear of the Said Danger for Duering the term of one year four field hands neamed as foallows: Mingo Suesand DillowSarling and Limbrick and likewise two horses with all farming Eutenshiels Set to til the Ground for which I the said Dangger Dothe oblige myself as an overseer to give the land Sufficient attendance with being a hand wit the negroes deuring that tarm being Expired and also has the Sixth part of all Grean I have put into the Grounds and also the fith pounds of tobacco throughout the Crop with also takeing Suffisent Cear of all stocks on the plantation belonging to the said above mentioned Graham to find fier wood and also is to have now when Calld for foar hundred weaght of beaf and a hundred of pork and Corn sufficient to Bread My family for Deuring the Crop being made.[13]

If any part of the bargain was broken, the whole was to be null and void, hence Graham could charge Dangger for the pork, corn, and so on due him under the contract.

Graham complained that Dangger failed to live up to his end of the bargain, and in fact destroyed many of the items left in his care. Graham submitted a list to the

Franklin County Court to support his complaint:

My Acount against Reaf Danger, March 4, 1786
to a Neagro Weagon and horses for one Day Uppon
    My Cost   £0/10/0
to One Mare going to My Stallon   0/15/0
to One freason he broak belonging to the three
    hors tree
to one Cleavis pin he lost
to too Axes, he burnt them and broak them
to tenn bushels of Corn he got from me
to One Sttear he took for fore hundread Waight
to One hundred Waight of pork he got
and to Damiges In Making of a Crop
and I for Warned him from taking his Cott away till
    I was sattisfied.

If Dangger wreaked such havoc in just a few months—losing equipment and burning axes—perhaps his ineptitude as an overseer explains why he was near the bottom of the Franklin County economic ladder. In 1786, according to the tax books, he did not own any land, slaves, horses, or cattle. He totally depended on his own labor for his living, provided someone would hire him. He quickly vanished from the county.

Archibald Graham, on the other hand, prospered. He owned 1,297 acres of land, four horses, and three cattle, and paid taxes on four slaves. The amount of taxes he paid placed him among the upper 7 percent of taxpayers in the county. Probably because Graham's land was all in one large tract, and unless he was absent frequently, he and Dangger lived and labored in close proximity to each other.

Many overseers worked for absentee landlords who either lived in another county or owned more than one operating farm in a county. On 4 January 1798 John Early, who lived in Franklin County, hired William Bradley, of Henry County, to oversee the work on Early's Henry County farm. Early lent Bradley five slaves, the farm tools necessary to make a crop, two plow horses, and one milk cow, and gave him three hundred pounds of pork, seven barrels of corn, one share of the tobacco made on the plantation, and one share of the grain. Early reserved to himself four and a half shares of the tobacco and five and a half shares of the grain. As a further incentive to Bradley to perform well, "Early (provided the said Bradley Behaves himself well) agrees to give him 150 weight of pork more in addition to the 300 weight."[14]

Franklin County's overseers, to judge from the scanty evidence available, seem not to have been any more respected by their employers than overseers throughout the South generally. (Of course, suit records are not the places where one would expect to find examples of employers who were pleased with their overseers.) No doubt there were many overseers who were judged worthy of their hire, performed their duties at least adequately, and moved on without leaving a trail of lawsuits behind them.[15]

The overseers hired in Franklin County, especially in the early years (when they are identified by occupation in a few records), were engaged largely as farm managers rather than as supervisors of slaves per se. They usually worked on farms with absentee owners, or managed one or more of several farms held by a single owner. In a county with relatively few slaves, landowner dissatisfaction with overseers may have been the result of a shortage of labor relative to the amount of work to be done, rather than incompetence.

The experience of Judge Fleming Saunders, who owned the Bleak Hill farm begun by his father, Peter Saunders, Sr., probably typified the experience of many absentee landowners. Saunders and his family lived on the farm immediately after his father's death but later moved to his wife's home—Flat Creek—in Campbell County. Although he visited the Bleak Hill property frequently, an overseer ran the farm. On one such visit in 1833 Saunders complained to his wife about the state of affairs:

> I have been very busy, found every thing much out of order, corn not cribed and the rough food very much wasted. I understand the overseer took no more interest in my matters and left home; every day adds new proof that man is not to be trusted.[16]

Two of Saunders's sons, Fleming Saunders, Jr., and Robert Chancellor Saunders, had better success in hiring an overseer for a farm they owned in Floyd County. James H. Roberts agreed to operate their farm on Greasy Creek for a year, beginning 18 December 1860, for $200 and

> also to find his board and washing. In case the said Roberts marries during the year other arrangements will be made. The said Roberts agrees upon his part to be industrious and attentive to said Saunders business, taking care of every thing and seeing that the servants are not neglected and all their needful wants are attended to. To be strictly economical and saving of every thing, Incurring no debts or disposing of no property whatsoever, where not specially directed. In case of dissatisfaction arising between the parties, it is further distinctly agreed that either party may brake the contract, the said

Left: *Walker McGhee plowing with horse. 1938 photo.* Right: *Scythe and Virginia-made wooden moldboard plow.* (Both: Blue Ridge Institute, Ferrum, Va.)

Saunders paying the said Roberts only for the time he has served and the said Roberts is required to give at least 2 weeks notice of his intention to leave.[17]

Roberts reported monthly to the brothers on affairs at the farm and appeared conscientious in his efforts to manage the place effectively. On 3 March 1861 he wrote,

> I am not agoing to Neglect the Plantation to Build the Kitchen, and If the Weather Remains like It is now, awhile longer I will be in time. I have had three Plows going for several days, I will get done Breaking up my corn land next week if nothing Prevents, and then I can start to sowing oats. I am not doing much at the fence But Will Work on It every chance. I am having the Manure piled up and there is a large quantity of It to Hall out. I have not sowed any Plaster Yet on the Clover, But the first Wet day comes I Will sow What I *have*. Twenty Two hundred lbs. is all I have got here. I Will send after some more as soon as I can get a little Straighter.
>
> Seed oats. Mr. Williamson says he thinks he can let me have them or Rather get me some for 25 cents per *Bushel*. It does not look like getting along Well to be buying oats for this place But We Will have it to do, for I have examined Whats here and I am confident they wont come up.
>
> The Hogs. I cant trade With Phillips for his he says he Will take 4 cents [per pound] But still he wont weigh them. He wants me to give him so much for the Lump. I know they will not bring as much as 4 cents a pound as he ask for them, and thats the Reason he Wont Weigh them, he knows It himself. If I cant get them at a fare price I Will not Pay anything more than they are Worth certain. Burnett steer is firstrate. I would hate to take Fifty Dollars for him now. All the Cattle are looking Very Well, Better than they did When You Were here. I never lost but one lamb. I have Twelve now thats out of danger.[18]

By the end of April 1861 the secession of Virginia from the Union and the threat of war occupied much of Roberts's attention, but he dutifully reported to Fleming Saunders on the state of the farm:

> Every thing is doing Well on the place. I shall make out Very Well With What Food I have. The Beef Cattle is getting in Very good order. I made the fence though the grass field some time back. I am making railes to do up another fence at this time and cleaning [up] together. I have not got as much corn land as I Wish to have planted. Dont you think it would be best to clean the Mill field up every chance We have. I Will shear the sheep this Week. Do you want the Wool sent to Lynchburg the first chance. I am sorry I bought them shoats now, considering the condision the Country is now in. By being very Saveing I think We might sell some Little corn. I cant take 50 cents a Bushel. We have Eleven Milch Cows. Several has been to see if they could Buy one. All has young calves But 3. I Hardly no where to sow any Buck Wheat at. I have been thinking to clean up the Hill side above the pine spring Next to the New fence We made. I Will start to coultering over my corn next Week if Fit. The first I planted Will soon be up. The Weather has been Beautiful for the last 8 or 10 days and the clover looks Flourishing.[19]

Obviously the need for work went on unchanged, war or no war.

The average size of Franklin County farms, likewise, remained remarkably stable. The 1786 land tax books reveal that 561 landowners—both residents and nonresidents—owned tracts of between 10 and 12,000 acres, and that the typical tract was just over 298 acres.[20] In 1850, according to the agricultural census conducted that year,[21] 1,309 landowners (presumably residents) owned tracts that totaled 351,877 acres, for an average of 269 acres per tract. Between 1786 and 1850, then, the size of the average Franklin County farm declined by 29 acres, or almost 10 percent, while the number of landowners had increased by more than 233 percent. By 1860, according to the agricultural census, the landowners had increased in number by about 12 percent to 1,484. They owned tracts that totaled 406,812.5 acres (a rise of more than 15 percent since 1850). The average farm size had grown slightly to 274 acres.

These numbers reveal several trends in Franklin County's agricultural history between 1786 and 1860. The increases in landownership during the earliest years most likely were due to newcomers arriving in the county and buying land. As the nineteenth century continued, however, the change can be attributed to a rise in the population from native births. The number of acres under ownership changed as vacant lands were acquired by grant and purchase and developed for agriculture. Farms declined in size as the population grew more rapidly than the available land, thereby increasing demand and causing the subdivision of family farms. The fact that the average farm size remained little changed in the ten years before the Civil War, as opposed to a 10 percent decline in the preceding sixty-four years, shows that these trends were beginning to stabilize.

The amount of land available for farm use was limited, however. Present-day Franklin County contains about 721 square miles, or 461,440 acres. In 1786 the landowners of Franklin County paid taxes on a total of 222,861.5 acres, or a little less than half the total. By 1850 Franklin's farmers owned 351,877 acres of land (about three-quarters of the county), and in 1860 the total had risen to 406,812.5, or almost 90 percent of the available area.

It is not possible to determine the ratio in 1786 of improved to unimproved land—acreage actually producing crops as opposed to forest—because the land taxes only record the total number of acres in each tract. No doubt a high percentage of each farm was unimproved. By 1850 the ratio was 36 percent improved acres to 64 percent unimproved. Ten years later the ratio was virtually unchanged: 38 percent to 62 percent. In other words, between 35 and 40 percent of the typical antebellum Franklin County farm was planted in crops, while between 60 and 65 percent was in woodlots or untended fields.

Most Franklin County farms during the antebellum period were general farms in the sense that they had a mixture of livestock and such crops as wheat, corn, oats, and flax. Almost everyone grew at least some tobacco as a cash crop, although a few farmers managed to get along without it.

Franklin County livestock consisted largely of horses, cattle, oxen, sheep, and swine, but some farmers may have kept more exotic animals. When John Boswell died in 1841 the inventory of his estate included among the horses and cattle a "Buffaloe Cow & Calf," two "Buffaloe" bulls, and a "Buffaloe Yearling."[22] (Of course, the word buffalo might refer to a color rather than the animal.) Later in the century mules, which at first farmers considered exotic, became more popular for plowing and general farm labor, and oxen slowly disappeared. By

1833 the demand and the price of mules had risen, as Judge Fleming Saunders reported to his wife:

> I will endeavour to provide the mules for your mother and will give directions to purchase them at the mount [Rocky Mount?] if they can be had. I understand from the best authority that mules have risen Very much.[23]

At first the cattle and swine ranged freely through the woods and fields to forage for themselves, but soon they were confined by fences. During the free-range era each farmer distinguished his wandering livestock from his neighbor's by the use of earcrops, and sometimes brands, that often were registered with the county court. On 6 April 1789, for example, John Cook registered his earmark ("a crop and under cut in the right ear and a slit in the left"); Thomas Hill did the same on 3 April 1804 ("a crop in each Ear and two Slits in each Ear").[24]

Although area residents raised much of their own livestock, sometimes the demand outstripped the supply. In 1823, for example, there appeared to be a general shortage of hogs for slaughter. Judge Fleming Saunders wrote advice to his mother-in-law in Campbell County:

> I think the article of pork will be Scarce, six Dollars Cash has been given here and the article is in demand. Mr. Hosten has promised to get on as fast as possible, and I hope you will be able to judge immediately whether you can supply yourself from the Western drovers, and if you cannot send Daniel up and I can now certainly get for you [hogs] at five Dollars neat.[25]

Franklin County was one of the principal tobacco-producing counties in Virginia during the antebellum period. By 1860 the Tidewater lagged the Piedmont in tobacco production. The Virginia tobacco belt stretched generally from the Blue Ridge east to the fall line and from the Potomac River south to the North Carolina boundary line.[26] Franklin County farmers shipped some of their tobacco to the Danville, Lynchburg, and Richmond markets, while local manufacturers purchased the rest. Indeed, local sales were preferred, to lower the risk of damage en route, provided the Franklin County manufacturers would pay a suitable price. In 1860, for example, Peter Saunders, Jr., of Bleak Hill, wrote to his brother,

Tobacco crop at Law homeplace, Glade Hill. 1920s photo. (Blue Ridge Institute, Ferrum, Va.)

I shall be able to sell all my flour at home at a price equal to what I could get for it in Lynchburg. Our tobacconists are buying tobacco rather slowly and in their offers for all except good wrappers, are considerably under last years prices. I have offered my crop for $8.00 round, but doubt whether any of them will give it. I think my crop taken all together is better than any I have had for several years past. I may have to send [it] to Lynchburg.[27]

Typical of such Piedmont counties, Franklin's tobacco production increased dramatically between 1850 and 1860, more than doubling from 1,081,464 pounds to 2,643,434 pounds. There were sharp advances in the production of several other major crops as well. Wheat production almost doubled, from 76,850 bushels to 124,396 bushels. More oats were harvested: 187,842 bushels in 1850 and 226,804 bushels in 1860. Curiously, the number of bushels of corn harvested declined from 411,908 in 1850 to 367,587 in 1860.

Perhaps the drop in corn production can be explained in part by the corresponding decrease in the number of cattle in the county between 1850 and 1860. Although the population of milk cows rose slightly, from 4,505 to 4,654, that of other cattle fell from 8,512 to 6,170. The number of hogs declined, too, from 26,805 to 20,261. On the other hand, there were about as many horses in 1860 as in 1850 (3,649 and 3,524, respectively); working oxen increased from 521 to 959, while the number of asses and mules more than doubled during the decade, from 125 to 304. The sheep population increased from 9,411 to 10,040.

To judge from the statistics, Franklin County's residents were not great vegetable eaters, unless the quantities of vegetables grown were underreported. The number of bushels of peas and beans picked dropped from 1,893 in 1850 to 1,418 in 1860. Buckwheat declined from 870 bushels to 393. Fewer sweet potatoes were grown in 1860 than in 1850 (12,146 from 15,988), while the less nutritious Irish potato increased in popularity (from 19,645 bushels to 27,013). The value of the fruit harvest rose dramatically, from $555 in 1850 to $17,307 in 1860, giving the first indication of the apple industry that would develop after the Civil War.

A few farmers raised, in addition to the staples, some crops that were unusual for the area. Almost six thousand bushels of rye and four hundred bushels of buckwheat were grown in 1860, as well as approximately two hundred bushels of barley and nine pounds of hops. Beer production was not recorded—nor was that of whiskey—but ninety-four gallons of wine were produced. Thirty-three pounds of maple sugar and seventy-three gallons of molasses were made. Besides the butter that was churned on virtually every farm, the production of cheese in 1860 amounted to more than eight hundred pounds. P. F. Brumley harvested the county's most unusual crop: four pounds of silk cocoons.

Several statistics indicate that the decade before the Civil War was a prosperous time for many Franklin County farmers. The value of the county's farms increased by 124 percent between 1850 and 1860, compared with a 71.8 percent increase for the entire state (including present-day West Virginia).[28] The value of Franklin County livestock rose by 41 percent during the same period; across the state the increase was 42 percent. The production of tobacco increased by 144 percent in Franklin County, while it rose by 118 percent throughout Virginia.

Based on the 1850 census figures, then, the typical Franklin County farm contained 269 acres, about a hundred of which were improved. On that hundred acres the average farmer grew 315 bushels of corn, 144 bushels of oats, 59 bushels of wheat, and 826 pounds of tobacco. It was the unusual farmer who plowed with either oxen or mules; most owned about three horses. The average farmer also had three milk cows, six other cattle, twenty hogs, and seven sheep.

Some idea of the crops and income of a small antebellum farmer can be gained from the 1841 estate inventory of Elisha Watkins. Among the crops were fifty-eight barrels of corn valued at $116; five stacks of "Blade fodder" worth $9; a crop of "Top fodder" at $3.75; $2 worth of shucks; three stacks of oats valued at $9; $2 worth of cabbage; a crop of cotton valued at $1; flax worth twenty-five cents; and his crop of tobacco valued at $30.[29]

In March 1851 a newcomer to the county described its agricultural character in a letter to his brother:

> In regard to this part of Virginia, this is quite a different looking Country from the Valley which I have been living in since the summer of forty-three. This is a verry hilly section of country. The land has naturally been a good strong Slate Soil but has been worked down to be poor in many places. The Land in quality is much inferior to the land in the Valley which is Limestone land. This is far from being a handsome country. This county abounds with numerous rivers none of which are very large. The Staunton river runs on the north side of the county and the Dan river heads in this county. Pig River runs within half mile of this place, yet I have not been to see it. Blackwater river is about 9 miles west of us. And Maggodee is some seven or eight miles distant. The principal crops are Tobacco & Corn with some oats & Rye. This county is wel watered with springs and fine water powers can be had on the Streams for any kind of manufacturing.[30]

Until the early nineteenth century most farmers practiced the intensive cultivation of crops. If the land deteriorated, as it quickly did when tobacco was the principal crop, the farmer moved on to other fields, perhaps to a new county or state. As the century progressed, however, experiment-minded farmers such as Thomas Jefferson and Edmund Ruffin proved that crop rotation and the regular fertilizing of land could keep it productive. Magazines and societies dedicated to the promotion of progressive-farming practices sprang up around Virginia during the antebellum period. Often, however, those who reaped the benefit of the societies and the new knowledge were in the upper levels of society; it took many years and less expensive tools for these new methods to trickle down to the lower elements of society. In the meantime, many of the affluent increased their wealth while the poor became poorer.

Moses Greer Booth, a justice on the county court who built the handsome Booth-Lovelace House in 1857, stood at the wealthy end of the spectrum. In 1850 he owned 970 acres, of which 500 were improved and 470 unimproved; the value of his farm was $7,000. He had $200 worth of farm equipment. His livestock included 12 horses, 2 mules, 20 milk cows, 55 other cattle, 160 sheep, and 175 swine, all worth $2,550. During the year Booth grew 650 bushels of wheat, 1,500 each of corn and oats, 5 of peas and beans, 100 of Irish potatoes, and 10 tons of hay, but no tobacco. His sheep produced 400 pounds of wool and his milk cows 300 pounds of butter, and he slaughtered $1,350 worth of animals.[31]

His labor force consisted of sixteen slaves, eight males and eight females who ranged in age from two to sixty.[32]

By 1860 Booth had 700 acres under cultivation, while 1,300 lay unimproved; his farm was valued at $40,000 and he owned $500 worth of equipment. He had 8 horses, 2 mules, 14 milk cows (which produced 500 pounds of butter), 2 working oxen, 20 other cattle, 100 sheep, and 75 swine, all of which were valued at $2,500; $1,000 worth of livestock was slaughtered during the year. The sheep produced 250 pounds of wool. Booth still grew no tobacco on his farm; his crops included 2,000 bushels of wheat, 3,500 each of corn and oats, 30 of peas and beans, 500 of Irish potatoes, 50 of sweet potatoes, 12 of clover seed, and 25 tons of hay. He gathered 100 pounds of honey and had no home manufactures worth mentioning.[33] Later in the 1860s he grew apples and his apple brandy won first prize at the Lynchburg Agricultural Fair.[34] By concentrating on crop production instead of livestock Booth became wealthy enough to purchase ready-made virtually everything he needed to clothe himself and furnish his new Greek Revival–Italianate mansion that still stands at the foot of Windy Gap Mountain. He also increased the number of slaves that he owned to thirty. Seventeen of them were males and thirteen females; they ranged in age from two months to forty-five, indicating that Booth probably had sold some of his slaves and purchased others.[35]

Edward Short, a neighbor of Booth, was at the other end of the scale. He owned no slaves, and his farm consisted of only seventy acres. Just twenty acres were cultivated, fifty were unimproved, and the farm was worth but $200. Short owned only $3 in farm equipment. His livestock consisted of three horses, two milk cows, five other cattle, and ten swine, all worth $150. During the year he grew 10 bushels of wheat, 200 of corn, 150 of oats, 5 of Irish and 10 of sweet potatoes, 3 of flaxseed, 10 pounds of flax, and 2,000 of tobacco. His milk cows produced seventy-five pounds of butter and he slaughtered $15 worth of animals during the year. Short's home manufactures were valued at $10.

By 1860 Short's situation had worsened. His landholdings had shrunk to fifteen improved acres worth $150; his farm equipment still was valued at only $3. His livestock was reduced to a horse and four swine worth $38. He grew eleven bushels of wheat, sixty of corn, five of Irish potatoes, one of flaxseed, and five pounds of flax. His cash crop, tobacco, amounted to 375 pounds. He slaughtered $30 worth of animals during the year and again produced $10 in home manufactures. He was barely surviving.

In contrast to either economic extreme was Powell M. Wade, a middle-class farmer who in 1850 owned a 400-acre farm, half of which was planted in crops. Wade's farm was valued at $2,300, and he owned $75 of farm equipment and machinery. He had four horses, three milk cows, sixteen other cattle, twenty sheep, and seventy-five swine; the total value of his livestock was $475, and he had slaughtered an additional $600 worth. During the year the 200 acres he cultivated produced 100 bushels of wheat, 36 bushels of rye, 950 bushels of corn, 640 bushels of oats, 30 bushels each of Irish and sweet potatoes, and 1,600 pounds of tobacco. His sheep yielded 100 pounds of wool, and his milk cows gave enough milk for 700 pounds of butter. The value of his home manufactures was $20.[36] Wade was a slave owner, with five male and seven female slaves in his household; they ranged in age from three to forty.[37]

By 1860 Wade had purchased 200 additional acres; 250 acres were under cultivation and 350 were unimproved. The farm's value had increased to $6,000, but the machinery was still worth only $75. Wade's livestock consisted of six horses, six milk cows, two working oxen, eight other cattle, sixteen sheep (which produced thirty pounds of wool), and thirty swine, for a total value of $715; he slaughtered $250 worth of livestock during the year. His crops included 400 bushels of wheat, 250 of corn, 400 of oats, 30 of Irish potatoes, 4 tons of hay, 40 pounds of flax, 6 bushels of flaxseed, and 2,000 pounds of tobacco. His milk cows produced 300 pounds of butter. Wade also kept bees; they gave him 5 pounds of beeswax and 40 of honey. The value of his home manufactures rose to $50.[38] During the decade Wade's lot had improved slightly and his farm became more diversified, although he grew more wheat and tobacco at the expense of corn and oats. He also acquired more slaves; in 1860 he owned sixteen, who ranged from two months to forty-five years of age.[39] The increase in number over 1850 from twelve to sixteen may have been due to childbirths rather than to purchases of slaves by Wade.

The relative prosperity of Franklin County farmers was in spite of, rather than because of, the transportation systems used to market their produce. Poor roads, hilly country, frequent streams, and long distances to major markets such as Lynchburg and Danville frustrated farmers no matter what their economic class. Not until almost midcentury did the internal improvement trend reach Franklin County, and even then its residents benefited little, regardless of occupation.

The colonial road system that existed when the county was formed consisted largely of traces and ruts. Even in the early nineteenth century, such travelers as the itinerant peddler quoted in the last chapter could lose their way easily, especially at night. Daytime travel was only slightly less difficult, particularly during foul weather, as Judge Fleming Saunders reported to his wife in 1835 after he rode from Campbell County to Bleak Hill in Franklin County:

> Although our trip was as usually is the case, interrupted with intolerably bad roads and difficulties in crossing the Water courses, no doubt you will be gratified to hear precisely how we got along. The roads in some places were so muddy, and the mud so stiff, that it seemed our horse would stick fast, and Staunton [River] was so high we had to ferry it [rather than ford it on horseback].[40]

No state road system existed; each county was responsible for creating and maintaining its own roads. Franklin County's early court order books, as in other counties, are replete with entries for the surveying, construction, or maintenance of roads. At its second meeting in February 1786, for instance, the court instructed William Rentfro, William Mavity, and Thomas Hale "to review a Rd. from the House of Colo. Peter Saunders the Nearest and best Way to the Washing. Iron Works [probably present-day Route 40]."[41] At the same meeting the court appointed Peter Wood to be the surveyor, or maintenance superintendent, of the road "from the Fork Roads Below Peter Hollands to Hails Ford and from thence to the Oposite Shore." The court also designated many of the residents who lived near the road as work gangs under Wood's authority to "Clear and keep the same in Repair."[42]

The system was inherently inefficient, and the roads frequently were in such a state of disrepair that attempts were made to turn the county's rivers into highways of commerce. James Callaway proposed the first such attempt in a petition to the General Assembly in 1796. He wrote that

> the improving the navigation of Pig River from the mouth of the said River to Washington Iron Works in the County of Franklin, would be attended with great convenience to your pe[ti]tioners and a number of other Citizens who live convenient thereto. Your Petitioners have made an experiment on the said River, by a Boat with Eighteen or nineteen hundred weight of Iron which was taken in and transported from the said Forge to Staunton River with but little obstruction.[43]

Although the General Assembly passed a bill authorizing the work and appointing trustees to raise money, the enormous cost of deepening Pigg River was enough to dissuade most potential investors. The job also required manual labor—a difficult and expensive undertaking. In 1799 another group of citizens sought the improvement of the Blackwater and Staunton rivers. They pointed out to the General Assembly that if the rivers were dredged and deepened,

> they would be enabled to Carry to Market the produce of their farms at a much less expence and more expedition than by Land through a hilly Country as is the present mode at an enormous expence. . . . Agriculture and Commerce would flourish amongst us.[44]

Again, their hopes foundered on the expense of the project, which they reluctantly abandoned.

Clearly, projects such as river improvement or road construction were too expensive to be undertaken solely by private stock companies. The participation of the state government—particularly through disbursements from the state treasury—was essential. Finally persuaded of the need, the General Assembly passed an act on 5 February 1816 to establish the Fund for Internal Improvement. The act created the Board of Public Works to oversee the fund and provided the mechanism for investing public money in private companies. After three-fifths of the stock issued by an internal improvement company had been purchased by private investors, the Board of Public Works used the fund to buy the other two-fifths, thereby completing the financing of the project.

The first such internal improvement to affect Franklin County was the Pittsylvania, Franklin, and Botetourt Turnpike, which the General Assembly incorporated on 7 April 1838. The road began in Danville, entered southeastern Franklin County along the old Snow Creek Road (present-day Routes 652 and 646), passed through Rocky Mount, Boones Mill, and Big Lick, and ended at Fincastle. The stockholders elected Dr. Richard M. Taliaferro president of the company, and Pleasant Dickinson, Giles W. B. Hale, James Shanks, and Robert T. Woods served as its first directors; Samuel H. Woods was the treasurer. Among the company's largest stockholders with at least twenty shares each were John Arthur, James Lanier, Fleming Saunders, James Shanks, John A. Smith, George P. Tayloe, John H. Wade, and Robert W. Williams.[45]

The route of the turnpike was surveyed quickly in 1838, but it took more than three years for the road to be built, at a cost of more than $26,000. Before the first fiscal year ended on 30 September 1839, three sections of the road, including more than twenty-seven miles from Rocky Mount to Big Lick, had been let to contractors at an average cost of $292.52 per mile. Five miles, from Rocky Mount to Blackwater River, had been completed and received by the company. Among the contractors were John Arthur, James W. Eubank, John A. Smith, Henry Taliaferro, and Robert Townes. By 27 December 1841 most of the turnpike was constructed. In Franklin County only five miles remained to be built; this section had not been put under contract for lack of funds.

A shortage of pennies for making change for tolls also affected the company. President Taliaferro complained to the Board of Public Works on 6 April 1841, "We are at a sad loss about cents for change. Have endeavoured to procure some at Lynchburg, and Petersburg, and failed, except for a small amount at the last named place."[46] Pennies and nickels were needed because of the amounts charged for toll: persons, five cents a head, and the same for horses and cattle; hogs, one cent each; tobacco, five cents a hogshead; four-wheeled vehicles, twenty-five cents apiece; and two-wheeled vehicles, ten cents each.[47]

Nine years later the company was virtually out of business. John Wade, who became a director after the resignation of Giles W. B. Hale, wrote to James Brown, Jr., the secretary of the Board of Public Works, on 16 September 1850, inquiring whether the company had forfeited its charter. Apparently the president had

Map of Pittsylvania, Franklin, and Botetourt Turnpike at Rocky Mount, 1838. (Virginia State Library and Archives.)

neglected for several years to make an annual report to the board, in violation of the act of incorporation. If the charter had been forfeited, Wade asked, could the company then collect tolls? He reported that over most of the road "the gates are all thrown open & has been for I believe Two or three years."[48] On one stretch of the road in Botetourt County, however, the tollgate had been repaired and tolls were still being collected. The travelers who had to pay there were making charges of unfairness.

The Pittsylvania, Franklin, and Botetourt Turnpike connected Franklin County with Danville and the markets of Southside Virginia to the east, and the upper Valley of Virginia to the north. Some Franklin County residents, particularly those in the western part of the county, thought there ought to be a better connection to Southwest Virginia as well. In 1847 the Rocky Mount Turnpike Company was incorporated to answer their needs.

The creation of the turnpike was due in part to three petitions submitted to the General Assembly in 1844 and 1848 from Franklin County residents. The first, which was submitted by Edmund Tate, asked for the improvement of an existing road that crossed the Blue Ridge into Floyd County at Daniels Run, just to the north of the eventual route of the Rocky Mount Turnpike; the petition was rejected for technical reasons.[49] Four years later a large number of Franklin County citizens submitted two new petitions asking that a more southerly route be chosen for the Southwestern Turnpike extension, which was under construction in Botetourt County. Instead of building the extension, which was to run from Buchanan to Salem, through the northwestern part of the county, one set of petitioners asked that it be constructed so as to pass through Big Lick,

the point where they strike the valley road, and altho the road is made more especially in defference to the interest of the So. West, still we think, as the improvement is made from the publick treasurary, it is but right that our convenience should be consulted, when by doing so the main object for which the rode was undertaken is unaffected.[50]

The second group of petitioners made a similar point, but also noted that

the outlet for all their agricultural produce has been and probably will continue to be to the James River, meeting it heretofore at Lynchburg, but that should the State Road be run on a line accessible to them much of the production of the County, will reach the Canal at Buckannan.[51]

Partly in response to the petitions, the General Assembly in 1847 incorporated a joint stock venture, the Rocky Mount Turnpike Company. The stockholders held their first meeting in Lynchburg on 21 October 1847, when the company organized itself and elected Major Samuel Hale, of Franklin County, as president. The stockholders chose John W. Dudley, of Lynchburg, to serve as treasurer and secretary, and elected a board of directors that included Alexander Irvine, of Bedford County, Harvey Deshius, of Floyd County, Judge Norborne M. Taliaferro, of Franklin County, and Henry Davis and John T. Davis, of Lynchburg.[52]

Despite the company's name, its office was in Lynchburg. The route selected for the road began in Lynchburg, ran southwesterly to the Staunton River, followed present-day Route 122 to Rocky Mount, then ran along Route 640 to conclude at Jacksonville (present-day Floyd), in Floyd County. On 19 February 1848 the General Assembly authorized the extension of the turnpike from Jacksonville to the Southwestern Turnpike in Smyth County.

From its beginning the turnpike faced financial difficulties because of underfunding. In a report issued to stockholders on 27 October 1849 the company admitted that it had been forced to alter the proposed route surveyed during the preceding year. The company intended to cross Staunton River at Radford Ford, just below Merriman Run in Franklin County, but the property owners there had claimed such exorbitant damages that the river crossing had to be shifted to Halesford. The company had begun construction of a 251-foot-long bridge at that point; the bridge would stand twenty-three and a half feet above low water when completed.

Another financial crisis, the report continued, had been created when the extension of the turnpike was authorized. None of the county courts west of Franklin County had authorized the opening of stock subscription books, and therefore the funds necessary to construct the road had not been collected. Apparently the counties feared that the funds might be used to build portions of the road not within their boundaries. The shortfall left,

> at least for a time, one of the fairest and richest sections of the state destitute of the most common facilities for transportation. The evil it is hoped is temporary and that however deep the apathy it will gradually be shaken off.[53]

Financial problems continued to plague the company. On 1 December 1849 a contract was let to Nowlin and Mosely to construct the eighteen-mile-long stretch of road between Staunton River and Rocky Mount, and also for a bridge over Gills Creek, where there was no convenient ford. There were no funds, however, to build bridges over Maggodee Creek and Blackwater River; instead, the route of the road had been planned to take advantage of available fords until the company could pay for bridges.[54]

Whether the bridges ever were constructed is uncertain. By 1854 the company was so strapped financially that it sold a five-mile-long stretch of the road, known as the "mountain section," to the state.[55] The section extended from Ivy Hill in western Franklin County to the road's intersection with the Floyd Courthouse and Hillsville Turnpike in Floyd County.

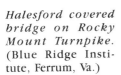

Halesford covered bridge on Rocky Mount Turnpike. (Blue Ridge Institute, Ferrum, Va.)

Even the sale of part of the road did not solve the company's problems. By 1859 it virtually had dissolved. The directors failed to attend meetings, so that it was almost impossible to assemble a quorum to examine and settle any accounts. The attorney general of Virginia sued the company for neglecting to reports its receipts and expenditures in accordance with its charter, but according to the company secretary, there was no money to pay any judgment that might be made against it:

We have allready been Compelled to pledge the future receipts of our road to Mr. Samuel Hale who was this day [12 February 1859] elected by the Board as President & Superintendent of this Road with authority to put the Road in Order that we may receive Tolls, the gates having been forced open Since 1 June 1858.[56]

At least a few of the gates still were manned in May 1861, when Peter Saunders, Jr., proposed to send one of his servants from Bleak Hill to Rocky Mount.

Cornelius says that Cupid only gave him one dollar yesterday on parting with him saying that he had used up the remainder in paying toll. I dont know how many gates are on the road, but 25 cents would be the maximum of the toll allowed by law at each gate and I dont think that the rates are fully up to the limit of the law. I shall furnish Cornelius with one dollar and 25 cents and food enough to last him down.[57]

The history of the Pittsylvania, Franklin, and Botetourt Turnpike Company and the Rocky Mount Turnpike Company is typical of antebellum turnpike companies generally. Founded amid high hopes, the companies soon discovered that the expenses of construction and maintenance were too great to be borne by stock subscriptions and tolls. In most cases the roads eventually were abandoned and their maintenance assumed by the counties they traversed. Those few companies that survived the financial stresses of the antebellum era failed to withstand the Civil War, during which the counties took them over.

The railroad companies fared better. Whereas turnpikes, for the most part, were too expensive to turn a profit for their investors, railroads—which had the advantage of being newly invented and therefore popular—were far more economical to operate. The expense of construction was more than offset by the high rates charged for the railroads' services, enabling the companies to make large profits.

Before the Civil War Franklin's citizens were unsuccessful in their attempts to attract a railroad to the county. In 1854 a petition was sent to the General Assembly signed by residents of Pittsylvania, Henry, Patrick, Franklin, and Campbell. The petitioners requested

a charter for a Railroad, from Lynchburg, our accustomed market, to a point upon the Virginia and North Carolina line, in or near the direction of the mouth of Smith's River . . . [and] a short link, of about thirty or thirty-five miles, connecting its Southern terminus with the North Carolina Central [Rail]Road.[58]

They also pointed out that

> the region of country they inhabit, has a good soil, a fine climate, an
> industrious and intelligent population, but is without good roads; and parts
> of it are far from market, so that agricultural pursuits therein are unprofit-
> able. They further represent that the portion of the region referred to, which
> borders on North Carolina, besides having a highly productive soil, yielding
> abundant crops of Tobacco and grain, contains extensive fields of Coal and
> Iron, but such is the expense and delay of transportation, that those
> necessaries which will not bear a high rate cannot be brought in competi-
> tion with the Coal and Iron found upon navigable waters, or in the vicinity
> of Improvements which can afford a cheaper transportation.

Although a bill was drafted, it died in committee. Not until 1859 was a similar
petition again presented to the General Assembly, with the information that the
legislature of North Carolina had chartered a branch line from the North Carolina
Central Railroad to the boundary with Virginia. The petitioners asked that a
railroad company be created to connect that branch line with the Virginia and
Tennessee Railroad in Lynchburg; the new road would pass through the counties
of Campbell, Bedford, Franklin, and Henry. In the petitioners' opinion it would

> result in great benefits to the Country through which it would pass, and to
> the State at large. It would form an important link in the great chain formed
> by the Piedmont lines of improvement. It would penetrate a populous and
> productive Country the Staples of which are tobacco and wheat, and thus
> become an important feeder to the James River and Kanawha Canal.[59]

Again a bill was written, but the war disrupted plans for construction. Businessmen, industrialists, and farmers alike remained dependent upon the roads and
turnpikes, poor though they were, for access to towns and markets. Franklin
County finally received the benefits of rail transportation in 1878, with the
creation of the Franklin and Pittsylvania Railroad Company.

During the antebellum period—indeed until well into the twentieth century
—the principal business of Franklin County, as in most of the United States, was
farming. That occupation, often conducted miles from towns or villages, meant
that families and neighbors relied on each other for mutual assistance, entertainment, and emotional support whenever loneliness and hard labor proved wearing
on their spirits. Religious revivals, weddings, funerals, dances, harvests, corn
shuckings, quilting bees, court days, and other rituals and public events brought
neighbors into contact to renew a sense of community. For emotional and
sometimes financial support, however, nothing was better than the family
network: husbands, wives, children, siblings, parents, grandparents, aunts,
uncles, cousins, and in-laws. The work, the hardships, the closeness, the
separateness, and the frustrations engendered by the farmer's world resulted in a
system of relationships and a way of life that have disappeared in much of the
country but that continue in many forms in Franklin County even today.

EIGHT

Domestic Life

The early settlers of Franklin County generally consisted of Germans and Scotch-Irish from Pennsylvania and Englishmen and their African slaves from eastern Virginia. Most of the Germans and Scotch-Irish came south into the area by way of the Great Wagon Road from Philadelphia up the Valley of Virginia to the western Carolinas. They tended to settle along the trace of the road that passed through Franklin County, particularly in the northern and western parts of the county. The English, in contrast, settled largely in the eastern and southern portions of the county, reflecting their emigration westward from the upper Piedmont and Southside of Virginia. Many emigrants, especially in the middle and late eighteenth century, merely passed through Franklin County on their way to greener pastures, or remained for perhaps a generation.

The settlers tended to come in groups rather than singly: families and neighbors often moved together. Frequently near neighbors in eastern counties remained near neighbors in their new county as well. Newcomers tended to bring with them from their old homes as much as they could carry, not only of personal possessions but of folkways and customs as well. They uprooted themselves in the hope of better opportunities, but they found comfort in a strange land by clinging to their recent past. The speech patterns of Appalachian and Blue Ridge inhabitants, which are considered by some to be reminiscent of Elizabethan English, exemplify this tendency. More recent opinion holds that the mountain speech is instead an amalgam of the different ethnic groups that have occupied the area. No matter which view is correct, the slowness with which speech patterns change corresponds to the tenacity with which people grasped their other habits of life.

Among their most important possessions were their networks of family and friends. These groups provided financial as well as emotional support. They, together with the customs shared by the members of the group, furnished each individual with a stable framework for living in a new county among strangers. Most of the white residents of Franklin County, despite their ethnic diversity, shared a commonality of law and custom as Americans that enabled them to live

147

together as a community. They also shared important beliefs: those relating to family life and child care.

In general, according to scholars of family history, in the late eighteenth and early nineteenth centuries families became more "child-centered." Parents increasingly accepted the proposition that children have lives and world views unique to childhood, and are not merely miniature adults. The idea of childhood as a recognizable time of life with its own special problems and wonders gained currency. Fathers as well as mothers adored their children, bragged about their development in letters to friends and relatives, were gripped by fear and worry when their children fell ill, and were virtually inconsolable when they died. Of course, earlier generations of parents also loved their children, but the diaries and correspondence left by those of the last few centuries reveal levels of emotion that are largely absent from earlier records.

On 19 May 1814 Alice Watts, of Flat Creek plantation in Campbell County, married Judge Fleming Saunders, of Bleak Hill in Franklin County. The couple moved to Bleak Hill and soon were immersed in the busy life of a wealthy, rural family with many slaves and a multiplicity of business and farming ventures. By October 1814 Alice Saunders also found herself pregnant, as she happily informed her mother in a letter:

> Come up after Christmas and stay until March or April, and I will return and stay some Months with you in the spring. If nothing happens, I shall require your good nursing in the spring. My situation no longer admits of a doubt, and I enjoy very good health indeed taking all things into consideration.[1]

An expectant mother often returned to her parents' home for the actual childbirth and remained there for several months afterward. Pregnancy was seen, in essence, as a form of illness requiring care and recuperation.

At first Alice Saunders continued to feel well except for occasional "colds." In her next letter to her mother she wrote that "yesterday evening," during a spell of good weather,

> I availed myself of the opportunity to go hunting with Mr. Saunders. I walked nearly two miles without the least inconvenience to myself. I find the more exercise I take, the better I feel after it. I am never the least indisposed, except a headache now and then, which I feel pretty much today.[2]

By mid-January 1815, however, Alice Saunders's health had deteriorated significantly, and she wrote her mother that she was suffering from the influenza that had been rampant among their slaves:

> I was taken . . . precisely as all the negroes were, with a violent chill, pain in my head and back. Mr. S. made me go to bed directly. . . . In two or three days I got perfectly well again.[3]

At the end of the month, though, she wrote that "I am generally so unwell, that my spirits are frequently very bad."[4] Apparently this pregnancy ended in miscarriage or stillbirth.

Alice Saunders became pregnant again, and on 31 March 1816 bore a girl she named Mary Elizabeth. She gave birth to her next child, Sarah, on 16 July 1817, to her third, William, on 18 January 1820, and to Edward on 4 November 1821. The first three died as children: Mary Elizabeth on 8 December 1825, Sarah late in 1818, and William on 24 May 1821. Her fourth child, Edward, died a young man in 1843. The next five children (Peter, born 1823; Ann Maria, born 1825; Robert Chancellor, born 1827; Fleming, born 1829; and Louisa Morris, born 1833) all lived to adulthood.[5]

The death of William Saunders, aged sixteen months, struck Alice Saunders especially hard, as she wrote to her mother a month after his death:

> I hope my dearest Mother has not thought me neglectful in not writing for such a length of time. My beloved Mother if you knew in what a state of mind I have been in for the last six weeks you could not blame me. The heavy and irreparable misfortune which we have experienced, has bowed me to the earth. Oh! so unexpected and attended with such afflictive circumstances was the stroke that time can never efface the impression which it has made upon my heart. My darling child's sufferings for more than a week before he left us, were sufficient to melt the coldest heart—indeed I never witnessed greater feeling for a dear sufferer than appeared to be generally experienced. But his afflictions are at an end—and to be united with him in that glorious mansion, which he now inhabits is the greatest object of my heart. Until he became too low to notice any thing, he never suffered me to leave him for a moment, and none but a parent can know with what anguish I watched by him without the consolation of believing that his sufferings were relieved for a moment. It is not right in me my dear Mother, to excite your feelings by dwelling upon this heart rending subject, but upon no other am I capable of writing or thinking at this time. I know, as a Christian, I ought to resign my darling child to the giver of all Good without a murmur, but I find it impossible to overcome my feelings at once.
>
> His dear image is constantly in my mind accompanied by such tender recollections that my heart often feels ready to burst. I hope I do not neglect the only means of procuring resignation to my fate—prayer and my bible seem to afford me more relief than anything in the world.[6]

Four years later, in 1825, Mary Elizabeth Saunders died, not long after her sister Ann was born. A grieving Alice Saunders gave her new daughter the middle name Maria in memory of her first-born child and wrote to her mother a few months later that

> My dear little Mary [Ann Maria] is one of the most playful forward Children I think I ever had. She sits alone perfectly well. I sometimes flatter myself that she is somewhat like the dear Angel after whom she is named, but it is perhaps only the force of imagination.[7]

She added that the funeral sermon for Mary Elizabeth Saunders had not yet been preached:

> We have been disappointed in procuring a Preacher to attend here this month as was expected and are compelled to put it off until the first Sunday

in June. Mr. Taylor of Halifax has promised to come out in August, but I cannot bear the idea of defering it until then, indeed I shall not feel willing to leave home until that melancholy proof of affection was bestowed on my dear sainted child.[8]

Nineteenth-century parents, as those before them, often lost at least one child in infancy or childhood, usually to illness. During the colonial period children typically lost one, or perhaps both parents, before they themselves reached adulthood. After the turn of the nineteenth century families increasingly were able to count on one parent—and perhaps both—surviving until the children were grown. Women were far less likely to survive than men, of course, given the rigors of frequent pregnancies and childbirth. Many children in the early nineteenth century spent part of their youth under the authority of a stepparent, usually a stepmother. Even so, the family unit often remained warm and nurturing.

Probably a third to a half of all children born did not survive their childhoods. Accidents also ended young lives. On 9 January 1789, for example, a coroner's jury met at Peter Geerheart's house to investigate the death of his son, John Geerheart, an "Infant" (a young person under the age of eighteen). The jury decided that "by Accident happening in the hands of the said John Gearheart he was killed suddenly by the fireing off a Smooth Gun which Gave him a Mortal wound in the Right Temple."[9]

Eighteenth- and nineteenth-century parents generally doted on their children. Judge Fleming Saunders often concluded his letters to his family in a manner typical of the day:

I hope little Edward has recovered and that his mother is relieved from her great anxiety. Kiss my children most affectionately for me and tell the two little girls I will have them some Chesnuts got and sent to them if the frost has not hurt them. . . . Give my love to all the family. I am your most affectionate husband, Fleming Saunders.[10]

Saunders, like most fathers, could not refrain from giving his children fatherly advice whenever the opportunity presented itself. On 13 March 1834 he wrote to fifteen-year-old Edward, who with his eleven-year-old brother, Peter, attended New London Academy:

After your mother leaves your Grand mama's [Flat Creek, near New London] I shall feel very uneasy about you and Peter. Pray take good care of yourself, always thoughtful in your conduct, and even then you will not be secure from danger and accidents. I wish you my son always to keep in mind how pleasant it is to a parent to have a prudent and wise child, and on the other hand how distressing it is to have an imprudent and indiscreet one, [who is] regardless of all moral duty and perfectly indifferent about education.

My son, youth is the time to lay a foundation for moral worth and future good Character, and I hope you will bear in mind that the single false step made in boyhood follows a man through life. It is of the utmost conse-quence that you should acquire an early habit for study, [and] lay up on your boy hood a store of information, the effect of which will give you an insatiable taste for more. Knowledge when associated with correct moral principles and good manners never fails to secure to him who possesses those qualities many friends who will be useful to him through life.

I wish you to be punctual in all your dealings, kind in your feelings to every one, doing at all times as you would be done by. I hope you will all times guard against injuring the feelings unnecessarily of any of your school fellows, either by harsh words or harsh conduct. Never resent any thing too quick, but be patient and firm in all your conduct. Never deny any thing you say or do and if wrong frankly ask for forgiveness. I hope you will encourage no feelings of pride, but be humble, firm and steady in your conduct, be neat and not gaudy in your dress, [and] keep your person also clean. Remember me to your Cousin William, your teacher, Nat Burwell, and your particular friends. Don't forget Frank. Write me as often as you can. I am your affectionate Father, Fleming Saunders.

If you should want any money, your mother can give it [to] you.[11]

Parents also happily reported their children's achievements, large and small, to their adoring grandparents. While Alice Saunders wrote a letter to her mother in 1826, her then-four-and-a-half-year-old son Edward ran into the room and interrupted her:

Edward has just come down and says I must tell Grand-Mama he is [a]head in spelling. He has kept that status ever since friday [5 May]. You would be surprised to hear how well the dear little fellow reads. Peter has improved smartly in his talking, and very often says "he wants to see dan Ma [Grandma] so bad." Mr. S. desires to be affectionately remembered to you. The girls also send a great deal of love to yourself and the family.[12]

Children exhausted their parents then as now. Writing to her mother five months after the birth of Edward, Alice Saunders noted,

I have no idea that you would know Edward now, he has fattened so much, and unfortunately so much flesh has entirely supplanted what little beauty he had to boast of, when he left you last Winter. I have to feed him three or four times a day, for I find I begin to lose ground very fast in point of strength. Until I get my cup of coffee in the morning, I am not worth a button.[13]

Although her children exhausted her, Alice Saunders remained by any standard an affectionate and loving mother to her children. Some other young people were not so fortunately reared. There are few indications among Franklin County's records of the abuse or maltreatment of children, however, and those are ambiguous at best. There were different standards in the late eighteenth and early nineteenth centuries for the treatment of children than there are now. For instance, orphaned children often joined the labor system at an early age. What would be classified as mistreatment today was accepted as normal then.

Perhaps the earliest Franklin County record that hints at the mistreatment of children by their parents was created on 4 February 1788, when the court ordered "that Jeremiah Halcomb and Ann Short be Summond to appear before the Court in April Next to Shew cause why their Children may not be Bound out."[14] Nothing further was recorded relating to this matter, which may have indicated that these two, presumably single parents, were incapable of supporting their children financially. The court may have issued its order because the children were about to become potential expenses to the county, rather than because of any overt sympathy for their plight. The court implied that if the parents could not care for them, then the overseers of the poor would apprentice them to a tradesman or farmer. Foster homes, orphanages, or any organized system of public charity for children simply did not exist.

The men who constituted the court of Franklin County were not heartless, however, but were bound by the customs and attitudes of their time. They did not hesitate to rule when customs or laws were violated, as occurred in 1803. On 7 November the court acted when it appeared

> by the oath of Jane Burton that Tubal Burton her infant child not two years old, has been illegally & inhumanely taken from her, and bound to William Hodges, Sr., it is therefore ordered that the said William Hodges restore the said child to his mother, and that he be discharged from his Indenture.[15]

The justices agreed that two years of age was too young to begin a career as an apprentice. The Virginia General Assembly, however, set no legal limit.

Apprenticeship was seen as one of the most humane ways available to protect a child, assuming that no relative or friend could provide care. In 1808 the court removed a girl from what must have been a depraved and violent home environment and placed her in an apprenticeship. The court

> ordered that the overseers of the poor bind Sally Slater (an Infant, the Daughter of Edmund S. Slater, a man who appears to the court, to be of dissolute and worthless manners, and not likely to bring up his child in honest courses) to David Dischong, untill She attains the age of Eighteen years.[16]

A month later, on 4 August 1808, the court ordered Edmund S. Slater to jail until he filed a $100 peace bond to guarantee his good behavior toward David Dischong, whom he must have threatened.[17]

Bald Knob Furniture Factory workers, including children. Post-1906 photo. (Blue Ridge Institute, Ferrum, Va.)

If a child was orphaned or if one parent (usually the father) died—particularly if the child was to inherit property upon attaining its majority—the court appointed a guardian to care for the child and its property. Guardianship was a solemn legal obligation requiring the posting of a sizable bond and the annual accounting by the guardian of the child's estate to the court.

Sometimes a parent named the child's guardian in his will. Often, however, the court made the appointment. When several children in the same family were orphaned, frequently guardians shared the responsibility for their care. On 8 April 1788, for instance, the court appointed guardians for the four orphans of John Pinckard: Nathan Ryan as guardian for John Pinckard, Jr., William Ryan for Churfott Pinckard, and Samuel Patterson for Thomas and Jane Pinckard.[18] The Pinckard children were not without parents, however. The occasion for appointing guardians was the marriage of their widowed mother, Jean or Jane Pinckard, on 12 March 1788 to Samuel Patterson.[19] Perhaps Patterson was wealthy enough to post a guardian's bond for only two of the children (Thomas and Jane), requiring the court to appoint the Ryans to manage the estates of John and Churfott. The children most likely resided with their mother and new stepfather.

The children of the poor, by contrast, were more likely to be separated physically and apprenticed. Thus on 6 March 1788, the overseers of the poor bound out two orphans of John Miller: Sarah Miller to George Medley and Peter Miller to Baley Carter.[20]

Upon reaching the age of fourteen, children could choose their own guardians. On 7 December 1789, for example, Dicey Greer, the daughter of Thomas Greer, appeared before the Franklin County Court and chose Thomas Dismass as her guardian. Dismass then entered the courtroom and filed a bond to guarantee the faithful performance of his duties.[21] Sometimes a child chose for its guardian a person who clearly was a relative, as when Jonas Turner, the orphan of James Turner, selected William Turner on 4 January 1790.[22]

Occasionally a guardian of special character assumed a responsibility that would have daunted many others. On 3 February 1806, for instance, John Hill accepted the guardianship of the eight children of his deceased kinsman, Isaac Hill:

Castillo Hill, Barber Hill, & Betsey Hill, Children of Isaac Hill deceased who arc of lawful agc for that purpose come into Court & choose John Hill as their Guardian, and the Court thereupon proceeded to appoint the said John Hill Guardian of Nancy Hill, John Hill, Isaac Hill, Winney Hill, & William Hill, other Children of the said Isaac Hill deceased, who are under age.[23]

A guardian cared for the child and managed his or her assets until the child became a legal adult at the age of twenty-one. The court allowed the guardian to reimburse himself from the estate for the child's clothing, education, travel, and so forth. When the ward finally attained his or her majority, the guardian presented the accounts of the estate to a committee for final settlement, and the remainder of the estate was turned over to the new adult. For example, the court of Franklin County, on 6 June 1803,

ordered that Stephen Smith, Fleming Saunders, Nathaniel H. Claiborne, and

Caleb Tate, or any three of them state & settle the account current of Tho. Hale with Patsey Casey Daughter of James Turner deced. who hath attained the age of twenty one years, & who was one of the Wards of the said Tho. Hale.[24]

Even though Patsey Turner obviously had married before reaching adulthood, that did not alter the obligation of her guardian.

Parents as well as guardians had a legal obligation to support the children under their care, of course, whether or not the parents were married. The little public welfare or charity that was available during the late eighteenth and early nineteenth centuries consisted largely of an occasional one-time payment made by the county from its coffers to a destitute mother. Legally, if either one or both parents did not tend to their child's financial needs, the child was put to work—apprenticed—for its own support.

In the case of a child born out of wedlock—called a bastard in the unabashed legal language of the day—the court's principal concern was that it not become an expense to the county. Fathers, when they could be identified, were compelled to support their children, "legitimate" or not. Thus on 4 August 1788 Samuel McCoy filed a bond with the overseers of the poor to pay £3 per year in quarterly payments for the support of a child he fathered with Tabitha Jones, and a record of the transaction was duly entered in the court order book for all to see, complete with the names of the father and mother.[25] Tabitha Jones, interestingly enough, was not "ruined" by the experience. She married Richard Hale about 24 October 1788.[26] Similarly, on 3 November 1788 John Luttrell filed a bond, at the rate of £6 a year for six years, to guarantee the support of a child he had with Sarah Elliott.[27] He married Elliott about 13 November 1788.[28] In each of these cases the child ended up living with two parents in the same household.

By contrast, the county court on 6 October 1788 ordered that William Frame, the "bastard child" of Happy Frame, be apprenticed to Lewis Bryant through the overseers of the poor.[29] The boy was therefore reared in a household that did not include—as far as is known—either of his natural parents.

A child fathered out of wedlock by a parent who was a member of a family prominent in Franklin County had a chance for a better life than one born to poor parents, provided that the parent accepted his responsibility. For example, in the case of Jane Jones Saunders, who was born about 1799 or 1800, the name of her mother is not known, but her father was Peter Saunders, Jr. Perhaps because he took the child under his care, there was no grand jury presentment for bastardy recorded in the county court order books.

Jane Jones Saunders was raised in the house of her bachelor father, who never married, and acted as his hostess. According to Saunders family tradition, her mother had appeared on her father's doorstep one day with the baby, thrust her into Peter Saunders's arms, and said, "Here—she's yours, so you raise her." Peter Saunders admitted his paternity in 1840 when he wrote in his last will and testament about "my natural daughter Jane J. Saunders who now resides with me." Although earlier the word "natural" simply had meant "my own," by 1840 its meaning had changed to "illegitimate; born out of wedlock; as, a *natural* son." The Saunders family accepted Jane Jones Saunders; she was referred to fondly as "Cousin Jane."[30]

Had Peter Saunders, Jr., not taken responsibility for his daughter, Jane Jones Saunders might well have been apprenticed if her mother had been unable to support her. Orphans, children born out of wedlock, and children whose mothers were unable to support them often were bound out. On 7 September 1801, for instance, the county court entered the following orders: "Ordered that the Overseers of the poor do bind Amos Ray, a bastard Child of Rebecka Ray, to Crisley Peters"; "Ordered that Mary Hixon an Orphan Child 8 years Old Daughter of Susannah Hixon be bound to Andrew Real by the Overseers of the poor"; "Ordered that the Overseers of the poor bind William Perdue to Gideon Roach."[31]

Although most of the persons to whom the children were bound treated them decently enough by the standards of the day, there were exceptions to the rule. In such cases, apprenticed children had only the court to depend on to save them from abuse. On 6 July 1801, for example, the court acted to protect William Barber, who filed a complaint

> by Edward Barber his next friend. It is ordered that Peter Livesay be summoned to appear here at the next Court to answer the Complaint of the said William Barber an apprentice for maltreatment & to shew cause why the said William should not be taken from him by the overseers of the poor and bound to some other Person.[32]

No further record of the case was found, which may indicate that the complaint was resolved.

A more complicated case of maltreatment surfaced in 1803. A boy named William Dent earlier had been apprenticed to a German resident named John Picklesimer (also spelled Beckleshymer) by the overseers of the poor. On 6 June 1803 the county court ordered Picklesimer—who was about to move out of the state—to appear at the next court meeting to show why Dent's indenture should not be canceled. During the next month, however, another issue arose, and on 4 July, when Picklesimer appeared, he was ordered to show cause why Dent "should not be taken from him for maltreatment." Whether Picklesimer was mistreating Dent or not, on 5 September the court decreed that he

> be inhibited from carrying the said apprentice with him, that his Indentures be considered as null and Void, and that the said overseers of the poor take the said apprentice into their care, and again bind him to whom they shall think fit, until he attains the age of twentyone years.

Picklesimer remained in the state. In September 1805 Dent's sister, Caty, was taken from Picklesimer and bound to Walter McGregor. Apparently the overseers bound William Dent to a new master—John Wilson—anyway, for when Wilson moved from the state in 1805, the court ordered that Dent be apprenticed to John Miller.[33]

Both of the Dent orphans survived their childhoods, married, and raised families of their own. William Dent married Elizabeth Fishburn on 7 February 1831;[34] in the 1850 census he was listed as a farmer with seven children and real estate worth $960.[35] Catherine Dent married Henry Love on 26 March 1814.[36] By

1850 he was dead, but she lived with seven children on a farm valued at $600.[37]

As described earlier, the Franklin County Court intervened on the occasions when children of too tender years were indentured. In 1808, the court ordered that "Ursula Holland surrender up to Nancy Pratt her Child Betsey & that the Indentures of the said Child to the said Ursula be null & void."[38] No reason was specified, and it is interesting that the child had been apprenticed to a woman.

Free black children also were bound as apprentices. On 6 January 1807 the court ordered the overseers of the poor to bind John and Isham Shavers to Benjamin Shavers (all the parties were free blacks). More than a year and a half later, however, the Franklin County Court ordered that

> Isham Shavers, an orphan child of colour formerly bound to Benjamin Shavers be bound to John Hale by the overseers of the poor—and that John Shavers who is in the same situation be bound to Thomas Hale, Jr., it appearing to the satisfaction of the court, that the said Benjamin Shavers is in a State of fugitation [has fled from justice], and is not likely to bring up the said orphans in honest courses.[39]

Although some orphaned children were left only with the protection afforded by the legal system and the county court, many others received tangible personal property when their parents died. In addition, living parents who had the means often made gifts to their children of land, slaves, or other property. Such a gift generally was viewed as a share of the parent's estate, not as a gesture made in addition to a share. In these cases the child who had received the property as a gift might be left only a dollar or some other token in the parent's will; sometimes later descendants conclude wrongly that their ancestor had been disowned or disinherited.

In 1791, for instance, John Starkey gave 134 acres to his son Jonathan Starkey, "in Consideration of the great Love and affection I bear to my Son."[40] William Toney, Sr., demonstrated considerably less sentimentality in 1795 when he gave his son Edmund Toney 120 acres "in Consideration of his duty . . . as his father."[41]

Often such gifts were provisional: usually the child agreed to accept the property in exchange for supporting his aged or infirm parents. In 1796 John Pitner sold most of his property to Michael Pitner for the nominal sum of £10 and "also for the board Maintenance and Support both food and clothes for himself as also for his Wife to be found them by the said Michael Pitner who is their son." In return young Pitner received one hundred acres, "also one bay horse and a red cow and white faced Heifer and all the household furniture and Plantation tools and Utencils."[42]

Sometimes relatives or friends were so close that they gave each other substantial gifts. John Via, Sr., presented his "loving cousin," William Martin, thirty acres on Rennet (Runnet) Bag Creek in 1804.[43] In 1789 Jacob Cradler, because of his love, goodwill, and affection toward his "Loving friend John Bowman and for the Better Maintenance and Livelyhood of him the said Jacob Cradler," put his trust in Bowman, giving him two tracts of land. Cradler also gave him "one Brown Mare five head of Neat Cattle and every other utensil of mine that Belongs to said Lands also all Bonds Notes of hand and all other obligations Writtings for the Benefit of the aforesaid John Bowman."[44]

Neither friendship nor family connections kept residents of Franklin County, like Virginians everywhere, from suing one another if they felt the need. Plaintiffs who initiated lawsuits against other family members usually disputed the division of property that followed the death of a parent or spouse. In November 1791, for example, Elizabeth Lyon Johns and her husband, Robert Johns, sued Mary Lyon, her widowed mother, for the possession of a slave girl named Luce whom Mary Lyon refused to turn over to her daughter.[45] Elizabeth Johns avowed that Elisha Lyon, her father, had promised her verbally before his death in 1787 that if she would remain single and "employ her labor and attention to his use" he would bequeath Luce to her. She stayed with her father for five and a half years, she said, between the time she came of age and when she married Robert Johns, and during that time she "lost several opportunities of employing herself to great advantage." She also maintained that Elisha Lyon told her husband at about the time of their wedding that although the slave Luce belonged to Elizabeth, the elder Lyon was "to have the use of her [Luce] during his life." Later Elisha Lyon "borrowed" £30 from Robert Johns and declined to pay it back, observing "as he had given your Orator's wife a negroe he ought to keep the money to make his bargain tolerbly good."

Mary Lyon countered by asserting that her husband had never given Elizabeth Johns a slave despite his daughter's attempts at persuasion. She was supported in her contention by Alexander Rose, who wrote in a deposition on 8 January 1791 that

> on a Curtin Day he hapned to be at Robert Johns Some time after Joseph Greer and Faney Lyon was mareid [about 1 May 1786[46]] & Robert Johns wife told him that her Dady had Given a Negro boy to Joseph Greer and Said that he Never Give her a Negro but Said that Charley Rorax had been there and She had Got him to write a Leter to her father. That they were about Going to Georgia & She Expected her father would Come There & his being a tenderharted man would Give her one.

Friends as well as families sometimes fell out with each other over debts or property disputes. On 4 September 1791 John Bell described a dispute between two friends to which he was a witness:

> A fue days after Joseph SpearPint Left living with John Prilliman he came to my Hous & tould me Jacob Prilliman sener Was owing of him & asked me to set Down his account for him & I did[.] the Account was ry & wheat to the amount of Twelve & six pence as well as I rember. Then he told me, to give Prilliman Credit for six shilling that he paid Thomas Brunte [Prunty] for him & a bushel of Corn which was two shilling & a Quart of brande one shilling & six penc & the ballance due to spearpint was Two shillings & six pence[.] he asked me To take the account to Prilliman & ask him for the ballance for he said he never intended to goe on ther plantation again[.] I went to Prilliman & he said the account he beleved was right but he wanted to se sperpint[.] some time after that I was at Prillimans & spearpint came There & he fell out with old Jacob Prilliman & abuesed him veri much & the old man did not seam to regard it much & spearpint went away in a Great rage[.] in about a weak after Spearpint Came to Prillimans again & seamed very

humbel & I heard him Tell the old man that he was sorre [he] had fell out
With him & desiered to be friens with him. The old man ansers well
Spearpint Told him he oed Peter Helm two Bushels of ry & if he would pay
Helm The ry & give him a pint of brande & they would make friens & be clear
of each other of all dues dels & demands from the begining of the world to
that day. I beleve the settelment was about jun in the year 1790.[47]

Evidently Spearpoint had worked for Prilliman for at least six months. During that
time he had pulled flax, cleared two acres of land, and split 1,450 rails for
fencing, in addition to his other duties on Prilliman's farm.

Sometimes family disputes resulted in violence. Little data exists concerning
domestic violence, except for the occasional entry in the county court order
books. In February 1786, for instance, Elizabeth Archer sued her husband,
William Archer, for an unspecified breach of the peace.[48] On 7 February 1803
William Starkey appeared before the Franklin County Court to take out a peace
bond for $500 to guarantee his good behavior; his wife had complained of "ill
treatment" at his hands.[49]

Suicide, or violence against oneself—rarely mentioned in the county records—occurred occasionally. On 15 March 1793 Mark Sheridan was found dead
in his house with his throat cut. Thomas Hale, the county coroner, summoned a
twelve-man jury, who assembled at the house to view the body and determine the
cause of death. The jury concluded that Sheridan had committed suicide by
slitting his own throat with a razor (valued at one shilling) by holding it in his
right hand and inflicting a wound "of the Breath of four Inches and the depth of
ten Inches."[50] In 1848 a despondent young man named Lafayette N. Hatcher took
his life after writing a suicide note intended for his parents that subsequently was
recorded as his last will and testament. "I have come to the conclusion," he
wrote,

that there is no pleasure in this life for me. I therefore take this rope and put
an end to my life. I don't want one tear shead for me, but rejois that I have
left this trublsome world. I have no hope of heaven at all, for I feel that I am
a sinner and a vill one to. Give Judson my histry and tell him to be a good
boy. Edmund I give my horse & saddle. Take good care of him. I also give you
all my clothes that you will ware. Sell the corn and pay my debts. Mar [Ma]
kiss little Tommy for me and don't let him forget that he once had a brother
Lafayette. Mar, you and Pa must not greave for me, I am to proud to be poor
and I had rather die. Tell all the children farewell. I want Robert McGuffin to
make me a plain Walnut Coffin, and I wish to [be] buried at the back of the
broom corn patch. I have drove up a garden path were I wish [to] lie. Get Mr.
Floyd to Preach my Funeral Sunday. Tell him to sing the 126 hymn in the
prayer book.
　　How short the race our friend has run,
　　Cut down in all his bloom.
Mary you must sing, 'tis delight without alloy.
　　So Farewell one and all.
I wish to be buried with the clothes I have on. Put my cap on and don't cut
my whiskers off.[51]

Although there were no psychologists or psychiatrists to help those who were mentally ill or in despair, aid was available from a variety of other sources. Besides one's family and friends, ministers and their congregations offered consolation and advice. As the century progressed, fraternal organizations were established to provide secular fellowship for their congenial members. On 20 January 1852, for example, the Rocky Mount Masonic Lodge No. 75 was chartered. James Dinwiddie was the Master; J. E. McCrery, Senior Warden; and Samuel Hale, Junior Warden.[52]

Suicides, lawsuits, and apprenticeships were hardly the stuff of everyday life for most eighteenth- and nineteenth-century Franklin County residents, however. Most of them went about their normal affairs, raising crops and children, enjoying friends and family, conducting their businesses, and ordering their lives in ways that suited them. They endured poverty, lack of privacy, sickness and pain, and a more-than-occasional acquaintance with death. They lived for the most part without public assistance, a room of one's own, medical care and pain relievers, and hospitals and nursing homes to hide the dying from their sight. They relied on their relatives and companions, their laws and customs, and their religious faith to see them through life's challenges. Most of all, they relied upon their families.

When nineteenth-century Virginians wrote or spoke of "family" they really referred to what is commonly called the "extended family": a sprawling network of parents, children, grandparents, siblings, in-laws, aunts, uncles, and cousins, often referred to collectively as "connections." The connections traded visits (often months in length), servants, children, livestock, and gossip almost as if they shared them in a common household.

Extended family listening to Bible reading, Callaway. (Blue Ridge Institute, Ferrum, Va.)

They assisted each other in times of illness or other disasters. In July 1829 Alice Saunders described the sicknesses that swept through the families of their "connections" and the efforts the family members made to help:

> I intended writing immediately after your Father returned, but about a week before, Robert [her two-year-old son] had been taken very sick, and continued to decline so rapidly for three weeks that we became very

doubtful whether you would ever see the dear little fellow again in this world. He has had a violent bowel complaint which for some time appeared to be the flux. Last friday was a week, we did not think he could survive it long, but when the Dr. got here he had become better. Yesterday and today he has attempted to walk a little. His appetite has become ravenous, and he makes Martha take him to the closset a dozen times a day to get bacon. He generally seizes on the whole piece and brings it to me. If he was not by nature one of the best children in the world, he would be dreadfully spoiled, for every thing about the House idolizes him. I hardly think you would know him now, he is so much reduced, but with care I hope he will soon be as well as ever. He is excessively fond of riding on horseback, and we have him exercised whenever it is cool enough in that way. Yesterday evening I rode with him as far as Mrs. Webbs and back again before dark. Miss Charlotte [Grimes, a schoolteacher] went over, and we accompanied her. We were called upon to witness a very distressing scene three days ago, the buriel of Sam Hairston's little Daughter. You saw her last Spring. The flux took her off in two weeks, and it would have made your heart ache to have seen its afflicted parents. Mrs. Hairston's Father come over to assist in nursing the child, and I am told he is extremely ill with the same complaint. The Dr. has not left him for three days. Colo. Ingles [Samuel Saunders's father-in-law] relapsed about ten days since and was nearer dying than ever. A Messenger got here about midnight, informing us of his situation. Mr. Saunders could not leave Robert to go over, but several of the family paid him a visit. Sister Hale staid with the Major [Samuel Saunders] while Mary [Ingles Saunders, his wife] was gone. They left the old Gentleman somewhat better though not able to raise his head from his pillow. The Dr. told me he was more perfectly resigned and happy at the prospect before him than any person he had ever seen. Sister Hale and all the connections who went over to see him staid all night with us on their return, the most fatigued poor souls you ever saw. Judith [Hairston] could scarcely sit up long enough to eat her supper. Jane [Jones Saunders] was taken extremely ill the night she got home with bilious cholick, and continued so for several days. I expect they were very much alarmed at her situation, for your Cousin John was sent in great haste two or three times to S. Hairston's for the Dr. She is now able to walk about again.[53]

Families preferred, of course, to get together for extended visits and for happier occasions. In 1834, for example, Alice Saunders wrote to her son Peter Saunders, Jr., who at age eleven was on a lengthy visit to his grandmother Watts's plantation at Flat Creek, to describe the wedding of cousin John Hale and her ride back to Rocky Mount and then Bleak Hill:

I was prevailed upon to visit your Aunt Hale's about the time of his marriage, and rendered her every assistance in giving them a handsome supper. She had prepared more nice cake, etc., than I ever saw for a private party, and when the table was set out covered with nice things, it looked very handsome. There were very few beside the connections, and the next morning we all left her immediately after breakfast. John brought his wife on to the C[ourt] House, and said he should sit to hard work without delay! Cousin Jane's carriage broke down, which gave us a pretty smart alarm, but it did not turn over, and we soon got out in safety. Fortunately Colo. Early's carriage was in company, and I got a very comfortable seat in it, until the other was repaired, which was easily done as soon as it could be gotten to a blacksmith's shop. The same evening I come on home with [her daughters] Ann and Louisa, and found your Father and the boys [Edward, Robert, and Fleming] (who had come on the day before) quite well. I felt very happy to get back in safety, and thought my quiet home much more pleasant after being in a bustle, and going through so much fatigue.[54]

Boys skinnydipping in Ferrum area. Swimming holes have provided farm children with an escape from the summer heat for generations. (Blue Ridge Institute, Ferrum, Va.)

Weddings and long visits served to relieve the tedium of everyday life in the country, at least for the women and children of the family. Visitors also put a burden, however pleasant, on the host to provide hospitality for his guests. Whether the host's house was large or small, whether the traveler was a peddler or a friend, the rules of hospitality and the lack of inns required a householder to supply food, drink, and accommodations to travelers who needed them. Usually guests announced their impending arrival beforehand, through letters or messages carried by friends or servants. Sometimes they arrived unexpectedly, however, and suffered the consequences when their hosts were unprepared. Alice W. Saunders related such an incident in a December 1814 letter to her mother:

> Never, but once before, did I suffer as much with the cold, as I did the day we left you. The wind was piercing, and blew immediately in our faces too, which made it infinitely more disagreeable. We stopped to warm very frequently, and owing to our losing a good deal of time we were unable to get to Mr. Hale's that night. We had to beg quarters at Booker Preston's (who married Kity H.) and there we met with cold comfort indeed. He was from home and the negroes so free that it was with difficulty we could get a fire. We had not eaten a mouthful of dinner, and nothing upon the face of the earth could they give us but a little broiled pork and cornbread.[55]

Alice Saunders often provided hospitality to friends and relatives at Bleak Hill, even after the house burned down in 1830. She wrote her daughter Sarah that the family had to use slave cabins as quarters for themselves and their guests:

We enjoy very good health in our little cabbin, and upon the whole seem to get on better than you would imagine. You would hardly believe it, but we have more company in our small cabbin, than usual, and last Wednesday Harriet, Jane and Judith came up and spent a day and night. Their intention was to return in the evening, but it proved a very rainy day, and they had to take their lodgings in Abbey's cabbin. I had a bedstead which the Major [Samuel Saunders] had sent us, and a small bed fixed up for them, and they lodged more comfortably than I expected. They diverted themselves a good deal at our small cabbin, and little fixments. I can do very well with my own family, but when three or four visitors come, I scarcely know how to manage. Your Father is fixing up the other two cabbins, and when we get them white washed and scoured out, they will be quite snug.[56]

Holland-Duncan House. 1988 photo. (Virginia Department of Historic Resources.)

Traditional birthplace of Jubal A. Early. 1988 photo. (Virginia Department of Historic Resources.)

Although log dwellings or cabins such as slaves lived in had once been the common housing stock of the county, particularly during the late eighteenth century, by the early nineteenth century they were largely supplanted by two-story frame or brick I-houses. The I-house, of which the Holland-Duncan House and The Farm are typical examples, generally has a central hall running from front to rear on each floor, with a room on each side and exterior end chimneys. It is usually symmetrical, with one or two windows on each side of a central entrance door. This basic I-house plan has been little altered over two centuries and remains the most popular vernacular dwelling type in the United States. Every modern residential development boasting "colonial" or "traditional" houses contains what are essentially I-houses.

Franklin County's antebellum dwellings varied in style and degree of grandeur. Peter Saunders, Jr., lived in a fairly modest I-house, unlike some of his equally wealthy contemporaries. In the 1820s he altered the three-room, story-and-a-half dwelling of James Callaway at the ironworks, the site of the county's first court, by raising it to two stories. The half-story roof was removed and a full second floor was constructed in its place. The central room on the first floor was narrowed by moving each of the two partitions between it and the rooms, one on either end in toward the center by a couple of feet. To the central room was added a staircase that led to the second floor, which had a corresponding central hall with two rooms, one on either side. Thus the modest late-eighteenth-century house at the ironworks became a modest, typical I-house of the early nineteenth century.[57] Here Peter Saunders, Jr., and his daughter lived for more than twenty years.

Others of Saunders's contemporaries built their houses in a similarly simple style. According to local tradition, Joab Early (the father of Jubal Anderson Early), who was commissioned a justice on 24 February 1827, built his dwelling about 1814. Here, supposedly, his son was born in 1816. The house may have evolved from a two-story, frame, side-passage-plan form to a two-story, central-passage-plan house with two rooms on each floor and an exterior chimney on each end. Its present appearance suggests a dwelling of the 1820s or 1830s.[58]

Cyrus Price House. 1968 photo. (Virginia Department of Historic Resources.)

In general, however, the well-to-do farmers of the antebellum period constructed somewhat more elaborate houses than their fathers and grandfathers, often using brick instead of wood. Cyrus Price, for example, who was commissioned a justice on 23 December 1839, built his two-story house of brick about 1835. The bricks were laid in Flemish bond; the four-bay facade of the house features an off-center entrance with a single window to the left of the door and two to the right. At the roofline is a molded brick cornice with elaborate dentil work. There is a two-story wing of brick attached to the left rear of the house, making it L-shaped. The fact that the wing also was constructed in Flemish bond and has the same cornice as the main part of the house may indicate that the entire structure was built at once instead of in two different phases. There are three exterior chimneys, two on the ends of the front section and one on the end of the wing. Inside, the house exhibits the usual central-passage plan, with a center hall and staircase separating a room to either side; this plan is repeated upstairs. The rear wing has one room on each floor.[59]

The Peter Saunders house of the 1820s and the somewhat more elaborate Price house of a decade later illustrate the slow evolution in taste of the members of Franklin County's elite, who preferred the simple I-house form. Wood was replaced with brick, the detailing of the cornice became more elaborate, and a rear wing appeared, but the essential style of each house was Federal, and the central-passage plan was used in both cases. As the end of the antebellum period approached, however, the architectural preference of the county's elite underwent further change.

An excellent example of this change is the Booth-Lovelace House, which is basically a Greek Revival structure with Italianate details. The house, which is almost square in shape, was constructed in 1858 for Moses Greer Booth, a county justice.[60] A wood-frame, two-story dwelling covered in weatherboards, the house is situated on the top of a hill with views of rolling farmlands and wooded hillsides. The three-bay facade is topped by a hipped roof so low in profile that it is virtually invisible from the ground. The front door, with an elaborate rectangular transom above it, is flanked by a pair of three-pane sidelights. The entrance is protected by a Greek Revival–style, one-story porch with four paired, square Doric columns and matching pairs of pilasters on either side of the front door. The eaves of both the porch and the roof are supported by sawed Italianate brackets. Similar, though smaller, porches shelter subsidiary entrances on each side of the house.

The Booth-Lovelace House possesses one of the most elegant interiors of its period in the county. All the doors and windows are framed by symmetrically molded, light-oak-stained wooden trim with bull's-eye corner blocks. The entrance hall contains a staircase to the right. At the rear of the entrance hall a service hall with staircase leads to the left. Both staircases feature heavily turned walnut balusters (two to a tread) and tapered octagonal newels. Of the four rooms that open off the halls on the first floor, the most elaborate is the parlor to the left of the entrance. It has two alcoves (one with a door opening into the entrance hall), intricate cornice and ceiling moldings, and a carved black marble mantel. The other mantels in the house are of marbled wood. The floor plan is repeated upstairs, where there are four bedrooms.[61]

The house presently standing at Bleak Hill, in the southwestern part of the county, is virtually contemporaneous with the Booth-Lovelace House but is a more sophisticated Italianate essay in brick. It was constructed by Peter Saunders, Jr., between 1855 and 1857 to replace at last the earlier house built by his father, Judge Fleming Saunders, that burned in 1830. On 22 March 1856, as the house entered its final phases of construction, it too almost burned down when a chimney caught fire. Peter Saunders related the episode to his mother:

Last evening I was startled by the cry of fire and on going out found the roof of the chimney in a blaze. Fortunately it was discovered before it had progressed far and as [there] happened to be a number of persons about the new house and ladders very convenient we soon succeeded in extinguishing it, although the wind at the time was blowing furiously. As not much damage was done I am almost glad that it happened. It will make all hands more careful and watchful about the place.

I am afraid that you are all two careless at Flat Creek. If that house should catch you have but little chance of extinguishing it. Shingle roofs after they get old catch very easily. You ought to keep a ladder always about the house and during the windy and dry weather of spring more care and watchfulness should be manifested.[62]

Booth-Lovelace House exterior (above) *and parlor* (below). *1989 photos.* (Virginia Department of Historic Resources.)

The Bleak Hill house and many of its outbuildings still stand on its hill overlooking fields and forests with the mountains as a background. Constructed in an L shape, the house with its projecting front faces the mountains to the west. A wooden one-story porch with simple Doric columns protects the western entrance and stretches across the facade from the projecting pavilion on the

Bleak Hill, front (west) elevation. 1988 photo. (Virginia Department of Historic Resources.)

northern end of the house. The pavilion has a single bay on each floor; the window on the first floor has three roundheaded openings separated by Doric pilasters, while the second-floor window has two similar openings. The recessed part of the house is two bays in width, with two windows on the second floor above the entrance door and its flanking window. The windows on the western facade's second floor are roundheaded like those on the pavilion, but the rest of the windows (including the one on the first floor of the west elevation) have flat tops. The house is covered with a standing-seam-metal roof supported by heavy sawed brackets under the eaves. Bleak Hill still has several of its outbuildings and retains its integrity as a large, remotely located hill-country farm.[63]

In the early nineteenth century, when most people could grow or easily purchase most of their food, hunting and gathering became a pastime rather than a necessity. Jonathan Cundiff noted in his diary that he shot passenger pigeons with little trouble: "[13 November 1820] the pegions came very plenty and we killed at 9 shoots 42."[64] Now extinct, passenger pigeons once flew in flocks so huge that they darkened the sky and toppled trees with their weight when they roosted.

Alice Watts Saunders wrote her sister on 26 September 1814 and described searching for hazelnuts during an outing that went awry:

> The day before yesterday Mr. Saunders and myself accompanied by his Brother Robert, took a trip of about twenty miles over the mountains in search of hazlenuts. We carried two servants with sack bags, confident that we should fill them both, but our long ride was almost for nothing, for we got only about a gallon altogether. I was sadly disappointed, for I had made up my mind to send my friends a good supply. It was a trip of disasters, for we were constantly getting lost, and what made it worse it was raining too. I

fared but badly, for in going through the woods I got my bonnet torn almost entirely to pieces. That begins to be the most miserable looking Country in the world. It must be wretchedly cold and dreary in the winter season.[65]

Many people, to the contrary, found the mountains a welcome relief, especially as a refuge from the heat of summer. Travel to spas or hot springs resorts, popular in Virginia since the eighteenth century, reached its peak in the decades before the Civil War. The counties of Alleghany, Bath, Botetourt, Monroe, Montgomery, and Rockbridge were home to such spas as the Red, White, Blue, and Yellow Sulphur Springs; the Warm and Hot Springs; the Healing and Sweet Springs; and the Rockbridge Alum Springs. Virginians—as well as residents of other states —flocked to the spas by the thousands, seeking not only good health but good times.

Each of the springs had its advocates, and the competition among the spas was fierce. In 1833 Henry T. Callaway, of Franklin County, wrote a testimonial to the efficacy of the Hot Springs that was published with others by the proprietor in *The Invalid's Guide:*

In the month of January, 1806, during my attendance on the Virginia Legislature, of which I was then a member, I was very sorely afflicted with an attack of inflammatory rheumatism, and about the 1st of July in the same year, after the disease had assumed a chronic state, I arrived at the Hot Springs in Virginia, much debilitated, requiring two persons to put me in and take me out of a carriage. I remained at the Springs sixty-three days, using the bath once every day except three. I was weighed the day I got to the Springs, and also on the day I left them, and if I was correctly weighed, I gained sixty pounds in weight in sixty-three days, and remained free from that complaint for upwards of twenty years.[66]

Callaway wrote a second testimonial describing graphically the attack of "Bilious Fever" from which he suffered in 1826, as well as a recurrence of the rheumatism in 1831. At the beginning of July 1832, he wrote,

I went to the Hot Springs, barely able to sit up, and used the waters freely, drinking and bathing, until the 30th of August [1826], when I left them, much relieved in every way. The ensuing summer I again returned to the Hot Springs, and used the waters by drinking and bathing, until the last of August, when I returned home entirely relieved of bowel disease, and nearly so of my rheumatism. I have again this summer visited these Springs, where I have been for three weeks using the waters as before, and believe myself entirely relieved of all my complaints, except a little stiffness in my hips and back.[67]

Peter Saunders, Jr., wrote his mother, Alice Saunders, in August 1856 from the Sweet Springs in Monroe County. He seemed as interested in the society there as in the healing powers of the springs. "We reached this place," he wrote,

on Thursday last [21 August], found it very full, but succeeded in getting quite comfortable quarters. They have now as many visitors as they are prepared to accommodate. We have met some old acquaintances, though most of the company are strangers. Many of them are from the south. Dr. Walker and his bride are here and seemed glad to see us. The place has been very much improved since I was here last. The accommodations are very good and we have the prospect of spending our time pleasantly. I came here with a bad cold and have only taken two baths as yet. Of course I can't have yet derived much benefit. I am in hopes that I will improve rapidly here. . . . Cousin Carter Gwathmey is now at the Red and Sweet Springs. We saw him a day or two since. He is looking much better than when I saw him last, though his health is far from being restored. I heard yesterday for the first time that cousin Betty Scott was at the White Sulphur. I was sorry to learn at the same time that she did not think herself any benefitted by the use of the water.[68]

Some entertainments were found closer to home. Among the unusual amusements that came to country people by the early nineteenth century were traveling shows and circuses. Jonathan Cundiff, who lived just across Staunton River in Bedford County, reported that he attended a circus two days in a row: "at nite [17 January 1823] went to the grocery and see the show and the master walked the wier and the bare spell and tell the time of nite by a watch. . . . [18 January] at nite went to the grocery and see them act again."[69] The next day he returned to watch the circus pack up and leave. In 1829–1830 the Franklin County Court licensed two "Exhibitors of Public Shows"—Alfred Cole and Company and Sizer Mead and Company—the latter of which was a traveling circus that no doubt attracted a large audience.[70]

Traveling shows, circuses, and visits to hot springs constituted some of the welcome respites from the everyday existence of rural life. Farming and business aside, that existence revolved around the extended family, and the anchor of the family—according to the mores of the times—was the woman in her role as wife and mother.

NINE

The Women's Sphere

The eighteenth- and nineteenth-century woman was trapped in a paradox: on the one hand adored by men and set on a pedestal, and on the other bound by customs and laws to fixed roles largely designed for them by men. By and large those roles revolved around the family, home, and church. Women were excluded from public life and the world of work outside the home. They were expected to be devoted to their families and to worthy causes, and to be subservient to their husbands and to men generally, at least in public.

Traditionally, when a woman married she moved from her own family's home to the place where her husband wished to live. Many women, however, did not go willingly and virtually mourned the loss of their familiar surroundings. For example, before Alice Watts married Judge Fleming Saunders on 19 May 1814 she lived on her parents' farm, called Flat Creek, in Campbell County, near present-day Evington. After her marriage she moved to southwestern Franklin County, near Bleak Hill. To judge from her letters to her family she found the place bleak indeed and longed for her former home. She may also have found her new role as a plantation mistress overwhelming, as a letter of 26 September 1814 revealed:

> This is the first leisure moment I have had for two days past, and I now feel infinite pleasure in the idea of having an uninterupted communication with you this morning. It is, to me, the greatest relief in the world, when I have been in the society of persons for whom I have no particular regard, to retire and carry on a silent conversation with one to whom I am particularly attached. You have no idea My dear Sister how solitary I have felt for a week past. My mornings are generally spent entirely alone, and it is at such moments I wish most for the society of Flat Creek, and the prattle of the dear little children. Of an evening if Mr. Saunders is out, and every thing profoundly silent, my imagination invariably wanders to Mama's fireside, where every individual is portrayed with the most affectionate interest. But I must dismiss this subject or I shall have a miserable fit of the Blues today.[1]

A few weeks later she returned to the subject in a letter to her mother, who was

169

a widow. Noting that her sisters had just left their mother at Flat Creek after a long visit, she added,

> While you had my Sisters with you, it seemed to me I could bear to be separated from you much better than I can now, when I could relieve in some degree your solitary situation. My wish to live near you my dear Mama increases daily, and every preparation which is made for a final settling hear, distresses me very much. But it is my duty if Mr. Saunders cannot be prevailed upon to move, to make myself as contented as I can. . . . Come up after Christmas and stay until March or April, and I will return and stay some Months with you in the spring.[2]

More than two years later Alice Saunders remained unsuccessful in persuading her husband to move, as she wrote to her mother:

> I feel excessively disappointed that the proposed exchange of the Counties has met with no success. I can conceive no good reason whatever that Judge S. could have in objecting to the alteration. I reflect upon it sometimes until I become quite depressed in spirits. The idea of spending the rest of my days in this part of the world is extremely disagreeable to me. I have already lived longer here than I wished; but we are by our natures poor discon[ten]ted creatures, and perhaps it would be the same case were I to go any where else.[3]

Eventually Alice Saunders got her wish and moved back to Flat Creek when the house at Bleak Hill burned down in January 1830, and after the family had lived for a while in the surviving outbuildings, including some of the slave cabins. Judge Fleming Saunders kept up the Bleak Hill farm as he traveled his circuit, but it was his son, Peter Saunders, Jr., who completed the present Italianate-style brick structure in 1857.

Circumscribed though they were by law and custom, women did more than manage households and bear children. They did not serve on juries, but they testified as witnesses in lawsuits and filed their own suits when the need arose. The earliest example of Franklin County women serving as witnesses occurred in the case of *Johnson* v. *Doggett*, when the court on 9 November 1786 allowed two

Women feeding chickens. Left: *Mary Davis, Redwood.* Right: *Julia Law, Glade Hill. Ca. 1920s photos.* (Blue Ridge Institute, Ferrum, Va.)

days' worth of expenses to Martha Miller and Mary Hartwell for their attendance.[5] On 6 March 1787 two women, Milley Thomas and Frances Thorp, obtained judgments in court against John Livesay and William Toney, respectively.[6] In May 1787 Rachel Jones sued Mary Webb for slander for saying that Jones had given false testimony in a sworn affidavit before Major Mark Rentfro. Although Rachel Jones sought £100 in damages, the jury awarded her only one shilling.[7]

Most lawsuits either were settled out of court or went to judgment fairly quickly. Occasionally, for women as for men, an especially acrimonious suit would drag on for years, spawning other suits and taking on the character of a vendetta. Such was the case with Penelope Guthrey, the widow of Henry Guthrey, who became embroiled with her neighbor, the litigious John Hook.

Henry Guthrey wrote his will on 20 October 1785; it was presented for probate on 3 July 1786. The brief document reads in part:

> I leave and Bequeath to my affectionate wife Penelope all my Estate both real and Personal during her Widdowhood. at her marriage or Death to be Sold and Equally Divided amongst my Children To Wit Mary, Agg, James, John, David, Salley, Ann, Penelope, Molly, Henry, Benjamin, & Ruth.[8]

Guthrey's estate consisted of six slaves, three horses, ten head of cattle, nineteen hogs, farm equipment, a "Silver Spoon & Candle Stick," five beds, a loom, five chairs, two tables, and cooking equipment and kitchen furniture.[9] His farm was composed of three hundred acres of land in two tracts, one of two hundred and the other of one hundred acres.[10]

The estate immediately was encumbered with lawsuits, however, including at least one by her next-door neighbor John Hook. Penelope Guthrey was compelled to file security bonds as administratrix of her husband's estate; the weight of them virtually bankrupted her. The county court decreed that if she failed "to give Such Security, it is ordered by the Court that John Hook and Rich'd Booth, her Securitys, Take Possession on the s'd Decedents Estate agreeable to the Inventory."[11] In May 1788 she filed a bond to give John Hook countersecurity for the administration of her husband's estate, and was told by the court that she was responsible for any interest that accrued by virtue of Hook's pursuing his suit against her.[12] In 1790 she appeared before the court to give countersecurity to Rachel Goggin, the administratrix of the estate of Stephen Goggin, deceased, who earlier had done the same for her. The court ordered Guthrey either to find the means to file a bond or to deliver her late husband's estate to Rachel Goggin.[13]

None of Penelope Guthrey's tribulations appeared to dampen her spirit, however. In 1791, when John Hook sued the Guthrey estate for a monetary claim, Penelope Guthrey countersued Hook for cutting down a tree on her property and for building a fence on her land.[14] Thomas Parker, who in the fall of 1787 began working for Hook, deposed on 10 December 1790 that at that time Hook told him to take some axes and "a Negro fellow," James, with him and go find John Guthrey (Penelope's son, who also was her overseer) and get him to show them a gum tree on Mrs. Guthrey's land. Hook said she had given him the tree and they were to chop it down to make planks and yokes. Parker walked to Mrs. Guthrey's house and "hollowed from the fence." She came out of the house and told him to see an old black woman on the way to John Guthrey's house, who would show them the way. They found John, who pointed out the tree to them, and they cut it down. Parker and James went back the next day to finish their work and encountered Mrs. Guthrey, who asked them where they were going. When they told her, "Mrs. Guthry then smiling asked this deponent who gave Mr. Hook the Gum tree." Parker said he did not know, but John Guthrey had showed them the tree willingly enough and he thought from her behavior earlier that she was willing for Hook to have it. Later she told Parker she was going to sue Hook over it; he said it was not worth her while, "that the tree would not have stood long, it being rotted at the root and six foot of it so decayed that it could not be used." She said she would not sue Hook were it not for the fact that Hook was suing her. Thomas Hunt also made a deposition on 10 December 1790, in which he stated that he was with Penelope Guthrey and John Hook at David Guthrey's house when Hook asked her why she did not simply put the tree on her account; she replied "she never would have brought such a suit if he the said John Hook had not sued her." Hunt and Nathan Tate, a surveyor, ran the lines of Hook's land and found his fence was all on his own land, not Guthrey's. Both suits were dismissed at the plaintiffs' costs.

The final victory in this war of lawsuits went to Penelope Guthrey. In November 1791 she convinced a jury that John Hook had cheated her.[15] She asserted that her late husband and Hook had conducted considerable business and that Hook was in debt to Guthrey for £100. Shortly before her husband's death Hook "made payment of a Negroe at the price of Eighty pounds," leaving a balance of £20. After Henry Guthrey died, Hook treated Penelope Guthrey with "Friendship & favour" and "she Trusted solely to the honesty & candor of the said Hook" because he was acting "more a Guardian of her, a Widow, than any thing else." As a result she was careless in keeping her accounts with Hook and let herself be talked by his storekeeper into signing a paper that caused her to lose some of her rights. The jury found in her favor.

Like Penelope Guthrey, many late-eighteenth-century women were scarcely shrinking violets, regardless of their inferior status before the law. Aliannah Hill, the daughter of Thomas Hill, filed a complaint on 7 March 1787 against Benjamin Hale "for an Insult offered her on the Highway."[16] The Franklin County Court ordered Hale to put up a £25 bond to guarantee his appearance before the next grand jury, which met on 7 May. He was indicted and filed another bond for £10 against his appearance at the August meeting of the county court. On 9 August the case was heard and Aliannah Hill was awarded an unspecified judgment against Benjamin Hale.[17] On 8 May 1787 Joanna Sheridan, the wife of Philip Sheridan, filed a complaint against William Griffith, also for "an Insult on the Highway."[18] She was content, however, to have Griffith taken into custody until he put up a bond for his good behavior.

Although disagreements and insults often led to lawsuits, occasionally they resulted in violence. On 30 March 1790, for example, Mary Jones swore in an affidavit made before Thomas Hale that she had "good cause to apprehend that John Brammer will beat Wound or Evilly treat her Children to the Great Deanger and risk of there lives." Hale ordered Brammer arrested and bound over for his good behavior, which occurred on 1 April. Four days later Brammer had Stephen Smith swear out a warrant on William and Susannah Griffith and Thomas and Mary Jones, charging them with "Trespass, Assault and Battery and false Imprisonment." Brammer swore that the defendants assaulted and injured him. Notes made on the reverse of a court summons include the following phrases: "Hairs parted from his head"; "drew hatchett & knife"; "run the knife through the officers Clothes." A jury eventually awarded Brammer £5 in damages.[19]

Usually the threat of violence was enough to cause the aggrieved party to ask a justice or the county court to require a peace bond of the other party. A typical instance occurred on 3 November 1788, when

> Eliza. Greer having Craved the Peace Agt. Noel Battles, the said Battles came into Court with Charles Sebrett his Security and Ack'd themselves Severally Indebted to the Com. Wealth that is to say the sd. Battles in the sum of £10 & his Securitys in the sum of £5 to be Levied on their Respective Goods & Chattles, Land & Tenements on the Condition the said Battles does not act with good behavior for one year & a Day Especially to the said Eliza. Greer.[20]

Few instances of spousal abuse were recorded in Franklin County, although there were occasional hints. On 1 September 1806, for example, Polly Hatcher persuaded the county court to order her husband, Henry Hatcher, to file a peace bond in the amount of $200 to guarantee his good behavior toward her.[21]

Women sometimes feared violence from other women, as when Margaret Stephens complained to the county court on 4 January 1790 concerning threats made against her by Elizabeth Rentfro. Rentfro came into court and, with Peter Saunders, Sr., acting as her security, took out bonds for her good behavior in the amounts of £30 for her and £20 for Saunders. The bonds were to be forfeited if Rentfro failed to act peaceably toward the citizens of Virginia for twelve months and a day—and especially toward Margaret Stephens.[22]

Sometimes women found themselves in court accused of crimes, although such cases were rare. On 13 July 1808, for example, the court examined Rebecca Amos and her daughter Sally on suspicion of having stolen "from John Spoon Eight Handkerchiefs, Two new thread Shifts, two thread Shirts, one Table Cloth, four pounds of machined cotton, one pound of Spun cotton, one Gallon of Salt, one choat out of the Pen, two cotton Petticoats & sundry other articles the property of the said John Spoon on the fourth day of this month."[23] After the evidence was presented, however, the court found the women not guilty.

Women rarely committed murder; when they did, however, children were the usual victims. The typical murderer was a woman with a child born out of wedlock, and she probably was motivated by shame, poverty, fear of public opinion, or some combination of the three. On 29 July 1800, for example, the Franklin County Court examined Sarah Vincent, a "single woman of said County, on suspicion of murdering or destroying her Bastard Child."[24] She pleaded not guilty, but the court found her guilty and remanded her to the district court for further trial on 15 September 1800. Several witnesses filed depositions with the county court. Mary Coger swore "that last harvest was a year she heard Sarah Vincent say she was at that time Two months gone with Child," and that later "she heard Sarah Vincent say she was Delivered of a Child." Frankey Kelly reported that Sarah Vincent "told her she had lost [miscarried] a Child, & that if it came to its full time it would be born on the 29th of February; that she saw the said Vincent & believed her to be pregnant." Susannah Kelly said that Vincent called on her "to milk her Cows & Complained she was sick, which she did & after going into the house where said Vincent lives, she found her in Bed, who told her she was Delivered of a Child, which was laid on a bench under a Dresser wraped in a pettycoat." Leah Kingary revealed that "she Discovered a hole in the Ground near the house where Sarah Vincent lived which she supposed to be intended for a Grave to bury a Child in of which she was Delivered a short time before; that she found a shift at the place belonging to a Child which Sarah Vincent claimed." At the September trial, however, the district court ordered Vincent "discharged from her Imprisonment" when the grand jury returned her indictment as "not a True Bill."[25] Perhaps the grand jury decided that the evidence, which was circumstantial and seemed as much to support a death by miscarriage as by murder, did not justify the indictment.

To investigate an instance of murder committed by several women, a coroner's jury met on 4 September 1809 to conduct an inquest on the body of a female child said to have been born of Mary Ann Jones, alias Mary Ann Roberts. The inquest was held at the dwelling of Richard Mullins, where the child was lying dead, to determine the cause of death. The jury found that Mary Ann Jones, alias Roberts, a spinster; Amelia Barns, spinster; and Keziah Mullins, spinster, "not fearing God," assaulted the infant and strangled her to death.[26]

No statistics exist to show how common were births out of wedlock, or how many brides were pregnant on their wedding day. Although singleness was looked at askance, marriage, as most texts for wedding ceremonies point out, was not an institution to be entered into lightly. Neither were engagements, as Jackson Griffith found out when he jilted Rebecca Quigley in 1799 to marry Catherine Sigmon. In April 1800 Quigley sued Griffith for breach of contract; a jury awarded her £18 in damages. She married Elias Leffew about 28 June 1802.[27]

When a wedding was held, parents who could afford to do so sometimes provided a dowry for the bride, although it usually was in the name of the groom. On 6 August 1792, for example, Gasper Howser gave 105 acres of land on Chestnut Creek to Abraham Stover "of his Free Good Will and pleasure . . . as a Dowry with his daughter Catherine now wife to said Abraham Stover."[28]

Often when a woman inherited a share of her deceased parent's estate, it was her husband who profited. Jane Pinckard, a daughter of John Pinckard, who died in 1788, married Charles Smith about 8 November 1790.[29] A year later, on 14 November 1791, her husband "Settled with Hugh Innes late a Guardian to Jean Pinkard Orphan of John Pinkard Decs'd and now my Wife and Received full satisfaction."[30] No doubt Jane Smith might have been more satisfied had she received the money instead of her husband.

Then as now, husbands and wives disagreed occasionally on a variety of subjects ranging from religion to child rearing. Society expected wives to yield to their husbands' wishes in most matters and keep within their own spheres of influence, as Judge Fleming Saunders expressed in a letter to his wife in 1833:

> You say as far as in you lies, you are much disposed to become a bright and shining Christian. May God grant you success is the sincere prayer of your affectionate husband, but beware that you do not mistake the Course, recollecting that all of us are Called upon to perform duties, each in our particular and appropriate sphere, and that we often neglect those duties by

interfering with duties in other spheres. The very existence of society depends upon a due observance of our appropriate duties and whenever we get beyond our sphere, disorder and confusion is the consequence.[31]

When wives became irretrievably dissatisfied with their husbands, or vice versa, separations sometimes followed. On rare occasions couples obtained divorces; before 1827 only the General Assembly could grant a complete divorce, which it almost never did. A separation agreement, called a "bed and board" separation, was more common. The agreement severed most of the bonds of matrimony but did not allow either party to remarry.

One such separation agreement was recorded in Franklin County in 1791. The couple was William and Kazia Poteet, who drew up an agreement on 7 December 1790:

the said Kazia do agree and Covenent with the said William Putteet to Raliquene and withdraw herself from his Bed and Bord and further to Disclaim all and every Indowment or Dower to which she was Intitled in Consequence of their Marriage Contract as follows . . . to give and Confirm to the Said Kazia one Bay Mare Saddle and Bridle on Father Bed and Furniture Two hundred weight of pork one Pott one Puter Dish Twelve Bushels of Corn one pare of Stilards one Cow and Calf Two Sheep one Chest one Bible and one Flax wheel with her wearing aperal to the use of the said Kazia as her own Proper Goods.[32]

A separation agreement was difficult to obtain when one party in the marriage abandoned the other. On 4 November 1801 Elizabeth Wimmer appeared before the Franklin County Court: "having made oath that her Husband Jacob Wimmer hath gone away & left her, Leave is Granted her to Sue by John Miller her next friend the said Wimmer for a Separate mantainance."[33]

Some women, against all odds, pursued a complete divorce with petitions to the General Assembly. Catherine Willis made two unsuccessful attempts, in 1807 and 1810, to obtain a divorce from her husband, Joseph Willis, who had abandoned her.[34] She wrote in her petitions that she had married Willis in 1802 in Pendleton County and moved with him to Franklin County about 1804. He soon abandoned her and their three children and moved to Ohio, where he was reported to have married again. Catherine Willis wrote that when her husband left her

he made way with all the property of every kind that he got by his intermarriage with her, and when he went off gave no notice of the place to which he intended to go so as to enable your petitioner to follow him. . . . [In addition] her said husband being very much in debt when he went off all the little property she has acquired since from time to time has been taken from her to satisfy her said husband's debts[.] even her [spinning] wheels and cards have been sold with which she was endeavouring honestly to maintain herself & her children.

She added that Joseph Willis "was in the habit of abusing her most wreatchedly, having tied her and whiped her frequently." Her charges were supported by affidavits signed by thirty-five neighbors in 1807 and twenty-one in 1810.

Despite Catherine Willis's story and the testimony of her friends and neighbors, the General Assembly denied her petitions without explanation. (Later, according to the marriage bond records of Franklin County, she married Peter Boon in 1817 and Peter Sigmon in 1819.[35][4] Perhaps Joseph Willis had died, or else she decided that if he could remarry without benefit of divorce, so could she.)

Phoebe Baker also failed in her attempt to obtain a divorce for abandonment. Born Phoebe J. Crews, she had married Jehu John Meadows in 1833.[36] He died in 1840,[37] and in December 1844 she married Pleasant Baker, of Bedford County. Her first husband, she wrote, had given her in his will,

> for and during her life, one hundred acres of land, on which land were all necessary buildings, his household, & kitchen furniture, plantation utensils, and stocks consisting of horses, Cattle, sheep, & hogs, and Six valuable slaves, all of which property at the death of your petitioner were by said will to go to and be the property of his three children born to him, said Jehu Meadows, by your petitioner. Your petitioner, states that the provision above made for her by her former husband, was amply sufficient to support and educate her three children and support herself.[38]

After she married Baker, however, her new husband

> gave himself up to the most loose and immoral propensities, and indicated a determination, to sell your petitioners interest, in the property, left her for life . . . [and] after staying with her about fourteen days the said Pleasant Baker left her and the last she heard of him, he was in Pulaski County, making his way westward.

Out of fear for the loss of her property and the risk to the welfare of her children, Phoebe Baker asked the General Assembly to spare her from "being reduced to want by this profligate man, . . . by divorce or one sort or another." As in the instance of Catherine Willis, however, the legislature denied her petition.

Men were no more successful at obtaining divorces for abandonment than were women. On 16 December 1842 John Bondurant filed a bitter petition with the General Assembly asking for a divorce from his wife, the former Nancy Finney.[39] He had married her in November 1828, he wrote, and had for many years lived peaceably with her. They had four children, two of whom had died. He asserted that

> his conduct to the said Nancy was at all times, until as will be hereinafter stated she became unworthy of it, kind and affectionate. He provided a comfortable home, furnished his family with everything necessary to their comfort, and observed on his own part a course of conduct marked by honesty, industry, and sobriety, to insure to them a respectable station in society.

Suddenly, in February 1841, Nancy Bondurant began to show a change in her feelings toward him. "He was at a loss to what to attribute this change upon her part. He knew that he had given no cause for it in his own conduct." When he addressed her on the subject she pleaded illness; his reaction was to have her treated by physicians. So matters continued until the fall of 1841, when it became obvious

to your petitioner and others that the said Nancy had established a criminal connexion with a certain Charles Richards, himself a married man. Indeed they had carried things so far that a plan was agreed between [them] that they should run off together. . . . [Then Bondurant] charged the fact of her criminal conduct on the said Nancy and she shamelessly admitted it and declared that it had existed & continued for a year.

Apparently John Bondurant had been the last man in his neighborhood to learn of his wife's affair. John Cook wrote in an affidavit that in August 1840 he had gone to the house of his kinsman Benjamin F. Cook and found Nancy Bondurant and Charles Richards

entirely alone as said Benjamin F. Cook was an unmarried man and not at home. This affiant presently noticed the shamefull & disgusting familiarity that was going on betwixt the parties. He then took a Chair and some news papers and went to the farther end of the poarch and commenced reading but Kept his mind & eye Occasionally upon the said Richards & Bondurant. They finally retired into a back room and he [neither] saw nor heard nothing more of them for the Space of fifteen or twenty minutes. They again came into the poarch and observed that they had been examining a new map of the United States which this affiant is confident was not the case as the map was so near him that he must have heard their voices or the sound of their feet. This affiant was then under the impression and that impression still remains that in their absence they were guilty of the grossest improprieties.[40]

Nancy Bondurant did in fact abandon her husband and children; Richards had left before her. She was quite bold and unrepentant about her actions and intentions. Isham Belcher reported that a few days before she left she told him that she was leaving for Tennessee. Belcher then asked her whether she was

guilty of what she was charged with (Vice, of having commited adultery & having illicit intercours with Charles Richards and abandoning her husband) And She answered that She had and that their Criminal Communication had been carried on for a length of time.[41]

John Bondurant asked the General Assembly to dissolve his marriage, writing that he

cannot consent again to live with a woman who has brought shame & disgrace upon her family. He cannot consent to allow his children to be contaminated by the association of an abandoned prostitute, to be raised up by her, and perhaps to be ruined by her example.

His claims were supported by the signatures of dozens of his neighbors but, as in the cases of Catherine Willis and Phoebe Baker, the General Assembly denied his petition.

No matter how compelling the petition, they all possess the flaw of giving only one side of the issue. This is particularly true in the case of abandonment, when the other spouse was no longer around to contest the claims made in the petition. No doubt there was much more to the story of John and Nancy Bondurant than was revealed in his petition. Perhaps Nancy Bondurant was in the midst of what is known in modern times as a "mid-life crisis," or perhaps John Bondurant was not the kind and generous man he portrayed himself to be. The complete story will never be known.

This is not quite the case with Franklin County's most notorious antebellum divorce petition—and the only one that was granted by the General Assembly. The incident that prompted the divorce proceeding involved attempted murder by an apparently mentally ill, drug-addicted member of a prominent Franklin County family, the Tates, and proved such a scandal that a genealogy of that family compiled as recently as 1936 omitted the very existence of the offending party, Mildred C. Tate.[42]

The Tates were related by blood or marriage to several families that dominated the political and social life of Franklin County from its formation until the mid-nineteenth century, as well as Bedford and Campbell counties. Those families included the Callaways, the Steptoes, the Inneses, the Earlys, and the Saunderses. Edmund Tate, the father of Mildred C. Tate, was a tavern owner in Rocky Mount who rose to the rank of colonel in the Franklin County militia. He died in 1829, aged about seventy.

A young attorney named William B. Williams, a native of Pittsylvania County, was living with Colonel Tate's family in his tavern when he died. Williams, having been treated kindly by the family, attended to their needs and took the youngest son under his care to raise and educate. In the meantime Williams fell in love with Mildred, Colonel Tate's eldest daughter. By 1830 his infatuation was well known in Franklin County, as Judith Hale wrote to her cousin in Campbell County:

> Thare is no such thing as Mildred Tate being engaged to Mr. Williams. He is very attentive to her. I believe he is anxious to marry her if he could get her consent. That he never will do in my opinion. Mildred has become very handsome and a quite interesting girl.[43]

Williams proposed marriage, but Mildred Tate rejected him and he resolved

> to discontinue his addresses, forming a fixed purpose of mind (which he announced to many of his friends) never to renew them, unless the most unequivocal indications were afforded on the part of the said Mildred of a change of sentiment.[44]

Mildred Tate did change her mind and accept Williams's proposal near the end of December 1832. The wedding date was set for 24 January 1833.

The nuptials were performed as planned and the festivities were held at the tavern, which had been purchased after Edmund Tate's death by Colonel Thomas Hale, until the evening of 25 January, when most of the guests departed. The building still contained several persons besides the bride and groom. Williams had contracted a cold, and on the newlyweds' retirement to their chamber, his wife prepared him a potion to drink that she represented as burned Baitman's Drops—no doubt sold as a sure cure for the common cold. The potion, however, proved to be laudanum, an opium-derived sedative in liquid form.

And so to bed. Mrs. Williams locked their chamber door, and her husband described the ensuing events with some delicacy:

> On retiring to bed the Said Mildred representing herself as greatly fatigued, insisted that she should be permitted to Sleep; at the same time insisting that your petitioner should compose himself to Sleep.
>
> This however he was prevented (as he supposes from the novelty of his Situation) from doing. She, however, placing herself on the further part of the bed, lay entirely still until almost eleven Oclock, when pretending to Wake up, and finding your petitioner awake, She represented that she had had a singular dream, that his hair was becoming Gray; and the manner of restoring its Colour had been discovered to her; and asked if she might make the experiment. Your petitioner, though conceiving it to be an idle fancy, yet willing to indulge her, Consented.
>
> And she arose from the bed, causing your petitioner to turn his face from her, and to promise not to look at her. This he agreed to do, imagining that all this had been conceived by her, to save her delicacy on an occasion, for which he then supposed, she had risen from her bed, needless here to be more than alluded to. Shortly after, she returned to the bedside with a phial the bottom of which he has since ascertained had been previously broken off by her, and placing the mouth of it in his ear, caused him to hold it upright with his hand, Saying at the same time she was coming with her Medicine, which she represented to be cologne. She then returned to the fire, and coming to the bed with a quantity of Molten lead, deliberately poured it through the phial into the ear of your petitioner. Your petitioner feeling the Shock turned suddenly over, and She fled at the same moment screaming from the room.

Mildred Williams, after unlocking the door, ran to the bedroom door of tavernkeeper Thomas Hale, who was fast asleep. He reported that he was

> alarmed by a Scream and a loud knocking at his Chamber door, that he immediately arose & opened the door. When he discovered Mrs. Williams who, appeared to be under the influence of extreme terror, that she Cried out immediately that her dear husband was dead or dying. He immediately went up to the room occupied by Col. Williams, who he found lying upon his back with his head and Shoulders somewhat raised and making efforts with his hands to raise himself up in the bed. That he was pale and appeared to this affiant to be in the act of dying and he supposed was under the influence of some kind of fit. That he caught hold of him and Shook him and Slapped him on the face. This affiant asked him what was the matter. He replied She has Murdered me. At this Moment she Mrs. Williams came to the room, and immediately ran up to Col. Williams and embraced him and expressed much satisfaction that he was still alive. She then threw the bed cover over his head and insisted that this affiant and his Wife should leave the room, stating that she wished to be alone with her dear husband. Col.

Williams took the cover off of his head. At that time this affiant found particles of a broken phial in the Bed and enquired of Col. Williams, what he had been doing with it, or what he had taken. She answered (before he could reply) that you know my dear husband you tried to kill me, that you went to the fire and threw the phial at my head, and that you have killed yourself. He then spoke, denying any attempt upon her life, and requested the affiant to examine his ear, which he did and found it filled with lead. This discovery seemed to afford him relief, as he said all the damage to be apprehended was already done, or known.

At this moment She manifesting the appearance of extreme agony, threw up her hands, saying that she did love her husband and fell back upon the Bed.[45]

The householders summoned Dr. Richard M. Taliaferro, who extracted the remaining lead from Williams's ear. Taliaferro also found that some of the skin had been burned off Williams's head behind his ear, exposing the bone of his skull.

Mildred Williams was removed to another room. The next day her brother James C. Tate took her to the nearby home of Robert H. Colhoun and his wife, Elizabeth, where she remained for more than a week. Elizabeth Colhoun's opinion was that not only was Mrs. Williams "not in her right mind," but she doubted whether she also "has any recollection of her marriage." Robert Colhoun reported that when he saw Mildred Williams a few days before her marriage, she "conducted herself so, as to produce the impression that she had lost her senses, or her modesty." He observed at that time "something remarkable both in her deportment and appearance" and that after the murder attempt "she seemed for some days to be labouring under mental alienation, and [he] does not think she has yet recovered."[46]

Several theories—two of them involving drug abuse—were advanced to explain Mrs. Williams's bizarre behavior. Thomas Hale thought she "had been in the habit of using Laudanum, and believes She was under its influence at the time" of her attack on her husband. Hale's wife, Harriet, reported that she knew nothing of Mrs. Williams's use of laudanum. However, Mrs. Hale noted that she herself had twice

procured opium [in the form of a cake or bar] for her own use, which except a small portion, was taken by some person from her drawer. This was three weeks before the Wedding. She observed her [Mrs. Williams] frequently take something from her pocket, and bite a part of it, and return it again, which the affiant supposed to be Candy, but does not know, thinks it might have been opium.[47]

Burwell C. Keatts, Armistead L. Burwell, and Michael D. Holland all testified that they had supplied Mrs. Williams with laudanum shortly before her wedding. Keatts wrote that she had

been in the habit for the last eight or nine Months of purchasing Laudanum of him frequently, sometimes one ounce at a time, sometimes less. He thinks the last She got of him was about the first week in January last at which time she got an ounce phial full. She always alledging She used it either for the tooth or head ache. On the 25th January last she asked this affiant to Send her some Laudanum, alledging she had Spilled the last She had got, at the same time stating she had the tooth ache, & at the same time Shewing a decayed tooth. This affiant forgot to Send the Laudanum as requested, but a messenger came to the Store about dark and asked for the Laudanum, and Mr. Holland (a young man in the affiants employ) Sent about 1/4 of an ounce.[48]

Besides possible drug abuse, mental illness was also suggested by several witnesses as an explanation for Mrs. Williams's behavior. Michael D. Holland recalled that about Christmastide he attended a postengagement party at which Mildred Tate was present and

appeared to be lively and cheerful, dancing and amusing herself with the company then assembled, for some time, when she took a seat near him, and leaned her head upon her hands. [He] asked her if she had a cold. She replied no, that it was something in her head. He then questioned her further, and she replied that her brain was affected, at the same time exhibiting a wildness of the eye, or rather a maniac stare, which startled him. He asked her if she was deranged, to which she made no direct reply, but endeavoured to explain the affection of her head or brain. [He] then said, that with the prospect before her, she ought to be very happy. She replied, happy? No. Never. . . . [He] was so shocked by her conversation and appearance, that he left the room. . . . [A week or so later] she complained of the affection of her head, and went on to say, that it was not pain, neither was it cold, for she had cured that the preceeding night, in her usual manner of late, by crying.[49]

Mildred Tate's mood swings also had been observed by Burwell C. Keatts, who

occasionally discovered an unusual depression of Spirits in the said Mildred, and at other times an unusual Cheerfulness. He once or twice saw her Weeping, on an other occasion she informed him she had been crying nearly all the night before; on being asked wherefore she was Weeping, She Smiled and Said it helped her head, saying she had a Cold & head ache.[50]

What may have in fact prompted Mildred Tate's depression was an engagement that she broke in order to marry Williams. Michael D. Holland thought that "a mutual attachment had existed between Miss Tate and a Young gentleman, which had been formed some time back." John S. Hale thought

that an engagement existed between Miss Tate and another young gentleman up to the time of her engagement with Col. Williams, and that her breach of that engagement was a subject of extreme regret upon her part, that he heard her observe she had written a letter, she would not write again if she could recall it. And he doubts not that the circumstance affected her materially.[51]

Mildred Tate's brother and guardian, James C. Tate, corroborated Williams's assertion that he had not pursued Mildred against her wishes, but had behaved as a gentleman. On the other hand, Mildred clearly was not competent to assent to a marriage, in her brother's opinion. He believed that she not only had no recollection of the events that occurred on the evening of 25 January, but also could not even remember that she had been married. Tate wrote that "upon being asked, if she was willing that a divorce should take place she replied and said that if she was married she ardently wished that it should be obtained."[52]

On 12 February 1833 Tate wrote Samuel Hale and Wiley P. Woods, Franklin County's representatives in the House of Delegates, in support of William B. Williams's divorce petition. Tate asked the two to enlist the aid of their fellow delegates from the area: Thomas Preston and Edmund Pate, of Bedford County; George W. Wilson, of Botetourt County; Jacob Helms, of Floyd County; Samuel McCamant, of Grayson County; Peyton Gravely, of Henry County; Isaac Adams, of Patrick County; and Vincent Witcher and William Swanson, of Pittsylvania County. He also urged them to speak to Benjamin W. S. Cabell, the senator representing Henry, Patrick, and Pittsylvania counties, and David McComas, the senator for Grayson, Smyth, Tazewell, and Wythe counties.

James C. Tate clearly was heartbroken over the incident. "It is useless for me," he wrote, "to attempt a description of my feelings to you, you can imagine as well as I can describe them, tho' I am firm and collected."[53] He concluded with the observation that there were "grounds for a divorce on either side, [for] it is evident to me that when the vows were passed Mildred was non Compos mentis [not of sound mind]."

On 7 March 1833 the General Assembly passed an act declaring

That the marriage lately solemnized between William B. Williams, of the county of Franklin, and Mildred C. his wife, formerly Mildred C. Tate, shall be, and the same is hereby dissolved, and the said Williams forever divorced from the said Mildred; and that all right, interest or claim of the said Mildred in or to the estate, real or personal, of the said Williams, or any part thereof, shall cease and determine henceforth and forever.[54]

William B. Williams, who apparently never remarried, continued to serve on the Franklin County bench for many years. Mildred C. Tate vanished from the records of Franklin County. She did remarry, however, and by 1836 was living with her husband, Dr. Edmond Tompson, in Jackson, Tennessee. The Tompsons had nine children.[55]

It is interesting that the Williams-Tate marriage, which involved broken hearts, drugs, insanity, and attempted murder, was dissolved by an act of the legislature that largely addressed property rights in dry legal language. No matter that every marriage, whether successful or not, was based on emotion, the law was cerebral and narrow in its focus.

The law's foundation was a concept of "fairness" that appeared reasonable on paper, especially where estates were concerned. A husband's estate, in the event he died intestate (without a will), was to be equally divided among his children, after his widow had been allocated a one-third portion of it. In addition, a widow whose husband left a will could renounce it if she disliked its terms and demand her one-third share.

When Charles H. English died in 1837 without a will, for example, he was survived by his widow, Lucy English, whom he had married in February 1833.[56] He left a substantial estate, including more than four hundred acres of land, one slave girl, one horse, six head of cattle, seventeen hogs, a bee stand and bees, a still, a clock, a gold watch, a looking glass, nine chairs, a bureau, a walnut table, and three beds.[57]4 Before his estate was settled Lucy English married William Brown in January 1840.[58] On 4 September 1848 Lucy Brown received her "third," or dower share, of Charles H. English's tract of land. The tract contained 135 acres—mostly in woodlands—and the house, which was depicted on the surveyor's plat as a three-bay, three-story, gable-roofed structure with a chimney on each end and surrounded by a picket fence.[59]

Occasionally a widow objected to the provisions of her husband's will and renounced it in favor of her dower third. On 4 February 1788, for instance,

> Mary Lyon came into Court and Renounce Benifitt of Elisha Lyon's Will, her Husband Deceased, and Prayd the Benefitt of the Law, whereupon it is ordered by the Court that John Smith, John Hook, Jonathan Richardson, and Gwinn Dudley, or any three of them, pay the third part of the s'd Lyons Estate to the said Widow agreeable to Law.[60]

In Lyon's will, which he had written on 27 January 1787, he lent the Widowhood and at her Marrag or Decese to be Equally Divided Amongst my Children Begotten by her and the Rest of my Estate to be Divided amongst my Children."[61]

By the standards of the time Elisha Lyon's will, which was typical of most of the wills written by men during the eighteenth and nineteenth centuries (Henry Guthrey's, mentioned earlier, is another example), was considered to be "fair." According to the terms of most wills, the widow generally retained the homeplace for her use during her lifetime or until she remarried; when either event transpired the farm was then to be sold and the proceeds divided equally among the children. If a man owned several tracts of land besides the homeplace, or many slaves, he might distribute them equitably among his children, or order that his property be sold and the money parceled out equally.

Despite the principle of "fairness," however, the system was inherently unfair to women because they could not control their property. The laws were designed to protect heirs, to keep estates from being broken up and the proceeds squandered, but not to protect women, whom men presumed to have no business sense. A widow encumbered with an unproductive farm could not sell part of it and put the money into another investment, because it had only been "lent" to her for her lifetime. On 5 November 1793, for instance, Elizabeth Dickenson, the widow and administratrix of John Dickenson, Franklin County's first surveyor, petitioned the General Assembly for permission to sell part of the land he left her for the benefit of their children. The legislature refused.[62]

By renouncing her husband's will, Mary Lyon hoped to control her own property. On 6 November 1788 the Franklin County Court ordered John Smith, Peter Holland, John Divers, and Daniel Ward (or any three of them) to select the dower of Mary Lyon.[63] The inventory of Elisha Lyon's estate, which the men appraised on 29 November 1788, showed that he had been prosperous. He owned six slaves (three women, two boys, and a girl), two horses, twelve head of cattle, two sheep, four beds, two tables, two chests, two trunks, a gun, and the usual farm equipment.[64]1 On 2 April 1789 the committee allotted Mary Lyon her dower third: two slaves (a woman and a boy), one horse, four head of cattle, two sheep, a bed, kitchen furniture, a chest, a trunk, and various "Working Tools."[65]

When Mary Lyon remarried a few years later, to James Watson about 29 August 1792,[66] at least she had some property that was her own and not her new husband's.

How did the wills written by women differ, if at all, from those written by men? The first woman's will in Franklin County was written by Mary Ann Estes on 18 November 1789 and recorded on 7 June 1790. She divided her property among one son, two daughters, two granddaughters, and one grandson. The division hardly was equitable, however: her son received her horse, all her cattle, four slaves, and the residue of her estate after the distribution to her daughters and grandchildren. Mrs. Estes left one slave each to one daughter, a grandson, and a granddaughter, and one bed each to her other daughter and granddaughter.[67] The remainder of her estate consisted of a sidesaddle, cooking and eating utensils, a table, and a washtub.[68]

The next woman's will to be recorded was written by Lucy Brown on 5 April 1797 and recorded in July 1797. Her will was just as "fair" as any man's: she gave her clothing to her five daughters and one colt apiece to her two sons. She directed that the money "arising from the Sale of my Estate Shal [be] Equally Divided and put to Interest for [all seven of] my Children until they Come of age to Recieve their Legacee."[69] Unlike Mary Ann Estes, Lucy Brown operated her own farm; her estate consisted of farm tools as well as the usual household furniture.[70] She also owned a "Corner Cubord" and "som old Books."

When Margaret Martin died between 1830 and 1832, she left a will that clearly favored her female children and grandchildren. Martin gave her daughter Sally Doughton $30 and a slave named Grace; after Sally Doughton's death the slave was to go to her daughter, Permelia Doughton. She also gave her daughter Polly Dabney a slave girl named Jane and ordered that the remainder of her property be divided equally among her other children (one male and six females). The inequity of this distribution becomes apparent when the inventory and appraisal of Margaret Martin's estate and its subsequent settlement are considered. The slave woman Grace, age thirty-eight, was appraised at $100, and Jane or Jinney, age eighteen, was valued at $300. The remainder of Martin's estate, which consisted of six head of cattle and assorted cookware, was valued at a mere $35.99. After various debts owed the estate were collected, however, each child was due to receive $31.69 in cash—an amount that did not approach the value of the slaves.[71]

Frances Sutherland wrote her will in 1845; it was probated three years later. Her estate consisted principally of four slaves, a tract of land, livestock (horses, cattle, sheep, and hogs), household and kitchen furniture, farm equipment, crops (corn, wheat, oats, and tobacco), her share in the estate of her deceased son, Joseph Sutherland, and any money in her possession as well as debts owed her. She left one-seventh shares to her grandchildren. She also left shares to one of her daughters-in-law and two of her daughters, but she left nothing to her sons or sons-in-law, who presumably had already inherited from her late husband.[72]

Women also were generous with their property during their lifetimes, especially to other females. In May 1798, for example, Ruth Hairston gave "one negro girl named Janty which is about ten or Eleven years old which negro Girl I purchased of George Hairston and all her Increase" to Jenny Rentfro, wife of Joshua Rentfro, of Patrick County. This gift was made because of her "natural love and affection" for Jenny Rentfro, and for $1.00.[73] In 1803 Ruth Hairston made several gifts to Elizabeth H. Rowland and Patsey H. Rowland because of her natural affection for them, and for $1.00: to Elizabeth, a slave woman Sarah and a boy Hiram, a sorrel horse, a bridle, a saddle, seven head of cattle, and a good bed and furniture; to Patsey, a slave boy Jim, a sorrel mare, a bridle, a saddle, seven head of cattle, and a good feather bed and furniture.[74]

Ruth Hairston was a wealthy woman who was able to indulge her generous nature. Most women did not have the means to follow her example, particularly those who were relatively unprosperous widows. Every slave, every head of livestock was essential to women who wished to preserve their independence. The alternative—a mixed blessing that was often unavoidable—was remarriage, especially for widows with young children or those with little means of support. Other than farming or teaching, women were effectively denied the opportunity to support themselves.

Women were, for the most part, excluded from the business world, particularly in the late eighteenth century. Occasionally a widow would take over her husband's business, such as an ordinary or tavern. Very few women, however, conducted a trade or profession. Most women who moved beyond their traditional roles as wives or mothers into the "world of work" remained nonetheless within a traditional woman's sphere, usually at home.

Elizabeth J. Woods was an exception. She was appointed postmistress of the office at Cooper's on 21 February 1845 and acted in that position until Robert Wright assumed it on 22 September 1846. Woods did not "inherit" the office

Midwife Sallie Philpott (seated) *with Elisa June Pinkard* (left) *and unidentified friend* (right). *Ca. 1900 photo.* (Blue Ridge Institute, Ferrum, Va.)

from a deceased husband who had held it previously, as was often the case. Ann J. Greer, on the other hand, did take over the postmastership at Rocky Mount that her husband Thomas S. Greer held before his death. She assumed the post on 27 October 1848 and kept it until 5 November 1851 when William B. Noble took her place.[75]

Milly Thomas, as an example of a woman in a more typical and traditional role, leased one of her female slaves to John Livesay on 28 September 1784 and entered into a standard business arrangement with him. He agreed to pay before 28 September 1785 £7 for the hire of the slave, and also to provide her with clothes and pay the tax on her, which was to be deducted from the rental fee. In March 1787, after Livesay neglected to live up to his end of the agreement, Milly Thomas sued and won a judgment against him.[76]

Women also entered into rental agreements with men. Benjamin Skinner Duvall swore out an attachment against Susannah Barton on 11 October 1790. She had leased a plantation from him for the rent of twelve barrels of corn payable on 30 November 1790, but he had reason to believe she was going to abscond before the rent was due. Apparently the two settled the dispute amicably, because Duvall dropped the suit.[77]

Women's lives revolved around home and the family—a circumscribed world wherein men allowed them considerable authority as the upholders of moral standards. In this role women were assisted by, and they in turn influenced, religious institutions and schools.

TEN

Churches and Schools

During the colonial period there was only one established, tax-supported, officially recognized church in Virginia: the Church of England. All others, in the eyes of the colonial government, were dissenters and therefore, because of the close connection between church and state, politically suspect. Dissenters were subject to civil penalties for their beliefs, particularly if they attempted to espouse them publicly. Some were jailed or harassed by mobs, or both. The persecutions were more likely to occur in the settled parts of Virginia—Tidewater, for instance—where the Church of England was in firm control, than in the less-settled regions such as the Valley and the upper Piedmont. For this reason most dissenters established their settlements in the western part of the colony, often not far from the migratory route, the Great Wagon Road. Along this road traveled the members of many dissenting sects: Quakers, Baptists, German Baptists, Presbyterians, and Methodists. More than a few of them settled in present-day Franklin County.

Many of the mid-eighteenth-century settlers of the Franklin County area who came from eastern Virginia were members of the Church of England. The church in the West probably was more tolerant than its counterpart in the East, however, because its members were likely outnumbered by the dissenters. They also lived on scattered farms, seldom saw a minister, and in some cases resettled after a few years. Many of the eastern Virginians for the first time not only encountered unfamiliar religious sects, but sects that were dominated by non-English nationalities as well, in particular Scotch-Irish Presbyterians and German Baptists.

As some groups left Franklin County and others remained behind, eventually the religious landscape in the county came to be dominated by a few dissenting sects in the late eighteenth and early to mid-nineteenth centuries. The established church virtually disappeared. Originally, the Church of England was organized in the Franklin County area in 1752 when Antrim Parish and Halifax County were formed. Six new churches, one of them on Pigg River, were built, as well as a chapel at Snow Creek. In 1769, two years after the formation of Camden Parish and Pittsylvania County, the new vestry ordered the construction of

187

another church on Snow Creek near the chapel. A chapel was also built on Story Creek in 1771. The first minister of the new parish seems to have been James Stevenson; the Reverend Lewis Guilliam succeeded him in 1771. Guilliam, an apparent loyalist during the revolutionary war, may have departed for England in 1777, leaving the parish without a minister.[1] The church never quite recovered from the effects of the Revolution—especially the disestablishment in 1786—and by 1840 "there were only eight communicants, and they all females, in the three counties of Pittsylvania, Franklin, and Henry."[2]

The German Baptists—also known variously as Mennonites, Tunkers, Dunkers, Dunkards, and Brethren—on the other hand, thrived, as did the various other dissenting denominations. The two largest non-German (generally English) groups were the Baptist denomination, which grew largely from roots in the North Carolina Piedmont and in Pittsylvania County, and the Methodists. By 1850 the Methodists had fourteen churches in the county valued (with other church property) at $3,500 and capable of accommodating 3,300 worshipers. At the same time the Baptists had ten churches valued at $2,250 with a capacity of 2,550, while there was one Dunkard church valued at $2,000 that could hold 1,500 members. By 1860 the Dunkard church had been replaced by a smaller one (capacity 500), but the value of the sect's property remained at $2,000. The Methodists that year had nine churches that held 4,100 members, and the value of the church property was $7,550. The Baptists had seven churches appraised at $1,850 that could accommodate 2,700 worshipers.[3]

Among the first groups of dissenters to settle in present-day Franklin County in any numbers were the German Baptists, today called the Brethren. Hundreds of them had been passing through the area for years. In 1753 one group of Moravians included a diarist who kept a record of the trek from Pennsylvania to the settlements around present-day Winston-Salem, North Carolina. Although small congregations had been established in the Valley of Virginia, most were temporary. Church historians consider the site of the first permanent settlement of Brethren in Virginia—established in the late 1750s or early 1760s—to be near Holmans Creek in present-day Shenandoah County. The second permanent settlement in Virginia was founded, according to church tradition, about 1765 in what is now Franklin County.[4]

About 1700, these participants in the German Baptist movement attempted to breathe new life into what some believed was a moribund Lutheran church, the state church of Germany. Some reform-minded Lutherans abandoned the established church altogether to form new sects; they were called separatists. The most important separatist in the development of the Brethren was Alexander Mack, Sr. (1679–1735), of Schriesheim. In 1706 he fled to Schwarzenau to escape persecution. There, in August 1708, he and seven of his followers baptized each other in the Eder River by trine immersion—immersing, or "dunking," a candidate for baptism three times in the name of the Trinity. The group became a congregational community known as the New Baptists of Schwarzenau.

Mack and his congregation lived in Schwarzenau until about 1720, when poverty and a decrease in religious toleration prompted them to move to the Netherlands; one group of his adherents, led by Peter Becker, had immigrated to Pennsylvania in 1719. In 1729 Mack and about half the Brethren in the Netherlands joined Becker in Germantown, Pennsylvania. Mack spent the remainder of his life there, preaching and leading his congregation. By the time of his death in 1735, the German Baptists were thriving in several settlements in Pennsylvania.

Soon the German Baptist movement, which included sects other than Mack's, spread south along the Great Wagon Road. By the late 1730s the first, temporary Brethren settlements were established in the Shenandoah Valley. The German Baptists had reached western North Carolina by the early 1750s. About 1765 Jacob Miller established the second permanent Brethren settlement in Virginia in present-day Franklin County.

Miller is an elusive figure, both in the history of the Brethren and in the early history of Franklin County. Apparently he was born either in Germany or in Franklin County, Pennsylvania, about 1735. He may have been baptized as a Brethren in 1762, then lived briefly in Maryland. He came to present-day Franklin County about 1765 and established a congregation on the upper waters of the Blackwater River. Miller traveled widely throughout Southwest Virginia, preaching and organizing new congregations. About 1800 he and part of his Dunkard congregation moved to the Miami Valley in Ohio, working there and in Indiana. He died in 1815.[5]

Miller was closely associated, in his work in Virginia, with an English convert named William Smith. Miller had been licensed in Franklin County on 2 June 1794 to perform marriages as a minister; Smith was likewise licensed, as a minister with the "Baptist Dunkard Church," on 6 June 1803.[6] Long before then, however, the two men had traveled together throughout southwestern Virginia. They preached as a team, with Miller delivering his sermons in German and Smith in English. Smith actually lived in what is now Floyd County. He is alleged to have been an Englishman who came to America as a soldier during the revolutionary war, remained after hostilities ended, and was converted by Miller.[7]

Miller, Smith, and their fellow Brethren ministers promulgated certain beliefs of the Brethren that set them apart. They believed that only adults, not infants, should be baptized. A baptism should not be performed by sprinkling but by trine immersion. The early Brethren were nonconformists; they refused to adapt their unique religious practices and beliefs to the standards set by other, more traditional denominations. The Brethren were convinced that a creed, or doctrinal statement with the force of law, would stifle the further development of the

Barnhardt Family (Dunkers), in plain dress. (Blue Ridge Institute, Ferrum, Va.)

church. They preferred to discuss doctrinal matters at their annual meeting. They also were nonresisters, subscribing wholeheartedly to the ancient Christian stance against violence and war. The early Brethren advocated the simple life, with an emphasis on plainness, humility, neatness, and wholesome living.

The principle of simplicity carried over into their worship gatherings and architecture. For many years there were no Brethren churches; members gathered in each others' houses. As congregations grew larger, however, the need for special places of worship resulted in the construction of plain meetinghouses. The first such meetinghouse in Franklin County was built in 1848. Although the brick church was large, one hundred feet by forty feet, presumably it was relatively plain. The principle of simplicity no doubt applied to Brethren domestic architecture as well, although identifiable examples in Franklin County have not survived. The Germantown Brick Church of 1848 is overwhelmed by later additions.[8]

One principle, promulgated at the 1797 annual meeting held in Franklin County, clearly set the Brethren apart from society, particularly in Virginia. This principle stated that slaveholding was wrong and one could not be a member in good standing if one owned slaves. At subsequent annual meetings Brethren leaders continued to exhort members to free their slaves, indicating that some Brethren found it difficult to live up to this principle. The Brethren were not abolitionists, however; the principle of nonresistance, which was derived from Christ's command to "Resist not evil," prevented them from openly advocating the abolition of slavery. Rather, they opted to set an example for others to follow if they chose. This fine distinction may have been lost on the Brethren's slaveholding neighbors, particularly as American society became increasingly polarized over the slavery issue during the antebellum period. At the very beginning of the Civil War, despite the Franklin County Dunkards' historical opposition to war and slaveholding, local secessionists considered them "all right"[9] as far as their loyalty to the Confederate cause was concerned.

The Baptists are another religious denomination that has been active in Franklin County for about the same length of time as the Brethren—perhaps even longer. The English Baptists were separatists from the Church of England who also embraced the baptism of adult believers. They were considered dangerous and were persecuted both in England and in the colonies because they espoused religious freedom and independent thought. Although Baptists were active in England in the early 1600s, they were little noticed in the colonies until the Great Awakening, the era of spiritual revival and reawakening that swept through the North American colonies, especially New England, between 1720 and 1760. The evangelizing methods of the Baptists made them an anathema to the Church of England authorities, especially in Virginia, where persecution kept their numbers small.

In 1760 there were only four Baptist churches in Virginia, with a total membership of 143.[10] Two of the churches, Ketocton in Loudoun County and Mill Creek in Shenandoah County, had 49 members between them. Another, the oldest and smallest in the colony, was Burleigh in Isle of Wight County, with 20 members. The newest and largest congregation with more than half the Baptists in Virginia—74 members—was established in 1760 at Dan River in Pittsylvania County.

The Dan River church was created largely because of the efforts of North Carolina Baptist Daniel Marshall. Marshall and Dutton Lane, an immigrant to Virginia from Maryland, preached in Pittsylvania County, where they were joined by two brothers, Joseph and William Murphy. The preachers converted Samuel Harris, a wealthy Pittsylvania County planter and lay reader in the Church of England, in 1759. This conversion was a major coup: Harris was a solid citizen, a member of the House of Burgesses, a county justice, and a colonel of the militia who commanded Fort Mayo. Harris became an itinerant minister and was associated with the establishment of at least twenty-five Baptist churches in Virginia between 1767 and 1791. No doubt his work and travels carried him into nearby Franklin County.

Seven Baptist churches were established in Franklin County between 1761 and 1790. The first was the Blackwater church, which was created in 1761 on Miry Branch of Blackwater River (near present-day Fairmont Baptist Church) and abandoned about 1785. Next was the first Snow Creek Chapel church, which was organized about 1771. In 1773 a congregation built the Pigg River church near the head of the river. The Gills Creek church flourished about 1774. Another church was established on Rennet (Runnet) Bag Creek about 1787 but only existed for a couple of years. At about the same time a congregation created the Staunton church. In 1788 a second church was established on Snow Creek; it survived until about 1860.[11]

The Baptists spread their faith rapidly by evangelizing. The principle of free thought that they espoused fitted nicely with the revolutionary principles that gained currency in the 1760s and 1770s. Both ways of thinking also aroused opposition from the Church of England and political conservatives. In some quarters, religious and political liberty went hand in hand; in other quarters—particularly in the Church of England—that notion was cause for concern. Most Baptists, in addition, devoutly believed in the separation of church and state.

The principles of religious freedom and the separation of church and state were not a natural product of the Revolution but were the result of a long campaign led, from within the governmental and societal power structure, by Thomas Jefferson. The degree to which each colony allowed any religious denomination other than the established church varied widely; two of the least tolerant colonies were Massachusetts and Virginia, and the most tolerant was Pennsylvania. Members of the dominant sect in Virginia—the Church of England—frequently practiced violence against dissenters. For their part, members of minority sects sometimes disrupted Anglican church services to proselytize. Religious intolerance was embedded in and protected by both English and colonial law.

Although the idea of religious freedom received support throughout the revolutionary era, many of the old laws remained on the books. Jefferson, in his *Notes on the State of Virginia,* described an act, still in effect in 1781, that was passed by the House of Burgesses in 1705. The statute levied extreme penalties on anyone who denied the existence of God or who said that there was more than one God. Commenting on this and similar acts, Jefferson wrote that

our rulers can have authority over such natural rights only as we have submitted to them. The rights of conscience we never submitted, we could not submit. We are answerable for them to our God. The legitimate powers of government extend to such acts only as are injurious to others. But it does me no injury for my neighbour to say there are twenty gods, or no god. It neither picks my pocket nor breaks my leg.[12]

Not everyone agreed, including Jefferson's fellow revolutionary Patrick Henry, who strongly opposed the disestablishment of the Church of England. James Madison outmaneuvered Henry, however, and guided Jefferson's "Act for establishing Religious Freedom" through the General Assembly. That act, which formed the essence of the First Amendment to the Constitution of the United States in 1789, declared that

no man shall be compelled to frequent or support any religious worship, place or ministry whatsoever, nor shall be enforced, restrained, molested, or burthened in his body or goods, nor shall otherwise suffer on account of his religious opinions or belief; but that all men shall be free to profess, and by argument to maintain, their opinions in matters of religion, and that the same shall in no wise diminish, enlarge, or affect their civil capacities.[13]

Jefferson's act finally was approved by Virginia's legislature in January 1786, the same month that Franklin County was organized. It was a coincidence of course, but a pleasant one nonetheless, that religious freedom was proclaimed simultaneously with the creation of Franklin County, which had long been the scene of so much religious diversity.

On 27 October 1785, just a few months before the passage of Jefferson's act, the General Assembly received a petition from the inhabitants of Henry County, which at that time included part of present-day Franklin County. The petition opposed a proposed act of the legislature that had been published for comment by the public; the act would have allowed teachers of the Christian religion to be paid out of a special tax levied by the state. Most of those who signed the petition, fittingly enough, were Baptists—members of a sect that had suffered more persecution than any other in Virginia during the years just prior to the revolutionary war. Taking a strong stand for the separation of church and state, the petitioners couched their arguments in language that Jefferson would have approved of:

Certain it is that the Blessed Author of Our Reledgion supported And maintain'd his gospel in the World for several Hundred years not Only without the aid of Civill power but against all the powers of the Earth. . . . That Reledgeous Establishment and Government is linkd together and that the latter cannot Subsist without the Former is Something new. Witness The State of Pensilvenai wherein no such Establishment Hath taken place their goverment Stands firm & which of the neighbouring states has better members of Bright Morals and more Upright Caracters. That it is against Our bill of rights, which says all Men by nature are born Equally free so no person In this commonwealth Shall Enjoy Exclusive prevelledges Or Emmoluments Except it be for Services rendered the state. . . . Finaly, if such tax is against the spirit of the Gospel, If Christ has for Several hundred years not only Without the aid of civil power but Against all the powers of the world

Supported it, if Establishment has never Been a means of prospering the gospel, if no more Faithfull men would be Cald into the ministry, If it would not Revive decayed Relidgeon and stop The groth of Deism or serve the purposes of government, And if Against the Bill of Rights which your pititoners firmly believe, they trust the wisdom And Uprightness of your Honourable house Will leave them Entirely free in matters of Reledgeon And the Manner of Supporting its Ministers.[14]

Although this petition could not have been the sole reason for the final approval of Jefferson's act, it no doubt contributed to the sense of public support for the act's passage. Among its signers were several residents of Franklin County: Benjamin Cook, William Cannaday, Joel Estes, Edgecomb Guilliams, Peter Hairston, Robert Hairston, William Mavity, Thomas Prunty, Isaac Rentfro, Jesse Rentfro, Stanhope Richeson, and Micajah Stone.

Besides the Baptists and the Brethren, a third Franklin County denomination benefited from religious freedom: the Methodists. Methodism began in the 1720s and 1730s as a reform movement within the Church of England led by John Wesley, an Anglican cleric. Seeking to regenerate interest in the church, Wesley preached outdoors, fostered discussion groups, and traveled widely.

On his voyage to Georgia in 1735, Wesley found that some of his shipmates were Moravians, a pre-Reformation Protestant denomination that originated in Bohemia in the 1450s. Since the 1720s the Moravians had been dominated by Count Nicholas Ludwig Zinzendorf, who visited the American colonies in 1741. Wesley was so taken with the obvious piety of the Moravians that he began at once to learn German so that he could converse with them. The simplicity of their faith, which stood in such contrast to Wesley's own intellectualism, moved him deeply and altered his message significantly. He spoke and corresponded with Moravians for years, meeting with Zinzendorf at his estate and in London. So close were Wesley's feelings for the Moravians that he hoped they could unite in a common denomination, but it did not happen.[15]

The Methodists were reformers within the Church of England, not separatists. The American Revolution, however, effectively separated the colonial Methodists from their English counterparts—including Wesley himself, who was a staunch Royalist. As the war progressed the Methodists united with the Baptists in seeking the separation of church and state. After the treaty of peace was signed with Great Britain in 1783, the American Methodists formed the Methodist Episcopal church. The new church thrived as its ministers rode their circuits, held outdoor services and revivals that evolved into protracted camp meetings, and spread their message using sermons and hymns.

The missionary zeal of the ministers yielded rapid results. By 1791, for instance, at least five Methodist ministers had been licensed to perform marriages in Franklin County: William Heath, Rice Haggard, Benjamin Barnes, Daniel Southall, and Henry Merrett.[16] The number of Methodists in the county by the end of the century probably approximated that of the Baptists.

One of the Methodist circuit riders who preached in Franklin County was the eccentric divine, Lorenzo Dow. Dow reported in his journal that he passed through the county on 28–29 March 1804, after he first preached at a protracted camp meeting near New London. There "Colonel [James] Callaway and a number of respectable gentlemen used their endeavors to protect our peaceable privileges"; feeling ill afterward, Dow rode to Franklin County

> in great misery eleven miles and spoke to hundreds, an hour by sun in the morning. Thence to Franklin court house at twelve o'clock, and some were offended, but good I trust was done. In the evening I spoke twelve miles off; but was grieved with the family; could not eat with them, but next morning quitted them betimes, and went to Henry court house: spoke to about fifteen hundred people; and stayed with general [Joseph] Martin at night; where we had a good time.[17]

Franklin County experienced little of the violent friction among religious denominations such as Dow hinted at when he mentioned that Callaway and others had protected his camp meeting. One intriguing exception occurred on 4 August 1802. The county court summoned William Perdue and Benjamin Ward "to appear here on the first day of November Court next, to shew cause why an Information should not be filed against them on the Presentment of the Grand Jury, for disturbing religious Worship."[18] The court dismissed its order on 2 November 1802.[19] It was not stated whose religious worship was disturbed, or if the court dismissed the order for lack of evidence.

No act proclaiming freedom of religion could, by itself, sweep away old attitudes and prejudices. The Henry County petitioners of 1785, for example, appeared less tolerant of what they termed the "groth of Deism"—a system of eighteenth-century religious thought that denied the interference of the Creator with the natural laws of the universe, and to which Jefferson subscribed. In March 1786, only two months after the passage of Jefferson's act for religious freedom, John Early (a member of the House of Delegates and a future Franklin County militia officer, court justice, and sheriff) entered the following disclaimer in the county records: "I have been by Some persons Accused with DEASAM But I Believe the Scriptures of the Old and New Testament to be True and I put my faith and Confidence therein."[20] Presumably Early believed his declaration would assist him in his political career.

Just as the public attitude toward toleration and religious freedom changed over time, so too did the beliefs of the members of the different denominations toward their own doctrines. The Brethren altered their concept of nonresistance, the Baptists and Brethren were challenged by organizational changes, and all the county's denominations were shaken by the same slavery question that divided the nation.

Brethren church members submitted several petitions to the General Assembly that documented their changing attitudes toward nonresistance. They submitted their earliest petition on the subject of military service in 1799, when the United States was in the midst of an undeclared naval war with France, its ally during the revolutionary war. Napoléon I had just come to power in France and fears of a general war were widespread. The German Baptists of Franklin County reflected that concern:

> The Petition of the people resident in Franklin County Calld. Tunkers pray that for their Consciencious scruples they may be Exempt from performing

Military duty but as they do not wish to shrink from Supporting Government they are willing that in addition to their proportions of the Revenue tax any thus Scrupelous and having a Certificate of Connection with sd. Church may be taxed 2 Dollars each per year as an equivlent for such Military Service Required of them but in case of invasion or insurrection they are then Willing to bear a part as other militia.[21]

The signers included John Becklehimer, John Becklehimer, Jr., John Boon, Joseph Flora, Henry Ikenberry, Peter Ikenberry, Jacob Kingery, Jacob Kinsey, Jacob Miller, Isaac Nave (Nafe), Jacob Nave, Jacob Nave, Jr., Michael Peters, and Stephen Peters. Interestingly enough, the Brethren's objection to military service did not extend to slave insurrections or actual invasions by foreign powers. The General Assembly rejected the petition.

In 1813, during the War of 1812 and after the United States had been invaded by British forces in the Great Lakes, the Brethren in Franklin and Montgomery counties united in a petition to the General Assembly. Their attitude having changed since 1799, they objected to a newly passed act concerning the militia that imposed heavy taxes and penalties on those who did not serve. The petitioners declared that

> we cannt feel a freedom to take up armes for the purpose of taking the Lives of any of the human race, even of those who may seem disposd. to distroy us. Feeling ourselves bound by that Sacred authority by which we are commanded not to resist evil . . . We beg Leave however to sogest that we do not Expect, nor even wish to be exempt from bearing an equil portion of the burthens of the times, wheather as it relates to the Suport of Civil Government or the releif of the distressed of every discription of our fellow Citizens. But [we are] advisd. that the Law providing for the Organising and Calling forth the Militia if left to opperate in its present form will Subject us to such penalties as must enevetably terminate in a Short time in the utter reduction of our little property and Consequently leave our families without the means of subsistence.[22]

The petitioners asked for relief from the provisions of the militia act, but the General Assembly rejected their request.

The United States was not at war in 1826 when the next petition from the Brethren arrived at the State Capitol. Once again the petitioners' complaint was centered on the most recent version of the militia act. The petition was signed by Isaac Nafe (Nave) and John Barnan, "Ministers in the Tunker church by order of the whole church":

> belonging to the profession of Christians usually denominated Tunkers and Menonists according to our understanding of the Holy Scriptures we cannot feel ourselves justifiable in bearing arms or engaging in war. . . . Your Memorialists do not presume to ask of the General Assembly any particular privileges or exemptions, and we hope that we may not be considered obtrusive in earnestly praying, that we may not be burthened with any penalties on account of our concientious non-conformity of the provisions of the Militia Laws now demanded by the public welfare.[23]

The part of the militia act that the Brethren found oppressive not only levied heavy penalties on those who would not march with the militia when ordered, but also enrolled them in the ranks of the next militia division to be called out for active duty. They believed that this provision locked them into a vicious circle.

The Brethren were not alone. Their petition was supported by another, prepared by non-Germans who were for the most part the sons of the county's founders: Moses Greer, Jr., Peter Saunders, Jr., Samuel Saunders, Samuel Hale, Thomas Bailey Greer, Asa Holland, John Clay, Robert Innes, Jubal Early, William Callaway, Henry Carper, Edmund Tate, and Nathaniel H. Claiborne. After restating the main points of the Brethren's memorial, these petitioners concluded with the statement that they "do hereby express our conviction that such an alteration would be just and salutery in its consequence." The General Assembly took no action on either petition, and the Brethren had little relief from the militia laws of Virginia until the Civil War began.

Despite the failure of the petitions, however, they are significant for revealing the changes in the views of nonresistance held by Franklin County Brethren. Whereas in 1799 they appeared willing to take up arms in case of invasion or insurrection, by the time they submitted the petitions of 1813 and 1826 the Brethren's convictions had hardened. It is also significant that non-Germans, presumably Methodists and Baptists, supported the Brethren's right to their opinion even though they did not share it themselves.

The Franklin County Brethren repaid the favor to the Baptists in the 1840s, although by then the two groups were on common ground in their opinions. When the Baptist congregations were organized in the eighteenth century, each one regarded itself as independent of all the others. Each was responsible for the support of its own minister; there was no all-encompassing Baptist organization to oversee the churches or ensure doctrinal homogeneity. Instead the churches gradually introduced something akin to the annual meeting of the Brethren, at which questions of doctrine would be debated and, it was hoped, resolved. Instead of just one annual meeting for the whole state, however, the churches in the various regions of the state formed themselves into associations—Franklin County was in the Strawberry Association. The groups then reorganized themselves as the number of congregations increased, or as controversies and disagreements caused them to separate.

Although an individual congregation was capable of certain actions, some decisions required a larger structure to execute them and assure uniformity. To fund missionaries, for instance, or to finance the publication of religious tracts, demanded some form of an institutionalized church organization—exactly what the Baptists and Brethren had separated from in the first place.

The mission movement of the early nineteenth century caused a serious schism among Baptists. The movement needed ministers who could devote most of their time to traveling and preaching, rather than remain in one location, and it required an organization to raise the money to support them. To some Baptists —and many in Franklin County—those who encouraged the movement were guilty of "hierling, money-getting views."[24] In the 1820s the controversy caused most of the antimission churches in Franklin and Henry counties to leave the Strawberry Association and form the Pigg River Association. A promission minister explained that in his opinion many of his antimission counterparts there were good men, of narrow views and scanty information. They were apprehensive that missionary efforts would take the work of human salvation out of God's hands and transfer all its glory to men, not considering that the same objection, and with equal force, or rather inconclusiveness, might be urged against all means employed for the salvation of sinners. Most of the churches in Franklin and Henry counties withdrew from the Strawberry Association, and organized the Pig River Association, a body most earnestly and successfully devoted to doing nothing.[25]

In December 1844 the Pigg River Association Baptists and the Franklin County Brethren submitted nearly identical petitions to the General Assembly within a few days of each other. The petitions were in the handwriting of the same person: Theodrick F. Webb, a Baptist minister. The petitioners objected to the efforts of Eli Ball, the editor of the Baptist newspaper the *Christian Advocate*, and other missionary Baptist ministers to obtain from the General Assembly an act enabling religious educational institutions to hold property given or bequeathed to them.

Once again Baptists (they styled themselves "Old School") and Brethren couched their arguments in terms of the separation of church and state. The Baptists wrote that they opposed any additional laws that by supporting religious organizations would

strengthen a religious aristocracy, or have a tendency to unite church and state, or to encourage even an idea that false benevolence, or religion, is to receive the fostering care of any legislation whatever, further than [what] is now abundantly extended. . . . We are apprehensive that our number may be represented as small and even contemptible, yet we claim to be the same patriot Baptists that contributed so conspicuously to secure religious toleration in Va. with Thos. Jefferson, Patrick Henry [*sic*], and James Madison at their head. . . . We have felt ourselves called upon in presenting this counter petition to set fourth our views and wishes briefly, that the publick may be disabused, and that our silence may not be construed into acquiescence.[26]

The Brethren wanted to make it clear that they did not

wish to be understood as being opposed to human learning, as this seems to be considered by many as the only alternative. No. We hope you in your wisdom will promote education by rendering it any constitutional aid in your power; believing that our temporal hapiness and prosperity in a good degree depends on it, and that it tends to strengthen our political fabric, which we ardently desire to be rendered permanent.[27]

The Brethren petition was signed by Isaac Nafe, Sr., John Barnan, Sr., Abraham Barnhart, Isaac Nafe, Jr., George Nafe, Abraham Nafe, Joel Peters, Jacob Peters, Samuel Frantz, Joel Fisher, Jacob Nafe, and John Flora. The Baptist petition was signed by four ministers representing eight churches with three hundred members: Theodrick F. Webb, George W. Kelly, Moses Greer, Jr., and Arnold Walker.

The controversy over missions became so well known that it aroused comment from members of other denominations. Judge Fleming Saunders, for example,

although a devout Episcopalian, had strong antimission feelings that he shared
with his wife, who apparently disagreed with him. In 1832 the judge wrote of an
incident involving a Baptist preacher named Tinsley, who

> went to Norfolk sometime ago, whether for pleasure or the cause of religion
> I cannot tell, but on his return he stayed a few days in Powhatan at the house
> of a respectable Widow, who was said to be much pleased with him (using a
> mild word). The Brethren and friends of religion had a collection made for
> him and no doubt he was fully reimbursed his expenses and Cost in his
> pocket. Can this system be right and propper which goes to reward each
> pretender in the country at the expense of the home staying and industrious
> part of the community.[28]

Of the early Franklin County ministers of any denomination, the only one
described at any length is Moses Greer, Jr. (1768–1848), one of the antimission
Baptist signers of the 1844 petition. Jeremiah Bell Jeter, a missionary Baptist
minister who was a native of Bedford County, mentioned Greer in his memoirs:

> Among my early acquaintances in the ministry was Elder Moses Greer, of
> Franklin county, Va. He was of a highly respectable family [a son of justice
> Moses Greer, Sr.], and fully sustained its respectability. He was rather above
> the ordinary stature, quite lean, and very plain in his dress, as were all the
> preachers of his region. His manners were simple and unaffected. He was
> past the meridian of life when [Daniel] Witt and myself were entering on our
> ministry [about 1822]. He was of very tender feelings, rarely failing to
> mingle a profusion of tears with his prayers and exhortations. He was a clear,
> sound preacher, and as free from ambition as could well be desired. In a
> small circuit in his county he passed his life in unostentatious efforts to do
> good. In his latter years he was led off from the main body of the Baptist
> denomination by the anti-mission faction. Let him not be severely censured
> for this. His means of information were very limited, and the missionary
> work, as it was presented to him by the leaders of the faction, seemed to be a
> very evil thing. I record, with gratitude and pleasure, this testimonial of his
> hospitality and kindness to me, when, as a stripling and a stranger, I visited
> his neighborhood.[29]

Jeter described Greer's preaching techniques, which were typical of some of
the backcountry preachers of his day: intoning and spiritualizing. Of Greer's
intoning, or delivering his sermons in a singsong monotone, Jeter wrote,

> he carried this art to the highest perfection. He sung his hymns, prayers,
> sermons, and exhortations all in the same tune, and a most mournful tune it
> was. No one not greatly given to levity could hear it without solemnity. All
> in sympathy with the intoner had their hearts stirred within them. If a
> stranger, unacquainted with his language, had heard his intonations he
> would have concluded that the old man was in fearful distress.[30]

A preacher who spiritualized saw religious symbolism in every word of Scripture
and expounded on its meaning at considerable length. Jeter quoted Greer's
attitude on the subject:

"I believe," he said—I remember his words well—"that every tex' (a common pronunciation in that day) in the Bible; and not only every tex', but every word; and not only every word, but every letter; and not only every letter, but every crook and dot of every letter, has a spiritual meaning." Beyond that theory it is not possible for human ingenuity to go. The excellent brother did not deem himself skilled in discerning the spiritual import of the Scriptures. He was careful not to venture in the ocean of divine truth much beyond his depth. When he allegorized the Scriptures, he was cautious to find in them only such truths as were generally received by evangelical Christians. It was wonderful how the spiritualizers did mix up in their sermons things true and fanciful, things spiritual and material, and they were generally accounted ingenious and wise in proportion as they gave the widest range to their imaginations and drew their sermons from the most unpromising sources.[31]

Greer's spiritualism stood in stark contrast to the intellectual approach to the Scriptures. Judge Fleming Saunders, for example, praised his wife for reading the Bible every day, but warned her that in order to understand it "correctly,"

you ought always to keep in view the time when, the place where, the reason why and the people to whom the words were said, and it will not do to form opinions from detached text, but the whole scriptures must be taken together.

I feel perfectly satisfied that if you read the word of God understandingly, and Compare it with the doctrines generally preached from the pulpit, you will readily discover a considerable discrepancy between the two. The Church has their hobbies, and no doubt they push them too far and it will finally tend to the injury of the cause of God. . . . I feel inclined to write more upon this subject but knowing your impressions generally about my religious notions, I will stop for the present.[32]

The conservative views espoused by Greer and his fellow preachers in the Pigg River Association did not win the day in 1844, but that did not deter them from petitioning again on the same subject four years later. Greer led the signers for the association; the others were Stephen Wood and Theodrick F. Webb. This time they were joined not by another denomination but by another antimission association of Baptist churches, the New River Association, which also submitted a petition to the General Assembly on 15 January 1848. The petitioners for New River were ministers Jesse Jones, Joshua Adams, Nathaniel Thompson, Jesse Corn, James Ingrum, and James Joys.

Once again the petitioners opposed a law to give religious denominations what they termed "corporate priviledges," fearing that it might re-create the hierarchies they had separated from years earlier. The Franklin County ministers asserted

That the proposed law would be fraught with danger to our Civil and religious liberties. That it would open the door to corruption and priestcraft. That it seeks to deprive orphans of their just rights. To Conect Church and state, and to build up religious aristocracies. First then as baptists we claim no connection with nor fellowship for the faith or

practice of the general association of Missionary baptists, nor are we sorry to
have an opportunity of disavowing their designs, and of disowning them, by
which means we desire to rid the name of baptist from the s[t]igma of
seeking legislative patronage.[33]

The ministers of the New River Association admitted

that it is right for the preachers to derive some assistance for there
ministerial labours yet it should be given to the persons them selves as there
needcessity may require and that By the hand of the doner himself and not to
be given in trust into the hands of those we know not to be applied as they
may think proper under the Specious name of benevolence or sending the
Gospel to the heathen.[34]

Once more the petitions languished in legislative committees. The antimission
Baptists, however numerous they may have been in Franklin County and the
western parts of Virginia, drifted quickly out of the mainstream of Virginia
Baptists in the nineteenth century.

As the missionary movement divided the Baptists, the issue of slavery divided
Baptists and Methodists just as it split American society during the first half of the
nineteenth century. The Brethren's beliefs diverged over the resolution against
slaveholding that was adopted at the annual meeting held in Franklin County in
1797. Other denominations, including the Baptists, debated the issue of slavery
in the late eighteenth and early nineteenth centuries and usually concluded that
the institution was evil and demeaned both slave and master. Often some form of
gradual emancipation was urged upon church members.

Over time, however, the aggressiveness of northern abolitionists, the defen-
siveness of southern slave owners, and incidents such as Nat Turner's Rebellion—the slaveholder's worst nightmare come to life—together with the retaliation that followed the rebellion's suppression, combined to harden attitudes in
the two sections of the country. As northerners and southerners drifted apart, so
too did many of the churches.

The Methodists divided first. At the annual meeting of the General Conference
held in New York during May and June 1844 the subject of slavery was debated at
length. When the views of northern and southern members became irreconcil-
able, the conference adopted a plan of separation that created the Methodist
Episcopal Church, South. The first meeting of the Southern Conference was held
in Louisville, Kentucky, during May 1845.[35]

For the Baptists the split occurred in May 1845, when the southern Baptists
held a convention in Augusta, Georgia. The preceding February, the board of the
Home Mission Society had met in Boston, and announced that it disapproved of
appointing slaveholders as missionaries. Reacting both to this specific incident
and to the abolitionist movement in general, the delegates in Augusta organized
the Southern Baptist Convention. The members voted to separate from the
Triennial Convention—the national organization—and establish their own policies.[36]

Despite the disunity within the Methodist and Baptist denominations, or
perhaps because of it, each group established several churches in Franklin
County during the antebellum period. All of the congregations were members of

the southern wings of their churches. Any divisions that occurred within the Baptist congregations largely were over the mission movement. Town Creek Baptist Church, for example, split after the Pigg River Association passed a resolution in 1832 declaring its nonfellowship with the missionary Baptists. There were enough supporters of the mission movement within the church to organize the Providence Missionary Baptist Church in 1833. Other churches were established as congregations outgrew their facilities. Fairmont Baptist Church and Story Creek Baptist Church were organized in 1855. Among the Methodist churches established during the antebellum period were those at Rocky Mount (1845), Gogginsville (1855), and Pleasant Hill (1857).[37]

Fairmont Baptist Church. 1988 photo. (Virginia Department of Historic Resources.)

Two other denominations, the Presbyterians and the Disciples of Christ, established toeholds in the county before the Civil War. The Presbyterians, who were relatively few in number, established Chestnut Chapel near present-day Sydnorsville in the early 1800s. Before then, Presbyterian ministers had visited the county, as in June 1790 when William Hill, Cary Allen, and Matthew Lyle preached several sermons as they rode east to west across Franklin County. They started at Captain Robert Woods's residence near Chestnut Mountain, then John Martin's nearby "at Mr. John Dickenson's, on Pig River—at Iron Creek—at Mr. Turner's, on Fawn Creek—at the meeting house near Capt. Hairston's, [and] the funeral sermon of old Captain Hairston." After many years and repeated visits by itinerant ministers, the Presbyterians in the county became numerous enough to form a congregation. In 1850, under the leadership of the Reverend Robert Gray, they organized a church in the same area as the old Chestnut Chapel.[38]

The Disciples of Christ organized in the county just before the Civil War, when in 1859 a congregation established the Snow Creek Christian Church under the leadership of G. W. Abell. The Disciples of Christ had begun in 1832 when the followers of Alexander Campbell, a Baptist minister who sought the unity of all Christians based on the restoration of primitive Christianity, joined with the New Light Christian Church of Barton W. Stone.[39]

During the antebellum period church buildings often served several denominations that took turns using the facility—hence the term "Union church." (Even the courthouse was used for services from time to time.) In Rocky Mount, county court clerk Robert A. Scott sponsored the construction of a frame Methodist church in 1845. Scott served as church steward, Sunday school superintendent, and occasional preacher.[40] A Pennsylvanian newly arrived in the town in 1851 noted that "there is four denominations hear that all preach in the same church the Presbateariams the Baptist sometimes, the Piscapalions and the Methadist South."[41]

Both the Methodists and many of the Baptists were active in the Sunday school movement of the early nineteenth century. John Wesley and his friends had been members of Bible study groups in England during the early eighteenth century. By the 1820s the Sunday school movement had attracted the attention of Baptist leaders, particularly those who supported missions. Sunday schools, which were centered on the study and discussion of the Bible, probably promoted literacy among church members who otherwise would have had no education at all.

Before the adoption of the Virginia Constitution of 1869 there was no system of free public primary and secondary education in the state. Schooling was considered a private and local matter, and the state played no part in setting the curriculum. In 1810 the General Assembly established the Literary Fund to help finance the construction of local schools through direct loans to localities, but there was no law requiring students to attend. Attendance depended on the enthusiasm of both parents and children, the weather, and the seasonal require- ments of the crops. The business of making a living for the entire family took precedence over formal education.

Most citizens, however, admitted to the importance of education. They agreed that almost all white males needed to be able to read, write, and cipher to a certain minimum degree of competence. Females, they thought, had less need for such abilities, and slaves and free blacks were better off without them. Wealthy white parents hired tutors for their children, while those of lesser means banded together to establish community schools and the poor generally had no instruc- tion whatever.

As early as January 1755 a survey mentioned a "School House on Fox Run a Branch of Black Water River."[42] At least one private school was in operation in Franklin County by 1787, when Robert Jones taught either Zachary Warren or Warren's children. Warren owed Jones £3 for the course of instruction: he paid off his debt in cash, with half a pound of flax, by mending a pair of shoes, and by cutting leather for shoes. He still owed more than £2 in 1790, when Jones sued him for the balance.[43]

Samuel King was another early Franklin County schoolteacher. In 1790 he charged David Beheler £3 for "Teaching 3 Children 10 Months Each."[44] Like Robert Jones, King was not paid and took Beheler to court. Apparently they quickly reached an agreement because the case was dismissed.

By 1794 schooling in Franklin County had become somewhat more sophisti- cated. A teacher with the unlikely name of Amariah Phares offered his services "at the rate of Twenty five Shillings pr Scholar in Cash, and for board one Bushel of Corn and Eight pounds of Bacon pr Scholar for the yeare."[45] Jones and King may have been part-time or amateur teachers, but Phares had the air of a professional.

Another teacher named Daniel French held classes at about the same time as Phares. In 1795 French purchased a tract of 150 acres on Indian Run from John McMillian, but McMillian left the county without executing a deed to convey the land to him. In September 1799 French sought relief from the county court and submitted a variety of receipts to prove that he had paid for the land. Among his papers was a receipt from McMillian for money received "Decr. 17 day 1795 of Daniel French Schoolmaster."[46]

Schools are mentioned occasionally as landmarks in early Franklin County records. The court minutes for 6 December 1802, for example, noted that

> The persons appd. to view the nearest & best Way for a public Road from where the former Road turned out above Brown's Store, to Peter Booth's new School House made Report, whereupon it is ordered that the Road be established agreeable to the said Report & that Daniel Brown be appd. overseer to open the same.[47]

Frequently private or local schoolhouses were constructed on some part of a farmer's property that had fallen into disuse, such as an old, worn-out field. This practice gave rise to the term "old-field schools."

The family of Judge Fleming Saunders sponsored a private school at Bleak Hill for their daughters and those of their relatives by 1825. Saunders's wife, Alice W. Saunders, wrote that her sister Betsy

> promised to send Mary over to School the first of December to go one Session to Charlotte Grimes. She commences school about that time. She is staying with me at this time, and pays very strict attention to the Girls. Sister Woods left Sarah with me and they are kept pretty closely engaged by Miss Charlotte. We calculate on having a larger school of little Girls then we had last session. Mr. S. thinks it best not to take any Boys.[48]

Four years later, in 1829, Alice Saunders wrote that she had heard that

> the inhabitants at Rocky Mount have engaged a Mr. Chapel and his Lady to teach School there, the next session commencing the first of May. I have a great deal of work to do, finding Mr. Woods's Children for school. I shall make no arrangements for Sarah until Mr. Saunders returns. I am not particularly anxious to place her in a little Village like that to acquire her education.[49]

Bleak Hill schoolhouse. 1988 photo. (Virginia Department of Historic Resources.)

Apparently the village school did not succeed. In June 1829, just a month after the session began, Alice Saunders wrote that

> Miss Charlotte has returned to the County and is employed by the Major [Samuel Saunders], Brother Peter [Saunders] and Mr. Woods to teach school at the C. House as soon [as] they get a house built for her. Mrs. Chapel is getting very much out of repute.[50]

In 1829 the General Assembly passed an act creating a system of free district schools for the education of poor children. Money for the schools came in part from private subscription (three-fifths) and partly from county quotas from the Literary Fund (two-fifths). The county school commissioners divided the county into districts and applied the funds to constructing the schools. Subsequently, the school and one acre of the land it stood on were conveyed to the president and board of directors of the Literary Fund. Franklin County became one of three counties in the state to adopt the system (Monroe and Washington were the others).[51]

The county built at least two district schools during the antebellum period. On 13 May 1830 Samuel H. Woods sold an acre of land, with an existing schoolhouse, to the president and directors of the Literary Fund for one dollar. The land was located on the south fork of Chestnut Creek. Three years later, in September 1833, David and Sally Fralin followed Woods's example with an acre, which also contained a schoolhouse, on Pigg River near Fralin's Ford. In both cases the property was to be used "for the purpose of a district school or such other school as shall be hereafter authorised or established by law."[52]

Although many early-nineteenth-century schoolteachers were men, teaching increasingly became a woman's profession during the antebellum period. One woman, Sarah S. Gray, operated a school in Franklin County in 1840 and 1841 that was contracted for by several families in the community. She wrote in a petition to the General Assembly in 1843 that she

> resorted to this employment with the view of supporting herself being left an orphan without any estate. She conducted the school in a manner entirely satisfactory to her Employers devoting her time to the advancement of the children committed to her care. In the neighbourhood of her school were many children of poor parents entirely unable to send them to school. [She] was induced on the advice of her patrons to receive them into her school as poor children not doubting but that she would be paid out of the [Literary] fund wisely appropriated by the Legislature for their Education.[53]

Unfortunately Sarah Gray ran afoul of the procedures and bureaucracy that administered the Literary Fund. She was unaware that she was supposed to have had the poor children "entered as scholars by a school commissioner" (Dr. Richard M. Taliaferro) before she could apply for reimbursement. Because she failed to do this—although she could account for the number of days each child attended her school—the county refused to pay her. Both Taliaferro and Peter D. Holland, one of the county court justices, signed Sarah Gray's invoice. The General Assembly, however, passed no act in her behalf.

Sarah Gray included with her petition her report for the schooling received by each poor child. The school session for 1840 ran for five months and ended on 12 December. The children who attended that session were Elizabeth Booth (aged ten), Juliana Jackson (ten), Louisa Jackson (twelve), Maria Jackson (eight), and John Hundley (nine). Their attendance during the session varied from thirty-two to seventy-five days. Gray taught them "Elementary Spelling" and reading, using an "elementary" book and the "New York Reader No. 1."

Gray's school session for 1841 lasted four months and ended on 23 December. Louisa Jackson did not return for this session, but the other children came back; in addition, Henry Bailey sent three of his daughters, Mary, Louisa, and Susan (aged eleven, nine, and seven). The number of days in attendance ranged from twenty-nine for the Jacksons to eighty-five for the Bailey girls. The same texts were used, but the course of instruction included "Orthography," or penmanship and spelling.

Although there were several elementary schools in Franklin County before the Civil War, there were no academies or colleges. The closest academy, which combined elements of a high school and a college, was New London Academy in Bedford County. The institution had an excellent reputation and attracted students from all parts of Virginia. Judge Fleming Saunders sent his sons Edward and Peter to the school for part of the second session of 1835 and the first session of 1836 (each session was six months long). The fees for board and tuition, as well as for three books, amounted to $190.25. Saunders paid his bill in cash, by donating a book to the school library, and by giving the kitchen four bushels of meal, six hams, and twenty-five pounds of venison.[54]

He also subjected his sons to the stern discipline of the schoolteachers. In March 1836 Saunders wrote fourteen-year-old Edward that he had received a letter from him,

> and I was truly sorry to learn that you and some of your school fellows had fallen out, and that your teacher had found it necessary to Slap your Jaws. . . . It was very unpleasant to hear you had complained of your teacher and had used harsh words towards him, words that ought not to be used by one boy towards another, by one gentleman to another nor upon no account by a pupil to his instructor. Mr. Dabney is the son of a Gentleman and Lady of the first respectability, and esteemed by all who know him, a just man and a man of honor.[55]

In 1826 a few prominent "farmers & planters" of Franklin County petitioned the General Assembly for permission to raise money for an academy by means of a lottery. They complained that the falling price of tobacco, their cash crop, furnished "but few of them with the means of educating their children at Colleges, and other seminaries of learning at a distance," thereby frustrating their desire to give their children a liberal education, "so that when they take their stand among the future men of their country, they may be useful members of society." The petitioners asked that half a dozen or more "discreet persons" in the county be authorized to hold a lottery to raise the $15,000 necessary to establish the academy. These trustees should also be "authorized to prescribe the rules to be observed, the Languages, arts, & sciences to be taught thereat, and all such acts as may be necessary to advance the prosperity of the institution."[56] Apparently, however, the General Assembly passed no enabling legislation.

By 1850, according to social statistics compiled by the Census Bureau, there were sixteen schools in the county, each with one teacher, and a total of 700 pupils. Only $950 were allocated from public funds for education. By 1860 there were twenty schools and twenty teachers, but only 370 pupils; public funding, on the other hand, had risen to $2,500. Isaac Cannaday, who reported the 1860 statistics for the United States census, wrote that "There is no established institution of learning in my district. Common schools are not to be found at any one place of longer duration than a few months."[57]

The 1850 census of inhabitants lists seventeen schoolteachers, three women and fourteen men (perhaps one of the teachers was not active when the social statistics were compiled). Seven of their schools were not in session: Charlotte Grimes, aged sixty; James Milano, forty-eight, who was born in Delaware; Orlando Simpson, fifty-two; Thomas Bird, thirty-four; Lewis Hale, forty-eight; Alexander T. Ferguson, twenty-five; and John Hogan, fifty-nine. The figures for the ten schools that were in session when the census taker appeared suggest that mid-nineteenth-century teachers did not have a particularly easy job. The average class size was about twenty-six pupils. The ages of the students, however, ranged from six to twenty-seven. Schoolteacher Edgar G. Jett, aged forty-three, had the smallest class (and probably the smallest income): seven students aged eight to twelve, including four girls and three boys. Green Pinkard, only twenty-five years old himself, had thirty-five students (fourteen girls and twenty-one boys) between ages six and twenty-five. Sarah A. Jones, twenty, taught twenty-one students between the ages of seven and seventeen (twelve girls and nine boys). Henry B. Johnson was fifty-six years old and taught thirty-four students (eighteen girls and sixteen boys) aged eight to twenty. Edward Preston was the oldest male teacher at sixty; twenty-two students, twelve girls and ten boys aged seven to nineteen, attended his school. Zachary Dewitt, aged forty, had twenty-eight students aged eight to twenty-five, nine girls and nineteen boys. Joseph P. Godfry, aged forty-five, taught nineteen students aged eleven to twenty-one, eight girls and eleven boys. Buford Wills, who was forty-five, had the second largest school: forty-nine students (twelve girls and thirty-seven boys) aged seven to twenty-two. Jesse McGee, thirty-one years old, had the largest class, which contained twenty girls and thirty boys aged seven to twenty-five. Letitia J. Baldwin, a twenty-four-year-old resident of Rocky Mount whose husband, Robert Baldwin, was a physician, operated a school for girls. She had twenty-one students whose ages ranged from eight to twenty-seven.

The churches and schools of Franklin County attempted to instill in the members of all the segments of society that they could reach acceptable standards of morality and learning. Schools as well as churches were regarded as places for the instruction of moral responsibility. Thomas Jefferson, in proposing a system of public education in the 1780s, suggested that it was the agency by which students might have "the first elements of morality"

instilled into their minds; such as, when further developed as their judgments advance in strength, may teach them how to work out their own greatest happiness, by shewing them that it does not depend on the condition of life in which chance has placed them, but is always the result of a good conscience, good health, occupation, and freedom in all just pursuits.[58]

Not everyone benefited from moral instruction, of course, and not every citizen engaged in "just pursuits." There were those in Franklin County who, because of choice or circumstance, engaged in criminal behavior. Those who were caught and convicted found themselves in the grasp of a criminal system that appeared harsh, yet by the standards of the day often was impartial. The convicted criminals who experienced the system firsthand received a rapid and rigorous education.

ELEVEN

Social Problems

The Franklin County Court met on the first Monday of each month to exercise its authority as the local judicial and executive body. It appointed county officers, listened as lawyers argued their cases, directed the improvement of roads, approved the selection of guardians, ordered legal documents recorded, and awaited with some interest the presentments or indictments issued by the grand jury.

In the eighteenth and early nineteenth centuries the grand jury and the county court served as guardians of public morals. Grand juries issued indictments for a variety of offenses both illegal and immoral. Such offenses as the failure of a road superintendent to oversee repairs, as well as cohabiting without benefit of clergy, adultery, bearing children out of wedlock, public drunkenness, fighting, gambling, and selling liquor without a license (especially to slaves) were affronts for which citizens were routinely haled before the county court.

The juries also showed a particular fascination with "profane oaths." On 4 May 1801, for example, Elisha Adams was presented by a grand jury "for profane swearing three oaths on this day in Callaway's Tavern, by the information of Abraham Jones and Thomas Walton two of this body."[1] Pleasant and Philemon Saunders each were fined $3.32 on 2 November 1802 for swearing four profane oaths apiece.[2] When Elisha Adams was fined ten shillings and costs on 5 November 1804 for swearing two profane oaths, he promptly launched another one at the court. He was "further fined 5/ for swearing one profane oath in the presence of the court, & the Shff. is ordered to confine him in the Stocks for the space of ten Minutes."[3]

Citizens also took each other to court for a variety of offenses against individual sensibilities. The most common offense was questioning another person's honor. Some historians believe that one of the many differences between northerners and southerners is that the former believe in the dignity of the individual while the latter believe in personal honor. The code of individual dignity assumes that each person has a worthy core or essence that remains unclouded by the opinions of others; the southern code of honor asserts, in effect, that a person is what others

209

think he or she is, and that one's worth in the eyes of society is reduced if one's reputation is sullied. This is thought to account for the popularity of dueling and fighting in southern society. In Franklin County there is no evidence of dueling, some evidence of fighting, and an abundance of lawsuits in which one citizen accused another of slander.

In May 1792, for instance, Samuel Davis sued Samuel Patterson because the former alleged that the latter had said Davis was "a dambd. rogue, and that he could prove it by good witnesses and that he stole a caz of wine from his father and gave it to his negros." The suit was dismissed after the parties made up their differences.[4]

Another suit for slander went to trial in August 1795. Burwell Rives had said of Arthur Edwards that he "was a damned rogue and had [infected?] his (the Deft meaning) negro with a collera and afterwards caught it himself." The jury decided, however, "that the plaintiffs character is not Injured. Therefore we find for him one penny Damages."[5]

Even former members of the House of Delegates were not immune from slanderous statements. In 1800 Ashford Napier, who had represented Franklin County during the General Assembly session of 1791, accused John Kindley of slandering him by saying he was "connected with Harse theives and would have been in Jail if you had not been blind (Meaning that the Plt had agreed with Harse theives to aid and assist them in the crime of Harsestealing for part of the stolen property)."[6] Napier and Kindley settled out of court.

Because of the sanctity of one's name and reputation in the community, some conscientious individuals went to great lengths to clear a person who had been falsely accused. Such an instance occurred in August 1798 when a report circulated that a John Boswell had stolen a paper of pins from William Dickenson's store. Dickenson himself (as well as Bedford County resident John Pate) wrote a sworn affidavit to set the record straight. Boswell, Dickenson wrote, was not in the store when the pins were taken, but came in about three hours later. At about that time the pins were discovered missing and everyone in the store was searched. Shortly afterward the pins were found outside, hidden between a box and a corner of the house. Dickenson thought that someone had placed them there and planned to remove them when he started home. After a while Boswell went outside, found the pins, put them in his pocket, and came back inside. He asked Major Terry if the pins had been found, and was told that they had been but were then left in place to see if the thief would take them when he went home. Boswell returned the pins and "mentioned to Cornelius Pate that he was afraid he had done Rong." Dickenson wanted the community to know that he was satisfied that Boswell had not stolen the pins in the first place and had no plan to keep them.[7]

Most people usually considered slander and thievery to be the responsibility of the perpetrator. Society was not to blame, it was thought, nor was the victim. Often, however, an exception was made for the wrongdoer under the influence of alcohol, particularly when injury or death was the result of overindulgence.

Although the connection between alcohol and carelessness or violence was obvious to most persons, there was little public support for regulating the consumption of alcoholic beverages during the antebellum period. Most people believed that drinking was manly and that drunkenness was almost inevitable.

They considered drinking to be socially acceptable unless a man, under the influence, neglected his family or business or committed an act of violence. Otherwise, casualties were accepted with a shrug. On 3 December 1804, for instance, a coroner's jury held an inquisition on the body of Joseph Young at the house of John Early. The jury decided that Young had died accidentally by falling out of Early's house—presumably out of a window or doorway—when in "a state of intoxication, and fractured his scull."[8]

Males began drinking at an early age. Jeremiah Bell Jeter, a Baptist minister who was a native of neighboring Bedford County, revealed in his memoirs that when still a child, "I drank as did other boys. When I was a little over eight years old [about 1810], I heard a wagon-boy, somewhat older than I, say: 'I have not drunk a drop of spirit for three years.' I had no acquaintance with him, but instantly resolved that I would follow his example."[9] Jeter's young friends thought him very peculiar when he thereafter declined alcoholic beverages.

Those who advocated the prohibition of liquor sales and consumption were viewed with suspicion during the antebellum period, so prevalent was the opposite opinion. Mary S. Watts, for example, poked fun at the temperance movement in an 1830 letter to her cousin Sarah W. Saunders, who lived in Lynchburg:

> Have you joined the "Temperence Society"? It is the fashion of the day for Ladies to join whether they indulge in *strong drink* or not. I have very old fashioned notions on the subject, and do not intend joining, even if *I* were ever so willing *Pa* would put a *"nay"* to the plan.
>
> I should like to know how many societies they will have before they get *tired;* they have already the Anti Swearing, Anti Eating (which by the by I should not much like to join) and Anti Lottery, societies and in the last paper I saw that an "Anti Wife Whipping society" had been instituted, probably by some poor dames whose Husbands spared not the rod. But I expect you are tired of Societies, and indeed I can't imagine what put them into my head this evening.[10]

Temperance societies were a northern phenomenon that spread southward, and southern members often were suspected of having abolitionist sympathies. Slowly, however, "respectable" citizens concerned about the deadly effect on society of overindulgence in alcohol began to adopt the opinions of the temperance advocates. In 1854 several like-minded Franklin County residents signed a petition to the General Assembly. They considered themselves and the people of Virginia to be

> greatly aggrieved and injured by the traffic in ardent spirits and other intoxicating liquors: That such liquors have produced, and are continually producing throughout this commonwealth, an amount of pecuniary waste and loss, of destruction of property, of injury to health and morals, of domestic misery, and of violence, pauperism, crime, and death, greater than any one, or than all put together, of the many practices forbidden by the present laws of Virginia: That the making and sale of liquors, being the manifest and easily removable cause of their widely-spread hurtfulness, should no more be permitted than the many other practices which are

sternly prohibited, though none of them are nearly so mischievous as the liquor traffic: That to tolerate that traffic any longer, is unworthy of the wisdom, humanity, and justice of a State, desirous, as she is bound, when it is practicable, to protect her people against wrong and evil: And that your petitioners deem [it] quite practicable, by judicious legislation, to avert from them and their countrymen, the mischiefs above alluded to.[11]

The petitioners closed with a plea that the General Assembly pass a law prohibiting "the sale or barter of any intoxicating liquor, except for sacramental, medicinal and mechanical uses." They suggested that the law be submitted to the voters in a referendum, with a form of reverse local option to be applied:

if a majority of them in every county and city shall approve the law, it shall be in force throughout the State; but if approved by majorities in some only of the counties and cities, it shall be in force in those counties and cities only.

The petition was signed by William T. Hancock, Pleasant Brown, William E. Duncan, A. Holland, Thomas Holland, H. S. Wright, Smithson G. Holley, J. D. Meador, B. N. Hutcheson, Peter L. Hancock, Washington C. Mitchell, James H. Wilson, William B. Arthur, James S. Turner, and William P. Flowers. Their program was not adopted until the next century.

Gambling was another popular indulgence during the antebellum period. Although the law often frowned upon cards and other games of chance, they were common throughout all levels of society. References to gambling often were casual, as in 1783 when George Griffith, who owed money to Thomas Miller, asked his gambling partner Joshua Wilson to "Please to Pay to Thomas Millar five Pound out of my acount of our Gaiming money and in so doing you Much oblige your friend George Griffith."[12]

Horse racing was the sporting event that provided the most excitement for gamblers and spectators alike in Franklin County. As early as 1763 there were "Race paths" near Chestnut Creek, while a 1774 Pittsylvania County road order mentioned "Standefer's Track" near Blackwater River (presumably at James Standifer's house of French and Indian War battle fame).[13] There was a racetrack at Rocky Mount in the late eighteenth and early nineteenth centuries, between the village and Grassy Hill (roughly in the vicinity of the Main Street–Pell Avenue intersection).[14] The *American Turf Register and Sporting Magazine* reported on races held there. In April 1834 James C. Tate wrote about on the fall meeting at Rocky Mount in 1833. The races began on Thursday, 10 October 1833, and lasted for three days. Two one-mile heats were run the first day in the Sweepstake Colt Race—winning times were two minutes and one-half second for the first race and two minutes flat for the second. On 11 October three heats were held for the Jockey Club Purse, and the winning times were four minutes and one-half second, three minutes fifty-nine seconds, and four minutes nine seconds.

On the third day three one-mile heats for the Proprietor's Purse were run; the winning times were two minutes four seconds, two minutes five seconds, and two minutes thirteen seconds. Four horses constituted the field for the first race: William Terry's Clar de Kitchen, John P. White's Fanny Kemble, William Garth's

Morgiana, and Thomas Hale's Sally Jeter. By the third heat only Morgiana and Sally Jeter remained. Tate reported that

> at the word go the third time Sally took the lead, hard pressed by Morgiana, they running locked for the first half mile, when Sally acting with the same urbanity of manners towards her [Morgiana] as towards Fanny Kemble on a former occasion, very politely bid her adieu also, and came out about twenty steps ahead. Upon this occasion the rain had been so great in the morning and continuing until 12 o'clock, that the track was literally a quagmire.[15]

Both the general public and the court often winked at drinking and gambling as long as people were discreet and did not behave as public nuisances. The court could not ignore such blatant violations as selling liquor to slaves, of course, nor could it overlook attacks on its dignity occasionally aimed by citizens emboldened by strong drink or sheer contrariness. In February 1786, for example, the court fined Holden McGee for "having offered an Contempt." The court remitted that fine but imposed another for drunkenness and "Profeng [profane] Luncy [?] in the face of the Court."[16]

The court sometimes used other incentives besides fines to discourage verbal abuse. On 3 November 1787 it not only fined Baldwin Rowland £10 for behaving contemptuously to the court but also ordered the sheriff to put him in the stocks for one hour.[17] Likewise, David Hughes was confined to the stocks for half an hour on 5 May 1788 "for an Insult offered to the Court."[18]

Court day was traditionally when citizens from all over the county assembled to attend the court sessions, watch the militia drill, trade horses, and discuss politics. Friends gathered at the tavern near the courthouse for a libation or two. Enemies encountered each other as well, and when the discussions of politics or lawsuits grew a bit too exuberant, fisticuffs often resulted.

Fights in the early nineteenth century were noted for their brutal, no-holds-barred nature. Biting, kicking, and eye-gouging were common. In some of the livelier frontier settlements there was scarcely a man to be found who was not missing an eye, an ear, or part of his nose. As a traveling minister, the Reverend William Hill, observed at a Franklin County court day on 6 September 1790:

> I . . . felt much concerned to see my poor fellow mortals drinking and degrading themselves below the brutes that perish, and to hear them cursing and swearing, and using the very language of hell. Some were stripping and fighting, and tearing each other to pieces like incarnate devils.[19]

Fighting was not considered much more than a nuisance by the authorities, unless the public peace was seriously disturbed, someone was badly injured, or a county court session was disrupted. During the early years of the Republic county officials resented any behavior that smacked of civil disobedience.

On 2 July 1787, for example, John Chitwood was fined £10 and ordered to jail until he paid the fine and took out a peace bond, for opposing

the Sheriff of this County in the Collection of the Publick Taxes, and for

Declaring himself Determined not to pay his Own Taxes, and Also for resisting the Sheriff and Continuing to Stand in Opposition and also for saying he Ought to go to Gaol, but that the Court nor all their friends Could not Carry him there.[20]

On 6 May 1788 the court fined Jeremiah Early, Jubal Early, and John Sullins each £10 for giving "a Contempt to the Order of the Court and for their Rid'ous [riotous] behavior and that they be Comm[itte]d to Custody till Paid and Costs and to give Security for their Good behavior."[21] The next day, however, the court remitted the fines of Jeremiah Early and John Sullins; presumably Jubal Early was required to pay his fine.[22]

The court did not forgive other transgressors so easily. On 4 January 1802 the court

Ordered that Charles Divin be fined ten dollars for behaving contumeliously and disorderly before the Court, and insulting the State's attorney in the presence of the court and repeatedly interrupting the court in the transaction of business before them and that he be commitd. to the custody of the Sh[eriff] till the same be paid.[23]

Later on the same day the court fined Divin another $25 for "repeatedly coming into Court, interrupting & violently stoping the business before the same, by swearing in their presence repeatedly."[24]

The next day's court proceedings may explain Divin's behavior. James Board appeared before the justices to answer the charge that on 28 November 1801 he

bit of[f] part of the Lip of Charles Divin [in a fight], with intention in so doing the said Charles Divin to maim and disfigure. . . . It appearing to the Court that the mittimus by which the said James Board has been committed for examination does not charge him with any offence of a feloneous nature, it is considered by the court that the said James Board for that reason be discharged.[25]

Perhaps Divin was outraged because he thought Board had escaped justice on a technicality. On 1 March 1802 the court relented and remitted the fines it had imposed on Divin.[26]

Some citizens disrupted the court proceedings from outside the courthouse, by having fights, loud arguments, or "riots" in the courtyard. On 7 March 1803, for instance, the justices ordered "that Elisha Adams be fined two dollars for raising an affray with John Guinn in the Court yard, and that he be committed to the custody of the Sheriff till he shall have paid the same."[27] On 6 May 1807, noted the county clerk, "George McCollister having behaved in a disorderly manner & raised a riot in the hearing of the Court, to the disturbance of its proceedings, It is ordered that for his offence, the Sheriff put him in the Stocks for fifteen minutes."[28]

In 1801 one county resident angered the justices by his misbehavior both outside and inside the courtroom:

David Ross having in the hearing of the court raised a riot and thereby having prevented the court for some time from doing the ordinary business of the county and being brought into court for the purpose of giving Security for his good behavior, and having contemptiously broke out of the court house, the court proceeded to consider what should be done with him for said contempt & it was ordered that he be committed to Jail and be kept there untill tomorrow morning 10 Oclk and after that till he give security for his good behavior for 12 months, himself in the sum of one hundred Dollars and two securities in the sum of 50 Dols. each.[29]

Many of the arguments that erupted in the courtyard were fueled by the liquor that was readily available at the tavern next door to the courthouse. The early nineteenth century was a hard-drinking age, and there were virtually no restrictions on the use of liquor except for its unlicensed sale. License fees were a major source of revenue for localities and a means of exercising control over public behavior. There also were penalties for public intoxication and some awareness of the links between liquor and violence.

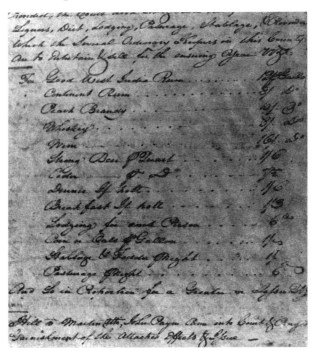

Tavern rates from 1786 Franklin County court order book. (Virginia State Library and Archives.)

In 1842 the Franklin County Court fined Henry G. Hopkins $40 and court costs for selling ardent spirits without a license. Three years later Hopkins petitioned the General Assembly to remit his fine because he was a poor man with a large family (eight children) and had been unaware that he was breaking the law. He claimed that the principal witness against him, his neighbor James Wright, had given conflicting testimony. The truth of the matter, wrote Hopkins, was that soon after he had purchased some liquor for his own use, Wright "sent his son to your petitioner's house with a request to let him have a portion of the said spirits, alleging that his family was sick and that he wanted the spirits for medicinal purposes."[30] Hopkins admitted that he expected remuneration from Wright to cover the cost of the gallon that he sent home with Wright's son, but he was not paid. The General Assembly was unsympathetic; it rejected Hopkins's petition.

Another Franklin County resident, Daniel Wray, was convicted in 1856 of selling spirits for consumption on the premises without a license. He protested to the General Assembly that when he paid his fee to the sheriff for an ordinary license, he was issued instead only a retail license, which did not allow on-site consumption, without his being aware of the difference. He too sought a rebate of his fine and court costs, but to no avail.[31]

Persons accused of crimes of violence or errors in judgment that led them into trouble often used intoxication as an excuse or as a mitigating factor. Sometimes the court accepted the claim, as in the case of Jonathan Richeson, one of the Franklin County justices who, in 1787,

> had been Represented to the Court as a Person who had Declared himself Against the Payment of the Publick Taxes. On Consideration whereof and after examining Divers Witnesses the Court are of Opinion that the said Richardson was rather Intoxicated and Expressed great Concern for what he had Said, Therefore in the Opinion of the Court he stands Excused and that the Same be Certifyed to his Excelly the Governor.[32]

No one accused of forgery or counterfeiting blamed intoxication; those crimes called for a steady hand and a cool head. Such crimes were rare, with forgery the more common of the two. In 1790 a jury found William Martin, Jr., guilty of forging the name of Alexander Ferguson to an order on the inspectors at the Rocky Ridge warehouse for three hogsheads of tobacco belonging to Ferguson.[33] Thomas Arthur, a county court justice, was accused in 1791 of forging another man's name to a legal document in a suit that was pending; he was never tried for the offense.[34] In 1804, however, the Franklin County Court acquitted James Holcom of forging an order in the name of James Young on Samuel Saunders.[35] (This was similar to attempting to pass a bad check.) Even more serious than forging another person's signature was the manufacture of spurious coins and currency. In 1793 Solomon Stansbury was caught with a set of types for stamping coins but was acquitted by the Franklin County Court apparently because he had not actually done anything with it.[36] Many of the county's residents petitioned the General Assembly in 1835 for the release from the penitentiary of Henry T. Clinton, who had been confined for passing counterfeit money. The petitioners insisted that Clinton was a "weak simple ignorant Man" who was duped by a confidence man named John Fisher. The legislature referred the petition to a committee, where it languished until the end of the session, when it died.[37]

Forgery and counterfeiting were, in a sense, forms of stealing—of obtaining something of value without paying for it. Out-and-out thievery was more common, although some enterprising individuals were tempted by both methods. Thomas Richardson, a laborer, was tried for forgery as well as for stealing in 1807. In the first instance he was accused of having "Stolen from William Curtain Two pair of shoes of the Value of four dollars" on 14 April 1807; when he was found guilty the Franklin County Court sentenced him to "receive fifteen lashes on his bare back . . . immediately . . . and that the Sheriff of this County carry him to the common Whipping post, and inflict the same & then discharge him."[38] Next he was tried before the district court for having forged the name of Abraham Rorer to a note for $60 and feloniously passing it to Joseph Mays. This time he was acquitted.[39]

Sometimes thieves stole money directly from their victims rather than attempting forgery. In 1786 Robert and Rebecca Edmonds were tried

> on Suspicion of Stealing from Charles Doughton a Squirril Skin Purse and in it One doubloon, a Joannis, eight Joannesses, & One Guinea On Monday night the 4th Day of this Inst. [September] at Rocky Mount. [He pleaded guilty and was sentenced to] Stand One half Hour in the Pillory, receive 39 Lashes on his Bare Back & have Both Ears Croped.[40]

Because no witnesses testified against Rebecca Edmonds, she was discharged from custody and presumably went home with her whipped and mangled husband.

Horse stealing and cattle rustling were not just phenomena of the Old West, but were common in the Old East as well. In March 1786, for example, the Franklin County Court tried William Dillingham for stealing a mare from Walter Bernard, a colt from Violet Hill, and a steer from Edward Richards. The court found him not guilty.[41] In August 1786 the court found John Barnett guilty of stealing one horse each from John Marr and Thomas Hale, and "Also by force of Arms Robing Samuel Durst [a potter who lived on Story Creek] of a Great Coat & Sundry Other Goods."[42] Barnett pleaded guilty and was ordered to stand trial before the General Court.

Stealing such clothing as a greatcoat was unusual, but several other instances are known. In June 1787, according to testimony, Benjamin Hensley broke into the house of Oliver Orr and stole a greatcoat and some other items. When Orr found the coat in Hensley's possession five months later, Hensley maintained that he "Won it at Cards of a person unknown to him."[43] The court declined to believe Hensley and ordered him tried by the General Court.

In contrast with stealing clothes for personal use, most horse and cattle thieves sold their booty to unsuspecting citizens. Occasionally, however, there were exceptions. In 1788 James Martin was charged with stealing and killing two hogs belonging to Joshua Dillingham; Martin was acquitted by the court.[44] The justices likewise found James Philips not guilty of "having feloneously killed and converted to his own use a Heifer the property of Thomas Jackson" in 1803.[45]

Among the horse-and-clothing thieves of Franklin County, only one has been written about at any length: Joseph Thompson Hare, alias Thomas Hunt, also called "Hare the Highwayman." The documented facts of his brief criminal career in the county are few. The county court arraigned Hare under the name of Thomas Hunt on 19 November 1806 for stealing, on 8 November, "one eagle-colored horse, four hundred and fifty Spanish Milled Dollars and sundry wearing apparel, the property of Robert Bumpass."[46] The court ordered him held in the county jail for trial in the district court. That trial took place on 15 April 1807 and the court rendered its verdict two days later, finding "Joseph Hare, alias Thomas

Hunt, late of the County of Franklin, Taylor [tailor] . . . guilty of the horse-stealing aforesaid . . . [and] he shall undergo confinement in the penitentiary house to be eight years."[47] Hare arrived at the Virginia State Penitentiary under guard on 28 April.[48]

"Hare Robbing the Traveller." (The Life and Adventures of Joseph T. Hare, the Bold Robber and Highwayman, With 16 Elegant and Spirited Engravings [New York: H. Long and Brother, 1847].)

HARE ROBBING THE TRAVELLER.

The undocumented stories about Hare were greatly embellished, supposedly by Hare himself, and published as *The Dying Confession of Joseph Hare, alias, Joseph Thompson Hare* in 1818. They also appear in an early "dime novel," *The Life and Adventures of Joseph T. Hare, the Bold Robber and Highwayman, With 16 Elegant and Spirited Engravings* that was published in 1847.[49] According to Hare, he was born in Chester County, Pennsylvania, in 1780. Although he came from a good family he proved a troublesome child and became a juvenile delinquent, at age sixteen robbing a neighbor. His father disowned him, and young Hare wandered from one large city to another, bent on a life of crime. By Hare's account he lived a life of high adventure, alternating criminal acts of cruelty with moments of gallantry and suffering from unrequited love. After a particularly successful robbery in which he is said to have relieved a rich Spaniard of $4,000, Hare moved on to Knoxville, Tennessee, then decided to wend his way on horseback to Richmond, Virginia, because of a promise of some easy money there. "At Abingdon," Hare wrote,

> I fell in with a drover of Franklin county [Robert Bumpass], who was on his way home from Kentucky, where he had been on a trading excursion, and on a pretty profitable one, too, as I thought, from the display which he made of his money. The devilish infatuation of my previous course of life seized possession of me, and in despite of all my previous resolutions, and of the important prospects which I had at Richmond, I determined to rob him. With this view, I kept in his company, but though I felt a secret repugnance to the act, and experienced a gloom of mind that I ought to have taken as a forewarning of my fate, I could not shake off the fascination which had seized me, but still kept on, like an ox going to the slaughter, as the Scripture says, or "a fool to the correction of the stocks."
> The warning clung to me so well, that I had even followed the drover to within fifteen miles of the Court House, in Franklin county, before I could

make up my mind to carry out the purpose, which I had performed with so much alacrity in many instances before, but stimulated by the blind confidence of a long career of wicked fortune, I suddenly resolved, and dashing up to his side, half mad with my own irresolution, I fiercely demanded of him his money or his life.

He hesitated for a moment, and then paid me over, with trembling hands, the sum of four hundred and fifty dollars, which he declared was all he had.—Without pausing to test his declarations by a search, or even to disarm him, I seized the money with eager haste, and turning my horse, struck in my spurs, and galloped away as if flying from the most sharp and inveterate pursuit. I turned my head but once in my flight, and then beheld the drover gazing after me as if undecided whether to give chase or no.

I plunged my spurs still deeper in my horse's side, and watched his strides with the intense interest of apprehension. I cannot account for the extraordinary feelings which had seized possession of me, unless it was a warning from some mysterious and supernatural power, or a forerunner of what was about to happen. I felt like a man under the influence of some hideous nightmare, and every time I urged my beast to speed, it seemed to me as if a crowd of fiends were whistling in my course, and on the point of laying their avenging grasp upon my shoulder. I rode and rode, without one moment's disposition to hold up, and when the powers of my tired animal began to flag, I kept moving forward in my saddle, like a steersman in a boat, in the hope that that would aid my motion. While proceeding in this way, a thing occurred, from the recollection of which I shrink, even in this dreadful hour.

The moon had risen during my flight, and about nine o'clock, which was the third hour of my race, she was an hour high, and, consequently, bright and full. I had been galloping through a long stretch of narrow road, the bordering trees of which shut out her beams, and left the surface of the path in gloom.—Suddenly I merged into an open rise, and there, in her silvery light, stood, right across the road, a pure white horse—immovable as marble, and so white that it almost seemed to be radiating light. I was a little startled by the first glance at the apparition, but expecting it to give way, I pressed towards it. But it did not stir, but stood with its small graceful head stretched out, its tail slightly raised, as if in a listening attitude, and its ears cocked sharply forward and strained towards the moon, on which its gaze seemed to be unwaveringly fixed. When within almost six feet of it, my horse suddenly recoiled upon his haunches, and, opening his nostrils with affright, gave a short cry of terror, and attempted to turn around. I trembled in my saddle as if struck with a sudden ague, but not daring to return into the gloom behind, I closed my eyes, bent my head, and driving my sharp heels deep into my horse's side, pressed onward at the fearful object. My steed took but one plunge, and then landed on its fore-feet, firmly resolved not to budge another inch. I opened my eyes, and the apparition had disappeared.—But an instant had elapsed and no trace of it was left. My most superstitious terrors were then confirmed, and I feared to go forward over the charmed space where the strange figure had stood. I recollected a roadside inn which I had passed a mile behind, and touching my rein, my horse turned swiftly round, and obeyed the summons with a fleeter heel than he had shown previous to his fatigue.

. . . The vision was the cause of my arrest, for during the night, a party of

fifteen men, consisting of the drover's friends, surrounded the house and
bore me off to Franklin county prison.

   . . . I think this white horse was Christ, and that he came to warn me of my
sins and to make me fear and repent.[50]

Hare's account of his robbery of Bumpass differed somewhat from the evidence
presented at his arraignment and trial before the district court; Hare's version left
Bumpass clothed and on horseback, rather than naked and afoot. The location was
less specific than local tradition, which held that the robbery and encounter with
the spectral horse took place somewhere on the road between Chestnut Mountain
and Turkeycock Mountain. Finally, Hare accused a Franklin County constable and
magistrate (both unnamed) of robbing him of the $4,000 he had stolen from the
Spaniard.[51]

After the trial, Hare served at least five years of his sentence before the governor
pardoned him for good behavior, according to his purported memoirs.[52] Hare
moved to Baltimore and worked for a time as a harness maker. Soon, however, he
resumed his life of crime, robbing wayfarers as far north as Canada. In 1817 Hare
joined a bandit gang that included his brother Lewis Hare, and they robbed a mail
coach near Havre de Grace, Maryland. The escapade ended his career, for he and
one of the other gangsters were hanged on 10 September 1818.

Robbers such as Hare sometimes acted in concert in Franklin County as well as
elsewhere. In June 1788 the Franklin County Court examined Reuben Pursel and
James Lynn, who were accused of stealing two of Thomas Arthur's horses. It found
both men guilty and remanded them to the custody of the sheriff for further trial
before the General Court.[53]

Sometimes whites and blacks cooperated to commit crimes, as when Aris
Vaughan and Salem, a slave belonging to Archibald Gordon, appeared before the
Franklin County Court for breaking into Daniel Brown's lumber house in 1789.
The court acquitted Vaughan and convicted Salem, who received thirty-nine
lashes at the whipping post.[54]

On another occasion, in 1804, Brice Richardson appeared before the court to
answer charges of having aided and abetted several blacks

in burglariously breaking and entering the Dwelling House of Happy Tally,
Widow of this county, on the night of Saturday the fifth day of this month,
and taking from thence a negro boy, the Property of the said Happy Tally.[55]

The court acquitted both Richardson and the unnamed blacks. Their motives are
not known. Were they planning to steal the child and sell him? Was one of them a
parent of Happy Tally's slave boy? The record is silent.

The use of legal technicalities to the advantage of the accused is nothing new.
In 1805 the court examined Thomas Quigley, who was charged with having

taken, Stolen, and carried away, a quantity of fodder of the value of three
Shillings, the property of Thomas Jones. . . . his Counsel objected to being
examined by the Court, on the following grounds, first that the warrant by
which the Sheriff summoned and convened the Court, does not [as] the
words of the Law require the Sheriff to [do] Summon eight magistrates at
least. Secondly because Thomas Thompson one of the members of the Court

was not present when the Court was opened; although he was legally Summoned, and took his Seat before the Examination commenced, there being only four members independent of the said Thomas Thompson, but these objections are overruled by the Court.[56]

Quigley's legal maneuvering did him little good: the court judged him guilty.

Even if the court found the accused not guilty, suspicion sometimes clung to him, especially if the acquittal resulted from a lack of evidence. Jesse Estes appeared before the Franklin County Court in 1806 and expressed concern for his reputation after the court had acquitted him of "having feloniously taken, stolen and carried away the sum of forty pounds, ten shillings and seven pence, in Gold and Silver, the property of John James of the said County, on or about the first of February last past."[57] The court obligingly ordered that it "be entered on record that this acquittal is by the unanimous opinion of the Court, not a Shadow of Suspicion appearing to them against the said Jesse Estes."

Sometimes the accusation of criminal behavior resulted from a personal animosity between the alleged victim and the accused. After the court found John Burgess not guilty of breaking into the house of John Prewitt and stealing linen, shoe buckles, and cash in 1789, for instance, the justices ordered Prewitt—not Burgess—to file a bond pledging his good behavior toward Burgess.[58] This suggests that Prewitt may have falsely accused Burgess of the burglary.

A man who falsely accused or insulted another courted a lawsuit or personal violence. Thomas Prunty sued Thomas Jones in 1789, two years after an incident in which, according to Jones, Prunty

in a gearing [jeering] insulting manner offered [Jones] a Bowl to Drink with him. Your Orator not willing to receive the insult which he conceives the said Prunty intended, resented it by striking the Bowl out of his hand. On which trifling circumstance the said Prunty instituted a suit, as your Orator verily believes he was seeking some occassion to do.[59]

The custom of the time was to pass a small bowl of punch around the table, and each man would take a drink. Jones responded to Prunty's social gaffe with a countersuit but a jury awarded damages to Prunty.

Sometimes what began as a friendly social gathering turned into a melee. On 20 December 1786 a group of men were playing whist, a popular card game, at William Thompson's house when a fight erupted between two of his guests, Edward Wilson and John England. The two began to argue, according to one witness, because

there appeared to be a fals Deal, that Mr. Wilson got a Kandle to Count the tricks, that upon Sarching Wilson found a Card Between Mr. Inglands feet which Caused a Quarrel, and that John Ingland did strike and assault the said Edward Wilson.[60]

England hit Wilson three or four times before Wilson could resist. Meanwhile, another guest named Ostin Shoat started hitting Wilson's wife, Sarah, and then assaulted their son Thomas Wilson. George Moore, who was also present, swore in a deposition that he had heard England say before the fight began "that he would Whip some one that Night." Wilson sued England, but the court dismissed the case.

Almost ten years later, in June 1795, a wedding at the house of William Mavity served as the occasion for a brawl between Hugh O'Neal and—once again—Thomas Prunty, who seemed to have a knack for irritating his fellow partygoers. In a deposition filed during the lawsuit that followed the festivities, Jonas Turner related that

> Sometime late in the Evening this Deponent with Thomas Prunty the Pl[aintif]f had a candle in his hand looking for the Plfs. bridle And After Serching in the Cornhouse went into the Kitchen where Nancy Oneal the Def[enden]ts Wife and Old Mrs. Mavity were siting and as this Deponent and the Plf. Prunty entered the House, the Defts. Wife asked what we were looking for. I answered we were looking for a Bridle. She replied as your Deponent recollects in these Words, "Damn you Neither of you are worth a bridle." On which She rose up and Walking towards the Plf. as well as this Deponent recollects Uttered these Words "Damn your fat belly Prunty." The Defts. wife was Speaking but a Very Short time to the Plf. when the Defendant came in and Struck his Wife and then Advancing to the Said Prunty Struck him Several Strokes. After which he Jerked the Plg. down on his belly, and as the Plf. Arose the Deft. Struck him under the ear, which appeared to be Very hard, on which the Plf. called on this Deponent to take him off which he did. And that it Appeared to this Deponent that no Just cause by Action or Jesture on the part of the Plf. was Offered to the Def. or to his Wife, And that after they were Apart and Peace in some Measure restored, the Plf. asked the Def. what Injury he had done him that he treated him in that Manner. On which the Def. Answer'd "Damn you dont ask me." This Deponent further Saith that sometime Afterwards he saw the Plf. fall down and Roll over and Said he did not know but his Scull was broke. And Giving James Young a relation of the Abuse he had received.[61]

This deposition probably did not do full justice to the truth of the affray. No one seemed concerned that the first person O'Neal hit was Mrs. O'Neal. There was no mention of liquor, either, but the episode bore all the marks of a drunken brawl. The jury evidently reached the same conclusion; it ruled that each party should pay his own court costs and awarded Prunty one penny damages.

The wording of indictments in assault cases often was more dramatic than the actual event. In November 1786, for example, Samuel Dillion charged that Barnett, Elijah, Elisha, Hezekiah, Isham (Jr.), Isham (Sr.), John, and William Blankenship, with "Swords, Clubs, Fists upon the said plaintiff . . . an assault did make and him did beat wound and Ill treat so that of his life it was greatly despaired."[62] Either Dillion exaggerated or the Blankenships were remarkably inept; eventually his suit—for £500 in damages—was dismissed.

Just as men committed violence on other men, women sometimes beat other women, as when the Franklin County Court on 3 August 1789 ordered Sarah Musgrove to appear to answer a charge of assault and battery against Jane Sellers.[63] And men threatened or hit women or children; on 30 March 1790 Mary Jones swore before a justice of the peace that she had "good cause to apprehend that John Brammer will beat Wound or Evilly treat her Children to the Great Deanger and risk of there lives."[64] Sometimes the threat of violence was vague, as when Mary Jones complained in 1803 of Thomas Arrington's "threats & menaces" against her; he filed a $100 peace bond.[65]

Rape, the ultimate male violence against a woman, was either rare or underreported because instances seldom appeared in the court order books. One assault, however, was reported on 1 December 1800 when the Franklin County Court examined John Allen Hancock for aiding in the rape of Jemima Douglas on 4 October 1800. The court remanded him to the district court for further trial and fixed his bond at $5,000.[66]

Murders were rare in Franklin County. Occasionally one spouse took the life of the other—or attempted to, as in the 1833 case of William B. Williams and his bride, Mildred C. Tate. Sometimes a master beat a slave to death, for example, when John Via, Jr., killed his slave Jane in 1807. Seldom was there a person killed with no likely suspect in view. On 6 February 1809, however, a coroner's jury that convened at the house of William Brizendine concluded that Joel Farris had been murdered there on 21 January by "some person unknown." The killer had assaulted Farris, hit him on his back near his right side, and also broken his neck, killing him.[67]

Just before the Civil War there occurred the most notorious killing in the history of the county, the Witcher-Clement gunfight at Dickinson's store on 25 February 1860. The store was located in the southeastern part of the county, not far from the Pittsylvania County line. It stood just across present-day Route 646 from the Brown-Law House, which served as an ordinary and stagecoach stop.

The Witcher family, which lived near Callands in Pittsylvania County, was a prominent one.[68] Vincent Witcher, the patriarch of the clan, served in the General Assembly for more than twenty years: as a member of the House of Delegates from 1823 to 1854 (except for the sessions of 1829–1830, 1833–1834, 1838, and 1839–1843) and in the Senate from 1845 to 1853 (except for the session of 1849–1850, when he was out of office, and 1850–1851, when he again served in the House of Delegates). His granddaughter, Victoria Smith, married James Clement, of Franklin County, in the late 1850s. The Clement family was as prominent as the Witcher. James Clement's father, George C. Clement, a noted Franklin County physician, graduated from Hampden-Sydney College and the medical school of the University of Pennsylvania. His large, five-bay brick house

Dr. George Clements house, Mountain View. Late-19th-century photo. (Blue Ridge Institute, Ferrum, Va.)

still stands near Penhook; behind the house are buried his three sons who were killed at Dickinson's store.

When James Clement married Victoria Smith, both families—who were friends as well as distant neighbors—were pleased at the match. For a time the couple was happy; a daughter, Lelia Maude Clement, was born in 1858. Apparently, however, Victoria Clement's continued friendship with a pair of her former suitors aroused her husband's jealousy. Angry arguments and threats of violence caused Victoria Clement to flee to a neighbor's house early in March 1859; she initiated divorce proceedings soon thereafter.

Because every antebellum divorce required an act of the General Assembly, the aggrieved party generally attempted to compile as much evidence against the offender as possible. The usual method was to obtain depositions from one's friends and supporters; the law, however, required that the other party be notified that depositions would be taken and thereby be provided an opportunity to respond. Sometimes the parties gathered at the courthouse or a nearby tavern or store. On the morning of 25 February 1860 the Witchers and the Clements met at Dickinson's store in its back room, which doubled as a counting room and a post office.

Perhaps because of all the threats and angry words that had been uttered earlier, each side came with concealed knives and pistols, ready for a fight. The small room was jammed with Witchers, Clements, their deponents, and county justice Robert Mitchell. Vincent Witcher, aged seventy-one, was accompanied by his son Addison Witcher, his grandsons John A. Smith and Vincent Oliver Smith, and his son-in-law Samuel Swanson. The three sons of Dr. George C. Clement—James, Ralph, and William Clement—also were there, as well as about eight deponents for the two sides. Addison Witcher questioned them for Victoria Clement, and Ralph Clement represented his brother James.

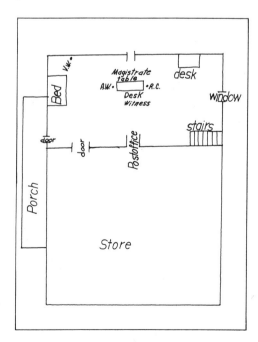

Sketch of interior of Dickinson's Store. (Bicentennial Reflections [N.p.: Franklin County Bicentennial Commission, 1986], 46. Reprinted with permission.)

About noon Elizabeth Bennett had just begun her testimony when trouble erupted. Vincent Witcher made a sharp remark to Ralph Clement, he responded, and suddenly gunshots rang out. Just who fired first is not known; at the later trial some witnesses stated it was Vincent Witcher, but one witness who was across the room swore that James Clement fired his pistol first. When the smoke cleared James and William Clement were dead, and Ralph Clement lay dying; James Smith was wounded in the shoulder. The county coroner found that "James Clement came to his death by wounds, five in number, made with a pistol, two in the breast, three in the back and shoulder" and that William Clement, in addition to having been shot six times, had received five stab wounds in his neck, shoulder, abdomen, breast, and back, and that these alone could have killed him.[69]

Between 15 and 23 March 1860 a five-judge panel of the Franklin County Court sat in Rocky Mount to consider the evidence against Vincent Witcher, Addison Witcher, John A. Smith, Vincent Oliver Smith, and Samuel Swanson, who stood charged with having "wilfully, deliberately and with premeditation murder[ed] and kill[ed] Ralph A. Clement, James R. Clement & William C. Clement."[70] The prospect of a trial excited the townspeople, as Peter Saunders, Jr., of Bleak Hill, learned when he arrived in Rocky Mount on business

> Old Capt. Witcher and four others are now in our jail to be examined for the murder of the Clements. The examination before the magistrates court is expected to commence to-morrow. I am not well posted as to the particulars but hear that the parties expect to be discharged by the examining court.[71]

The judges were Richard M. Taliaferro, Robert Bush, Moses C. Greer, Jonathan H. McNiel, and Isaac Cannaday. William M. Tredway represented the defendants, who insisted they had returned fire in self-defense after James Clement began shooting. Because there was no proof of who fired the first shot, and because the charge of premeditation was not supported by the evidence, the panel voted three to two "that there is not probable cause for charging the said prisoners with the offense aforesaid, and doth order that they be acquited and discharged of the said offense,"[72] thereby terminating the case.

Peter Saunders, Jr., commented on the case in a letter to his brother:

> You will probably have seen from the papers before this reaches you, notice of the acquital of the Witchers by the examining court. The trial excited great interest in the community. Although it lasted for more than a week a good many people of the country quit their business and attended it through. I heard only a part of the evidence and a portion of the speeches. So far as I know I believe the action of the court is generally approved by those acquainted [with] the facts. It was a dreadful killing, but the affair seems to have been commenced by the Clements and Captain Witcher and his friends seem to have acted at first upon self defence, though in the progress of the fight, they may have gone beyond the strict limits of self defence. I feel confident that if sent on to further trial they would all have been acquitted by a jury.[73]

The controversy surrounding the killing, however, has lasted in Franklin County long after the gunfire ceased, with considerable debate over the question of who shot first. No one is any closer to answering that question now than in 1860.

Had the Witchers been convicted of murder, they might have been executed or sentenced to long terms in the State Penitentiary in Richmond. Between the eighteenth and mid-nineteenth centuries a considerable evolution of thought with regard to punishment had occurred. Until the turn of the nineteenth century there was no penitentiary or state prison in Virginia. Persons convicted of crimes by county courts were punished immediately after trial and released. The punishments ranged from confinement in the stocks to whipping, branding, and ear-cropping. Jails were used primarily for confinement before trial, not for punishment afterwards.

By the end of the eighteenth century, however, the idea of doing penance for one's crimes gained acceptance among modern thinkers who believed a convict should be confined in a solitary cell, there to reflect on his misdeeds and resolve to live on the right side of the law after his release. The concept of rehabilitation did not exist; there were few opportunities for work while in prison and usually the authorities enforced a code of silence. As the nineteenth century continued this new method of correction proved no more effective than the old. Gradually as hopelessness pervaded the system, the concept of doing penance was abandoned but nothing was substituted in its place. Instead, the prisoners were seen as almost less than human and—particularly after the Civil War—as a source of cheap labor for industries, farms, and public projects.

As with the correctional system, the law enforcement system was cumbersome and inefficient. Each county relied on an antiquated structure involving a sheriff, deputy sheriffs, and constables, supplemented by citizen participation either singly or in groups.

Sometimes a law enforcement officer needed to call for help. A constable, for example, asked the county court for assistance in 1803 when he attempted to arrest Thomas Cheatham but failed. The court, finding that Cheatham "stands out in opposition & resists the Efforts of the Constable to arrest him . . . ordered that the Constable be instructed to take the Power of the county [the militia or a posse] in order to aid him in Executing the said Warrant."[74]

The state reimbursed private citizens who arrested suspects or transported them to jail. In 1811, for instance, Richard Stockton, a Franklin County inhabitant, pursued a horse thief all the way to Wythe County before capturing him. The thief, Anderson Barker, was tried and convicted, but the judge who heard the case refused to allow Stockton the $20 reward posted for Barker's capture and conviction,

> because he was not the first who laid hold of the horse theif and not because his testimony was meterial to his conviction. . . . it is true a Mr. Evans of Wythe was the first who siezed the prisoner, but [Stockton] employed Evans to assist him.[75]

Stockton petitioned the General Assembly to allow his claim and the legislature agreed.

In March 1857 Fielding Jones, an accused murderer, escaped from the Nelson County jail. The governor offered a $100 reward for his capture, and James B.

Cannaday, of Franklin County, succeeded in apprehending him. He received the reward but also submitted to the state auditor of public accounts a bill for $123.34 for his expenses. Cannaday's expenses included money paid to five other men who assisted him, mileage for conveying Jones from Long Branch in Franklin County to the Nelson County jail and returning, the services of James H. Griffith as a guard, the use of several horses for seven days, and other expenses, such as

> 1 meal at Christiansburg, .50; fee to jailor of Montgomery County for receiving said Jones into his jail one night for safe keeping, .80; Rail Road fare for prisoner from Christiansburg to Lynchburg, $3.45; fee of Jailer at Lynchburg receiving prisoner one night for safe keeping, .80; Stage fare from Lynchburg to Nelson Ct. House and one meal, $3.00.[76]

When the auditor refused to reimburse Cannaday, he appealed to the General Assembly, which agreed to allow $80.30 of the expenses he sought. His case provides a glimpse into the intricate workings of the criminal justice system in antebellum Virginia.

The system of the day did not include licensed bail bondsmen. A prisoner awaiting trial remained in jail unless his family or friends could post his bond. If the defendant failed to appear for trial the bond was forfeited; usually the person who posted the bond could not recover his money. Sometimes the money was recovered if fraud was involved, but most such efforts proved fruitless.

In 1841 Melville Talbot and Sampson D. Patterson posted bail in Lynchburg for William Kyle, who had been convicted of operating an illegal gambling game (faro) at the tavern of Hopkins Nowlin at Rocky Mount. Kyle's bond, which was financed by Talbot and Patterson, supposedly guaranteed his appearance for sentencing. On the appointed day, however, Kyle could not be found; he had fled the state. Patterson also disappeared, leaving Talbot responsible for the entire sum. Various judgments were levied against Talbot by several courts, and Talbot ultimately appealed to the General Assembly for relief. The legislature, however, refused to intervene in the judicial process and rejected Talbot's appeal.[77]

The jail that confined the highwayman Hare, the gambler William Kyle, the murderer Fielding Jones, and the horse thief Anderson Barker, also held the mentally ill—or "lunatics," as they were called—of Franklin County, at least until they could be accepted into the overcrowded state mental hospitals. In 1770 the first mental hospital in America was established in Williamsburg. The Public Hospital or Eastern Lunatic Asylum (now Eastern State Hospital) opened in 1773 and remained the only such institution in Virginia until Western State Hospital, in Staunton, opened in 1828.

In the eighteenth and nineteenth centuries, of course, even less was known about mental illness than in modern times. Typical diagnoses included "disappointment in love," and alcoholics and senile geriatric cases received the same care as the truly mentally ill. Confining mentally ill persons in county jails, a common practice throughout the state during the antebellum period, was not considered cruel. Although the accommodations were no doubt spartan, at least the inmate was not wandering about, unable to fend for himself—he was sheltered and fed. He received no treatment, of course, and his care was the least expensive that could be provided.

The county court did demonstrate concern for these jail inmates by attending to their special needs when they were called to the justices' attention. In April 1858, for example, the Franklin County jail held Charles Bishop, who had been "regularly declared a lunatic by a Commission of Lunacy composed of three Justices of the peace of this County" and jailed until he could be transferred to one of the state hospitals. When Bishop became ill, however, and could not be moved, the court ordered the jailer to "make proper provisions for the care and maintenance of the said Bishop and that Dr. Thomas B. Greer do visit and attend upon the said Bishop and render him such medical assistance and treatment as he shall require."[78]

A mentally ill person depended on his friends and neighbors. Because he was incapable of managing his affairs, some concerned friend or relative had to step in and make sure that the county court appointed a committee of responsible citizens to tend to his property, pay his bills, and so forth. An ill but prosperous person, such as Ashford Napier at the turn of the nineteenth century, might be cared for at his own home or someone else's; a poor or unmanageable patient probably ended up at a state hospital.

As with the mentally ill, the poor of Franklin County largely depended on their more prosperous relatives and friends for their support. As there was no welfare system or organized private charities, a poor or infirm person with no one to assist him or her generally begged for assistance from the county court. Such assistance came grudgingly, because the court was tightfisted about spending public money. In 1850, for example, the county supported forty paupers at an annual cost of $1,017, or $25.43 per person—about seven cents a day for each pauper. By 1860 the county supported sixty paupers over the course of the year for $1,607, or $26.78 for each person (about seven and a third cents a day).[79]

The official reaction to the unemployed poor generally took one of two forms: to indenture them to tradesmen or to push them beyond the county's borders. Those who could not be put to work or forced out faced life in the county poorhouse, an institution that dated from the early nineteenth century. As with most poorhouses, the one in Franklin County was located in the countryside and operated as a farm, so that it might be somewhat self-sufficient.

During the colonial period the Church of England cared for the poor. The church vestries distributed part of the money collected by the church either to the poor directly as a form of relief, or to other persons paid to house and feed the poor or infirm. After the revolutionary war and the disestablishment of the Church of England, the General Assembly authorized each county to create a committee called the overseers of the poor to replace the vestries in that function. Gradually the idea of concentrating the poor in workhouses or poorhouses gained acceptance, particularly among overseers of the poor, as a cost-effective means of caring for and controlling the poor and infirm. The public elected the overseers, who operated the poorhouse, bound out orphans and illegitimate children as apprentices, and accounted for the funds they distributed for the care of the poor.

Franklin County did not build its poorhouse or poor farm until after 1833, having suffered several false starts. In 1818 the county court "determined on building a Poor House and to let the building to the lowest bidder . . . but before the matter was carried into effect and the building erected the project was abandoned."[80] Next, William A. Burwell had provided in his 1821 will that if his son did not live to adulthood the county was to receive "a suitable piece of Land for a poor house," but, because his son lived to maturity, the county did not acquire the property. In February 1833 the Franklin County Court made the decision to proceed and appointed commissioners to find and purchase a tract of land. The commissioners reported in June that they had a verbal agreement to buy about 166 acres on the Pigg River from Meredith Dillion. The court approved the purchase and allocated $2,000 in county funds: $1,500 for the property and $500 for the construction of the poorhouse.[81]

The poorhouse envisioned by the court consisted of several buildings, not just one. The justices appointed Richard M. Taliaferro, William B. Williams, and Robert T. Woods as construction commissioners and ordered them to see

> that the house now occupied by Dillion be removed to a convenient site and rebuilt with a shed addition for a steward's house. They also direct that five buildings of one story each [be constructed] 34 feet by 16 with a chimney in the middle [to divide the building into two rooms], to be built of Bricks, the walls to be one brick thick, to be covered with shingles, floored with plank, and the Walls and ceiling plastered, the said buildings to be arranged in two rows, fronting each other, with a reasonable space between them, and the Steward's house placed at one end thereof.[82]

Residential unit at county poor farm, built after 1833. Mid-20th-century photo. (J. Francis Amos, Rocky Mount, Va.)

Strangely enough, the poor farm was built as directed but not on the Dillion property, which in fact was purchased by the court on 5 November 1833.[83] Even before the purchase the justices directed the commissioners to "rent or otherwise dispose of " the tract for the coming year; construction did not begin immediately and the justices wanted the county to derive some income from the land in the meantime.[84] The commissioners eventually built the poor farm several miles to the northwest of Rocky Mount, on the north bank of Blackwater River, just off present-day Route 737. After the poorhouse closed its doors in the late 1940s the buildings were demolished or altered as dwellings and the property became a general farm. Some of the structures still stand, built of brick laid in four-course

American bond. The contracter was Silas Heston, who had constructed the Jeffersonian courthouse in 1831.

In the 1850 census the farm had twenty-six occupants ranging in age from eight months to eighty-five years. Twelve of them were adults in their twenties or older, and the remainder were children. Five of the occupants were black. At least one of the white men was boarded out, probably because he was capable of performing some labor, and his caretaker was paid $20 a year for his trouble.[85]

The presence of blacks in the county poorhouse is a reminder that the days of slavery also were the days before racial segregation as it gradually came to be institutionalized, codified, and practiced after the Civil War. Blacks and whites lived and worked cheek by jowl; they did not live in separate neighborhoods, nor did they travel one in the front and the other in the rear of the same railroad car. There existed an enormous gulf, the gulf between those who had freedom and those who did not, but that separation was a legal and not a physical one. Black paupers lived much the same as white paupers—not very well. In the poorhouse those who had nothing at all lived more equally regardless of race, perhaps, than anyone else in society. If paupers no matter what color found themselves relegated to the lower rungs of the social ladder because of their dependence upon public charity, blacks in a white, slaveholding society were at or near the bottom rung in terms of freedom.

TWELVE

Life at the Bottom: Slaves and Free Blacks

One early fall day in 1791, several white men stood talking in William Lee's farmyard in Bedford County. Three of the men—David Morgan, Thomas Prunty, and James Stone—were Franklin County residents. Morgan's farm wagon also stood in Lee's yard, and seated in the wagon was a family of seven black slaves, Sampson, his wife, and their five children. Morgan and Lee were about to conclude a transaction commonplace throughout the South: the exchange of money for human beings. Once the exchange had been made, Morgan and his new property would ride together to Morgan's farm in Franklin County, and the slave family would continue its life of servitude under a new master.

While the white men haggled nearby, the thoughts of Sampson and his family probably turned on two subjects: what kind of master Morgan might be, and the home and friends they were leaving against their will. One of Sampson's daughters, Betty (who was twelve or thirteen years old), faced leaving the only home she had ever known and, as James Stone later put it,

> appearing to be averse to going with Morgan began to cry and . . . Mr. Lee offered to take the Negroe again of Mr. Morgan to which the sd. Morgan assented, when the girl got out of the Waggon. But the other Negroes, to wit, the father & mother insisting to keep thar child, the sd. Morgan again directed her to get in the Waggon, & Morgan had them carried off.[1]

If Sampson hoped his family might remain together he soon was disillusioned, however. On his way home, Morgan stopped the wagon at the house of Moses and Elizabeth Ray and ordered Betty to get out, for it was his intention to lease her to the Rays. Elizabeth Ray noticed that Betty limped when she climbed down from the wagon but did not dissuade her husband from leasing the girl at the rate of

231

seven pounds ten shillings, which was about the going rate for a grown woman. When after a few days Betty's limp still remained, Elizabeth Ray asserted,

> I asked her to Shew me the wond [wound] that made her Lame and She Did so I Shaw a [*illegible*] & old Skare [scar] it appeared to be whare hur hip and thy [thigh] Joind it was a large Sunken place and . . . if the Said negro was Ever to have a Child it wold render hur Totallery incapable of service.[2]

That the Rays were willing to rent a girl from David Morgan at the rate usually paid for a woman most likely meant that slave labor was scarce in their part of Franklin County. That did not mean, however, that they did not expect good value for their money. When Elizabeth Ray discovered the truth about Betty's limp, she and her husband demanded that Morgan reduce his rate. He agreed to a rate of five pounds ten shillings. Nevertheless, the Rays soon decided that Betty simply could not do the work expected of her, that she was worth no more than her "victuals and Cloaths," and that in fact they did not want her even if she were presented as a gift.[3] They returned Betty to Morgan, who admitted that a partially disabled slave "will not hire for more than about half the price such Negroes would, if sound."[4]

David Morgan was convinced he had been cheated by William Lee, who had deceived him not only about Betty, but also about her father, Sampson. Morgan freely admitted at the time of his dealings with Lee that he "was no judge of negroes" and was compelled to take Lee's word for the state of their health. When he noticed that Betty

> halted as she walked David Morgan asked said Lee what was the cause of her Lameness. Said Lee Told him it was Occationed by a hurt She got in a Craddle when she was an Infant which Caused one of the Sinews of [her] leg to Shrink and that it did her no damage now and that he never had put her to any busness more than Toting water and such Like Chores about the house and that he had often observed her when Romping and playing to be as active as any Child about the house. Then David Morgan went into the field where the Old negros was at work. When he Returned he asked William Lee if there was not something the matter with the old negroe man [Sampson]. William Lee answered I thought to have mentioned and it had like to have slipped my memmory that I have heard him often Complean when Rooling Logs and toting fodder and such like Labour complean of a Little Rupture [hernia] in his grine [groin] but it never hurt his Service.[5]

Lee said that Sampson, "in cases of hard service," and in cloudy weather, "was obliged to ware a Tress [truss]."[6]

Morgan also attempted some sharp dealing. Soon after his purchase of Sampson and his family from Lee, Morgan sold a slave named Nell—possibly Sampson's wife or one of his daughters—to George Mabry, Sr., of Patrick County. After the Rays returned Betty to him, Morgan attempted to trade her for Nell, but Mabry observed her disability and declined. Morgan then offered him Betty and thirty pounds, but to no avail; even the offer of thirty pounds and Sampson was refused. Mabry said that he would not have taken forty pounds and either Betty or Sampson for Nell.[7]

William Lee's response to the accusations that he knowingly sold what Morgan and the others insisted were damaged goods was, in effect, to blame the slaves. He retorted that he had been open and frank in discussing Betty's lameness and Sampson's rupture, and that these disabilities had not prevented either slave from working while he owned them. He admitted that Sampson's hernia hurt him if he was overworked, but that he could work well in moderation. Lee also maintained that he had offered to take the slaves back if they proved unsatisfactory. Not only had Morgan declined the offer, he said, but he had also praised Sampson's performance.[8] Lee seemed to suggest that either Morgan and the Rays were managing the slaves improperly, or else the slaves were pretending to be more disabled than they were in reality.

The story of Sampson, Nell, Betty, and their family illustrates, among other things, the near-total control slave owners enjoyed over their human property, and the near-total lack of control that slaves had over their lives. If a slaveholder wished, for example, he could sell, trade, give away, or lease any or all of his slaves to another white farmer. In 1937 a former slave recalled the trauma of being sold at age nine, with two of her cousins, to a slave trader passing through Powhatan County on his way to the slave market in Richmond. At the market Benjamin Tinsley, who later moved to Franklin County, negotiated with the trader:

> After dey talked a long time, he said he wanted me. I thought when dey was talkin' dat he was goina take all of us. When be bought me an' started to take me off, I ax him if he was goina take all of us. He said no. De trader said he was goina carry dem down in Georgia. I started cryin'. Massa Tinsley asked what I was cryin' for. I said I didn' want to leave my cousins. He said he didn' want dem an' den he carried me on off. I never did see my cousins no mo'. . . . Some years after de War one of my daughters carried me back down to Powhatan County on de James River to see if I could find my mother. After we got dere, dey tol' me my mother had been dead three years.[9]

A slave owner could keep the slave family together or split it asunder. He could treat his slaves well or poorly; he could overwork them or allow them adequate rest; if they disobeyed him his options ranged from cajoling them into doing his will to beating them to a point just short of death; and if he were so inclined he could sexually assault any of the women at any time. If he were to kill one of his slaves, or abuse one of them so badly that his neighbors complained, he faced arrest and trial before an "impartial" jury of his fellow white males.

A slave such as Sampson had no more rights than the horses that pulled the wagon in which he sat. The slaves, like the horses, were valuable to their owners only for their labor. Although most slaves worked in fields or as house servants in Franklin County, others labored in tobacco factories, brickyards, or as carpenters, masons, and blacksmiths. Whatever their work, only the slave owner reaped the benefits. Sometimes, though, the owner of a slave who was a skilled craftsman allowed him to keep at least part of his earnings as an incentive to work harder.

Common sense also suggested that unless the owner was below the standard for the average slaveholder, the slaves would be housed, fed, and clothed adequately enough, which was to say in a fairly perfunctory manner. The housing would be crude and uncomfortable (probably a drafty, dirt-floored log cabin such as the first white settlers threw together for a season or two); the food would consist largely of cornmeal, sweet potatoes, molasses, and stews made with the poorer cuts of pork; and the clothing would be one "suit" per year (in what was probably an extraordinary example, five yards of cotton for shirts, seven yards of oznaburg for britches, a pair of stockings, and one pair of shoes for each man;[10] enough cloth for a few dresses for each woman).

Slave cabin at Marshall Waid farm on Chestnut Creek near Sydnorsville. (Blue Ridge Institute, Ferrum, Va.)

If a slave fell ill his owner usually dosed him with home remedies. Years later the memory of these cure-alls had not faded from the mind of one former slave, who recalled that the slaveholder's wife "had three kinds of medicine that would cure everything":

> One was vinegar nail, one rosin pills and the other was tar. When we had aches or pains in the stomach or the back she would make us drink "vinegar nail" which was made by getting about a pound of square cut iron nails and put them in a jug with a lot of vinegar, then at night we had to take two rosin pills. These pills were made of raw pine rosin. When we had the tooth ache or the ear ache she would fill the tooth or ear full of tar. We never had a doctor.[11]

Occasionally a slave owner summoned a doctor to treat his slaves if they declined almost to the point of death or failed to respond to treatment; preventive medicine was almost unheard of. Alice W. Saunders despaired of the life of one of her slaves in 1814: "Mr. S. thinks it highly probable we shall lose that negroe woman Jenny. She was extremely ill when he was over, and had a little upstart who knew nothing of his business to attend on her. Sister Morris has lost two."[12] Slaves contracted a wide variety of diseases; Dr. Henry Dillard made a call in 1861, for example, to the slave quarters on a farm where he "treated child with secondary Syphilis at the quarters."[13]

Slave owners granted their servants some leisure time and occasional encouragements. Generally they allowed their slaves a small plot of land to cultivate for their own use. They provided them passes to walk from one farm to another for short visits. They allowed them to earn and keep money from extra work. A slave might save enough money eventually to purchase his own freedom; once free, he could then save part of his wages toward the purchase of his wife or his children. Christmas, when farm work slackened anyway, was about the only holiday of the year for most slaves. During the Christmas season a generous owner might give his servants extra days off, hand out bonuses of cash or food, and forgive transgressions.

The leasing of such slaves as Betty was a very common practice in Franklin County before the Civil War. Perhaps the small size of the average farm and the high price of slaves excluded most farmers from the ranks of slaveholders. In 1786, for instance, more than 76 percent of Franklin County residents did not pay taxes on any slaves; of the remaining 24 percent, three-quarters of them were taxed for five slaves or fewer. By 1800 more than 82 percent of residents paid no taxes on slaves. Only about 18 percent of residents were so taxed, and of those about 88 percent paid taxes on five or fewer slaves.[14]

The phrase "paid taxes" is significant because renters of slaves usually were responsible for paying the personal property taxes on them. That is, the person who paid the tax on a slave was not necessarily a slave owner; he may only have leased the slave. Moreover, the tax books do not reflect short-term leasing arrangements between slaveholders and nonowners, such as for a harvest, house and barn construction, or other short-term projects. The tax figures demonstrate, however, that there was a decline in the use of slaves, whether through ownership or long-term leasing, of 6 percent between 1786 and 1800. This decline may indicate that slavery was not as profitable or as popular in Franklin County as it was in the eastern part of the state, at least in the late eighteenth century.

Census figures, however, contradict this trend over the long run. In 1790 Franklin County's population was 6,842; of that number, 5,735 were white, 34 were free blacks, and 1,073 were slaves. Proportionally, 84 percent of the population were whites, half of one percent were free blacks, and just under 16 percent were slaves. By 1860, out of 20,098 inhabitants, there were 13,642 whites, 105 free blacks, and 6,351 slaves. On the eve of the Civil War, then, the proportions had shifted dramatically: 68 percent of the population was white, half a percent free black, and just under 32 percent slave. In other words, the proportion of slaves to whites in the county had doubled, while the actual number of slaves had increased sixfold. Clearly, in Franklin County as in much of the South, whites found slavery a profitable system of labor.[15]

The personal property tax records of 1861 support this conclusion. Among all Franklin County taxpayers, too, the proportion of persons who paid taxes on slaves had increased to 25 percent in 1861 from 18 percent in 1800. Of this group, one-third paid taxes on only one slave, while fully 77 percent paid for five slaves or fewer. Only fourteen slave owners (less than 2 percent) paid taxes on twenty slaves or more: John Patterson, Owen Price, and John Wade, Sr. (twenty); Abram T. Holland (twenty-two); Samuel Hale (twenty-three); Walter C. Callaway and William H. Edwards (twenty-four); Jane Jones Saunders (twenty-nine); Peter M. Guerrant (thirty-one); James S. Callaway and Thomas C. Callaway (thirty-four); Harvey Clayton (thirty-five); John S. Hale (fifty-four); and Peter Saunders,

Jr. (sixty-five). The county remained, then, one in which the vast majority of residents owned no slaves, while those who did generally owned fewer than five. Many nonslaveholders followed the long-established practice of leasing slaves; support for the system remained deeply entrenched.[16]

While David Morgan leased Betty in 1791 to Moses Ray for one year at seven pounds ten shillings, the other details of the rental agreement are not known. They probably differed little, however, from those agreed to by Milly Thomas and John Livesay in 1784: Livesay leased a woman slave from Thomas on 28 September 1784 and was to pay seven pounds for her hire before 28 September 1785. He also had to provide clothes for the slave and pay the tax on her, which was then deducted from the rental fee.[17] In another instance, on 20 November 1794 William Ryan and Thomas Sherwood hired a slave woman named Moll from the estate of Thomas Pinckard for one year. They agreed to pay the estate seven pounds fifteen shillings in addition to the tax, provide Moll with clothes, and support her child.[18]

Some farmers derived a considerable income from leasing out their slaves when they were not needed for work at home. Judge Fleming Saunders, for example, complained in 1833 that

> I have not been able as yet to hire out the usual number of young negroes, but still hope to do it, although little encouragement is given me to do so, they are generally returned badly clothed and without any pay. I have settled three plantations entirely under the management of negroes, how it may turn out I cannot say, but badly no doubt.[19]

On 23 January 1862 Fleming Saunders, Jr., the judge's son, leased one of his slaves, "a little negro girl Betsy Ann," to A. J. ("Jack") Shelton, who agreed

> to pay on the 25th Dec. 1862 the Sum of twelve dollars. I have further agreed to feed and treat her well, furnishing her a comfortable place to sleep. Also I am to furnish her with a summer and a winter suit of clothes complete, the summer dress of good cotton oznaburg and the winter dress of good home made Linsey and a pair of stockings and a pair of good sowed shoes at the end of the year.[20]

Apparently the arrangement did not prove suitable to Shelton, for a note on the back of the agreement reads "The girl was sent home Easter Sunday 20th April 1862."

Slave owners routinely used their servants as collateral for loans. For example, in July 1785 Isaac Rentfro struck a deal with William Walton for two slaves owned by Walton. Rentfro signed a mortgage in which Walton financed his purchase of

> one Negro Woman Named Rachel, and one Negro boy Named Bob [probably Rachel's son], and doth agree with the Sd Walton that In case, the above sd Money is not paid by the Above Mentioned time [25 December 1785] that I will deliver up the Sd Negro wench and boy imediately unto the Sd Walton to be Sot up at Public Vendue and Sold for Ready Cash.[21]

In another case a master used his slave as currency in kind. James Parbury agreed to pay Thomas Hutchings "a negro of the first rate" for value received of Hutchings (about £150 worth). When he failed to comply he was sued; the jury decided the case in the plaintiff's favor in August 1787.[22]

Slave owners occasionally sold their servants to satisfy court judgments. In 1803, for example, Samuel Hairston (the guardian for Jubal Early's orphans) won a judgment against Leonard Cheatham that included an attachment of some of Cheatham's property, in this case a slave girl named China. The Franklin County Court issued an order on 8 March 1803 that China be sold and the money from her sale be turned over to Hairston.[23] Presumably the sale took place and China was separated from her family and friends because Leonard Cheatham did not pay his debts.

The death of a master was viewed with concern by his slaves because to settle his estate they might be sold, or distributed among his heirs, thereby breaking up families. After Judge Fleming Saunders died on 23 May 1858, his executors disposed of part of his estate the next year, including many of the slaves. In a letter written to his brother Fleming on 28 July 1859 Peter Saunders, Jr., of Bleak Hill, described his efforts to purchase many of his father's slaves in order to keep them in the family. To arrange the necessary financing he had to visit a bank in Abingdon, and returned just in time for the sale:

> I did not much expect a sale of any of the negroes to take place last Monday and had not quite completed my pecuniary arrangements. I succeeded however as well as I had any right to expect and finding when I got to Abingdon that I could arrange to raise what money I wanted we thought it best to let the sale of twenty five of the negroes take place. I bought sixteen of them in for Ma Ma at an aggregate price of $9,115.00. I got $5,000.00 from the Bank at Salem and used $3,000.00 of the money provided by you in Lynchburg. I gave my check whilst in Abingdon for this amount on the Virginia Bank, and in order to be sure that the money was provided for the check I ran down on the cars from Roanoke on yesterday and attended to it in person. I returned the same evening only staying in Lynchburg 1 1/2 hours. I think it is a great relief for Ann and Mr. Preston that the negroes were sold. I bought in those that they wanted and the others were purchased by unexceptionable masters and in families. The traders did not get any of them. James and his family were not sold and it will require three or four thousand dollars for their purchase. I valued them at twenty nine hundred, but am afraid that they will sell for more. I dont think that it will be advisable for Ma Ma to buy more than Jane's family. The other negroes and all the personal property will be sold on the 4th Monday in next month.[24]

Not all slaves acquiesced quietly in their lives of involuntary servitude. Some chose among the various means of passive and active resistance available to them to protest their condition. Sampson and Betty, for instance, were suspected of using their disabilities to avoid work—probably the most common form of resistance. Such "strikes" were used rather than outright sabotage, since everyone on the farm, even the slaves, benefited from a good crop in an era of subsistence farming; likewise, everyone suffered if the crop was poor.

Some slaves were bold enough to threaten trouble overtly. One such instance was reported by William S. Morris in 1848 in a letter to his uncle, Judge Fleming

Saunders. Apparently Morris, who was in Lynchburg, was accompanied by a slave named Booker that belonged to his uncle. Judge Saunders's son Peter wrote Morris asking for the return of Booker, whom Morris had leased to a third party named Ives. Booker objected to returning to Franklin County, and Morris described the disagreement in his letter:

> About a week since I received a letter from Peter in which he desired me to send Booker to Franklin, and accordingly as soon as I could get him from Ives, with whom I had conditionally promised he could stay until the first of September, I sent him to Flat Creek [Judge Saunders's home in Campbell County], with Uncle Peter [Saunders, the judge's brother], who happened to be here in a marketing expedition, with the direction to get a horse there and proceed directly to Franklin. I think you are acting wisely to take him away from here, for although he has been sober generally, for the last month as far as I could judge, yet I can put no confidence in him and he is very much inclined to be idle. I could not get Ives to take him by the month or for the rest of the year at anything like a fair price, and I had determined to send him home, if I had not gotten Peter's letter, unless he would take him for a definite period at a definite price. I think it very probable, from the manifest reluctance with which he left here, and some expressions which he let slip, that he will come back here again, or stay at Flat Creek. If he comes back here, I shall inform him of your wishes for him to go to Abingdon and if he should refuse which would not surprise me, I shall put him in the charge either of some waggoner, or send him by some one going over in the Stage, peaceably if it can be done, forcibly if necessary. I have no idea of your being annoyed and put to inconvenience by a head strong negro if I can prevent it. I wrote to Peter yesterday, and informed him that I had complied with his letter, and expressed the belief that Booker would not get further than F. Creek unless he was compelled.[25]

The next level of resistance, which Booker had threatened, was running away. When Betty cried and refused to climb into David Morgan's wagon, Morgan acceded quickly to Lee's suggestion that he leave her behind, most likely because he knew that if she went unwillingly she might run away. If she had run off, Betty probably would have returned to the Lee farm in Bedford County—which she considered home—but some slaves ran away to be free. The chance of permanent freedom was slim, for patrols of whites kept a sharp eye out for black strangers. The best way for an escaped slave to remain free was to head for a free western state or territory or, if that was too far to roam, to slip into the free black community of a large Virginia city and attempt to blend in. First, however, there were miles of open countryside to negotiate and dozens of white patrollers to avoid. If captured, the slave was confined to jail, his or her description was advertised in the state's newspapers, and eventually the owner claimed and punished the slave. If the owner never came, then the slave was sold at public auction to a new owner.

Most slaveholders attempted to prevent runaways by making the slave's life bearable enough that he or she would lack the motivation to take to the roads. The most effective means of preventing runaways, however, was to keep slave families together. Most slave owners recognized the importance of this tactic and broke up families only when, in their view, there was an economic necessity.

Sometimes the dynamics were complicated. In 1814 Alice Saunders described how her husband, Judge Fleming Saunders, attempted to keep slave families together while distributing his work force among several farms:

> Mr. Saunders went over to Botetourt last week, and had less trouble about the Negroes than he calculated on. Absolum was the only one that made the smallest objection, and he disliked leaving his children by a negroe woman of my Brothers, though he will not acknowledge her as his wife. He has parted from poor old Martha. Lew has a wife belonging to Patty, who Mr. S. has promised to hire or purchase as my Brother may think proper. He will not agree to be sold, and is very anxious for Mr. S. to buy his wife. She is a negroe under a very good character, and Mr. S. is willing to give her full value. He will write to Brother upon the subject as soon as we hear he has gotten home.[26]

Although marriages between slaves were not recognized by the law, both master and slave acknowledged them. Slave marriages contributed to the stability of the plantation—from the master's viewpoint—and doubtless made the slave less apt to run away. For the slaves, the fact that the marriage was extralegal meant little because they had virtually no rights before the law anyway. At least marriage gave them a small share of autonomy within an almost totally oppressive system of life and labor.

Slave husbands and wives gave ample evidence of their devotion to each other. On 30 April 1861 James H. Roberts, the Floyd County farm overseer for Fleming and Robert Saunders, wrote of a slave whose wife had been transferred to Flat Creek plantation in Campbell County and was due to return: "If Lidney dont get Home soon I think Sparel Will certainly Have a Fit about her. I Believe she is about everything he is Thinking about now."[27] Sparrel took matters into his own hands a few days later when his wife still had not returned, as Roberts wrote on 9 May:

> Sparrel started Down to Campbell after his Wife last Friday night and met them in Franklin. I Was right smartly Freted at his going away and saying nothing about it. He taken Horse Bridle and Saddle and put out. He had been asking me to let him go for some time and I Would't consent to it and he told [me] some Morning I Would't find him on the place. He is all right since his Wife come.[28]

Judge Saunders and his wife, like other slaveholders, did not hesitate to sell several slaves when they believed it necessary. In 1817 Alice Saunders observed that her husband was

> just as much engaged about his plantation as if he had no Overseer at all. He generally goes out a little after eight, and I never see him again until about three in the evening. His negroes are pretty much dissatisfied with their new Overseer. He makes them work rather harder than they have been accustomed to. Mr. S. sold Nelly and her family a few days ago to a Dutchman not far from Brother's plantation. I was somewhat opposed to her Childrens going with her, particularly the eldest, but he thought they would fare better with people who would think it to their interest to take care of them

than w[ith] Negroes. I expect our Cook will go next. She has been giving herself some high airs lately.[29]

At the same time, slaveholders such as Judge Saunders routinely included their slaves under the affectionate umbrella of "family." Writing to his wife in 1835, Saunders told her,

I found upon getting home, things and matters in as good condition as I could have expected. The family with the exception of Moses and Doshe, well, the former had been Very sick, but says he is getting better, the latter Complaining of her leg, etc., etc. . . . Tell Fleming [their five-year-old son] Moses is too sick to make his wagon and that he must come up and see about it himself.[30]

Some slaves saw themselves as members of their master's family while others did not. The last resort of a desperate slave was violence, whether against himself, another slave, the possessions of white people, or white people themselves. Slave suicides are not reflected in the county records; so stringent were the laws against crimes and violence committed by slaves, however, that virtually any such act was one of suicide.

The murder of one slave by another was rare, but not unknown. It probably arose from the many tensions of slave life, particularly the strain of confinement in close quarters with the same people day after day. Sometimes one slave was accused of murdering another when the cause of death was not known, as in the case of Sarah, a slave of Samuel Hairston, who was charged with the murder of another of his slaves (also named Sarah), in September 1801. She pleaded not guilty before the Franklin County Court and was acquitted.[31] This case indicates that there was at least some chance of justice for slaves.

Other cases point to the opposite conclusion, however. On 3 January 1791 the Franklin County Court tried Aris Vaughan for being in collusion with a slave named Salem (the property of Archibald Gordon). Salem was accused of breaking into Daniel Brown's lumber house on the night of 6 April 1789 and stealing a new man's saddle, a pair of saddlebags, a sack bag, and six yards of tow linen. Vaughan pleaded not guilty; after examining witnesses, the court acquitted him. Salem also pleaded not guilty, but after the court examined more witnesses it found him guilty and ordered the sheriff to give him thirty-nine lashes on his bare back at the whipping post.[32] Taken at face value the case shows that the white man Vaughan "got away with it" while the slave Salem paid the price, but it is impossible to be certain because the evidence against each of them was not recorded.

Certainly, according to the standards of the day, Salem was fortunate to have endured only a whipping. Crimes against the property of white people often were punished by death. On 3 February 1824, for example, a female slave named Nancy, who belonged to Tyree G. Newbill, was convicted of burning the barn, cornhouse, wagon house, and chaff house of William Brooks on 22 January 1824. The Franklin County Court sentenced her to be hanged "at the usual place of execution" on 2 April, but she was reprieved on 17 February for transportation to Liberia. The state reimbursed her owner $250 for depriving him of his property.[33]

Judge Fleming Saunders described an incident at Bleak Hill that suggests the terror the white man's system of justice held for most slaves. On 6 April 1833 he was writing a letter to his wife when he was startled

> by an alarm given that Lewis Bottom [one of his slaves] had drowned himself. It seems the day before yesterday some person in the night set the school house on fire. Shortly after breakfast on the same day, and after I had gone to my Brother's the Major [Samuel Saunders], the Col. [Samuel Hairston] his Father and Brother comes over to my house, charges Daniel with it, and takes him to Compare and examine the tract, etc. In the evening when I returned from my Brother's Daniel makes great Complaint of the Col., etc., for which I gave him but little satisfaction, stating the general character of the negroes justify the charge or rather induced the making of it. The Col. came over yesterday morning to the mill to see me upon the subject. I told him I was very sorry he had not sent for me and enabled me to be present at the examination. He said he regreted my absence too, but something prevented. He said he was satisfied from the circumstances that Daniel was guilty. I told him I could not think so, that Daniel was by no means vindictive in his temper, that I did not pretend to say he was the best negroe I had but that he would not [commit] an act of that description, and the same time observing I had a settlement to make with Lewis and Abram, a little rascally of a mill boy was present, slipped over to where Lewis was at work and told him I intended to cut him all to pieces, whereupon he cleared out, and when I was writing [you] Tommy who was in the crib, said he heard as he supposed Anthony hallo out that Lewis Bottom had drowned himself in the race. He came runing to the house scared to death and put the whole plantation in alarm. Search was made but Lewis could not be found.[34]

Three days later the crisis passed, as Saunders reported that

> Lewis Bottom came home Saturday night and pretended to be deranged which I soon cured. Col. Hairston is now satisfied the schoolhouse was burnt by some of his own people, why it was done I cannot say. I hope it will give you pleasure to tell you in all those crosses I was never once out of temper, although I have had enough to provoke any human being.[35]

Of course, the irritations that plagued Saunders were less a matter of life and death than the accusation against Daniel, or the fear that gripped Lewis Bottom.

Although Saunders often seemed short-tempered with his servants, he and his wife and children had a genuine affection for some of them. The servants they preferred were probably those who "behaved" and appeared most obsequious and dutiful. Their master expected Daniel and Lewis Bottom to do his bidding, sometimes by traveling considerable distances, without supervision. In 1860, hearing that both slaves had died, Peter Saunders, Jr., wrote to his brother Fleming Saunders to commiserate:

> We were truly sorry to hear of Daniel's death, though a brief note of Ann, had somewhat prepared me for it. It is seldom that we see a better, and more faithful servant than he was. In him and Lewis, you have sustained a heavy loss at Flat Creek and I fear that their influence upon the other servants will be very much missed. There has been a good deal of laying up amongst the

servants here [Bleak Hill], though generally their complaints have not been very serious. There have been one or two cases of severe sore-throats.[36]

The overt relations between slave owners and slaves ran the gamut from cordial affection to anger and hatred. Sometimes slaves in their rage resorted to violence against their masters, almost always as a futile act of desperation. The most serious crime a slave could commit was one of assaulting a white person. This was the ultimate act of resistance for which the full fury of the white-controlled legal and judicial system was reserved. Perhaps the unforgivable crime, in the eyes of whites, was the rape of a white woman. Retribution was swift: Jack, a slave owned by Jubal Early, allegedly raped Mrs. Sarah Hickerson on 16 October 1794; on 25 October he was tried and condemned by the Franklin County Court, and on 28 November he was executed.[37] Likewise, a slave named Anthony, who belonged to William Ferguson, was condemned on 15 September 1817 to hang for the rape of Juriah Young. The sentence was carried out on 14 November "between the hours of twelve and two O'Clock . . . at the usual place of execution."[38] Even attempted rape merited the death penalty in the eyes of the white majority. On 3 May 1830 the Franklin County Court sentenced Henry, a slave of John W. Lumsden, to hang for that crime; the sentence was executed on 25 June.[39]

Behind the harshness of the laws against slave crime was, of course, the white Virginian's fear of slave insurrection. The example that burned itself into every white mind was the slave uprising in Santo Domingo in the 1790s when more than sixty thousand people were killed. In 1800 a rebellion was planned in Henrico County but collapsed when a slave betrayed its leader, Gabriel Prosser. The slaveholder's worst nightmare came true in August 1831 when a group of slaves in Southampton County revolted under the leadership of a slave preacher named Nat Turner. More than sixty whites were murdered in the night by slaves who during the day had seemed docile enough to their masters. In the frenzy of retribution that followed, more than one hundred slaves were killed and Turner and twelve of his followers were hanged.

It is difficult to underestimate the panic, hysteria, and paranoia that gripped white Virginia in the wake of Nat Turner's Rebellion. It is also difficult to overestimate the importance of the rebellion to North-South relations and the coming of the Civil War: it truly was a point on which the history of the country turned. Before Nat Turner struck, many southerners viewed slavery as a "troublesome burden" that might be lifted by a gradual emancipation that they believed would be as liberating to the masters as to the slaves. Others saw the institution as a "necessary evil" that was essential to the current economy of the South but that might be obliterated in the misty future. After the rebellion, however, conservatives touted slavery as a "positive good" that kept the savage blacks properly subservient to white masters. Before the insurrection the slave laws were strict but afterward they achieved new levels of oppressiveness; the rights of free blacks were severely limited; abolitionist literature was censored and its possession became a crime; and the debate in the South over slavery was silenced.

On the other hand, an enlightened mind in the governor's chair, John Floyd, attempted during the months following the rebellion to lead the General Assembly toward the gradual, if not the immediate, abolition of slavery. He reasoned that the only certain way to prevent similar slaughters in the future was to rid the state of the evil institution that had spawned them, not to add to its oppressiveness by enacting harsher laws. His view, unfortunately, was overwhelmed by the conservatives in the legislature, and Virginia and the South turned down the long road to war.

After the hysteria over Nat Turner's Rebellion subsided, the lives of most slaves went on much as before. Most of them labored as agricultural workers. They tended crops, raised livestock, cooked, cleaned house, and did general chores around the farm. A few worked at a trade or in industry, at the Washington Iron Works or as blacksmiths or carpenters. In the 1780s and 1790s, for example, a slave named George, who was owned by Henry Loving, was "by trade a carpenter" and was hired by John Hook to build a barn for him.[40] Besides paying for George's clothes and taxes, Hook agreed to lease him from Loving for £39 per year—or roughly five times the rate for an unskilled slave such as Betty. Highly skilled slaves were rare because the demand for their skills often enabled them to earn enough extra money to purchase their freedom.

Skilled or semiskilled slaves whose owners hired them out were better prepared for true freedom when it came in 1865 than those who spent their lives in farm labor at home. Booker T. Washington's stepfather, Washington Ferguson, for example, worked at the Kanawha saltworks in present-day West Virginia, at tobacco factories, and on railroad construction gangs. His master, Josiah Ferguson, found him to be a troublemaker and hired out his labor rather than have him around the farm, which was across the road from the Burroughs farm. When the Civil War ended, Washington Ferguson, who had run away to the saltworks, was able to send for young Booker and the rest of his family and support them because of his earlier experience with the free labor market.[41]

Little is known of the everyday details of slaves' lives in Franklin County. Slaves were forbidden to read and write, so few left letters or diaries describing their lives. To judge from the evidence left by travelers and white slaveholders, the slaves' routines consisted of long days of labor in the fields, farm chores, and household duties. Some aspects of slave life in Franklin County from the slaves' point of view, however, were revealed in three interviews with former slaves between 1937 and 1940: Baily Cunningham, Martha Showvely, and Martha Zeigler. The interviews were conducted by a black, William T. Lee, and two whites, I. M. Warren and Essie W. Smith, as participants in the Federal Writers' Project during the Great Depression.[42] And one of Franklin County's most famous sons, Booker T. Washington, wrote briefly about his childhood as a slave on the farm of James Burroughs in his autobiography, *Up From Slavery*.

Baily Cunningham confirmed that slave diets varied as little as the daily work. Often the slaves baked their cornmeal into hoecakes or ashcakes that were doused with molasses before being eaten, while they combined pork and vegetables into a stew. Certain vegetables may have been introduced or retained in the American cuisine because slaves preferred them: okra, turnip greens, black-eyed peas, eggplant, watermelons, and peanuts. A number of slave-created recipes have remained popular, especially those for the soupy stews known as gumbos. Slaves also supplemented their diets with fish they caught and wild animals they trapped or, occasionally, were allowed to hunt.[43]

According to Cunningham, whose master, "Bemis" (probably Parmenas) English, owned a farm about eleven miles from Rocky Mount,

We ate twice a day, about sunup and at sundown. All the work hands ate in the cabins and all the children took their *cymblin* [squash] *soup bowl* to the big kitchen and got it full of cabbage soup, then we were allowed to go [to] the table where the white folks ate and get the crumbs from the table. We sat on the ground around the quarters to eat with wooden spoons. Rations were given to the field hands every Monday morning. They would go to the smokehouse and the misses would give us some meal and meat in our sack. We were allowed to go to the garden or field and get cabbage, potatoes and corn or any other vegetables and cook in our shanties. We had plenty to eat. We had a large iron baker with a lid to bake bread and potatoes and a large iron kettle to boil things in. On Saturday morning we would go to the smokehouse and get some flour and a piece of meat with a bone so we could have a hoe-cake for dinner on Sunday. Sometimes we had plenty of milk and coffee.[44]

Booker T. Washington, in contrast, wrote that he could not recall

a single instance during my childhood or early boyhood when our entire family sat down to the table together, and God's blessing was asked, and the family ate a meal in a civilized manner. On the plantation . . . meals were gotten by the children very much as dumb animals get theirs. It was a piece of bread here and a scrap of meat there. It was a cup of milk at one time and some potatoes at another. Sometimes a portion of our family would eat out of the skillet or pot, while some one else would eat from a tin plate held on the knees, and often using nothing but the hands with which to hold the food.[45]

Cunningham's clothing, until he was twenty years old (he was probably born about 1838), consisted of what he called "shirt tails": "It was a long garment that came down to the knees. The boys and girls never wore but one garment even in the winter time. It was made large and out of cotton, flax, or wool on the old loom which was kept going all the year."[46] He insisted that he "never had on 'britches' or a suit of clothes . . . [and] never had a hat or shoes until I was twenty." The field-workers, on the other hand, "had wooden sole shoes, the wooden bottom was made of maple, the size of the foot, one half inch thick or thicker and the leather

Slave shoe or clog, from Bremo, Fluvanna County. (The Museum of the Confederacy.)

nailed to the wood. Our master had lots of sheep and the wool was made into yarn and we had yarn socks in the winter."[47]

Booker T. Washington, in remembering his childhood as a slave in Franklin County, agreed with Cunningham about the clothing they wore. "The first pair of shoes that I recall wearing," he wrote,

> were wooden ones. They had rough leather on the top, but the bottoms, which were about an inch thick, were of wood. When I walked they made a fearful noise, and besides this there were very inconvenient, since there was no yielding to the natural pressure of the foot. . . . The most trying ordeal that I was forced to endure as a slave boy, however, was the wearing of a flax shirt. [Because the fabric was so rough, putting on a new shirt was] almost equal to the feeling that one would experience if he had a dozen or more chestnut burrs, or a hundred small pin-points, in contact with his flesh. . . . Until I had grown to be quite a youth this single garment was all that I wore.[48]

According to Cunningham the slaves on the English farm lived more comfortably than most because their master was wealthy. He described their housing as

> log cabins, some had one room and some had two rooms, and board floors. . . . The cabins were covered with boards [from English's sawmill], nailed on and had stick-and-mud chimneys. We had home-made beds, corded, with mattresses made of linen filled with straw, and pillows the same and a woolen or cotton blanket. We had home-made tables and chairs with wooden bottoms. . . . The cabins were built in two rows not very far from the misses big house. My mother kept house for the our misses and looked after the quarters and reported anything going wrong to the misses.[49]

The lot of Booker T. Washington, his mother, and his brother and sister may have been more typical of slaves in the county:

> I was born in a typical log cabin, about fourteen by sixteen feet square. . . . [It] was not only our living-place, but was also used as the kitchen for the plantation. My mother was the plantation cook. The cabin was without glass windows; it had only openings in the side which let in the light, and also the cold, chilly air of winter. There was a door to the cabin—that is, something that was called a door—but the uncertain hinges by which it was hung, and the large cracks in it, to say nothing of the fact that it was too small, made the room a very uncomfortable one. . . . There was no wooden floor in our cabin, the naked earth being used as a floor. . . . While the poorly built cabin caused us to suffer with cold in the winter, the heat from the open fireplace in summer was equally trying. . . . I cannot remember having slept in a bed . . . [we children instead] had a pallet on the dirt floor, or, to be more correct, we slept in and on a bundle of filthy rags laid upon the dirt floor.[50]

The slaves' recreational opportunities generally were limited to such entertainment they devised within the confines of their quarters: religious services if the whites allowed them, visits to friends and relatives on nearby farms, and working as a group or in families on their private vegetable plots. These activities on their home farms were monitored by the slaveholder and his family. Gatherings of neighborhood slaves for religious services, dances, or friendly visits were closely regulated both by the civil authorities and the slave owners, however. By 1850 the laws of Virginia decreed that if

> any person knowingly permit a slave, not belonging to him, to remain on his plantation, lot or tenement, above four hours at one time, without leave of the owner or manager of such slave, he shall be fined three dollars; and any person who shall so permit more than five such slaves to be at one time on his plantation, lot or tenement, shall be fined one dollar for each slave above that number, and such assemblage shall be deemed an unlawful assembly.
>
> The object of the first clause of this section is to protect private rights, by preventing persons from knowingly permitting the slaves of others to tarry on their premises, without the owner's leave, for an unreasonable time. The object of the last clause is to guard the public against assemblages which might be dangerous to the peace or injurious to morals in a much shorter time than four hours.[51]

Reconstruction of Booker T. Washington's birthplace cabin at the Booker T. Washington National Monument. 1968 photo. (Virginia Department of Historic Resources.)

All the laws and supervision did not prevent the slaves from getting together occasionally for dances and visits, however. Indeed the slave owners probably realized that these events acted as a safety valve. In December 1794, a few days after Christmas, a traveler passing through the county on the Great Wagon Road remarked in his journal that he had stopped at the "Widow Forgesons [probably Elizabeth Ferguson, widow of John Ferguson, who died in 1789 or 1790] where we met with about 30 Negroes at a Ball in what they Call a Negro house."[52] Baily Cunningham remembered that before the Civil War the adult slaves

> had big dances at night, sometimes. Somebody would play the fiddles and some the banjo and sometimes had a drum. We did the "buck dance." A boy and girl would hold hands and jump up and down and swing around keeping time with the music. We would dance awhile then go to the other room and

drink coffee, corn whisky or apple brandy, sometimes some of us would get drunk. We would dance and play all night but had to be ready to work next day. We had to get a pass from our master or misses to go to the dance [on another farm], as we were afraid the "Patty Rolers" [slave patrollers] would get us. The master would have eight or ten men on horses watching and any one caught without a pass was taken up and punished, sometimes whipped.[53]

Martha Showvely also recalled the dances: "De white folks 'lowed us to have dances on Sat'day nights. I 'member dere was a man named Lewis Cain who used to play de banjo an' call de figgers for de dances."[54]

In contrast, Booker T. Washington once was asked what he remembered of the "sports and pastimes that I engaged in during my youth." He was shocked to realize that

until that question was asked it had never occurred to me that there was no period of my life that was devoted to play. From the time that I can remember anything, almost every day of my life has been occupied in some kind of labour.[55]

Worship services held for slaves had to be supervised by a white man to ensure that the slaves were not surreptitiously teaching one another to read and write. Baily Cunningham recalled that the slaves on the English farm "never went to school or to church."[56] A slave could not purchase liquor, or sell anything to a white man, without the consent of his owner. A tavern owner who violated either of these edicts could lose his license. In addition, no slave could hire himself out without the consent of his owner, although slaveholders frequently hired out extra slaves. Baily Cunningham, for example, was leased "to a man running a hotel in Lynchburg when he was twenty years old"; he also reported that "all the field hands our master did not need on the plantation were sold (hired out) to the tobacco factories at Lynchburg."[57]

White people, in Franklin County as elsewhere in the South, largely took for granted the institution of slavery and the restrictions on the activities of slaves. Aside from the Brethren, who generally kept their opposition to slavery to themselves, most white county residents spent little time thinking about the institution whether or not they owned slaves. They seldom uttered opinions about slavery in private correspondence, much less in public. After the Revolution, in some parts of the South, there was a wave of manumissions as revolutionaries suffered crises of conscience over the disparity between their own newly won freedom and the lack of it for most American blacks. If there were any such crises and manumissions in Franklin County, however, they were not recorded.

There were manumissions in Franklin County, although the motives for them are not clear. The first recorded "freeing" of slaves was instead the recognition of a legal fact. After Colonel John Early died in the summer of 1804 at the age of forty-seven, his will revealed that several of his servants were in reality free blacks and not slaves.

I give & bequeath to my three natural Sons, Samech, Jubal, and Melchizedech, all the residue of my Estate both real and personal, to be

equally divided to them by my Executors, except the following negroes to
wit: Hannah and her Six Children, namely, Bacchus, Ruth, Courtes [Curtis],
Betty, James, and Sam, who it is my last Will and desire shall be free, as
Hannah was born free, the Children consequently are.[58]

Because Virginia law did not recognize slave marriages, the status of the mother
determined the status of her children: if she was a slave, so were her children;
likewise, the offspring of a free black mother also were free. Early's will was
probated on 3 September 1804. On 1 October, in accordance with the laws of
Virginia, Hannah's six children appeared before county court justice Moses
Greer, Sr., and he registered them as "free Negroes":

No. 1. Bacchus aged 32 years, a bright Mulatto, with straight hair, five feet
eight Inches high, with a Scar on his right cheek, emancipated by John
Early's Will proved in Franklin Court.
No. 2. Ruth aged 30 years, a Dark Mulatto, with curled hair, five feet 3¼
Inches high, Emancipated as above.
No. 3. Betty, aged 26 years, a Very bright Mullatto, with Straight hair, five
feet four Inches high, Emancipated as above.
No. 4. James aged 23 years, a bright Mullatto with straight hair, five feet 10½
Inches high, with a Scar over the right eye, Emancipated as above.
No. 5. Coutis [Curtis] aged 28 years, a Dark Mullatto, with Curled hair, Six
feet high, with a wound, or Scar on the third Finger of the left hand,
Emancipated as above.
No. 6. Sam aged 21 years, a bright Mullatto with straight hair & Grey eyes,
five feet 9½ Inches high, Emancipated as above.[59]

The registration of Hannah's children shows them to be typical of most
emancipated slaves: they were "mulatto," which meant in the legal parlance of
the day that they had "one fourth part, or more, of negro blood."[60] It was another
way—the preferred way, to whites—of saying that Hannah's children had white
ancestors as well as black, perhaps a white father or grandfather. Most emancipated slaves, indeed most free blacks who were freeborn, were mulattoes. By law,
a free mulatto was subject to the same restrictions as a free person of African
ancestry only. In some cases, however, mulattoes or their children who were
light-skinned enough eventually "passed" for white, as suggested by the gradual
disappearance of racial indicators for a few free blacks in tax and census
records.[61]

Only a handful of white Franklin County slave owners freed their slaves,
usually after the owner's death through the provisions of his will. William A.
Burwell, one of the two men to serve in the United States Congress from the
county during the early nineteenth century, provided for the emancipation of his
slaves in his 1821 will. According to his will, however, the slaves would only be
freed if his son did not live to adulthood, if they remained in bondage for two or
three years first to earn money to support themselves, and if they left Virginia for
the western United States within five years. Because Burwell's son survived, the
emancipation did not occur. Burwell added the following to the end of his will,
though: "I must beg my Executors to treat my Slaves with strick justice & see that
they are never treated with barbarity."[62]

John Wray wrote a will in November 1832, little more than a year after Nat Turner's Rebellion, that provided for the eventual emancipation of his slaves. Unfortunately for the slaves, more than twenty-five years passed before their manumission became a reality. Their emancipation did not occur until 31 May 1858, after the death of Wray's widow. Fourteen slaves survived to claim their freedom.[63]

Catherine B. Leftwich liberated her slaves in her will, which was probated in January 1853. It was January 1857, however, before the Franklin County Court ordered "that an authenticated copy of the said Will be furnished each one of the following named negroes with a description of their persons." The freed slaves were Terry (aged about twenty-five); Louis (about thirty-five); Alexander (about thirty-one); Alexander's wife, Milly (about twenty-four); and their children Mary Jane (seven), James (two), and George W. (eleven months).[64]

Two slave owners, Henry T. Callaway and William Callaway, emancipated their slaves with deeds of manumission. William Callaway emancipated six of his slaves in this way on 15 April 1850.[65] On 10 January 1851 Henry T. Callaway wrote a deed in which he freed his slave David[66]—but only after Callaway's death, which did not occur until 1853.[67] Although the county court permitted David Callaway to remain in Virginia, it denied William Callaway's former slaves that privilege.[68]

Some slaves sued for their freedom and won. On 4 March 1805, for instance, a slave named Mingo appeared before the Franklin County Court to argue that he should be freed.

> On the motion of Mingo & on his petition presentd. to the Court stating his Claim to freedom under the Laws of this Com. Wealth, his case was referd. to Nathl. H. Claiborne & Fleming Saunders Gent. practicing atto[rney]s in this court, who thereupon reported that in their opinion he is entitled to his freedom. It is therefore ordered that he have leave to Sue Mary Austin who holds him in Slavery, in forma pauperis, and the said F. Saunders & N. H. Claiborne are assigned to him as counsel, and it ordered that he remain in Custody of the Sheriff of this county until he gives him bond & security in the sum of £3 in this court, or with the Clerk thereof with condition to have him forth coming to answer the Jud[gment] of this Court, and that the said Mary Austin do not maltreat or abuse him in consequence of this suit, but allow him reasonable time after his having given such Bond & security, to go to the office, to take out [subpoenas] for his witness, and to do whatever else shall be necessary for procuring Testimony.[69]

A year later, on 4 March 1806, Mingo won his freedom. A jury was sworn to hear the case of *Mingo (a Pauper)* v. *Mary Austin* and

> to enquire into the Plaintiff's right to his freedom, and of the Damages which he hath Sustained by occasion of the Defendant's detaining him in Slavery, to wit, Nathan Greer, Joseph Greer, Obediah White, Benjamin Booth, Burwell Rives, Joseph Hembrick, David Robertson, Martin Woody, Asa Hodges, William Clay, John Ferguson, & Amos Hundley, returned a Verdict that the Plaintiff is a free man & not a Slave, and that he hath sustained Damages by occasion of the Defendant's detaining him in Slavery to one cent, besides his

costs. Therefore It is considered by the Court that the Plaintiff is a free man
& not a Slave, & that he recover against the Defendant, his damages aforesaid
in form aforesaid assessed, and his costs by him about his suit in this behalf
expended.[70]

Although the damages to Mingo for more than a year in slavery were considered
by the jury only to be worth a penny, the former slave had not won a hollow
victory. The suit cost him nothing, because Mary Austin was required to pay his
attorneys' fees and other court costs. Had that award not been made, Mingo would
have begun his life as a free man hopelessly (for him) in debt. Most important,
Mingo won his freedom. As a free black resident of a slave state, however, Mingo
could be said to have traded one set of insoluble problems and stifling
restrictions for another.

Indeed, after 1806 Mingo could not remain in Virginia—where he probably
had family and friends still in bondage—without the permission of the county
court. Obtaining permission was a complicated process that required him to
provide character witnesses, petition the court, and post a notice on the
courthouse door. If the court denied him permission to remain in the state he had
to leave within a year; if permission to remain was granted he was registered by
the court (as in the case of John Early's emancipated slaves) and given a copy of
the registration to serve as an identification paper. If Mingo left the state he could
never return; likewise, free black friends and family members living outside
Virginia could not move into the state to be with him. He was required to pay a
special tax on himself and he had to renew his registration at least every five
years.

The restrictions and special laws were more than a hint that free blacks were
not wanted in Virginia; those acts were intended to be just short of an eviction
notice. Ironically, there were harsher laws concerning free blacks in the Upper
South, of which Virginia was a part, than in such Deep South states as South
Carolina and Louisiana. From the slave owners' perspective, for freedom to
beckon runaways to the nearby states of Pennsylvania and Ohio was bad enough;
for their property to be further tempted by the example of free blacks in their
midst was almost intolerable. For many whites the phrase "free black" was a
contradiction in terms, just as the phrase "black slave" was redundant.

Free blacks were subject to harassment by any white who was so inclined. They
could be arrested by any white person and confined to jail if found without proof
of their freedom. George Welch suffered such a fate in 1803. The court minutes of
1 August 1803 reported that

a mulatto man who calls himself George Welch thirty years old about five
feet six Inches high, with a blemish in his left Groin, who had been
committed to the Jail of this county for want of Credentials of his Freedom,
was this day brought before the Court, and it appearing from the Testimony
of John Windle, that the said George Welch was born of Free Parents in the
State of Pennsylvania, and that he served his time with the father of him the
said John Windle, by Indentures executed in the said state, It is the opinion
of the court that the said George is a free man & not a slave. Therefore it is
considered that he be discharged from imprisonment, and be registered,
No. 2 in this county.[71]

Sometimes free blacks were enslaved against their will. Deborah Payne, for example, was a free black woman who was brought from Maryland and enslaved by one Leonora Smith, then sold several times. Among her owners were William Davenport, who sold her to Thomas Livesey, of Franklin County, who then sold her to Walter Guild, of Pittsylvania County. On 23 May 1787 she proved her free status to the Pittsylvania County Court, which ordered her released from bondage. After she moved to Franklin County, on 15 July 1802 she recorded her certificate of freedom and registered in accordance with the law.[72]

The record concerning Deborah Payne does not reveal how she was brought from Maryland to Virginia in the first place, but kidnappings of free blacks for sale as slaves were not unknown. On 14 August 1807 the Franklin County Court examined Chapman Stewart "on Suspicion of his having feloneously taken & carried away, one free negro Woman, named Fanny Scott, to sell as a Slave."[73] Stewart was acquitted; the fate of Fanny Scott was not mentioned.

Many free blacks, because of the laws, fled the state, or at least Franklin County. Mingo, for example, probably moved away; no record of his registration was found. Other free blacks migrated to Virginia's large towns and cities: Alexandria, Danville, Norfolk, Richmond. In this they followed the example of free blacks throughout the South who discovered greater freedom in the cities, where they could merge with a large free black population, than in the countryside, where they were easily noticed and made the targets of harassment and resentment. The census records reveal the increases and declines in the free black population of Franklin County before the Civil War: 1790, 34; 1800, 27; 1810, 86; 1820, 143; 1830, 195; 1840, 174; 1850, 66; 1860, 105.[74]

Obviously, some free blacks chose to remain in the rural areas they knew as home. Despite all the laws and hostility that cast a shadow over their lives, free blacks enjoyed some of the protections afforded any citizen. Slave marriages existed only in the minds of the slaves and by the sufferance of their owners. Free blacks, on the other hand, could have "real" marriages, and their children were born free. They could not vote, but they could own land and personal property— even slaves. They could not serve on juries or testify against whites, but they could dispose of their property using wills and deeds; their property was subject to the same protections under the law as that of whites.

Several families of free blacks lived in Franklin County during the antebellum period. Among the most numerous was the family of Beverly; they intermarried mostly with the Shavers (also spelled Chavis) family. Other family names included Cuff, Dunning, Early, Freeman, Frog, Gee, Green, Kennon, Marrs, Saunders, Shilling, and Smithers or Smothers. At least two of the free blacks of Franklin County fought for their country in the revolutionary war: Sylvester Beverly and Will Cuff. Sally Dunning, a free black, was Congressman Adam Clayton Powell's grandmother.[75]

Some free blacks themselves owned slaves. Whether in some cases the slaves actually were the spouses or children of their owners, however, remains unclear. Strangely enough, there were advantages to be derived under the antebellum legal system from the ownership of one spouse by another. Whereas free blacks were encouraged to leave Virginia, the laws discouraged the transportation of slaves beyond state lines unless they were sold. If one spouse owned another, then, the laws actually assisted them in keeping the family together in Virginia, particularly if their neighbors considered them man and wife (whether or not a "legal" wedding had occurred).

A known case of the ownership of one spouse by another was that of Nelly Green, who owned her "man & husband Phill called Phill Wood,"[76] and who willed him to four of her children when she died between 1834, when she wrote her will, and 1838, the year it was probated. Although Phill Wood technically was the slave of Nelly Green their true relationship was made clear by Green's use of the word *husband* and by her insistence that her property "remain together as it now is in the care & under the management of my said man & husband Phill during his natural life for the benefit comfort & Support of him & all my children."

Nelly Green named seven children in her will (Sam, Abraham, Lucy, Mariah, Isaac, Jacob, and Jesse) and one grandchild, John. She left her husband Phill to only four of her children, however (Sam, Abraham, Lucy, and Mariah), and declared that, in the unlikely event that all four of these children predeceased Phill, "it is my will & desire that he should be Emancipated provided it should be possible & conformable to the Laws of the State of Virginia." If the laws permitted Phill Wood to remain in Virginia with his family, then he was to be freed, otherwise he should remain the slave of her children.

Nelly Green's freedom was of greater legal consequence to her family than the status of Phill Wood because her children were free. In order to safeguard their free status, and to comply with the laws of Virginia, the children of Nelly Green as well as the children of other free blacks appeared before the county court to be registered. In 1805, for example, the court clerk noted the registration of "John Cousins a Black man free by birth, Twenty four years old, about five feet, nine Inches high" and also certified "that Abraham Marrs, about twenty two years of age, a Dark Mulatto, was born of Free parents and that he is entitled to his freedom under the Laws of this Com[mon]Wealth."[77]

Samuel Boyd, a free black, also owned slaves when he died in June 1831. In addition, he was the father of slaves owned by other masters—white men—and he provided for his children in a complicated will he wrote just before his death. He emancipated two of his own slaves who apparently were unrelated to him: "negro man Jesse commonly called Ferguson's Jesse" and "Leana the wife of Squire commonly called Squire Callaway."[78] He left his household items to his wife Agnes and some cattle and hogs to Perlina Stewart. He directed that most of the rest of his property be divided

> amongst my Seven Children to Wit my son Simon a slave in the possession of and the property of Capt. William Crump, My son Abram and my two Daughters Ama and Cassandra in the possession and in the property of Robert Waid and my sons Stephen & Samuel, the property of the heirs of Charles Waids deceased and my Son Spencer the property of John F. Waid which three last Children are under the management of the said John F. Waid.[79]

Although former slaves may have been free of compulsory servitude in the eyes of the law, that same legal system effectively kept most of them in a state of dependence on white largess. Twenty-six of the 105 free blacks identified in the

1860 census schedules, for instance, lived in white households. Of the sixteen separate black families identified in 1860, ten were headed by females; such families had less opportunity for economic prosperity than those headed by grown, laboring men.[80] Even free black families headed by men were not especially prosperous: few owned much taxable personal property, and even fewer owned land. Only seven free blacks listed in the 1860 census owned real estate: William Ingram ($500); Keziah Smithers ($400); Bluford Rayford ($200); Lucinda Fry ($350); Pitchegrue Fry, a tobacco roller ($300); John Stewart, a shopkeeper ($200); and William Turner, a blacksmith ($300).

Free blacks held a narrow range of occupations. In 1860 three were listed in the census as laborers (Henry Foley, Murph Burwell, and James Hale). Three others were listed as servants (Ann Choice, Susan Stewart, and America Newberry). There also were three carpenters (Stephen Dunnings, Matthew Hix, and Jacob Colthard). Two free blacks were blacksmiths (William Turner and a Smithers whose first name was not given). Celia Foley was listed as a tenant farmer, John Stewart as a shopkeeper, Pitchegrue Fry as a tobacco roller, and Adam Dunnings as a farmer (although he owned no land).

In 1860 the roles of slaves and free blacks in Franklin County, as elsewhere in Virginia, were graven in stone and were almost identical. Both groups faced a life of labor for others—whether as slaves or as free servants and laborers—rather than for themselves. They were subjected to restrictive laws no white man would have tolerated. They were essentially powerless and voiceless. If their status was to change, it could only happen because of the generosity of white men—or because of a conflagration that would consume the old society and its laws. The changes came in a conflagration called the Civil War.

THIRTEEN

Civil War

The election of Abraham Lincoln as president of the United States in November 1860 precipitated the secession crisis that erupted the next month. Perceived by most Southerners as virulently antislavery, in fact Lincoln was only moderately so. As in the case of the American Revolution nearly a century earlier, however, appearance dominated reality. Disbelieving Lincoln's conciliatory inaugural address, secessionists gained the ascendancy in one state convention after another, and gradually the Southern Confederacy was formed as each state seceded: South Carolina first on 20 December 1860, then Mississippi, Florida, Alabama, Georgia, Louisiana, and Texas. Against the wishes of Virginia governor John Letcher, in January 1861 the General Assembly approved a bill calling for a special convention to meet in Richmond in February to consider secession. The convention assembled on 13 February, and its members heatedly debated the issue.

On 16 April 1861, the day before Virginia seceded from the Union, Franklin County delegate Jubal A. Early rose to address the convention. Strongly opposed to secession, Early spoke briefly but prophetically of its effects:

> I have sat in my seat all day, and imagined that I could see a ball of flame hanging over this body. Without meaning to reflect upon the motives and the conduct of gentlemen, I have felt as if a great crime was about being perpetrated against the cause of liberty and civilization. . . . I cannot permit the occasion to pass, when an ordinance of secession has [been introduced to] this body, without expressing my feelings upon it in addition to casting my vote against it. It may be that such a vote, which I feel bound to give, shall draw upon me some censure. I trust I shall have manhood and firmness enough to endure, because the course I propose to pursue I feel to be in the interest of my country, in the interest of my State, and in the interest of the cause of liberty itself. What must be the result, the inevitable result of this proceeding? War, sir—such a war as this country has never seen, or, until recently, has never dreamed of.[1]

The civil war that Early foresaw was not at first fought to free the slaves, or to bring the fruits of liberty to free blacks. The North pursued the war to prevent, by military means, the political division of the United States into two separate countries. The South fought, once it had seceded from the federal Union, to preserve what it regarded as its independent nationhood.

The spirit of secession, much as the spirit of independence almost a century earlier, did not blossom overnight. Just as many of the revolutionaries of 1776 argued for reconciliation with the mother country rather than separation, so a number of future Confederate leaders—such as Robert E. Lee and Jubal A. Early—opposed secession until it became a reality. Early, who with Peter Saunders, Sr. (son of Samuel Saunders), represented Franklin County in the Convention of 1861, said in the same speech quoted above:

> During the progress of this Convention, we have frequently referred to the example of our fathers in the Revolution. They took no precipitate course of action. They protested and remonstrated for years. They had their armies in the field twelve months before they decided upon the final act of separation from the British Government. . . . I see no reason why we should act more precipitately than those men whose true devotion to country, and whose patriotism is a common theme among all of us.[2]

Early admitted that his pro-Union views were not shared by the majority of his Franklin County constituents, "who are opposed to me in sentiment" on the subject of disunion.[3] The opinions of Peter Saunders, Sr., are not known, because unlike Early he gave no speeches during the convention and indeed was absent most of the time because of illness. Presumably, however, he agreed with Early's positions, as in every instance but one he voted with Early when he was present. After the war he wrote that he opposed secession.[4]

Early spoke often and vividly during the convention, and laced his speeches with homespun anecdotes to make his point. The majority of his fellow delegates disagreed with Early's slow and cautious approach to breaking up the Union— particularly after the engagement at Fort Sumter and President Abraham Lincoln's call for troops to suppress the insurrection. Early and the other delegates frequently engaged in heated debate, and twice Early found himself on the edge of a challenge to a duel.[5] On the second occasion Early apologized to the convention and to the delegate he had inadvertently insulted:

> Some gentlemen who are friends of mine, in whom I have great confidence, have represented to me that perhaps I was not fully aware of the purport of the language I have used. I am not accustomed to speak in a deliberative body, and, in fact, I am not much accustomed to speak in any way, and I know that very frequently my ideas get ahead of my language. If I used language which would bear the construction which my friends tell me they understood, it was language I did not intend to use. . . . I intended the language to be applied in a political [not personal] sense. If I used any expression that would have any other construction, it was because I have not a command of language to express my ideas.[6]

Armed conflicts between members were avoided as the convention prepared for the greater conflict soon to come. After Lincoln's call for troops, the convention passed the secession ordinance on 17 April 1861. Although Early voted against it, he did sign the document. Back home in Franklin County, war fever raged among much of the population, as Dr. Thomas Bailey Greer reported in a letter to his "General & friend J. A. Early" on 25 April:

> I drop you a line in haste simply to say that We are all looking to you as our leader & as you will not probably be back soon, to say that I will look to & take care of all that concerns you here [referring most likely to Early's white mistress, Julia A. McNeal or McNelly, and their children]. You may rely upon it, they shall not want for any thing whatever. I will see to it as long as I am here. I will go out tomorrow & see. We are all united here now. Resistance eternal resistance is our unanimous voice. Several efforts are being made here for several volunteer companies. I think Joe Hambrick will complete a good company by next Saturday [Hambrick raised the Franklin Rifles, which became Company B, 24th Regiment Virginia Infantry]. Morgan is also making an effort. The boys here are all going. Great anxiety is expressed here to hear from you. We have not exactly learned your position as regards secession but we all see that you are preparing to defend Va. We have heard that you voted ag[ains]t Secession but signed the Ordinance. We are all satisfied at it, be it as it may & even the Dutch [Dunkards] are all right. I saw Ben Wray today & he is strong for resistance & say he will write forthwith for his Nephews in Indiana to come home & by the Southern routes. I should dislike very much to be drafted as a private as I think there would be a good deal of *surgical skill badly employed*. Cant you drop me a line. I am resolved to spend what I have got & all I have made for our army. The people here are so resolved. We had a big meeting here yesterday & speeches by Irvine, Hambrick, Mitchell, Taylor, Taliaferro, & Peter G[?]. The latter subscribed $500 for volunteers & more if necessary, Peter Guerrant the same amount & Jas. & Peter Callaway several hundred. Do you think there would be any likelihood of my being able to get a position as surgeon any where? I have got all the outfit [equipment]. I shall try to be satisfied any way & do my best for my country.[7]

Greer remained in the county during the war and served in various civil capacities, including that of overseer of the poor.

Jubal Early, on the other hand, became Franklin County's most famous soldier. Born to Joab and Ruth Early on 3 November 1816, he entered West Point in 1833.[8] He soon exhibited the crustiness and acid tongue for which he later became renowned. In 1836 a fellow cadet, Lewis Addison Armistead, was expelled for breaking a mess-hall plate over Early's head, an incident no doubt provoked by some sharp comment from Early.[9] (Armistead later led many Franklin County soldiers over the stone wall at the climax of Pickett's Charge at Gettysburg.) Early graduated eighteenth in his class the following year and was commissioned a second lieutenant in the 3d Regiment United States Artillery. Following a brief, unhappy sojourn in Florida during the Seminole War, Early resigned his commission and returned to Franklin County to study law.

Early read law under Norborne M. Taliaferro in Rocky Mount. Admitted to the bar in 1840, he quickly gained a reputation as an able, quick-witted lawyer.

According to local tradition his law office, a small frame structure now standing on the grounds of The Grove, was moved after 1907 from its original site on Main Street. Early probably rented the office from Thomas S. Greer, who owned the lot; Samuel S. Bright bought the lot about 1860 and used the building for his saddle and harness business.[10]

One of the best-known of Early's legal cases involved a slave boy named Silas, who was owned by Mary Brooks. She was involved in a dispute regarding her inheritance from her deceased husband when on 12 August 1859 Silas apparently burned down the Franklin County jail. Perhaps a fear of being sold away from his family prompted the arson (the sale of Mary Brooks's slaves was in fact approved by the Franklin County Court on 22 October 1859). At any rate, the court appointed Jubal Early as Silas's counsel and tried him on 3 January 1860. He pleaded not guilty but was convicted; Early argued eloquently on his behalf and convinced the court to sentence Silas to transportation "beyond the limits of the United States" rather than to death, the usual penalty. A guard escorted Silas by stage and rail to the State Penitentiary in Richmond, and on 21 January 1860 handed him over to prison officials, who noted that he was "heavily and expensively ironed." On 13 February 1860 Governor Henry A. Wise commuted Silas's sentence to "labor on the public works for life." The state compensated Mary Brooks $1,200 for the loss of her slave.[11]

Early entered politics briefly and served as one of Franklin County's representatives in the House of Delegates during the session of 1841–1842. He settled into his law practice and lived in Rocky Mount at Hay Turnbull's hotel until the voters elected him to the Convention of 1861. He changed his residence to the Hale House hotel, which stood on Main Street opposite the present-day Price-Perdue building, when he returned to the county a year later to recover from combat wounds.

After Virginia seceded, Early accepted an appointment as colonel of the 24th Regiment Virginia Infantry, which contained two companies raised in Franklin County. Early presented a striking appearance. He stood almost six feet tall but seemed shorter because of the painful arthritis that had afflicted him since the war with Mexico and caused him to stoop. Not yet forty-five when the Civil War began, Early seemed much older; his beard was prematurely gray and he shuffled when he walked. He drank occasionally, chewed tobacco, and laced streams of expectorated juice with a profanity so colorful and inventive that no one who heard it ever forgot it. (One of his more printable epithets for Union soldiers was "Blue-Butts.")

John S. Wise, who saw Early when he was home in the summer of 1862, wrote a word picture that not only portrayed him at the height of his fame but also summarized the opinions of his Franklin County neighbors:

> He was a singular being. . . . At the time of which I write, he was the hero of Franklin County, and, although he professed to despise popularity and to be defiant of public opinion, it was plain that he enjoyed his military distinction. It had done much to soften old-time asperities, and blot out from the memory of his neighbors certain facts in his private life which had, prior to the war, alienated from him many of his own class [presumably his alleged keeping of black and white mistresses]. In fact, I doubt not he was a

happier man then than he had been for many a year before, or was at a later period, when he became more or less a social and political Ishmaelite.

He was eccentric in many ways,—eccentric in appearance, in voice, in manner of speech. . . . His voice was a piping treble, and he talked with a long-drawn whine or drawl. His opinions were expressed unreservedly, and he was most emphatic and denunciatory, and startlingly profane.

His likes and dislikes he announced without hesitation, and, as he was filled with strong and bitter opinions, his conversation was always racy and pungent. His views were not always correct, or just, or broad; but his wit was quick, his satire biting, his expressions were vigorous, and he was interestingly lurid and picturesque.

With his admiring throng about him on the tavern porch, on summer evenings in 1862, General Early, in my opinion, said things about his superiors, the Confederate leaders, civic and military, and their conduct of affairs, sufficient to have convicted him a hundred times over before any court-martial. But his criticisms never extended to General Robert E. Lee. For Lee he seemed to have a regard and esteem and high opinion felt by him for no one else. Although General Lee had but recently been called to the command of the army, he predicted his great future with unerring judgment.[12]

Early was said to be the only man who ever dared to swear in the presence of Lee; Lee referred to Early fondly as "My bad old man." His troops called him, among other terms of endearment, "Old Jube," "Old Jubilee," and "Old Lop Ear" (because of his large ears). Early's penchant for sarcasm made him enemies; generally he was respected but not liked. On one occasion Early's stern Presbyterian commander, Major General Thomas J. ("Stonewall") Jackson, sent him a brusque message asking why Jackson had observed stragglers in the rear of Early's division. Early responded tartly: "General Early's compliments to General Jackson, and he takes pleasure in informing him that he saw so many stragglers in rear of my Division to-day, probably because he rode in rear of my Division." Jackson smiled; the only other man who could have amused him with an impertinent note was J. E. B. Stuart.[13]

Early's superiors tolerated his sarcasm and profanity because his leadership ability and personal bravery were beyond reproach. He led his regiment so adeptly at the First Battle of Manassas (Bull Run) that he was quickly promoted to brigadier general. Wounded and hospitalized at the Battle of Williamsburg on 5 May 1862, Early gave up his command to recuperate at home but soon obtained another under Stonewall Jackson. He suffered heavy casualties at Malvern Hill, but later fought well at Cedar Mountain, the Second Battle of Manassas, and Sharpsburg (Antietam).

After another successful exhibition by Early at Fredericksburg in December 1862, Lee promoted him to major general. Despite his many achievements, however, Early had some shortcomings as a commander. He had little regard for the cavalry. Sometimes he committed his troops, or refused to commit them, without reconnoitering adequately, as in 1862 at Williamsburg, in 1863 during the Battle of Chancellorsville, and in 1864 at the Wilderness and Bethesda Church. Early performed well during the Gettysburg campaign and at many other battles, however, and Lee, who had great confidence in Early's abilities, promoted him to lieutenant general in May 1864.

In June 1864 Lee assigned Early command of an army in the Shenandoah Valley. The Valley was strategically important for several reasons. It ran from northeast, within a short march of Washington, to southwest, and was bordered by steep ridges with occasional gaps that opened into the Piedmont. A Confederate force could enter the Valley in safety near its southern end and emerge at its northern end close to the Union capital. If a Federal force could occupy the Valley it could not only prevent this but could also pass eastward through the gaps to strike the Confederates in the rear. In addition, the Valley was the major grain-producing region of Virginia; it was vital to the Confederate food supply. Lee dispatched Early with instructions to clear the Valley of the Union force under Lieutenant General David Hunter.

Early first encountered Hunter at Lynchburg on 18–19 June, as Hunter attempted to strike at Lee's western supply lines. Hunter fled toward West Virginia and escaped Early after a final engagement at Hanging Rock in Roanoke County, not far from Early's home. Having thus removed the Union threat in the Valley, Early then gained fame for his raids into Maryland and Pennsylvania, particularly for the Battle of Monocacy, Maryland, on 9 July, and his subsequent actions around the defenses of Washington, when many frightened residents of the capital thought its capture was imminent. Late in the same month troops under Early burned the town of Chambersburg, Pennsylvania, when its citizens refused to pay reparations for property destroyed by the Union army in the Shenandoah Valley.

Some of Early's midsummer successes came not against Hunter, who had been relieved later in the summer, but against his replacement, Major General Philip H. Sheridan. At first the new Union commander was wary, but after his army grew to two and a half times the size of Early's, Sheridan attacked vigorously and routed Early's army at the Third Battle of Winchester on 19 September 1864. One disaster quickly followed another, from Cedar Creek one month later to the Battle of Waynesboro on 2 March 1865. The press wondered if Early had been drinking and compared him most unfavorably with his deified former commander, the great Stonewall, who had swept the Valley clean of the Union army in 1862. Early, though, unlike Jackson, faced skilled Union commanders who possessed a clear superiority in men and supplies. Jackson's army numbered about 17,000 and he usually faced no more than 20,000 second-line Union troops. During Jackson's Valley campaign of 1862 he lost about 2,750 men while the North lost about 5,500. In 1864 Early lost 10,000 men while Sheridan lost around 15,000. Jackson was famous for his long marches in the Valley; during his two-and-a-half-month campaign in 1862 he and his "foot cavalry" covered almost 650 miles. During a four-month period in 1864 Early's army marched more than 1,500 miles. Jackson fought ten battles or engagements and several smaller actions. Early fought seventy-five battles and skirmishes. A North Carolina woman assessed Early's performance more accurately than the press when she confided to her diary, "Gen. Early is sober & his disasters in the Valley were attributable to his want of men. The wonder is that he did so much."[14]

After his final defeat at Waynesboro, Early rode southwest to Abingdon, where he attempted to assemble another army. On 29 March 1865 Lee, realizing that everyone but him lacked confidence in Early, relieved him from command and ordered him home to Franklin County. Early left Abingdon on the afternoon of 30 March and arrived in the evening at Marion, where he was bedridden for several days with a bad cold. He later recalled that when

> I was in a condition to be moved, I was carried on the railroad to Wytheville, and was proceeding thence to my home, in an ambulance under the care of a surgeon, when I received, most unexpectedly, the news of the surrender of General Lee's army. Without the slightest feeling of irreverence, I will say, that the sound of the last trump would not have been more unwelcome to my ears.[15]

Early stopped briefly in Lynchburg, where in May a report circulated that he had died. The *Lynchburg Virginian* corrected the story, acknowledging that

> Gen. Early was in this city a short time since, in excellent health, having entirely recovered from his late indisposition. He left here with the intention of repairing to a distant portion of the country, after sojourning for a few days at his home in Franklin county, and we have since learned that he has set out on his journey. He carries with him the best wishes of a host of warm personal friends and admiring countrymen.[16]

As soon as he recovered fully, Early headed south and west, intending to join the army of Lieutenant General E. Kirby Smith, commander of the Trans-Mississippi Department. Smith surrendered on 26 May 1865, however, before Early could reach him. After an arduous journey on horseback that took him from Franklin County through North Carolina, South Carolina, Georgia, Alabama, Mississippi, Arkansas, and Texas, Early boarded a ship for Havana, Cuba. After sojourns in Bimini and Mexico, he subsequently settled in Toronto, Ontario. While in Canada he began his literary career, producing a volume on the last year of the war in an effort to explain his defeat in the Valley. In 1869 Early returned to Virginia and lived the rest of his life in Lynchburg, where he resumed the practice of law. He died there on 2 March 1894 at the house of his niece, Ruth Hairston Early.

Since Early's death historians largely have rehabilitated his reputation as a capable and audacious, if sometimes reckless, field commander. Lee himself wrote Early a kind letter the day after he relieved him of command, noting approvingly that he "exhibited during his whole service high intelligence, sagacity, bravery and untiring devotion to the cause in which he enlisted."[17] Early's devotion to the cause only intensified after the end of the war. Through his own writings, such as *A Memoir of the Last Year of the War* (1866) and the posthumous *Autobiographical Sketch*, Early created his reputation as the prototypical "unreconstructed Rebel"—a final irony, considering his early and sincere opposition to secession.

Given Early's personality and reputation, there is a strong oral tradition in Franklin County concerning his exploits at the end of the war. According to one story, for example, immediately after the assassination of Lincoln, Early made a speech indicating his approval of the murder, which resulted in an attempt by Union troops to arrest him. Early hid in the garret of Watt Callaway's house about five miles from Rocky Mount and was protected by the family, particularly by a servant named Surry. One day a troop of soldiers rode into the yard and asked Surry if Early were about. Surry pointed down the road and convinced them Early had just ridden away; as soon as the troop galloped off in pursuit, Surry summoned the general from his hiding place and suggested he ride away in the opposite direction. Early took his advice, thus beginning the journey that eventually took him to Canada. Other county sites where Early is alleged to have concealed himself from Union cavalrymen include the John S. Hale house, The Grove, and the Saunders home, The Farm.[18]

When the Civil War began, Early was one of the few Franklin County men of service age who had had any experience with regular army life and warfare. Most Confederate soldiers had at least a fleeting acquaintance with military drill and organization because of their service in the county militia. By the beginning of the Civil War militia officers were elected by their men rather than appointed by the county court; otherwise, the militia system had not changed since the revolutionary war. Generally, each county organized its militia into a regiment or two, and each regiment usually consisted of one or two battalions. Four companies made up a battalion. Despite the militia's organization, however, its members were no more ready for combat than their counterparts of a century earlier. The Confederate leadership looked to such experienced former Union officers as Robert E. Lee to whip its nascent army into shape.

As the letter from Thomas Bailey Greer to Jubal Early indicated, enthusiasm for secession and war, although no substitute for experience, ran high in Franklin County. Men joined military units at such a rate that the number of recruits soon outran the supplies available for them. Mattie Brown described the situation in a letter of 30 May 1861 to her friend Lizzie:

> I don't think that there has been many weddings in this neighborhood since you left here. The people are thinking about something else besides marrying. Now they are thinking about fighting the Yankeys. Dick has volunteered and gone to fight. He left here last Sunday was a week ago. He is now in Lynchburg. Pa received a letter from him yesterday. He said he was well & enjoying himself finely. He gave his likeness to I & sister that he had taken in his uniform. Jim & Henry Brown volunteered last Saturday in Captain Hatcher's Company. I don't know when they will leave, not in less time than a month I know for they have not got their uniforms yet nor don't know when they will for they can't get such material as they want greys mixt. and the other companies that has gone has taken all the cloth that was made and those things have to wate. . . . You never saw as many more boqets give in your life as was give to Capt. Hambrick. He had his arms full. I sent one of his soldiers one of the prettiest ones. . . . Two companies have left Franklin and two more nearly ready to leave and they was making up two more so you may know the young men are getting very scarce in Franklin.[19]

James H. Roberts, the overseer of Fleming and Robert Saunders's farm in Floyd County, wrote to Fleming Saunders on 30 April 1861 of the effect of secession:

> A great Many People has not plowed any yet. They are excited so they dont no What to be at. Every Body is in a buzz of excitement. I have Never for the

first time felt afraid. I no that our gallent Enemy [army—Roberts himself obviously was excited] Will conquer the mercenary soldiers of Lincoln. Yet I no that much Blood Will be spilled and Many Precious lives Will be lost. Yet We shall come out conquerors. Va. has at last gone out of the Union, and had she gone out Two months ago all this blood shed might have been avoided. I Were at the [Floyd County] C[ourt] H[ouse] last Saturday to the General Muster, great deal of excitement. There they made several Volunteer Companys expecting now every day to be called for. General Preston, and Mr. Wade of Montgomery addressed the people and it seem to be a very serious time With the most of their Listeners. I Would like to Belong to Capt. R[obert] C. Saunders company, the Best Kind, But I have Volunteered up here and Will start When called for. I had rather stay at Home, But if my service is needed I Will give them all the fight I have. If I should go some one ought to take my place on your Farm, But I hope I Will never be called for.[20]

Roberts did leave the farm, for on 24 June 1861 the Saunders brothers signed an agreement with Edward M. Burruss for his services as overseer.[21]

Although at the beginning of the Civil War, men from the same county often made up large parts of battalions and regiments, that soon changed as the Confederate army was organized and reorganized. Thus the infantry and cavalry companies raised in Franklin County were quickly scattered throughout several regiments. This dispersal was not popular with the troops. In July 1861, for example, the members of Company K (a Franklin County unit), which had been attached to the 42d Regiment Virginia Infantry, petitioned unsuccessfully to be removed and added to the 24th Regiment. Company K, known as the Franklin Invincibles, was enlisted on 17 June 1861 at Rocky Mount. Its captains were, successively, Samuel Hale, Jr. (1861–1862), Samuel H. Saunders (1862), and James W. Helm (1862–1865).[22]

Franklin County contributed two companies to the 24th Regiment Virginia Infantry, of which Colonel Jubal A. Early was the first commander. Company B, the Franklin Rifles, was recruited and led by Captain Joseph A. Hambrick, an 1857 graduate of the Virginia Military Institute and a local lawyer. The company was mustered into service on 28 May 1861 in Lynchburg; Hambrick served as its captain until he was promoted to major in 1863. Captain John J. Bernard assumed command but resigned in September 1864.

The 24th Regiment's Company D, the Early Guards, was raised and commanded by Captain Thomas Skelton Taylor, another graduate of the Virginia Military Institute (class of 1857). Captain Taylor and his company were mustered into service at Lynchburg on 11 June 1861. Taylor served as captain until October 1861, when he died of typhoid fever. Captain Mordecai Cook took his place until May 1862; illness forced him to leave the service. Captain Fleming Saunders commanded the company until August 1863, when he resigned and Captain Peter B. Booth replaced him.

The 57th Regiment Virginia Infantry had three companies of Franklin County men: Company B, the Franklin Sharpshooters (enlisted 15 June 1861); Company C, the Franklin Fireaters (enlisted 21 June 1861); and Company G, the Ladies Guard (enlisted 13 July 1861). The captains of the Franklin County companies were: Company B, Waddy T. James (1861–1862), John H. Smith (1862–1863), and John L. Ward (1863–1865); Company C, Edward T. Bridges (1861), David P.

Heckman (1862–1863), and Charles H. Jones (1863–1865); Company G, William Patterson (1861), Benjamin H. Wade (1861–1862), and Daniel Arrington (1862–1863). Wade became lieutenant colonel of the regiment and died at Gettysburg, the highest-ranking officer from Franklin County to be killed.

At first the companies were part of Major Elisha F. Keen's Battalion Virginia Volunteers. By October 1861, however, they had been formed into the 57th Regiment Virginia Infantry with Colonel Lewis Addison Armistead as its commander. Armistead served as colonel until he was promoted to brigadier general on 1 April 1862 (the regiment was assigned to his brigade); Keen replaced him as colonel but resigned in July 1862 and was succeeded by Colonel David Dyer. He served until January 1863, when he resigned and was replaced by Colonel John B. Magruder, who was mortally wounded at Gettysburg on 3 July 1863. Colonel Clement R. Fontaine assumed command of the regiment until the surrender at Appomattox on 9 April 1865.

Franklin County recruits made up Company A, 37th Battalion Virginia Cavalry, which was organized on 2 August 1862. The company was led initially by Captain James R. Claiborne, then by Captain George T. Williams.

Three companies were raised in Franklin County for the 10th Regiment Virginia Cavalry. Company A, Caskie's Mounted Rangers, was mustered into Confederate service on 9 June 1861. Its first captain was Robert A. Caskie (1861–1863) and its second was Edwin A. Fulcher. Company C was organized on 20 March 1862 and led successively by Captains William W. Flood, Nathaniel Richerson, and William A. B. Wingfield. Company K, the Texas Rangers or Rosser's Mounted Rangers, was organized on 1 June 1861; its captains were J. Travis Rosser, James L. Dickson, and William L. Graham.[23]

The 2d Regiment Virginia Cavalry (until October 1861 the 30th Regiment Virginia Volunteers) included a company recruited principally from Franklin County: the Franklin Rangers, raised by Captain Giles W. H. Hale, which was enrolled on 20 May 1861 and later became Company D. Colonel Thomas Taylor Munford, a Richmond native, commanded the 2d Virginia Cavalry for most of the war.[24]

Other Franklin County residents served in various other units during the war.

Sgt. Sparrel Dudley, Company E ("Franklin Guards"), 58th Regiment Virginia Infantry, holding locally made bowie knife. (Blue Ridge Institute, Ferrum, Va.)

They included the 19th and 21st cavalry regiments, as well as the 34th, 36th, 43d, 51st, 53d, and 58th infantry regiments. Perhaps two thousand men served from the county altogether, and their regiments fought in every major campaign of the war in Virginia, Maryland, and Pennsylvania. More than three hundred of them died: about eighty-five in action or from wounds, forty or so while prisoners of war, and the remainder (roughly 60 percent) of disease while in camps.[25]

At the beginning of the war the Union and Confederate armies in Virginia jockeyed for position while they built up their forces and supplies. Each army initially avoided major engagements and spent much of its time reconnoitering and fighting small skirmishes.

At first the 2d Virginia Cavalry, for example, saw duty in the Shenandoah Valley and western Virginia as pickets, raiders, and guards. Moses L. Booth wrote an account on 12 July 1861 of what must have been his first combat experience. Captain Hale and twenty of his men were on patrol near Harpers Ferry, hoping to intercept Union couriers, when suddenly

> Zip Zip—went the bullets directly over our heads. . . . We struck up a brisk run thinking soon to pass the enemy. But presently the bullets commenced whistling around us like hail stones and every step we took they came thicker & thicker. The enemy were about 500 yds. from us on the other side of the Potomac. Sometimes the balls would cut great limbs from directly over our heads, sometimes they would strike the rocks & spatter in our faces. We run thus for three quarters of a mile perfectly exposed to a raking fire from the enemy before we could find a road or path that we could get up the mountain. At last however, we struck a hog path and up it we went. We stopped in about 3/4 mile from the river to see if we had lost any of our men or had got hurt. Strange to say there was no damage done to any of us though our poor horses were nearly all barefooted & broken down. While we were there the balls would drop around us. There must have been in all five hundred shots fired at us. Whole Co's [companies] would open on us at a time & how we escaped unharmed is for Divine Providence & not for us to say. The bullets would pass under our horses over us & level with us. I know one passed in 12 ins. of me. Those Yankees have most splendid weapons. Their Minie Rifles (the kind that they were firing at us) will kill a man one mile & a half. Oh! to hear one coming so near to you will make the very blood stop in your Veins. They don't sound like any other ball & wherever they strike death is sure to follow. . . . I never wish to be in another such a scrape. I would not have cared for it could we have returned the fire, but that was impossible. They had two or three thousand men at the place and were under cover. We only 20—perfectly exposed.[26]

The combination of fear and excitement that Booth described was typical for a young soldier seeing his first combat. A year later he was elected second lieutenant in Company D. Sadly, Booth died in a cavalry skirmish on 28 May 1864, in Henrico County; he was only twenty-three.

As the armies of the North and South assembled, trained, and skirmished, both sides evolved grand strategies that affected their conduct of the war and dictated offensive or defensive actions as the conflict ground on. Lincoln's objective was to preserve the Union. He sought to do this by destroying the Confederate army in the field, breaking its lines of communication and supply, seizing its capital, and denying foreign governments the opportunity to recognize it as an independent nation.

The Confederate objective, under President Jefferson Davis, was to survive as an independent nation. To do this its army needed to avoid destruction, to inflict such casualties upon the Union army that the North would grow weary of the fight, to disrupt the Union lines of communication and supply, to threaten if not seize its capital, and to create an aura of legitimacy for its government so that it would be recognized (and supported) by foreign powers.

Both armies followed a routine that alternated campaigns and battles with periods of relative inactivity. Fighting was essentially a fair-weather activity: the armies maneuvered and engaged each other in the spring, summer, and fall, while encamping for the winter and restricting their activities to reconnoitering, skirmishing, and replenishing supplies and manpower.

Soon after it enlisted in 1861, Jubal Early's 24th Regiment loaded itself on railroad cars and rode to Manassas Junction. From there it marched to Occoquon. Throughout most of June and July the 24th Regiment marched back and forth between Manassas Junction and Occoquon as the Confederate army maneuvered and prepared for the anticipated Union invasion of Virginia. Finally, on 21 July 1861, a battle developed for control of the railroad center at Manassas Junction; it became known as the First Battle of Manassas. The Union army commanded by Brigadier General Irvin McDowell attacked the Confederate army led by Brigadier General P. G. T. Beauregard, but was routed. The battle became an overwhelming victory for the Confederate army, but the 24th Regiment largely played a

Left: *Lt. Moses L. Booth, Troop D ("Franklin Rangers"), 2d Virginia Cavalry.* Right: *Booth's tombstone near Taylors Store. Booth died in a cavalry engagement at Union Church, in Henrico County, near Richmond.* (John Booth Joplin, Rocky Mount, Va.)

supporting role. It had, at least, faced artillery and musket fire and held its assigned positions. Lincoln immediately replaced McDowell with Major General George B. McClellan, a superb organizer, and both armies spent the rest of the year skirmishing or encamped between Richmond and Washington.

Many of the Union soldiers captured in the battle were confined in Richmond, where they became the objects of curiosity. One member of Franklin County's Company B, 57th Regiment Virginia Infantry, Private William D. Young, wrote his sister on 15 August 1861 to let her know that he was well and had arrived safely in Richmond to train. Otherwise, he reported,

> there is not much news to write; there is a great many Soldiers here some twenty or thirty thousand. There is near about twenty hundred Yankees in prison. I have seen some of them, they look very savage.[27]

Until the spring of 1862 the 24th Regiment served in Northern Virginia, either in camp or on picket duty. George W. Finney, a second lieutenant in Company D, wrote a letter to his mother on 6 September 1861 and described the routine at Camp Ellis, near Washington, D.C.:

> I am still enjoying my health very well, but very much fatigued at this time. We have performed very heavy duty for the last week or two. I have not sleep any for several days and nights but still I enjoyed very good health considering the exposure I have gone under since I entered into camp life. I have been down in sight of Washington on a skirmish expedition in full sight of the enemy. We had several skirmishing fights with them & several shots exchanged. None of our boys got hurt. We killed and taken prisoners some 15 or 20 of them.[28]

In April the regiment moved to Richmond to man the defenses there. The inactivity took a heavy toll on the regiment from disease; probably half the unit suffered from one illness or another in the months following the First Battle of Manassas.

During the winter of 1861–1862 most of the Confederate army entrenched itself at Yorktown and Norfolk under the command of General Joseph E. Johnston. In March 1862 McClellan moved his huge army to Fort Monroe and began in April to make a slow assault on Richmond in what became known as the Peninsula campaign. In the face of McClellan's ponderous advance, Johnston began to withdraw toward Richmond in early May. Lincoln, who wanted a victory, repeatedly urged McClellan to attack Johnston's rear guard. McClellan finally complied on 5 May 1862, at the Battle of Williamsburg.

The 24th Regiment marched from Yorktown toward Williamsburg on 3 May, in heavy downpours of rain. The men bivouacked on the green at the College of William and Mary until the early morning of 5 May. As the battle developed outside the town, the regiment was not committed until the late afternoon. Jubal Early commanded the brigade of which the 24th Regiment was a part. He was given the task of overcoming what was thought to be a Union battery that had been harassing the Confederate left flank. Early personally led his massed brigade in a charge of more than a mile through swampy forests. He later received criticism for not having sent skirmishers ahead of the brigade to report on the terrain and locate the Union forces more precisely. If he had done so, he would have discovered that they were attacking not only a battery, but ten guns in a fortified position supported by five regiments of infantry. By the time the 24th Regiment emerged from the woods in front of the Union position, it was alone; the other regiments in the brigade had gotten lost or detained in the heavy forest. With Early in the lead, the 24th Regiment charged the Union guns in an unsupported assault. The charge was as fruitless as it was heroic: Early and several other officers were wounded, others killed; the total number of killed, wounded, or missing amounted to 189; and the Union position was not taken. At the end of the day the regiment joined the general withdrawal of Johnston's army to the defenses around Richmond. Early went home to Franklin County to recover from his wounds, which consisted of two bullets in his shoulder. Despite his wounds Early had fought until he was so weakened by loss of blood that he had to be removed from the field. His courage and determination increased his stature in Lee's eyes as well as those of his men.

On 31 May Johnston attacked McClellan at Seven Pines, east of Richmond, in an indecisive battle in which the 24th Regiment took part. The encounter stopped McClellan on the outskirts of the capital and resulted in the wounding of Johnston. President Davis replaced him with General Robert E. Lee, who immediately began strengthening the eastern defenses of Richmond with such vigor that the newspaper wits dubbed him the "king of spades."

What the armchair strategists did not understand was that Lee, an engineer, realized that a strongly fortified capital could be defended by relatively few men, which would enable him to take his outnumbered army on the offensive against McClellan. This he did in a blizzard of assaults between 25 June and 1 July that was known as the Seven Days' campaign. One battle followed another as Lee pushed McClellan back down the Peninsula: Oak Grove (25 June), Mechanicsville (26 June), Gaines's Mill (27 June), Allen's Farm and Savage's Station (29 June), and White Oak Swamp (30 June). The campaign ended in a Confederate defeat at Malvern Hill (1 July) but Lee had attained his objective. Richmond was saved and McClellan made what he called a strategic withdrawal and others termed a "great skedaddle." Lincoln replaced him with Major General John Pope.

The 24th Regiment saw little action during the campaign until 30 June and the Battle of White Oak Swamp. Brigadier General James Lawson Kemper's brigade, of which the regiment was a part, succeeded in capturing and holding for a time some strongly defended Union breastworks, but a sharp counterattack dislodged the Confederates.

The 57th Regiment, with its three Franklin County companies, saw its first action during the Seven Days' campaign; previously the regiment had spent most of its time either in camp or on marches from one bivouac to another near Suffolk. Near the end of May 1862 the regiment joined the main army east of Richmond as it stalled the Union approach to the Confederate capital. The regiment received its baptism of fire on the last day of the campaign at the Battle of Malvern Hill. Owing largely to a lack of communication among several battlefield commanders, the 57th Regiment took part in an unsupported assault against strong Union artillery positions on the crest of Malvern Hill, and suffered severe casualties.

Lee succeeded in driving McClellan from the gates of Richmond in part because he had summoned to his army the force commanded by Stonewall

Jackson. Jackson had spent the winter in the Shenandoah Valley after the First Battle of Manassas, where he had earned his sobriquet by holding firm a defensive line on Henry Hill. During March and the first half of April 1862 Jackson swept the Valley clean of Union troops in a brilliant campaign that made him the first great hero of the Confederacy. He did not do so well immediately after he joined Lee, perhaps because of exhaustion. Indeed, the Seven Days' campaign succeeded despite complicated battle plans, foggy orders, and a general lack of coordination among Lee's generals.

During the summer and fall of 1861 the 42d Regiment had served largely in western Virginia; in December it marched to Winchester to join Jackson. The regiment served in Jackson's Shenandoah Valley campaign, notably at the First Battle of Kernstown on 23 March 1862 and at Cross Keys on 8 June. At the end of the month the regiment took part in the Seven Days' campaign to the east of Richmond that ended the Union army's threat to the capital for the time being.

Lee and his army moved north toward Washington to menace the Union capital in return. The next major engagement for the 42d Regiment was at Cedar Mountain, in Culpeper County, on 9 August. Although Jackson held the field, he very nearly suffered a defeat even though his troops outnumbered his Union adversaries. At the subsequent Second Battle of Manassas (29 August), the 42d Regiment bore the brunt of the pompous Pope's piecemeal attacks as Jackson defended a railroad cut. The 24th Regiment spent most of the battle protecting an artillery battery. After Lee's brilliant victory, Jackson's exhausted division pursued Pope's retreating army and attacked it at Chantilly in an unsuccessful attempt to destroy it. The 24th Regiment also took part at Chantilly and captured one of Pope's batteries in a sharp action. A frustrated Lincoln replaced Pope with McClellan, hoping that his former army commander had acquired aggressiveness since the Peninsula campaign.

Lee, on the other hand, had aggression to spare. Buoyed by his most recent success, he invaded the North to embarrass and demoralize the Union army and gain foreign recognition of the Confederate government. Moving into western Maryland, Lee encountered McClellan's army at Sharpsburg, along Antietam Creek. Jackson, who with the 42d Regiment had been dispatched by Lee to seize Harpers Ferry, rejoined the main army in time for the Battle of Sharpsburg on 17 September 1862, in what turned into the bloodiest single engagement of the war. The day's fighting may have cost the 42d Regiment almost half its men in casualties. Although Lee held the field he was unable to continue his invasion and returned to Virginia by way of the Shenandoah Valley. The failure of Lee's campaign not only meant that his other objectives were unrealized, but it also gave Lincoln the impetus he needed to issue his preliminary Emancipation Proclamation on 22 September. From this point on the destruction of slavery became a Northern objective as important as the preservation of the Union. Lincoln also replaced McClellan for the second and last time, with Major General Ambrose E. Burnside.

Lee and Burnside met in an unusual winter battle at Fredericksburg on 13 December 1862. The 42d Regiment suffered relatively few casualties and the 24th Regiment saw limited action. The climax of the engagement came when Burnside's brave soldiers hurled themselves against Lieutenant General James Longstreet's position on Marye's Heights in a futile attack that decimated the

Union ranks. Burnside's replacement, Major General Joseph Hooker, arrived about a month later. Both armies went into winter quarters until the following spring.

In April 1863 Lincoln visited Hooker and urged him to defeat Lee in one grand battle. Hooker put most of his army in motion on 27 April, leaving part of it at Fredericksburg to hold down the Confederates near the town, and crossed the Rappahannock River to sweep around Lee's army to the west and envelop it near the community of Chancellorsville. Lee, outnumbered two to one, divided his force and sent Jackson on a quick march to strike Hooker's left flank. The battle raged over three days, from 2 to 4 May, and in the end Lee had emerged victorious from what many historians consider his most brilliant battle. The cost to Lee was almost unbearably high, however: Jackson was wounded by his own troops while conducting a reconnaissance and died of pneumonia eight days later.

Lee withdrew his army west toward Culpeper while the Union army recuperated. Once again, Lee used a major victory as a springboard for an invasion of the North. Early in June he began moving his army to the Valley to resume the attack on Pennsylvania that had ended the previous year at Sharpsburg. This year it would end at Gettysburg.

The Gettysburg campaign began with a clash of cavalry on 9 June at Brandy Station, just east of Culpeper. Several Franklin County cavalry companies, including those in the 10th Virginia Cavalry, took part. As with most cavalry regiments at the beginning of the war, the 10th Virginia spent much of its time on picket duty or patrols. By the summer of 1862 the regiment was assigned to the newly created brigade commanded by Brigadier General Wade Hampton. The brigade pursued McClellan's retreating army during the Seven Days' battles and thereafter; following the Second Battle of Manassas it rejoined Lee's army for the Sharpsburg campaign. In Maryland Hampton's brigade screened and supported the infantry but was not closely engaged. It did fight a skirmish at Barnesville, Maryland, on 9 September, however.[29]

The regiment battled the 6th Regiment Pennsylvania Cavalry at Emmitsburg, Maryland, on 11 October. By November 1862 another army reorganization placed the 10th Virginia Cavalry under the command of Brigadier General William H. F. ("Rooney") Lee, the second son of Robert E. Lee. For the rest of the war the regiment remained in Lee's brigade.[30]

The 10th Regiment spent much of the winter of 1862–1863 in the vicinity of Fredericksburg. In January 1863, however, it patrolled the Shenandoah Valley with most of Lee's brigade. At Chancellorsville in May 1863 the cavalry fought in the thick of the action and captured the essential crossroads there.[31]

By early June the regiment was encamped near Brandy Station, in Culpeper County. On 8 June it took part in the grand cavalry review staged by Major General J. E. B. Stuart for Robert E. Lee's benefit just to the west of Brandy Station. The next day a reconnaissance in force by the Union cavalry corps surprised Stuart and resulted in the Battle of Brandy Station, the largest cavalry battle on American soil in its history, in which about twenty thousand cavalrymen were engaged. Rooney Lee's brigade fought for most of the day north of Brandy Station near the Hazel River. In the late afternoon, as his father watched from a nearby house, Lee led his brigade in a charge that ended abruptly for him when he received a serious wound in his leg. Colonel John R. Chambliss, Jr., assumed command and continued the attack until the Union force withdrew across the Rappahannock River at sundown, ending the battle.

Between 9 June and 1 August 1863, when the 10th Virginia Cavalry fought again at Brandy Station in a smaller action, it lost eight killed, sixty-nine wounded, and an unspecified number missing or captured. The losses resulted not only from the Battle of Gettysburg (one killed, nine wounded, and two missing), but also from other actions at Aldie, Middleburg, and Upperville in Virginia, and at Hagerstown, Williamsport, Funkstown, and Boonsborough in Maryland.[32]

Discovering Lee's army in motion after the Battle of Brandy Station, the Union army pursued, though at a respectful distance to the east, close by Washington. As it marched into Pennsylvania, it acquired yet another commander, Major General George Gordon Meade. Three days later, on 1 July, the two armies collided at Gettysburg. Throughout the battle the Union force held the better terrain, frustrating Lee. The 42d Regiment, for example, made several unsuccessful attacks on the strong Union position on Culp's Hill. The regiment saw its heaviest fighting there on the evening of 2 July, when the Union forces repulsed its night assault on the breastworks.

Lee did not have the entire Army of Northern Virginia at Gettysburg when the battle began. The division commanded by Major General George E. Pickett, for example, followed the main army and encamped near Chambersburg, Pennsylvania, by late June. The division included the 24th Regiment and the 57th Regiment, which had seen only limited action at the Second Battle of Manassas and remained largely in support at Harpers Ferry and Sharpsburg. In October 1862 the 57th Regiment had been attached to the brigade commanded by Brigadier General Lewis A. Armistead.

In February and March 1863 the 24th Regiment had marched to Richmond and Prince George Court House, then traveled by rail to Kinston, North Carolina. The regiment moved again by rail to Tidewater Virginia in April, entrenching itself near Suffolk. In May the 24th Regiment marched first to Richmond, then to Taylorsville, in Hanover County, where it trained and was resupplied for the Gettysburg campaign. On 8 June the regiment left its camp at Taylorsville and marched to Culpeper Court House, then followed the main army with the rest of Pickett's division.

Early on the morning of 2 July Pickett's division began its march to Gettysburg and bivouacked late in the afternoon a few miles short of the battlefield. At 3:00 A.M. on 3 July the division resumed its march; it arrived behind Seminary Ridge at Gettysburg, out of the sight of Union observers, five hours later. Ordered to lie quietly, the men nonetheless rose and doffed their hats as Pickett, Longstreet, and Lee inspected their lines. Lee had made his fateful decision to send Pickett's division against the center of the Union line on Cemetery Ridge in a desperate attempt to break the line and turn the tide of the battle after attacks on the Union flanks had failed during the previous two days.

At 1:00 P.M. the Confederate artillery on Seminary Ridge opened a furious barrage on the Union lines a mile away on Cemetery Ridge; the Union gunners returned fire. The Confederate bombardment lasted for almost two hours but did little damage as most of the rounds overshot their target. At 3:00 the firing stopped and the battleground was strangely silent. Behind Seminary Ridge

Pickett's division had formed in two parallel lines, one behind the other, facing
east toward Cemetery Hill. Armistead's brigade, with the 57th Regiment,
constituted the left center of the second line; the 24th Regiment stood in the first
line in front of and to the right of the 57th. Smoke from the artillery duel had so
shrouded the battlefield that visibility was at first obscured. Lee and Longstreet
gave their commands, and the division marched in its perfect lines through the
haze and down the hill to the wheat field below. Pickett's Charge was under way.

Pickett's Charge. (Kathleen R.
Georg and John W. Busey, *Noth-
ing But Glory: Pickett's Divi-
sion at Gettysburg* [Hightstown,
N.J.: Longstreet House, 1987].
Reprinted with permission.)

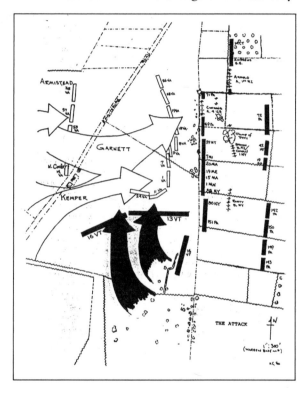

It was an awesome sight to the soldiers on both sides—thirteen thousand men
in two neat rows (the first almost a mile in length), marching through the wheat
fields toward the silent Union guns. As the Confederates neared the halfway point
at the Emmitsburg road the Union artillery opened fire, not only from Cemetery
Ridge but from Little Round Top to the south. Pickett's lines took fire from the
front and from the right flank as well; Armistead's and Kemper's brigades, on the
right of Pickett's division, bore the brunt. The artillery fire devastated the ranks:
by the time Pickett's division neared Cemetery Ridge the lines had shrunk from a
mile in length to less than half a mile as the gaps caused by fallen men were filled.
On the heights above, Union soldiers chanted "Fredericksburg! Fredericksburg!"
while their gunners took revenge for the debacle at Marye's Heights.

As Pickett's front line neared the stone wall atop the ridge, the Union line
erupted in flame and smoke as both artillery and infantry fired a volley in unison,
at point-blank range. The blast of canister and musket balls cut down hundreds of
the attackers and stalled the charge so that the second line passed through the
first. Few of the survivors in the 24th Regiment pressed forward over the wall;

most staggered back toward Seminary Ridge. There they lay, exhausted, as Lee gazed mournfully at them. When Brigadier General Kemper, who had been seriously wounded in the charge, was carried by on a litter, Lee asked him if there was anything he could do for him. Kemper replied through his pain, "Yes, General Lee, do full justice to this division for its work today." Lee said he would.

Meanwhile, against the very heart of the Union line at a jog in the stone wall known as the Angle, came Armistead's brigade, with Armistead himself in the lead—the last Confederate brigadier still on the field unwounded. He drew his sword and held his hat aloft on its tip so his men would know where he was. Behind Armistead and slightly to his left was the 57th Regiment, led by Colonel John B. Magruder. Just before the regiment reached the wall Magruder shouted, "They are ours!" and fell mortally wounded with two bullets that crossed in his chest as he stood atop the wall. Armistead vaulted the stone wall, waving his sword and hat and yelling, "Follow me, boys; give them the cold steel." As he placed his hand on a cannon barrel Armistead was mortally wounded. He died two days later, in a Union hospital.

Some of the 150 or 200 soldiers—many of them Franklin County men—who followed Armistead over the stone wall (the "high water mark of the Confederacy") were quickly surrounded and killed or captured. The colors of the 57th Regiment fell on a Union cannon and were captured. The few survivors not taken prisoner made their way back to Seminary Ridge, where perhaps some of them heard Lee assume responsibility for the disaster, saying it was all his fault. The casualty rate was enormous: Armistead's brigade lost more than 70 percent killed, wounded, or captured, while the 57th Regiment's casualties may have been almost 75 percent. The 24th Regiment suffered a loss of 160 (out of 442 engaged) during Pickett's Charge—a casualty rate of more than 36 percent.[33]

"Give Them the Cold Steel!" Brig. Gen. Lewis A. Armistead leads survivors of Pickett's Charge, many of them Franklin County men, over the stone wall at the "high water mark of the Confederacy." Regimental flags visible in the painting are (left to right) *38th, 56th, and 53d.* (Don Troiani, Historical Art Prints, Ltd., Southbury, Conn. Reprinted with permission.)

After the failure of Pickett's Charge, a grieving Lee led his army back to Virginia. Union general Meade followed too slowly and the Confederates escaped to Orange County, where they made their winter quarters. By mid-September 1863 Kemper's brigade, with the 24th Regiment, had encamped in Hanover County. In early January 1864 the regiment moved by rail to North Carolina once again. For the next four months it saw duty in Goldsboro and Kinston and assisted in the capture of Plymouth. On 8 May the regiment boarded a train once more and returned to Virginia.

During the winter of 1863–1864 Rooney Lee's cavalry served on picket duty. On 9 May 1864 Major General Philip H. Sheridan and twelve thousand Union cavalrymen headed toward Richmond. To oppose them Stuart could muster only about forty-five hundred men. The two cavalries met at Yellow Tavern north of the capital on 11 May, and during the battle a snap shot from the revolver of a Union trooper mortally wounded Stuart, who died the next day in Richmond. Chambliss's brigade, including the 10th Virginia Cavalry, fought at Yellow Tavern and at Trevilian Station in mid-June.

Meade remained in command of the Army of the Potomac, but during the winter Lincoln appointed Lieutenant General Ulysses S. Grant, the conqueror of Vicksburg, as commander of the entire Union army. At last Lincoln had found a general who could get the job done. Grant came east at once to join the army at its winter camp in Culpeper County and supervise its subsequent campaigns. On 4 May 1864 Grant and his army crossed the Rapidan River and attempted a maneuver that would occupy him until April 1865: to turn the right flank of Robert E. Lee's army and position his own army between Lee and Richmond. To accomplish this maneuver Grant's army had to pass through a tangled woodland called the Wilderness that lay uncomfortably near the site of Lee's great victory at Chancellorsville. The aggressive Lee, outnumbered as usual, struck Grant while he was pushing through the forest and used the dense woods to his advantage. The 42d Regiment was engaged early, bearing the brunt of the Union attack on the Confederate right flank. The line nearly broke but finally held when reinforcements arrived. The 42d Regiment withdrew and saw little fighting for the rest of the day.

The result, after two days of battle (5–6 May), was a tactical victory for Lee, who had stymied Grant's maneuver. Much to Lee's surprise, however, Grant did not—as had all his predecessors—withdraw his army to lick his wounds and await his replacement. Instead he turned south once more and pressed on toward Richmond, forcing Lee to assume a defensive posture. Moving ever southward, Grant turned west to fight Lee again (Spotsylvania Court House, 8–19 May) and again (North Anna River, 23–26 May) and again (Cold Harbor, 1–3 June).

By 10 May the 42d Regiment occupied part of a fortified salient or breastworks, called the Mule Shoe, near Spotsylvania Court House. A daring Union attack in the evening penetrated the salient but was stopped by a sharp counterattack. In order to guard against such surprises, the Confederates established a picket line, or advance guard, about a third of a mile in front of the salient. On 11 May the 42d Regiment served on picket duty. At about 4:30 the next morning, as the regiment was being relieved, the Union army corps commanded by Major General Winfield Scott Hancock attacked the salient through the picket line. The regiment barely escaped to the relative safety of the salient. Soon, however, the attackers overwhelmed the salient and killed or captured most of the division of which the regiment was a part. Corporal Charles L. Russell, 93d New York Infantry Regiment, captured the regiment's battle flag, a feat for which he was awarded the Medal of Honor. The 42d Regiment almost ceased to exist.

After the Battle of Cold Harbor Grant crossed the James River and marched his army to Petersburg. Lee reinforced the city to prevent its capture and a possible attack on Richmond from the south, and the two armies settled down to a siege that lasted from June 1864 to April 1865.

The siege was hardly static, however. In June 1864 Lee dispatched Early to the Shenandoah Valley to keep his western lines of supply open and to threaten Washington in an attempt to draw off part of Grant's army. Grant countered by placing Sheridan in charge of a large Union force—evidence of the North's superiority in equipment and numbers of men—without reducing his own army. A remnant of the 42d Regiment continued to function as part of Early's division. It saw action in several of the principal battles of Early's Valley campaigns, including the Second Battle of Kernstown (24 July 1864), the Third Battle of Winchester (19 September), Fisher's Hill (22 September), and Cedar Creek (19 October). At the beginning of December the regiment moved by train from the Valley east to Petersburg.

The 37th Battalion Virginia Cavalry, which joined Early at Lynchburg in June 1864, had spent most of the campaign seasons of 1862 and 1863 raiding and skirmishing in West Virginia. In October 1863 it was assigned to the cavalry brigade led by Brigadier General William E. ("Grumble") Jones, an able if surly commander from Southwest Virginia. At first the battalion served with Jones in Tennessee, then marched with him to Southwest Virginia and Kentucky. It saw action in the Battle of Jonesville, in Lee County, on 3 January 1864. In the spring the battalion marched down the Valley to Staunton, reaching it soon after Jones, who had come to the area earlier with most of his brigade, was killed in the nearby Battle of Piedmont against the Union force commanded by General David Hunter. Soon incorporated into Early's division, the 37th Battalion took part in the fighting around Lynchburg in mid-June 1864.

In July it marched with the rest of Early's division to the outskirts of Washington, D.C., and raided the countryside almost to Baltimore. On 30 July the battalion participated in one of the most notorious actions of the war, the burning of Chambersburg, Pennsylvania. Early had ordered Brigadier General John McCausland to capture the town using two brigades (one of which included the 37th Battalion) and to demand $100,000 in gold or $500,000 in paper money as retribution for the destruction wrought by Hunter in the Valley of Virginia. When the citizens refused to pay, McCausland ordered the town burned; the fire destroyed more than four hundred buildings, almost three-quarters of which were dwellings.

For the remainder of the war the battalion served with Early's dwindling division in the Valley as it retreated before the superior numbers of Union troops commanded by Sheridan. The 37th Battalion took part in several battles in the Valley campaign, most notably the Third Battle of Winchester (19 September) and Fisher's Hill (22 September). The battalion had been joined during the campaign by the 2d Virginia Cavalry, which had performed well in the Gettysburg campaign, particularly in fighting near Ashby's Gap. It broke and ran at Tom's

Brook (9 October 1864), however, when it faced overwhelming odds. By the late winter of 1864–1865 the 37th Battalion virtually had disintegrated. Finally it disbanded on 22 April 1865 near Buchanan, in Botetourt County.

After Sheridan defeated Early at Waynesboro on 2 March 1865, he joined Grant at Petersburg. Grant persisted in his efforts to get around Lee's right flank. His perseverance culminated in the defeat of Pickett's division at Five Forks, a strategic road intersection southwest of Petersburg, on 1 April.

Pickett had retained the 57th Regiment in his division after the Battle of Gettysburg. His command spent most of the remainder of 1863 in camp recovering from the Gettysburg campaign, and later undertook light duty in Kinston, North Carolina. In February 1864 Pickett tried and failed to capture New Bern. Soon thereafter the division marched to Richmond and manned the city's defensive lines.

After being ordered to Drewry's Bluff, in Chesterfield County, in May, the 57th Regiment took part in the Battle of Chester Station on 10 May. Six days later the division, including both the 24th and 57th regiments, took part in the Second Battle of Drewry's Bluff, which temporarily halted the Union army under Major General Benjamin F. Butler in its advance toward Richmond and Petersburg. Charging out of its fortification called Fort Darling, the 24th Regiment supported Brigadier General Archibald Gracie, Jr., and his Alabama brigade, which had been thrown back by the Union defense. The 24th and 11th regiments broke through the Federal lines, inflicting heavy losses on the enemy. The cost to the 24th Regiment was severe, however: more than 50 percent killed or wounded. Among those who died in Richmond hospitals was Major Joseph A. Hambrick, the young Franklin County lawyer who had raised the 24th Regiment's Company B at the very beginning of the war.

Aside from occasional skirmishes in the vicinity of Richmond, Pickett's division saw little action for the rest of the year. By mid-July 1864 it was dug in on the Howlett Line, part of the Richmond-Petersburg defenses, where it remained through the ensuing winter.

For the rest of the war the 10th Virginia Cavalry personnel served as pickets and as raiders against the Union army threatening Richmond and Petersburg. On 16

Battle flag of 10th Virginia Cavalry. (Massachusetts Commandery, Military Order of the Loyal Legion, U.S. Army Military History Institute, Carlisle, Pa.)

August a Pennsylvania cavalryman mortally wounded Chambliss during a skirmish on the Charles City Road to the east of Richmond. Colonel Richard L. T. Beale, of the 9th Regiment Virginia Cavalry, soon assumed command of the brigade of which the 10th Cavalry was a part.

In early 1865 the Confederate cavalry continued its defense of Petersburg and Richmond. After Lee abandoned those cities in April the cavalry covered his retreat to the west. Probably, as was the case with most other cavalry regiments, few troopers of the 10th Regiment surrendered at Appomattox; most just slipped away before the end and headed home.

Late in March 1865 Pickett marched his division southwest of Petersburg to Five Forks, in Dinwiddie County, to reinforce the right flank of Lee's defensive line. On 1 April, as Pickett enjoyed a shad bake behind his lines, the Union cavalry suddenly attacked. Pickett rode through heavy gunfire to organize the defense but it was too late. The Confederate right flank had crumpled under the assault, which enabled the Union army to roll up Lee's lines toward Petersburg. More than two hundred men of the 57th Regiment were captured at Five Forks.

This defeat, combined with a massive Union assault on the city's defenses the next day, compelled Lee to abandon Petersburg and Richmond. His forces depleted by hunger and desertions, Lee and his army fled west in the direction of Lynchburg, with Grant and Sheridan in pursuit. They caught up with Lee at Saylers Creek on 6 April and captured a quarter of his army in an afternoon. Two days later Grant's army surrounded Lee and the Army of Northern Virginia near Appomattox Court House.

Grant, knowing the end was near and in the midst of an exchange of notes with Lee, had been suffering from a tension-produced migraine headache for two days. On the morning of 9 April, Palm Sunday, Lee failed in his attempt at a breakout through the encircling Union army. Grumbling that he would "rather die a thousand deaths," Lee sent Grant the note he had been waiting for: Lee would surrender the Army of Northern Virginia. Grant's headache vanished instantly. He and Lee met at the house of Wilmer McLean in the village of Appomattox Court House and ended the Civil War in Virginia. The surrender ceremonies were held on 12 April, as the Army of Northern Virginia marched from its bivouac into legend.

Among the men who surrendered were fifty-eight officers and men of the 42d Regiment, the remainder of the 57th Regiment, and twenty-three officers and men of the 24th Regiment. The 2d Virginia Cavalry Regiment escaped the trap and rode to Lynchburg, where it disbanded on 10 April after learning of Lee's surrender.[34]

The reduced numbers of men in the regiments at the end was due in part to battle casualties, but also to desertions, as many soldiers headed for home rather than risk becoming the last victim of a lost war. Disease played a large role as well, particularly when the soldiers encamped during the war. Camps were both a blessing and a curse to the men. A newly established camp afforded weary veterans a place of rest and, sometimes, of comfort compared to the rigors of the campaign. During a long winter encampment the soldiers often constructed huts of logs with stone, brick, or stick-and-mud chimneys. While in camp the officers used the opportunity to improve the men's skills by what the soldiers quickly came to regard as endless drilling. The peacefulness of camp life quickly turned to tedium. Boredom reduced morale and increased the number of soldiers absent without leave (AWOL), as well as outright deserters.

A greater curse than boredom, however, was disease. Epidemics of measles, smallpox, dysentery, malaria, and pneumonia swept through the camps and caused more deaths than combat. The lack of sanitation, as well as ignorance of insect-borne diseases, contributed to the toll. To cite but one of thousands of examples, on 19 October 1861 two brothers, William D. Young and George O. Young, wrote their sister from Camp Belcher, which was located in a "nice old field" east of Richmond. They reported that

> we are as well as we ever was only we arnt quite as Strong as we was before we was Sick. . . . We have some sick men & some of them are very bad off. We have lost eight of Company. John Leshure & John Brammer is dead. I wrote you word that they was mending & died here. . . . Dennis P. Stanly said that he saw the Doct. when came back that attended on them & he Said they Both was Ded.[35]

King D. Richards wrote his family from several camps and entrenched positions during the first two years of the war and described the illnesses that swept through the ranks. From Norfolk, 19 April 1862: "There is so many sick men here that they have a bad chance to be out of doors too. The sickness is mostly measles and mumps." From Drewry's Bluff, 7 June 1862: "Our Regiment is very sickly at this time. Out of 1200 or 1300 men we only have about 600 reported for duty. The measles is the worst disease that we have in the army. In fact it kills more persons than any other disease that is subject to the army."[36]

The soldiers also suffered from chronic shortages of supplies, including arms, ammunition, horses, and clothing. Often they had to rely on their mothers and sisters for the last-named article. Second Lieutenant George W. Finney, of Company D, 24th Regiment Virginia Infantry, wrote his mother on 6 September 1861 to ask for clothing. He was very specific:

> Four shirts bluish flanel two of them the other two lincy if you cannot get any blue flanel get them all lincey also get me two pair of drawers blue flanell. If you can not get any mix blue flanel cotton cloth will do. Obtain for me and send them by John A pair of strong boots No. 8 1/2 or 9 also send me 2 or 3 pair of socks with these things I think I can go comfortably through the winter. . . . Tell Babe to make my shirts strong and nice get blue or brown colors I mean the flanel & make me two pockets in the bosom also run a black stripe down the brest make it uniform I want the flanel very nice. Black stripe round the edges of the pockets make the bosom as you like you know best how to make it to be uniform.[37]

Shortages, disease, defeat—all contributed to a general decline in morale among many soldiers, particularly those who lived in trenches or camps for long periods of time. Inactivity bred discontent. Griping always has been the prerogative of the private soldier, no matter what the war, but a lack of action—particularly when combined with the other, insoluble problems affecting the Southern army—was especially conducive to defeatism and desertion.

The army attempted to boost morale by granting furloughs when possible so soldiers could make brief visits home. King D. Richards, frustrated because he wanted to see his wife and baby over Christmas 1862, wrote in 1863 that "it was entirely out of my power to come with out running away and I don't want to do that if there is any possible chance to avoid it. But if they don't give me a furlough after a while I am going to take a French one [AWOL] for sure."[38] George H. T. Greer, a member of Jubal Early's staff, received a furlough for Christmas 1862 after the Battle of Fredericksburg. He rode one train to Richmond, another to Lynchburg, and a third to Big Lick, where he found he had missed the day's stage to Rocky Mount. It was Christmas Eve, Greer wrote in his diary, and

> finding no other conveyance I set out [on foot] with my knapsack on my back for home, determined to reach it if possible today. I happened however to meet with Nick Boone about 13 miles from home who kindly lent me a horse to ride down to Uncle Moses [Greer]. After eating half a dozen of Mrs. Boone's fine pippins I started. When I arrived at Uncle Moses I found that my cousin had ridden all his trusty horses on Christmassing but Jake Webb being a [*illegible*] good fellow would not let me refuse the loan of his horse, which he was riding. I made town in about two hours, a distance of 10 miles. When I reached home, to my surprise I found my Aunts family in great distress over the death of Henry Carper, who had died about one hour before I arrived.[39]

If Greer was a bit surprised to find that life (and death) went on at home as usual in his absence, the civilians at home were equally shocked by the effect of war on their sons and brothers. The stagecoach that Greer had missed carried them off to the war and brought them home again, changed. John S. Wise described the contrast:

> Tom, Dick, and Harry, the new recruits bound for the front, proud in their new and misfit uniforms, seized mother, wife, sister, or sweetheart in their arms, kissed them, bade them have no fear, and scrambled lightly to the top [of the stage]. . . . [When the stage returned] there was young So-and-so, with his empty sleeve. A year ago he had left the place, and passed safely through all the earlier battles; but at Malvern Hill a grapeshot mutilated his left arm. Amputation followed, and now, after a long time in hospital, here he was, home again, pale and bleached, with an honorable discharge in his pocket, and maimed for life. And there, collapsed upon the rear seat, more dead than alive, too weak to move save with the assistance of friends, was a poor, wan fellow, whom nobody knew at first. How pitiful he seemed, as they helped him forth, his eyes sunken yet restless, his weak arms clinging about their necks, his limbs scarce able to support his weight, his frame racked by paroxysms of violent coughing! "Who is it?" passed from mouth to mouth. "Good God!" exclaimed some one at the whispered reply, "it can't be! That is not Jimmie Thompson. What! Not old man Hugh Thompson's son, down on Pig River? Why, man alive, I knew the boy well. He was one of the likeliest boys in this whole county. Surely, that ar skeleton can't be him!" But it was. The exposure of camp life had done for poor Jimmie what bullets had failed to do.[40]

Some soldiers were sent home to die but others, such as Jubal Early, came home to recover from wounds. One famous soldier who visited Franklin County in the course of recuperation was Major Heros von Borcke, the colorful Prussian giant who served on Stuart's staff. He received a terrible wound during an engagement at Upperville on 16 June 1863: a bullet struck his neck and passed down into his chest, lodging in his lung. Surviving almost miraculously, von Borcke became a near invalid in Richmond until 1864, when he spent

> the summer and autumn in light duties, inspections, &c., filling up the rest of my time with visits to friends in the mountains of Virginia, where my poor suffering lungs had the benefit of the cool aromatic breezes.[41]

Among the friends von Borcke visited was the family of his comrade on Stuart's staff, Chiswell Dabney, at Vaucluse, the Dabney home near Lynchburg. Dabney's sister, Elizabeth, was the wife of Peter Saunders, Jr., the master of Bleak Hill in Franklin County, and von Borcke spent time there as well.[42]

For a soldier who returned whole or at least in good health, however, the quiet time at home was somehow more precious and appreciated because he knew it would pass quickly. George Greer wrote of the pleasure of awakening in his own bed on Christmas Day 1862:

> No harsh toned bugle awakes me from my dreams of home, no thundering of artillery or deadly rattle of musketry startles me from my repose on this Christmas morning. I can hardly realize that I am again at home, amid the scenes and among the friends of my youth—
> "Home again! Home again!"
> How entirely different is this day from the Christmas days of my early days. Christmas morning was then the "ne plus ultra" day of the year, the joy alike of the young, old, white & black. Then the firing of cannon, the shooting of guns and the rapid "pop-pop-pop" of firecrackers awoke us to the realization of the anniversary of our Blessed Savior.
> Now all thoughts are absorbed in the war, the cannon roars and the muskets rattle afar on the borders of Virginia, carrying with every discharge some "quondam" Christmas celebrator to that "bourne from whence no traveler returns." . . . I attended preaching this morning, Mr. Greg being the minister. Saw all my friends, among whom was —————, who I was particularly glad to see. I feel like one in a trance, to see my friends, whom I've so long wished to see, around me, just as they were in days gone by.[43]

Greer next returned home almost a year later, on 5 October 1863, after losing an arm in an artillery duel at Somerville Ford, Virginia, on 14 September. By early November he was able to walk around town comfortably. He reported a festive Christmas party in the building that housed the office of the county clerk, where he was a deputy:

> This Christmas bids fair to be one of unusual gayety and pleasure. Already numerous parties or in other words "shin digs" are spoken of. I stayed last night with Joe Noble, and arose this morning [Christmas] at 2 o'clock in order to be at an egg nog at brother's room, above the Clerk's Office. Upon assembling there we found a goodly crowd, to wit: Jas. Greer, Jimmie Carper, G. Frank Board, Bob Blackwell, Copeland Wingfield & John I. Saunders. The egg nog was "alright" about day, and the crowd having

betaken bounteously commenced a scene of the wildest revelry. Jimmie Carper, John Saunders & Copeland Wingfield were soon tight and the rest quite lively.[44]

This was probably the last Christmas in Virginia during the war that would "bid fair to be one of unusual gayety." Soon casualties, shortages, and lost battles would combine to lower the morale of civilian and soldier alike. One manifestation of a decline in morale among the troops exhibited itself in an increasing tendency to fraternize with the enemy. At the beginning of the war many soldiers held attitudes similar to those of Private William D. Young, of the 57th Regiment, who thought that the imprisoned Yankees he saw in Richmond looked "savage." It was also common to denigrate the fighting abilities of the enemy on the one hand, and on the other to give succor to wounded or captured adversaries. The latter, after all, was perfectly in keeping with the Southern code of chivalry. Fraternization across the battlefield, however, was particularly dangerous to morale because it humanized the enemy a soldier might be called on to kill the next day, and ultimately sapped his will to fight and kill.

Private James L. Finney, of Company D, 24th Regiment Virginia Infantry, reported instances of fraternization in a letter he wrote on 23 September 1864. "We are very well fortified," he wrote,

on this line extending from Richmond to Petersburg where our division is. The enemy is also well fortified on our front. Our Picketts are very near each other some parts of the line not exceeding forty yards. Though the Picketts are on very good terms trading & talking with each other, swapping papers etc., though it is contrary to orders to have any communication with them. Were our men caught communicating with them they would be severely punished though ketching is before Hanging.[45]

One offense that often resulted in hanging—or shooting—was desertion. Soldiers frequently went AWOL for short periods of time, usually to escape the boredom of camp life. Sometimes they left to go home to plant, plow, or harvest crops. The authorities often excused such absences, particularly in the early stages of the war and if the unit was not in a combat environment. True desertion, or going over to the enemy, was unforgivable and the outcome was usually execution. Toward the end of the war, however, what had previously been excused became regarded as desertion; the manpower shortage meant that every soldier was essential, whether in combat or on a defensive line.

Often men listed as deserters were in reality AWOL to make a brief visit home or harvest crops, then return to the army. Sometimes, however, they had such other intentions as a life of crime. In September 1863 a Franklin County resident on Story Creek complained that "the deserters have been playing the wild up here burning houses and commiting other depredations."[46] On 14 September 1863 the *Lynchburg Virginian* described a group of deserters who had formed a bandit gang in Franklin County:

A large band of deserters were captured in Franklin County, a few days ago, by the Enrolling officer of that county and his guards assisted by some citizens. It appears that there were a large number of deserters in that county, and that they had been banded together for offensive and defensive operations by an outlaw named Goodson, who was once sentenced to the State Penitentiary but broke jail and has since escaped arrest by taking refuge among the mountains and living out of doors. Under the lead of this character, the deserters had commenced pillaging and robbing the people, breaking open houses and committing other depredations, preparing for Winter by laying in supplies of provisions and clothing. It is said that they had actually erected in the mountains a sort of fort in which they designed to defend themselves, if attacked, against all authority civil or military. But their career has been brought to a close.

Capt. Ridgeway, enrolling Officer for Franklin county, determined to break up the band, and for this purpose organized his detachment and such volunteers as he could get, placed guards at the passes of the mountains, to prevent escape, and hunted down these deserters, capturing between sixty and seventy of their number. Four of his own men were wounded. Two of the deserters are reported killed, but this is not known to be certainly the fact. The outlaw, Goodson, made his escape but the people declare their determination not to relax their efforts for his capture until he is brought to justice.

The example of Capt. Ridgeway and the people of Franklin might be profitably followed in other counties and neighborhoods. It will require strong and prompt measures to rid the country of this great nuisance, deserters.[47]

The group included at least two local men, James P. Saul and William Robert Saul, brothers who had deserted from Company K, 42d Regiment.[48] A second newspaper report published two days later revealed that

Two deserters, named Saul, brothers, were shot in Franklin County Monday [actually Saturday, 12 September] by citizens. They had perpetrated acts of incendiarism and other outrages, when the citizens of the neighborhood rose up and executed summary vengeance on the offenders. The mountain regions of that county are said to be infested with deserters who commit all manner of depredations. Vigorous steps are now being taken for their arrest both by the military and civil authorities, and many have already been brought to justice. Enrolling officer Ridgeway is much commended for his vigilance.[49]

A week and a half later the Lynchburg newspaper reprinted a more-detailed account of the crime, capture, and execution of the deserters than was first published in the *Danville Register* on 18 September:

In the early part of last week, a band of deserters went to the plantations of three individuals, Monroe Thompson, Harvey Thompson, and Mrs. Hays, a widow lady, and burned their barns, with the crops contained in them, together with their hay, oats and everything else they could set fire to, the object evidently being to destroy all the property they could get in reach of. The people having ascertained that these incendiaries were living in a cave about eight miles from Franklin Court House, armed at once, surrounded and succeeded in capturing them on Friday night last [11 September]. On Saturday, three of these deserters thus taken, who were known to be guilty of burning the barns, &c., viz: Robert Saul, James Saul, and a man named Patterson, were brought forward for trial before a jury of the citizens who had taken the matter in hand, and, the evidence being deemed conclusive of their guilt, they were, without any regular process of law, condemned to be shot.

On Saturday evening the two Sauls were conducted by a large body of citizens into an old field and executed in military style; Patterson, having turned evidence against them, was sent to jail and now awaits further consideration. Fifty-one guns were fired at the two criminals who were shot, but no person belonging to the army took a hand in the execution, the affair being managed and conducted wholly by citizens of the county. The men confessed their guilt previous to the execution.[50]

A newspaper editorialist complimented the Franklin County vigilantes, noting that about forty of the captured deserters had been sent to Lynchburg on 26 September.[51] Unfortunately, the executions did not stop deserters from preying on civilians. A year later, in Floyd County, a resident described many of the same crimes:

There are so many deserters in Floyd now and are committing all kinds of depredations & breaking in peoples houses and taking everything they want, about three weeks ago a crowd of about twenty come here. Come in the house, plundered in the drawers took all they wanted, then made Pa get & go to the store. Took nearly everything they wanted, made all the threats that ever men could make, cursed & cut up. They have taken about fifteen thousand dollars from Pa in the last month. I don't know what will become of us all if they aint stoped. They have taken all Henry Bishops gold and silver. Also I hear they have taken fifteen hundred dollars in silver from Mr. Mangafs, they have been to about nearly every house in the neighborhood, and all over the County, is the same way. I do wish they all could be caught. They almost ruin all the people, & will if they are let alone. . . . We are here with no man on the place, but two black boys. We feel lonely, if the deserters should come now, I dont know what we would do.[52]

The army tried and sometimes executed deserters when it caught them. In mid-November 1863 a firing squad executed three soldiers of the 42d Regiment for "desertion, under repeated and aggravated circumstances." Six brigades of infantry marched to the execution ground to witness the event. The three deserters knelt with their backs to stakes, and after being tied to the stakes were blindfolded. One of them, Private Reuben Cooper, of Company K, "wept unabashedly and aroused sympathy among the observers." To add to the horror of the situation, the first volley failed to kill the three men and one or two more were required before they were pronounced dead.[53]

Private James L. Finney, of Company D, 24th Regiment Virginia Infantry, wrote on 23 September 1864 that he had witnessed an execution for desertion:

Well I must tell you one of the most saddest scenes I have witnessed since the war of which occured a few days ago in the fifty seventh Regt. That was a man tied to a stake and shot to death. The offence was desertion. Oh what an awfull sight, Let who will see it. I understand Peter C. Law is or was brought back to his Co. Yesterday. I am fearfull his sentence will be a hard one. I think there is but little Desertion now from our Army some occasionally go to the Yanks from our Regt.[54]

Peter C. Law, a private in Company G, 57th Regiment, went AWOL on 22 May 1864 and was returned to his unit on 23 September. He was not executed, and survived to surrender with his regiment at Appomattox Court House.[55] Ironically, James L. Finney himself provided ample evidence that executions failed to stop desertions. He deserted his unit in February 1865.[56]

By March 1865 all but the most optimistic in the army knew that the end was near. Rather than be among the last to die in a losing cause, many soldiers deserted—not to the Union lines, but to begin the long walk home. Private William Turner, Jr., of Company B, 57th Regiment, described the increasing attrition rate in a letter written to his parents on 13 March 1865:

> The solgers is low down moas out of hart tha air tiered out amos and starve out wrashing [ration] is neair nothing not half a nuff for a man a tawl the Solgers sees hard times wee got marching orders nite be fore last the men wrun a way by gangs thirty 35 left the 57 regemt forty 48 left the 53 regment sixty five left the 38 regment that nite the men is runing a way by gangs everywheair.[57]

The civilian population also despaired. William D. Stone, a cavalryman, wrote his sister Sue on 25 March 1865 and tried to boost her spirits as well as his own.

> You spoke of being despondent and low spirited. Let not the shadows of fate cast their gloom over you, but be ever hopeful that at some future day, not far distant, the blessing of an honorable and lasting peace will illumine the southern skies and gladden the hearts of our soldiers as well as the girls at home, who will no doubt welcome their sweethearts back again with their most bewitching smiles.[58]

Back home, the soldiers' families and friends in Franklin County had been dreaming of peace—and hoping for victory—for four years, ever since the men had marched off to war. A letter written in 1861 by a family in Floyd County to one in Franklin County expressed the attitudes of local secessionists:

> The people seams to think it is for the best for the North and south to Divide as a house Divided a gainst its self can not stand [quoting Lincoln's inaugural address] i had rather they would go on Withe the war that to bee under lincons administration or any Black republican administration even if it causes four years war, all the talk is volenteeringe with the people. We have thre companys of volenteers in floid [Floyd County] there is upwards of twenty in our neighbourhood nearly every young man and some married men volenteered in floid and even the Boys wante to volenteer. We can hardly keep William and Sparrels William from volenteering and goinge to war we are for cecession nearly to a man. if in piece we will rejoice if not By the force of arms. I glory in the Determination of the South. Death or Victory. No more on that head.[59]

As soon as the Ordinance of Secession was passed on 17 April 1861, it severed the political ties that connected the United States and the commonwealth of Virginia and absolved her citizens of any allegiance to the national government in Washington, D.C. The effects of the ordinance soon were reflected in the official acts of local government; on 7 May, when George H. T. Greer became a deputy clerk of the Franklin County Court, he "took the Oaths required by law (except the Oath to support the Constitution of the United States)."[60]

Virginia's leaders in the convention and the General Assembly, once other legislatures began passing resolutions and ordinances to raise troops, moved slowly down the same path. The state's leaders knew that secession meant war. Preparations for war gathered momentum when on 19 January 1861 the General Assembly passed an act authorizing the local courts to arm their respective militia. The law resulted in a flurry of activity around the state as courts met to decide how to pay for arms and supplies. On 6 May 1861 the Franklin County Court accordingly pledged "the faith of the County to make an appropriation of at least ten thousand dollars to arm and equip the volunteers which may be called into the service of the State from this County during the present difficulties."[61] On the same day the court also "ordered that the Volenteer Companies organized or which may organize in this County, have the priviledge of occupying the Court house while they are here."[62] The justices met again on 3 June to consider the provisions of the act and decided to issue $50,000 worth of bonds to arm and supply the militia. The funds, the justices ordered, were to be used "for arming and equipping the volunteers from this County and for procuring necessaries for the families of such of them as shall need assistance."[63]

As the war progressed the government found itself raising taxes to increase revenues to prosecute the war. In 1862 the General Assembly, like the United States Congress, after some debate levied a tax on distilleries. Henry Dillard wrote to Christopher Y. Thomas, the state senator whose district included Franklin County, on 25 January 1862 regarding the proposed tax:

> Professional business has dwindled down to nothing—and having a large quantity of grain on hand at my plantation I have determined to distill it into whiskey. If the Legislature taxes the business, it will reduce to some extent the price of grain, and only enable the North Carolinians who make a great quantity of whiskey to monopolise the market at the most exorbitant prices. More than that, there are not half as many distilleries going into production as are reported to be in progress. Not a single establishment has been started in Franklin with more than two stills. Yet it is reported that many large ones are going to work. You may rely on it, it is not true. I shall of course cheerfully submit to any tax, but I really do think it a doubtful policy to tax distillers.[64]

Dillard hardly was prophetic and he may have been less knowledgeable about the number of local stills than he thought. The Franklin County tax returns for just the period of May–September 1863, for example, listed seventy distillers who produced 7,672 gallons of whiskey and brandy. Individual production ranged from two gallons to six hundred. Among the largest producers were James R. Dillion (600 gallons), Tyree T. Dillion (500), Sparrel Dudley (217), Nathaniel Angle (200), Lydia Divers (200), James A. Dudley (200), William R. Dudley

(200), and Daniel P. Hellar (200). The new tax raised more than $2,000 in revenue.[65]

Not only did the tax fail to suppress the distilling industry, but distillers expanded their activities. In his message to the General Assembly on 7 December 1864, Governor William Smith bemoaned its ill effects upon the war effort:

> The recent crop of apples was the most abundant we have had for many years, and would have furnished a large amount of healthy succulents and an ample supply of vinegar, so essential as an anti-scorbutic for our soldiers. But a frenzy, almost, seems to have seized upon the people for converting this fine crop into brandy, which, in its effects upon our army, is most pernicious.[66]

Besides struggling with the consequences of new taxes and an abundance of brandy, once Virginia became part of a new country—the Confederate States of America—its citizens found themselves adapting to a government that had many similarities to their former one. It possessed a congress with an upper and lower house, a president, a vice-president, cabinet secretaries, an army, a navy, and a system of currency. The confusion wrought by the change to a new monetary system afforded the unscrupulous an opportunity to make a profit at the expense of their less-sophisticated fellow citizens. On 5 May 1862, for example, Sampson Jones appeared before the Franklin County Court to answer charges that he did "falsely and feloniously pretend and represent to Creed Standley that he would give him small notes for a fifty dollar Confederate States note and did by these means . . . obtain from the said Creed Standley a Confederate States note for fifty dollars."[67] He was remanded to jail and eventually ordered to stand trial before the circuit court.

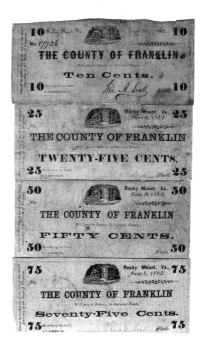

Franklin County fractional notes. (J. Francis Amos, Rocky Mount, Va.)

To muddle the monetary scene further, Franklin County issued its own currency. On 3 June 1862 the county court authorized the printing of $15,000 in paper money, in denominations of less than a dollar: seventy-five, fifty, twenty-five, and ten cents. It gave Robert A. Scott, the county clerk, the chore of having the notes printed, signing his name on all of them, and putting them in circulation; for his services, he received 2 percent of them, or $300. To obtain the county's currency, citizens had to exchange "Treasury notes of the Confederate States or of the State of Virginia, or current notes of the Banks of this State or of any of the states of this Confederacy."[68] The county government, as with its state and Confederate counterparts, struggled to maintain its fiscal footing.

Much of the money raised by issuing the new notes was used to support the wives, children, widows, and orphans of county soldiers in the service of the Confederacy. With increasing numbers of men absent from home and with farming and other types of equipment in short supply, many families that had been scraping by slipped into poverty. One man in nearby Pittsylvania County recalled having to do without, even to the point of wearing the kind of shoes slaves wore:

> I also remember how that such things as coffee, tea, sugar and sole leather could not be shipped in and how we drank rye and wheat coffee without sugar; and how we wore wooden bottom shoes with upper leather tacked to the bottoms. These shoes were made to fit the foot out of sassafras or willow wood and ironed off with narrow strips of iron to keep the wood from wearing out. These shoes were dry but cold and noisy. We had to wear home-made clothing and home-made shoes altogether.[69]

The county government soon stepped in to see that its sons, who were suffering the inevitable hardships of military life, at least did not have to worry that their families were starving. Even to maintain the needy at subsistence levels, however, depleted the county coffers drastically.

At first the number of persons receiving public assistance was not large. The court divided the county into nine districts; in December 1862 there were 56 persons in the first district who relied on public assistance.[70] By October 1864, however, the number for the district had swelled to 232, and the total for the county amounted to about 2,300.[71]

By the end of the war local governments found it almost impossible to provide for their indigent citizens. On 2 January 1865 the Franklin County Court ordered its clerk to notify

> the proper authorities of the Confederate States Government, that this County is now supporting between 1900 and 2000 Indigent persons of soldiers families, and the number steadily increasing, that the Court has now about 1000 bushels of grain on hand for their support, and that in the opinion of the Court it will require at least 6000 bushels more grain for their maintainance till next harvest, than they now have or [*illegible*] in their opinion if procured by purchase or impressment.[72]

If the roughly 2,000 men serving in the Confederate army were deducted from the 1860 white population of 13,642, then about 17 percent of those remaining were supported by the county.

Even before the county began distributing money to needy citizens, however, it illustrated its concern over its wounded soldiers. On 7 July 1862 the court appointed Robert Gray, George C. Menifee, Hay Turnbull, James M. W. Leftwich, and Henry F. English as a committee to visit "any Battlefield, Hospital, or other place where any wounded soldier from this County in the service of the Confederate States, may be, and to see that all such soldiers are properly cared for and attended to."[73] On 4 August the committee, which apparently had visited the hospitals in Richmond, returned its report to the court.

The county justices had to address the health needs of the civilian population as well as the soldiers. On 5 January 1863 the court was informed that several persons living near Alexander Ingram were infected with smallpox. It ordered that a vacant house formerly occupied by Elijah Hix (deceased) be turned into a hospital and that smallpox patients be quarantined there. The court assigned Peter Saunders, Sr., the task of moving the patients to the new hospital and arranging for their care.[74]

With many able-bodied white men absent in the army, the Confederate authorities decided to use slave labor for military construction projects. On 3 October 1862 the General Assembly passed an act authorizing the governor to impress slaves to labor for the public defense. Governor John Letcher soon issued a proclamation requiring the justices of each county to compile the information necessary to put the law into effect. The Franklin County Court devoted several sessions to this task, beginning on 12 December 1862. At its first session it ordered its members to

> enroll in their respective Magisterial Districts all male slaves between the ages of 18 & 45 years—that they in making out said roll, state the names of the owners, the names of the slaves, that they also report upon the physical condition of such slaves as the owner may claim to be unfit for such service.[75]

On 20 December the justices returned their rolls to the court and formally made the requisition for the governor. Two hundred and ninety-nine slaves were impressed from 240 slaveholders. John S. Hale had the most slaves impressed (nine), while Peter Saunders, Sr., and John I. Saunders contributed six slaves each. Most slave owners lost only one slave to the war effort.[76] Not all slaveholders, however, acquiesced quietly in the impressment of their property; Peter Saunders, Sr., for example, petitioned the court on 19 December 1862 to

> exempt his slaves from the requisition of the Governor of this Commonwealth for slaves to be used for the public defense, upon the grounds that his slaves are engaged in making iron for Billharts [Bilharz], Hall and Co. of Pittsylvania County and John S. Brown of this County to be used by them in making guns for the Confederate States. The said Peter Saunders Sr. proved the said facts to the satisfaction of the Court, but the Court refused to exempt said slaves from said requisition, upon the grounds that this Court has no power under the law to make said exemption and it is ordered that these facts be certified to the Military authorities of the Confederate States at Richmond.[77]

Whether his slaves were impressed or not, Saunders continued to manufacture iron, and sold some to Henry County in December 1864 for unspecified repairs.[78]

The impressment of slave labor continued throughout the war. As late as 3 April 1865 the Franklin County Court convened once more to order the justices to compile lists of slaves to labor on fortifications and other public works.[79] Six days later the war ended at Appomattox.

Many of the physical necessities of life were in short supply during the war and were rationed. One product was salt, which was essential for the preservation of meat in the years before refrigeration. The state set up an agency to purchase large quantities of salt for military use and for distribution to private citizens. Until the agency was established, however, private citizens had to scramble to secure supplies of salt adequate for their own use. The county government stepped in on 2 June 1862 to see that its citizens' needs were met. The county court appointed John A. Smith to serve as contractor and ordered him to purchase, using county funds, ten thousand bushels of salt from Stewart Buchanan and Company, lessees of the Preston and King Salt Works in Washington County, "for distribution by sale amongst the people of this County."[80] Smith was to include in the sale price not only the cost of the salt but also the charges for its transportation to Franklin County. He was to sell the salt by "allowing to each individual so many pounds of salt to each member of his family white and black as will make an equal distribution amongst all the citizens." So much government red tape obstructed Smith in the pursuit of his duty that the court on 6 April 1863 observed that he finally had been able to procure the salt only by using $8,000 of his own money. The county's response to Smith's sense of duty was to increase his compensation from $400 to $600.[81]

On 30 March 1863 the General Assembly passed an act to provide for the production and distribution of salt to the civilian population. The act required that each county appoint an agent to carry out its provisions; on 7 July 1863 the Franklin County Court appointed John D. Noble, whose duties were essentially the same as Smith's had been. This time, however, the county issued bonds to raise the necessary funds and required Noble to sell them.[82] A month later, however, Noble resigned in a dispute over the number of locations in the county at which

Bilharz, Hall & Co. carbines. (John M. Murphy, La Jolla, Calif.)

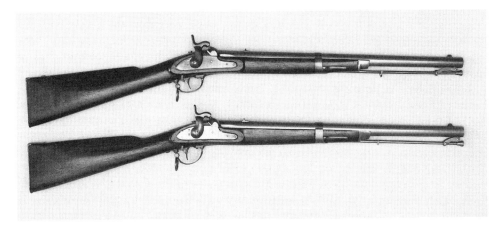

he was to offer the salt for sale. He apparently wanted fewer sites than the court, which appointed George C. Menifee in his place. The justices also noted that John A. Smith had died recently without fulfilling all his duties under their earlier order. Some of the salt he had purchased was still in the hands of the manufacturers, while much of it was in storage at the Big Lick depot or at various places in Franklin County. The court ordered Menifee to tend to Smith's unfinished business as well as his own duties.[83] Menifee did so well that he reported to the court on 4 January 1864 that he actually had a surplus of funds on hand. The court ordered him to pay the balance to Robert A. Scott for the benefit of indigent soldiers and their families.[84] Menifee continued in the position throughout the war; in November 1864 the county justices allowed him fifteen cents per bushel of salt distributed as compensation for his services.[85]

Shortages and financial difficulties plagued local governments as the war ground toward its end. Eventually Franklin County found itself barely able to support impoverished soldiers and their families by distributing cash from its coffers. Instead, it returned to the practice of a century earlier during the revolutionary war and began to impress wheat, flour, and corn from its less-impoverished citizens. John D. Noble, who previously had acted as the county's salt agent, was the justices' choice for this unpleasant duty.[86] On 4 April 1864 the court had appointed Noble to be the county's commercial agent under a recently passed act of the General Assembly that provided for the purchase and distribution to the public of cotton, cotton yarns, cotton clothing, and hand cards.[87] The purpose of the act was to encourage the home manufacture of clothing and other cotton products; this gave support to the Southern cotton growers and reduced the dependence of Virginians on "foreign" products.

Noble had posted a large bond to guarantee the faithful exercise of his duties, which required him to handle sizable sums of money. He also was responsible for the equitable distribution of scarce resources, particularly with regard to the county's needy citizens. In the midst of his task, however, Noble was conscripted into the army in mid-October 1864, which threw the distribution system into a state of near chaos. Noble had made investments and planned for the parceling out of food and cotton, but he was the only person in the county who understood the system he administered. Once the county's justices learned that he had been drafted, they also found that he had been rejected for field duty because of physical disabilities and assigned to lighter tasks. The court immediately requested Governor William ("Extra Billy") Smith to seek an exemption for Noble from the Confederate States War Department so that he could return to his duties as commercial agent for the county.[88] Noble soon was released from military service; he was carrying out his functions as agent as late as 6 March 1865.[89]

Despite the activities of individuals such as Noble, Franklin County continued by and large its peaceful, tranquil ways, war or no war. John S. Wise, a son of former governor Henry A. Wise, described the county in his book *The End of an Era*. The governor sent his family to the safety of remote Franklin County in 1862 as the war threatened the eastern part of the state. John S. Wise recalled that

Rocky Mount, our place of refuge [in 1862], was a typical Virginia mountain village. Even at this present time [1897–1898], when it has its railroad and telegraph, one in search of seclusion from the outside world might safely select it for his purpose. Month after month, year after year, roll by without other things to vary its monotony than the horse-tradings, or public speakings, or private brawls of court days, or an occasional religious "revival."[90]

The Wise family traveled by stagecoach through Big Lick to Franklin County. John S. Wise evidently was unused to life in the mountains, and was surprised by the differences between his new home and the Piedmont and Tidewater regions of the state.

Twenty-eight miles of travel over such a route [the road from Big Lick to Rocky Mount] seems much more than the measured distance, and carried us indeed into a new class of population, as distinct from that which we left behind as if an ocean instead of a mountain range had separated the two communities. Soon the broad pastures and fields of grain had disappeared. In their place were rough, hillside lots, with patches of buckwheat or tobacco. Instead of the stately brick houses standing in groves on handsome knolls, all that we saw of human habitations were log-houses far apart upon the mountain sides, or in the hollows far below us. . . . Up, up, up,—until the mountain side fell far below our track; down, down, down,—until our wheels ground into, and our horses scattered about their feet, the broken slate of a roaring stream. Now, following the sycamores along its banks, with here a patch of arable land and its mountain cabin, whence a woman smoking a pipe, and innumerable tow-headed children hanging about her skirts, eyed us silently; and there another roadside cabin, with hollyhocks and sunflowers and bee-hives in the yard, the sound of a spinning-wheel from within, a sleeping cat in the window, and a cur dog on the doorstep; here a carry-log, with patient team drawn aside upon the narrow road to let us pass, the strapping teamster in his shirtsleeve, with trousers stuck into his cowhide boots, leaning against his load so intent in scrutiny of us that he barely noticed our salutation; here a bearded man, clad in homespun and a broad slouched hat, riding leisurely along on his broad-backed, quiet horse, carrying the inevitable saddle-bags of the mountaineer.[91]

Wise described the village of Rocky Mount as a small, rough town:

[At Rocky Mount] the stage road, after passing our house, entered the main street of the village, which was a rocky lane upon a sharp decline, with stores and houses scattered on either side, terminating at an inclosure where stood the court house, clerk's office, and county jail. Halfway down this street was the tavern, an antiquated structure, with a porch extending along its entire front, its brick pillars supporting a second story overhanging the porch. This porch, which was almost on a level with the street, was provided with an ample supply of benches and cane-bottom chairs. At one end of it, suspended in a frame, was the tavern bell, whose almost continual clang was signal for grooms to take or fetch horses, or summons to meals.

The tavern porch was the rallying-point of the town: hither all news came; here all news was discussed; hence all news was disseminated. From this spot the daily stage departed in the morning. Here villagers and country folk assembled in the day and waited in the evening; and to this spot came the stage in the evening, bearing the mail, the war news, and such citizens as had been absent, visitors who drifted in, or soldiers returning sick, wounded, or on furlough.[92]

Early House tavern (right) on Main Street, Rocky Mount, facing north. Note stepping-stones in street. Late-19th-century photo. (Blue Ridge Institute, Ferrum, Va.)

Not every civilian in Franklin County, however, supported the war or viewed a Confederate loss as a tragedy. The Brethren—the "Dutch" of whom Thomas Bailey Greer wrote to Early in May 1861—by and large stood by their pacifist principles and refused military service. They did so often at a cost to themselves not only in terms of money but with a loss in goodwill among their neighbors, many of whom suspected the Brethren of being Unionists.

The Virginia government was willing to excuse members of the Brethren from military service, provided each man either hired a substitute to serve in his place or paid a fine of $500 plus 2 percent of the assessed value of his taxable property. Most of the Brethren paid the fine to the state, but after the Confederate government took command of the state's army they found themselves subject to a Confederate conscription act. Eventually the Confederate government also exempted the Brethren from military service but not before many Brethren were drafted. In April and May 1863 thirty-six Franklin County Brethren who had been conscripted sought to have their fines remitted by the state; perhaps they intended to pay them to the Confederate authorities, since the Confederate conscription act exempted Brethren from service under the same provisions as the earlier state law.[93]

The Brethren leaders in Virginia, particularly Elder John Kline, who was a spokesman for the Shenandoah Valley congregations, did not hesitate to petition and confront state or Confederate officials concerning their members' nonresistance principles. Many of the Brethren also really were Unionists at heart, although they generally practiced a careful neutrality—a fine distinction often lost on their ardently Confederate neighbors. Although it is not clear whether any Franklin County Brethren were persecuted for their principles, others were. On 15 June 1864 Confederate soldiers murdered Elder John Kline in Rockingham County by shooting him in the back as he rode home alone after visiting a friend.[94]

Some Franklin County residents were Unionists and did what they could to support the Northern cause, including service in the Union army. One was encountered in 1863 in a Chester, Pennsylvania, hospital where wounded Confederates captured at Gettysburg were treated. He was, according to the Southern soldier who wrote about him,

> a doctor, a Virginia renegade from Franklin county, who was insulting, mean and cowardly, and how could it be otherwise with a renegade—a man too cowardly to fight on either side, but sought to protect his worthless hide and scalp from bullets by getting employment in the bomb proof department far away from danger. The boys gave him many a hard thrust—said many mean things to him they would never have thought of saying to a brave man, conscientiously opposed to us.[95]

Black Southerners, of course, had a special reason to hope for a Union victory. On 22 September 1862 President Abraham Lincoln issued a preliminary Emancipation Proclamation. It decreed that on 1 January 1863 all slaves in states still in rebellion would be free; another proclamation issued on that date declared the first one in effect. Because the proclamations only pertained to states in rebellion, however, it hardly had the force of a law of the land. It did encourage slaves to leave their masters and follow the Union army as it passed by, and thousands did so. Franklin County's slaves, though, were deep in Confederate-held territory; the Union army was many miles away, but no doubt a few slaves attempted to flee to it. The remainder had to wait for the war's end.

The end finally came, and with it came freedom. Booker T. Washington described the scene on the Burroughs farm when a Federal officer announced the death of slavery and the Old South:

> The night before the eventful day, word was sent to the slave quarters to the effect that something unusual was going to take place at the "big house" the next morning. There was little, if any, sleep that night. All was excitement and expectancy. Early the next morning word was sent to all the slaves, old and young, to gather at the house. In company with my mother, brother, and sister, and a large number of other slaves, I went to the master's house. . . . The most distinct thing that I now recall in connection with the scene was that some man who seemed to be a stranger (a United States officer, I presume) made a little speech and then read a rather long paper—the Emancipation Proclamation, I think. After the reading we were told that we were all free, and could go when and where we pleased. My mother, who was standing by my side, leaned over and kissed her children, while tears of joy ran down her cheeks. She explained to us what it all meant, that this was the day for which she had been so long praying, but fearing that she would never live to see.
>
> For some minutes there was great rejoicing, and thanksgiving, and wild scenes of ecstasy . . . [that] lasted but for a brief period, for I noticed that by the time they returned to their cabins there was a change in their feelings. The great responsibility of being free, of having charge of themselves, of having to think and plan for themselves and their children, seemed to take possession of them. It was very much like suddenly turning a youth of ten or twelve years out into the world to provide for himself. In a few hours the great questions with which the Anglo-Saxon race had been grappling for

centuries had been thrown upon these people to be solved. These were the
questions of a home, a living, the rearing of children, education, citizenship, and the establishment and support of churches. Was it any wonder that
within a few hours the wild rejoicing ceased and a feeling of deep gloom
seemed to pervade the slave quarters? To some it seemed that, now that they
were in actual possession of it, freedom was a more serious thing than they
had expected to find it.[96]

And what of the Burroughs family, whose world had altered its dimensions just
as radically in its own way as that of the slaves? Washington recalled that as the
Federal officer spoke,

> All of our master's family were either standing or seated on the veranda of
> the house, where they could see what was to take place and hear what was
> said. There was a feeling of deep interest, or perhaps sadness, on their faces,
> but not bitterness. As I now recall the impression they made upon me, they
> did not at the moment seem to be sad because of the loss of property, but
> rather because of parting with those whom they had reared and who were in
> many ways very close to them. . . . [In the hearts of many older slaves] there
> was a strange and peculiar attachment to "old Marster" and "old Missus,"
> and to their children, which they found it hard to think of breaking off. With
> these they had spent in some cases nearly a half-century, and it was no light
> thing to think of parting. Gradually, one by one, stealthily at first, the older
> slaves began to wander from the slave quarters back to the "big house" to
> have a whispered conversation with their former owners as to the future.[97]

At the Burroughs plantation both former slaves and former masters accepted
the reality of the changed situation and sought rational ways with which to deal
with it. Others, however, were not so reasonable. It might have been an omen that
at the first Franklin County Court meeting held after the war's end, on 1 May
1865, the only two mentions of black-white relations were in regard to violence.
In the first case, "Stephen, a slave the property of Elizabeth Via," was accused of

*Burroughs "big house"
(burned mid-20th centu-
ry) at Booker T. Washing-
ton National Monument.*
(Blue Ridge Institute, Ferrum, Va.)

murdering "John Boyd, Jr., alias John Via" on 27 December 1864. In the second case, "Eleanor, a slave the property of Cary Gray," was charged with having burned down Gray's house on 23 March 1865. It is unclear whether these postwar references to Stephen and Eleanor as slaves were made regarding their status when they allegedly committed their crimes, or whether it demonstrated some unwillingness on the part of the justices to accept the new order of things.[98]

At the same court meeting, the justices sounded an ominous note when they observed that

> it having been represented to the Court that acts of lawlessness are frequent in the County, it is ordered that the persons hereinafter named be appointed a special County police under the 201st Chapter of the Code of Va. The persons so appointed are authorized and directed to make out in each of their respective magisterial Districts a Roll of so many persons as they may deem necessary as a posse for the execution of the powers conferred upon them by law, and it shall be the duty of the persons so enrolled and notified of their enrollment to hold themselves in readiness to meet promptly whenever summoned by any of the police, to assist in making the arrest of any person ordered by them [the police] and to give aid in suppressing or preventing any violations of the laws.[99]

Soon enough, however, law and order throughout the South, including Franklin County, would be out of the hands of posses and under the control of what Southerners viewed as a Union army of occupation.

Franklin County suffered little, at least physically, as a result of the Civil War. It not only escaped combat except for some minor raids at the end of the war by the Union cavalry of Major General George Stoneman, it also did not fall victim to the scorched-earth policy applied by Sheridan to the Shenandoah Valley or by Sherman to Georgia on his famed March to the Sea. The county's wounds instead were psychological and emotional.

Part of Stoneman's cavalry passed through Franklin County and Rocky Mount, headed south, on 6 April. The next day the 10th Michigan Cavalry and part of the 15th Pennsylvania Volunteer Cavalry passed through Cannaday Gap from Christiansburg on their way to Martinsville, where they fought a skirmish the next day. A battalion of the 15th Pennsylvania, commanded by Major William Wagner, rode through the county on 10 April, the day after Lee's surrender. It had camped in Franklin County at Halesford on the evening of 9 April after a skirmish in Bedford County with bushwhackers—small groups of armed men who shot at them from long range or attacked the rear of the column on horseback. On 10 April the troopers

> left camp at 8 A.M., in a hard rain, marched over a mountain [Grassy Hill], passed through Franklin Court House, Va., and marched to within seven miles of Henry Court House, where we halted and fed. . . . We marched fifty-five miles, from A.M. of the 10th to A.M. of the 11th.[100]

Many of the stories of looting and plundering by Union soldiers arose from the federal policy of having the fast-moving cavalrymen live off the land rather than burden themselves with supply trains. Officially, the soldiers were supposed to take from civilians only foodstuffs, replacement horses, and the like, but in fact some stealing of valuables occurred when the attention of officers wandered. It is interesting that most accounts related through oral tradition by Southern civilians stress the Union troopers' fascination with family silver, while the accounts written by the soldiers themselves generally mention only clothes, horses, and above all food. For example, the chronicler of the exploits of the detachment of Pennsylvania cavalry that rode through Cannaday Gap on 7 April related that

> while we are now experts at mountain climbing, it gives us no pleasure. It was late at night when we went into camp, too tired to get supper. We seize all the horses as we go along, and get so many, that as those in the column become exhausted, a fresh one is at hand, and the exhausted one is abandoned. . . . If we are working hard we are living well. There are chickens, ham, eggs and biscuit for the men and plenty of forage for the horses. Captured some stockings, which were intended for the rebel army.[101]

On the other hand, it is doubtful that many cavalrymen reported the taking of silver and other valuables from unarmed civilians when it did occur.

Besides being hungry, the Union troopers no doubt were angry because of constant harassment by the bushwhackers. Such attacks probably explain some of the surly and suspicious soldiers encountered by civilians.

Although many of the oral traditions reporting encounters between civilians and the supposedly silver-obsessed blue-clad cavalry seem apocryphal, some have the ring of truth. For example, it is certain that the battalion of Pennsylvania cavalry led by Major William Wagner rode from Halesford to Rocky Mount by way of present-day Route 122 on 10 April 1865. (There is a unit history in which the expedition was mentioned by several of the cavalrymen, as well as the official report of Major Wagner himself.) Taking that route, the battalion would have passed by the Holland-Duncan House, now a bed-and-breakfast accommodation. The house, which was the home of Asa Holland, his family, and his son-in-law William E. Duncan, also served as a post office, with Asa Holland as postmaster.

According to Holland family tradition,[102] the neighborhood had been awash for some time with rumors about the impending arrival of the Yankees. On the morning of 10 April 1865 Peter D. Holland, Llewellyn Powell, and his son John Powell encountered the Union cavalrymen crossing Staunton River at Halesford. They galloped away, pursued by the cavalrymen, who no doubt thought they were bushwhackers. The three men, latter-day Paul Reveres, gave the alarm at each house they rode by, including the Holland-Duncan House. One of the Duncan children, Lula, who was about four years old, grabbed a biscuit from the pantry and raced to the attic to watch for the Yankees from a safe window. Captain Charles B. Duncan, a Confederate officer home on furlough, was riding to the house for a visit when one of the servants ran into the road and waved him off. Just after he rode away the Union men, who approached from both the front and back, surrounded the house.

Asa Holland marched bravely into the road, presented himself to "Major Wagner" as the owner of the house, and demanded that the officer post a guard to protect his family and his property (no doubt he already had heard of the Yankee hunger for silver). Wagner replied that "there was no necessity for a guard as this was a Government Depot and he intended to halt, feed his men and take possession of the Confederate property." Holland denied the accusation and accompanied Wagner as he searched the premises, including several large trunks that were locked, as well as the office in the yard. Wagner found no Confederate property and seemed almost apologetic as he explained that a man in Bedford County had given him the information. The family tradition asserts that there were in fact a box of swords at another house owned by Asa Holland in Pittsylvania County and that perhaps the informant simply confused the two. Or perhaps he knew that Holland was a postmaster under the Confederate government and assumed that his Franklin County house was used for more than a post office.

Meanwhile, Wagner's men searched for cold pies and other victuals. They were disappointed when they were told that in this house the pies were baked fresh every day and there were no leftovers. The men carried away all the meat and cornbread they could not eat at once, but overlooked some corn hidden in a nearby tobacco barn. They also missed some horses that were grazing in distant pastures, while they rode off with two that a servant was unable to conceal. According to family tradition,

> the officer apologized for taking the provisions, but said he was obliged to have something to feed his men on, and in fact, if he did not he could not control them. They went off, taking along the two horses they had found, but one of these (a mare) returned the next morning. She was not in condition to work as they had been told and it seemed they must have let her go. The other was never recovered but it was said that he threw the man who rode him and was so contrary that they let him go too.[103]

As the arrival of Union troops and the stories about them indicated, Franklin County was part of a defeated and occupied land. Even more important—although perhaps few of its inhabitants fully grasped the fact—a way of life had vanished utterly: "gone with the wind," as the novel's title suggests. Whether one viewed what was gone with nostalgic longing or with thankful dismissal depended largely upon one's skin color and previous status. For both white and black, master and former slave, the old world, with all its roles, customs, folkways, laws, and penalties had been replaced by a new world without slavery—a world that both races would find demanded new roles, customs, and laws. Adjusting to that new world (the first of the several New Souths that have come and gone since) would be a painful experience for white and black alike. The whites would have to come to grips with defeat, and the blacks would have to learn to be free.

Despite the early forebodings, in one sense the end of the war had brought freedom to white masters as well as to black slaves: the whites were released from the bondage of responsibility. Gradually, too, the bonds of that perverse, paternalistic affection that sometimes linked master and slave were dissolved and replaced by the ties of economic necessity. The former slaves needed to work for their own livelihoods and their former masters needed their labor.

The law of the land decreed the end of slavery and freedom for all Americans.

Outside the realm of law, however, stood a byzantine social system that continued to recognize and enforce the old rules of subservience and superiority. For a brief period—Reconstruction—those rules were suspended by the occupying army of Federal troops and officeholders. With the end of Reconstruction in the South as a whole in 1877, however, white conservatives reenacted the old social rules with a vengeance, and the era of Jim Crow segregation began. Jim Crow did not end until the era of the civil rights struggle of the 1960s. Between those two eras, white and black Virginians walked a long and tortuous road together.

FOURTEEN

Reconstruction, Freedmen, and the New Social Order

With Confederate general Robert E. Lee's surrender to Union general Ulysses S. Grant at Appomattox on 9 April 1865, four years of civil war came to an end. The South, and especially Virginia, faced the prospect of rebuilding its homes, factories, and economy with much of its youth dead or disabled, its economy destroyed, and its countryside devastated. Virginia had been the site of three-fourths of all the fighting during the war, its prewar internal improvements debt amounted to $37 million, and with the destruction of its financial institutions and the loss of its slaves, the commonwealth's future looked particularly bleak. For the newly freed bondsmen, however, the future held both promise and apprehension. On the one hand, four years of civil war had broken the chains of involuntary servitude to white masters. On the other, freedmen now faced the challenges inherent in their newfound liberty: making a living, acquiring property, especially land, and exercising the franchise. They would also have to confront the obstacles created by whites who sought to transform a society that had been based on black slave labor to one based on free labor that was largely segregated.

With the assassination of President Abraham Lincoln on 14 April, Andrew Johnson became president and at the end of May began Presidential Reconstruction, or, as he preferred it, "Restoration." But Reconstruction did not go smoothly as President Johnson and the Radical Republican members of the United States Congress differed in their approaches to restoring the South to full partnership in the Union. The president believed that the South was part of a federation and that the newly won freedom of blacks did not require special protection, whereas the Radicals maintained that the South had committed "state suicide" and must be punished before being allowed back into the Union.[1] In the ensuing struggle between the president and the Radical Republicans in Congress, the latter proved the stronger party and shunted aside Johnson's Presidential Reconstruction in

299

favor of forced Congressional Reconstruction. Not satisfied with southern adherence to Johnson's "mild" Reconstruction policies, Congress passed a series of Reconstruction acts beginning in March 1867 that divided the South into five military districts and placed a Union army general in each district to ensure that the Thirteenth and Fourteenth amendments to the U.S. Constitution (ending slavery and granting citizenship to the freedmen) were ratified, that each state passed a new constitution to enfranchise blacks, and that blacks' civil rights (under the Civil Rights Act of 1866 and the Fourteenth Amendment) were protected. Virginia became the First Military District under the command of General John M. Schofield.[2]

The war itself had barely touched Franklin County in a firsthand way, several incursions in April 1865 by the Federal cavalry under command of Major General George Stoneman that passed through the Halesford and Rocky Mount areas being the only Union troop visits to the county. But in the aftermath of war, the United States Army stayed to oversee the Reconstruction of the South. A U.S. Army lieutenant was stationed at Rocky Mount and assigned the primary duties of teaching blacks their civic responsibilities, finding them employment and enforcing fair labor agreements, providing them the necessities of life, and generally looking after their interests. Under the auspices of the Bureau of Refugees, Freedmen, and Abandoned Lands (the Freedmen's Bureau), which had been created by Congress on 3 March 1865,[3] First Lieutenants James K. Warden, William F. DeKnight, Newton Whitten, and Augustus R. Egbert served successively as assistant superintendents of the Freedmen's Bureau for Franklin County during the years of the bureau's activities in Virginia, which concluded on 1 January 1869. While each man brought a different perspective to his work, the majority found that "the Freedmen in this county seem to be getting along as well as they are almost anywhere else, and the feeling existing between them and the Whites, appears, comparatively, more harmonious than in many other localities."[4]

Even so, of the four William F. DeKnight appeared to be the most outspoken about the condition of the freedmen, especially regarding native whites' treatment of them and attitudes about them. James K. Warden, who served in Franklin until July 1866, generally reported that conditions between the two races were good, but he noticed a deterioration toward the end of his stay when a number of Union troops were withdrawn. DeKnight observed race relations from August 1866 until November 1867 as Presidential Reconstruction "failed" and Congressional Reconstruction took effect. He was followed briefly by Newton Whitten who echoed the sentiment of his two predecessors that the native whites only paid lip service to freedom for the slaves because of the Union army's presence in Franklin. The final assistant commissioner in Franklin, Augustus R. Egbert, expressed opinions that differed from the other three who had shown varying degrees of sympathy for the freedmen's situation in postwar Franklin. Egbert concluded that "the *natural indolence* of *the race*" hampered the freedmen's progress and, in his opinion, it was the county's poor whites who were suffering the most.

Writing from Halesford to her parents in early July 1865, M. F. ("Fannie") Burroughs gave the native white's view of the situation in Franklin under military rule:

Times have come to that, that people hardly know what to do. The negroes are considered free by *Military law*. Some of them are behaving now as well as they did before & some of them are cutting up on a high horse. Some rejoice in their freedom & some are cut down about it but as a general thing they remain with their Marsters & we have heard lately that they are bound to keep them until next April. Some think they will never be free & some think they will. One thing certain the most of them are ruined & the next thing will be to send them off.

The Yankees pass in small numbers all most every week along the turnpike. They have been at Rocky Mount for a month & are getting very tired of the blacks behavior they are called upon so often to settle a difficulty between them.[5]

In neighboring Henry County, white attitudes about the end of slavery were no different from Fannie Burroughs's. George W. Booker, member of the "House of Delegates (So called)," writing to a friend in Henry, related to him that "one of the young Gravelys—a grand son of Mr. Jabez Gravely—told me, that his grand father did not believe that slavery had gone up till the Comr. of the Revenue in listing his property, refused to list his negroes as slaves."[6]

In the immediate aftermath of war, farmers who had depended on slave labor found themselves faced with the prospect of hiring newly freed slaves to work for them. And indeed by 1870 more than half of Franklin's black citizens who worked were listed in the census as farm laborers, generally for white landowners. Throughout the state in 1865 farmers assembled in county or district meetings to set a wage scale for the freedmen. The farmers generally agreed to pay $5 per month and board for physically fit men and $3 per month with board for boys and women. On 24 July 1865, Franklin's farmers met and issued a statement about wages:

Whilst we recognize the propriety and necessity of giving employment to the negroes and of encouraging them to industry and good conduct by fair and reasonable rewards for their labor, still, in consequence of the many difficulties surrounding the subject, we deem it wholly impractical at this time to fix any regular standard of wages for labor—each case must necessarily be governed by the circumstances attending it, and in the present unsettled and prostrated condition of the finances and business of the country, laborers must be content with moderate wages or go without employment.[7]

One farmer who wrote of his experiences in hiring freedmen as laborers was future Franklin County school superintendent William E. Duncan. When he returned home from war, Duncan took over the operation of one of his father-in-law's farms at Sandy Level in Pittsylvania County, about six miles east of Penhook. Duncan had been a schoolteacher prior to the war (operating Halesford Academy by 1857) and evidently had had little experience running a farm. Between 1865 and 1874, Duncan wrote a series of letters to his father-in-law, Asa Holland, prominent Halesford farmer and merchant, detailing his difficulties adjusting to an unfamiliar life in the postwar world.[8]

Although Duncan spoke of conditions in Pittsylvania County, perhaps his comments applied equally to life in Franklin. In late 1865 Duncan told Asa Holland of the unsettled situation regarding his using freedmen as laborers: "The negroes give me some trouble. They do but little work. I think the sooner we can learn to do without them the better it will be for all of us." A week later Duncan complained to Holland that "the negroes are worse in this county than Franklin." Within the month Duncan reported that "the [uprooted] negroes are passing through the country and stealing every thing they can lay their hands on," but Duncan told his father-in-law that he would have to see Holland in person to give him the full picture. Duncan asked Holland to send the barrel of molasses Holland had been keeping for him as "the negroes have eaten nearly all I had here."[9]

Two years later Duncan's attitude had not changed: "I am every day more fully convinced of the importance of getting rid of all the negroes. They are always destroying something on the plantation and about the house. I look forward to living another year without them with a great deal of pleasure" as he had "no domestics to whom [he] could safely entrust any thing." Duncan's attitude about paying wages to freedmen was equally harsh. Most farmers in Pittsylvania County still did not pay standing wages, and Duncan personally did not know any black man that he would be willing to pay $75 and rations to have work for him. "I am thoroughly cured of paying standing wages, and I dont believe you can make any thing by paying $75 and rations," he wrote to a Captain Craft to whom he wished to sell a mule and a horse, "but you may succeed better than I have."[10]

Peter Saunders, Jr., at Bleak Hill in Franklin County, echoed to some extent the sentiments of William E. Duncan in several 1866 letters to members of his family. In three letters to his mother written in May, September, and November 1866, Saunders repeated that while he wanted to add some buildings to his plantation and sow some wheat before winter as well as to complete other jobs, he also wanted "to save labor especially during the winter" as he did "not want to be burdened with many hirelings" employed "during the bad weather." In May he reported that he was occupied in supervising his "farming operations. The negroes work pretty well & so far I have gotten along smoothly with them. I dont expect to make much but hope to meet expenses. Melinda has returned to us as a nurse & Betty [his wife] finds her a great comfort. The girl we had in her place was a poor chance."[11]

One of the primary goals of blacks during Reconstruction was the acquisition of land and other property.[12] The 1860 census had recorded 105 free blacks living in Franklin County, along with 6,351 slaves. Of the free blacks one woman was tenant farming, and seven others (including two women) owned real estate valued at $2,250 and personal property worth $1,450. Another four had some personal property but no land; indeed, one, Mathews Hix, a carpenter, owned $3,300 in personal property. Of the seven landowners, eighty-four-year-old Keziah Smithers held fifteen acres worth $400 (in the 1850 census her land had been worth $80). And sixty-year-old Lucinda Fry owned $350 worth of land. Ten years later, and five years after emancipation, 48 blacks in a total black population of 5,996 owned land valued at $26,651. At the same time, 1,613 freedmen worked as farm laborers. The black population owned personal property valued at $16,555.[13] Thus while William E. Duncan and some other native whites believed that the freedmen were disinclined to work, in fact most of them were gainfully employed and an increasing number were acquiring land with the money they earned.

Indeed, subdistrict Freedman's Bureau commander William F. DeKnight reported in September 1866 that generally speaking most freedmen were engaged in sharecropping on yearly contracts, although some were working for themselves. Those who sharecropped lived on someone else's land, raised crops, and gave a percentage of those crops to the landowner as rent. The majority of blacks were "industriously at work," and while all of the arable land was not under cultivation DeKnight hoped that as each crop produced more profit more land would be put under cultivation. DeKnight thought that sharecropping was giving "fair satisfaction" especially from tobacco.[14]

Of course, DeKnight did not find the perfect situation in Franklin with regard to race relations. He discovered that it was "difficult for a great many of the whites to realize the changed condition of affairs" and noted that blacks who attempted "to gainsay the assertion of a White" would be considered insolent and their conduct would not be tolerated. Conversely, whites who used "any immoderate language, however extreme, . . . would never be regarded as affording excuse, even for retort." For most contracts between whites and blacks a major provision was that any sign of insolence on the part of the black would result in the immediate termination of the contract with consequent "loss of the entire fruits of his labor up to that time and regardless of the sacrifice of his prospects for the future, at perhaps the very worst season of the year." Thus "evil-disposed" or "unjustly domineering" employers could wreak havoc with the freedmen and subject themselves to violent retaliation. In court contests between aggrieved freedmen and "privileged" whites, DeKnight had no faith that the justice system would work to the advantage of the freedmen. But, in fact, no cases of outrageous injustice to the freedmen were reported to Colonel Orlando Brown, assistant commissioner of the Freedmen's Bureau for Virginia.[15]

In addition to ensuring that freedmen were fed and clothed, the Freedmen's Bureau was also responsible for seeing that the emancipated blacks were given fair treatment in judicial proceedings. In April 1866, Warden reported that he had witnessed several civil court cases involving blacks and he was "satisfied that it is the intention on the part of those in authority to deal with all parties in a manner perfectly just and fair. No fault can be found."[16] A month later, however, he encountered a case in which a white and a black were accused of horse theft, tried, and convicted—"both appearing *equally guilty*"—but the white man received a sentence of one year in the state penitentiary, whereas the black man was sentenced to five years. Warden believed that an injustice may have occurred, but on the other hand the black man's jury might have given the white man five years if it had heard his case. Thus Warden wanted the governor to make the sentences the same.[17]

Several months later, after William F. DeKnight had become assistant superintendent in Rocky Mount, he reported three cases of freedmen before the law: the first involved a man and a woman accused of larceny who were to be remanded to the grand jury but because the grand jury was not in session the commonwealth's attorney quashed the proceedings. In the second case, Henry Fry had been arrested in Pittsylvania County for "stealing" his son from James Patterson in Franklin and keeping him two weeks at E. C. Dodson's (Dodson reported this activity). DeKnight found that the boy had indeed been bound to Patterson and thus the $42 bond Fry had had to give a justice of the peace was in accordance with Virginia law. And finally DeKnight received a complaint from the steward of the local poorhouse that a black man employed at the place had been found in bed with a white, female pauper. The black man had been suspected of this behavior before being caught and warned against it. However, Justice of the Peace John I. Saunders discussed the matter with the commonwealth's attorney, William T. Taliaferro, and decided that Saunders did not have the authority to take the accused before the grand jury.[18] In a later report DeKnight elaborated on the case saying that the woman already had two illegitimate children—one white and one black—and that the steward of the poorhouse beat her for her indiscretion in this case. Soon thereafter, she took her children and left, saying that she had found some other place to live. The accused black, however, was to be indicted by the grand jury for his "offense." DeKnight believed that in all fairness if the man were indicted, the woman should be too.[19]

This was not the only case of miscegenation that DeKnight found. In October 1866 he mentioned the case of a white woman, reputedly a property holder and owner of several slaves, who was indicted in mid-October for cohabiting with a black man (also indicted) with whom she had lived for about twenty years and by whom she had had several children.[20]

Although DeKnight did not report numerous cases of ill-treatment of the freedmen, he did find at least one disturbing incident involving a black woman and a white man. On 1 September 1866, Martha Wright complained to DeKnight of the abuse she had suffered two days earlier. She had gone to the house of "Daniel Padue" on 30 August in company with a white woman to clear her name "of a false charge of having misrepresented some commonplace language of his, by which a misunderstanding had resulted between another family and his." Perdue ordered her to leave, and when she did not exit quickly enough to suit him, he beat her and then chained her hands together and hung her in a tree with her feet just off the ground. Despite the entreaties of Martha Wright's husband (who arrived just as she was being hung up) and others, Perdue refused to release her from about 10:00 A.M. until about two hours before sundown. When he finally did release her, he threatened "that if he ever caught her on his place again, that 'he would blow powder and shot in her, as long as he could find her.' " Perdue was also reported to have stated that he could not get her to leave because of her violent behavior, "as if the same force employed to do that [hang her up], was not sufficient to eject her."[21]

DeKnight referred the case to Mr. Hopkins, justice of the peace, recommending that Perdue be bound over to keep the peace and taken before the next grand jury to be indicted. If nothing was done, however, DeKnight warned Hopkins that Perdue would be taken into military custody. A month later, however, DeKnight demonstrated that so far as the military in Franklin County was concerned it had no real power to rectify wrongs against blacks. Perdue had sworn out a warrant against Martha Wright, asserting that she had insisted on coming to his place after she had been forbidden three times to do so. Thus when Hopkins saw the case, he dismissed the charges against Perdue and caused Wright to be bound over to keep the peace. Indeed, DeKnight's power seemed to be limited to giving legal advice to the freedmen and writing letters to the justices of the peace and the magistrates asking that corrective action be taken in such cases of evident injustice between whites and blacks. But when such action was not taken, DeKnight apparently let the matter drop.[22] It was no doubt reports like this one that helped bring an end to Presidential Reconstruction and the beginning of Congressional Reconstruction.

For the first seven months of 1866, Assistant Superintendent James K. Warden reported that the situation vis-à-vis whites and blacks was generally good. For January 1866 he stated that "since my entrance upon my duties . . . I have seen nothing to indicate any thing save the kindest feeling toward the freedmen except perhaps in a few undesirable cases." Each month until July he found things improving, the freedmen working "well" with "a disposition on the part of both classes, each to deal justly fairly and faithfully with the other." But in July Warden discovered that, although the situation was still "passably good," before "the withdrawal of so many troops, there was a more general justice toward the freedmen, altho nothing of an overt nature has taken place as yet."[23]

William F. DeKnight arrived in Franklin in August 1866 to relieve Warden and found that the situation in the county "compare[d] generally, not unfavorably with that existing in some other sections" and in fact was "comparatively more harmonious than in many other localities." He reported that a group of five huts on Grassy Hill inhabited by white prostitutes as well as white and black men had just been torn down by the owners as the residents would not work and were so "thievish" that they "had long since become a pest to the country." The women were physically as strong as the men, but after their huts were burned they maintained they had no means to go elsewhere. DeKnight remarked that "money to some extent, was furnished, to assist them" with the result that "no personal violence" or complaints were observed thereafter.

A month later, however, he reported that two of the women who had lived in the huts had come to him saying that they had been offered small amounts of money to leave the place but had refused to do so. Instead they used some boards to make a kind of shed near their small vegetable garden. DeKnight told them to call on the nearest magistrate for redress of any wrong they believed they had suffered. A little while later the women returned to say that they had called on the presiding justice of the county, Thomas H. Bernard, who told them he had no use for "Yankees" or for anyone who relied on the military for help, that DeKnight had been sent there "to attend to the 'Niggers,' and if they, the two white women, pleased to place themselves on a level with the niggers," they could just go back to DeKnight as he, Bernard, would do nothing for them. They and other poor white women who had asked DeKnight for assistance, however, were not covered by the provisions of the Freedmen's Bureau Act and thus DeKnight could do nothing for them either. Not unexpectedly, feeling against "Yankees" was "still very bitter" and only fear of the consequences kept one citizen from "killing every Yankee that comes in the place."[24]

One of the major objectives of northern philanthropic societies and the Freedmen's Bureau was to establish schools to educate the newly freed citizens. DeKnight no doubt was sorry to learn that sentiment against freedmen's schools was present when he had to report that one of the leading men of the county had said that no white male teacher who came would find a place to live and any white female teacher would be treated like a "whore." One of the two hotelkeepers in Rocky Mount stated that he would board such teachers at his hotel if his other boarders did not object. Of course, he felt certain that those boarders would object.[25] At the end of February 1867, however, DeKnight could report that a Miss Harkrider,[26] an impoverished daughter of the former jailer, was trying to start a school for black children. But because she was a white native she was considered a traitor to the county, and DeKnight thought that only the presence of the U.S. Army and himself kept her from being run out of town.[27]

In a special report of 15 October 1866 regarding education, DeKnight had stated that a black woman who lived about a mile from Rocky Mount had offered part of her land for a schoolhouse, rent-free, but $250 would be needed to erect the building. As of the end of February 1867 nothing had been done, to DeKnight's knowledge, to raise the money. Moreover, he had reported in December 1866 to Brigadier General Orlando Brown that another site about seven miles from Rocky Mount containing two buildings that could be converted for a school was available at a cost of $300. He asked that the Freedmen's Bureau purchase the property and received a reply from the Reverend Ralza M. Manly, superintendent of education for the Freedmen's Bureau, that it was not the policy of the bureau to buy real estate. Furthermore, no money would be forthcoming for schooling until "responsible parties" undertook "the regular maintenance of a school." Unfortunately, according to DeKnight, there was "no White person in the County who will, and no Colored who can assume any such responsibility." Thus, unless the Freedmen's Bureau stepped in to help there would be no school for black children. By way of example, DeKnight cited the report he had made earlier on schools wherein he had stated that $20 per month could be raised among the black citizens to support a school. As of the end of October 1866, however, only $9 of $45 that had been subscribed had been paid to the "Treasurer" appointed to receive the school moneys and as of 28 February 1867 no more had been collected. Indeed some of the blacks had moved away, others had lost interest or become discouraged, or found they did not have the wherewithal to help sustain a school, so that the president of the school association could not even convene a meeting to discuss the situation further. DeKnight had to report he "very seriously regret[ted] this collapse of a most laudable project."[28]

In March 1867 after passage of the First Reconstruction Act, DeKnight found conditions in Franklin in "such a peculiar transition, as to be difficult of appreciation." He perceived that the freedmen were really beginning to feel free for the first time,

> while the more intelligent appear to realize to the fullest extent the serious and important responsibility which has thus suddenly been devolved upon them; and they are no doubt sufficiently competent to direct the minds of the less enlightened.

DeKnight observed that the white population, on the other hand, was "more sore now than ever." Some few were still conciliatory but more (even those who had been disfranchised) were declaring that they would never vote again so long as the blacks had the franchise. There were only a few true Union men in the county, he thought, and they were mostly Dunkards who could not hold public office because of their religious beliefs, nor had they had much experience of slaves.

Thus the Dunkards did not care much one way or the other, according to DeKnight, about the "great measure [the First Reconstruction Act]."[29]

Elizabeth Dabney Saunders, the wife of Peter Saunders, Jr., who had served in the Virginia General Assembly during the war, probably represented the opinion of much of the white population when she wrote to her brother-in-law on 23 March 1867 that "Mr. Saunders is quite despairing about his farming operations, & what with that and the prospects of the Country, I believe he is more low spirited than I ever saw him. I would be so glad if we could emigrate to some land where the name of Yankee would be 'tabooed,' but unfortunately our necessities tie us down to this miserable one, where we have yet to see or rather feel the worst, I suppose, of what our enemies intend to inflict on us."[30]

In the next several reports, DeKnight described conditions in Franklin as improving, mostly, he believed, because of the presence of the military to protect the freedmen and restrain the whites' resentment. As he had been ordered to do, DeKnight spent some of his time instructing the freedmen in their rights and responsibilities. He preached moderation in all things,

> the cultivation of kindly feelings on all sides; the abandonment, as visionary, of any inordinate hopes, which will most likely never to be realized; the persevering in continued industry, &c.; and I also, while endeavoring to explain to them the necessity for firmness, and that they should totally disregard all idea of fear, tell them that they must just now preserve a perfect state of quietude and avoid all causes of disturbance whatsoever.

DeKnight reported that the freedmen were following his advice and he expected them to continue to do so.[31]

By the end of June 1867, DeKnight was also able to report progress on the education question. He attributed the happy turn of events to the passage of the first two Reconstruction acts and noted that because of those acts some whites who had previously been favorably disposed toward the freedmen had been "somewhat emboldened" early in June and had come forward and established as an educational institution a black Sunday school. The new school was located at Gogginsville, six miles north of Rocky Mount, and had forty-six members. A week later another Sunday school was opened at Rocky Mount with approximately one hundred scholars of all ages. The Gogginsville school had requested books and the Rocky Mount school needed them as well.

> Of course I have done all in my power to bring about this happy result; and now that the work has been entered on, I will strive to the utmost of my ability—especially if the *Books* can be *obtained* to merge it into a day school also.

DeKnight could not be wholly convinced that the whites were motivated by pure altruism, and indeed they might have just wanted to convince the freedmen that they were the freedmen's only true friends. But if someone locally did not institute schooling for the blacks the federal authorities would have to do so, which would leave the whites "still further alienate[d] from . . . the feelings of their late dependents." Whatever the reason, DeKnight wanted to take advantage of any opportunity offered him.[32]

In his July report, DeKnight noted that the two schools were progressing well. The blacks were greatly interested in these schools and it was a common sight for black women to be observed poring over their books. The Richmond branch of the American Tract Society had sent a load of books the first of July in response to his 11 June request, and two weeks later he had asked them for books for the second school. Since there seemed to be a sentiment to establish day schools, DeKnight stated that he was trying to cooperate "with the movers." But he also reported that he had discovered some of the would-be teachers were more interested in their own "aggrandizement" than in the welfare of the freedmen.[33]

On 10 June 1867 General John M. Schofield, commander of the First Military District, issued an order to begin the registration of enfranchised whites and the freedmen to vote for or against a state constitutional convention and for delegates to such a convention if it was approved. When registration was completed 121,271 whites and 106,105 blacks had been enrolled to vote. The Freedmen's Bureau played a large role in registering blacks "since agents were considered derelict in performance of their duties if any freedman, through ignorance, failed to register."[34] In compliance with his instructions, DeKnight reported that he had chosen three or more black men in each district and instructed them about their voting rights. He then directed them to tell the others about their civic duties. DeKnight was frustrated however by two rulings of the Virginia attorney general that caused some unidentified whites to tell the blacks that the whole thing was "a mistake about their being 'put on the Board' " and that the whites planned to get the blacks drunk on election day and cause the latter to vote the way the former wanted.[35]

At the end of July 1867, DeKnight reported that the efforts to register the freedmen had been successful and the blacks were discussing possible candidates to a constitutional convention. DeKnight had heard of those who said they did not

Booker T. Washington speaking in Louisiana, 1915. (National Park Service.)

trust anyone from the area and wished they could vote for a "Yankee." According to DeKnight, the poorer whites there felt the same way. There were no nonmilitary "Yankees" in Franklin, however, so DeKnight counseled the new voters to cast their ballots for the best man or men in the county. He found no evidence of white interference in the registration process, which had totaled 3,052 voters: 1,997 whites and 1,055 blacks. Three blacks had been rejected, two for being minors, and the third for being a nonresident. Approximately 380 more whites could have registered than did and 55 more blacks did register than were expected. Because DeKnight anticipated that the poorer whites would vote with the freedmen, he expected them to decide the election outcome.[36]

With the beginning of Congressional Reconstruction in 1867, "politics emerged as the principal focus of black aspirations" and a wave of traveling speakers, both white and black, traversed the South to carry the Republican message to the hinterlands.[37] The Congressional Republican Committee sent Dr. H. J. Brown (a northern black) to deliver an address on 24 August regarding Reconstruction in Franklin County. Dr. Brown had spoken on 16 August at Liberty in Bedford County where "W. H. R." wrote Brown was doing "great work, and his arguments are forcible, clear, and convincing; and he must annoy Democracy *terribly.*"[38] Moving on, Brown spoke at Salem on 23 August and then headed for Rocky Mount. Assistant Superintendent DeKnight reported to his superiors a rumor that Dr. Brown was shot at twice while on his way to Rocky Mount from Salem, but DeKnight could not prove it.

At the same time that Dr. Brown was speaking to area citizens, the Union Republican party, which had been called to the Franklin meeting by Peter Saunders, Sr., a Unionist member of the Virginia (Secession) Convention of 1861 and a state senator,[39] intended to nominate Republican candidates for the state constitutional convention after Brown's speech. Brown had persuaded Saunders, at DeKnight's recommendation, to preside over the meeting, along with two other white county residents. "The Doctors Speech was naturally most unqualifiedly condemned, and both he and his hearers cordially and equally execrated" by outraged white Franklin citizens, and Saunders and his associates "were afterwards very severely censured for having had any connection with the affair." Each of the county's nine magisterial districts had been asked to send two black and two white representatives to the meeting but some districts sent as many as nine whites and two blacks and other districts sent no one at all. Thus those attending could not decide on candidates to the convention, especially as some of the whites had clearly been sent by other than Republicans. Saunders recommended that they adjourn the meeting until after the order for the election had been issued and try again. He then left and while those still present were considering his proposal his cousin Peter Saunders, Jr.,[40] of Bleak Hill, recommend that a meeting be held on 7 September to be attended by anyone of any party to nominate convention candidates. DeKnight noted that "the term 'Conservative' is the mildest and most liberal that can be applied" to Saunders, Jr., but strangely enough even the black representatives fell in with his suggestion and agreed to the 7 September meeting. DeKnight expressed his dismay at this situation in his 31 August report to Orlando Brown, noting that he had warned the blacks before the meeting not to be seduced by any outside parties.

The Colored People, now that they see where they are drifting to, regret their false step; and as Mr. Saunders *Sr* (the Republican) declares he will have nothing to do with the proposed meeting, the Colored people and Republicans are left without any one who is capable and confident enough to organize their party.[41]

DeKnight lamented the fact that there seemed to be no leader for the Republican party in Franklin. He saw evidence that the conservative whites planned to take over the Republican party and cause the blacks to vote as the conservatives desired. DeKnight felt handicapped by his perception of his authority:

But, while in the discharge of my duty I endeavor, to the best of my ability, to properly instruct, advise, and, as far as consistent, cooperate with the colored, and loyal White people, it is my understanding that I can take no open part in the organizing of political parties.

Created in the North as "a middle-class patriotic club" during the Civil War, the Union League emerged in the postwar era "as the political voice of impoverished freedmen"[42] and local units of the League sprang up throughout the South. Franklin County was no exception. Writing in the *Great Republic*, journal of the Union League, "C. H." noted that Franklin's League members had organized their Council (the local organizational unit of the Union League)[43] on 7 August 1867 with one hundred thirty members. C. H. held the same opinion as DeKnight about the motives of Conservative whites regarding the freedmen's registering to vote:

We anticipate serious opposition from the enemies of the Government, of which there are many here. They possess most of the property, and will intimidate laborers, both white and colored, and prevent them if possible from attaching themselves to our organization. But whatever the opposition may be, we are going to try and increase our roll of members at the rate of two hundred per week.[44]

Trouble came immediately and from an unexpected quarter, when the members tried to have a flag made for themselves. After securing a model from DeKnight, one of the members

undertook to have one made. In doing so he got a White tailor (a Mr. Wm. E. Andrews) to assist him. The latter named person, being in the Store of a Mr. Davis Ayers, was in the Act of sewing on the stars, when a Mr. John Saunders, of Bedford County, at the time on a visit here, entering, demanded to know what was being done. He was told that they were making a United States Flag. His reply was—"Damn the United States Flag! I wish that it, and who ever attempted to make such a thing, were landed in hell; and if ever any one were to attempt to raise it over me, I would send them there damn quick" — or words to that effect.

Someone asked the freedman trying to secure the flag if the blacks planned to resume the war—"which seemed [to DeKnight] to mean that the bare fact of their exhibiting the flag, would inevitably bring about such a result." Thus DeKnight had John Saunders arrested and bound over at a time and place chosen by the commanding general to answer for Saunders's insults to the United States flag. This prompt action, DeKnight reported, resulted in a cessation of overt contempt and the sight of "the Emblem of the Nation float[ing] proudly, free from insult or molestation" at the Republican meeting the next day, 24 August.[45]

Nevertheless, the couple who were responsible for making the flag received word "that they were both hated on its account," he for purchasing the material for it and she for helping to sew it. DeKnight reported that he heard "a Mr. 'Giles Hale,' white, of course, say, that he had the greatest enmity for, and utterly despised it; and when he saw it brought out he could hardly restrain his aversion."[46]

Hale figured in further Union League activities soon thereafter when at the conclusion of a League meeting a fight broke out between a black man and a poor white man. Instead of arresting both parties for disturbing the peace, Giles W. B. Hale, "one of the so called better class,"[47] according to DeKnight, waded into the fight on the black man's side. As county jailer and deputy sheriff, Hale protected his employee by threatening to shoot anyone who touched the black or himself. DeKnight concluded that Hale should be removed from office for failing to do his duty by arresting both men.

Efforts to organize a branch of the Republican party continued to suffer from "outside interference" as well. Another meeting took place in September 1867 with a registrar at large appointed from Richmond present to address the gathering. He did not speak long before Peter Hale and William Burwell began to "cross question" him "very understandably" about why blacks could not vote in New York

> whence the Registrar hailed, and at length proceeded to denounce him as being an enemy of the negroes, whom they accused him of wishing to deceive, pronounced themselves, as usual, their only true friends, and went on to declare that he should not be allowed to continue, &c.

DeKnight was sent for and made Hale and Burwell leave. Nevertheless by the end of September DeKnight had to report that no delegates had been chosen for the potential constitutional convention.[48]

By 12 October when registration ended three more blacks had been added to the rolls, bringing the total black registration to 1,091. At the 22 October election 911 of them voted, 900 for the convention and 11 against. Many whites and about twenty blacks showed up at the polls, however, who had not registered to vote. Some of the blacks thought that attending Union League meetings meant they were automatically registered to vote, and others, although the facts had been explained to them, still presented themselves at the wrong polling places and thus could not cast their ballots. The black vote alone could have elected the candidates to the convention,[49] but a few whites voted with them. The delegates chosen were W. F. B. Taylor and M. F. Robertson. Taylor received 112 white and 834 black votes for a total of 946, and Robertson secured 167 white and 794 black votes for a 961 total. There were nine regular candidates in the field with votes cast for fourteen people. R. J. Webb, an independent candidate and "a good Union man" was not elected, perhaps because he was "said to have been harsh to his slaves." A conservative ("Rebel") candidate, James Patterson, garnered 359 votes, 2 of them from blacks. As he had been disfranchised, DeKnight stopped Patterson's running but upon receiving orders on the night of 19 October had to allow him back into the race. DeKnight believed that if he had not interfered, Patterson would have won with a white majority. Taylor had been nominated by the Republican party and the Union League of Patrick County, while Franklin's Union League supported and elected Robertson, "in lieu of a more suitable candidate; he, while not belonging to any party, still advocating proper and liberal measures."[50]

DeKnight reported that the election went smoothly and the blacks "behaved in the most exemplary manner." In fact, he decided that racial feelings on both sides had seemed "pleasant" and noted that he had heard no complaints to that date of any whites taking "wrong action" against the freedmen. He attributed the lack of complaints "entirely to the force of circumstances." DeKnight concluded, however, that "a large class of the whites feel quite sore over this [election] result."[51]

A month later Newton Whitten made his report, after taking over command in Rocky Mount from William DeKnight. Noting some "slight estrangement" between the races, especially on the part of the whites from the recent election, Whitten attributed such a reaction to the fact that the freedmen had been

> given their suffrage in opposition to the larger portion of the whites in the county. But this feeling could hardly have failed to attend an exciting political revolution as this has been where the once master and slave met on an equality at the ballot box.

Whitten thought that these feelings of estrangement would be of short duration, however. In particular, he had heard of no incidents of retaliation against blacks who had voted contrary to their white employers' preferences.[52]

At the end of December, Whitten sent in his last report from Rocky Mount to Orlando Brown. He stated that he had checked carefully to be sure that no black had been fired from his job because of his vote in October. Despite his failure to find any such occurrence, Whitten averred,

> it must not be understood, as indicative of any liberality or concession on the part of the whites toward the freedmen, relative to the right of suffrage of the latter for such is not the fact. Capital and labor are so evenly balanced in this section that the former could not dispense with the latter without serious injury. Furthermore, the fear of future legislation has a good effect in counteracting any oppressive action of this nature, and these facts alone probably prevent the discharge of the freedmen to some extent, and not any political change in the view of the whites in the county.[53]

The last assistant commissioner for Franklin County arrived in January 1868 and he took a different view from the others of black-white relations in the county. Augustus R. Egbert found that the blacks showed an unwillingness to enter labor contracts with whites and attributed their hesitation both to distrust of whites whom the blacks thought would not pay what was owed when the crops were harvested and to what he termed "the *natural indolence* of *the race*." Egbert noted that the freedmen "work no more than is absolutely necessary—(& even when agreements are made the freed people work very irregularly) partly, no doubt because of the uncertainty of payment, & partly because they feel that they *had* to *work* when *slaves* & *now* that they are *free* they do not *choose to*—This feeling will last for a time—& is natural."[54]

Another factor that disturbed the process of making contracts, Egbert reported, was

> the fact that the laws of Virginia *bind* the *white man* & *not* the *negro* when a *verbal* contract is made—Evilly disposed persons, therefore, frequently persuade the freed people that they have been hiring for too little & that they can get more at such & such a place—or, that they will not be well treated. Hence they break their engagements & hire to another—This most frequently occurs with regard to the hiring of children.[55]

But Egbert also pointed out his discovery concerning the nature of society in Franklin:

> It must be borne in mind that this section of the country is very different from the other parts of the State—there were here during the war a large, comparatively, population of Union people—very little aristocracy—& the war feeling not so bitter—These things may acct. in a measure for there being so little difficulty between the two races—The uncertainty of the political aspect of affairs, too, has its influence.
> Taken altogether, I think the comparative situation of the freed-people here better than in many other parts of the State as compared with the Whites—
> The country is so poor agriculturally that it will require a long time to become prosperous—& the freedman will rise if educational advantages be afforded him—in the scale of humanity furt[h]er than the country will recover from its present prostrations.[56]

Schooling the freedmen also occupied Egbert's attention. Only if the Freedmen's Bureau stepped in with financial aid could the freedmen be educated— "the *only* means by which the Status of the negro can be improved"—as the freedmen themselves were "*too poor*" to raise enough money even to build a schoolhouse. Blacks were vitally interested in educating their children, but "on the Bureau then falls the onus of the matter—It has become a mere question of Dollars & cents & in this view of the question they [the bureau officials] must decide the matter."[57]

A month later, Egbert reiterated his call for the bureau's financial assistance to educate the freedmen and pointed out "they know that the Bureau has furnished with school house & teachers—gratis—in *other counties* & *they are willing she should do the same here.*" Moreover, the bureau could expect to support black education in Franklin for "a very long time"; and if no such aid was forthcoming, little could be done for the blacks. Egbert, however, had heard that a black woman was teaching black children to read at Charles B. Reynolds's place in an old cabin there. She was reportedly charging one dollar per child per month and had about sixteen pupils. There would be a hundred, said the informant, if the school were free.[58]

Interestingly enough, Egbert thought that the poor whites were suffering most of any group in Franklin. While there were "*loud complaints* of *Hard times* among all classes" and certainly the blacks did and would "suffer to some extent," Egbert thought their suffering was not more than the poor whites, who were the only ones to "come on the county" in his last reporting period. Expressing an attitude typical of the time, Egbert noted that "nothing but actual experience & necessity will appeal to the reason of the Freed people with sufficient force to impress on their minds the necessity for economy and prudent living." Egbert enumerated several of the "hundred" reasons why some freedmen did not want to work, including failure to adhere to contracts with whites, laziness, and unauthorized absences from work to attend political meetings, especially at harvest and other busy times. Few of the freedmen, however, earned enough to pay for more than food and clothes and many of them were "improvident & will mire in debt": they did not discover how great their debts were until time to make the payment. But "the poor whites deceive them a great deal & stir up a feeling against the able employers—induce them to work for them, to exchange substantials for apple brandy." Egbert declared that he had not found too many instances of this deceit, however.[59]

Egbert also reported in March 1868 on the status of freedmen before the courts and noted that in one case of assault involving whites only as defendants, a black was serving as "an important witness." In fact, in December 1867, Newton Whitten had recounted two trials of blacks wherein the blacks had been allowed to give evidence "and I believe full weight was given to their testimony and the law relating there to carried out in good faith."[60] Egbert also found, among others in the February and March courts of 1868, two cases of whites assaulting and one shooting at blacks, four petit larcenies, three misdemeanors, and one lewd cohabitation. Egbert concluded that the action of the court toward blacks had been "perfectly fair."[61]

From March until June 1868 Egbert reported that the conditions he had found in March still existed. For the final six months of the year, he submitted no further reports. By 1869 the Freedmen's Bureau and the Union officers had left Franklin County while the state of Virginia went about the completion of the process of being readmitted to the federal Union. The constitutional convention that met in Richmond from 3 December 1867 until 16 April 1868 created a new state constitution that brought Virginia more nearly into compliance with Congressional Reconstruction guidelines. The constitution, known familiarly as the Underwood Constitution for the convention's president, John C. Underwood, a federal judge from New York, introduced universal manhood suffrage, the secret ballot, and a statewide system of public schools. But the new constitution also disfranchised many former Confederates and replaced Virginia's traditional system of county government controlled by justices of the peace with a New England–style township system. Because of widespread opposition to these last two provisions, a compromise committee persuaded President Ulysses S. Grant to place the last two items separately before the voters. The result was an overwhelming approval of the constitution itself, rejection of the final two planks, and Virginia's readmission to the Union. In November 1869 Virginians again elected a governor for the first time since 1864, and Reconstruction came to an end.[62]

In November 1866 William F. DeKnight had reported to Orlando Brown that an unfortunate precedent may have been set when Justice of the Peace Thomas H. Bernard granted a license for freedman John P. DeHaven to marry. Since there was "no lack of regularly ordained ministers," DeKnight feared that such an indiscretion might "operate to divest that rite of somewhat of its solemnity [as] it d[id] not leave as distinct a line of demarkation between the past system that ha[d] prevailed, and the present that should obtain." That is, DeKnight wanted the freedmen to have religious wedding ceremonies so as to ensure that the marriages would last, in contrast to slave marriages that were not conducted by religious authorities but informally sanctioned by the slave master. Contrary to DeKnight's fears in this case, however, it is clear that Bernard was simply legalizing an existing common law marriage. Indeed, from the 1870 census it appears that John P. DeHaven was a fairly prosperous farmer with a stable family life. At the age of fifty-two, he owned 100 acres of land (75 of it improved and 25 of it forested), his farm was worth $500 and his personal property $250. DeHaven and his wife, Elizabeth, had eight children ranging in age from four to twenty-one, four of whom worked as farm laborers. The household also included a twenty-two-year-old farm laborer and his two young children as well as three more young DeHaven girls whose relationship to the others is not clear. In addition, DeHaven owned a horse, four cows and two oxen, three sheep, five hogs, altogether worth $200, as well as farm machinery valued at $40. By August when the census was taken he had raised 20 bushels of winter wheat, 200 bushels of Indian corn, 100 bushels of oats, 780 pounds of tobacco, 50 bushels of Irish potatoes, 3 tons of hay, 10 pounds of flax, and 3 bushels of flaxseed. He and his family had also produced 100 pounds of butter and 20 gallons of sorghum molasses. The value of his animals slaughtered was $50 and the estimated value of all of his farm products including animals purchased was $450.[63]

In 1860 there had been 105 free blacks in Franklin and 6,351 slaves, with a white population of 13,642.[64] In 1870 Franklin's total population was 18,264 and of that number 5,996 were black, constituting 33 percent of the county's inhabitants. More than half of the black population was described in the census with some type of occupation (or in 144 cases "no occupation," mostly for those older citizens who had "retired," and another 157 "at home," primarily teenagers). Of those 3,074 who worked, there were 1,613 farm laborers, 94 cooks, 265 domestic servants, and 887 women keeping house. It is interesting to note that so many of Franklin's black women had been able to join "the nineteenth century's 'cult of domesticity,' which defined the home as a woman's proper sphere,"[65] since before the war most slave women had worked in the fields along with the slave men.

Of the other occupations represented by blacks in 1870, there were 17 blacksmiths, 26 working in tobacco factories, 5 carpenters, 1 wheelwright, 1 collier, 1 hammerman, 1 working in a forge, 2 hostlers, 5 millers, 1 nurse, 11 wagoners, 1 gardener, 2 shoemakers, 2 hotel waiters, 1 hotel cook, and 1 at school. Another 59 were farmers.[66] Five of the 59 farmers lived in the Glade Hill section of Franklin County and may constitute a representative sample of the entire group.

There were 2,550 people living in Glade Hill and 188 of them were farmers. The 183 white farmers owned 50,662 acres worth $160,200, and the 5 black farmers owned 1,765 acres worth $2,500. Thus the average white farmer's land was worth $3.16 per acre, while the average black's was $1.42 per acre, with less of his acreage in improved land than the average white's. Other categories find closer parallels between whites and blacks, however. For the value of each man's livestock, the average for the blacks was $236 and for whites $240; and for the estimated value of all farm products (mostly crops) the blacks' average was $865 apiece while the whites' was $885. Of individual crops, the black average for tobacco was 1,980 pounds as compared to 1,397 for whites; 230 bushels of Indian corn to the whites' 195; 33 bushels of winter wheat to the whites' 31; but 106 bushels of oats to the whites' 124; no rye to the whites' 3 bushels; and 75 pounds of butter to the whites' 132.[67]

It was clear in 1870 that the pattern of black life in Franklin did not differ substantially from that of much of the rest of the state with black populations. Fifty-two percent of the employed blacks were engaged as farm laborers, with another 12 percent serving as domestic servants or cooks, the traditional roles that blacks had held from soon after their arrival in the colony in 1619. But there was some hope for the future. At least two of the black farmers owned land worth about $1,000 and a third, Creed Williams, held land valued at $5,000. These three stood out from the rest as well in the estimated value of their farm products: $700 for Stephen Warren and $1,430 for Lewis Walker, both of Glade Hill; and $1,053 for Creed and Harriett Williams, of Long Branch. Thus much had been accomplished, especially in the freeing of 6,351 slaves, but much was left to do.[68]

FIFTEEN

Rocky Mount Comes of Age

In Virginia before the Civil War a courthouse town such as Rocky Mount and a county's mercantile center usually were one and the same; the town came into being because the court met there and the crowds that came to court also came to buy the necessities of life. In turn the mercantile activities of the town both required and attracted turnpikes as merchants and their customers clamored for better transportation. People and goods, however, could move no faster than a horse could trot, which meant that a customer in a hurry was forced to buy locally. A rough ride to Rocky Mount was endurable and relatively convenient, whereas a similar ride to Lynchburg called for an effort too great for many to make. The coming of the iron horse, which could run all day at ten miles an hour, suddenly expanded the potential market for each customer. Lynchburg and Danville could be just about as convenient to a Franklin County resident as Rocky Mount if a railroad station was nearby. The challenge for the county was to attract a railroad line.

The Civil War destroyed the viability of the antebellum internal improvement system in Virginia and ultimately the state sold its interest in all but one internal improvement company. Most of the joint stock companies, such as the Rocky Mount Turnpike Company and the Pittsylvania, Franklin, and Botetourt Turnpike Company, that had funded and constructed the state's network of turnpikes and canals were out of business. The costs of maintaining the turnpikes almost always exceeded revenues and all but a few of them became part of county road systems; the canals could not compete with the faster, more efficient railroads.

After the war the railroads, which had proved their worth in shuttling troops and supplies during the conflict, emerged as the dominant form of transportation in the country. On 10 May 1869 the crews laying track for the Union Pacific and Central Pacific railroads linked their lines near Promontory, Utah, completing the first transcontinental railroad. Now the country was united by a rudimentary rail system that could transport more goods and people from coast to coast—and do it much faster—than any boat or stagecoach. Every town and market center suddenly seemed closer to every other center, and the competition for railroad service grew fierce. Towns that sprang up around rail junctions prospered, while others not as fortunately situated withered and died.

Rocky Mount's first attempt after the Civil War to attract a railroad, as with those before it, was unsuccessful. Early in 1872 supporters of a narrow-gauge railroad between Liberty, in Bedford County, and Rocky Mount wrote that

> the country through which the proposed road will pass is a splendid section of the State, and if its resources were opened up, would attract the attention of emigrants of the very best class. It is one of the finest tobacco growing regions in the world, and can produce "yaller kivers" [covers or wrappers] equal to those of Pittsylvania or anywhere.[1]

The General Assembly cooperated by passing an act on 23 March 1872 that incorporated the Liberty and Rocky Mount Narrow Gauge Railroad Company. The act named twenty-one directors, eleven at Liberty and ten at Rocky Mount. The latter included Moses G. Booth, B. M. Hatcher, Peter Saunders, George H. C. Greer, George E. Dennis, Hughes Dillard, J. W. Hartwell, James C. English, John S. Hale, and J. C. Ferguson. Despite the passage of the act, however, the road never was built. Whereas before the war enthusiasm and capital were plentiful enough to justify the construction of a railroad from almost any population center to any other, afterwards that was no longer enough. The enthusiasm still existed but the capital was scarce. Before a community could attract a railroad, it required something extra to offer: a prime location or some resource unavailable elsewhere.[2]

The success of Big Lick as a rail center in the 1880s provided the model for other towns to follow. One railroad—the Norfolk and Western (formerly the Virginia and Tennessee)—already passed through the community when the attempt was made to attract a second in 1881. The Norfolk and Western was about to extend its line to the newly opened Pocahontas coal mines. Meanwhile, the Shenandoah Valley Railroad was approaching the Big Lick end of the Valley but was about to be diverted from Buchanan to Lynchburg, the site of the headquarters of the Norfolk and Western Railroad. Several citizens of Big Lick, led by John C. Moomaw, became convinced that their town would make a better terminus for the road; after a meeting of interested citizens on 21 April 1881 that raised enough funds to purchase the right-of-way into the town, Moomaw rode to a meeting of the road's board of directors in Lexington and persuaded them to his point of view. Not only did the Shenandoah Valley Railroad come to Big Lick, but in 1883 the Norfolk and Western Railroad also moved its headquarters there from Lynchburg. Big Lick became the hub of railroading in Southwest Virginia.[3]

The transformation of Big Lick into Roanoke showed what could be wrought with a railroad. In April 1881 the village of Big Lick had a population of about seven hundred. By 1884 the village had grown to a city of almost five thousand. The railroad made the difference. Although not every village could attain the size of a city, railroad or no railroad, each county through which a rail line passed could expect a bit more prosperity. Franklin County eventually reaped the benefits that resulted from the junction of two railroads at Rocky Mount: the

Franklin and Pittsylvania Railroad and the Roanoke and Southern line of the Norfolk and Western Railroad.

The Franklin and Pittsylvania Railroad received its charter from the General Assembly on 12 March 1878. The impetus for the road was the purchase in 1877 of Franklin County iron mines by the Pennsylvania Steel Company. In Pittsylvania County other mines, mostly of barite and manganese, had been developed near Pittsville on the Lynchburg-Danville Division of the Southern Railroad. The Franklin and Pittsylvania Railroad linked the two mining areas.[4]

The route was just under thirty-six miles long and took until 1880 to complete. It ran approximately along present-day Route 40 from Gretna (then called Franklin Junction) through the Pittsylvania County communities of Farmer, Pittsville, Toshes, Sandy Level, and Angle, then into Franklin County and through Penhook, Novelty, Union Hall, Glade Hill, Redwood, and into Rocky Mount.

Franklin and Pittsylvania Railroad depot in Rocky Mount. Early-20th-century photo. (Blue Ridge Institute, Ferrum, Va.)

Franklin and Pittsylvania Railroad "one and only" engine and crew. Standing, left to right: *unidentified brakeman, Mr. Haskins, Mr. Mayhew (conductor), Clifton Doss (engineer).* Above, left to right: *M. I. Scruggs, unidentified fireman, Mr. Haskins's daughter. 1920 photo. (Bicentennial Reflections* [N.p.: Franklin County Bicentennial Commission, 1986], 58. Reprinted with permission.)

According to a 1915 schedule, a one-way trip from start to finish took just under three hours.

In 1880, then, Rocky Mount was linked by an east-west line to a railroad—the Southern—that ran north and south through Lynchburg and Danville. Before the century ended another branch line, the Roanoke and Southern, tied Rocky Mount directly to a north-south route.

The Roanoke and Southern Railroad was conceived in 1886 as a branch line of the Norfolk and Western Railroad from Roanoke to Winston-Salem, North Carolina. Incorporated in Virginia on 12 February 1886 and in North Carolina eleven days later, the railroad was not completed until 1892. When finished it stretched 123 miles from Roanoke, through Rocky Mount to Martinsville, and on to Winston-Salem. The line was exceptionally crooked, however, because of the hilly country through which it ran. The rambling route earned the line its nickname, the Punkin Vine.[5]

Just as Big Lick competed with other Valley towns for railroad business, so did Rocky Mount for the Roanoke and Southern Railroad. On 14 June 1890 the citizens of Rocky Mount approved a bond referendum for $20,000 to attract the railroad to their town. Apparently there was some opposition to the issue, for on 22 February a writer for the *Roanoke Daily Times* pointed out that the construction of the branch line to the south would give Roanoke

> transportation facilities with Franklin and Henry counties, which raise the finest tobacco of any section of the globe, and also with Danville and the "bright belt" of North Carolina. All of the tobacco that is shipped to Lynchburg from the first named counties, has to go over two roads, and it takes about four days for a farmer to make a trip, dispose of his crop and return home.[6]

The writer stressed that the proposed road would enable a Franklin County farmer to ride to Roanoke, sell his crop, and return home all in the same day.

Map showing railroad lines through Rocky Mount. (Poor's Manual of the Railroads of the United States, 1913 [New York: Poor's Railroad Manual Co., 1913].)

At about the same time a writer in the *Henry County Bulletin* urged his neighbors in Franklin County to approve the referendum, under the headline "Good Advice, A Sensible Talk to the People of Franklin County":

Should they decline to aid in the construction of the work from which they expect so many benefits, simply because the road is to be built anyhow, then they may have to wait a long time for its blessings. What right would Franklin people have to ask favors of a railroad company whom they had snubbed in its incipiency? What right would they have to ask for the location of a depot, for special rates on freight, or for anything the company might be able to give, if they refuse to aid in its construction, when to do so, would not increase their taxes one cent? . . . It has become the custom of railroads to advertise and point out the advantages of the country through which they run. Could Franklin County expect the railroad people to make the same effort on their behalf, should they fail to vote for the subscription, as for the communities from which they have drawn support?[7]

Whether the eloquence of this particular writer swayed the "Franklin people" is unclear, but the vote that approved the $20,000 referendum was reported later as "unanimous." Supposedly enthusiasm for the project was so high that the people of Rocky Mount gladly would have voted five times that amount.[8]

Despite this enthusiasm, however, the terrain almost caused the road to bypass Rocky Mount. In August 1890 two construction engineers surveying various routes through the county from Roanoke to Martinsville admitted that they were examining three possible routes, one through Rocky Mount and two to the west of it. Even as late as September the most that the chief engineer of the railroad would admit was that the line might pass near the town. On 25 October 1890, however, the Roanoke paper carried the jubilant report from Rocky Mount that

Col. Crocker, chief of the corps operating on the line between this place and Roanoke, has made one of the most successful pieces of engineering in the last few days ever accomplished in this country. He has succeeded in running a beautiful line around the end of Grassy Hill, near this place, securing an easy grade and reducing the cost of construction over the middle route immensely.[9]

Essie Smith, who for many years served as Rocky Mount's librarian, recalled the excitement when the line was completed:

You have to remember that the country about us was largely wilderness. We had no contact with the outside world but the little Danville and Pittsylvania Railroad from Rocky Mount to Franklin Junction, now Gretna.
   So when the Roanoke and Southern folks came and the contractors (Allen and Moseley, Fortune Brothers, I believe), there was real excitement. I remember especially a great ball that the engineers gave when the line was completed. Major Andrew Onderdonk, the chief engineer, was there and Colonel [F. H.] Fries [one of the early supporters of the line]. . . . It was a gay occasion but a sad one, too, because it meant all of these people would be leaving and they had meant a lot to the town.[10]

Perhaps because the Franklin and Pittsylvania Railroad gained a reputation for being slow and irregular, it was referred to ironically as the "Fast and Perfect." Even the company admitted its faults: the same 1915 schedule that showed the Gretna-to-Rocky Mount trip as a three-hour journey noted in the fine print that "the time and connections shown are not guaranteed"; the fine print did not explain that most delays were due to derailments. According to one of the many stories about the railroad, one day a train approaching Penhook stopped when the engineer noticed a minister walking near the track. When offered a ride to the village, the minister declined because he was in a hurry. The railroad's customers also noted with tongue-in-cheek pride that although the line was not as long as some others, it was generally about as wide.

Derailments were a problem. Occasionally an engine jumped the tracks and came to rest in some farmer's cornfield. Injuries, fortunately, seldom were serious. Once a derailment occurred just as the train pulled into the Rocky Mount station; the passenger cars almost tipped over, throwing some of the standing travelers toward the exits. A salesman remarked that although he had enjoyed the ride to that point, he disliked the company's method of unloading passengers.

Both railroads began as independent companies but were quickly absorbed into the larger lines. The Southern Railroad leased the Franklin and Pittsylvania Railroad for thirty-four years after its construction; when the lease expired in 1914 the two counties assumed custody of the road, which once again became independent. Unfortunately, the line was unprofitable and the officers filed for bankruptcy in 1921. A year later Nathaniel P. Angle purchased the line. Angle, perhaps the leading businessman in Rocky Mount, hoped to keep Franklin County's "own" railroad in operation, but in 1932 he admitted defeat and closed down the line. The Punkin Vine line, or Roanoke and Southern branch of the Norfolk and Western Railroad, has continued to operate to the present day. The Norfolk and Western leased it beginning in 1892.

Despite its success in attracting two railroads, Rocky Mount did not become another Roanoke. The railroads were branch lines, not trunk lines, and Rocky Mount was not suitably located, as was Roanoke, at the crossroads for rail

Franklin and Pittsylvania Railroad derailment. (Blue Ridge Institute, Ferrum, Va.)

transportation among Southwest Virginia, the Valley, and the Piedmont. Nonetheless, the freight and passenger depot at the junction in Rocky Mount contributed to the increased prosperity enjoyed by the town in the late nineteenth century.

The General Assembly had incorporated the town of Rocky Mount, the boundaries of which were to extend a half mile in every direction from the courthouse, by an act passed on 17 February 1873. The legislature appointed Giles W. B. Hale, Hughes Dillard, Thomas B. Greer, John I. Saunders, William E. Andrews, Hugh Nelson, and Robert A. Scott as trustees for the town. It empowered them to elect a mayor from among their membership and to appoint a town sergeant, a police force, and other necessary town officers. The old town of Mount Pleasant, which had been formed in 1804 over the objections of Robert Hill and James Callaway, was absorbed into the new town of Rocky Mount.[11]

Robert A. Scott was the first mayor of Rocky Mount, and served from 1873 to 10 July 1876, when Giles W. B. Hale succeeded him.[12] When the trustees (or town council) replaced Mayor Scott with Hale in 1876 they passed a resolution assuring Scott that he had their respect

> for the able, impartial and just manner in which he has discharged the duties of the office of Mayor since the organization of the Corporation of Rocky Mount, and that in his retirement he carries with him the kindest feelings and best wishes of his brethren of the Council.[13]

Hale resigned on 27 March 1877 and Jesse Prunty succeeded him. The council elected Hale again on 8 July 1878 and he resigned on 1 August 1879; James H. Binford was elected in his place. Binford served until 1 July 1880, when Scott again was chosen. On 20 September 1880 Scott resigned and once more Jesse Prunty won election. Scott was elected mayor pro tem on 21 June 1882, perhaps because Prunty was ill or absent.[14]

During the first few years of the town's history following incorporation, the council members and other officers devoted most of their efforts to improving Rocky Mount's condition and keeping it clean and safe. Harkening back to the early days of county government, for instance, on 4 September 1873 the council passed an ordinance requiring all men between the ages of sixteen and sixty to work on the roads and streets of the town for two days a year or pay a fine of $1 for each day missed. In February 1874 a committee was appointed to oversee the construction of plank sidewalks in the business district.[15] As time passed other

Antebellum Saunders covered bridge, Pigg River, Rocky Mount. Demolished 1939. (Blue Ridge Institute, Ferrum, Va.)

improvements were made to enhance transportation, such as the construction in 1928 of a new concrete bridge over Pigg River. Late in 1939 the old wooden covered bridge nearby, which according to tradition had been constructed by Peter Saunders, Jr., just before the Civil War, and which had not carried motor traffic since the new bridge was built, was approved for demolition. Apparently there was concern that the old bridge might collapse in a flood and damage the new one downstream.[16]

The council members considered animal control and sanitation as important duties; on 29 January 1874 the mayor appointed a committee of three to select locations for "horse racks" as well as a pen for hogs found roaming at large in the town. On the same day another committee assumed responsibility for examining alleys and backyards for garbage and other "unsightly matter." Property owners who did not clean up their grounds when ordered were required to pay a $5 fine.[17]

Noise and its abatement concerned the council. On 28 April 1882 the council killed the joy of small boys when it ruled that anyone who affixed tin cans or other noisy items to dogs or other animals and created a disturbance that frightened the horses could be arrested and fined.[18]

A memorable disturbance took place in the 1880s when a circus came to town. Braxton Bragg Tyree, a county resident who was in his early teens at the time, stood watching as the circus workers fed the animals. He later recalled that he

> saw a man go to a lion's cage to feed it and as he opened the door the lion jumped out. A yoke of oxen was hitched to a post near by and the lion jumped on one of the oxen and the oxen ran away, wagon and all. The lion then headed for Bald Knob, the circus men after it with a net and spears. They were on horses as well as on foot. The lion headed back toward town and every one was excited as there were no telephones at that time to warn people. It was on the main street and people were shooting at it and it finally went into a blacksmith shop where an old negro man was working. He gave the lion the whole shop and headed for the loft, where he staid until the lion was captured. They ran a spear into his mouth until they could get a rope around his neck and get him back into the cage.[19]

No doubt the uproar thrilled every little boy in town.

Rocky Mount enjoyed the same power to issue licenses as had the county. On 4 August 1874 the council imposed a $2 annual license tax upon resident auctioneers; vendors of goods, wares, and merchandise; lawyers; doctors; dentists; druggists; and bankers. Restaurateurs paid $5 a year. The council also taxed vendors of saddles and harnesses; jewelers; insurance agents; notions and fancy goods sellers; patent medicine salesmen; and photographers.[20]

The town government took steps to reduce crime and trespassing. On 30 March 1874 the council forbade loitering in the alleys, lots, or outhouses "of any housekeeper" after dark, as well as frequenting at night "the back lots and servant houses of housekeepers in this village." In each case the mayor could levy fines for violations.[21]

As the town grew its amenities slowly improved. In 1872, for example, the Franklin Bank had been incorporated. (The Gogginsville Savings Bank had been incorporated in 1850 but it is unclear whether it ever actually engaged in business.) Around the turn of the century local newspapers advertised the First National Bank of Rocky Mount, the Angle and Company dry goods store, Peak and Angle (furniture dealers and undertakers), and the Hotel Rocky Mount. By 1908 the *Franklin Chronicle* noted that "Rocky Mount is progressing in many ways. Our houses are all occupied and there are no vacant buildings of any kind. What we need now is, first, street lights, and secondly, more and better sidewalks."[22]

Part of the council's concerns resulted from the fear of fire that it shared with the public. Given the close proximity of flammable buildings to one another, the lack of zoning or construction codes, and the use of fire for light and heating, periodic disasters were bound to happen. The best the citizens could hope for was that vigilance and the primitive fire-fighting equipment of the day would prevent fires from spreading beyond a few buildings. The council did what it could by appointing a committee to look into the danger of fire in the new town. On 5 February 1874, for example, the committee reported that several rooms in the Franklin Hotel were "in a dangerous condition in consequence of the state of the roofs." The council ordered that two of the rooms "be recovered in new shingles or other safe material" and that no fires be lighted in the rooms until the repairs were made. It also decided that another chimney was too low and ordered it raised to "at least three feet above the comb" of the roof.[23]

Outbuildings also were a matter of concern. Both the house of Mary Ann Hodges and her smokehouse, as well as Ferdinand Turnbull's kitchen (which stood on the site of the present Greer and Melesco law office), seemed to the council to have unsafe roofs. In February 1874 it ordered the owners to make the necessary repairs and not to light any fires in the meantime.[24]

The strategy of observation and repair generally worked. In the nineteenth century, Rocky Mount never suffered a truly devastating fire as a result of accident or carelessness. What did occur, however, was even more frightening: a fire allegedly set by arsonists. The story of that fire is a convoluted tale involving both politics and racial conflicts.

During the Reconstruction era the lot of the freedmen generally improved. They had freedom, a few opportunities for education, some economic leverage, and many of the rights of citizenship. To some conservative whites, however, who for the first time had to reckon with the political and economic power of blacks, matters had gone too far too fast. In the end, the conservative white Southerners who had lost the Civil War were victorious in Reconstruction. One by one the statehouses and governor's mansions of the former Confederacy fell to the white conservatives who proceeded to roll back as many as they could of the new freedoms enjoyed by blacks.

These political battles continued for many years—from the end of the war to the end of the century—and the fortunes of conservatives and liberals ebbed and flowed as first one side and then the other gained the upper hand for a few years. In Virginia the "final" victory of the conservatives came with the adoption of the Constitution of 1902 that effectively disfranchised the black population. That victory endured until the defeat of Massive Resistance in the 1960s.

After the end of the Civil War white politicians found their old parties and alliances in disarray. New parties formed, at first, around economic issues, particularly those involving the payment of the state debt. Most of the outstanding debt was incurred during the antebellum era when the state issued bonds to pay for its internal improvement program. Ironically, however, most of those improvements had been constructed in what became West Virginia. Along with the question of West Virginia's paying its one-third share of the debt was that of whether Virginia should assume responsibility for all of the remaining two-thirds or readjust it and pay less as other states of the former Confederacy had decided to do. Those who wanted to pay all of Virginia's share (to avoid alienating northern and foreign bondholders) became known as Funders, because they supported the full funding of the debt by Virginia. The second group called themselves Readjusters. They believed the state's share of the debt should be readjusted since the state was bankrupt and had no hope of recovery otherwise. In general, the Funders tended to be the state's more prosperous and influential citizens— businessmen and planters—and the Readjusters attracted small farmers and merchants.

The Funders dominated state government throughout the 1870s. The Readjusters were led by such divergent personalities as the colorful and controversial General William Mahone, a former Confederate general who was president of the Atlantic, Mississippi, and Ohio Railroad Company, and the Reverend John E. Massey, a Baptist minister who served during this period as a delegate and state senator from Albemarle County. In some ways the Readjuster movement was the child of Massey; Mahone was Massey's recruit. Soon, however, Mahone began to dominate the movement and he and Massey became political enemies.

Mahone was a talented politician who had much in common with the "bosses" of the later nineteenth and early twentieth centuries. His friends thought him autocratic and his enemies considered him a dictator. Under his iron hand the Readjusters became an early version of a political machine.

Late in the 1870s Mahone realized that if he ever was to succeed in capturing the state government he would have to form a coalition with black voters to give him the numerical superiority he needed. Although he and his white supporters were more "liberal" than their opponents, they were not much more so, and his coalition party proved extremely controversial among white voters. It succeeded in its goal, however, when the Readjusters won enough seats in the General Assembly in the 1877 election to force considerable concessions from the gubernatorial administration of Frederick W. M. Holliday (1878–1882). Mahone himself was elected to the United States Senate two years later and served from 1881 to 1887. His election was in large part the result of the cooperation of the Republican party in Virginia; Mahone soon became a Republican himself. Although he spent most of the decade in Washington, D.C., Mahone maintained his tight control over affairs in Virginia, leading his opponents to complain of the infection of "Mahoneism." Such former allies as John E. Massey abandoned him completely when he joined the Republicans.

Massey, meanwhile, went from one political success to another during the 1880s, with the exception of not obtaining the nomination for governor in 1881. This largely was because he was not Mahone's choice for the nomination—which did not endear Mahone to the Baptist minister. Massey sided with the conservative Democrats and won election to the office of auditor of public accounts in 1881 and then served as lieutenant governor from 1886 to 1890 under Governor Fitzhugh Lee.

Franklin County was Readjuster country. In the off-year General Assembly election of 1879, when the Readjusters secured even more seats, Franklin County's voters sided with them.[25] By the gubernatorial election of 1889, however, the county had become solidly Democratic—at least among the white electorate, who voted overwhelmingly for Philip W. McKinney.[26] Massey, who was one of the most eloquent speakers in the state, stumped hard for McKinney. Mahone, the Republican candidate, who had a high-pitched, squeaky voice, spoke for himself wherever he could. Often the two men shared the same platform and delivered their speeches one after the other.

On the afternoon of 7 October 1889 Massey and Mahone arrived in Rocky Mount to campaign. With the election only a month away (5 November), there was great excitement and people flocked to the town. The largest building in the heart of town, the Franklin Warehouse (near the present-day Presbyterian church) owned by J. H. Binford and Giles W. B. Hale, was selected as the site of the rally. A large and enthusiastic crowd of cigar-chewing Democratic party supporters arrived early and packed the place to hear their man, effectively shutting out Mahone's crowd—much of which was black—from the arena. Later that night, at about 1:00 A.M. and long after the throngs had dispersed, the warehouse burned down.

The fire spread and destroyed twenty-two buildings in uptown Rocky Mount, both businesses and dwellings. The town council hired John Wren's National Police Detective Agency, a Richmond firm, to investigate the cause of the fire, which was assumed by the councilmen and many others to have been arson. On 1 November five local blacks were arrested: George Early, William Brown, Nannie Woods, Bird Woods, and Morgan Dickenson. All except Dickenson were eventually brought to trial.

As often was true when exciting events led to court actions, the case was tried as much in the newspapers as in the courtroom. According to one such account, among the evidence presented at the arraignment of George Early was the report that he had

> "in a jubilant humor, a day after the fire told a white citizen that they had a fire down town when Massey spoke here before, and every time Massey comes here the town is set afire, and it's done again." He also said that he and two others of Billy Mahone's boys poured one and a half gallons of oil on the warehouse and burned the d——d town. The investigation has developed a terrible condition of affairs here, and the white men see the necessity of defending their homes and firesides against Mahoneism.[27]

When a lynch mob formed, the law enforcement officers packed Early on a train and moved him to Lynchburg for his own protection. According to the black newspaper the *Richmond Planet*, the move occurred after

> George Early was taken from jail [in Rocky Mount] by a crowd of men and dragged behind a horse and buggy with shots flying around his head, and was told if he did not acknowledge that the other prisoners did the burning he he [*sic*] would be killed. The men then built a fire around him and told him that if he did not admit that he did the burning he would be consumed.[28]

Early made a confession to his escort on 2 November as they rode to Lynchburg. A newspaper reported that he implicated the other suspects when he said

> that he saw Bud [Bird] Woods (colored) pour the oil on the warehouse, and Bill Brown (colored) touch the match, and "then we went out by the alley and over the fence by Sims's stables, and on down by the back of the depot, by Mrs. Manor's, to my house, so that it would appear that we were at my house at the frolic [dance]. We all agreed to swear that we were at my house at the frolic at the time." He also said it was done because Massey spoke in the warehouse and Mahone was not allowed to speak in it.[29]

Another motive prompted the arson as well, according to the newspapers and several white witnesses. On 7 October a black man named Henry Smith had been arrested for disorderly conduct. A crowd of his friends followed him and the white officer to the jail, protesting all the way. George Early and William Brown were in the crowd, and Early demanded to be allowed to pay Smith's fine so he would not have to be jailed. When he was refused, Early swore he would have Smith out of jail by 2:00 P.M. or burn down the town. Some witnesses reported that they heard Early say

> that the negro had no show in that town, and had had none since it was incorporated, nineteen years before; that he had offered to pay Smith's fine, but nothing would do but they must put him in jail; and that he added: "I will have him out of there or burn the d——d town before morning."[30]

At the trial of Early and the others, which took place in December 1889, his confession and statements were used as evidence. All the defendants were convicted and sentenced in July 1890 to hang; George Early, Bird Woods, and Nannie Woods on 22 August 1890 and William Brown on 19 September 1890. They filed several appeals with the Virginia Supreme Court of Appeals, but to no immediate avail; Governor McKinney did, however, grant Nannie Woods a stay of execution until 19 September. On 22 August 1890 George Early and Bird Woods were executed at 10:56 A.M. in the basement of the county jail before about twenty-five witnesses. Before he was hanged Woods denied his guilt, saying that he "was arrested on the 2nd of November on a charge of burning the town, but before God I am as innocent of that charge as an angel. I bear no malice in my heart towards any one, and my soul is going straight to Heaven."[31] Early spoke along the same lines, saying

> that when he confessed he lied; that both white and colored had lied on him; that he had forgiven all, and wanted all to meet him in Heaven; that God had forgiven him—not for the burning, of which he was innocent, but for other sins which he had committed.[32]

Both Nannie Woods and William Brown delayed their executions by continued appeals. William Brown's appeals resulted in a new trial's being ordered by the Virginia Supreme Court of Appeals in its decision handed down on 11 December 1890. The court ruled, surprisingly, and tragically too late for two of the defendants, that the "facts stated by the Commonwealth's witnesses do not fully and satisfactorily prove that the fire which burned the warehouse, and from which it was communicated to other buildings in the town, was of incendiary origin; and they do not exclude the hypothesis that the fire may have originated from accidental causes."[33]

The court continued:

> The record shows, by the witnesses for the prosecution, that there had been held in that warehouse that day a large and promiscuous crowd of excited listeners and spectators at a public political meeting, and the Commonwealth's witness, himself, speaks of his anxiety and apprehension of the danger of fire from the "cigar stubb," or anything else with fire on it, being left in the warehouse; though, indeed, he does not speak of any liability of a conflagration from "fire-water," or whiskey—the twin-abomination and concomitant of tobacco.[34]

One witness, Giles W. B. Hale, a co-owner of the warehouse, testified that he thought the fire had been set because when he saw it both the inside and outside of the building was burning. P. C. Clarke said that he had gone into the warehouse after Massey spoke specifically to see whether or not any lighted cigars were left in it; he saw none and left the door open when he departed. Two other men testified that they crawled under the warehouse about a week before the fire to recapture a tame fox and saw no flammable material around.[35]

The court found that none of the foregoing testimony proved arson one way or the other. It also ruled that the testimony of A. R. Binford, which had been presented in court as the best proof of arson, was to the contrary the most unbelievable. Binford testified

> that when he got to the fire it was very small; could have put it out with two buckets of water, but was uneasy about his brother, who was sick near by, and went back to see about him; that he was satisfied that the fire was the work of an incendiary; that he found a plank torn off—he did not know how long it had been torn off—the warehouse, the northwest corner, about ten or twelve inches wide; that he put his head in through the hold and saw where oil had been poured along the planks or beams to a pile of trash which was not on fire; that there was a black charred mark or line made by the fire from the inside of the warehouse, where he stood, to the said pile of trash which was about 18 feet out towards the centre of the warehouse; that he had no reason for thinking that any oil had been used, except from the appearance of the charred mark aforesaid.
>
> This witness, who thrust his head in through a hole only ten or twelve inches wide, and saw the fire in a pile of trash, "very small," and which he could have put out with two buckets of water, so lost his head, that, though he had presence of mind to mark the minute observations of which he testifies, he, yet, instead of putting out the fire, "very small," or at least calling for help, ran away from the place, to look after a sick brother; never reflecting that, by putting out the fire, in its very small beginning, in a pile of trash lying on the floor of the warehouse (which he says he could easily have done), he could have saved the warehouse and the other houses which took fire from it.[36]

The court also cited the uncontradicted testimony of a witness named Bowman that during the political meeting "much smoking was indulged in by the audience, and that cigar stubs were recklessly thrown around by the crowd."[37]

The court ordered a new trial for Brown because it was convinced that the commonwealth had not proved that the cause of the fire was arson. In Richmond the black newspaper the *Richmond Planet* commented that

> [t]his is a terrible arraignment of the jury that passed upon these cases. It tells in no uncertain tones the prejudiced conditions existing in that community, and makes one wish in vain for the resurrection of those human beings hanged for a crime which possibly they never committed.[38]

Brown underwent a new trial in August 1891 and again was convicted, based largely on the testimony of two black detectives. He appealed his conviction, and the Virginia Supreme Court of Appeals handed down another reversal on 10 November 1892. In its written opinion the high court left no doubt of its disgust with the detectives who investigated the causes of the fire in 1889. Two of the detectives, Henry Edwards and Robert Clay, were blacks employed by John Wren. The court was particularly offended by

> the statement of the hired *detective*, Henry Edwards, of admissions of the accused, which, he says, were made to him at or about the time of the occurrence of the fire, and which were, he says, taken down, at the time, in a written memorandum made by him, of the existence of which he never spoke upon [earlier] and which he claims now, for the first time, to have remembered and found . . . to convict the prisoner, and to attest his own detestable calling. And, also, the evidence of Robert Clay, another negro detective, the hired creature of Henry Edwards, of admissions alleged to have been made to him . . . by the prisoner, in jail. This hired and subservient agent and creature, Robert Clay, was put into the cell of the prisoner (by whose authority, or with whose permission or collusion does not appear), and was kept there for three days and four nights, ostensibly as a murderer; and he says himself "He, the prisoner, asked me if I was guilty of the murder? *I told him I was.*" Without dilating upon the modern iniquity and illegal inquisition of forcing prisoners (innocent in the eyes of the law, helpless in their cells, suffering the loss of liberty, and separated from their families and friends) to undergo attempts made upon their lives by reptile spies, whose paid and professional undertaking is to *furnish* ready-made and requisite *admissions* of guilt, it is enough to say that the new evidence is totally insufficient to warrant the conviction of the prisoner. . . . Of course, it was the *undertaking* of these detectives to *furnish* evidence to hang the prisoner; but not only are the so-called admissions of the prisoner insufficient to warrant the taking of the life of the prisoner, but they admit of an innocent construction; while Clay, the hired tool of the spy and detective, Edwards, expressly and squarely admits that he deliberately and unqualifiedly *lied*.[39]

Apparently the prosecutors gave up after the court's ruling and did not try Brown again.

Nannie Woods also escaped the gallows. Governor McKinney commuted

Woods's sentence to life imprisonment on 16 September 1890; Governor Charles T. O'Ferrall, convinced of her innocence by "the judge, clerk, mayor and many prominent citizens," pardoned her on 30 January 1895.[40]

Were the accused guilty? Were they all innocent, the victims of politics and racism? What possessed George Early first to admit his guilt and implicate the others, then to recant? Was he frightened into his admissions by the lynch mob? Most likely none of these questions ever will be resolved satisfactorily, and the case will continue to be debated.

It is interesting, however, to compare the great fire in Rocky Mount with another incident that occurred six years earlier, in 1883, just three days (instead of a month) before an election. On 3 November a race riot took place in Danville; it began as a street brawl and escalated until several persons were killed or wounded. Governor William E. Cameron called out the militia and soon restored order. The Democrats, however, publicized the incident widely; they charged black supporters of Mahone with starting it and were in turn accused of being the secret instigators. Regardless of the truth, the conservative Democrats reaped the benefit as they captured two-thirds of the seats in the statehouse from the Readjusters, riding a wave of antiblack sentiment following the riot. As Mahone's biographer put it, "The decisive victory, without doubt, was due in large measure to the timely occurrence of the Danville Riot."[41] Could the Rocky Mount fire have been a similarly "timely occurrence" designed to sway the election of 1889? If so, the result was the same as the Democrat McKinney won the office handily.

Rocky Mount, looking north on Main Street toward Chronicle Building (formerly the Early House hotel), about 1910. (Blue Ridge Institute, Ferrum, Va.)

Franklin County remained a Democratic party stronghold through the mid-twentieth century. At the time of the fire the county's delegate to the General Assembly was a young Democrat, Edward Watts Saunders, who was serving his second term. He first was elected in 1887 and served until 1901; during the session of 1899–1901 he presided as Speaker of the House of Delegates. Born 20 October 1860, Saunders was the son of Peter Saunders, Jr., and Elizabeth Dabney Saunders, of Bleak Hill, and the grandson of Judge Fleming Saunders. Educated at Bellvue Academy in Bedford County (the motto of which was "Learn or Leave") and at the University of Virginia, Saunders practiced law in Rocky Mount and resided at The Grove. Upon his election in 1887 he replaced his father, who had served during the Civil War (1861–1863) and again from 1883 to 1887.

Edward Watts Saunders combined a career as an elected official with service as a jurist. He was appointed judge of the Fourth Judicial Circuit in 1901 and of the Seventh Judicial Circuit in 1904. Two years later he won election to the United States House of Representatives, in place of Claude A. Swanson, who was elected Virginia's governor, and served until 1920, when he was elected to the Virginia Supreme Court of Appeals. He died on 16 December 1921 and was buried in High Street Cemetery in Rocky Mount.[42]

Aside from Rocky Mount's contribution of resident Saunders to the political life of the state, the town figured little in state or national politics in the late nineteenth and early twentieth centuries, except anecdotally. One such story involved Carter Glass, of Lynchburg, the author of Virginia's 1902 constitution, congressman (1902–1918), secretary of the treasury under President Woodrow Wilson (1918–1920), and U.S. senator (1920–1946). One afternoon in October 1910, Glass found himself in Rocky Mount with no way to get to Roanoke, where he needed to catch a train, the Memphis Special, that evening. H. L. Davis, a local blacksmith who owned a 1905 White Steamer automobile, offered to give the congressman a ride for $10, free if he arrived too late for the train. The manufacturer claimed a top speed of seventy-five miles per hour for the car, and Davis recalled later that he was sure he attained that speed on some stretches of the road. Bouncing over the rough surfaces, splashing through creeks, and careening around hairpin curves in the mountains, Davis soon reduced Glass to a state of nervous prostration. Just after Davis narrowly avoided tumbling the car into a ravine, Glass yelled at him to slow down because "it isn't going to do you any good to make that train and find me dead in the back seat." Davis shouted back, "Our contract doesn't say anything about getting you there alive." They made the train but, according to the story, Glass was so weakened by the experience that Davis had to carry his bags.[43]

One of Edward Watts Saunders's sons, Peter Saunders, followed his father into public service. Young Saunders, born on 1 August 1890 in Rocky Mount, was educated at Hampden-Sydney College and Washington and Lee University, where he received his law degree. He practiced law in Rocky Mount from 1914 to 1922, owned and edited the *Franklin Chronicle* from 1918 to 1929, and was chairman of the county's Democratic party from 1918 until his death in 1945. In 1922 Governor E. Lee Trinkle appointed Saunders his executive secretary, a post he held through the administrations of Trinkle, Harry F. Byrd, Sr. (Saunders was a staunch supporter of the Byrd "organization"), John Garland Pollard, and George C. Peery. He served simultaneously as secretary of the commonwealth from 1927 until January 1938, when the newly inaugurated Governor James H. Price declined to reappoint him. State Attorney General A. P. Staples also appointed him chairman of the Board of Motion Picture Censors. When Governor Colgate W. Darden, Jr., took office in January 1942, he reappointed Saunders as his secretary. Saunders died of a heart attack in his room at the Hotel John Marshall in Richmond, where he had lived for many years, on 24 July 1945.[44]

In contrast with the Saunderses father and son, most residents of Rocky Mount played no part in state politics. The town retained its role as the center of political and economic life in the county and prospered in its quiet way. Rocky Mount remained the local market for the sale of agricultural products and farm supplies despite the presence of the railroads.

SIXTEEN

Business and Industry

Although a predominantly agricultural county, Franklin has also traditionally included some industries in its economic life. From the colonial period until 1851, the Washington Iron Works played an active role, shipping its products as far south as South Carolina. In 1836 Franklin also boasted tailors, saddlers, cabinetmakers, blacksmiths, a boot and shoe manufacturer, a weekly newspaper printed in Rocky Mount, tanneries, and a tobacco manufacturer. In 1852 there were forty-seven "manufacturing establishments" in the county, as well as twenty-seven merchants. In the post–Civil War period country stores continued to constitute a major factor in Franklin's business life. The 1871–1872 Virginia business directory found 21 country stores located throughout the county, a decrease of 6 over the number listed in the 1852 Virginia business directory. But the number of country stores, called general merchants in the later Virginia business directories, soon increased beyond the prewar figure and by 1897 had reached 59, almost doubled by 1906 to 109, and attained 115 by 1917.[1]

One such general merchant was J. B. Brooks, a black man who established his Brooks and Company in Rocky Mount in 1898. By 1943 the store had been serving the county "for more than 44 years and enjoy[ing] the esteem of a large group of patrons both white and colored of the town and county." By then, too, Brooks and Company was one of the oldest in Rocky Mount "in years of continuous service in the town and county." Samuel M. Phelps and Lee M. Waid had bought the company in 1913 with $1,000 that Phelps borrowed and repaid within two years. Filmore Brooks served as the third partner in the enterprise for two years before leaving the business, which by 1943 had shown a "noteworthy and steady growth. Not only has the company served as a distributing concern for staple and fancy groceries, fresh fruits and vegetables, but also as a local cattle market of considerable size through their slaughter house in which they process veal, beef and mutton, purchased or on the hoof, into fancy dressed home-killed meats."

333

The owners took an active role in the county's civic life: Lee Waid (who had worked in West Virginia's coal fields before returning to Franklin in 1913) served as secretary of the Franklin County Colored School Board, member of the local lodge of black Odd Fellows, deacon at the black First Baptist Church, and assistant in the juvenile division of the Trial Justice Court. Sam Phelps (who had received his degree from Virginia State College [now University], taught two years in Franklin, and kept Filmore Brooks's books before buying the company) was a past master of the black Odd Fellows Lodge, a deacon in the First Baptist Church, and an owner and operator of Midway Cleaners. Samuel Waid Phelps, "younger associate in the business" and Sam Phelps's son, was prominent in young people's activities and scoutmaster of the black Boy Scout troop. Jordan Hicks, one of the oldest meatcutters and butchers in Rocky Mount, had charge of processing cattle and sheep for the company. He had gone to work there when Brooks and Company opened in 1898. Situated on the corner of West Court Street and Main Street, "Brooks and Company has admirably lived up to their slogan, 'The Busy Corner,' in their many years of service here," the *Franklin News-Post* writer concluded. "Located as they are next to the Bankers Trust Company and across from the court house, they are easily accessible to the throng of buyers who make Rocky Mount their buying center."[2]

Both Lee Waid and Samuel Phelps had long and distinguished careers as Franklin County civic leaders. A wing of the Franklin Memorial Hospital was named in Waid's honor in the 1950s and the Franklin County Training School was renamed Lee M. Waid School and dedicated in his memory in 1959. Sam Phelps served as president of the local National Association for the Advancement of Colored People and the Parent-Teachers Association for twenty years, was one of the founders of the black Boy Scout program, and an executive member of the Boy Scouts Algonquin District for many years. In addition to Brooks and Company,

Brooks and Co., interior. Left to right: *Ira Phelps, Earnest Holland, owners Lee M. Waid and Sam Phelps.* (Blue Ridge Institute, Ferrum, Va.)

Phelps and Waid also jointly owned the Midway Cleaners, and engaged in real estate and farming. Brooks and Company was sold to the Bankers Trust Company in 1958. Lee M. Waid died in 1957 and Sam Phelps in 1974. In 1970 Phelps's only son, Waid Phelps, became the first black elected to the Rocky Mount Town Council and served until his death in 1985.[3]

Although they lived in a predominantly agricultural county, many late-nineteenth- and early-twentieth-century Franklin County farmers combined husbandry with industry in order to earn an adequate livelihood. Thus the farmer raised a crop (usually including some tobacco as well as wheat, corn, and vegetables) and perhaps cut wood for crossties for the lumber industry or railroads in the county, or gathered tanbark for the county's tanneries, or worked part-time at a warehouse, or added blacksmithing to the farming. But if it was necessary, he engaged in whatever nonfarm activity was required to make a living.

One of these sources of extra income for Franklin's farmers came from supplying tanbark to the county's various tanneries. For the two-year period 1918–1919, for example, James H. Waid collected almost eighteen dollars for his tanbark. Braxton Bragg Tyree described the use made of tanbark when he recalled that his father purchased leather to make shoes for the family from the Bernard Tannery. "It was located near where Tip Hudson's house now stands [on Tanyard Road in Rocky Mount]. They tanned the beef hides in vats, or tanks. They used a substance from oak bark. They used black oak, red oak and chestnut oak."[4]

Tyree recalled years later that the 1890s were hard economically for Franklin County farmers (especially after the panic of 1893) and tobacco did not bring in much income. Thus some men cut crossties for the railroads and others sought tanbark for the tanneries. "This was very cheap labor and you had to take Nat Angle's 'brass checks' for that. He stood in well with the railroads and the tanneries and you had to sell to him and the only place you could spend his 'brass checks' was at his store. This is the reason I left Virginia and went to South Dakota where I could make better wages."[5]

On the other hand, the story of Robert Lee Kent, of Wirtz, demonstrates the opposite approach to economic success. Born in the Halesford area of the county in 1875, Kent in 1895 became a clerk on a yearly contract at the store at Halesford. By 1900 he had bought the store. Within nine years he had sold that store, moved to the community of Taylors Store where he served as postmaster, married, and in 1909 purchased another store at Wirtz. It was "the typical country store of the era. If he didn't have what the customer wanted, and he usually did, he would get it." He supplied the community's needs from the cradle to the grave for cash, credit, or "barter for everything from chickens, eggs, butter, etc. all the way to pulpwood, tanbark, or entire farm crops." Kent also acquired 400 acres of land at Wirtz and raised cattle, grain, tomatoes, and apples (in the orchard of one thousand trees he set out). And he built and ran a cannery that produced "as many as 30,000 cases of canned tomatoes in a peak year."[6]

At the same time, Kent became a director of the Peoples National Bank in Rocky Mount in 1908, and in association with Nathaniel P. Angle, a major Franklin County entrepreneur, he gained a seat on the board of directors as a charter stockholder of every enterprise Angle started. In the 1930s Kent purchased the Hale property on Main Street in Rocky Mount and in 1937 built the Mount Theater. From then until he retired at the age of ninety in 1965, Kent generally managed the theater himself. At his death Kent had been in business for seventy-one years and a bank board member for sixty.[7]

Not every businessman could match Kent's success story, however. But over the half-century from 1870 to 1920, Franklin witnessed a growth in its business life as new companies emerged and old ones disappeared. The 1870 United States census found a number of industries in Franklin: thirty-three gristmills, twenty-five blacksmiths, seven tanneries, one saddle- and harness maker, two shoe- and bootmakers, seven sawmills, one dyeing and wool-carding factory (which produced 2,000 yards of cloth and 5,600 rolls of wool), three (legal) distillers (who made a total of 4,860 gallons of apple brandy: the 1871–1872 Virginia business directory listed Maxey A. Pope at Rocky Mount as a distiller and rectifyer, and Jonathan N. McNeil at Rocky Mount as a wine manufacturer), and four tobacco manufacturers (who produced 95,680 pounds of tobacco, 36,000 pounds of tobacco stems, and 167 boxes of tobacco).[8] The 1871–1872 Virginia business directory named four tobacco-related businessmen: John Hale, Jr., at Rocky Mount, a tobacco-leaf dealer; W. A. and F. K. Brown at Dickinson (by 1927, W. A. Brown's tobacco company had moved from Dickinson to Martinsville and in that year became part of the Sparrow-Gravely Company[9]); Carper and Printz at Rocky Mount, tobacco manufacturers; and W. G. and J. W. McGhee at Snow Creek, tobacconists (retailers). In the 1880 census, however, there were listed only eleven blacksmiths, five wheelwrights, six tanneries, eleven sawmills, twenty-seven gristmills, three boot- and shoemakers, two cabinetmakers, and three tobacco manufacturers (two making tobacco products and the third tobacco boxes).[10]

Contrasting the figures given in the industry census returns were those found in the Virginia business directories. Because a businessman had to request (and probably pay) to be included in the business directory, many more businesses are listed in the census records than in the directories for a comparable period. For instance, the Virginia business directory for 1871–1872 listed only seven blacksmiths (Stephen Tate at Gogginsville, King Tate at Rocky Mount, Samuel B. and Richard Fisher and Jacob Hurtman at Taylors Store, and Warren Ellis and Thomas T. Fralens at Union Hall) as compared to twenty-five in the 1870 industry schedule of the U.S. census. The 1871–1872 directory also included one iron founder (Ammon and Smith, of Snow Hill), four gristmills (J. A. White at Dickinson, Jacob Taylor at Rocky Mount, and James Hutts and the firm of Zeigler and Angle at Union Hall: there were thirty-three in the 1870 industry census), three companies selling trunks, saddles, and harnesses (Samuel G. Bright, Alfred S. Hughes, and William H. Keeny, all at Rocky Mount), another selling lamps and oils (Pope, Dudley, and Bernard at Rocky Mount), one millwright (A. T. Carter at Dickinson), a painter (presumably of houses: William C. Smithers at Rocky Mount), two boot- and shoemakers (Keeny and Davis at Rocky Mount and James K. Ellis at Union Hall), three carpenters and builders (John S. Semones at Dickinson, William L. Wells at Taylors Store, and John H. Morgan at Union Hall), one "mason builder" (Thomas C. McBride at Rocky Mount) three saw- and planing mills (John K. Zeigler at Dickinson, Jacob Taylor at Rocky Mount, and Zeigler and Angle at Union Hall: there were seven sawmills in the 1870 industry census), a tailor (William E. Andrews at Rocky Mount), two tanners and curriers (Charles E. Bernard in Rocky Mount, and C[reed] and W. E. Bernard at Union Hall: there were seven tanneries in the census), and two wheelwrights (Samuel Henser at Taylors Store and Thomas Hutts at Union Hall). The county's one cabinetmaker (Nicholas Cassell, of Rocky Mount) was also its only undertaker. There was one hotel (the Early House in Rocky Mount) and a restaurant run by Mrs. L. D. Horn, of Gogginsville. The county had two dentists (B. A. James at Dickinson and W. Y. Irons at Rocky Mount) and five physicians (John W. Poindexter at Dickinson, Thomas B. Greer and Jacob W. Webb at Rocky Mount, S. G. Reese at Taylors Store, and Benjamin Williams at Union Hall: there had been ten physicians listed in 1852), as well as seven lawyers or law firms(A. H. Dillard, Peter H. Dillard, George E. Dennis, G. H. I. Greer, Gilmer and Nelson, Edmund Irvine, and William A. Taliaferro, all of Rocky Mount: there had been six lawyers listed in 1852). The 1871–1872 directory, however, recorded no dressmakers, druggists, milliners, newspapers, saloons, watchmakers, or jewelers.[11]

In the antebellum period, however, Franklin had had a newspaper—in about 1834 the *Franklin Whig*, located in Rocky Mount, became the first newspaper published in the county. It was established by the Reverend Matthew H. Jackson (a Presbyterian) and Colton Cabanass. The publication office was located on Maple Street in Maria Turnbull's house, now the site of T. Keister Greer's and David Melesco's law office.[12] While the 1871–1872 Virginia business directory found no county newspapers, that omission was filled in about October 1872 when Randolph Dickinson began publication of the first *Franklin Gazette*. It continued until the spring of 1876 when W. R. Murrell and W. A. Belcher bought the paper and changed its name to the *Virginia Monitor*, which merged a few months later into the *Conservative*, owned by W. A. and C. J. Griffin, at Salem. In about August 1876, Gabriel Banks and W. I. Boone started the second *Franklin Gazette*, which in 1877 was described in the business directory as being owned and edited by Boone and John W. Stump in Rocky Mount. Ownership of the *Gazette* changed several times over the next eleven years, Banks selling out to William Bush, Bush in turn to Stump, of Bedford County, stump to W. A. Belcher and Abraham Hancock, who in turn sold it to G. London Scott, of Amherst, in 1880. In 1888 Frasier Otey Hoffman, of Bedford County, acquired the *Gazette* and

Blacksmith Jesse F. Fralin with J. S. O. Hodges. Ca. 1912 photo. (Blue Ridge Institute, Ferrum, Va.)

changed its name to the *Franklin Times*. Described as a Democratic paper, the *Times* was published on Thursdays. Within three years, another Democratic paper had joined the *Times*, this one the *Daily Times*, published at Handy. Both papers still operated in 1897, the *Daily Times* under the management of W. R. Prillaman as a weekly. Sometime thereafter, Hoffman began a rival newspaper, the *Franklin Democrat*, "on account of some dissension on political questions." But by 1899, Hoffman had resumed the editorship of the *Times* and merged the two papers into the *Times-Democrat*, which he edited with his wife Branch Douglas Hoffman, "Literary & Associate Editor."[13]

Competition emerged in Rocky Mount in 1905 with the introduction of the *Franklin Chronicle*, edited by A. W. Robbins. Although the *Handy Daily Times* had lapsed, by 1906 E. G. Coleman was editing the *Franklin Rural Events*, a Democratic weekly, at Glade Hill. Interestingly enough, E. G. Coleman had become a musical-instruments store owner at Rocky Mount by 1911 and his *Rural Events* was no longer published. The competition also proved too stiff for F. O. Hoffman as his *Times-Democrat* had ceased publication by 1917. The *Chronicle* had changed ownership, now being edited by C. B. Willis, who also advertised himself as a publisher. Presumably A. W. Robbins was the owner of the Robbins Printing Works, located in Rocky Mount by 1917 as well. In 1916 Robbins had advertised that he was a wholesale dealer in subscriptions to papers and magazines (except the daily papers of Roanoke and Lynchburg).[14] On 20 September 1923, the *County News* began publication, but merged with the *Chronicle* in 1929 to form the *County News and Chronicle*. Sol Goodman, of Martinsville, organized the *Franklin News-Post* in 1935, and a year later the new owner, William Barnes, merged it with the *County News and Chronicle* to form the *News-Post and Chronicle*, the latter name dropped sometime later. Pennsylvanian Earle M. Forsythe bought the *News-Post* in 1936 and ran it until 1950 when he sold it back to William Barnes. After Barnes died in 1952, Kermit W. Salyer purchased the Post Publishing Corporation and sold it in 1981.

The third *Franklin Gazette* began operation in 1938, became the property of Kermit Salyer in 1958, and ceased publication in 1968. T. Keister Greer, Flanders Callaway, Allen O. Woody, Jr., and Malcolm Coe organized the *Franklin County Times* in 1968 and sold it in 1973 to three former employees of the *News-Post*. In 1981 a new corporation, Franklin County Newspapers, bought both newspapers, and ended publication of the *County Times*. The county is presently served by the *News-Post*, published triweekly.[15]

Several businesses that operated in Franklin County in the postwar period but virtually ceased operation with the coming of automobiles were saddle- and harness makers, blacksmiths and wheelwrights, coach- and wagonmakers, and livery stables. For instance, according to the Virginia business directories, Franklin's saddle- and harness makers began small in 1871 with three, grew to a high of fifteen by 1893, and fell again to three by 1917. Combining blacksmiths and wheelwrights into one category, the business directories listed nine in Franklin in 1871. Until 1906, the directories did not include this category again, but in that year found forty blacksmiths and wheelwrights in the county. That number dropped to twenty-five in 1911 and twenty-one in 1917.

One of Franklin's blacksmiths was Toney Ross, born in Henry County in about 1858, the son of Andy and Rose Estrige Ross, who were probably slaves. Toney

Ross married B. Hollandsworth in 1884 and came alone to Franklin County to the Coles Creek area to find carpentry work. Before he could build a log cabin for his wife, however, she died in a fire at their home in Henry County. Ross built himself a blacksmith shop in Franklin "equipped with anvil, bellows, heavy tables where the lumber was cut to make hounds for a wagon or do a complete making of spokes to go into the wheel and iron rim to hold it together." In 1885 he married Ella Virginia Holland, with whom he had eleven children, nine of whom survived to adulthood. With the money he earned as a blacksmith as well as from farming, Ross bought twenty-five acres in 1900 from W. T. Holland and Samuel Smith and constructed a three-room log cabin for his wife and family, using a broad ax to hew the logs and building the chimneys with flint rocks.[16]

Scattered accounts from several years of Toney Ross's blacksmith ledger survive that give a revealing glimpse into the everyday affairs of a small businessman. Ross received twenty-five cents apiece for making such items as a firedog, shovel, harrow teeth, colter, and swingletree—a swinging bar to which the traces of a harness are fastened. For shoeing horses he was paid as little as twenty cents or as much as $1.60. Similarly, shoeing a mule brought him variously nineteen cents to one dollar. For what he called "blacksmithing" he made as little as a nickel (in 1904) to as much as $3.60 (in 1912). Ross also made or repaired mattocks, plows, harrows, hamhooks, pots, horse- and mule shoes, "bull tungs," axles, and hooks for a drag. In addition, he did wagon, buggy, and "shop" work, fitted wheels, and sharpened plows and other implements. None of these activities paid him more than $3.60 and usually only about forty cents. Nevertheless, after his death on 22 January 1913, his family was able to maintain his land so that five generations have lived there "and added more to it for which Mr. Toney Ross labored so hard to secure."[17]

Nine coach- and wagonmakers operated in Franklin in 1884, the first year they were listed in the business directory, reached a high of thirty-five in 1893, dropped to twenty-six in 1897, and ceased to appear in the business directories thereafter. From 1884 to 1897 there were either one or two livery stables listed in the county and located in Rocky Mount. In 1906 the county had six livery stables: three at Rocky Mount, one at Ferrum, another at Union Hall, and one at Boones Mill. In a 1908 newspaper advertisement, the Rocky Mount Livery Company ("Scott & Byrd, Proprietors") noted that "our hacks meet all trains for purpose of conveying people to points off the railroad. Look out for them on arrival at depot."[18] By 1911, seven livery stables served the county, now five at Rocky Mount, one at Union Hall, and one at Halesford. Six years later, Rocky Mount had only three livery stables, Boones Mill one, and Henry one.

At the same time the Rocky Mount Motor Company, dealer in automobiles, made its first appearance in the 1917 business directory, along with three garages: the Rocky Mount Motor Company again, Goode Motor Company at Henry, and Boones Mill Motor Company. In 1916 the Rocky Mount Motor Company advertised the Ford, "the Universal Car," which it sold at prices ranging from $390 to $740 for the town car.[19] Eleven years later, Rocky Mount's Central Garage, Inc., announced for sale the Hudson Super-Six whose "principle" was "freed to the limit" and noted that the automobile allowed a "Fast Get-away and performance so smooth that only a *stop watch* shows how swift." Prices ranged from $1,285 to $1,850 for a seven-passenger sedan.[20]

In 1926 the *County News* announced the "Exit [of] the Horse" as it discussed the U.S. Census Bureau's figures for horses and mules raised in the country in 1920 and 1925. In that five-year period the number of horses had decreased from 19.8 million to 16.5 million with an 11 percent drop in the number of two-year-old or older horses at work on farms, as well as a decline of 52 percent of young horses under two years of age. The writer concluded that the figures showing the decline in young horses

> plainly indicate that the farmers have finally recognized the superiority of the motor and the tractor over horse-drawn vehicles. No longer are horses being bred on the same large scale to haul wagons to market, or to draw plows in the fields. The faster and more powerful motors can do the work more rapidly and at less cost.

The writer decided, however, that while the horse was losing its place as a work animal on the farm it would never "be as extinct as the dinosaur" because the horse had "been an indispensable factor in the building of the nation" and "contributed in no small way to the development of civilization and the stability of the republic." In Franklin there had been 5,034 horses and 1,563 mules in 1909–1910; the number of horses had increased to 5,502 in 1920 and mules to 2,323; but by 1925 there were only 4,500 horses and 2,280 mules and by 1945 the decline had reached 1,775 horses and colts and 1,513 mules.[21]

Milling of various types occupied a significant place in Franklin's economic life. For instance, according to the U.S. census and the Virginia business directories the number of saw- and planing mills in Franklin grew from seven in 1870 to a high of forty-two in 1897 and then declined to twelve by 1917. The directory in 1890 described Franklin's major timbers as being pine, oak, hickory, walnut, and chestnut. According to the business directories, the county entered the timber business between 1893 and 1897 when Giles W. B. Hale at Rocky Mount and Franklin Log and Lumber Company at Ferrum began operation. By 1906, Franklin had two stave manufacturers, Ferrum Stave Manufacturing Company and Foster Stave Company at Nola. In fact, the Ferrum Stave Company had been in business as early as 1899, when it reported to the *Franklin Times-Democrat* at the end of September that it had "done a large business this season, having shipped about 55 cars bark and 35 cars staves."[22] By 1911 there were eight stave manufacturers in the county, but the number fell to three by 1917. By 1906 as well, Franklin had seventeen lumber dealers, one in Rocky Mount, four in the Rocky Mount area, three at Sydnorsville, one each in Snow Creek, Hernando, Taylors Store, Boones Mill, Hardy's Ford, Callaway, Penhook, the Union Hall area, and the Leatherwood area. That number fell to eleven lumber dealers in 1911 but rose again to fourteen in 1917. In fact, one source of extra income for the county's farmers derived from supplying crossties to lumber dealers. James H. Waid received $29.95 in 1919 for crossties.[23] After the Norfolk and Western Railroad Company completed its line to Ferrum in 1892, "Ferrum became the largest shipping point on this railway for logs, lumber, cross-ties, barrel staves, tanbark, manufactured lumber products and oak and locust pins and brackets for telephone and telegraphic industries." Indeed, using some of these raw materials, Thomas B. Stanley, R. E. Weaver, J. V. Chapman, and J. V. Webb started Ferrum

Veneer in 1937. Writing in 1955, Pedro T. Slone recalled that "it was an interesting sight" to observe wagons standing in line along the railroad siding and being unloaded of tanbark and crossties. The wagon's occupants closest to the one being unloaded would help so that no one had to wait too long. "Sometimes a two-horse load would bring as much as five dollars." Since railroad ties usually brought twenty-five cents and each wagon could hold about ten ties, the owner usually earned $2.50 per wagonload. "Most of the merchants bought tan-bark and cross ties, and there was considerable rivalry among them to buy when a load entered the village."[24] Boones Mill was home to another company that produced brackets, the American Pin and Bracket Company, formed in 1923. Until it ceased operation in the 1930s, the company made locust insulating pins and oak brackets.[25]

Two of Franklin County's early lumber dealers were Nathaniel P. Angle and Jack Garst. Nathaniel Peter Angle was born on a farm in southwestern Franklin County, near Ferrum, on 16 September 1861. His parents—Nathaniel Angle, of Franklin County, and Sarah Frances Wills, of Bedford County—married in Franklin County about 18 November 1852. Nathaniel P. Angle was the third of ten children (six boys and four girls).[26] Angle began his career as a schoolteacher, but, as soon as he had earned enough money to do so, he moved to Lebanon, Ohio, and attended Piedmont Business College. In the 1880s he returned to Franklin County and entered the leaf tobacco business; tobacco manufacturing was one of the county's major industries in the postbellum period. Nathaniel Angle took an exceedingly active role in Franklin business and industry and as he prospered extended his business interests into fields other than tobacco. By the early twentieth century

Bailey Helms sawmill. Ca. 1900. (Mrs. Elizabeth Cooper, Callaway, Va.)

Ferrum Depot. Above tracks, left to right: *depot, cannery, and Ferrum Mercantile store.* Below tracks: (left) *Paul Simms's packing house;* (far right) *Hurt and Co.* (Blue Ridge Institute, Ferrum, Va.)

he had established in Rocky Mount a department store, a hardware store, a furniture store, the Rocky Mount Grocery and Milling Company, and the Rocky Mount Motor Company. Angle constructed a Masonic temple and donated land for a public school. He became president of two banks and in 1924 he purchased a local railroad company. He also owned the Rocky Mount Hotel; a local newspaper, the *County News* (1923); and the Angle Silk Mill (1929), as well as his major business, the Bald Knob Furniture Company, which he organized in 1903.[27] Local oral tradition states that on the day of Angle's funeral, a visitor to Rocky Mount asked why everything in town was closed and was told "Rocky Mount is a one-horse town and the horse just died."[28]

Jack Garst, born 5 May 1863, was the son of George Garst and his second wife, Mary Frances Lockett, whom he had married on 14 June 1855. George Garst

Left: *Corn and grain mills established by Jacob Boon in the mid-1780s.* Below: *Partial view of Boones Mill, looking north. Photos ca. 1920.* (Blue Ridge Institute, Ferrum, Va.)

operated the Garst Mill three miles west of Roanoke and Cave Spring on Mud Lick Creek in Roanoke County. The elder Garst's mill was a combination grist- and sawmill, "with a capacity of 35 barrels of flour and 20 bushels of cornmeal per day. George did only custom sawing."[29] Jack Garst married Rosa Belle Angell at Boones Mill in 1898, operated his father's mill for about five years, and then moved to the Boones Mill area of Franklin County in 1906 and entered a partnership in the corn- and flour-milling firm of Angell and Garst (which was his alone by 1911). He also began his lumber dealership there at the same time. By 1917, Garst had sold the flour mill and instead owned a sawmill. He was described in 1924 as being "in business on an extensive scale." At that time he was a contractor for the bark used in extracts and canning, manufactured "great quantities of telegraph poles and railroad ties," owned and operated five sawmills, and in some years shipped as many as "one thousand carloads of lumber and timber product." By 1940, however, he only owned two mills and leased two others, cutting mostly hardwoods; he was "interested in the pulpwood business." During his long career, he also engaged in farming, contracting, and banking. When he died in January 1941, Garst was described as being "the largest shipper of cord wood in this section of the country." Moreover, railroad officials recognized him as the first to ship on the Winston-Salem branch of the Norfolk and Western Railroad after the line was built through Franklin, according to the *News-Post*. At his death, Garst was vice-president of the Farmers and Merchants Bank at Boones Mill and associated with the Boones Mill Supply Company among other enterprises.[30]

Garst was only one in a long series of flour and corn millers in Franklin County. In 1871, according to the business directory, Franklin had four gristmills (the 1870 census found thirty-three) but saw that number grow to a high of sixty-seven in 1897 before declining to sixteen in 1917. Franklin had also had one millwright in 1871 and twenty by 1897, but only two in 1911 and none in 1917. One of the county's early mills was constructed by Jacob Boon, first cousin of Daniel Boone, in 1782 on Maggodee Creek. From that beginning the town of Boones Mill grew and flourished. Boon's corn and flour mills stood in the town at least to the late 1800s and the flour mill operated into the 1920s.[31] Perhaps the earliest mill in Franklin County was that erected by James Rentfro before 1753.

During the 1880s and 1890s Virginia entered a building boom as new railroad lines to the southwest opened the coal fields to eastern ports and exposed new areas to commerce. In the financially destitute postwar period, work had begun slowly in resuming the antebellum program of Virginia railroad construction. By the early 1880s, however, the Shenandoah Valley Railroad, chartered in Virginia in 1867, had reached Waynesboro from Hagerstown, Maryland, with Pennsylvania backing, and was ready to connect up with the Norfolk and Western Railroad then serving the iron ore deposits on the western side of the Blue Ridge Mountain. In order to reach the coal fields in southwestern Virginia and West Virginia, the Shenandoah Valley Railroad needed a western terminal at a site that already served the N&W. The company chose the town of Big Lick in 1881, and soon thereafter the community experienced the building boom that had affected other sites on the railroad's network. Big Lick was renamed Roanoke in 1882 and the next year N&W moved its headquarters there from Lynchburg.[32]

Partly as a result of the proximity of the railroad, and Roanoke's growth and incorporation as a city in 1884, the building boom soon reached Rocky Mount. In 1884–1885 the county had two "carpenters and contractors" (R. A. Hoal and Menefee, Skinner, and Company, both at Rocky Mount) and no land agents. By 1890 there were two land agents (J. C. Greer at Rocky Mount and S. C. Kennett at Reverie) and still two "carpenters and builders" (J. M. Menefee and T. T. Wade, both at Rocky Mount). Three years later the situation had changed radically: now twenty-nine carpenters and builders plied their trade throughout the county, one each at Hardy's Ford, Mingo, Penhook, Felicia, Hunter's Hall, Ramsey, Sydnorsville, High Peak, and Rocky Mount, and two each at Shady Grove, Ferrum, Naff, Pigg River, Joel, Waidsboro, Kennett, Handy, Villa, and Shooting Creek. Moreover, there were now seven land agents, two at Handy, and one each at Rocky Mount, Shady Grove, Naff, Shooting Creek, and Ferrum.

The number of carpenters and builders had grown to thirty-four in 1897 but there were only three land agents listed (one each at Handy, Shooting Creek, and Ferrum). By 1906 thirty-nine carpenters and builders operated in Franklin, but there were no land agents. In 1911 twenty-four carpenters and builders served the county and W. C. Menefee was listed as being in real estate in Rocky Mount. The boom had clearly ended by 1917 when the county had only seven contractors and builders and two real estate agents. W. C. Menefee still operated along with A. W. Robbins, who had previously been editor of the *Franklin Chronicle*. Robbins, in fact, advertised in a January 1917 *Chronicle* that he had a "good tobacco farm!" for sale located within a mile and a half of two railroad stations and cheap at $12.50 per acre.[33]

Other industries associated with the building and lumber trades grew up in Franklin by the late 1890s. In 1884 Franklin had one hardware store, Garrett and Sims, at Rocky Mount. In 1890 J. N. Montgomery had taken over as owner of the only hardware store in the county. By 1893 he had been joined by Menefee Brothers at Endicott. Four years later there were four hardware stores in the county, two at Rocky Mount (J. N. Montgomery and Franklin Hardware Company) and one each at Hardy's Ford and at Eddy. By 1906 only J. N. Montgomery and Franklin Hardware Company operated in the county. By 1911, however, Angle and Company had joined the others at Rocky Mount, H. H. Hancock operated at Halesford, and S. W. Thomas at Endicott. The county still had five hardware stores in 1917 and now two plumbers as well (J. N. Montgomery and Company and W. W. Scott, both at Rocky Mount). Another company that J. N. Montgomery owned was the Rocky Mount Ice, Coal, and Wood Company, which he and George W. Altice sold to Z. T. Perdue and Allen D. Simpson on 26 March 1926.[34]

In addition, painters finally reappeared in the business directories in 1911 after the one listed in 1871 had disappeared by 1877. There were four painters in 1911, two at Nola, one at Sago, and one at Endicott. By 1917 five painters worked in the county including Peter Saunders at Rocky Mount. The first Franklin furniture store mentioned in the business directory was that of Peak and Angle, located in Rocky Mount and listed in 1897–1898. By 1906, the county had five furniture dealers: Angle and Company and Peak and Angle at Rocky Mount, B. M. Goode at Alumine, Hancock and Divers at Halesford, and T. H. Rakes at Shooting Creek. In 1911 there were seven furniture dealers in the county and Bald Knob Furniture Company was listed for the first time as a furniture manufacturer. Six years later the county had nine furniture dealers.

Described as being "the largest and most important manufacturing industry in Franklin county, and one of the largest in the Piedmont plateau," the Bald Knob Furniture Company was organized in 1903. The State Corporation Commission incorporated the company in 1907, and by 1910 the enterprise employed some sixty-five workers and provided electricity to the town of Rocky Mount. Sixteen years later, the number of employees had risen to 275. The company manufactured and sold "a superior grade of bedroom furniture which f[ound] ready sale in practically every state in the Union." Using great amounts of local poplar and chestnut woods, "which add[ed] materially to the value of the industry as a home enterprise," the plant produced furniture that was described in 1926 as being "artistic in design, superior in workmanship and reasonably priced." In 1927 the company announced that it would have a work force of six hundred men "upon completion of factory No. 2."[35] Although the company suffered in the depression of the 1930s especially when the shipping and finishing departments burned in 1932, it recovered, in part because of a government loan that allowed completion of a new plant, and continued operations. During World War II, for instance, the Bald Knob Furniture Company reported the construction of a new water system by April 1942 that supplied all water requirements except drinking fountains from its own mains. The company had a million-gallon dam and 116,000-gallon reserve built on a twenty-acre tract of the Angle estate. The water came from a branch that had supplied water for the locomotives of the old Franklin and Pittsylvania Railroad. Bald Knob had also built a powerhouse, and the company believed it was ready to compete with other furniture makers throughout the country.[36]

Indeed Bald Knob was clearly successful, as a *News-Post* article in late December 1943 noted that the company had declared a 3 percent dividend to its shareholders out of the previous year's earnings; it was having an "exceptionally good" year and the prospects for growth seemed excellent. This had been the first year for some time that a dividend had been paid.[37] By 1940 the number of employees had reached 340. The company manufactured in addition to bedroom furniture, dining-room furniture, tables, chairs, chests of drawers, and night-

Bald Knob Furniture Co. Ca. 1920 photo. (Blue Ridge Institute, Ferrum, Va.)

stands. James N. Montgomery became president of Bald Knob after the death of Nathaniel Angle in 1936 and served in that capacity until the company was sold to the Lane Furniture Manufacturing Company in 1957.[38]

Three other furniture companies operated in the county. The first was the Grassy Hill Furniture Company, founded in 1926 at Rocky Mount to manufacture antique reproductions, as well as to refinish old furniture. Among the founders of Grassy Hill Furniture was William L. Cooper, whose son George in 1952 started Cooper Wood Products, Inc., now located near Grassy Hill. In the late 1930s, Homer Murray established the Novelty Furniture Company at Boones Mill. His company produced footstools that were sent to New York to be covered by women there with tops they had needlepointed. During World War II, Novelty also manufactured brackets for poles for the British and file handles for the U.S. government. A third furniture manufacturer, the Greer Furniture Company, also operated in the county in the early twentieth century.[39]

Other industries that operated in Franklin over the years were associated with the minerals found in the county. From early in its history, Franklin County had had ironworks, the Washington Iron Works established in 1773 being the most prominent until its destruction in a flood in 1851. In 1880 the Pennsylvania Steel Company, of Steelton, Pennsylvania, leased from John Hale the Franklin mine, a half mile northwest of Rocky Mount, after a branch of the Virginia Midland Railroad reached the area and made it feasible to extract the iron ore. The mine had previously been worked by Robert H. and Peter Saunders in 1861 and earlier supplied them with ore for the Washington Iron Works. The Pennsylvania Steel Company had taken a twenty-year lease on 3,000 acres in the Franklin-Pittsylvania County area and within two years the Pittsville Iron Mines, located in Pittsylvania County eight miles from Franklin Junction (now Gretna), had supplied "10,000 tons of Excellent iron ore to the Bessemer Steel Works, near Harrisburg, Pa." In 1880 as well "several leases of iron land [were] made by companies in the southern portions of Franklin Co."[40]

In the 1884–1885 Virginia business directory Thomas Martin's iron mine at Roberta near Henry was the only one listed. But the directories noted in 1890–1891 that Martin's mine had been joined by four other iron mines: the E. Barksdale and the Hairston Mines, both at Waidsboro, J. T. Moorehead's mine at Roberta, and Saunders Mines at Young's Store. Seven mines operated in 1893: John Barksdale, J. Shelton, and S. G. King, all at Handy; the Hairston Mines at Waidsboro; T. B. Martin and J. T. Moorehead, each at Roberta; and again the Saunders Mine at Young's Store. By 1897, there were just four iron mines still in operation: T. B. Martin and J. T. Moorehead continued their respective operations at Roberta, as did the Saunders Mine, now listed at Nola, along with the Brown Hill Mining Company at Ferrum. But by the time of the 1900 census, the only persons associated with iron mine–related activities were two iron miners, both probably working in the Fayersville iron mines in Patrick County.[41] In 1892, H. B. C. Nitze had published an article in which he noted that the Pennsylvania Steel Company had abandoned its mining operations outside of Rocky Mount, presumably because of the cost of transportation. Although "the deposit exists in a long, low ridge, parallel to the 'Grassy Hills,' " Nitze observed that "the outcrop is very distinct and has been stripped to a great extent by the Pennsylvania Steel Company." He found on examination of the mine that despite there being a number of old shafts, all were filled with water so that he could not examine them. In fact, the Virginia Development Company put down the last shaft to a depth of seventy-five feet and that too had filled with water.[42]

Franklin had had one iron founder in 1871 (Ammon and Smith at Snow Hill, southeast of Sydnorsville), two in 1890 (combined in a category with machinists) along with two separate machinists, four iron founders and machinists in 1893 and 1897, but neither iron founders nor machinists listed by 1906. There were six machinists listed in 1911, however, but only one, J. L. Perdue in Rocky Mount, in 1917, along with R. W. Pedigo, an iron founder and machinist at Figsboro.

For a while in the last years of the nineteenth century, slate quarries operated in the county: in 1890 C. J. Saunders had one at Waidsboro, and in 1893 John Barksdale operated the Stuarts Knob slate quarry at Handy (at the same time he was also working an iron mine at Handy). These operations must not have been profitable as no quarries were listed thereafter in the business directories.

Despite the disappearance of quarries from the business directories, Franklin boasted a flagstone quarry that operated from antebellum times until the 1940s. In the antebellum period John S. Hale owned the flagstone quarry, located in Rocky Mount west of Needmore, and used slaves to quarry some of the stone. After his death in 1872, his widow, Margaret J. Hale, sold the property to William Crump Smithers, who hired workers at fifty cents a day to quarry the flagstone by hand. In 1884 Major Jedediah Hotchkiss collected some of Smithers's granite to be used at a Virginia minerals and ores exhibit at the New Orleans Exposition.[43] By the early decades of the twentieth century, however, Smithers's sons installed modern quarrying equipment and began extracting as much flagstone in one day as could be hand-quarried in weeks. Much of the flagstone used throughout Rocky Mount came from the Hale-Smithers quarry, especially in sidewalks, private house and garden walks, house chimneys, tombstones, and the town's Trinity Episcopal Church.[44]

Coal mining also occurred for a short time in Franklin. Two coal mines were listed in the business directory in 1893, those of Elisha Akers and Lem Ingraham, both at Handy. In 1897 Mine Branch at Handy and W. Bennett's at Boones Mill were in operation, but no coal mines appeared in the business directories thereafter. Another short-lived mining activity in the late 1800s was the search for gold in Franklin County. In 1858 the *Bedford Democrat* had reported that a Dr. Grasty, who had been trying to find gold in Orange County, had decided to move to Franklin instead because he discovered three dollars worth of gold on the land of Captain Stephen Preston in Franklin. The newspaper described Grasty as being "very sanguine of success, in the gold mining business" in Franklin. Presumably Grasty achieved no success as nothing further is known of him. When Professor William M. Fontaine visited in May and June 1882 on an exploration of the geology and mineral resources of the area, he reported that between the Pigg River and Rocky Mount numerous veins of quartz existed, some of which "seem[ed] to be of a character favorable for the occurrence of gold." Indeed, he expressed himself unsurprised to hear that "alluvial gold had been found at several points" between the river and Rocky Mount. He concluded that "the gold veins, or original deposits, do not appear to have been found. So far as I could learn, the gold found did not occur in quantities that would pay for working in the way search was carried on for it."[45]

Perhaps Fontaine's report spurred new interest in attempting to mine gold in Franklin, as in 1893 the Virginia business directory found three gold mines in Franklin, two at Handy operated by Randolph Jones and by F. M. Prillaman, and a third at Waidsboro that someone named Sexton was running. Evidently, none of these gold mines were productive as the category does not appear in any subsequent business directories. In the late 1930s S. H. Ellis discovered gold and silver in a mine on the banks of Maggodee Creek near Boones Mill. Mineralogists who assayed the mine's dirt declared that Ellis might be able to obtain as much as $20 per ton of the quartz.[46] But again, gold mining apparently failed to become a major activity in the county.

Fontaine also found an excellent quality of asbestos about two miles east of Rocky Mount and noted that "about a car load of the material had been raised and ship[p]ed." When the asbestos first came out it was in rods of perhaps as much as five feet in length, but with a tendency to break up into shorter rods. "Fibre a foot long may be easily obtained. This locality well deserves to be thoroughly examined." No further exploration of the asbestos seems to have been made, however. And while Fontaine found copper deposits on Grassy Hill he observed that "obscure pits and excavations are found that have not been made within the memory of any one, and no one can give anything more than a conjectural explanation of them." Perhaps the copper had been exploited by Colonel John Chiswell during the Revolution.[47]

The mining of soapstone, talc, and mica began in Franklin early in the twentieth century and by 1914 Henry Mining Company was producing among other things soapstone griddles, small electrical insulator units, and soapstone foot warmers. As the company did not prove to be profitable, it was sold about 1916 to Franklin Soapstone Products Corporation, which operated the plant until the autumn of 1918, primarily pulverizing the soapstone for various uses. Operations ceased, however, in late 1918 and did not resume until June 1920 when the Blue Ridge Talc Company bought the enterprise and rebuilt, modernized, and enlarged the plant. In 1926, J. G. Claiborne reported that Blue Ridge Talc was producing 95 percent of the soapstone used in foundry facings in the United States and Canada. While 75 percent of the company's output went to the foundry trade, the remaining pulverized soapstone was used in lubricants and insecticides, and as filling in paints, sealing waxes, and plastic cements. The company also produced the largest amount "of mineral colors in the state of Virginia," consisting of cement and mortar colors and paint pigment. The company sold most of the paint pigment throughout the United States, and exported it to Canada, England, and Cuba.[48]

In the late 1800s Snow Creek residents were bringing mica sheets into Rocky Mount for sale, but because the area was inaccessible to railroad transportation, the mica mines were not "worked profitably" in the 1890s. In the twentieth century the Chestnut Mountain Mica Company began operation on land it had bought from George K. Cooper, who first developed the mica deposits around 1909. Cooper tried to interest a group of men in southwestern Virginia in operating the mine on a large scale but was unsuccessful. A group of men from Danville next bought the property and in 1915 H. C. Fields, of the Chestnut

Mountain Mica Company, acquired the mine, further developed it, and sold it by 1926 to the Clinchfield Mica Corporation, headquartered in New York.[49]

During World War II the Carrolton Corporation, of New York, began mining an eight-acre flint-rock tract near Wirtz. The flint was sent to the steel mills near Parkersburg, West Virginia, and other northern sites to be used as flux in the heat treatment of high-quality steel in electric furnaces. Between thirty and forty men worked in the county from February until 1 June 1942, going north for the summer, and returning to the county for the autumn and winter.[50]

Although Bath County, Virginia, home of Warm, Hot, and Healing Springs, is perhaps one of the best-known areas in the state for spring waters, the Rocky Mount vicinity was not without its own mineral waters and by 1926 Shoaf Springs, west of town, was home to the Rocky Mount Lithia–Magnesia Springs Bottling House. Anticipating a popular demand, the owner built a hotel, shelters, fountains, and rock walkways. Nevertheless, the hoped-for crowds of spa-goers never materialized. Instead the Norfolk and Western dining cars for years featured Deep Rock bottled water from the springs. Another beverage, requiring carbonated water, Coca-Cola was bottled by Harry, Moton, and Crump Menefee on North Franklin Street in Rocky Mount from 1919 until 1945 when the Rocky Mount Bottling Company, by then located on Franklin Street at Floyd Avenue, closed.[51]

Another industry that existed in Franklin during the later years of the nineteenth century was that of wool manufacturing. By 1890 two woolen mills operated in the county: Piedmont Woolen Mill at Callaway and J. W. Wortz's mill

Above: *Rocky Mount Camping Grounds and Bungalow Hotel at Shoaf Springs.* (Blue Ridge Institute, Ferrum, Va.) Right: *Hotel Rocky Mount with auditorium at right.* (J. Francis Amos, Rocky Mount, Va.)

at Villa. In addition, from at least 1884, W. W. St. Clair at Gogginsville had functioned as a wool dealer. Six years later there were five wool dealers and nine in 1897, along with a third woolen mill: Callaways at Waidsboro. In 1906 there were no wool dealers and only James A. Martin at Callaway still operated the Piedmont Woolen Mill.

Martin's Woolen Mill at Callaway. Ca. 1900 photo. (Blue Ridge Institute, Ferrum, Va.)

Martin began the company in 1880, buying the necessary machinery for the mill in Philadelphia, and, according to his daughter Carrie Pedigo, stopping en route to attend Grover Cleveland's inauguration in Washington, D.C. (which occurred in March 1881). Martin's two cousins, R. A. and P. C. Martin ran the mill, with James A. as general manager, Robert A. as bookkeeper, and Philip C. ("Buck") as purchasing agent, traveling the countryside to obtain the wool from farmers in a nine-county area. Buck Martin used a schooner-type wagon pulled by two virtually identical mules. Any child who could distinguish which mule was which "was considered highly intelligent." Children were also enthused when Buck returned from Craig County after a wool-gathering trip, according to James A. Martin's daughter, as maple syrup was made in Craig. The children "would follow the wool-laden wagon for miles."[52]

Manufacturing blankets, dresses, pants, and other woolen items, Piedmont Mills operated until 1907, when competition forced Martin to sell it. After the farmer had gathered the wool into a bed sheet pinned with thorns, Buck Martin carried the wool to the factory, where the company kept half of what was produced and the farmer received the other half made up as he desired. The company featured a storeroom where non-sheep-owning citizens could buy the finished goods. Most people, however, brought in their own material to be made into whatever garments they wished. With fifteen to twenty employees, the mill could process one hundred pounds of wool per day. City clothing stores hastened the demise of Piedmont Woolen Mills.[53]

Among other businesses related to agriculture that operated in Franklin were cattle dealers, sellers of agricultural implements, canneries, fertilizer dealers, and lime manufacturers. Cattle dealers first appeared in the 1890 Virginia business directory when thirty-two were listed. That number had decreased to twenty-five in 1893 and twenty-three in 1897. For 1906 the category of cattle dealer was not included. In 1911 there were thirteen livestock dealers in the county and in 1917 nine. Sellers of agricultural implements first appeared in the business directory of 1890 when there were four of them, including Nathaniel Angle at Waidsboro and Garrett and Sims at Rocky Mount. That number held steady for 1893, fell to two in 1897 and 1906, but grew to five in 1911 and to eleven in 1917. Only once were fertilizer dealers listed as a separate category, in 1906, J. H. Dudley and Son at Union Hall and Peak and Angle at Rocky Mount. Lime manufacturers made an appearance in three of the business directories, 1890 through 1897, F. Cook and M. Parell both at Shady Grove for all three directories.[54]

The first cannery appeared in the 1897 business directory: H. Ikenberry and Sons at Rocky Mount. In 1906 only W. M. Kesler and Company at Boones Mill was listed, but in 1911 fourteen canneries had begun to operate in the county, two each at Boones Mill and Wirtz, one each at Callaway, Dillons Mill, Endicott, Rocky Mount, Sontag, Sydnorsville, and Waidsboro, and three at Nola. The business had really expanded by 1917 when thirty-one canneries appeared in the business directory, six at Wirtz alone, five at Boones Mill, and four at Callaway, with three at Naffs, two each at Dillons Mill, Ferrum, Glade Hill, and Rocky Mount, and one each at Endicott, Henry, Scruggs, Taylors Store, and Union Hall. Two of the canning companies at Ferrum, Ferrum Supply Company and Hurt Canning Company (operated by John K. Hurt), later joined by George A. Menefee's cannery, "processed tomatoes, apples, blackberries and peaches and sold them through brokerage houses in Roanoke and Bluefield," West Virginia. "Ferrum became the shipping and distribution outlet for the western part of Franklin, eastern Floyd and southwestern Patrick counties."[55]

Two other categories related to horticulture that appeared at various times in the business directories were florists and nurserymen. M. F. Hurt at Waidsboro was first listed as a florist in the 1884 business directory. Six years later Mrs. E. C. Price at Naffs ran the only florist shop specified in the directory. In 1893, however, the county boasted seven florists: Mary R. Bowling at Handy, Mary Matthews at Waidsboro, Maggie Naff at Naffs, Mrs. E. C. Price now at Rocky Mount, and three men, J. E. Cox at Mingo, James Potete at Taylors Store, and Byrd Smith at Shooting Creek. Mrs. J. L. Abshire had opened a florist shop at Boones Mill by 1897, as had Mrs. M. E. Bowman at Taccio. Mary R. Bowling, Mrs. E. C. Price, and Byrd Smith still ran their businesses in 1897. They had been joined by J. W. Angle at Waidsboro and H. C. Harrison at Redwood. The business directories for 1906 and 1911 did not contain the florist category, but in 1917 B. M. Buckhorn at Ferrum appeared as the only florist given for the county. For nurserymen, however, their only appearances in the business directories came in the 1890s, J. W. Hickman at Sophronia and W. M. Kestler at Red Plains in 1890, W. M. Kestler alone in 1893 and 1897.

Women operated businesses in Franklin at least by 1871 and thereafter, engaging in a variety of pursuits, not all of which were considered feminine. For instance, in 1906 Mary DeWitt at Sydnorsville was listed in the Virginia business directory as a tanner. Mrs. Eliza Garvin at Sydnorsville ran a country store by 1871 and Mrs. L. D. Horn a restaurant at Gogginsville. Women did not again appear as restaurateurs until 1917 when Mrs. Fannie Allen and a Mrs. Campbell were both running restaurants at Rocky Mount. A black female restaurateur who did not appear in the business directories was Mrs. Ollie Hopkins. She operated a successful establishment at the corner of Court and Warren streets in Rocky

Mount that was especially popular on court days. Her food was described as being delicious, and "the country people thought [her restaurant] had the best 'eaten' in town." Mrs. Hopkins also operated a boardinghouse in the upper floor of her home, but both businesses were for whites only.[56]

By 1877 Franklin had two milliners, Miss E. C. Lavender and Mrs. Isabella Scott, both at Rocky Mount. Miss Lavender continued to appear in the business directories through 1884 but not thereafter. Mrs. Scott, on the other hand, appeared in the directories through 1893. There were five milliners in Rocky Mount in 1897 but none that can be identified from the directories as women. By 1906, however, Mrs. S. E. Ramsey at Alumine and Miss Eva Saunders and Company at Rocky Mount were both listed as milliners. In fact, in a 1903 Rocky Mount newspaper advertisement, Miss Saunders announced her "Spring and Summer Millinery, White Goods, Notions, &c." and that she was the successor to George T. Horne, who moved his business to Roanoke by 1910.[57] Mrs. A. M. Bowman at Boones Mill and Mrs. S. E. Brodie at Henry were listed as milliners in the 1911 business directory, but there were no milliners given in the 1917 directory. Mrs. Bowman advertised in November 1908 that she had fall millinery and cloaks. "Don't you think it is time for the Fall Hat and Cloak!" she asked her customers.[58]

Other occupations that drew women were hotels, grist- and sawmills, schools, music teaching, groceries, and florist shops. By 1880 Mrs. E. L. Helm kept a hotel at Helm's Store (now Helm), which she continued into the mid-1890s. Other female hoteliers listed for Franklin at various times were Mrs. Susan M. Belcher who was operating a hotel at Mingo by 1893 (she was not listed in 1897, however) and Mrs. S. M. Young at Henry in 1911. In 1917 boardinghouses were given for the first time and the directory found six women engaged in that business along with three men: Mrs. G. C. Campbell, Mrs. M. E. Horne, and Mrs. J. R. Robertson at Rocky Mount; Mrs. S. E. Turner at Boones Mill; Mrs. J. A. Martin at Callaway; and Mrs. Mary L. Eggleston at Henry. The men were Ira D. Hoy at Boones Mill, Robert Skinnell at Ferrum, and G. Z. Doss at Penhook. Presumably Mrs. J. A. Martin was the wife of James A. Martin who had operated the Piedmont Woolen Mills until 1907.

The ranks of general merchants did not again include women after 1871 until the 1884 business directory, which listed Mrs. Eliza Howard at Rocky Mount, Miss Lockey W. Chitwood at Villa, and Mrs. D. T. Martin at Sydnorsville. Mrs. Martin and Miss Chitwood, now listed at Reverie, appeared in the 1890 directory. In 1893 only Miss Lockey Chitwood at Villa was listed, but in 1897 she had been joined by Mrs. E. K. Allen at Rocky Mount. In 1906 the Della Williams Company at Alumine was given as the only general merchant with which a woman's name was associated. But Mrs. N. C. Morris at Rocky Mount and Miss M. E. Perdue at Redwood appeared in the list as grocers. Five years later, Mrs. Ella Frith at Waidsboro and Bettie Mettes at Boones Mill, RFD 3, were named in the directory as general merchants. There was also Allie Zeigler at Rocky Mount. Mrs. Vinda King and Mrs. W. G. Turner, both at Henry, were the only women general merchants listed in the 1917 directory.

Mary Callaway appeared in the 1880 and 1884 directories as the manager of both a grist- and a sawmill, located at Callaway. In 1890 Mrs. M. A. Martin at Bonbrook operated both a corn and flour mill and a sawmill. Mrs. S. L. Saunders at Bruce ran a corn and flour mill. Thereafter only Mrs. M. A. Martin appeared as the proprietress of a corn and flour mill, at Bonbrook through 1897. No women appear in the directories as mill owners in the twentieth century.

In 1880 Milley Prillaman at Blackwater was listed as a brandy distiller but no other women ever appeared in this category. The 1884 directory named postmasters and postmistresses for the first time. In that year Mrs. P. D. Hairston was postmistress at Hunter's Hall, where she also ran a school; Hattie F. Brown served as postmistress for Rocky Mount and Sallie A. Young at Young's Store. Lockey Chitwood, who ran a general store at Villa, was also the postmistress there. Marshall Wingfield in his history of Franklin County listed as the earliest Franklin County postmistress, Mrs. Caroline Y. Semms at Rennet Bag, where the post office was established 29 August 1873.[59] In fact, the first postmistress in Franklin County appears to have been Elizabeth J. Woods, who received that office on 21 February 1845 and held the post a year and a half until Robert Wright assumed it in September 1846. The only other Franklin County woman found to have served as postmistress in the antebellum period was Ann J. Greer, who on 27 October 1848 took over the office after the death of her husband, Thomas S. Greer. She held the office until November 1851 when she was replaced by William B. Noble. Interestingly enough, in the immediate postwar period (January 1866–December 1867), fourteen women held the office of postmistress out of twenty-six post offices in Franklin County, eleven of them at the same time.[60] One explanation for this phenomenon may be that the men who otherwise would have continued as postmasters had been disqualified by their service to the Confederacy. The first woman listed as a notary public was Mary V. Hancock at Rocky Mount in 1906. Miss C. I. Blair at Rocky Mount appeared in that category in 1911.

Two other women who ran schools were Ida Angle at Villa, listed in 1890 and 1893, along with Miss F. Ross at Young's Store, who was still listed in 1897. By the early years of the twentieth century, the directories list only teachers, so that in 1906 there were thirty-eight female teachers given and in 1911 sixteen. The teacher category did not appear in the 1917 directory, nor did music teachers. In 1906 music teachers were listed for the first time. Elizabeth M. Brodie taught music at Snow Creek, Mrs. J. K. Hurt and Miss Annie Lee at Crawford, Mrs. G. R. Thomason at Taylors Store, and Miss Elsie White and Miss Kate St. Clair at Rocky Mount, RFD. Five years later, there were only three music teachers named: Miss Elizabeth Arthur at Wirtz, RFD 1, along with Miss Mattie Duncan and Mrs. J. P. Thompson at Halesford.

Franklin County has been home to various other businesses and industries such as the manufacture of Byrd's Oriental Balm beginning in 1877. The salve was produced by Wiley A. Byrd and Son ("vendor of medicine") at Glade Hill.[61] In 1917 a company was formed principally to manufacture Byrd's balm, the Blue Ridge Chemical Company, producing soaps, vinegar, syrup, various extracts, and other medicines as well. Located in the building that housed the Black Prince Overall Company, the Blue Ridge Chemical Company went up in flames along with Black Prince in 1926. Thereafter Zack Perdue made Byrd's Oriental Balm until he sold the operation.

Another pharmaceutical house that operated in the county was the J. Kyle Montague Medicine Company, chartered the year after the Blue Ridge Chemical Company. It produced Montague Liniment, Horse and Cattle Powder, Poultry

Powder, and Liver and Kidney Pills. Located in a two-story frame building at the foot of Scott Hill in Rocky Mount, the business apparently died out when Kendrick Broom Company moved into the building in 1928. Started by R. J. Kendrick who had taken over broom manufacturing from a Mr. Hall, the Kendrick Broom Company provided work for three people who made around twenty dozen corn brooms per day. After Kendrick drowned in 1936, the company closed.[62]

An additional industry that grew slowly in Franklin County until the early years of the twentieth century was the manufacture and sale of clothing. In the business directories of 1871, 1877, and 1880, William E. Andrews appeared as the only tailor in the county, with his business at Rocky Mount. At various times boot- and shoemakers were also listed: Keeny and Davis at Rocky Mount and James K. Ellis at Union Hall in 1871. James K. Ellis appeared again in the 1897 directory as a boot- and shoemaker at Union Hall. The category was not given in the 1877 through 1893 directories, nor after 1897. The first mention of clothiers came in the 1917 business directory with the listing of Angle and Company and Nathan Morris, both at Rocky Mount. That same directory saw the first mention as well of overall manufacturers, the Rocky Mount Overall Company, perhaps the first clothing manufacturer in the county. J. N. Montgomery and Company established the overall company in 1913 and ran it until 1920, when it was sold, reorganized, incorporated, and renamed the Black Prince Overall Company. Under the new ownership, the business was moved toward the end of 1926 to the Farmers Mercantile Store (owned by Nathaniel P. Angle), where fifteen employees produced overalls and overall jackets. In that year, J. G. Claiborne described the company:

> The plant is modern in equipment and produces products that are unsurpassed on the market, strictly high-grade goods and sold on the guarantee that they will be purchased by the trade or else the factory will cancel order and redeem shipment. All goods are sold direct to merchants. In addition to having a large output in Franklin county, the company enjoys a lucrative trade in other parts of Virginia and in North Carolina.[63]

But tragedy struck on 12 January 1927 when fire broke out about 7:15 A.M. and quickly spread to the third floor where eleven female employees of the Black Prince Overall Company were working. They were aged eighteen to twenty-five and most lived in the Rocky Mount area. The unfortunate women had only two means of escape, the elevator, where the fire seemed to be centered, and the third-floor windows, as there were no fire escapes. Panicking, the women ran to the windows and started to jump, despite warnings from the people on the street to wait for blankets and ladders. Among those who tried to break the women's fall, J. B. ("Ben") Morris, who owned a grocery store across the street, caught one (injuring his back in the process), but before he could arise another young woman landed on him and the woman he had just tried to save. Allen Simpson broke the fall of another, and Lee M. Waid attempted to assist several others. Because they were so panic-stricken, however, the young women began jumping en masse and those on the ground could do little to save them. The eleventh woman, Annie Brown, of Sydnorsville, probably fainted, as she fell back into the fire before she could get out of the window, and perished. A second victim, Lydia

Frith, died of her injuries that afternoon.[64] One eyewitness recalled that tobacco trucks were brought to carry the women to nearby homes where they could escape the bitter cold while waiting for ambulances to arrive from Roanoke, for there was no hospital in Rocky Mount then. "One girl was in such pain that she would scream each time we touched her. She was taken to Mr. and Mrs. L. M. Menefee's and we placed blankets and hot water bottles around her," the eyewitness later wrote—"Mr. Morris was the 'hero' of the day."[65]

One of the women who jumped to safety, Thelma Altice, later recalled the events for the *Roanoke Times*. She stated that she and ten others had been at work about thirty minutes when she left her sewing machine and started to the dressing room. Seeing the rear of the room filling with smoke she may have yelled "fire" but could not remember. At any rate, all of the others ran to the front of the building and opening a window began screaming for help. "Pandemonium reigned, and the young women instantly lost almost all control of themselves." Altice found that both the stairway and the elevator were filled with smoke and the front window was the only way left to exit. Dora Turner and Grace Hodges jumped from the window first. Altice then leapt out, grabbed a telephone wire, and swung to the second floor where the wire broke so that she landed on Ben Morris, who tried to catch her.[66]

After Altice regained her feet, two men led her away to a store. She could hear the screams of the others stop "and immediately the girls fell to the pavement, one after the other, making a terrible noise as they struck the sidewalk." When asked why Annie Brown did not jump, Altice replied that she believed that Brown suffered from fainting spells and "that while debating whether or not to jump for her life, she was overcome by smoke, which was pouring out the windows, and fainted, falling inside." Altice averred that the fire had made such headway that it burned the hair from the back of her head and also "seared" her left ear. "Several others also were slightly injured by the flames which rapidly crept upon them after the fire was discovered."[67]

Within two hours four buildings had been totally destroyed and five others damaged by smoke, fire, and water. The Farmers Mercantile Building, which housed the Rocky Mount Drug Company and the Morris Dry Goods Company on the first floor, stock storage on the second floor, and the Black Prince Overall Company on the third floor, was a total loss. J. N. Montgomery and Company's

Site of Black Prince Overall factory fire, Main Street. N Morris Department Store building next door still stands. 1927 photo. (Blue Ridge Institute, Ferrum, Va.)

hardware business, located in a building attached to one side of the Mercantile Building, also fell to the flames. Montgomery had had a building lost to fire on the same spot in 1887.[68]

The other two structures that completely burned were W. S. Smithers's Paint Shop and B. S. Parrish's Cash and Carry Grocery, both one-story frame buildings. Across the street the fire gutted B. L. Perdue's Cafe and badly damaged the building owned by W. C. Menefee that housed the Rocky Mount Bakery. J. B. Morris's grocery, the Presbyterian church, and Rakes Motor Company sustained less serious damage. Total damage amounted to $250,000, "a huge sum in 1927."[69]

Three days after the fire, Rocky Mount's mayor N. B. Hutcherson thanked everyone who had helped the fire's victims, especially those who sent the ambulances from Townes-Cawley Funeral Home, the Oakey undertakers, and the Red Cross of Roanoke that rushed the young women to the Lewis-Gale, Jefferson, and Roanoke hospitals: "To the above and all others who aided in any way in this, the saddest and most heart rending experience in the history of Rocky Mount, we desire to express deep appreciation."[70]

By 18 January, the *Roanoke Times* reported the "stricken town [was] back to normal." The cleanup process had begun and plans were announced for rebuilding. Nathaniel P. Angle, who owned the Farmers Mercantile Building and the two housing the Cash and Carry store and the Smithers Paint Shop, expected to reconstruct the three structures as soon as possible. He was joined in that ambition by J. N. Montgomery, who intended to rebuild his hardware business on its previous location. "The buildings will begin as soon as the weather conditions will permit, and all will be of brick and steel," the newspaper announced. Soon thereafter, the Black Prince Overall Company reopened in an auditorium on Oak Street.[71]

Another fabric manufactory that operated in Franklin was the Angle Silk Mills, Inc., which was chartered in June 1929. Nathaniel P. Angle, for whom it was named, served as president and treasurer until his death late in 1936. J. D. Pell was hired as manager of the mill, which he bought after Angle died. Originally the company manufactured silk and rayon fabric for use in women's clothing, but later ceased weaving silk and produced other materials instead. A second plant opened at Ferrum in 1947, and both plants became part of J. P. Stevens Company in 1959.[72]

In February 1937 fire once more struck Rocky Mount, ten years after the Black Prince Overall Company had burned in 1927. Ironically the blaze once again affected the Angle family. This time the conflagration apparently began in J. L. Ramsey's electrical shop, perhaps due to defective wiring, and in the process destroyed the Angle brick building, completed in 1916 by W. N. Angle, and an adjacent tobacco warehouse that belonged to the estate of Nathaniel P. Angle. Damage estimates were put at $96,500, most of which was only partially covered by insurance. Lost in the blaze along with the brick building and the warehouse were the Angle Hardware Company, Ramsey's electrical shop, Martin Jewelry, the third-story Angle building apartment of B. L. Angle, Jr., and the offices of W. H. Cobb, physician, and D. E. Stone, dentist. No one was injured in the fire but B. L. Angle, Jr., had had to carry his three-year-old son from the building and then return for his wife who had recently undergone an operation. It was the second fire for the warehouse, which had burned in 1884, but had been rebuilt the following year.[73]

With the onset of World War II in Europe, various county businesses began to gear up for increased production to meet anticipated government demand. "The first direct effect of the national defense program on business activity in Rocky Mount" was reported on 25 October 1940 "when Fred D. Vaughn, president of the Rocky Mount Manufacturing Company, announced that a 70 percent increase in payroll of the local concern would be made within the next 30 days." The company had been chartered in October 1939 as the town's newest industry and by October 1940 employed 225 men, with the expectation of adding 150 additional employees by 1 December. Manufacturing "R[oyal] O[ak] W[holesale] patented 'spring cushion' windows" the company had received orders from national defense agencies for thousands of the windows and Vaughn believed those orders would "tax our fullest capacity for months to come." He anticipated expanding the company into another part of the old Bald Knob Furniture Company building; the windows were wanted especially for "cantonments and military training bases in the eastern section of the country." Vaughn expected the company to grow indefinitely as it already had "exclusive rights in a large area including a large number of states in the east and promises to develop into a[n] enterprise that will surpass even the fondest hopes of the town and community."[74]

In July 1941 improvements at the factory were reported: a huge steam-driven generator had been installed so the local plant could make its own electricity, along with dry kiln equipment to provide 50 percent increased efficiency in the cross-ventilation over the present kiln system. The company also acquired a new sander, tenon machine, ripsaw, band saw, veneer splicer, and core machine to improve production and workmanship. Separate offices had been created for the president, general manager, secretary-treasurer, bookkeeping department, and shipping department, all controlled through a central information office. Orders looked good through the fall and thus promised a successful year, according to J. N. Montgomery, Jr., the new president.[75]

By April 1942, however, so many male employees at the Rocky Mount Manufacturing Company had left for the service that fifty women were hired to take the men's places. The women were employed in the glazing and screen departments "where nimble fingers and quick action are needed."[76] Undoubtedly they proved to be excellent replacements.

A U.S. Census Bureau report in March 1941 revealed that retail sales in Franklin County in 1939 had totaled $2,113,000. Of this amount fifty-seven food stores had sold $467,000; thirty-seven general stores including food, $260,000; seven general merchandise stores, $228,000; three apparel stores, $17,000; five automotive stores, $367,000; eighty filling stations, $328,000; four lumber, building, and hardware stores, $152,000; five drugstores, $67,000; fifty-one grocery-combination stores, $463,000; six restaurants-eateries, $52,000; and various other merchants for which no breakdown of sales was given, for a total of 194 "active proprietors of unincorporated businesses" with 196 the average number of employees and a total payroll of $153,000.[77]

Three years later, Z. Taylor Turner, owner and manager of the local Mick-or-Mack celebrated his ninth anniversary in business with the well-wishes of hundreds of his patrons. Known as "The Value Wizard" Turner had begun his career at a young age and had spent thirty-four years in retail and wholesale groceries. From a small start in June 1937 when he obtained a local franchise of the Mick-or-Mack chain organization, Turner had built the business by June 1944 to about $500,000 in retail and wholesale sales, "making it the largest independent store in Virginia."[78] In addition to groceries and meats Turner sold feed and supplies to the farmers, and according to a glowing article in the *News-Post*, his "pioneering work" had "been instrumental in making Mick or Mack a trading center that br[ought] thousands of people to Rocky Mount every month." By 1945, Turner's customers included not only Franklin residents but also those of surrounding counties, and he expected soon to reach the three-quarter-million mark in sales.[79]

In late June 1945 construction began on another industry in the county, the Franklin Veneer and Lumber Company, which was expected to be "one of the largest and most modern veneer plants in the South . . . as soon as priority orders for needed materials and equipment are received from governmental agencies." Organized by Thomas W. Greer, of Greer Lumber Company, R. E. Weaver, of Weaver Mirror Company, and Charles Carter Lee, commonwealth's attorney, the company was built on land east of Greer Lumber Company, near the State Highway Department office. Fifteen to twenty highly skilled men made plyboard for lend-lease shipment to England, France, Russia, China, and other war-torn countries, where the "cross-banding veneer" produced in Franklin would be used in building projects. Because of a large supply of lumber from Franklin and surrounding counties, the company anticipated producing about 100,000 feet of plyboard per day.[80] Wartime delays in receiving equipment prevented the company from opening in 1945, but by early January 1946, work was being completed on the dry kiln and "the massive, specially constructed-, cross-cut lathe" was expected shortly. Franklin Veneer and Lumber Company received its charter from the State Corporation Commission on 25 January 1946.[81]

As Franklin's businesses and industries entered 1946, the end of the Second World War promised that the new year would be "a hum-dinger, unless continuing labor strikes retard[ed] the manufacture and delivery of materials and merchandise." In the 4 January 1946 edition of the *News-Post* the editor canvassed several of the county's businessmen and reported "prospects [were] bright for [the] new year." Thomas W. Greer, of Greer Lumber Company, assessed the situation, stating, "We are now experiencing the greatest shortage of building materials I have ever seen in my life and if this [keeps?] up we will see a lot of building here during 1946."[82]

D. C. Vaughn, of the Rocky Mount Manufacturing Company, reported that his business was also being affected by lumbermen's strikes in the West and glassmakers' strikes in Pennsylvania, but he expected the disputes to be settled within the next six months at which time his company would "be in good shape for the next year—yes, three or four or five years." He continued, "We have more orders now [for the Royal Oak Wholesale patented 'spring cushion' windows] than we can fill and are having to turn down orders every day because of the lack of lumber and glass." In anticipation of a postwar boom in the building industry, Rocky Mount Manufacturing had taken out advertisements for the first time in "several internationally circulated 'home' magazines" and was receiving "thousands of inquiries . . . from prospective home builders in every state of the nation and several foreign countries." The company had also bought land near Ferrum where "a modern streamlined plant for top production" would be built as soon as materials became available. Certainly for Vaughn's company, 1946 promised to be a banner year.

Strikes among glassmakers also affected the Weaver Mirror Company. Robert E. Weaver, who had started the company in 1932,[83] discovered that his "only trouble" was "getting plate glass" and until the strikes were settled "conditions w[ould] be a real bottleneck. . . . We have more orders for mirrors than we can fill right now, and there are indications that good business will continue throughout the new year."[84]

The Bald Knob Furniture Company also expected a busy year. R. H. Robinson, of the company, noted, "We have all we can do for the next three or four months and prospects look good for the whole year." His sentiments were echoed by J. D. Pell, of Angle Silk Mills, who reported his company was "operating at capacity with three shifts and [he] anticipate[d] a continuation of good business throughout the new year." Because so much rayon had been diverted to the manufacture of automobile tire-casings during the war, his company had been experiencing a shortage, but Pell expected increased supplies to appear within a few months "and the local silk mills can then be assured of a larger supply of rayon than has been possible during the war years."

With an end of strikes and the increasing availability of goods and materials that the war had previously required, Franklin merchants also anticipated a good year. "When we can get the goods there will be no limit to the sales volume," one merchant asserted. Dealers in automobile tires and electrical home appliances indicated the same thing, "all that is needed is the goods to sell." Thus the county entered the postwar years with a bright mercantile future amid a climate of great optimism. For the county's other business—farming—the future was not as bright, however.

SEVENTEEN

Agriculture and Farm Life

Writing in the mid-1930s, Franklin County native Marshall Wingfield described a county that was mostly hilly and stony except for the land along the rivers and creeks. In his day and that of his ancestors much more labor was required to produce a relatively small harvest than became the case in the mid-twentieth century with the introduction of mechanized farm equipment. Wingfield wrote of a land of thin topsoil that washed away in a few short years after it had been plowed, leaving clay and rocks. But "the people have been healthful and the population has increased as rapidly as the soil has failed." In Wingfield's childhood, Franklin's major "crops" were tobacco and whiskey.[1]

For generations, Franklin farmers had raised corn and tobacco, followed by smaller harvests of wheat, oats, and rye, as well as some hay. In 1860, for example, the county's largest crop was tobacco (2.6 million pounds), followed by less than half a million bushels of Indian corn, a quarter of a million bushels of oats, and one hundred twenty-four thousand bushels of wheat.[2] Fifty years later, the tobacco and corn crops had more than doubled, but the oat and wheat output had been halved.[3] The agricultural life of the county changed again in another fifty years, by which time the tobacco production had dropped to 3.9 million pounds. And by 1987 that figure had fallen to 2.5 million pounds.[4]

Wingfield described a life of farming in the days before mechanization that was hard and long. The most labor-intensive activity was growing tobacco, since its plant beds required much more attention than any other plant's. Every year the farmer chose a new and fertile site, burned enough wood on the ground to kill the surface weeds and grasses, and pulverized the soil to a powderlike consistency. The farmer then sowed the tobacco seeds sometime in January, if not before Christmas. When spring came the farmer placed a shallow wall of logs and dirt around the beds and covered them with cheesecloth (also called plant-bed cloth) to keep the tobacco flies from killing the plants. Unless it rained frequently the plants had to be watered from a sprinkling can and also weeded as the burn did not go deep enough to kill all grasses.[5]

When the plants reached six to eight inches high, they were moved to rows three feet apart and each plant set in the ground three feet from the next in the row. If the rains known as "the tobacco season" did not arrive on time, the plants grew too large and were lost. Thus during such a delay, the farmer would haul water into the fields, set out the plants in dry earth, and water each one individually. In order to preserve the plants from cutworms it was necessary to worm the plants constantly. It was also necessary to hoe the plants constantly as well, because weeds and grass would quickly damage the tobacco. Wingfield pointed out that crabgrass formed the bane of every Franklin tobacco grower's existence, so that yearly each one cleared new ground for tobacco to try to escape the curse.[6]

When Wingfield was a boy in the 1890s, clearing the new tract of large trees was too much work for one man so each farmer would invite his neighbors to help him cut those trees into ten- or twelve-foot sections. The farmer would have already trimmed out the smaller trees and undergrowth and burned them, some of that burning having been done on the plant beds. "These cuttings cost the farmer nothing but a jug of whiskey, a big dinner, and the obligation to assist at similar cuttings all the men who had assisted him."[7]

Next the farmer "coltered" the ground, which consisted of using "a sharp piece of steel, about two inches wide and ten inches long, called a colter," and attaching it to a "single shovel" plow. Then using the two slowest and most placid mules he owned, the farmer attempted to till the soil. The job was made difficult by unbreakable roots that halted the team so suddenly that it was thrown back on its haunches, as well as other roots that broke, flew back, and barked the farmer on his shins. But unlike the misnamed "Farmer's Friend" plow whose handles were constantly hitting the farmer in the chest or under the chin when roots were caught, the coltering plow's handles just dipped when the plow struck a root. Wingfield, who had suffered many of "those sickening wallops in the solar plexus," believed "that if the Devil had given Job a Farmer's Friend plow, that gentleman, whose name is a synonym for patience, would hardly be supplying texts for sermons today."[8]

Once the ground had been coltered, the farmer used a drag harrow to collect the turf and separate it from the dirt. After collecting the turf into large piles and allowing the March winds to dry them for several days, the farmer next attached a "bull tongue" (a somewhat broader blade than a colter) to his single shovel plow and plowed crosswise over the colter furrows. Then he harrowed the land again and laid it off in furrows three feet apart and fertilized the ground. Before 1900 few farmers "listed" the ground to fertilize it; instead they made "hills"—mounds of soil created with a hoe over a handful of fertilizer. A strong farmer could make a thousand hills a day. In the early 1900s, the idea of listing became more popular; it consisted of making "a small sharp ridge" on each row by "running a plow on each side of the open furrow piling the dirt to the center" after the fertilizer had been sown in the furrows.[9]

After the tobacco plants grew too large for cutworms to be a problem, hornworms took over to attack the leaves. Hornworms (hawkmoth caterpillars) grew to be about four inches long and as big as a man's finger. They could eat as much as a silkworm and thus had to be picked off the plants and killed. This activity was considered child's work when Wingfield was a boy, "and a shuddery one for a child who was afraid of the wriggling, spitting things." Between hoeings and plowings, each plant had to be wormed as well, which meant a continual series of activities to bring the plants to harvest. Finally, each plant was "laid by," given its last working, and then "topped," leaving ten to fifteen leaves on a stalk. Once the top of the plant was removed "suckers" sprouted that had to be pinched off to avoid sapping the plant's strength.[10]

Before the early twentieth century tobacco was harvested by splitting the stalk to within six to eight inches from the ground and forking it over the tobacco stick (made of oak, about five feet long, holding six to eight plants). But with the increased demand for bright cigarette tobacco, the farmers began pulling the leaves from the stalk instead of cutting them. They then tied the leaves to the tobacco stick with twine, thus allowing even the top leaves to be used as bright tobacco. Formerly only the bottom leaves, which had begun to ripen when the plants were harvested, could be used as bright tobacco. When all of the tobacco had been tied, the farmers hung the sticks in the tobacco barns and left the tobacco to sit for several days to "yellow" before the fires were lit. For a day or two the fires were kept at about one hundred degrees Fahrenheit to "shrink" the tobacco and after that the temperature was gradually raised to about two hundred and forty degrees Fahrenheit until the tobacco was dry. The tobacco dried in about six to eight days and someone stayed at the barn at all times to tend the fires and maintain a proper temperature. In the late nineteenth century, professional "tobacco curers" traveled from barn to barn to perform the drying process, charging five dollars per barn for six to eight days of work. They "were elderly men, usually without farms or families—ne'er-do-wells who drifted from place to place." By Wingfield's childhood, they had mostly disappeared.[11]

When the curing season ended, the marketing season began. If a rainy period did not come to soften the tobacco leaves, the farmer had to cover the dirt floor of the barn with wet, green boughs "to get the tobacco 'in order.'" Later farmers hung the cured leaves on racks in pit barns—buildings with large open basements dug into the earth—to soften in the humid atmosphere so they could be handled without crumbling. After the leaves became soft and pliable, the farmer sorted them into about five or six hundred pounds of bundles and loaded his wagon for the trip to market. Wingfield and his family hauled their tobacco to Danville for sale, a trip of forty miles over bad roads that required spending a night cn route. They stayed either at "tobacco haulers camps" or beside a country store, whose owner, if enterprising, would have put up temporary stalls for the horses or mules and shelter for the men. After sleeping in one's wagon or in camp bunks, the Wingfields arose the next morning about 4:00 A.M., had breakfast, fed the horses, and resumed the journey.[12]

Upon arrival in Danville they unhitched the horses and took them to stalls under the tobacco warehouse. As a child, Wingfield never felt comfortable walking down narrow, four-hundred-foot aisles between rows of stalls "flanked on both sides by the heels of strange mules and horses!" He did not usually get much sleep at the warehouse either. After supper at a nearby restaurant or on the food they had brought, the Wingfields would retire to a partitioned area at one end of the warehouse that contained a stove and "sleeping racks." Usually, however, farmers who had not seen each other in a year spent the night catching up on all the news. Others who had been good family and churchgoing men the rest of the year sampled "such saloon goods as were not procurable at home. As a rule, there were several half-drunken farmers to make the night hideous with their maudlin songs and silly boastings."[13]

The tobacco had been packed for market according to its quality and when it was unloaded at the warehouse, each grade was weighed separately and placed on the warehouse floor. By Wingfield's time, professional pickers had ceased to operate so that each farmer graded his own tobacco before carrying it to market. The grades were divided as follows: first "lugs," the leaves that grew just off the ground and were full of sand holes; second, the bright leaves from the middle of the plant called "wrappers" (the finest leaves) as they were used to wrap the plugs that were pressed for chewing; and third, the "green tips" from the top of the plant that had not ripened before picking. There were also usually two more "in between" grades. Each pile of tobacco was marked with a tag affixed to a wooden peg the size of a pencil. The tag gave the weight and owner of the pile. "As the auctioneer walked down the line of piles 'crying the bids,' he was followed by clerks who added to the tags the amount paid for the piles, stating the price per pound as well as the total."[14]

It behooved each farmer to sell his tobacco at a warehouse's first sale so that he could start home sooner and perhaps arrive home with more of his money if he avoided all the patent medicine vendors, cardsharps, fortunetellers, shoddy-goods dealers, and horse traders who congregated for the sale. The first sale usually began around 8:00 A.M. and lasted about an hour, depending on the quality of tobacco on the floor. Then the same buyers, and occasionally the same auctioneer, would go to the next warehouse (if the town had more than one) and begin the process all over again. If a town had several warehouses (as did Danville), the warehousemen reached an agreement whereby the first sale rotated among the warehouses so each one received an equal chance to be first. Originally several long blasts on a ram's or cow's horn called the sellers to the auction, but by Wingfield's day a farm bell mounted on a twenty-foot pole pealed out the announcement to the crowds. Wingfield's father always went home with all of his money as he had worked too hard to squander the proceeds from a crop that, "he often said, required thirteen months of the year to grow and market."[15]

When the tobacco, as well as the corn, had been harvested, the farmers in the late autumn then put in wheat, rye, and oats. To clear a field of cornstalks, it was

Corn shocks along the north fork of the Blackwater River, in northwestern Franklin County. (Blue Ridge Institute, Ferrum, Va.)

necessary to cut and pile the stalks for burning. This, Wingfield lamented, was considered easy work and left primarily for the children to do, and they were kept out of school until the task was finished.

> I have chopped down these dead stalks until my arms, back, and shoulders ached. The hoe seemed to grow heavier as the day progressed, and by night it felt as if it were made of lead. At the end of the day there were often blisters in my hands which had been made by the friction of the hoe handle. Frequently, I went home too tired to eat, and so climbed the stairs and went supperless to bed. But the stalks had to be cut before I could go to school again.[16]

The smaller children followed along behind the older ones and gathered up the cut stalks for burning. Frequently, Wingfield wished that he could trade cutting for gathering, but since the latter was "a child's job" he would not sacrifice his emerging adulthood for such indignity. The happiest day of his cornstalk-cutting life was 24 October 1902 when he was nine years old. On that glorious day, word was brought to him that after four sisters a baby brother had finally been born. "I dropped my hoe and ran home with all the possible speed."[17]

Much harvesting in Franklin County was done cooperatively, especially the harvesting of wheat when a farmer would invite his neighbors to help and offer them a jug of brandy or whiskey as an incentive to great effort, while his wife and the neighboring women prepared a large supper. Of all the various cooperative farming activities that Wingfield remembered, he thought that corn shucking provided the merriest time for those involved. There was much less labor involved in corn shucking than in the reaping of wheat, which "was done during the hottest days of summer." After the corn had been brought in from the fields it was stored in rail pens in the shucking yard until the wheat-sowing season had ended. Beginning in the afternoon, all of the neighbors would gather to shuck the corn, usually finishing late at night. Wingfield recalled that if there was no moonlight, resinous pine knots, called lightwood, were wired to posts and set ablaze. They also used kerosene lanterns. If a farmer wanted to complete the whole process that night, he had his helpers divide the corn into long ears and nubbins, the latter to be fed later to the livestock. A partition divided the corncrib into two rooms, the back room for the long ears, and the smaller front room for the nubbins. If there were two or more rail pens holding the corn in equal amounts, the shuckers divided into groups to "shuck a race." The owner did not always gain by this contest as in the excitement to win "many would toss ears into the shucked pile without thoroughly husking them," leading the next day to his having to reshuck the corn. The "prize" everyone sought in the shucking process was a "sport" or red ear—"a signal for passing around the ever-present whiskey jug." In the years before Wingfield's birth, the older men recalled that discovering a red ear had entitled the finder to present it "to the lady of his choice in exchange for a kiss" at the party held after the shucking. By Wingfield's time, however, the men preferred passing the whiskey jug to stealing a kiss, the early twentieth century having ushered in the death of romance.[18] In fact, "after some of the men went to the jug a few times they wanted to sing." Braxton Bragg Tyree, who was born in 1871, years later recalled part of a song the men sang: "There is one thing the poor men seldom do, throw out the old corn to throw in the new. I don't know what my wife and children will do, we ate up the old corn and have very little new."[19]

Bowman family and oxen, near Six Mile Post. 1913 photo. (Blue Ridge Institute, Ferrum, Va.)

Along with community threshings and corn shuckings, county residents gathered for apple butter and molasses boilings. Pedro T. Slone, of Ferrum, who was born in 1879, wrote of life in Turners Creek Valley in the 1870s and detailed a story about his father and a neighbor who had jointly raised a crop of sugarcane. After the cane had boiled for a week, Slone's father and the neighbor planned on a neighborhood "candy pulling" the last night. The cane was boiled in pans set in a rock flue daubed with clay from a nearby hole in the ground, where the skimmings were poured. The neighbor decided to play a practical joke on some of the boys who were expected that night so he covered the skimmings hole with grass and sticks. "It was near the path to the spring from which they brought water. As he was hurrying from the spring with a bucket of water before the boys arrived, he tumbled into it himself."[20]

Both Marshall Wingfield and Braxton Bragg Tyree recalled another popular sport in Franklin's social life, the tournament, which derived from the Scotch-Irish ancestry of many county residents. Knights representing each community in the county dressed in "spectacular regalia and mounted on their well decorated horses made an imposing spectacle." Tyree described the course as consisting of "five poles, seven or eight feet tall, with an arm out from each pole containing a hook." Each hook in turn contained a ring "and a man on horseback carrying a lance, rode down a track beside these poles as fast as he could get his horse to go and would attempt to get the rings from the hooks." According to Tyree, the knights made five trips down the track and the one who snared the most rings won a crown that, Wingfield stated, the winner gave to the lady of his choice as the queen of the community he represented. The customary ending to the day's festivities was a ball with a grand march led by the winning knight and his lady. Tyree remembered that Ben Patterson won the last one Tyree attended. At the party afterward held at the home of William Riley Hutchinson, Patterson crowned Lily Hutchinson and subsequently made her his wife.[21]

One black Franklin County farmer kept a detailed list of his yearly income and two years of that record survive, for 1918–1919. By 1910, James H. Waid and his wife, Emma Muse Waid (whom he married in 1889), were the parents of eight children. Eight years later, two of the sons owned property of their own—John L.

with two tracts totaling twenty acres and worth $110, and William G. with one tract of thirty acres worth $75. James H. Waid himself owned 197 acres valued at $832.50, located in the Wirtz area of the county. Since William G. Waid's land did not include any buildings and lay by one tract of his father's, no doubt William (who was twenty-two in 1918) lived at home. In 1918 James H. Waid made $1,267.69 from his various farm activities. Most of Waid's transactions netted him from five to fifty dollars with an average of thirteen dollars. Six of his sales, however, returned from one hundred to one hundred eighty-five dollars: for wood, flour, corn, tomatoes, "w[?]," and butter. In addition, to these products, Waid sold the output of his vegetable garden and orchard (that he presumably did not need for family use), as well as straw, tanbark, chickens, hens, eggs, milk, and pigs. Waid also cut wheat and worked at the warehouse, which netted him $4.20. His income included another $5.75 that "Childress give mother" and $98.33 for that mysterious item listed as "w" that perhaps in this prohibition era was whiskey.[22]

Unusual example of a late-19th-century I-house with a triple gable across the front (Route 640). 1988 photo. (Virginia Department of Historic Resources.)

The next year, after World War I had ended, James H. Waid's income almost doubled to $2,318.65, much of the increase due to his sale of $928.20 worth of tobacco (a product that had not appeared on the 1918 account). The next largest returns came from flour ($209.70), butter ($158.30), and w[hiskey?] ($136.56). He also cut crossties to net $29.95. Waid evidently was a successful farmer as he earned enough from his farm activities to place at least three of his children in private school, paying $122.70 on 30 December 1920 for the tuition for Emma, Ruth, and Blanco at the Christiansburg Industrial Institute in Cambria, Virginia.[23]

As James H. Waid's 1918–1919 accounts show, no other crop for the small farmer brought as great a return as tobacco. Indeed, for many years the largest crop raised in Franklin County was tobacco. Despite the fact that much of the county consisted of hilly terrain, every section of the county until the last years of the nineteenth century saw the production of some tobacco. Most of the tobacco crops were sold in Danville or Lynchburg until at least the beginning of the twentieth century when Rocky Mount had gained its own tobacco warehouses where the farmers brought their tobacco. In the 1850 census, Middleton R. Hurt and John D. Booth were listed as tobacco manufacturers, and both combined this activity with running a general store.[24]

By 1860, Franklin County had seventeen tobacco factories, but that number slowly declined after the Civil War.[25] At one time or another, there were two tobacco factories at Snow Creek, two near Taylors Store, five at or near Shady Grove, one at Dickinson's Store, one near Gogginsville, one at Helm's Store, two near Callaway, one at Bonbrook, one at Union Hall, one at Hatchers, one at Glade Hill, and four in Rocky Mount.[26] In 1881–1882, for example, there were fifteen tobacco manufacturers in Franklin County: Lewis Becker and Sons and B. F. Bernard at Snow Creek; J. R. and F. R. Brown, J. P. Bondurant, F. Cook, G. W. Lester, and H. C. Lester, all at Shady Grove; W. A. Brown alone as well as W. A. and W. N. Brown, Jesse Prunty, and M. Ward, all at Rocky Mount; Dobyne and Willis along with S. B. Willis at Callaway; G. M. Helm and Brother at Helm's Store; and S. D. English at Union Hall.[27]

Among Franklin's tobacco manufacturers, Shelton and Watkins became the earliest manufacturers at Shady Grove, opening their factory in 1835. William A. Brown produced his famous "Brown's Log Cabin" tobacco at Dickinson's Store. John S. Hale operated one of the largest factories on the site of the Hotel Rocky Mount (now the Oak Manor Apartments) in Rocky Mount and employed more than one hundred slaves in the antebellum period.[28] Another early tobacco factory was at Algoma, then known as Ash Grove, and its "Monican" brand was sold in the Deep South. The company of Price and Hurt was probably the last tobacco factory in the county, producing Yellow Rose Smoking Tobacco.[29] The last tobacco manufacturer listed for Franklin County in the Virginia business directories was that of Tazewell Helm and Brother, at Rocky Mount, in 1897.[30]

The earliest warehouses found in the postwar Virginia business directories were those in the 1884–1885 edition, the Farmers Warehouse and Callaway's, both at Rocky Mount. By 1917, Rocky Mount had three tobacco warehouses: the

Left: *Farmers unloading tobacco at warehouse. Ca. 1920s photo.* Below: *Warehouse sale, Rocky Mount.* (Virginia Department of Historic Resources [left]; Blue Ridge Institute, Ferrum, Va. [below].)

Farmers, Garrett and Company, and Perdue and Company. Still another early twentieth-century tobacco warehouse there was the Banner Warehouse on Claiborne Street. The Franklin Warehouse was the last built (by 1942), and both the Farmers and Franklin warehouses closed in 1960.[31]

In 1926, the county newspaper, the *County News*, published a supplement that detailed some aspects of Franklin's tobacco culture. The writer noted that Franklin's soil was especially suited to growing tobacco and that unlike much of the rest of the state "the land is capable of producing the highest quality of dark tobacco as well as light grades." The eastern and southern sections of the county furnished the best smoking tobacco, while other areas grew the dark grade that was used for plug or chewing tobacco. The dark tobacco could be grown anywhere in the county as it did not need a special soil. Most of the county's tobacco was flue-cured, with only a small amount being air-cured as was customary among the burley-tobacco growers in Kentucky.[32]

Until 1930 the United States Census Bureau's agriculture census reports did not distinguish among the varieties of tobacco grown, so it was not until that year when the Census Bureau recounted that Franklin farmers had grown 1,733,000 pounds of flue-cured and 780,000 pounds of fire-cured tobacco. In 1920, the total tobacco poundage was 3,516,757, grown on 8,473 acres of land. The *County News* noted that tobacco was indeed the leading money crop, although in 1926 there were an estimated 20,000 acres more planted in corn and 10,000 acres more planted in wheat. In the 1920 census report, in fact, 598,663 bushels of corn had been raised on 31,606 acres and 21,699 bushels of wheat on 27,410 acres.[33]

The *County News* also reported that the local market had been seeing sales of more than 3 million pounds of tobacco on average, with more than 4 million pounds of the loose-leaf tobacco sold in a single season. Up to that time the average price had been $15 per hundred pounds with $20 per hundred expected that year.[34] Tobacco-sale activity in Rocky Mount during the five years of World War II may give a representative picture of such sales in the county, at least until 1960 when the last tobacco warehouses closed in Rocky Mount.

During World War II, despite wartime rationing and restrictions, Franklin County farmers enjoyed one of the better periods for tobacco sales. In 1941 the tobacco market opened in Rocky Mount with prices reaching a twenty-five-year high. The peak on opening day was $41 per hundred pounds with an average of $31.97. Franklin farmers received about forty thousand dollars the first day. When the season ended late in October, Cam Perdue, warehouse manager, opined that the farmers had done as well as the previous year but with less acreage. Rocky Mount had led all Old Belt markets with an average of $34.02 per hundred pounds, an increase of fifty cents over the previous year. In celebration, the Rocky Mount Tobacco Board of Trade held "a stag party at [the] Hotel Rocky Mount" on 31 October for buyers, sellers, auctioneers, warehouse staff members, and "a few invited guests." A "most delicious" fish dinner helped the participants enjoy themselves.[35]

The tobacco market in 1942 improved over that of 1941 with another high average for tobacco sold that reached $50 by early October. The growers were happy with the opening day's figures and proclaimed it the best season since 1919. The market opened a week early and was "expected to be one of the best money markets ever experienced [t]here." The opening day, however, caught many farmers by surprise; they had to rush to make the early date.[36]

Despite the rush, within twelve days as much tobacco was sold as had been marketed during the entire 1941 season. This activity was attributed to an "excellent set of buyers, the fine work of Auctioneer Dave Fulk, and the fact that every pile [was] sold the same day it [was] placed on the floor."[37] Once again Rocky Mount enjoyed an exceptional tobacco season, averaging $10.46 above the 1941 season with sales of 1,613,510 pounds for 1942, which was almost twice the 920,780 pounds of 1941.[38]

In June 1943 it was announced that tobacco farmers might have to use an "old tape measure" to calculate the distance to the closest tobacco market because the federal Office of Price Administration had said that only enough gasoline would be issued for tobacco farmers to get to the closest market. For Franklin those in the Rocky Mount area would have to go there and the others in the six-mile area on the Franklin-Henry County border would go to Martinsville.[39] In mid-September, the warehousemen prepared for the upcoming tobacco auction by pouring a new concrete floor in the Farmers Warehouse to avoid the earlier damage caused by heavy trucks. With John Davis as auctioneer, everyone expected another good year of sales because of an "exceptionally good crop of smoking tobacco" for Franklin county and surrounding areas, "which is of the proper type to bring good prices."[40]

Because of wartime restrictions, a farmer could not grow as much tobacco as he would have done during peacetime. Just before the 1943 auction season opened, 1,149 people had received their "tobacco marketing cards" for staying within the allotment for growing tobacco, and, therefore, they could participate in the upcoming tobacco sale. Approximately one hundred farmers who had grown too much tobacco, however, had to pay a fine before they obtained the white card allowing them to sell their tobacco.[41] When the market opened, farmers received $40.29 per hundred pounds and by midweek were getting $41.30. All grades of tobacco sold higher that year than before; in fact, medium grades went for $5 to $7 higher than 1942.[42] Indeed for the first two weeks of the tobacco market, Rocky Mount topped all other markets with an average of $43.46 per hundred and sales of 415,698 pounds of tobacco.[43]

For those farmers who had grown too much tobacco and had to pay fines before selling it, good news came in mid-October when the federal government increased allotments for flue-cured tobacco acreage for 1944. The *Franklin News-Post* attributed the increase to ever-growing numbers of cigarettes' being shipped to the U.S. military forces and to tobacco companies' dipping into surpluses that would soon be exhausted. Thus Franklin County farmers put an additional 661 acres into tobacco for a total of 3,308 acres on about 1,300 farms. In the previous year they had only received a 15-acre increase in the allotment along with a special 40-acre increase for which more than seven hundred farmers had made application the previous spring.[44]

The 1943 tobacco market season was extended, running from 30 September to 30 November as opposed to the 1942 season that had run from 22 September to 12 November. When the final figures for the season became available early in 1944, it was found that the Rocky Mount tobacco market was second in the state with an average of $42.06 per hundred pounds. Rocky Mount had been topped only by Danville, which averaged $42.81 per hundred. Martinsville, the other local market, had been sixth with an average of $40.20.[45]

For the 1944 tobacco market season, opening day became dependent on when the Georgia and Florida markets ceased the "marketing holiday" that was being held to obtain higher prices. At the end of July, Governor Colgate W. Darden called for a five-day postponement of Virginia's market opening because the Georgia and Florida markets had not yet opened. By September another reason for the delay had been added, the "present acute shortage of labor."[46] The market season finally began on 28 September when the coin toss for the first sales went to the Farmers downtown warehouse and the first two piles of tobacco brought $45, "a record price for first sale." Once again the opening day trend was well above the ceiling price of $43.50 and even very poor grades ran in the high thirties. "Old-timers here state that the opening day's sales were the best they had ever seen here from the standpoint of quantity and quality of the leaf, prices received, and the utter enthusiasm of the farmers." Cam Perdue, the local warehouse manager, thought he saw a greater representation of the surrounding area attending this market than he had ever seen before.[47]

By the middle of November common tobacco had "skyrocket[ed]" into the high thirties (usually it sold in the twenties) with the good cigarette type maintaining the previous week's high of $46 to $49 per hundred pounds. It was not even necessary to display much salesmanship that week as illustrated by the story of Frank Hutcherson, of Glade Hill, "who was called to jury duty and was unable to watch the floor sales. When he had completed his day's work at the court house, he found that two piles of 200 and 225 pounds he had left unattended had brought $46 a hundred."[48]

When the final reports for the 1944 tobacco sales came out in March 1945, it was found that the Rocky Mount market had handled 2,277,944 pounds, which was 342,078 pounds more than the 1943 total of 1,935,866. Moreover, the average price had been $42.56 per hundred pounds for a total sale of $969,514.25. For the state this had been the biggest year of tobacco sales since 1939, with the highest average prices paid since 1919. Finally, the 29 percent increase in value over 1943 was the greatest on record to date.[49]

The 1945 agricultural census found that Franklin had had 1,401 tobacco farms in 1940 but 1,283 in 1945. Fewer farmers were planting fewer acres in tobacco as well, 4,031 in 1945 as contrasted with 4,892 in 1940. Nevertheless the total number of pounds of tobacco raised had increased from 4,105,340 in 1940 to 4,134,600 in 1945. The value of that tobacco had risen from $492,641 in 1940 to $1,571,148 in 1945. By 1987, when the county had only 376 farms as compared with 4,205 in 1920 and 1,138 in 1978, 128 farms with sales of $10,000 or more were still raising tobacco, with a value of $3,194,000. There were, however, a total of 190 farms raising tobacco in 1987 with a total of 2,473,829 pounds. Increasingly, however, Franklin farmers had turned from tobacco raising to orchard products, grains, livestock, and dairies.[50]

While the southern and eastern sections of the county are well suited to tobacco, the northern and western areas lend themselves better to apple orchards. In 1860 Franklin's orchard products had been worth $17,307; by 1945 that figure had risen to $673,123. In the days before spraying for insects and knowledge of pruning and grafting, the county's orchards, especially its apple trees, were allowed to grow with little care. Marshall Wingfield nevertheless maintained that much of the fruit was still good enough to send to distant markets, although most of the apple crop was made into apple brandy. By 1903, however, the situation changed when Dr. Samuel S. Guerrant left his medical practice in Roanoke and returned to his ancestral home, Algoma, to engage in the apple-raising business, creating the county's largest apple orchard in the first half of the twentieth century. His progenitor, Peter Guerrant, had come to Franklin in the early nineteenth century and bought land where he immediately set out apple trees. When Marshall Wingfield recounted the story in the 1930s some of Peter Guerrant's trees were one hundred years old and still bearing fruit.[51]

Located at the foot of the Blue Ridge Mountains, about eleven miles from Callaway, Algoma, a large estate of 3,625 acres, by 1933 employed 180 people and shipped as many as twenty thousand barrels of apples a year, an increase of ten thousand barrels over 1926. Some years the entire crop was shipped to England. In 1926 two hundred acres of the then two-thousand-acre farm were planted in apple trees: one-half were pippins and the other half winesaps, Ben Davis, Yorks, Black Twig, and Delicious. From 1906 to 1926, Algoma had lost only one crop, and in only one year had the apples been damaged by hail, "a remarkable record." One of the pippin trees alone had produced more than twenty barrels of apples in one year. Indeed, it was said that Guerrant's "trees were always a thing of beauty at springtime and were annually viewed by countless persons."[52]

Algoma was almost a self-contained industry with its own planing and gristmill, sawmill, electric power, and blacksmith shop, described as being "as near self-sustaining as one can find in this day and age." The house itself featured different wood in each room from trees on the estate, which also boasted a swimming pool.[53] Algoma apples won many prizes including gold medals at the Saint Louis World's Fair of 1904 and at the Jamestown Exposition in 1907 as well as the Emerson Cup in 1907 and a $50 prize at the international apple show at Spokane, Washington, in 1926. Dr. Guerrant was especially proud of two letters he and his family had received concerning their apples. On 23 February 1865, General R. E. Lee wrote to Dr. Guerrant's mother thanking her for a barrel of apples from Algoma: "they are remarkably fine and in perfect preservation."[54] During Woodrow Wilson's term as U.S. president, Guerrant had sent him a barrel of apples for which Wilson thanked him, saying they "were especially good, because they were flavored with friendship."[55]

Algoma Orchards apple display. (J. H. Claiborne, comp. and ed., "Franklin County, Virginia: Historical and Industrial—Past, Present and Future," *County News*, supplement [(Rocky Mount, Va.), 1926], 11.)

The Franklin County Orchard Company owned another orchard in the county for about fifteen years, which was located about a mile and a half west of Rocky Mount. The company purchased 1,612 acres and in 1911 planted apple trees on 300 of its acres. The primary products from the orchard were vinegar and cider, with perhaps "a little 'moonshine' also." In 1928 the company sold the land in smaller tracts. The Teman family, of Kit Carson County, Colorado, bought 347 acres and started an egg farm, one of the first in the county. Sometime later Benjamin Maxey purchased the egg farm and opened an airfield.[56]

Today the largest apple orchard in Franklin is at Occanneechi Orchards, located northwest of Boones Mill. It was begun by Arthur High ("Buck") Garst and is presently run by his sons, Fred and Jack Garst, who increased the number of apple trees to thirty-five thousand on two hundred acres. Occanneechi apples are shipped to the eastern United States and the Midwest.[57] In 1978, the town of Boones Mill, which is surrounded by apple orchards and thus noted for its apples, organized its first annual Boones Mill Apple Festival. Conceived by Homer Murray, a lifelong resident of the town, the apple festival has continued to grow, and by the time of the county's bicentennial in 1986 was attracting as many as 6,000 visitors.[58]

In 1909, Franklin had more than one-quarter million orchard trees (apple, peach, pear, plum, and cherry) and harvested almost one hundred sixty-five thousand bushels of fruit. Of that total, 75 percent of the trees were apple, yielding 96 percent of the harvest. In 1920, the agricultural census found a 15 percent increase in the total number of fruit trees overall as well as a 15 percent increase in the total number of apples trees. The increase in yield of apples, however, was 42 percent, but now they constituted only 90 percent of the fruit total.[59]

Twenty years later Franklin had 2,655 farms raising apples and harvesting 263,000 bushels worth $176,120. Wartime inflation and increased production provided totals in 1945 of 287,000 bushels valued at $544,950. However, although 2,850 farms were now raising apples, there were 5 percent fewer trees. So in twenty-five years, the number of trees had declined 34 percent and the number of bushels harvested had increased by only 5 percent.[60]

Contrasting the agricultural census of 1954 with 1959 reveals that the number of farms with orchards had declined 90 percent to 297 over the 1945 total and by 1959 to 196. For apple orchards the number was 339 farms in 1954 and 198 in 1959. The number of trees had suffered a similar decline, to 68,086 in 1954 and 49,288 in 1959. By 1954, however, the number of bushels of apples harvested had risen to 302,926, a 5 percent increase over 1945, but by 1959, that figure had dropped to 166,412 bushels.[61]

In 1987, fifty-eight Franklin County farms accounted for a total of 1,024 acres in orchards. Of that number fifty-five farms had 929 acres in 68,847 apple trees and forty-six farms harvested 10,857,232 pounds of apples, or 226,192 bushels. Thus Franklin's apple orchards had surpassed the level of 1959 for apples harvested, but had not reached the 1945 peak of 302,926 bushels.[62]

Over time, livestock and poultry gained prominence in Franklin's agriculture, especially after the turn of the twentieth century when improved roads and railroads opened the county to the shipment of milk and butter. In 1860 Franklin had $503,103 worth of livestock, including 46,037 horses, mules, milch cows, oxen, other cattle, sheep, and swine, and the value of animals slaughtered was $164,531. The county produced 158,337 pounds of butter and 846 pounds of cheese. By 1884, the Virginia business directory had begun mentioning that Franklin paid "a great deal of attention" to "fine stock for market, and horses, milch cows and other cattle are shipped in large quantities. The dairy products pay well, nearly one-half million pounds of butter being made yearly."[63]

In the 1909–1910 agricultural census, Franklin County had 7,197 dairy cattle, with 23,288 calves, other cattle, horses, mules, swine, sheep, and goats sold or slaughtered for a value of $201,167 for animals sold and $183,457 for those slaughtered. In addition, 7,122 dairy cows had produced 2,104,538 gallons of milk, and Franklin farmers had sold 8,921 of those gallons. They had also sold 8,110 gallons of cream. Moreover, they had produced 781,302 pounds of butter and sold 163,046 pounds of it. Dairy products excluding home use of milk and cream were valued at $158,344, and Franklin's dairymen had received $40,176 for the sale of their dairy products, which did not include cheese.[64]

The Norfolk and Western Railroad began service to Franklin County in the early 1890s and within a decade carried Franklin's butter to Roanoke for sale. Later the railroad also carried milk to the city's dairies. For instance, W. P. Saunders, of Bleak Hill, the county's first Grade A dairyman, shipped his milk by railroad in 1914 from Ferrum to the Clover Creamery in Roanoke. By 1917 he was joined in that endeavor by B. T. Flora and J. A. Naff from Boones Mill. Within six years, 300 gallons of milk a day went to Roanoke from Boones Mill alone. Soon thereafter, in 1926, the national highway, Route 30 (now Route 220) opened and increasingly trucks transported the milk to Roanoke.[65]

The *County News* in 1926 reported that although Franklin County farmers had produced cheese as good as that found in Wisconsin or New York, they had found a better market for raw milk than for cheese and thus had stopped supplying the two local factories at Retreat and Dugwell, which then closed. While some farmers in the county were conducting dairying operations, many were not, so that the writer (a county native who was successfully dairying) recommended that local farmers give serious consideration to dairying and enlist the aid of the experts at Virginia Polytechnic Institute to begin the undertaking.[66] Several farmers who lived in the northwestern part of the county were trying to improve their dairying operations. They included B. F. Flora, J. A. Naff, C. G. Clingenpeel, and Samuel Bowman, who in 1911 had purchased the first registered Holstein bull in the county. A large shipment of dairy cattle from Ohio arrived in the county seven years later. By early 1941, the *County News* writer's plea for improving the county's dairying operation bore fruit when R. T. Hopkins, manager of the Southern Dairies Corporation at Christiansburg, visited Franklin soon after the new year to talk to local farmers about building a milk-receiving station and making Franklin "into a milk producing county on a commercial basis."[67]

It soon became clear that Franklin farmers could furnish an adequate supply of raw milk to sustain a bulk plant. By early February, approximately four hundred thirty farmers had expressed an interest in the proposed receiving station. Moreover, there were more than twenty-three hundred cows available with a daily output of about one thousand gallons. And if the milk station were built, Franklin's farmers planned a 45 percent increase in their herds with the expectation that their dairy output would soon exceed five times the amount the dairy officials required in early negotiations.[68]

In April 1941, Southern Dairies announced that it would indeed build the milk-receiving station. Because the tobacco market had been reduced by the loss of the export trade and the steady erosion of the tobacco-growing industry from Virginia to the Deep South during the past several years, "Franklin county farmers [were] doubly jubilant over the prospects of the development of another cash market for their farm products through the sale of milk at a local plant." During the wait for the new building a temporary receiving plant was set up locally.[69]

Within another month Southern Dairies reported plans to build the new receiving building on land owned by W. N. Shearer, the site of the old flour mill of the Rocky Mount Grocery and Milling Company, which had been destroyed by fire in April 1939. After delays caused by lack of parts that had to be redressed by the federal Office of Production Management, T. W. Greer, of Greer Lumber Company, local contractors who had won the bid and had hoped to have the building finished by 1 September 1941, completed the plant in time for court day, 2 March 1942.[70]

When the plant finally opened the expectation that an initial delivery of 300 pounds would make a good start was confounded by the fact that about 800 gallons (6,807 pounds of milk) were received on the first day. W. W. Austin brought in the first few gallons of milk before 7:00 A.M. as he went to work. G. P. Holland arrived second. The first ten people received special prizes of "handsome table electric lamps as gifts from the Southern Dairies Company."[71]

Over the next three years the milk-receiving plant grew and expanded its operation and building. Within five months of its opening, in fact, the *News-Post* reported that such a load of milk was being received at the plant that new cooling equipment was needed to take care of deliveries. The plant managers also planned to install an additional ammonia compressor as well. " 'The farmers of Franklin county are doing a wonderful job in building up their milk production,' stated Mr. Hopkins. From the results so far accomplished, says the Southern Dairies official, Franklin county should, in time, become one of the big milk producing counties of the state."[72]

In January 1943, at the Farm Mobilization Day in Franklin County the county's farmers were asked to increase 1943 milk production 8 percent over 1942. The county was already producing 80 percent as much as Botetourt and Roanoke counties combined and "ranks high among the best counties of the State." About 35 million pounds had been produced in Franklin in 1942 and an 8 percent increase would mean 37.8 million pounds for 1943 or 282,500 gallons.[73]

Soon thereafter, the Rocky Mount receiving plant added a second milk-tank truck, and by the end of July a high of 4,600 gallons had been reached for the week. The milk-receiving plant proved so successful in fact that by early December 1943 it expanded its operation to process Grade A milk; previously the plant had been processing only Grade C milk, used in powdered milk and other dairy products. The plant sent its first shipment of Grade A milk to Winston-Salem, North Carolina, where all such shipments were to be bottled for sale in the North Carolina market. W. P. Landreth, general manager of the Winston-Salem division of Southern Dairies, praised area farmers for the increase in their milk production from month to month, saying they were competitive with any market of its size in the country, "and with its continued growth during the next few years it will undoubtedly develop into one of the best cash crops for the farmers of Franklin county." As the 1926 dairy farmer had recommended, Franklin farmers also consulted with experts from VPI about buildings and other requirements for producing Grade A milk, which was paying 30 percent more in cash returns than Grade C. Many farmers expected to meet the Grade A requirement without spending more than $1,000 (which would require a building permit). At that time the Rocky Mount receiving plant was accepting about fifty-five hundred gallons of Grade C milk every other day, necessitating three milk trucks for transportation and greatly exceeding expectations for a market so recently opened.[74]

By the middle of 1944, operations had become so extensive that further improvements were made to the plant. The building was enlarged; a new conveyor was added on the building's north side so that the cans of milk could be delivered there; a receiving tank and can-washing machinery were moved to the opposite side of the structure to allow more equipment to be put in their places; and a cold storage room with cork walls for the Grade A milk was added. Finally, the plant installed a new deep well pump to bring cool water from 340 feet below the surface as more than 1.5 million gallons of cold water a month were required to cool the milk.[75]

The 1945 agricultural census compared dairy production in Franklin in 1940 and 1945 and found a substantial increase. In 1940 Franklin County farmers had produced 2,991,908 gallons of milk and sold 494,838 gallons of whole milk, along with 141,441 pounds of cream (butterfat) and 190,882 pounds of butter, for a value of $186,390. By 1945, those figures had risen to 4,627,439 gallons of milk produced and 2,224,629 gallons of whole milk sold, along with a decline to 111,286 pounds of cream (butterfat) and 105,679 pounds of butter, for a total value of $727,418. This constituted a 390 percent increase in the value of dairy products for the five-year period.[76]

In 1986, the bicentennial edition of the *Franklin News-Post* included a summary of the county's agricultural industry after two hundred years. From tobacco as traditionally the primary farm product, the predominant farm activity had become dairying along with the raising of beef cattle, and its attendant hay, corn silage, and corn crops. The 1987 agricultural census tells the story. The total sales for Franklin's agricultural products was $31,893,000. Of that sum, livestock, poultry, and their products furnished $26,362,000. Hay, silage, and field seeds produced an additional $148,000, with $121,000 for grains (including corn, wheat, soybeans, and oats). Fruits, nuts, and berries supplied $1,325,000 and nursery and greenhouse crops a further $175,000. Finally, Franklin had 376 farms totaling 111,380 acres, with an average of 296 acres per farm and an average of $85,000 in agricultural products per farm.[77] As the *News-Post* concluded, "these small farms constitute the county's most important industry."[78]

The decline in the numbers of farms serves to illustrate, however, the dramatic shift of people and occupations from a rural to a more urban environment during the twentieth century. The future of traditional agriculture in Franklin County, as elsewhere, is uncertain.

EIGHTEEN

Religion and Education

A s the Civil War produced turmoil and uncertainty, the years that followed proved no more stable. The old way of life had vanished and in its place a new one slowly evolved. During this period, as in other times of trouble, many people turned to their churches to renew their sense of direction and purpose.

Many new congregations were formed in Franklin County during the postwar years. In some cases they replaced older churches that had declined during the war. In other instances they reflected the growth of relatively new religious denominations that competed with the older Brethren, Methodist, and Baptist churches.

The Church of the Brethren prospered in the years following the Civil War. By the early 1870s its membership had outgrown the Germantown Brick Church of 1848 and organized two new congregations: Antioch eight miles northwest of Rocky Mount, and Bethlehem three miles west of Boones Mill. Each congregation built a new meetinghouse in 1873. The Antioch church was frame and the Bethlehem church was brick; today the Bethlehem meetinghouse still stands, although heavily altered. The congregation demolished the Antioch meeting-house in 1919 and built a new frame church; additions were constructed in 1948 and 1961.[1]

In the early 1880s several long-standing disagreements within the Church of the Brethren resulted in a schism. Members who wanted Sunday schools, Bible classes, and other innovations that more conservative members considered worldly gained control of the annual meeting. Those opposed to the new trends broke with the church in 1883 to form the Old Order Brethren. This split occurred mostly in southern Virginia, particularly among the Brick Church, Antioch, and Bethlehem congregations in Franklin County. Generally the members of each division continued to use the same meetinghouse for several years until new ones were built.[2] Presently there are three Old Order churches in the county, Bethlehem, Oak Hill, and Pigg River.

Another meetinghouse built by the Church of the Brethren was the Blackwater Chapel, about ten miles west of Boones Mill, which the church constructed around 1885 as a union church. Brethren, Presbyterians, Primitive Baptists, and Christians (Disciples of Christ) all used the chapel. The Brethren replaced it with the Monte Vista Church in 1921–1922. The Cedar Bluff meetinghouse, built in 1889 about four miles northwest of Boones Mill, also served several denominations, including Brethren, Baptists, Christians, and Methodists.[3]

As in the case of the Brethren congregations, the Baptists of Franklin County also enjoyed significant growth after the Civil War, especially the Missionary Baptists. Several of the postwar churches descended from the relatively few antebellum Baptist churches that remained mainstream, or promissory, in attitude (many were antimissionary).

The oldest such congregation in the county is Providence Baptist Church, which was organized on 18 November 1833 by former members of the Town Creek Baptist Church led by the elders John S. Lee and Ebner Anthony. For more than twenty years Providence Church stood alone, until Story Creek Baptist Church was established in 1855. The first Missionary Baptist church organized after the Civil War was Rocky Mount Baptist Church (1879); Mill Creek Baptist Church followed in 1885. Beulah Baptist Church, near Sontag, was organized in 1888 by former members of the Providence, Town Creek, and Rocky Mount churches. Scores of other Missionary Baptist congregations, black and white, have been organized over the years.[4]

Many Primitive Baptist churches, the theological descendants of the antebellum antimission churches, exist in Franklin County. One of the earliest congregations continues to occupy the former Anglican church of 1769 on Snow Creek.

Although the Anglican church had been the established church during the colonial period, Episcopalians were rare in Franklin County after the Revolution. Baptists took over both the Anglican churches, at Carolina Springs and at Snow Creek. By the 1840s, however, when Bishop William Meade asserted there were only eight communicants in three counties (Franklin, Henry, and Pittsylvania), two small Episcopal congregations developed in the county under the leadership of the Reverend Edmund Christian. No permanent ministers served them until 1858, when the Reverend John R. Lee, a graduate of the Virginia Seminary (1843), came to Rocky Mount. Two staunch Episcopalian families, the Hairstons and the Saunderses, built a small church near Bleak Hill after the Civil War; in 1881 the structure was consecrated as Ascension Church and was served by the minister of Trinity Church in Rocky Mount. The chapel's construction was due to the perseverance of Elizabeth Saunders, the wife of Peter Saunders, Jr., of Bleak Hill, and Prudence C. Hairston, wife of William Hairston, of Hunter's Hall. In the late 1890s Esom Sloan, who converted from the Brethren faith, built a small church and school later known as Saint Peter's-in-the-Mountains, in the same neighborhood.[5]

As the Episcopal church revived somewhat, the Methodist church continued to prosper. At least four churches were constructed before the Civil War: Rocky Mount (1845), Gogginsville (1855), Pleasant Hill (1857), and New Hope (1850s). Among the congregations established after the war were Flint Hill

(1870), Boones Mill (1887), Highland (1896), Saint James (1896), Bethany (1912), and Trinity (1912).[6]

Perhaps surprisingly—because the Scotch-Irish used the Great Wagon Road as well as the Germans—Presbyterians were scarce in Franklin County before the Civil War. Two congregations existed: one near Sydnorsville that may have been formed about 1790 and the second (much better documented) near Callaway. The Callaway congregation was organized on 15 September 1850 by the Reverend Robert Gray; among the founding members were Callaways, Hairstons, Woodses, and Burwells (the latter two families from the Sydnorsville congregation). On 21 September 1851 the congregation dedicated its new church. Piedmont Presbyterian Church still stands: a small brick meetinghouse-style structure with two doors in its gable-ended front. An unobtrusive later addition is attached to the rear of the building. After the Civil War other Presbyterian congregations were established: Rocky Mount (1877), Bonbrook (1897), and Blackwater (1924).[7]

St. James United Methodist Church, 1896. 1970 photo. (Virginia Department of Historic Resources.)

A congregation of the Disciples of Christ, or Christian church, was organized in 1859 as Snow Creek Christian Church. In 1862 two congregations, at Cool Springs and at Mount Ivy, were formed. Others followed after the war: Doe Run (1872), Pleasant View (1884), Forest Hill (1910), Rocky Mount (1917), and Boones Mill (1918).[8] Several of the congregations owed their establishment to the efforts of the Reverend T. J. Stone, a near-legendary minister of the late nineteenth century. A native of Carroll County, Stone spent forty years in the ministry and was a particular inspiration to young Marshall Wingfield.[9]

That Franklin County is a community of religious diversity and toleration was borne out by a church census conducted in Rocky Mount and published in 1941. Some 210 persons out of the 1,905 interviewed had no religious preference, but the remainder identified with fourteen different sects. They included 450 Baptists; 107 Primitive Baptists; 101 Brethren; 247 Disciples of Christ; 2 Catholics; 1 Dutch Reformed; 80 Episcopalians; 101 Holiness; 4 Jews; 548 Methodists; 2 Moravians; 8 Old Order Dunkards; 53 Presbyterians; and 1 Quaker.[10]

Believers did not restrict their activities to establishing new churches, but demonstrated a concern for education as well. The Episcopal, Methodist, and Presbyterian churches established mission schools in Franklin County soon after the turn of the twentieth century. The first, Saint Peter's-in-the-Mountains, was an Episcopal mission school begun in the 1890s by Esom Sloan. The Reverend William T. Roberts, who came to Trinity Church from Bruton Parish Church in 1902, encouraged the project. By 1907, when Miss Caryetta Davis took charge of the school, it had forty students and some resident teachers. A storm destroyed the church in 1914; it was rebuilt in stone, as was the school, between 1915 and 1921 and financed by Arthur C. Needles, president of the Norfolk and Western Railroad. The school, which included grades one through seven for mountain girls, closed in 1943; presently the building houses the Phoebe Needles Conference Center, operated by the Episcopal Diocese of Southwestern Virginia. During its life as a school the average enrollment was between a hundred and a hundred and fifty students. The conference center is located west of Rocky Mount near the intersection of Routes 640 and 748.[11]

Saint John's-in-the-Mountains Mission School originated as a Sunday school begun about 1909 by Ora Harrison, a public school teacher in the hill country. She enlisted the aid of the Reverend Roberts to construct a mission building completed in 1915. In 1921 the mission built a stone structure similar to that at Saint Peter's. It contained the school, chapel, auditorium, and community center. Saint John's stood about twenty-one miles southwest of Rocky Mount and, like Saint Peter's, primarily served mountain girls until it closed about 1937. It averaged between seventy-five and a hundred and twenty-five students.[12]

St. Peter's-in-the-Mountains: (left) *original church & school;* (below) *school interior.* (Virginia Department of Historic Resources.)

The Presbyterian church founded the Algoma Mission School in 1910 on property owned by Dr. Samuel S. Guerrant. At first the school occupied a one-room building, but by 1926 it was in a large, frame, eleven-room structure. The building contained classrooms, dormitory quarters for the children, and "home quarters" for the teachers; it also had a remarkable two-story porch across its front. The second story was Craftsman in style, with square wooden columns, while the first story was Tudor Revival, with pointed archways to support the upper floor. Three teachers taught an average of fifty children a day. Long abandoned, the building stood derelict and on the verge of collapse in 1970.[13]

In 1913 the Virginia Annual Conference of the Methodist Episcopal Church, South, organized a board of trustees to establish a school in the southern highlands. A committee of four, led by Dr. Benjamin M. Beckham, selected Ferrum as the site for the school. Beckham, who was to become the institution's first president, later wrote that Ferrum's location on a railroad line was a determining factor in its selection.[14]

The new school, which was named Ferrum Training School, opened for its first session on 15 September 1914 with six faculty members and ninety students. It served both as an elementary and a high school or academy. The popularity of the school resulted in the growth of the village of Ferrum, as the land between the railroad depot and the campus was laid out in lots. Soon the school administration

Left: *William Matt Feazell house, on site of Ferrum College, across Route 602 from Franklin Hall.* Below: *Early view of Ferrum College. Ca. 1930 photo.* (Blue Ridge Institute, Ferrum, Va.)

established branch schools, and by 1925 the enrollment had grown to about seven hundred fifty students. The competition from public high schools, however, prompted the board of trustees to change the school to a junior college at its spring meeting on 14 April 1926.[15]

Financial difficulties led to the temporary suspension of the junior college courses after the 1928–1929 school year. By 1940, however, the program had been so far revived that the trustees again changed the school's name, to Ferrum Training School–Junior College.[16] The Southern Association of Colleges and Schools accredited Ferrum in 1960 and thereafter the school experienced significant growth. Led by its president Dr. C. Ralph Arthur, the student population grew to more than a thousand. And continuing under the leadership of Dr. Joseph T. Hart at least eleven new buildings were constructed by the early 1970s. In 1974 Ferrum offered its first bachelor's degrees and in 1976 the school won accreditation as a four-year college by the Southern Association of Colleges and Schools. By 1990 Ferrum offered twenty-seven degree programs leading to bachelor's degrees.[17]

The general decline in church-supported primary and secondary education in the late nineteenth century resulted largely from the system of free public schools established by the Virginia Constitution of 1869. The schools themselves, however, did not spring into being overnight, and in fact there existed considerable statewide opposition to a centralized school system. Much of the philosophical opposition generally came from the wealthy, landed segment of society. Although the gentry supported the academies and colleges that catered to their own children, many of them also traditionally opposed education for the masses, especially when it was to be done at public expense. They objected too to the creation of a state bureaucracy to administer a standardized program of education. At issue was local control, not only of the schools but of the taxes that supported them. For several years the school issue was what would be called today a political football; support for it waxed and waned seemingly with each change of the government in Richmond. The school system, then, was not simply created (except on paper); rather, it slowly evolved during the period between 1870 and the end of the century. In Franklin County it had at least the tentative support of most of the population, according to Thomas H. Bernard, the county's first superintendent of schools, who reported that "many heretofore indifferent, if not hostile, are disposed to give the system a cordial support."[18]

Both the recently freed, illiterate blacks and the undereducated, impoverished whites desperately needed the new school system. In a letter written on 28 April 1875 W. C. Boyd, a black teacher at Halesford, commented on the deplorable state of learning in Franklin County:

> I am sure you don't have any *idea* what a bad condition [this part of Virginia] is in regards of an education; it is almost past all hopes; ignorance and poverty are walking hand in hand. No longer than today I have had a white lady come and ask me to back a letter for her. Since that is the case with these whites you may imagine how it is with the poor colored man who has never had an opportunity of being cultivated. It is true that they are free, but it reminds me more of the time when I was a slave than anything else. Its

master and mistress just as it was twenty years ago. . . . All of them are ignorant, white as well as the *black man*.[19]

Census data for 1870 tend to support Boyd's contentions. Franklin County, with a total population of 18,264 (both white and black), had 5,781 persons above age ten who could not read (32 percent of the total population) and 6,597 persons above ten years of age who could not write (36 percent).[20] Probably most of the illiterates were former slaves but many no doubt were whites for whom farm work had taken precedence over education.

The new system consisted of a state board of education that established policy and a superintendent of public instruction to carry it into effect. The county and city school systems, which implemented instructional policies at the local level, included a three-person board of trustees for each school district and a district superintendent over all the districts in the locality. The local superintendent's duties were to examine and appoint teachers, supervise the schools to ensure that the state board–approved textbooks and course of instruction were presented, and account for the receipt and distribution of funds.

On 23 November 1870 the State Board of Education appointed the first school trustees for each of Franklin County's nine districts (a tenth, Little Creek District, was added later). The trustees were: for Rocky Mount, George C. Menefee, Thomas L. Reynolds, and Edward J. Turner; Snow Creek, Elijah B. Wade, Thomas N. Bondurant, and Benjamin F. Cooper; Union Hall, William Powell, William Frith, and John N. Walker; Gills Creek, John W. Price, Benjamin G. Garrett, and Benjamin R. Hutcherson; Bonbrook, Moses G. Booth, David C. Cobb, and Paschal Meador; Maggodee, Jesse Dillion, John C. Hall, and William L. Bernard; Blackwater, Lewis H. Turnbull, Moses T. Greer, and Benjamin B. Webb; Long Branch, David P. Hickman, George T. Williams, and Stephen Thomas; and Brown Hill, George C. King, Thomas H. Prillaman, and Daniel P. Helms.[21]

For the next two decades the trustees and local school superintendents fought an uphill struggle to establish the legitimacy of the system. Thomas H. Bernard served from 1870 to 1872 as the first superintendent of schools for Franklin County under the new constitution. He was succeeded by William A. Griffith, who held office until 1876. Although Bernard and Griffith constructed several public schools in the county during their tenures, neither man was a professional educator.[22]

The next superintendent, however, was a teacher. William E. Duncan, who served two terms (1876–1881 and 1886–1889) held a degree from the University of Virginia in the schools of Latin, French, Spanish, and Moral and Natural Philosophy.[23] In 1852 he married Sallie Elizabeth Holland, a daughter of Asa Holland, who was a prominent merchant and farmer at Halesford. By 1857 Duncan had established Halesford Academy, at which he conducted two five-month sessions each year.[24] During the Civil War he served as a quartermaster with the Confederate artillery, and after the war he attempted—unsuccessfully—to make a living by farming some of his father-in-law's land at Sandy Level in Pittsylvania County. In 1874 he returned to Franklin County and established the Halesford Classical and Mathematical School. Seven years later, he constructed a small frame building on the west side of present-day Route 122, across from the Holland-Duncan House. The two-story brick dwelling, which was visited by Union cavalry at the end of the Civil War, was home first to Asa Holland (Duncan's father-in-law) and after his death to William and Sallie Duncan. It now serves as a bed-and-breakfast inn. In 1990 the schoolhouse was moved to Dudley Elementary School to save it from destruction; unfortunately an arsonist burned it down soon after.[25]

Duncan was an active and knowledgeable superintendent. During his tenure, according to several of his supporters, he did

> more for the education of the young people of this County than any other one man.
> While he was Supt. of the County . . . our Public Schools were greatly improved and the cause of Public Education highly successful.[26]

Not everyone admired Duncan, however. John S. Hale, one of the county's wealthy men who perhaps opposed the public school system, accused Duncan of having (during his first term)

> used his position as superintendant to promote his private school by agreeing with his pupils to give them "A" certificates as public school teachers, provided that the pupil would attend his school for the period of three months, said Duncan agreeing to wait for board & tuition till the teacher could make it by teaching in the public schools of the County. One person to whom he made the proposition is Edward Webb of Franklin Co. Va. who was utterly incompetent to teach any school.[27]

Duncan knew of the accusations against him and denied them vigorously. In a letter seeking the support of Franklin County delegate Peter Saunders, Jr., for his reappointment, Duncan wrote on 28 November 1885 that

> I was the one who was turned out of office to make room for the present incumbent [Bruce A. James, 1881–1886]. The Mahone Legislature removed me for no other reason except my political views.[28]

Duncan was but one of the many victims of the post–Civil War political system in Virginia, in which virtually every state governmental post was considered a political plum. Politicians who gained power used it blatantly to reward their

The Duncan School (demolished). 1970 photo. (Virginia Department of Historic Resources.)

friends and punish their enemies. They replaced incumbent officeholders with little concern for ability. No doubt Bruce A. James felt himself equally wronged when he was removed in 1886 and replaced by Duncan.

By the late 1880s, during Duncan's second term as superintendent, popular opinion throughout the state generally had shifted toward support of the public school system. In his annual report for the year ended 31 July 1888, in answer to a question from the state board concerning local support, Duncan responded that "public schools are much more popular than formerly, and public sentiment grows more favorable as better qualified teachers are employed."[29] The 1888 reports of other superintendents reflected a wide range of opinion among the public:

> Very favorable [Bedford County].
> There are still some good citizens in Roanoke who do not believe in public schools; but they offer no factious opposition and accept them as the inevitable [Roanoke County].
> Some warmly in favor of the Public School System, some Strongly opposed to it. The Mass of the people show but little interest [Nottoway County].

Duncan's report illustrates the still-rudimentary condition of elementary education in the county. He noted that there were 115 schoolhouses, of which 34 were log and 81 frame. None were of brick or stone construction. Only 10 of them had outhouses; the average school lot consisted of about an acre of land (presumably with some strategically located trees or bushes where outbuildings were lacking). Eighty-six of the schools had grounds that Duncan considered "suitable," and only 32 had furniture that he regarded as "good." Among the miscellaneous expenses that he reported for the year was $35.27 spent in the Union Hall District for "axes, buckets, brooms, etc."[30]

The State Board of Education apportioned funds among the localities, approved the textbooks used in the school system, and let bids for most school supplies. In 1871 Franklin County, with 7,239 children of school age (the fifth-largest school population in the state), received $1,809.75 as its proportion of state funds in the first of several apportionments conducted by the state board.[31] The board selected the following books: Guyot's *Introduction to the Study of Geography, Elementary Geography, Intermediate Geography*, and *Common School Geography*; Maury's *First Lessons in Geography, Intermediate Geography*, and *Manual of Geography*; Davies's *Primary Arithmetic, Intellectual Arithmetic, Elements of Written Arithmetic*, and *Practical Arithmetic*; Venable's *Primary Arithmetic, Mental Arithmetic, Elementary Arithmetic, Practical Arithmetic*, and *Higher Arithmetic*; Bullions's *School Grammar* and *Practical Grammar; Analysis and Parsing*; McGuffey's *New Eclectic Readers* (first through sixth); Harvey's *Elementary Grammar* and *English Grammar*; and Holmes's *Speller, Primer*, and *Readers* (first through fifth).[32] The board also let bids for such supplies and equipment as ink, inkstands, pens, slates, slate pencils, slate rubbers (erasers), blackboard crayons (chalks), blackboard rubbers, writing books, numeral frames, wall maps, outline maps, models, charts, globes, cards, and school registers, histories, and dictionaries.[33]

Duncan, in his report for 1888, described the official duties he had carried out in the course of the year. For his annual salary of $600 he worked 296 days. During the year he traveled 1,823 miles on official business, wrote 1,207 letters, attended 18 school board meetings, and paid 211 visits to schools. There were only 6 schools in the county he did not visit and he went to 48 of the schools only once. Over the previous twelve months he had held seven training sessions or "District Institutes" for the county's teachers, six for white teachers and one for blacks. Twenty-six blacks and a hundred and twenty whites attended the institutes.[34]

Duncan, as superintendent, licensed black as well as white teachers. Emma M. Muse, for example, received her third-class teacher's certificate from Duncan on 4 October 1888. The certificate stated that she was authorized to teach in the free public schools of Franklin County, "having furnished satisfactory evidence of good moral character and general fitness, and having this day passed a lawful examination . . . in the subjects and with the results indicated."[35] Her scores ranged between 74 and 76 out of 100 in reading, spelling, writing, arithmetic, geography, grammar, United States history, Virginia history, "Map-Drawing," and "Theory and Practice of Teaching." She signed her contract with the Franklin County Board of School Trustees on 29 October to teach for five months at the Powder Mill schoolhouse. The board fixed her salary at $18 per month provided the school maintained an average daily attendance of twenty students. If the attendance fell below that average, she would receive ninety cents a month for each student, unless there were fewer than ten, in which case the board would dismiss her and close the school. Her class roll for April 1889, fortunately for her salary, listed twenty-seven students, seventeen boys and ten girls.[36]

During the late nineteenth century the public schools faced some competition from private elementary and secondary schools. The statewide business directories published during the 1880s and 1890s list several such schools in the county. They included Mrs. Prudence C. Hairston's Piedmont Institute for Young Ladies at Hunter's Hall (1884–1885); Ida Angle and S. C. Angle at Villa (1890–1891); S. R. Drewry and B. E. Kesler at Sophronia (1890–1891); Miss F. Ross Young at Young's Store (1890–1891); Stuart's School near Shooting Creek (1893–1894); Knob Institute at Handy (1893–1894); Handy Academy at Handy (1897–1898); T. A. Walker's Piedmont Normal School at Rocky Mount (1897–1898); and U. C. Moore's Ferrum High School at Ferrum (1897–1898).[37]

Some private schools, such as the Mountain View Normal School, were established to train teachers for the public schools. Duncan's daughter Sallie W. Duncan served as assistant principal at Mountain View Normal School by 1891, while J. A. Barnhardt was the principal. The school held four-month sessions and offered classes in "Orthography, Etymology, Drawing, Penmanship, Political and Physical Geography, Virginia and U. S. History, English and Latin Grammar, American and English Literature, Physiology and Hygiene, Elocution, Rhetoric, Arithmetic and Algebra."[38] Barnhardt informed his prospective students that the

latest Normal Methods of Instruction will be pursued throughout every branch. Those desiring to teach will have an opportunity to grasp the best Methods of School Management. Special attention will be given to Drawing, Physiology and Hygiene as teachers are now required to teach these in the Public schools of Virginia.[39]

Other county school superintendents included Richard S. Brown (1889), W. O. Frith (1889–1901), H. D. Dillard (1901–1914), R. A. Prillaman (1917–1927), Harold W. Ramsey (1927–1968), C. I. Dillon, Jr. (1968–1984), and Leonard A. Gereau (1984–present). Ramsey's forty-one-year tenure was the longest and probably the most historic; during this period several teaching revolutions swept the nation along with the trauma of racial desegregation. During the 1925–1926 school year, just before Ramsey became superintendent, Franklin County's school enrollment was 6,758 (275 of which were high school students), with an average daily attendance of 4,885. There were 223 teachers. The county had 1 high school, 2 other schools teaching high school work, and 4 junior high schools. There also were 127 one-room schools, 26 two-room schools, and 10 consolidated schools.[40] By the time Ramsey retired in 1968 the school system was thoroughly modern.

The first high school constructed as such in Franklin County was completed in the summer of 1924. The school's amenities included drinking fountains, a gymnasium, and a cafeteria. A square brick structure that contained sixteen rooms, the high school served the county's needs for almost thirty years until it was replaced by the consolidated school in the early 1950s.[41]

By 1944 the county school board, under the leadership of superintendent Harold W. Ramsey, decided to consolidate the county's scattered schools and initiate a building campaign in Rocky Mount. After the Rocky Mount Graded School burned on 10 February 1944, the school board decided to use part of the insurance money to purchase a site located on Route 40 just to the east of town for the consolidated school, which was to include a new high school. According to Ramsey, the county needed a modern high school in Rocky Mount to accommodate about five hundred white high school students, as well as a county high school for about one hundred and fifty blacks. He estimated that the new white high school, if constructed with a gymnasium, an auditorium, and laboratory rooms, would cost about $250,000; the school for blacks, about $35,000. He suggested that the ideal situation "would be to bring all the [white] high school children of the county into one modern centralized school building where adequate facilities would be available for the education of all county children in a manner that would fit them for later life." The consolidation effort faced widespread opposition, however, and funds were unavailable because of the war. Ironically, once the war ended the need for expanded facilities became

Rocky Mount High School. (Blue Ridge Institute, Ferrum, Va.)

painfully obvious as returning servicemen swelled the ranks of high school students. The construction of the consolidated school, however, was not completed until 1953.[42]

The new consolidated school accepted only white students; blacks were generally taught, as they had been for years, in older, inferior structures. During the Reconstruction era blacks at first had no school buildings as such, but met in churches, houses, or log cabins to receive a rudimentary education. Early attempts to purchase land and finance schools met with little success largely because of white opposition. A few whites, such as Robert A. Scott, the clerk of the Franklin County Court, tried to assist the blacks by obtaining schoolbooks, but for most of the late nineteenth century blacks were forced to struggle against the odds to receive a little education.

The inequities were many and well known. In 1888, for example, Franklin County had seven graded schools in five of its ten school districts, five for whites (Rocky Mount, Blackwater [Callaway], Snow Creek [Sontag], Helm's Store, and Halesford) and two for blacks (Rocky Mount and Snow Creek [Sontag]). The principal at the Rocky Mount school for blacks, Laura C. Dehaven, supervised two teachers; Sontag's principal, Daniel M. Hughes, had only one. Ninety-four students enrolled at the Rocky Mount school and the average daily attendance was forty-two. At Sontag sixty-four students enrolled and about forty attended each day. In terms of average daily attendance compared to the average monthly enrollment, Rocky Mount had 62 percent attendance and Sontag 73 percent. The county expended forty-three cents a day for each student enrolled at Rocky Mount, and forty-one cents a day per student at Sontag.[43]

By contrast, the expense for white students at the other graded schools ranged from a low of fifty-six cents a day to a high of sixty-eight cents even though the attendance percentages were between 46 and 60 (compared with 62 to 73 for the black schools). The average daily attendance at the white schools ranged from twenty-five to forty-three pupils.[44]

In 1888 the total population of school-age children in Franklin County was 10,492 (7,010 whites and 3,482 blacks). The county had 148 schools (some in private homes), 117 for whites and 31 for blacks; in other words, two-thirds of the students (whites) were eligible for 80 percent of the schools, while one-third (blacks) made do with only 20 percent of the schools. The county had 148 teachers (58 white men, 59 white women, 17 black men, and 14 black women). Assuming that all the teachers taught only students of their own race, there were 112 potential black students for each black teacher, but only about 90 students for each white teacher. The teachers' average monthly salaries suffered from similar disparities. White men received $24.55, white women $23.86; black men received $19, black women $15.87.[45]

By the turn of the twentieth century more black schools had been constructed or given to the blacks when the whites left them for better quarters, as was the case with the Henry Fork School. Most black schools were one- and two-room buildings scattered around the county, however, and most students probably learned despite the facilities, not because of them. In 1902 the Pigg River Baptist Association appointed trustees to acquire land and construct buildings for a large, modern school for blacks on the edge of Rocky Mount near Bald Knob. Among the men and women who led the effort were William T. Walker, the

Reverend T. W. Brown, Lee M. Waid, Henry Smith, Zack Hopkins, and Mrs. Martha Brown. Soon the school was incorporated with fifteen, later twenty-five, trustees; its name was changed about 1915 from Rocky Mount School to Booker T. Washington Normal, Industrial, and Academic School.[46]

Appropriately, the new school was named for one of the county's most illustrious sons, a black educator of national importance. Not only did the name honor the man, it also reflected the fact that the school was his intellectual offspring, as were so many others of its time. Washington advocated black self-help through what would now be considered vocational education programs. He believed that black schools should prepare their students for the business of life by offering them training in mechanical or manual skills or trades, such as carpentry, joinery, and blacksmithing. In Washington's view, a traditional, "classical" education offered nothing of practical value to former slaves and their children. Before blacks could reap the benefits of that type of education, he believed, they first needed to acquire the economic skills long taken for granted by whites—skills that could only result from steady, useful, and uplifting work. Too many blacks, in the opinion of Washington, saw labor as demeaning—perhaps an understandable attitude produced by the demeaning experience of slavery, but one that ultimately was counterproductive of economic freedom. Washington viewed labor for one's own benefit as liberating and ennobling, not demeaning, and as the blacks' only hope of proving their self-discipline to skeptical whites.

Washington's philosophy enjoyed widespread popularity among members of the white establishment around the nation. In part this was true because it reinforced their own racial stereotyping: blacks, in their view, had no business receiving a classical education, not because other needs might be more pressing, but because they lacked the mental capacity to absorb and appreciate it. Conversely, they considered blacks well suited to manual rather than intellectual labor, as Washington, to their minds, advocated. If most blacks became laborers or craftsmen, they thought, it would be easier to keep them in their "place" than if they became lawyers and doctors and affluent businessmen. Washington's emphasis on self-reliance and cooperation among blacks, with its implications of isolation from the larger, white society, was embraced by the white advocates of racial segregation as proof that black leaders wanted segregation too. Eventually

Franklin County Training School class. 1941 photo. (Blue Ridge Institute, Ferrum, Va.)

many blacks began to regard Washington's philosophy as outdated at best, and as playing into the hands of whites who sought to exploit blacks at worst. Regardless of its merits or shortcomings, however, for many years Washington's ideas swayed black educators and their white supporters, as well as white bigots. To his credit, Washington's dream of self-reliance encouraged blacks to create their own educational establishment—one that remained largely under the control of blacks, even at the local level—whereas before they had been dependent totally on the largess of white politicians and school administrators.[47]

The black schools in Franklin County had their own black superintendent, Mrs. Minnie H. Moorman, by 1929. There were, however, far too few such schools to meet the educational needs of the black community. As the whites who controlled the purse strings for state and local funding directed more and more of those funds to upgrading white schools, the black educational establishment fell further and further behind. Buildings deteriorated, supplies ran short, and the underpayment of black teachers continued.

On 18 June 1940 the United States Circuit Court of Appeals for the Fourth Circuit, sitting in Asheville, North Carolina, ruled on a request by Melvin O. Alston, a black teacher in Norfolk, Virginia, who "sought to have nullified the salary differentials which were said to exist in the state."[48] The court decided that the salaries of blacks could not be less than those of whites "for teachers and principals of equal scholastic qualifications and teaching experience, performing essentially the same duties and services when those differentials are based solely on race or color." In Franklin County a committee of black school patrons including Samuel Phelps, the Reverend Morton H. Hopkins, H. G. Helms, and W. M. Haynes, representing the black parent-teachers association of the county, presented a petition on 13 January 1941 "asking the local school board to establish a salary schedule for teachers without regard to race or color. They also ask[ed] that steps be taken to begin the equalization by September, 1941, extending over a period of three years." The school board had anticipated their petition in December 1940 by directing School Superintendent Harold W. Ramsey to make a study of black teachers' salaries before the budget was made up for the next school year. He found that about $6,000 would be needed to meet the proposed salary increases, but because both the board and the black teachers wanted the increase to stretch over three years, this would mean an increase of $2,000 for the next year, $4,000 the following year, and $6,000 the third year. Ramsey submitted figures that showed black salaries were about $200 less than whites' or an average of $394 per year for a black teacher as compared with $594 for a white. With thirty-two black teachers in the county, he concluded, approximately $6,000 would correct the inequity.

Besides teachers' salaries, something else related to the schools occupied the thoughts of Franklin County's citizens in the 1940s: a disease called poliomyelitis, sometimes known as infantile paralysis. The disease caused the wasting away of the large muscles and even death; it was highly contagious and easily passed from one child to another, especially at school; and it struck terror into the hearts of parents. Until the development of the Salk vaccine in the 1950s, mothers and fathers viewed the approach of every school year with some foreboding. In 1944 the first polio victim in the county was black, the nine-month-old child of Walter and Sadie Jones, of Route 4, Rocky Mount, who died at the beginning of August. Four active cases were reported in Rocky Mount, Glade Hill, Callaway, and Endicott.[49]

For weeks the newspaper carried periodic reports of other cases and the community wondered if the schools would open as scheduled on 7 September. After two new cases were discovered in Boones Mill, school officials decided to postpone the opening for ten days, until 18 September. The fear of contagion arose not only from the fact that schoolchildren spent hours each day in close proximity in their classrooms, but also that more than 2,500 of them rode school buses that transported them about two thousand miles a day. When the schools at last opened attendance was normal. The first day for Boones Mill High School and the one- and two-room schools at Fairmont, Monte Vista, White Oak Ridge, and Adney's Gap was put off until 25 September because of their close proximity to Roanoke County, where several polio cases still were active.[50]

Although the end of polio was nowhere in sight in September 1944, at least the nation could see the end of World War II approaching. In another year it would be over, the soldiers would be coming home, and the country would shake off the last vestiges of the Great Depression and enter what for many would be an age of unprecedented prosperity that lasted for about four decades. That prosperity, and the changes that accompanied it, would also change much about Franklin County. Among the traditions that refused to die, however, was moonshining.

NINETEEN

Prohibition and Bootlegging in Franklin County

From the earliest days of the colony of Virginia, the settlers had attempted to make wine and spirituous liquor. Although first the Virginia Company of London and later the royal government supported wine making with offers of land and indentured servants, no winery became successful in the long-term in Virginia during the colonial period. In addition to the colonists' failure to cultivate the vines and graft sweeter-tasting European grapevines to hardy American stock, the plentifulness of imported wines and liquors, especially rum and brandy, discouraged homegrown wineries.[1] Captain George Thorpe, however, distilled the first grain alcohol from Indian corn on the James River in the early 1620s. Both the Virginia Company and Governor John Harvey soon thereafter accused the colonists of overindulgence in liquor. In fact, Harvey reported that "one half of the tobacco profits received by the planters was being spent on drink."[2]

In spite of efforts to control distilling and consumption, many individuals continued to own stills and make their own peach and apple brandy, hard and soft cider, wine, beer, rum, some grain whiskey, and applejack.[3] And as the Virginia colonists moved farther inland, access to imported alcohol became more difficult so that a dependence on homemade varieties took hold. Moreover, despite some concern for drinking, there seemed to be semiofficial sanction of such consumption at many public occasions, with the requisitioning of a gallon of brandy for any type of official meeting documented again and again.[4]

Despite such semiofficial sanctions, however, the British government imposed duties, for example, on molasses (1733) and, to help pay for the French and Indian War, on sugar (1764) and on liquor licenses (through the 1765 Stamp Act)—all essential to the manufacture or sale of spirits. Colonial outrage at such "taxation without representation" helped fan the flames of revolution.

After successfully concluding war with Great Britain (1775–1783), the United

States attempted a national government under the Articles of Confederation, which proved unsuccessful. On adoption of the United States Constitution in 1789 by most of the thirteen original colonies, the new government under first president George Washington looked for more successful ways to finance itself and pay for revolutionary war debts than the government under the Articles had found.

By 1791, however, the new secretary of the treasury Alexander Hamilton realized that measures put into place previously to raise revenues were inadequate to meet the interest on the national debt. He therefore proposed the revenue-raising Whiskey Act, placing an excise tax on stills and distilled alcohol, "articles . . . very productive of revenue because of their extensive consumption."[5] Vigorously challenged by those who disposed of excess grain by distilling it, the state legislatures of Maryland, North Carolina, and Virginia passed resolutions objecting to the Whiskey Act.[6] For the western areas of those states and Pennsylvania, in particular, roads to market were bad and few in number. Therefore, turning rye and corn into whiskey provided a means of transporting the product on horseback in small loads, instead of having to ship large amounts of the grain itself, thereby allowing the distiller to pay his debts. Because hard currency was required to pay the new excise tax and hard currency was almost nonexistent, and because there were so many farmers making distilled spirits on a small scale, it seemed to them—"the defenseless population of the interior"—that they had been unfairly singled out to finance the federal government "in order to relieve the commercial and importing interests of New England, to whom the tariff was inimical."[7]

Thus opposition to the excise tax continued to grow, with a Pittsburgh, Pennsylvania, convention adopting a protest to the tax on 21 August 1792 to which President Washington responded with a proclamation that the tax would be collected and warned against any opposition. Finally Shays's Rebellion broke out in western Pennsylvania in July 1794. Disgruntled farmers who opposed the whiskey tax burned tax collectors' homes and tarred and feathered revenue officers. In early August Washington called out a 12,900-man force from Virginia, Maryland, New Jersey, and Pennsylvania to suppress the rebellion. Led by Henry ("Light-horse Harry") Lee (great-grandfather of future Franklin County commonwealth's attorney Charles Carter Lee), the army put down the rebellion in November 1794.[8]

The whiskey tax was finally repealed in 1802 but reinstated in 1814 to pay for the debts incurred from the War of 1812. The tax was repealed again in 1817. Thereafter, until 1862 when the federal government enacted a new whiskey tax during the Civil War (which did not affect the Confederate states until the war's conclusion), local temperance societies that grew up by the 1830s led the fight against Demon Rum. One aspect of temperance that especially concerned local citizens and the states was that of serving alcohol to slaves. In North Carolina, legislation was passed as early as 1798 to prevent ordinary keepers and liquor retailers from "entertain[ing] slaves against the will of his master" with a penalty of losing one's liquor license. By 1833, the General Assembly of North Carolina had enacted bills making it illegal to sell liquor to slaves for any reason.[9] In Franklin County, those who retailed liquor without a license were subject to the penalty of the law. For instance, at the 6 November 1809 county court, the grand jury indicted Langston Cooper for retailing peach brandy without a license at Cook's old store on 14 October 1809, on information of Lewis Wingfield and Jacob Bondurant, "two of our Body."[10]

Throughout Virginia, approximately one hundred local temperance societies had sprung up in the 1820s and 1830s with a membership of about thirty-five thousand. General John Hartwell Cocke, of Fluvanna County, was elected president of the American Temperance Union in 1836. Joseph Martin's gazetteer, published that same year, noted that Union Hall in Franklin County boasted a "well organised temperance society." The Washingtonians, reformed alcoholics who "entertained" their audiences with stories of the horror of their days in the bottle, held mass meetings and parades throughout the commonwealth in the 1840s. And although the Washingtonians proved of short duration, fraternal temperance lodges followed in their footsteps to give Virginians another source for antidrinking activities. The Sons of Temperance gained a foothold during the 1850s and the Independent Order of Good Templars gathered a membership of thirteen thousand in Virginia after the Civil War.[11]

Combining with the Good Templars were the Methodist and Baptist churches throughout the state whose members formed 70 percent of the backbone of the temperance movement. For one hundred years the General Rules of the Methodist church had warned its members against "drunkenness or drinking spirituous liquors, unless in cases of necessity."[12] In 1899 the Virginia Conference announced that the only remedy for the evils of Demon Rum was prohibition. Strongly supporting that stand was the Woman's Christian Temperance Union, which joined forces in Virginia with the Baptists and Methodists in 1882. Led by national president Frances Willard, the WCTU formed local societies, sponsored essay and speech contests in the schools on temperance topics, established temperance instruction in Sunday schools, and held public meetings and marches to call attention to the need for national prohibition. By 1900 there were sixty-three local units in Virginia with more than twelve hundred members.[13] The organization that actually brought about statewide prohibition in Virginia was the Anti-Saloon League, organized in Richmond on 12 March 1901, six years after formation of the American Anti-Saloon League.

In the postwar years, local option had become the focus of Virginians' temperance efforts. In 1878, for instance, Montgomery County received authorization from the General Assembly to forbid liquor licenses in the college town of Blacksburg. Two years later the assembly allowed Loudoun, Warren, King George, and Clarke counties to hold local option referenda. Charlottesville led the fight for a general local option that the General Assembly enacted in 1886. For almost twenty years thereafter the local option remained in effect. Thus if one-fourth of the voters at a November election petitioned the appropriate court, a county, magisterial district, or corporation could hold a special election to determine if liquor licenses would be granted. By 1900, 27 of Virginia's 100 counties were dry, with one or more dry districts in an additional 28 counties.[14] Franklin was not one of them. Thereafter, led by the Virginia Anti-Saloon League, a concerted effort took place to persuade the General Assembly to restrict the liquor traffic. In 1903 the assembly obliged with the [William Hodges] Mann bill (a rider on the general revenue bill) that restricted licenses granted for rural saloons, resulting in the closure in 1903 of 530 saloons, more than one-third of the state's total. Moreover, by 1905 the Mann bill and local option had reduced the number of town and county saloons from 962 to 359, thus driving the saloon from forty-seven counties. And in 1908 House Speaker Richard Evelyn Byrd pushed through an act that effectively created prohibition in all areas except towns with a population of more than 500 and summer resorts. At the same time, the League showed such amazing success with the local option that 90 percent of the state's area and 70 percent of its population were dry by 1910.[15]

Nevertheless, in 1914 despite the fact that much of the state was dry, ten major cities, including Richmond and Norfolk, still had almost six hundred saloons. But the Virginia Anti-Saloon League, the WCTU, and the Methodist and Baptist churches and others still had as their goal the complete prohibition of alcohol throughout the commonwealth and in 1914 finally persuaded the General Assembly to allow a referendum so that the state's citizens could vote on statewide prohibition. The referendum was held on 22 September 1914 and the drys won with a vote of 94,251 to 63,886. Franklin County, which had remained wet until the end, voted 1,079 for prohibition and 1,373 against.[16] On 1 November 1916, the Mapp Act (named for Senator G. Walter Mapp, of Accomack County), became law and Virginia inaugurated statewide prohibition.[17]

The effect of the growing movement for prohibition in Franklin can be seen in the Virginia business directories for 1871–1872 through 1917. In the first directory, Franklin had listed no saloons, no wine and liquor retailers, and only one wine manufacturer, Jonathan M. McNeil, of Rocky Mount. In 1877–1878, William A. Brown, of Dickinson, was listed as a general merchant who also sold liquor, as he did in 1880–1881, but not thereafter. The business directory gave ten distillers of brandy in 1880–1881, three at Blackwater, one at Brown Hill, two at Long Branch, two at Otter Creek, one at "Running [Rennet] Bag," and one at Starry Creek. The number of distillers had increased to twenty-seven in 1884–1885, seventy-six in 1890–1891, and seventy-seven in 1893–1894. Four years later that number had started to decline, to seventy-one in 1897–1898, and precipitously thereafter, so that in 1906 there were sixteen distillers, in 1911 one, and in 1917 none.

The number of saloons followed a similar pattern. The first time saloons are listed in the business directory is in the 1897–1898 edition, when Franklin had four saloons, all located in Rocky Mount. In 1906 only one saloon remained in the county, at Rocky Mount, run by R. F. Rakes.[18] George L. Rakes, who had operated a saloon in Rocky Mount in 1897–1898, was now distilling liquor at Shooting Creek and continued to do so until at least 1906. A 1908 newspaper advertisement for A. B. Rakes, who ran a barroom next door to the First National Bank in Rocky Mount, noted that Rakes's whiskey was made in a copper still and he was offering it at a "Rock Bottom Price"—Royal Arch Corn Whiskey, four years old, at $1.75 per gallon or $0.90 per half-gallon. "If you don't think I will do what I say, come in my barroom and let me cite you. If anybody can beat my price on Copper Distilled Liquor and the age of my whiskey, let me know and I will do better than these prices." Rakes signed himself the "Whiskey Peoples Friend."[19] His competitor, A. S. Adams, proprietor of the Midway Saloon in Rocky Mount, did not try to beat Rakes's price; his Royal Arch Corn Whiskey sold for $2.50 a gallon and $1.50 a half-gallon. He advertised that "Mountain Corn Whiskey will be sold as cheap as it is sold in Rocky Mount or elsewhere, and I guarantee it to be as pure and good as is made." He concluded, "Call on me for Honest Liquors."[20] In 1911, R. F. Rakes still ran a Rocky Mount saloon, but by 1917 he was no longer in the business and the only Rakes listed as doing business in Rocky Mount was Rakes and Company, a general merchandise company and a hay, grain, and feed store.[21]

At the same time that the temperance movement began to gain effect in bringing about prohibition, the federal government in the post-Reconstruction period made the suppression of moonshiners a top priority. Whereas before the Civil War corn whiskey and applejack could be made legally, after the war federal excise taxes threatened to put illegal distillers out of business. In 1876 President Ulysses S. Grant placed Green B. Raum as commissioner of the internal revenue in charge of the effort to eradicate moonshining and Raum in turn sent a force of revenue agents to fight the battle. In 1878 the agents suffered their highest casualties (eight killed and seventeen wounded as compared with one killed and one wounded in the 1903–1904 fiscal year),[22] but by 1882 the IRS had achieved more than a 60 percent conviction rate of moonshiners and Raum concluded that the supremacy of the law had been established. Internal fighting, informers, personal and factional conflicts, all had played a part in disorganizing the moonshiners and contributing to the apparent federal success. The excise tax accounted for one-fifth to one-fourth of the entire federal tax revenue and thus members of both parties, Democrats and Republicans, continued to uphold enforcement. At the same time, moonshiner resistance persisted through the 1880s and 1890s, increasing dramatically after the panic of 1893 when the federal government raised the excise tax. Farmers who had not previously participated became active in the moonshine business. An early-twentieth-century writer, however, concluded that "modern moonshining is not nearly so romantic as the old time manufacture of 'mountain dew.' The 'shiner of old would defend his still with his life, and a 'location' and a raid meant a battle. Nowadays the moonshiner thinks discretion the better part of valor and when the revenue men find him out he decamps."[23] In 1898 the Republican administration increased the number of revenue agents, which in turn offered more effective control of moonshiners. But after 1900 when the individual states began to adopt strong prohibition laws, moonshining became much harder to stop.[24]

One area where moonshining has never been stopped is Franklin County. In January 1904 the *Roanoke Evening News* published an article signed by "J. L. G." describing one of the primary moonshining areas of the county:

Shootin' Creek and Runnet Bag in Floyd and Franklin counties, are the ideal localities for moonshining and blockading [presumably from Civil War usage "when contraband was rammed through coastal blockades"[25]]. The residents appreciate this and for many years have availed themselves of it. Situated in the foothills of the Blue Ridge, the country covered with a dense growth of laurel and ivy, permeated by numerous streams of the clearest, coldest water, apples and corn in abundance, nature seems to invite you to "jist make a doublin' or two for your own use." If I lived there I would moonshine, too, one couldn't help it.

The writer had recently spent a night in the area with "an old gentleman, who, with his boys, and his neighbors have moonshined for years." Despite the fact that the "revenue raiders" came sometimes and "cut" up their stills or "hauled [them] off " to the United States court, they continued the business, simply moving the still to another mountain gorge. A few days before the writer's visit the revenuers had come, and the men enjoyed retelling the story. "They are all expert shots," J. L. G. explained, "and could, if they wished, kill every raider who visits their mountain fastnesses, but they would not 'hurt a hair on his head.' " The old gentleman turned to the writer and said,

> Well, . . . I reckon you'r 'round' lookin' otter 'sessments ["the tax assessed by the government against the distiller for failure to account for the spirits he had produced, and against the blockader for failing to pay the specific tax for carrying on the business of a liquor dealer"] 'haint you? Well I'll be blest ef old Pack [Park] Agnew aint the all fird'st man atter 'sessments that ever I seen or heerd tell of. It peers to be all he studies 'bout, an' that 'tother old feller thar with him, old Beamer they call him, they say he's rank pizen too. I was over on 'tother side of the ridge at Bill's sto' 'tother day, an' a passel of us fellers was a settin' 'roun' jokin' when the mail boy rid up. He was tellin' us 'bout seein' a strange man down the way that he mistrusted was a revenue. He sed the stranger was a sayin' as how old Park took it powerful to heart 'bout his men bein' run outer here; oh they say he rar'd an' he pitched an' he froth'd, an 'lowed that he didn't have nary [a] dep'ty that was wuth a chaw o' tobacker, an' that he was aimin to cum up here hisself an' he would show who's who. You tell him to cum, to cum right here to my house, an' I'll do the best I kin by him an' his hoss. But my notion is old Park would'nt know a block still from a gov'ment still if he seed it.[26]

Four days later J. L. G., who seems to have been a government revenue agent after all, reported on his second visit to try again to collect the federal revenue tax from another moonshiner, this time an old woman, "a notorious blockader," who lived on the banks of the New River (in Pulaski County). Described as "typical of her class," she was, J. L. G. noted, "tall, raw-boned, angular and muscular, [with] iron gray hair, and a pair of black eyes, which could almost flash fire." A woman who had no use for revenuers and other busybodies:

> The moment I entered she began, and the last thing heard upon my retreat, was her voice, "What! you back here agin! I wish I may die if it don't beat all I ever seen or heerd tell of, a body can't turn 'roun' unless they run again' a revenue; they're thicker in huckleberries, a prowlin' a nosin' an' a pryin' into other folkses bizness. I reckin' you're back here again' 'bout that 'sessment old Park Agnew's bin a ritin' me 'bout? Well you go right back to old Park, jist as straight as yer laigs kin carry you, and tell him I haint sold no licker, an' don't owe no cussed 'sessment, an' haint got no money fer him. You tell him I say, he's got a devil in his heart biggun 'ary cliff on the river. Tell him I was down at Brush Creek meetin' house last Sunday an' heerd the circuit rider tellin' 'bout the devil as how he was chain'd down, but I don't b'lieve nary [a] word of it, I 'blieve he's loose, an' old Park is him. He's the wust one that's bin in office since the war. Now you mind an' tell him jist what I've tole you, an' if ever I lay my eyes on him, I aim to let him know what I think of him. An' don't you let me see you a prowlin' 'round here no more nuther."

And she hasn't.[27]

Perhaps typical of moonshine activity in Franklin was a series of reports in the *Roanoke Evening News* that detailed such activity in the county during a two-year period from 1903 through 1905. In the spring of 1903 "the notorious moonshiner, desperado and outlaw" Jeff Nowlin was arrested for moonshining and for trying to assassinate Deputy Marshal Wilson, of Radford. A posse led by Deputy Collector Tucker surrounded Nowlin's Shooting Creek home and captured him. Thereafter, bail was set so high that he could not make it, "hence he had to go to jail." Late in the year after two months in the Rocky Mount jail, Nowlin accompanied Deputy Marshal Zackfield B. Wade to Harrisonburg to be tried at the U.S. courthouse. The *Evening News* said of Nowlin that he "has been a desperate character and has given the officials a vast amount of trouble," but the officials thought he would get a long sentence and be put "where 'moonshine' can't be made."[28] In February 1904 Nowlin stood trial along with one Charlie Nowlin, who had been charged with failure to make proper entries in his books at the time he made brandy. If found guilty, Charlie Nowlin would lose forty gallons of brandy and all the appliances needed to make a distillery.[29] But the jury failed to agree and "the matter will come up at some future term of the court."[30] Evidently Jeff Nowlin escaped a verdict too—the court's at least.

A year and a half later, presumably before Jeff Nowlin could be tried again, his career came to an abrupt end: George McAlexander killed him in September 1905 and received a sentence of eighteen years in the state penitentiary. McAlexander escaped the ultimate penalty of hanging because of the "fact that he had been on a protracted drunk for the past five years, and his mind had become diseased from the excessive use of whiskey," a fact his counsel, Nicholas H.

Members of the Ingram family posing with their large turnip-type still on Thompson Ridge in southwestern Franklin County. (Blue Ridge Institute, Ferrum, Va.)

Hairston, of Roanoke, and Peter H. Dillard, of Rocky Mount, used "strongly in his favor." Interestingly enough, the cause of the murder was not moonshining per se but simply the product of the process. Several men including McAlexander had met one Sunday at Nowlin's to help lay a hearth. They had some whiskey to drink and soon a small disagreement broke out between Nowlin and McAlexander. Despite the fact that the altercation was broken up, McAlexander left vowing to kill Nowlin. He soon returned with a shotgun and blasted Nowlin "instantly" into eternity.[31]

Alcohol consumption played a role in another bizarre incident in Franklin early in 1904. "If any evidence were needed to prove that man is a totally depraved being, it would be found in the story of the death and burial of Ruth Rakes, wife of Jeff Rakes, of Franklin county, and the events subsequent thereto, including the courtship and marriage the second time of the husband of the dead woman," reported the *Roanoke Evening News* in its 1 February 1904 edition. Rakes was a prosperous farmer at Long Branch near Shooting Creek, an area long known as a center for "illicit distilleries which have been successfully operated in open violation of the revenue laws, and it has been dangerous ground for United States deputy marshals and revenue officers to tread for more than thirty years." Rakes himself was a member of a family "prominent in the community for years, and many of them have been directly identified with the element of moonshiners that have so successfully dominated this wild mountainous section."

Ruth Rakes died in mid-January after becoming "violently ill," but the cause of her death had not been determined by the time the *Evening News* learned of it, "and while no one dared to suggest that she died from other than natural causes, the action of the dead woman's husband was such as to set tongues to wagging." She was scarcely cold when her husband broke out the best flour that he had never let her touch and had prepared a "fine breakfast." Nailing up the flour barrel, Rakes left for Alumine, fifteen miles away, to get a coffin for his "old woman," after cursing neighbors who wanted to go for the coffin themselves. He "started off singing" and "at once proceeded to tank up on Franklin county 'moonshine.' " After buying the coffin and notifying all of the townspeople that he was now a widower, Rakes drove on to the railroad depot "where it is alleged that he publicly danced a jig on the depot platform." That duty performed, Rakes purchased a new suit at a clothing store where he announced his intention to wear the suit to his second wedding. Then laying in a fresh supply of liquor, he returned home, sitting on the coffin all the way and giving every appearance of going to "a frolic, instead of to the burial of his wife and the mother of his children." This impression was heightened by Rakes's singing of songs at the top of his voice—songs "typical of the mountain section in which he resides and [that] could in no way be considered as being of a sacred nature."

The neighbors soon realized that Rakes intended to find a new wife when he began querying the single women at his wife's funeral the next day just after the late Mrs. Rakes was laid to rest. Spurned by "one of the best known and most prominent young ladies of the neighborhood," he swore revenge and had to be forcibly restrained by "friends of the bereaved family" who persuaded him to take his five young children home. Not to be denied, Rakes spent the next week searching the countryside for a wife. In all he proposed to and was turned down by "at least thirty women, ranging in age from 14 to 35 years." He interviewed "every marriageable woman for miles around" until he found his late wife's niece on the eleventh day after Ruth Rakes's funeral. This intrepid woman had recently been divorced and until the court fees were paid she could not become the second Mrs. Rakes. Filling up again with moonshine, Rakes roared off to town to pay the fees and secure a marriage license. When he arrived home and attempted to show a neighbor the license, however, he discovered he did not have it. Rakes "saddled a fresh horse and rode at break-neck speed to Rocky Mount, where he obtained the coveted paper," and returned home to his second nuptials several hours late.[32] It is not recorded whether or not the second marriage was a success.

In mid-March 1904 a group of twenty mountaineers from Franklin and Floyd counties went on trial in the United States court in Lynchburg "for various infringements of the revenue laws," "illicit distilling," and "almost every technical point of law, including an attempt at murder of the marshal." When the train carrying the mountaineers, along with witnesses, traveled through Roanoke, a reporter for the *Evening News* noted that "they were jovial and feeling in the best of spirits."[33] They probably thought there was little chance of their conviction given the light sentences many moonshiners received.

A month later a probable informer came to an untimely end when he and his daughter were shot and killed from an ambush on 21 April while riding on horseback from Endicott to their home in the Rennet Bag section of the county. James Nowlin and the child were left beside the road with the girl's arms still around her father's neck. "Nowlin was known among illicit distillers as an informer [and "had given information about certain illicit stills"] and this is supposed to account for the murder."[34]

The *Franklin Times-Democrat* of 1 July 1904 contained a notice dated 17 May 1904 and signed by H. N. Dillard, Franklin County commonwealth's attorney, that the governor, Andrew J. Montague, had authorized a $500 reward "to any one who may arrest the murderer of James Nowlin and his little child and secure his conviction of the crime." Dillard further noted that "Nowlin and his child were shot from ambush on the creek known as Runnetbag, not far from Endicott, Franklin county, on Thursday, 21st day of April, 1904, while in the peaceful pursuits of a citizen."[35] But so far as is known, the crime was never brought home to the perpetrator.

Just two weeks after the deaths of the Nowlins, father and daughter, the *Evening News* reported that revenuers had destroyed several small stills in the county during the first week of May, but noted that "considerable difficulty is being felt in carrying on the raids successfully these days, as the long-distance 'phone is now in use through the mountain and this modern improvement is more to the advantage of the moonshiner than to the federal officers."[36]

On 4 August Captain Charles Gee, "raiding deputy collector of Richmond," Jesse J. Harris, U.S. deputy marshal of Roanoke, and two assistants, "Messrs. White and Pollard" made "an important raid" on an illegal still twelve miles south of Copper Hill in Franklin. The owner, Giles Shockey, a reputed Franklin County moonshiner, was a well-known farmer "of considerable wealth and standing in his community."[37] The agents destroyed a still with a 200-gallon capacity and eight fermenters found at two locations. Shockey had avoided capture before by continually moving his still from place to place and in fact had pulled the still out this time and hidden it in the woods. The agents had no trouble finding it, however, since the still was located near the site of the murder of James Nowlin and his daughter four months previously—an area the officers had already searched thoroughly. "The district is an exceedingly tough one, and so regarded by the officers. One moonshiner stated to the officers that he 'had put seven informers out of the way and had a grave dug for another.' " Despite the threat, Shockey appeared before U.S. Commissioner White two days later and was sent on to the grand jury. Shockey's Franklin and Floyd County friends stood security for him and he was released on $500 bail. Within several more days Deputy Marshal Harris arrested Daniel Walton at his home in Floyd County and charged him with being part owner of Giles Shockey's still. Walton too was released on $300 bail.[38]

Two weeks later, the *Roanoke Times* reported that Harris, Gee, and White had broken up a still in Bedford County located on a stream where "a corps of Tidewater engineers were surveying." While the moonshiner could not be arrested because he could not be found, "raiding deputy Gee, who is the only man authorized by law to destroy [a still], performed his duty in a most creditable manner." The writer concluded that "Harris is becoming a terror to moonshiners in the adjoining counties and they are now beginning to fear him."[39]

Two months later, Captain Charles Gee, U.S. deputy collector, led raids on Shooting and Rennet Bag creeks on 19 and 20 October. On Shooting Creek he and his men destroyed a 130-gallon still allegedly belonging to Asa McAlexander. In addition, Gee and U.S. Deputies Zackfield B. Wade and W. T. Webb broke up twelve fermenters with 2,400 gallons of beer and 400 gallons of "slop," all located in a wooden shed within fifty feet of the public highway. The still had apparently been in operation for about a year. The next day the same officers destroyed the still of S. E. Bolling and A. N. Wagner on Rennet Bag Creek—also a 130-gallon unit, with thirteen fermenters containing 2,600 gallons of beer, as well as malt, tubs, buckets, and other paraphernalia. Both men were sent to the grand jury in Danville but released in the meantime on $300 bail. During the previous few weeks, Captain Gee had destroyed seven illegal stills in Franklin and with the help of U.S. Deputy Marshal J. J. Harris had brought in "scores of law-breakers" from Franklin, Bedford, Campbell, and Floyd counties.[40]

Hosea Thomas's still on Shooting Creek. Left to right: Arthur Martin, Sparrell C. Rakes, T. P. ("Press") Martin, and Wiley Thomas. 1915 photo. (Blue Ridge Institute, Ferrum, Va.)

The life of the revenuer, however, was one of occasional extreme danger. At the end of October the "Moonshiners Put Up [a] Fight" in a battle at the aptly named Shooting Creek Gap. Officer Thomas Greer somehow became separated from his party and was nearly shot to death. The moonshiners fired more than forty rounds at him and wounded his horse so badly that the animal died. Greer's hat and coat were riddled with bullet holes. "The officer put up a desperate fight and it is doubtful whether he will again molest or venture into the enemy's country."[41]

The Nowlins figured in further moonshine activity in November 1904 when Captain Gee made a raid on a still at Nowlin's Mill on Shooting Creek. Again he destroyed a 130-gallon-capacity still with 2,000 gallons of beer ready for distribution. The moonshiners, worried by recent raids, had removed the still from a furnace and were taking it a short distance from the log building where it had been kept on Sam Nowlin's farm. Since they had received enough notice beforehand they all escaped to the mountains before the "officers could possibly reach them." This made the eighth still that Gee and his men had broken up in a month's time.[42]

A month later, U.S. Marshal Jesse Harris went back to Rennet Bag Creek and cut up two distilleries and captured Gorman [or Norman] Via, "one of the most noted moonshiners of that section." Although the first still was not in operation the agents were able to find a "small quantity of beer on hand" and the second one in full operation. They destroyed the 150-gallon still, about 2,000 gallons of beer, and "singlings." Via's friends tried to free him but Captain Gee and Deputy Marshal Z. B. Wade, of Rocky Mount, arrived in time to foil the would-be rescuers. Thus Via was placed in the Rocky Mount jail.[43]

Continuing their busy ways, two and a half weeks later, Gee and Harris made a raid on a still on Greasy Creek in Carroll County that was owned by William Marshall. The *Evening News* reported that "Captain Gee and Mr. Harris are making it warm for those who break the United States laws in this section of the state. Within the past six months they have destroyed a dozen or more illicit distillers."[44] In Pittsylvania County where the agents could not find the still they were after, a "little 'talk' " saved the day. U.S. Marshal J. J. Harris made his abortive raid in December at the farm of Sam Farmer but no amount of searching revealed the still despite "every evidence that an illicit still had recently been operated on the plantation." The newspaper account quaintly noted that Harris and his men gave the owner that little talk, "or, rather, put him through 'the third degree,' and immediately after their departure the moonshiner took the still and shipped it to the revenue agent in Wytheville. This is the first instance on record of where an illicit still was placed in the hands of the government officials in a similar manner."[45]

A prominent farmer presumably unconnected to moonshining became the object of moonshiner vengeance in January 1905 when he was called to the door of his home on the night of 15 January and "had hardly crossed the threshold before a volley was fired by a party and he fell to the ground dead," struck nineteen times. Perhaps the "party" was a moonshiner bent on paying him back for being an informer. In reporting this murder, however, the *Evening News* noted that the account could not be confirmed by press time.[46] Two days later the paper thought the story validated when "a gentleman who arrived in Roanoke yesterday confirmed the killing."[47] Henry Moore, however, was not dead, nor had anyone actually come to his door and fired at him. Thus it was a mystery to Moore and the *Evening News* how the story got out that he had been killed. Like Mark Twain the reports of Moore's demise were very much exaggerated as attested by the Reverend M. W. Royall who had been visiting Moore when the article about his death appeared in the newspaper. "They would both like very much to know who it was that sent the report out, as Mr. Moore objects seriously to being shot to death by midnight assassins without his knowledge."[48]

Deputy Marshal Zackfield B. Wade was not so lucky. He met his maker at the hands of black moonshiner Cephas Poindexter near Union Hall on 26 July 1905. Poindexter had been operating an illicit distillery for a long time and had been the object of constant scrutiny by officers of the law. Eventually, Deputy Wade got on his trail and "followed him through the brush." According to the newspaper's account, when Wade found the still he tried to arrest Poindexter, who was about to start the still: "When the officer called to the negro to halt, Poindexter, without turning, picked up a double-barrel shotgun that was at his hand and discharged the contents of one barrel at the officer." At Poindexter's trial, C. D. Williams testified that before he died Wade recounted the incident. "He said he had gone to C. Poindexter's house [not to his still] to arrest him, that Cephas Poindexter came out of the house and he called to him to halt. Cephas raised his gun & shot, saying 'Oh! Yes. Damn you. I would get you.' Then he (Wade) shot at him twice with his pistol before he fell but did not think he hit him." Help for Wade came immediately and he was put on a train for Rocky Mount but died just as the train pulled in. Poindexter was able to escape.[49]

The thirty-five-year-old Wade had been in the revenue business for seven years "and was very popular, but a terror to the many illicit distillers in this section." Poindexter had been working in West Virginia in the coal mines for the previous several months and had just returned home when Wade arrived with an old warrant for his arrest. After shooting Wade, Poindexter escaped to the woods while his father carried Wade to the Glade Hill station for the train trip to Rocky Mount. The younger Poindexter returned a while later to tell his wife he was leaving and she would never see him again. Governor Andrew J. Montague offered a reward of $250, which "served to inject new fire into the already excited citizens [of Franklin] and more posses were organized to hunt down the criminal." Three days later Sheriff David A. Nicholson and his posse reportedly surrounded Poindexter near Union Hall, but failed to capture him. Poindexter was "armed to the teeth with the double-barreled shotgun" he had used to kill Deputy Marshal Wade and "an ample supply of ammunition," as well as "a high grade revolver." He expected to die rather than surrender. The previous Sunday when he returned from West Virginia to Rocky Mount he had told a black minister, the Reverend Joseph Belcher, and later "a reputable white man," Sparrell Callaway, living in the vicinity of Union Hall, "that he would kill any revenue officer who approached him, and would give neither warning nor quarter." Wade had been able to fire a shot that grazed Poindexter's thumb before falling.[50]

Poindexter was finally captured on 30 July and taken to the Roanoke city jail "for safe keeping." A prominent Franklin farmer, sixty-year-old W. D. Haynes, described as "a man of unshaken nerve," had been riding his horse near his home when he stumbled upon Poindexter "sitting by the roadside with his shotgun across his knees, the muzzle pointing to the ground." Haynes saw Poindexter first and covered him with "a pair of vicious looking revolvers." The standoff ended when Poindexter agreed to the capture if Haynes would guarantee he would not be lynched. After disarming Poindexter, Haynes walked him five miles until they reached a place two miles from Rocky Mount where they were joined by two other men, one of whom went into town to get Deputy Sheriff J. P. Hodges and U.S. Deputy Collector Charles Gee. The officers soon arrived and shackled Poindexter, marching him seven miles to Wirtz where they all took the train for Roanoke. Arriving in Roanoke, the train was met by a party of several hundred people and Poindexter was led with difficulty to the city jail and searched. "He was then made to remove his shoes to make certain that no weapon . . . [was] concealed

Execution of Cephas Poindexter, the last hanging in Franklin County, 24 Nov. 1905. (Frank Lynch, Rocky Mount, Va.)

about the lower extremities. Nothing was found in the shoes except two tired feet." Poindexter had been living on huckleberries and roots since his escape and asked for a meal, which he soon received. In answer to the *Evening News* reporter's questions, Poindexter stated that he had never made moonshine and that he had shot in self-defense.[51]

Poindexter thought that his lawyer would be able to sustain a plea of self-defense and get him off, and indeed he and several members of his family testified that Wade shot first. In his testimony Poindexter stated that a man who turned out to be Wade came up just before daybreak and called to Poindexter to halt, "and I halted. He came up in a little place where the moon was shining and set in shooting. I asked him not to shoot. He shot twice and brought the pistol down to shoot again and I shot and his pistol went back from him. He did not shoot any more and I ran. I didn't know who it was. I had just come home from West Virginia. I had some money and I did not know who it was who had come there."[52] Nevertheless, the jury found him guilty and recommended the death penalty. His lawyer, Colonel J. W. Hartwell, asked for a new trial and was denied. After the Virginia Supreme Court turned down Poindexter's appeal for a writ of error and supersedeas and after two reprieves Poindexter was hanged at Rocky Mount on 24

November 1905, stating as his last words that he was guilty of the crime but thought the penalty was too severe as he had only acted in self-defense. "He was stoical all the time and never once weakened."[53]

Reward notice. Ca. 1918. (Prohibition Commission Records, Virginia State Library and Archives.)

NOTICE
$25.00 Reward

will be paid to anyone furnishing information leading to the arrest and conviction of any person caught operating a still in Franklin county, Virginia. Such information should be furnished to Mr. Archer G. Sims, State Prohibition Inspector at Endicott, Virginia.

No Reward will be paid for the capture of a still unless the party operating the same is arrested and convicted in the Franklin County Circuit Court.

J. SIDNEY PETERS,
Prohibition Commissioner of Virginia.

THIS OFFER EXPIRES FEBRUARY 28, 1918

Eleven years later in 1916 when most moonshine states including Virginia became dry, the moonshine business went into high gear and "general lawlessness reached its highest peak."[54] Nowhere was this more evident than in Franklin County. After the Mapp Act took effect in November 1916, the state of Virginia began prohibiting the manufacture and sale of "ardent spirits." Three years later the Eighteenth Amendment to the United States Constitution established prohibition nationwide and in 1920, with the passage of the Volstead Act, enforcement of nationwide prohibition began. In the period from 1 November 1920 until 30 June 1933 (prohibition was repealed in December 1933 when the Twenty-First Amendment to the Constitution took effect), Virginia's Department of Prohibition and local officials made a total of 186,207 arrests for bootlegging and related activities, seized 730,141.5 gallons of "ardent spirits," destroyed 33,009 stills, and confiscated 11,965 vehicles. During that same period, there were 1,669 arrests in Franklin County, 130,716.75 gallons of liquor seized, 3,909 stills destroyed, and 716 automobiles confiscated. Thus Franklin accounted for less than 1 percent of all arrests statewide, but 18 percent of the alcohol seized, 12 percent of the stills destroyed, and 6 percent of the vehicles taken.[55]

Two years later in 1935 the full extent of moonshining in Franklin became known during "the Franklin county whisky conspiracy case."[56] Prohibition had made illegal distilling and sales vastly profitable for such "entrepreneurs" as Chicagoan Al Capone, but as one witness at the Franklin conspiracy trial noted, "The Franklin county moonshiners were [also] greatly aided by the coming of national prohibition for the prices of liquor went up sharply."[57]

Between late October 1934 and early February 1935 a federal grand jury sitting at Harrisonburg heard testimony that resulted in indictments for conspiracy to

Approximate fluid contents 500 ml. No bacteriostatic or other preservatives added.

Internal contents of humidifier bottle sterile and non-pyrogenic.

Directions for Use

1. Remove humidifier adapter from package. Remove break-away "trigger" from bottle top by sharply pulling up on "trigger". Secure humidifier adapter to bottle by turning in a clockwise direction until adapter has been completely seated to the bottle top.

2. Attach the humidifier nut to the outlet of the flow meter. Remove break-away "trigger" from outlet of the humidifier with an upward snapping motion. Do not twist off.

3. Attach delivery tube to the outlet port of the humidifier.

4. To check audible relief alarm, set flow meter at 4 LPM, fold back and pinch tubing. A whistle will be heard: release tubing and proceed with therapy.

5. Adjust liter flow in accordance with doctor's prescription.

Warning: Read humidifier bottle label prior to use.

©Copyright 2003. Cardinal Health, Inc. or one of its subsidiaries. All rights reserved.

Manufactured under one or more of the following Patents: 4,367,182; 4,865,777; 391,171; 5,000,674

key excise taxes. Those local, state, and federal corporation. Several of former sheriff D. Wilson t, Deputy Sheriffs Henry mer Virginia House of s Attorney Charles Carter ite.[58] For two years prior estigators led by Colonel ke, one of the defense ania")[59] had looked into s in Franklin county, fifth he prohibition years."[60] autumn of 1928 when together a group of his Abshire, Charles L. Rakes, he county into districts, eputies to enlist people to se still operators, $25 per tion. Hodges had recently n for using liquor in an m a penitentiary term, he k of your future," Deputy which, Hodges replied, "To nwealth's attorney and also campaign and we've got to get our money back."[63]

John Lee's son Carter had been accused of being a ringleader in the conspiracy, but unfortunately for the prosecution's case against the younger Lee, Bridges was one of a string of witnesses with a grudge against Lee and his family. In 1923 Bridges had been prosecuted by John Lee for killing his own brother and brother-in-law and had to admit during his testimony that "he did not 'care a damn' what happened to the Lee family because John Lee . . . had prosecuted him 'too hard' " despite the fact that he had claimed self-defense and been acquitted.[64]

A theme that ran through the conspiracy trial testimony was the division of the protection money to include a share for "the other fellow up at the courthouse." But no one was ever identified as that "other fellow." In fact, Peter Hodges's son Wilson gave testimony that also helped the case of Commonwealth's Attorney Lee as the younger Hodges maintained that so far as he knew Lee was not "the other fellow"[65] and that "he did not know of Lee ever receiving a cent of protection money or having any knowledge of the activities in his office."[66]

It seems evident that vital testimony could have been provided by Deputy Sheriff Thomas Jefferson ("Jeff") Richards, who had acted as treasurer of the late sheriff's "granny fee" operation. But seventeen days before the grand jury began meeting in October 1934, Richards and a prisoner were ambushed and killed. Richards had left the home of Edgar A. Beckett, former state prohibition officer, about 9:15 P.M. on 12 October to escort the prisoner back to Rocky Mount. Both men stepped out of the car when the firing began. The prisoner was found about ten yards in front of the vehicle with seven slugs in his back. Richards still had his unused pistol in his hand and was lying on the driver's side with fifteen bullets, both shotgun and .45 caliber, mostly in his chest and only a few shots in his back. The car, a 1931 Ford roadster, had been riddled with buckshot and .45-caliber ammunition, including twelve bullets in the roof and twenty-four in the front windshield.[67] Both the prosecution and the defense questioned William McKinley Webb, unindicted coconspirator, about the killing during the conspiracy trial, but Webb denied emphatically that he was the murderer (he was first cousin to Richards, interestingly enough). Since the defense could not establish a definite link between the ambush and the trial, Judge John Paul disallowed any further discussion of Richards's death. At of the time of the trial no culprit had been found, but two years later two West Virginia men with no connection to this conspiracy were tried in Franklin County and found guilty of Richards's murder.[68]

Led by government prosecutors, Sterling Hutcheson, district attorney for the eastern district of Virginia, and Frank S. Tavenner, Jr., assistant district attorney for the western district of Virginia, the government continued to build its case from testimony by the three surviving Hodgeses, Wilson, Joe, Jr., and their mother, Bettie. They stated that Wilson had succeeded his father (who died in January 1930) as sheriff and continued the conspiracy that his father had reputedly created. Wilson "admitted receiving protection money, allowing stills to run under protection, letting liquor cars pass on the highways and selling captured whiskey." His brother Joe, Jr., and his mother substantiated the story that his mother and dying father were persuaded to let Wilson become sheriff by the deputies, the later judge P. H. Dillard, and Commonwealth's Attorney Carter Lee. The deputies gave as the reason for Wilson's succession that "it was not best to 'disturb the arrangement which they had.' " Wilson Hodges continued as sheriff until he was defeated for reelection by C. C. Jamison and left office on 1 January 1932.[69] The strain evidently became too great as he was drinking heavily, according to his mother's testimony, by the time he lost that primary to Jamison.[70]

Leonard L. Fralin and H. J. ("Jake") Wright, "two of the admitted big shots of the liquor business," continued the construction of the government's case by stating that they had operated with Peter Hodges's and his son's protection and had "paid regularly for the privilege." Alleged moonshiner Tom Cundiff's testimony, however, did little to advance the case when he was accused of hating Carter Lee and being willing to do anything to get back at the commonwealth's attorney. Even his assertion that a $39 check he gave Lee on 10 October 1933 was part payment of protection was contested by the defense, which declared that in fact it was payment of a fine and that Clerk of Court T. W. Carper had accepted it as such on 11 October.

In erecting the conspiracy structure the government introduced a parade of 176 witnesses "who told the jury of the huge extent of the liquor operations in the county." They related that many of them had been forced to join with large manufacturers in order to stay in business and "have good luck" as well as being compelled to pay a "granny fee" (the term apparently originating from the fact that old women acted as midwives and received a fee for delivering babies so when a still was "born" the law got a "granny fee"[71]) to county officers for protection.

Next a dozen rumrunners testified that they had moved more than a million gallons of whiskey out of the county during the period covered in the indictment. They had been assured of being "protected to the county line" by the dealers from whom they had obtained the whiskey and told how the liquor-laden automobiles had traveled in regular caravans at high speed from points in the county to Roanoke with "pilot" cars running interference to "ward off any officers that tried to stop them." The most fascinating rumrunner was coconspirator Mrs. Willie Carter Sharpe—the "queen of Roanoke rum runners"—who maintained that she had either hauled or piloted more than 220,000 gallons of whiskey out of Franklin County between 1926 and 1931, including a period between early May, the time she was arrested, and July 1931, when she stood trial for transporting liquor.[72]

It must have come as an extreme disappointment to all those in court, however, that the diamond Mrs. Sharpe reportedly wore in her teeth was no longer in evidence when she took the stand. The story she told was one fraught with interest nevertheless. Born in Floyd County, she had moved to Roanoke in 1918 and after several years and several moves she returned to Roanoke about 1922 where she worked in a five-and-dime before marrying the son of John Carter the "bootleg king of the city at that time." Sharpe began immediately to transport illicit whiskey from Floyd County, but a year after divorcing Floyd Carter she switched to Franklin County in 1926. Much of the time she merely piloted the liquor, driving a variety of automobiles but mostly a specially built machine designed for high speed that had steel fenders. She had acquired the car from Carroll Falwell in Lynchburg in exchange for 700 gallons of whiskey. Admitting that at one time a machine gun had been mounted on the vehicle, she maintained that the weapon was no longer there while she drove it.[73]

Sherwood Anderson, who covered the conspiracy trial at the request of Henry Morgenthau, secretary of the United States Treasury, wrote in *Liberty* magazine that after Willie Sharpe told her story on the stand she talked freely. "It was the excitement got me," she said. Most of the other rumrunners she had known were "kids who liked the excitement [too]."

> There were women, some of them of respectable families, who came to her—this after she had been in jail, had been in the newspapers. "They wanted the kick of it," she said. She refused to tell who they were. "Some of them had in their veins what you call the best blood of Virginia," she said.[74]

The government attorneys added statistical detail to the testimony by introducing evidence from the Norfolk and Western Railroad's files, as well as those of trucking lines and a wholesale distributing company, that from 1930 until 1935 a total of 37 tons of yeast, 16,920 tons of sugar, and thousands of tons of malt, meal, and other materials needed in the manufacture of whiskey had been shipped to the county.[75] The yeast consumption alone was more than nine times that of the city of Richmond, which had a population seven times greater than Franklin's. Further, more than a million five-gallon cans, most of the "noiseless" lacquered type made specifically for liquor, were sold in Franklin, many by Robert P. DeHart, of Shooting Creek, who pleaded nolo contendere.

The government took twenty-five days over a period of five weeks to build its case. The defense used sixteen days in its attempt to refute that case, calling sixty-nine of its own witnesses, for a total of four hundred witnesses for the trial. Introductory statements took a day and closing arguments and rebuttal another four apiece. Thus the trial lasted ten weeks, the longest trial on record in Virginia to that date except for the month-long treason trial of Aaron Burr held in Richmond beginning on 3 August 1807. The defense consisted originally of a dozen lawyers, reduced to ten after several defendants pleaded guilty or nolo contendere at the start of the trial. The attorneys were Samuel R. Price, T. Warren Messick, and R. Lee Carney, of Roanoke; John W. Carter, of Danville; Stephen D. Timberlake, Jr., and J. Wesley Taylor, of Staunton; Beverly A. Davis, Sr., and Jr., H. Dalton Dillard, and J. Bradie Allman, of Rocky Mount.

In his instructions to the jury at the conclusion of the defense's case, Judge John Paul explained to the jurors that their duty consisted of determining whether or not a conspiracy had existed to defraud the government of its tax on liquor and which defendants, if any, were active participants in such a plan. The fact that some of the defendants clearly operated stills and individually avoided the payment of excise taxes thereon, he said, was not proof of guilt in regard to the conspiracy charge.[76]

Regarding Charles Carter Lee, Judge Paul told the jury that Lee could not be found guilty "for any dereliction or irregularity in the performance of his duties as such under the laws of the State of Virginia. Much evidence has been introduced as to the manner in which Mr. Lee dealt with violations of the liquor laws, involving, as it is alleged, laxity in their enforcement and unreasonably light punishments, which in some instances were not in accord with the punishments prescribed by the state law." But Lee was not being tried for the manner in which he conducted the responsibilities of his office. Evidence of that conduct was "introduced" simply to allow the jury to determine if Lee was "guilty of the crime of conspiring or agreeing with other defendants to commit the offenses charged in this indictment." If the jury decided that Lee had conducted his office in a haphazard manner and allowed gross violations of the law to occur with insufficient punishment, these factors could be used to convict Lee of conspiracy but not of improper performance of his duties. This injunction applied to other officers of the law as well, the state prohibition officers, the federal prohibition officer, and the deputy sheriffs.

Judge Paul elaborated on the conspiracy and its participants by noting that the government was seeking to prove that beginning about September 1928 or thereafter, a number of people resident in Franklin County entered into an agreement to defraud the government and that among those involved were operators of distilleries making liquor and others transporting it for distribution and sale. Some of those involved, too, were county, state, and federal officers "who permitted or encouraged the making and removal of this illicit liquor by allowing it to be made and removed without interference." In so doing, these officers combined to violate the U.S. revenue laws. Moreover, testimony indicated "that the sheriff of Franklin county in conjunction with other defendants occupying positions as officers of the law established a plan by which persons were encouraged and permitted to engage in the manufacture of liquor, and evidence has been introduced showing the payment of protection money by those engaged in the liquor business to the officers of the law for the privilege of maintaining their operations." Evidence also showed that small, independent operators were put out of business by having their operations raided and their stills destroyed. Nevertheless the liquor dealers, "in order to stimulate and increase their business, were guaranteeing protection within Franklin county to those who purchased liquor from them, it being contended by the government that this was in pursuance of their agreement with the officers of the law for the protection of their customers."

In conclusion, Judge Paul told the jury all it had to do was to determine if a conspiracy existed and who were parties to it. The judge warned the jurors, however, to remember that evidence of guilt could be established not by testimony of perhaps unreliable coconspirators but only "by independent or direct proof, or by all the facts and circumstances of the case, which convinces you that a conspiracy existed and [if] the participation of a particular person in that conspiracy is also shown, then the declarations or statements of any co-conspirator is evidence against all of those shown to have been members of the conspiracy." Finally, the jury was not to be influenced by the failure of defendants to testify in their own behalf. They did not have to testify, and no determination of guilt was to be made by that failure, he said.

Judge Paul was followed by Assistant District Attorney Frank S. Tavenner, Jr., for the prosecution, who told the jury members that "your verdict will determine whether law and order shall prevail or whether these persons can continue to defy the government." Tavenner told the jury it was his belief that there had been overwhelming testimony to confirm that the late sheriff J. P. Hodges had organized the conspiracy after ouster proceedings began against him in 1928.[77] Even on his deathbed Hodges continued the conspiracy when his associates Edgar A. Beckett, Jeff Richards, Henry T. Abshire, and Charles L. Rakes came to ask Hodges and his wife to allow their "young son's becoming sheriff" to maintain the arrangement already in place. Wilson had known about the organization while still in business college in Roanoke as did his younger brother, Joe. "And they used him (Wilson) as a tool and when he had served his usefulness they put him out."

Tavenner noted that the jury had heard testimony from people who ordinarily observed a code of silence—"a great many people up there in the mountains who make a little liquor, but who otherwise are honest men." Of them, Tavenner said, " 'Those men up there in the mountains, although they have made a little liquor, are honest men—all the resources of 10 to 12 lawyers didn't shake a one of them and I venture to say in nine-tenths of the cases they wish they hadn't examined them. It was not an easy thing to do,' he declared, for these persons to come into court and testify about this matter because they were breaking a precedent and therefore 'I am convinced that you believed them.' " On the other hand, the "younger defendants represent a new era in crime," said Tavenner, "they purchased materials in the staggering quantities, organized their communities and drove people around them into the business. At last the people have spoken and from 50 to 75 of them have told you of paying protection while dealing under the big liquor barons." He averred that the jury could "wipe out the testimony of any 10 or 12 men in this case and it should not affect your decision."

Tavenner continued by pleading with the jury to "give the government back to the people of Franklin county and let them return to the natural pursuits of farming." He pointed out that if the 61,960 pounds of yeast received in three of the county's districts alone had been used in making loaves of bread, those loaves if stretched end to end would traverse 1,245 miles, from Roanoke to Omaha, Nebraska. "The 25,241,410 pounds of sugar, he asserted, would be enough for two tons per capita" if divided. And the million five-gallon cans sold in Franklin, if flattened out, would yield enough tin to roof 2,900 homes of "40 by 40 feet." If all of the 33,777,000 pounds of sugar used in the county from 1930 until early 1935 were spread out over the city of Roanoke with an area of 10.8 square miles, it would be three-quarters of an inch deep. The tax alone on the liquor the government had shown had been manufactured (well over one million gallons, not including the 220,000 gallons credited to Mrs. Willie Carter Sharpe), would have come to $5.5 million.[78]

Following Tavenner's remarks to the jury, the defense lawyers began their summations. Stephen D. Timberlake (in a four-hour address) defended Carter Lee, who earlier had explained in his own defense his method of conducting the operations of the commonwealth's attorney's office. Because it had proved so difficult to convict alleged bootleggers unless they were caught in the act of distilling illicit liquor, Lee told the jury, he had accepted a guilty plea from those arrested and collected a fine when the persons were brought into the courthouse instead of sending any of them on to a judge and jury. He used as his authority for this unusual approach the instructions of the late Franklin County judge Peter H. Dillard, who had recommended fines and suspended jail sentences, "later approved by the court," for those willing to plead guilty to possession where conviction for manufacturing was doubtful; former assistant state attorney general Thomas Whitehead, who had been in charge of Virginia's prohibition enforcement; and Governor John Garland Pollard, who had sent a letter to the state's commonwealth's attorneys dated 2 November 1932 asking them to reduce criminal costs to the state by accepting suspended sentences and probation for prisoners if possible and fewer confiscations of liquor cars to avoid storage costs.[79] Lee had added that he also followed this course because of crowded conditions in the Franklin County jail and because court cases became so backlogged that sometimes it took six months for those arrested to come to trial.[80]

Nevertheless, prosecuting attorney Sterling Hutcheson had elicited testimony to show that nowhere else did the commonwealth's attorney set and collect fines and fail to send the prisoners on for confirmation of the proceedings by a county judge. Lee had also simply collected fines from second-time (or more) offenders, which was not done anywhere else.[81] During his tenure as commonwealth's attorney, Carter Lee stated, he had achieved 475 convictions for prohibition cases, sent 26 people to the state penitentiary for violating the antiliquor law, and secured about 200 convictions for other crimes (not including the Rocky Mount mayor's court whose records had been lost or juvenile cases).[82] And in Lee's defense, a witness noted the Virginia Anti-Saloon League consensus that "the Franklin situation was in measure a result of lack of diligence on the part of officers, but that they felt Mr. Lee was always a 'vigorous prosecutor' of cases brought before him."[83] Thus Timberlake reminded the jury that while Charles Carter Lee, whom he believed was the object of much desire for revenge, had been mentioned in the testimony of government witnesses, nevertheless, of fifty coconspirators who had testified, Lee had prosecuted and convicted twenty-three of them as well as twenty-two others not named in the indictment. Finally,

Timberlake told the jury, "I ask of you only as a small measure of recompense to this boy [aged twenty-nine] for what he has suffered to reach a decision quickly, to return him to his wife and baby, and to the loving and loyal friends who are awaiting him. I leave you confident of your verdict."

The proceedings were enlivened by an eighteen-minute harangue from Beverly A. Davis, Sr., who pleaded for his client—an accused bootlegger—saying his client was "a simple mountaineer who didn't even know the meaning of the word conspiracy." Only the testimony of William McKinley Webb tied Davis's client to this mess, and "I'll face the issue fairly and squarely," he said. "Of course he's made liquor. Some of the witnesses told the truth when they said he did. He has made it like his daddy and his grand-daddy before him and he made it to buy winter clothing for his children. There he sits—a typical mountaineer—a good citizen, no matter what he had done, nobody can say he was ever in a conspiracy." Davis insisted that his client "never put a copper in sugar save to sweeten his wife's coffee." In answer to the question of whether or not the accused used yeast, Davis exclaimed, "Why, if my client was to find a pint of yeast in the road he wouldn't know what it was," while the courtroom "roared." Davis begged the jury to let his client "go back to his farm in the mountains and continue to live as he has before."

" 'Still making liquor?' inquired Judge John Paul with a laugh.

'No sir, he's had enough of making liquor after he gets out of here,' came back the attorney.

'Well, I just said that because you said you wanted him to live in the future as he had in the past,' explained the court."[84]

J. Bradie Allman "in his remarks admitted that liquor had been made in Franklin for generations, that it was probably being made when George Washington was in Pennsylvania under John Adams suppressing the whiskey rebellion, and contended that the topography of the county lends itself to the purpose." Allman said of J. P. Hodges, late sheriff, that the only honest thing he had ever done was to ask while he was on his deathbed that his son Wilson not be made sheriff, but Wilson as sheriff "carried on until the good people of Franklin county kicked him out in the street and ended the cesspool of iniquity that had been created in the sheriff's office."[85]

District Attorney Sterling Hutcheson, of Richmond, gave the concluding statement to the jury. He took four hours and fifteen minutes to summarize the government's case.[86] Hutcheson went through the testimony of those witnesses whom he believed demonstrated most accurately the government's case for conspiracy and answered another defense criticism as to why the government had not "done something about" the "monument of crime" that had been revealed, saying, "We have drilled holes in that monument and placed the dynamite in them and we have put the match in your hands—I ask a verdict of guilty against these defendants—the evidence demands it, the testimony has been strong, convincing and overwhelming."[87]

The Franklin County conspiracy case went to the jury at 3:10 P.M. on Saturday, 29 June 1935, after forty-nine days of evidence and argument. On 1 July the jury returned its verdict that a conspiracy did exist from September 1928 until February 1935 and that twenty of the twenty-three defendants were guilty thereof. Acquitted were Commonwealth's Attorney Charles Carter Lee and

Deputy Sheriffs Will Wray, of Henry, and Howard L. Maxey, of Ferrum.[88] Among those found guilty were Samuel O. White, of Huntington, West Virginia, under suspension from the Alcoholic Tax Unit and former federal prohibition agent stationed at Roanoke; Edgar A. Beckett, of Callaway, former state prohibition inspector; Henry T. Abshire, of Boones Mill, deputy sheriff; and David A. Nicholson, of Ferrum, former member of the General Assembly.[89]

When the jury brought in the verdict, the judge asked the courtroom to restrain any emotion while the verdict was read. Only one wife of a defendant wept, quietly. Charles Carter Lee "slumped down in his chair with a sigh and then smiled broadly." The judge took a small recess and invited the jurymen back to the law library while well-wishers and family members crowded around the three men who had been acquitted. "Even those who had been convicted added a word as the freed trio sought to express regrets to the others."[90]

Almost two weeks later Judge Paul passed sentence on those found guilty as well as the others who had pleaded nolo contendere. Among those the judge placed on probation was D. Wilson Hodges, son of the former sheriff Peter Hodges who originally had conceived of the conspiracy plan. Judge Paul noted that he gave the younger Hodges probation after he had "given [Hodges's case] a good deal of thought." He explained that the situation "of Mr. Hodges in particular is as unfortunate as any I know of. Here he was a young boy hardly turned 21, dropped into that situation and his whole life has been ruined by it. I feel sorry about the situation that was created."[91]

Following the conclusion of the trial, the editorial writer for the *Roanoke Times* commented on its outcome, saying that the fact "that there had been extensive moonshine and liquor-running operations in Franklin County for years was general knowledge." The government did not seek to prove the extent of moonshine activities in the county but to prove that a conspiracy "had existed with ramifications reaching into the political and social life of the county," and clearly did so to the satisfaction of the jury. The people of Franklin could feel satisfaction in the acquittal of their commonwealth's attorney, who when told of the extent of shipment into the county of yeast, malt, sugar, and other whiskey ingredients running into the millions of dollars, expressed "amazement at the extent of the liquor business in Franklin." The writer concluded:

> Now that the trial is over, it is in order to express the widespread sympathy which is felt, no doubt, for the law-abiding citizens of Franklin County in the stigma that has been placed on the good name of their county. Many of the very best and most useful citizens of Roanoke have come from Franklin County, contributing in marked degree to the upbuilding and development of this community. It goes without saying that a neighborly good will is felt, and with it an understanding of the peculiar problems of law enforcement under the conditions that have existed in Franklin.
>
> The verdict returned in the Federal court Monday afternoon furnishes, incidentally, a complete and crushing answer to those who mistakenly advocate a return to a so-called prohibition system under which a thoroughly organized and widespread traffic in liquor has enriched individuals and business concerns alike.

The *Richmond Times-Dispatch* came to the same conclusion as the *Roanoke*

Times about Prohibition. Stating that "it is a matter of gratification for Mr. Lee and the other two officers of the county [who] came out with clean hands," the editorialist stated that "the result gives color to the statement of Mr. Lee that the case against him was manufactured by persons whom he had prosecuted and who were taking that means to wreak their vengeance." With regard to the "noble experiment" of Prohibition, however, the writer agreed with the *Times*:

> Perhaps Franklin County did not deserve the high place the Wickersham commission gave it on the list of communities which flouted the prohibition law [the report had termed Franklin "one of the wettest spots in the United States"]. These proceedings in the Federal Court, however, indicate that the "noble experiment" was widely violated in that section. Yet it is possible that little more reverence was paid it in many other counties and cities in Virginia which have not come under the scrutiny of Federal investigators. Certainly, it was not difficult to obtain liquor in the vast majority of communities in the State. At times a whistle would almost bring bootleggers running from all directions. The plain truth is that prohibition did not prohibit.[92]

The ripples from the conspiracy trial did not end with the conviction of twenty of the defendants, however. Almost a year later, twenty-four people "were indicted at Harrisonburg for conspiring to influence the jury in the trial." Those indicted included two former federal prohibition agents, Edgar A. Beckett and Samuel O. White, who had already been found guilty in the conspiracy trial, along with Amos, Hugh, and Edd Rakes, Edgar T. Marshall (son of conspiracy trial juror Leander E. Marshall), David A. Nicholson (also found guilty in the previous trial), and C. Will Wray (former Franklin County deputy sheriff who had been found not guilty). One other now indicted committed suicide before he could be tried.[93]

From the time of the verdict in the July 1935 conspiracy trial, rumors had circulated that jury tampering had occurred and thus Colonel Thomas Bailey, of the federal Alcohol Tax Unit, had conducted an investigation resulting in the grand jury indictment on 31 March 1936. The charge included thirty-two overt acts constituting a conspiracy to affect the 1935 trial's outcome, primarily payments made by one defendant to another—specifically that Clifford Martin had paid Edd Rakes $1,100 and Claude Shively had paid Rakes $700 so that Rakes could in turn pay Hugh Rakes $300 to influence the jury in the conspiracy trial. According to the plan, if all of the defendants were convicted Martin and Shively would receive the balance of their payment from Edd Rakes, but if the defendants were not convicted Hugh Rakes would receive the entire amount. The final two overt acts consisted of the charges that Edd Rakes had returned almost $900 to Clifford Martin and about $450 to Claude Shively in July 1935. Conviction of the charge of conspiracy to tamper with a jury could result in sentences for each man of up to six years in prison and a fine of $5,000.[94]

A day after the story of the indictments had appeared in the press, an editorial writer with the *Norfolk Virginian-Pilot* reviewed the history of the Franklin County conspiracy trial and called on someone who could speak from a sociological and economical viewpoint to write a book about Franklin County. It should include a section on "the original unofficial investigation in prohibition days which led the investigators to characterize Franklin County as one of the worst liquor centers in the country" as well as the long-winded federal investigation that resulted in the July 1935 conspiracy trial of thirty-four persons, only three of whom were acquitted. There should also be included "the discovery by Federal Judge John Paul months later that a batch of those found guilty and sentenced were, under pretense of preparing their appeals, continuing the operations for which they have been convicted and were also participating actively in political campaigns" and his resultant order that they should go immediately to jail, ultimately upheld by the circuit court of appeals. There also should be a summary of the subsequent investigation of jury tampering rumors that had just resulted in the indictments of twenty-four persons, seventeen of them previously found guilty and one acquitted in the conspiracy trial. "If sustained, these charges will demonstrate that just as there were few limits to which the Franklin County liquor ring would not go to insure good business for itself by buying off officers of the law and cramping the style of competitors, so there were few limits to which it would not go to try to buy off the jury."

But the editorialist concluded that in writing this "extraordinary" tale, the author should try "to probe deep beneath the surface in an effort to understand first causes in Franklin County." It should be remembered that the

> people of Franklin County were not any worse in the beginning than people in other counties. A large number of them were lured by the easy profits from illegal liquor, and some of them were shrewd enough to organize it on a businesslike basis. The results are spread in the records of these court actions. It is an extraordinary picture of how men, once having become tangled up with such ventures, are becoming deeper and deeper entangled.[95]

By the time the trial began in mid-May 1936, three of the twenty-three still-living defendants indicted in March had recently completed their sentences from their previous convictions and were free on bond, while ten others were still being held in Floyd County where they had been brought from other prisons to await trial. In addition, most of those who had pleaded nolo contendere changed their pleas to guilty on the new trial's first day and some even testified for the government, for a total of eighteen guilty, three not guilty, and two nolo contendere pleas. Thus the three pleading not guilty, Amos Rakes, a Patrick County merchant living near the junction of Floyd and Franklin counties; David A. Nicholson, of Franklin County; and Edgar T. Marshall, of Forrest Hill, Maryland, were actually tried for conspiracy to commit jury tampering.[96]

After a week of testimony the judge gave the case to the jurors late on Friday afternoon, 22 May 1936. Speaking for the prosecution Assistant District Attorney Frank Tavenner, Jr., averred, "There is no red herring that can be dragged across the trail of crime in this case which will destroy the scent of the trail." In an hour and twenty minutes, Tavenner summarized the testimony and emphasized to the jury that this case was so serious because "the courts would be powerless if juries are rendered impotent." He asked the jury to find the three defendants, Edgar Marshall, Amos Rakes, and David Nicholson, guilty.[97]

When the jury returned its verdict on Saturday afternoon, it had followed

Tavenner's recommendation for Amos Rakes and Edgar Marshall but had acquitted David A. Nicholson. Judge Paul sentenced Amos Rakes to a term in the federal penitentiary at Atlanta of eighteen months with a $2,000 fine and gave Edgar Marshall the same eighteen-month sentence in Atlanta, but a $500 fine.[98]

Before passing sentence on those to whom he gave probation, Judge Paul announced that he was going to do something "which you probably didn't anticipate," and immediately sixty-six-year-old Henry T. Abshire, former Franklin County deputy sheriff, and Willard Hodges broke into tears and cried throughout "the remainder of the proceedings." Judge Paul confessed that perhaps he was "making a mistake" by putting them on probation, but he realized that the sentences they had received the previous summer had been severe enough and to impose more time "for this affair . . . might carry beyond the point where you deserve." Nevertheless, he said, he did not want them to think that he took their activities "lightly." Even so, Paul continued, "It appears none of you originated this plan, and that you were merely making some contributions to the fund. I haven't been inclined to view that with great harshness, since no actual jury tampering had occurred." To emphasize how seriously he took the crime of attempted jury tampering, however, he told those placed on probation that he would not recommend that those among them who had been sentenced for the liquor conspiracy should get parole.[99]

In summing up his opinion of the verdict the *Roanoke Times* editorial writer stated that the verdicts would "be hailed with approval and satisfaction by all right-thinking citizens who realize the seriousness of the offense." The writer also commended the judge for showing "mercy" to the thirteen who received probation, saying the judge's action "speaks well for his insight into the motives which led these unfortunate men into the predicament in which they found themselves as a result of their rash attempt to tamper with the processes of the Federal court." The editorialist approved of Judge Paul's reminder of how seriously he viewed attempted jury tampering when the judge said he considered it "about the most vicious thing we can think of if it ever becomes prevalent."[100]

At the same time, the *Times* writer refused to censure Franklin County's population for this situation, remarking that Franklin had "in it as fine and law-abiding citizens as can be found in any sub-division of the Commonwealth." Indeed, "some of Roanoke's best and most substantial citizens came from there and the ties between this city and Franklin County are particularly close and cordial." The editorialist, in fact, expected Franklin County "to right the situation and stamp out the disgraceful evils that have attended the operations of the liquor ring which has made that county its headquarters."

In conclusion, the *Times* congratulated Judge Paul for the "dignity, firmness and fairness" that he demonstrated during the trial and noted that the outcome of the trial would "go far to vindicate the might of the law in the eyes of the public" as well as to maintain "that confidence in the integrity and efficacy of the system which is of paramount importance if our courts are to continue to be instruments of justice as well as of law."

The *Roanoke World-News* agreed with the *Times* in its assessment of the trial, the people of Franklin County, and the responsibility of Franklin's citizens to stamp out the illegal liquor evil. The *World-News*, however, cautioned the inhabitants of the commonwealth as a whole, observing that the trial's lessons "applie[d] to other sections of the State as well, and should be especially pondered by those 'respectable' citizens who by their purchases of illicit liquor made possible a gigantic whiskey ring that not only demoralized officers, but that sought to affect by bribery the administration of justice."[101]

Perhaps the climax of the liquor and the jury-tampering conspiracy trials came almost a year after the jury reached its verdict in the latter trial with the convictions of two West Virginia men for the murder of Roanoke County deputy sheriff Clarence E. ("Big Boy") Simmons and Franklin County deputy sheriff Thomas J. ("Jeff") Richards. On 17 July 1936, Simmons was driving late at night on the road from Rocky Mount to Roanoke (Route 220). He died when he was hit by shotgun pellets fired at him from an automobile that pulled in behind him (.45-caliber bullets were also found at the scene). Simmons's passenger, Deputy Sheriff Charles E. Boone, was not injured and miraculously survived the incident, which caused Simmons's car to run into a ditch. Boone had been slumped in his seat sleeping and invisible to the killers but awoke when he heard the gunfire in time to grab the steering wheel and prevent the car from hitting a telegraph pole. Only the presence of another car on the road nearby kept the killers from staying to finish the job.[102]

The first newspaper reports of the shooting noted similarities between the ambush of Simmons and another that had occurred almost two years earlier. In October 1934, Franklin deputy sheriff Jeff Richards was transporting a prisoner, James Smith, at night on the same road as Simmons. Both men were shot under almost the same circumstances. The editorial writer at the *Roanoke Times* called the killing of Simmons "a deliberate challenge to the forces of law and order in this section and as such it must be met."

> Roanoke County is a law-abiding county, peopled in the main by law-abiding folk. It will not countenance so flagrant a crime against the good name and fair reputation of the county. Wherever the trail leads, whether to this city or to a neighboring county, it must be followed with grim and inexorable persistence. Roanoke is not Chicago and Roanoke County is not Cook County, Illinois. The methods of gangland must not be allowed to gain a foothold here.
>
> Officer Simmons' murderers must be apprehended and punished.[103]

On 20 July, Paul and Hubbard Duling, of Enon and Summersville, West Virginia, respectively, were arrested at their homes and charged with Deputy Simmons's murder. Roanoke County commonwealth's attorney Edward H. Richardson stated that the two Dulings had been "positively identified" as having pulled in behind Simmons and fired at his car. Richardson also linked the "assassination of Simmons" with "the death of John Franklin Duling another brother of the accused" who had died in December 1933 when he leapt from his car after having been chased from Boones Mill by Franklin County deputies T. J. Richards and Edgar A. Beckett to the Roanoke County line where Roanoke County deputies Clarence E. Simmons and C. J. Bradley joined the pursuit and shot out Duling's rear tire. In the aftermath of Frank Duling's death, his brothers had been heard by witnesses to declare their intention to seek revenge on Simmons as he "was responsible—he killed Frank."[104]

Indeed at the Dulings' first trial in Roanoke in September 1936 for the murder of Simmons, Frank Duling's sister-in-law testified that the night after his death she had accompanied her sister, Frank's wife, and three of Duling's brothers, Earl, Paul, and Hubbard, to Roanoke to identify Frank's body. At the same time the Dulings decided to seek Simmons and spent some time traveling the roads around Roanoke looking for him. Interestingly enough, they stopped at one point to ask a group of men talking to some law officers if any of them were Simmons, "adding that they 'were looking for [the] —— —— —— who killed their brother.' " They were unsuccessful that night in their search. Earl Duling, in fact, only lived two months longer than Frank, dying in a shootout with police near Beckley, West Virginia, in February 1934, during a liquor search.[105]

During the trial, Hubbard and Paul Duling's lawyers sought to show that the brothers were not in the Franklin-Roanoke area when the Simmons slaying took place but in fact were at home. Three relatives and ten friends testified that both Dulings were engaged in their usual activities at home and indeed one witness stated that he helped Hubbard, who ran a beer parlor and tourist camp, work a crossword puzzle between 10:00 and 11:00 P.M. on the night of the shooting. He was positive of the date because he remembered he could not drink that night as he planned to take a physical examination the next day at the Charleston Du Pont plant.[106]

The prosecution attempted to prove that Hubbard and Paul Duling did indeed kill Deputy Simmons and therefore called on witnesses who swore that they saw the Dulings sitting in their automobile outside of Uncle Tom's Barbecue, about a mile south of Roanoke, from 9:30 P.M. until 2:45 A.M. when Simmons drove by and the Dulings pulled out to follow him.[107] Despite all of the testimony, however, the first jury could not reach a verdict so it was dismissed and the Dulings were tried again in December 1936.

At the second trial, the lawyers had a difficult time impaneling a jury as many of the 300 prospective jurors had already formed an opinion about the case or objected to capital punishment. Finally, however, a jury was chosen. After listening to similar testimony as that given in the first trial (it was again brought out that Hubbard Duling had served time in the federal prison in Atlanta for "violation of the national prohibition law" and had transported liquor from Virginia to West Virginia), this second jury brought back a verdict of guilty of murder in the first degree. The jurors, however, imposed the least possible sentence for the crime, twenty years apiece in the state penitentiary.[108]

The *Roanoke Times* editorialist found the verdict puzzling and not to his inclination. It "savors too much of a compromise to be altogether to our liking."

Paul and Hubbard Duling in court just before hearing verdict. (Dorothy Cundiff, *Franklin County Yesterday & Today* [*1979*], 99. Reprinted with permission.)

Either the Dulings were guilty, as charged, or they were innocent men unjustly accused. If the former, they richly deserved the electric chair; if the latter, they were entitled to be set free. Loath as we are to find fault with the verdict of the jury, we cannot see it any other way.

Twenty years' imprisonment is insufficient punishment for men who would drive more than a hundred miles into another State to waylay and murder a county officer. On the other hand, it is a harsh and unjust sentence for men who had nothing whatever to do with the crime. However, it was the jury's responsibility and we have not the least doubt that they discharged their task to the very best of their ability and with an honest effort to serve the ends of justice.[109]

Contrary to the prosecution strategy used in Roanoke at the trial for Simmons's murder, Franklin County Commonwealth's Attorney Charles Carter Lee, at the first trial in February 1937 for T. J. Richards's killing, called a ballistics expert from the Federal Bureau of Investigation in Washington, D.C. He testified the shells that were used to kill Franklin County deputy sheriff Richards and his prisoner, James Smith, were fired from the same shotgun as that introduced in evidence as having belonged to the Dulings. Presiding judge Abram H. Hopkins sent for his own ballistics expert, chief of the bureau of identification of the Washington, D.C., metropolitan police, who came to the same conclusion. Nevertheless, the first jury (drawn from Franklin residents) also failed to agree on a verdict (it being "reliably" reported that the jury divided seven to five for conviction) and had to be dismissed.

Again the *Roanoke Times* editorialist expressed his disappointment at the outcome and noted:

The slaying of Simmons occurred under circumstances similar to those which attended the killing of Deputy Richards. Both officers were ambushed and killed on the highway. Both were alleged to have been suspected by the Dulings of killing two other brothers formerly engaged in illicit transportation of liquor. As in the Simmons case, the evidence against the defendants in the trial which ended at Rocky Mount yesterday was circumstantial.[110]

A new trial was set for April 1937 but did not take place because neither side could agree on a jury. The judge ordered a mistrial after more than two hundred twenty-five veniremen had been interviewed and the defense in a surprise move asked for that mistrial. When the jury had failed to agree in February Commonwealth's Attorney Lee had suggested a change of venue to which the defense counsel "objected strenuously."[111] At the final trial in May the jury came from Halifax County. After an eight-day trial the jury returned a verdict of guilty of first degree murder in the case of Richards and Smith and set the Dulings' punishment at ninety-nine years each in the state penitentiary.[112]

Once again the *Roanoke Times* editorialist surveyed the outcome of the trial and once again could not feel complete satisfaction. He believed that despite Hubbard Duling's statement of innocence to the contrary "public opinion will support the jury's conclusion and deem it a right and just verdict." He concluded that the ninety-nine-year sentences were "tantamount" to life sentences.

The crimes of which they have been convicted were among the most atrocious in this section of the State and while the evidence against them was purely circumstantial, it was so strong and conclusive as to leave no doubt of their guilt in the minds of the jurors.

Separately convicted of slaying two deputy sheriffs in neighboring counties, there is scant likelihood that any future Governor of Virginia will restore their freedom. Barring the improbable event of their escape, the Dulings will spend the rest of their days on earth behind prison bars.

Richards and Simmons have been avenged. The law has struck back at their slayers and justice has overtaken them. But they have received a break, nevertheless. They are very lucky men to have escaped the electric chair.[113]

The moonshiners and their way of life quickly became the subjects of study by historians. During the Great Depression, the Virginia Writers' Project of the federal Works Progress Administration paid local people to interview former slaves, businessmen, former Confederate soldiers, and others as part of an oral history program. Essie W. Smith, daughter of slain revenue agent Zackfield B. Wade, conducted interviews in Franklin County. Among those interviewees was a former bootlegger with whom Smith spoke in May 1939. "After much conversation and some judicious insinuations he finally confessed,"

I once did a little bootlegging. Most of the fine houses, and all of the comforts you find in the mountains come from selling brandy or whiskey on the side. Mountaineers don't figure like other people. They think if they have surplus apples and there is no market for them, and they would waste on the ground, it is all right to make them up into brandy for which there is always a ready sale and a good price. Money products around here are very scarce, and sometimes tobacco, the only money crop, barely pays the fertilizer bills, and there are some things, like taxes, which demand ready cash. When you haven't a single cent to meet these necessities it is a temptation to exercise a profession which demands only a little energy and secrecy. It's the same with corn. Sometimes this brings such a small price it is not worth hauling it to market, but made up into whiskey there is always a good margin of profit, for it is popular and salable at all times without any advertizing. Everybody buys it, and there is no penalty attached to drinking it, which is certainly far worse than making it.

The bootlegger explained that the mountaineers did not make the laws and instead grew up on ideas that originated with the formation of the United States. "A man who lives where water and air are both free has different ideas of freedom. He thinks he can use his corn and his apples in ways that are most profitable to himself, and that it is nobody's business except his own." He continued,

Of course all the bootleggers get caught eventually. Revenue officers cut up a few stills and send a few men to the penitentiary every year. They have to do this to keep their jobs. The men they send up are always far better than they, themselves, for I never knew a Revenue officer who did not drink too much to keep any other job. But after so many men got caught in that liquor conspiracy trial in this county, and I missed being arrested, I promised my wife I would never make another drop as long as I lived. I never did like the stuff anyhow. The smell of whiskey always made me sick.[114]

The bootlegger discussed some of his World War I service. "Yes, I was in France. You see I can serve my country even if I have been accused of not obeying some of her laws." In eighteen months, he "participated in three awful battles, the Argonne, San Mihiel, and the Meuse." The experience cured him of any liking of war: "I never want to see another war, or have my boy see one. There is no good side to fighting. I even hate to hear a band play." In concluding his remarks, the bootlegger expressed his hope that his son would grow up "to be a Christian, a Democrat and able to earn his living in peaceable pursuits, in a free country."

Sometimes when I go to sleep in my comfortable bed, and recall the days and nights in mud and trenches, I wonder if I can be the same man, and when I hear a knock at the door and know it is no one coming to arrest me I experience such waves of thankfulness that I almost shout. A good home, a good farm, a fine boy, plenty of feed in the barn, and things growing in profusion all around me, and above all a handsome wife—could any man ask for more?[115]

TWENTY

The World Wars

The First World War began in Europe on 28 June 1914 when Archduke Francis Ferdinand, crown prince of Austria, was assassinated in Serbia, and Austria-Hungary declared war on Serbia five days later. A month afterward Austria-Hungary's ally Germany declared war on Russia and France, soon followed by Austria-Hungary's war declaration against Russia as well. The United States government stated its intention to remain neutral. But German U-boat attacks against both American shipping and Americans on Allied ships, especially the sinking of the *Lusitania* on 7 May 1916, increased American demands for war. President Woodrow Wilson, however, did not want to enter a war and tried with every means at his disposal to avoid it. Finally, at the end of January 1917 Germany announced that it would begin unrestricted submarine warfare on 1 February so that any ship, whether neutral or not, would be sunk without warning, and then immediately proceeded to make its threat a reality. On 2 April 1917 President Wilson asked Congress to declare war on Germany, which the Senate did on 4 April, followed by the House two days later.[1]

Congress passed the Selective Service Act on 18 May authorizing the registration and drafting of men between the ages of twenty-one and thirty. Three weeks later on 5 June America's young men registered for the draft. For the entire war Franklin County sent 493 white and 98 black soldiers to the military.[2] Many Franklin soldiers did not wait to be drafted but instead volunteered, including "every boy in service from Rocky Mount." Two of the county men who enlisted, Buford Angle and Greenwood Garrett, epitomized "real patriotism"—Angle was underweight and Garrett underage. In spite of being turned down several times, both men eventually were accepted by the military and sent to France, fought and were wounded in battle, "but after the war reached home safe and sound."[3]

On 21 September 1917, the women and other citizens of Rocky Mount held a patriotic celebration for the county's draftees who were scheduled to leave that day or on 1 October for military camp. A large number of residents attended from throughout the county to hear patriotic speeches and the Roanoke Machine

Works band play "patriotic airs." The Jubal Early Chapter of the United Daughters of the Confederacy sponsored a second send-off featuring "bountiful refreshments," a piano solo and a vocal solo by Miss Myrtle Shoaf as well as another vocal solo by Miss Lulie Simms, and patriotic songs by a choir.[4]

Elliot B. McGuffin, of Callaway, the first Franklin County man accepted by the local draft board, led the initial group of enlistees when they left for camp on 22 September. He was also one of nineteen men the War Department chose from Camp Lee to attend the Quartermasters' Officers' Training School at Jacksonville, Florida, and he received the first commission by a man drafted in Franklin. B. C. Harrison led the second group of Franklin men who left for camp on 1 October 1917. Sent to France, he was wounded in battle, but arrived safely home after the war. The third contingent left under the command of William E. Jefferson, of Penhook, and was described as being "in good spirits at the prospects of training to fight the 'Fritzies.' " J. Bradie Allman, later a member of the House of Delegates and Rocky Mount mayor, led the fourth group of Franklin County draftees to camp. He, too, reached France and participated "in the fight."[5]

Among the few Franklin servicemen who died during the conflict, George Edgar Ramsey died at Camp Lee and was eventually buried at Henry. Several others returned home and later died of war-related wounds: Keva Campbell, John Jameson, George Laprade, Willie McBride, and L. O. Quarles.[6]

Those who received combat heroism awards included Private Charles N. Parcell, whose "extraordinary heroism in action near Nantillois, France, October 5, 1918" earned him the United States Distinguished Service Cross. While under heavy enemy fire, he succeeded in carrying messages from the platoon commander to squad leaders. The citation noted that "although twice wounded in the face by shrapnel, he continued his duties until ordered to the dressing station."[7] A newspaper account later related the circumstances under which Parcell received the Distinguished Service Cross along with the French croix de guerre. During the Battle of the Meuse-Argonne, "the final major battle of the war,"

Charles N. Parcell, Franklin County's most decorated soldier of World War I. (Sue Parcell Bindewald, Rocky Mount, Va.)

Parcell's Company D, 317th Infantry, 80th Division, came under heavy enemy machine-gun and shell fire while awaiting orders to advance. The "din of battle was so intense" that the officers realized their orders could not be heard. When plans to relay those orders to each corporal and from him to the men developed a hitch, "Parcell arose to the emergency. In full view of the Germans he ran down the line of the company and communicated the orders to each corporal. Six machine gun nests peppered diligently at Parcell, but he was not hit. He said the bullets were kicking up tufts of dirt all around him, and they sounded like a drove of bees around his head."[8]

Soon thereafter, his platoon became separated from its kitchens. Serving as the platoon's dispatch runner, "Parcell was sent over a desolate hill to look for the 'chow' wagons," but failed to find them. He did, however, find two men in U.S. uniforms, one of the 315th and the other of the 319th infantries, whom he queried about the location of the kitchens. As the men spoke with suspicious accents, Parcell "marched them to his commanding officer, who, incidentally, was the son of Secretary of the Treasury Carter Glass" (Captain Powell Glass). For this action, he received the Italian croix de guerre. The French Medaille Militaire was presented to him "for carrying dispatches on foot under shell and machine gun fire." Parcell received the shrapnel wounds in his face when a shell burst close by and a fragment lodged immediately under his right eye. Discharged from service in March 1919, Parcell returned home but soon entered the Marine Hospital at Wyman Park, Maryland, for treatment of an infected bone near his eye and complications caused by inhaling chlorine gas.[9] When his treatment was completed, Parcell returned to his farm in Franklin and later published a series of articles about his war experiences in the *Franklin County News*.[10]

Private Isaac F. Ingram also received the Distinguished Service Cross for his "extraordinary heroism in action near Samogneux, France, October 15th, 1918." Alone, he advanced using his automatic rifle to silence a hostile machine gun "whose fire was holding up the line." Ingram and Parcell were 2 of 156 Virginians to receive the Distinguished Service Cross during World War I.[11]

Posey Lee Webb won the croix de guerre for his heroic conduct at the Battle of Belleau Wood, France. "He participated in battle of Verdun Sector, wounded in breast at Belleau Woods, returned to his command, and was wounded in ankle by machine gun at the battle of Soissons." He was 1 of 217 Virginians so honored.

Two other Franklin County men were cited by their division commanders "for gallantry in action and especially meritorious services": Clarence Lumsden, of Boones Mill, and Alonzo R. Mathews, of Penhook. They were 2 of the 142 Virginians thus honored.

Because Franklin County is located so far from the coast it was not exposed to German submarine activity and other war threats that the Atlantic coastal areas and big cities experienced. Nevertheless, "the county suffered greatly in having to give up men for service; the homes were saddened by the absence of loved ones." At public meetings the men in service were especially missed. County families practiced "self-denial and sacrifice." Many homemakers resolved to buy no veal, to serve meat at only one meal per day, and to reduce sugar consumption. All actively supported "Hooverizing"—Herbert C. Hoover's program to control food production and distribution "so that armies and civilians" in Europe "might be adequately fed." Hoover persuaded the nation "to cut down waste and reduce consumption" with voluntary wheatless Mondays, meatless Tuesdays, and so forth, and, as a result, in 1918 the United States exported three times "the normal amounts of breadstuffs, meats, and sugar."[12]

One of the items shipped to Europe during the war was canned tomatoes from Franklin County. In a letter in the *Franklin Chronicle* from W. F. Mills to his wife, Mills stated "that he had eaten a can of tomatoes packed by Mr. Jack Garst of Boone Mill, Va," as had Edmund Roberts, of Rocky Mount. Gilbert Finke, of Salem, writing to his parents about Jack Garst's tomatoes that he had eaten, enclosed the proof—the label from the can, which "showed a beautiful picture of the Magodee Valley above Boone Mill, skirted by the Blue Ridge Mountains." Another soldier, W. Carey Coleman, though, wrote home that while he was glad the wheat crop was good, he certainly "would like to have one of [his mother's] good hot biscuits now. I know exactly how good it would go." Private Carroll T. Richards wrote his mother that he found nearly the same crops in France as they had at home. "We get plenty to eat. Have all kinds of vegetables, fish, beef, all kinds of desserts. It is cooked good."[13]

Another war-related activity that took place on the home front was the sale of Liberty bonds and war savings stamps. Nathaniel P. Angle served as county chairman of all of the men's Liberty bonds sales drives. Mrs. W. C. Menefee led the women in the second, third, and fourth bond drives, while Miss Ann Joplin chaired the Victory loan drive. In the third Liberty loan campaign the county exceeded its quota by $40,700.[14] For the entire Liberty bond campaign, the committees sold $750,000 worth of bonds, as well as $70,000 in war savings stamps.[15]

One way of gaining the support of the people for the war in the days before widespread radio use and before television was to send out speakers to rally the citizens. These "four-minute men" traversed the country and "let loose a barrage of oratory at movie houses and public gatherings."[16] Franklin County's "four-minute men" included Judges Edward Watts Saunders and John P. Lee, as well as Commonwealth's Attorney A. H. Hopkins.[17]

Franklin's citizens also supported the war by daily prayers for the soldiers and by attending special church services in honor of "our boys." During the war, the Bald Knob Furniture Company sounded the factory's whistle every day at noon as a signal for its hearers to stop their activities and pray for the soldiers. "A touching thing happened one day when a little girl, playing in her own front yard with a little friend, heard the whistle, and said to her little friend, 'Let us pray.' Down on their knees in front of the steps they went and with bowed heads and closed eyes they said: 'God bless our soldier men.' Such was the loyalty of even a little three-year-old child."[18]

County residents also established a local chapter of the American Red Cross. Twenty members organized a Red Cross first aid class in Rocky Mount in November 1916 with Dr. G. W. Hooker as instructor and Mrs. George Greer as president. During 1917 the group raised funds for the Red Cross and also completed the first aid course. On 22 October 1917, a meeting of people interested in Red Cross work convened at the home of Judge and Mrs. E. W. Saunders, followed about two weeks later by the formal organization of the Franklin County Red Cross Chapter.[19]

Mesdames J. C. Shearer, C. A. Johnson, and H. D. Dillard became chairwomen of the tobacco market solicitors, which was the main source for fund-raising. "Often the ladies were at the warehouses (Rocky Mount then had three warehouses) by 4 A. M. begging tobacco from the farmers as they unloaded. This tobacco was graded and sold for the Red Cross. The farmers were liberal in their contributions."[20]

One of the better-known activities of the Red Cross on the local level was the encouragement of knitting for the soldiers and sewing hospital gowns and related items. At war's end Franklin's needlewomen had produced 1,517 knitted and 1,112 sewn garments.[21]

In writing about Red Cross activities for the Virginia War History Commission, Mrs. W. C. Menefee noted that it would be impossible to list all Franklin County residents who "did their bit," but she did name some of those "in the rural districts who superintended and aided in every way possible to carry on the Red Cross work" including Dr. and Mrs. Samuel Guerrant. Misses Ette Davis, a teacher at Saint Peter's, and Ora Harrison, a teacher at Endicott, came in for special mention "for the way they worked in establishing a friendly feeling toward the Red Cross among the mountain people, many of whom were prejudiced against Red Cross work," a sentiment later shared by others after the Red Cross in World War II charged soldiers for its canteen operations, which were provided free by other agencies.[22]

Three other groups that aided Franklin County's war effort were the Jubal Early Chapter of the United Daughters of the Confederacy, the Odd Fellows, and the Masons. Both the Odd Fellows and the Masons lent their meeting halls free of charge as sites for entertaining the departing troops, and the Odd Fellows also allowed their hall to be used for Red Cross workroom activities. The Jubal Early Chapter of the UDC joined with the Red Cross to engage in other war work.[23]

When the final results were tallied at war's end, Franklin's Red Cross workers had raised $3,639.23 for materials to be made up for the soldiers; $5,000 in the war fund drive; approximately $500 in canteen contributions; and had produced 1,112 sewn garments and 1,517 knitted items, as well as 1,060 articles contributed to a linen shower.

After the armistice ending the war was signed on 11 November 1918, Washington asked for the names of those who had worked a certain number of hours per day for the Red Cross in order to give them badges of honor. Franklin's women decided not to single out anyone for fear of overlooking others who had made equal contributions. "Those who had done possibly more than others said: 'We do not want any distinction of honor for what we have done. It was done willingly and cheerfully, and that is all the praise that we want. If we were mentioned especially, some who deserve as much mention as we might be overlooked.' "

Walter L. Hopkins, a charter member of the General John J. Pershing Post No. 1 of the American Legion, Washington, D.C., gathered a group of Franklin County World War I veterans in March 1919 and from that meeting came Franklin's veterans' association, organized 7 April 1919. In June the members voted to unite with the national American Legion and on 1 July 1919, Franklin County's American Legion Post No. 6 was chartered as what was probably the first American Legion Post in Virginia and perhaps the second post in the United States. By October 1919 more than fifty men belonged to the post.[24]

In July 1920 Mrs. Walter L. Hopkins organized the Woman's Auxiliary of the Franklin County American Legion Post No. 6. She also served as the first president, along with Miss Ann Joplin as first vice-president.[25]

A year after the armistice on 15 November 1919 the United Daughters of the Confederacy and the Franklin Post of the American Legion held a grand reunion at the courthouse for Confederate and World War I veterans with a speech by W. L. Hopkins, a luncheon sponsored by the UDC at the Franklin warehouse, and a parade featuring the Norfolk and Western Band from Roanoke. Others who participated in the parade included the Confederate and World War I veterans, schoolchildren, Daughters of the Confederacy, and members of the Red Cross. State Senator Beverly A. Davis, Sr., and Congressman Edward Watts Saunders also addressed the gathering. The affair "was a great success and was enjoyed by all."[26]

Unfortunately for the United States and the world, "the war to end all wars" did not guarantee peace. The Treaty of Versailles that the Germans signed on 29 June 1919 left Germany with a huge war debt and stripped it of its colonies and military machine. Thus Germany found itself in a financially unstable state, unable to defend itself from outside aggression.[27] These conditions led to the rise of Adolf Hitler and the Nazi party, who promised to rearm Germany and make it financially strong once again.

As the 1930s came to an end, it became increasingly evident that the world was moving toward war once more. Beginning in 1936, three years after he took power, Adolf Hitler began to take back the territory he believed belonged historically to Germany. Earlier in the decade, Japan had invaded Manchuria in 1931, igniting the Second Sino-Japanese War. Finally, on 1 September 1939 the Wehrmacht marched into Poland and World War II began. It was not until 7 December 1941, however, when the Japanese staged a surprise morning raid against the United States Navy at Pearl Harbor, Hawaii, that the United States officially entered the war. Before 7 December 1941, the United States had unofficially joined the war by supplying Great Britain and the other allies with

Armistice Day parade in downtown Rocky Mount. (Blue Ridge Institute, Ferrum, Va.)

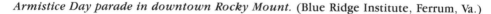

desperately needed ships and supplies, under the Lend-Lease program of 11 March 1941. Six months before the Lend-Lease program was initiated, Congress passed the Selective Service and Training Act of 1940. With the reinstitution of the draft and the U.S. entry into World War II a year later, life in Franklin (as in the country as a whole) changed dramatically. Because so many of its sons entered military service, job opportunities that had not previously existed opened for women. As the country moved further into a war economy, the United States embarked on drives to sell war bonds and stamps and to collect scrap metal, rubber, and other desperately needed materials. In addition, rationing of many of the necessities as well as the luxuries of life affected everyone on the home front.

When the national registration was held on 16 October 1940, twenty-one-year-old Willard Jess Underwood, of Callaway, was one of those throughout the nation who drew the number 158, and on 29 October when Secretary of War Henry L. Stimson drew numbers to initiate the draft he chose the number 158 first.[28] Thus Underwood became the first man in Franklin County called for the national draft.[29] By 8 November the county had been notified that the first draftees were to report to one of the two induction centers in Virginia (Roanoke or Richmond). The first draft call, which was to be held on 26 November, consisted of 122 Virginians with one from Franklin—Gerald Kendrick, aged twenty-one, of Rocky Mount—who had passed his physical.[30]

On 22 November, however, the *Franklin News-Post* reported that "peace-time history was made in Franklin County [that] week," when twenty-six-year-old John Henry Kirby, a black man, received "the honor of being the first volunteer to represent the county among those who report to Roanoke headquarters next Tuesday, November 26." A change in the status of qualification had removed Gerald Kendrick from being the first volunteer to go.[31] The day after Kirby reported to Roanoke, he arrived at Fort Meade, Maryland, for a year's training, the first of twenty-five volunteers to be accepted. On Tuesday morning, 26 November, the members of the draft board and a number of "interested persons" gave Kirby "a final 'good luck' sendoff." Upon leaving, Kirby told the draft board, "The president called for us and I would rather be a volunteer and go right away than to wait and be drafted later on." The newspaper found that Kirby "seemed to be in the highest spirits in anticipation of his year's training in camp."[32]

Readers of the *Franklin News-Post* were no doubt pleased to learn on 18 April 1941 that they were living in the Heart of Virginia. Correspondence reaching the local draft board that week concerned a man from Hardy who had registered in absentia for the selective service. In giving his address "the communication to the local board [gave] the address . . . as 'Heart of Virginia' and the postoffice department delivered the card to Rocky Mount without delay."[33]

By the first of May 1942, 1,856 Franklin County men had registered for the draft. "Many of them were bent and gray and came within the prescribed maximum age limit by only a few days or weeks. Others were fat and bald and declared they could fight as good as anyone . . . for a few minutes. Others carried the military carriage they had learned in the last World War, and declared they were ready and willing. But all were of the same mind . . . to do their best for their country." Among those who had registered were the judge of the circuit court, county officials, ministers, lawyers, doctors, bankers, farmers, and two members of the county draft board, as well as a factory worker, a common laborer, and a WPA worker.[34]

In July 1942, Mary Elizabeth Carroll, daughter of Mr. and Mrs. R. S. Carroll, of Rocky Mount, "ha[d] the distinction of being the first Franklin county girl to be chosen as a candidate for the officer personnel of the Women's Auxiliary Army Corps which ha[d] recently been organized." She had applied and taken the tests in Roanoke, which she passed; she then passed the physical examination at Camp Lee, and attended the final interviews at WAACs (later the Women's Army Corps) headquarters in Baltimore. After being accepted, Carroll went to Richmond to be sworn in and then to Fort Des Moines, Iowa, on 14 September to begin training. She was an honor graduate of Rocky Mount High School and of Farmville State Teachers College (now Longwood College) and had taught the previous year at Ferrum High School.[35] By January 1943, she was in Miami, Florida. Her sister, L. Virginia Carroll, had trained for the Women Accepted for Voluntary Emergency Service (WAVEs) at Smith College and was assigned to active duty in the United States Naval Reserve in January 1943. She had taught in the Petersburg and Princess Anne County schools before her enlistment.[36]

The second woman to join the WAACs was Doris Powell, daughter of Mr. and Mrs. Henry L. Powell, and granddaughter of Mr. and Mrs. Allen Powell, of Rocky Mount. She received her appointment from the Richmond office on 8 September 1942 and left soon thereafter for Fort Des Moines for her basic training. Powell was twenty-one years old, had graduated from Rocky Mount High School, and at the time of her appointment was working as a stenographer for Krogers in Roanoke.[37]

The first black woman from Franklin County mentioned in the *News-Post* as being in the WAACs was Nannie Victoria Smith, daughter of Lee Smith, of Rocky

Opal James (below left) *and H. Doretha Mack* (below right), *U.S. Army Nurse Corps. (Service Record Book of Men and Women of Rocky Mount, Va., and Community* [N.p.: V.F.W. Post No. 6002, n.d.].)

Mount, who had also completed her basic training at Fort Des Moines. Two of her brothers were in the army as well: Sergeant M. G. Smith and Private Curtis Williams Smith of the field artillery. Nannie Smith had been an employee of Midway Cleaners and had graduated from the County Training School before entering service.[38]

One unanticipated question that had confronted the local draft board by April 1941 was whether local men who had been convicted of making or transporting bootleg whiskey were to be disqualified from military service. The Richmond Selective Service Office had ruled that such men had to be classified as 4-F (in this case morally unfit). Of 100 men who had been classified 4-F in Franklin to that date, 25 had been convicted of felony moonshining. The ruling from Richmond stated that if men so classified were sent for induction anyway, they would be immediately rejected and others (more acceptable) would have to be sent to replace them.[39] Not surprisingly, "the blanket prohibition had been widely objected to in Virginia, particularly in the southwestern part of the state where old convictions for distilling in the prohibition period forced selective service boards to put many otherwise desirable men in class 4-F."[40] On 18 April 1941, General George C. Marshall, U.S. Army chief of staff, made a new ruling regarding felony convictions for moonshining in prohibition days that allowed those twenty-five Franklin men to be automatically reclassified as 1-A from 4-F. Because of the widespread objection to the felony ruling Marshall decided that with only one conviction a man was still eligible for military service, but if he had more than one felony conviction, had committed a "heinous" crime, was on parole or probation, or was under a suspended sentence he could not serve his country.[41]

In addition to moonshine convictions, the local draft board had to confront another problem. By the beginning of June more than one hundred Franklin County men had been rejected for military service because of illiteracy. The U.S. government was considering solving this problem by making the men go to night school. While the war was evolving into a machine war so that men with less than a fourth-grade education would not be of much use, "yet it is believed by some here," said the *News-Post*,

> that through the exercise of sharp wits and a cunning which could be well utilized, many of the non-intelligent group are possibly side-stepping military training. It is reported that one youth of Franklin county was asked by examiners how far he had gone in school [and replied], "Guess I've gone about two miles," or words to that effect.
>
> "Sometimes it takes smart people to be dumb," said one local citizen whose boy [was] already in the armed services.[42]

At the end of July the War Department announced that henceforth the injunction against men who did not have a fourth-grade education would be lifted and those "who c[ould] understand simple orders in English and who possess[ed] the ability to absorb military training rapidly" would be eligible for the draft. Ten percent of Virginia's potential inductees fell into this category, and 6 percent of them had signed with an *X*. At that time Virginia had no plans to institute remedial courses to prepare the undereducated for military service. Virginia's attitude may have resulted from the experience of neighboring North Carolina where twenty-three classes had to be "abandoned" as "the rejected candidates were 'a little too wise to go to [a] school which will prepare them to get into the army.' " A North Carolina educational official, J. E. Miller, added that "the illiterate youth who is eager to learn that he might serve his country is an unusual case."[43]

In time many Franklin County families would have several sons or sons and daughters in service. The first such family reported was that of L. G. Peters, of Wirtz, who had three sons in service by 12 March 1942.[44] Among Franklin County families with several sons in service by April 1942 was the Edward Turner family with three sons in the U.S. Army. Two other sons ages ten and two and a daughter were not yet serving.[45] In addition, Mrs. Marion Marshall, of Salem, formerly of Rocky Mount, was a six-star mother with three sons in the army, two in the Marines, and a son-in-law in the Army Air Force, all in service by March 1943.[46] By May 1943, Mr. and Mrs. W. T. Newman, of Wirtz, had a son, four grandsons, and sixteen nephews in service all over the world.[47] By December 1944, one Franklin County family had everybody in service except the wife and daughter; the father and three sons were in the navy.[48] Another family, the Wrights, lost three of seven sons, two in World War I and one in World War II.[49] Still another family had five sons in service by March 1945 and a sixth had fought in the First World War.[50]

In October 1941, Franklin County suffered its first war-related loss of life when Robert James Moore, son of Mr. and Mrs. Jesse Moore, of Penhook, died of pneumonia while undergoing basic training at Fort Bragg, North Carolina.[51] An editorial noted that "his honor [wa]s as great as if he had died on the field of battle for his country. He passed away in his line of duty, a soldier to the last."[52] The first man to be reported missing in action was Fireman First Class Stewart Herbert Stanley, the son of Mr. and Mrs. W. L. Stanley, of Ferrum. His family received word in early September, and the *News-Post* published the story on 11 September 1942, the day Stanley's ship "was struck from the Navy Register." He had been serving on the USS *Ingraham*, of the Atlantic Fleet, doing convoy escort duty between the United States, Iceland, and the United Kingdom for vessels carrying desperately needed supplies to the Allies "to stem Hitler's advance and to take the offensive." German U-boats constituted a constant threat, but the *Ingraham* went down in a fog off the coast of Nova Scotia on 22 August when it collided with the tanker *Chemung* while investigating a collision between the USS *Buck* and a merchant ship. Depth charges on the stern exploded, the *Ingraham* sank almost immediately, and all but eleven of the ship's crewmen died.[53] Soon after the fate of the *Ingraham* was reported on radio, one of Stanley's sisters called her parents from Panama, but "the phone conversation was censored so strictly that no mention was permitted of the name of the vessel, any circumstances known of the incident, or the boy's name other than his first name."[54]

The first Franklin County man to be killed in action was Ensign Frank E. Boone, who also died in August 1942, when the Japanese sank the cruiser USS *Quincy* during the battle for Guadalcanal.[55] The *Quincy* had sailed for the Pacific in July 1942. While preparing for the invasion of Guadalcanal the ship had destroyed some Japanese installations and an oil depot during the shelling of Lunga Point. After supporting the Marines who landed on 7 August, the *Quincy* took up patrol duties between Florida and Savo islands; early on 9 August the cruiser was sunk by heavy Japanese bombardment with all of her guns out of commission.[56]

Apparently Franklin's only black soldier known to have died in action in World

War II was Herbert Nash Lumpkins, the son of Mr. and Mrs. Obe Lumpkins, of Rocky Mount. He was killed at Normandy on 15 June 1944. Three other black soldiers, Cabell Muse, Rufus Taylor, and Webster Wade, also died in service.[57]

One of the shortages caused by the war was in medical service to county citizens. In June 1942 the county's physicians and dentists met with the Medical Officers Recruiting Board in Martinsville about the county's medical needs. President Roosevelt had established the Procurement and Assignment Service to balance civilian and military medical needs. There were six doctors in Franklin, four in Rocky Mount, one in Ferrum, and one in Boones Mill, as well as three dentists who practiced in Rocky Mount. Penhook's dentist had already left for military service,[58] and the Moneta, Bedford County, physician who had served a large area of Franklin was also in the military. But despite the county's wish that no more doctors would be drafted,[59] two of Rocky Mount's doctors entered the service in August 1942.[60] At the same time, Boones Mill's doctor died, but by 4 September Dr. Hugh H. Trout, chairman of the Medical Procurement and Assignment Service of Virginia, had found a replacement to work part-time in Boones Mill.[61] In August 1945 Major E. C. Jamison, U.S. Army Medical Corps, returned home to resume private practice. Dr. W. H. Cobbs had died unexpectedly and the remaining physicians in Franklin were so overworked that the county petitioned the military to release Dr. Jamison.[62]

At the end of June 1942 Franklin's delegate to the Virginia General Assembly, Virgil H. Goode, enlisted in the army and became the county's first elected official to join the armed forces. The Selective Service Act had exempted state legislators during their terms of office, as well as judges of circuit courts, the only two public officers so designated. Goode had "served two terms in the State legislature where his pleasing personality, unusual energy and proven ability in leadership ha[d] made him stand well with his colleagues." Taking a leading role in the sales of U.S. savings bonds, Goode was a member of the Radford Regional

Frank E. Boone, first combat casualty from Franklin County (below left) *and Herbert Nash Lumpkins, only known black casualty* (below right). *(Service Record Book of Men and Women of Rocky Mount, Va., and Community* [N.p.: V.F.W. Post No. 6002, n.d.].)

Defense and Franklin County Defense councils, as well as government appeal agent for Franklin under the Selective Service Act.[63]

Because Goode was initially assigned to duty at Camp Lee near Petersburg, he was able to attend the General Assembly sessions during the day while returning to the post at night. Eventually, however, his duties at Camp Lee became so time-consuming that he had to give up going into Richmond for the assembly. Thus in March 1944, the *News-Post* announced that Lieutenant Goode planned to turn over his pay and expenses to the county because he had not been able to attend all of the recent assembly sessions, the amount probably to be around $650.[64]

Since he was no longer able to serve as a legislator, Goode in May designated various organizations to receive his $655 salary and benefits from his assembly membership, including the Franklin County branch of the American Red Cross, Franklin Post No. 6 of the American Legion, the United Service Organizations, the Tuberculosis Association, the Virginia Cancer Foundation, local Lions, Men's, Woman's, and Ruritan clubs, county Boy and Girl Scout troops, and the school superintendent, Harold W. Ramsey, to buy flags for schools that did not have them. Goode had decided he wanted the county to have the use of his assembly pay rather than letting it go back into the state treasury or keeping it for personal use.[65]

In November 1942 the State Bar appointed Charles Carter Lee to be chairman of the Franklin County War Service Committee of the State Bar. The committee was intended to help men in service and their dependents, as well as to aid in the work of the Selective Service boards, Civilian Defense councils, local rationing boards, war bond and stamp committees, law officers of military posts, and other war service agencies.[66]

That same month the *News-Post* announced that the village of Henry had 18 percent of its population of 116 in the service: 21 men. If every area gave 18 percent of its population to the armed forces there would have been about 23,400,000 in service and from Franklin more than 4,500 instead of the 750 men and women who were then serving in the military.[67] By the middle of January 1943 the number had risen to more than 1,000.[68] In October 1943, 1,269 men had been drafted from Franklin: 1,100 white and 19 black; and several hundred had enlisted.[69] By the end of the war a total of 2,309 Franklin County men and women had served in the armed forces.[70]

After the declaration of war on Japan in December 1941, Commissioner of the Revenue Cam B. Perdue was named coordinator of Franklin County's Volunteer Emergency Service. A nine-member county emergency defense committee was chosen that included Franklin's member of the House of Delegates and common-wealth's attorney, the chairman of the board of supervisors, two local mayors, and the county sheriff. Soon thereafter various departments were organized, among them, fire, police, emergencies, nursing, utilities, and air raid warning services.[71] Commissioner Perdue even received offers to house children who might have to be evacuated from the Eastern Shore.[72]

All county residents, especially those between the ages of sixteen and sixty, were encouraged to sign up for volunteer work, and by 16 January 1942, a total of 1,719 local citizens had done so, "a record that ha[d] not been equalled in the state, so far as [wa]s known."[73] Indeed, the *News-Post* reported in March 1942 that Franklin was unique in registering 1,725 local citizens for civilian defense.

Moreover, the county had scheduled six first aid classes with 345 registrants, and classes were being organized to train volunteer firemen and policemen, while Rocky Mount had a class in operation already.[74]

Also in March 1942, the Black Civilian Defense Corps was organized and directors chosen for the auxiliary police; air raid wardens; auxiliary firemen; road repair crews; bomb, clearance, decontamination, and rescue squads; emergency food and housing; and the medical corps.[75]

At the behest of Governor Colgate W. Darden, on 2 June the Franklin County Game Protective Association met to form a county militia (or minutemen) under the auspices of the state adjutant general. The purpose of the militia was to "protect against saboteurs and raiding parties, destroying them or serving as a holding force, pending the arrival of fully equipped troops. Their function is that of armed combat." Only those eighteen years old or older and physically fit could participate; they also had to bring their own rifles or shotguns.[76] When the "Home Guard Company" was organized on 8 June 1942, forty-eight men signed up.[77]

"The first direct effect of the national defense program on business activity in Rocky Mount" had been reported on 25 October 1941 "when Fred D. Vaughn, president of the Rocky Mount Manufacturing Company, announced that a 70 per cent increase in payroll of the local concern would be made within the next 30 days." The company had been formed the year before as the town's newest industry and by October 1940 employed 225 men with the expectation of adding 150 additional employees by 1 December. Manufacturing "R[oyal] O[ak] W[holesale] patented 'spring cushion' windows," the company had received orders from national defense agencies for thousands of them, and Vaughn believed those orders would "tax our fullest capacity for months to come." He anticipated expanding the company into another part of the old Bald Knob Furniture Company building; the windows were wanted especially for "cantonments and military training bases in the eastern section of the country." Vaughn expected the company to grow indefinitely as it already had "exclusive rights in a large area including a large number of states in the east and promises to develop into a[n] enterprise that will surpass even the fondest hopes of the town and community."[78] By April 1942 so many male employees at the Rocky Mount Manufacturing Company had left for the service that fifty women were hired to take their places. The women were employed in the glazing and screen departments "where nimble fingers and quick action are needed."[79]

Another local manufacturer, the Bald Knob Furniture Company, reported the completion of a new water system by April 1942 that supplied all the water requirements except drinking fountains from its own mains. The company had a million-gallon dam and 116,000-gallon reserve built on a twenty-acre tract of the Angle estate a short distance northeast of the plant. A branch that had supplied water for the locomotives of the old Franklin and Pittsylvania Railroad now supplied the company. Bald Knob had also built a powerhouse and believed it was now ready to compete with other furniture makers throughout the country.[80]

The rationing of gasoline, foodstuffs, and other commodities affected the everyday life in the county as well as throughout the United States. Franklin County experienced the first example of this phenomenon on Sunday, 3 August 1941, when gasoline stations began conforming to an immediate 7:00 A.M. to

7:00 P.M. schedule. Only trucks, taxis, commercial cars, physicians, and ambulance drivers were exempt. On 5 August W. E. LaPrade, manager of Rocky Mount Motors, rigged up a bicycle for motorists who had been stranded and had to get somewhere in a hurry, after several out-of-town motorists had to spend Sunday night in Rocky Mount because of the new closing.[81]

On 15 May 1942, gasoline rationing for the duration of the war went into effect and 2,672 ration books were issued in Franklin County.[82] On that same day a price ceiling was imposed on just about everything Americans ate, wore, and used. Raw and unprocessed agricultural products were not affected (fluid milk and ice cream were controlled; flour was not, but cake mix was).[83] In July permanent gasoline rationing went into effect but with a week's delay to allow motorists time to organize "car pooling clubs."[84] On 21 July everyone filled their automobile tanks in anticipation of getting only four gallons a week thereafter so that at fifteen miles per gallon one could only drive 240 miles per month. Because most service station attendants had not punched the rationing cards during the temporary rationing period, 15 May–22 July 1942, motorists were able to prepare for the worst on 21 July when 119 dealers used 56,200 gallons to fill all of the tanks in the county.[85] Early in August local merchants did a big business in silk stockings, as the government was about to take over all surplus stocks of silk.[86]

The Japanese attack on Pearl Harbor took place three weeks before Christmas, but despite the shock of the attack shoppers in Franklin thronged the stores by the end of the next week. Christmas buying had suffered an initial setback but by 19 December the pace had increased, although Rocky Mount cut back on Christmas lights and other electrical decorations to save electricity for the war effort.[87]

Two years later the *Franklin News-Post* mentioned Christmas again, declaring that this holiday season would be the first under real wartime conditions; during the previous Christmas, the writer noted, there had still been enough left from prewar days that almost every gift need could be met. But in 1943 there were no rubber or metal toys and their "absence . . . [was] quite noticeable. Wooden and pasteboard items predominate[d]." Merchants received enough candy, however, to maintain some festive spirit. There was also sufficient tinsel and "highly colored wrappings" to make the gifts look decorative at any rate even if the recipient might not be receiving exactly what was wanted. Local merchants advertised that even enough wool goods were coming in so there would be plenty of hose, anklets, and socks, along with a sufficient amount of "attractive" yard goods and plenty of patterns to tempt each mother "to make her own and the kiddies' clothes as far as possible."[88]

One of the ways in which Franklin County supported the war effort of the United States was by raising money for the American Red Cross's war relief fund.[89] Between December 1941 and April 1945, Franklin County exceeded the Red Cross's quota by 51 percent. In March 1945, at that year's campaign fund-raising dinner in Rocky Mount, Private First Class W. Francis Gravely, who had been wounded in a breakthrough at Saint-Lô, praised the efforts of Red Cross workers who "carri[ed] cheer and comfort when it meant so much to the boys over there." After he was wounded he had received two pints of Red Cross blood plasma and four pints of blood and he planned to give that much blood back when he was able.[90]

During that same campaign Mrs. Christine Tyree, of Sontag, achieved individual fund-raising honors by collecting $171 from her neighbors, "sometimes walking as far as three miles to see one person."[91]

Franklin County also supported the American Red Cross in other ways. During the week of 3 October 1941, the local Red Cross chapter opened its sewing rooms. With several sewing machines and much material, local women volunteers made army and navy hospital gowns, operating-room gowns, robes and other garments for convalescents, and children's and babies' clothes to be sent to warring countries.

Franklin County women also aided in the American Red Cross's war effort by sewing surgical dressings, knitting sweaters and scarves, and making up kit bags for those in service. Each bag had the name of the Franklin County chapter on it and contained ten items: razor blades, shoestrings, pencils, writing paper and envelopes, playing cards, cigarettes, books of fiction, soap, box candy, and a sewing kit.

In January 1944 the local Red Cross women received a letter from two men who had gotten sweaters made by Franklin County needlewomen. One of them, Private First Class Walter Wisewicz, wrote to thank the women

> for the generous work you are doing, as we were given slipover sweaters the other day which were sent from your chapter, the Franklin county chapter, Virginia. I was fortunate to be one of many to get one. As we were out on bivouac, and indeed it sure was cold out, and as I slipped it on beneath my other clothing, believe me, I felt warmer, and right there my mind was made up to write and try to express my thanks and joy.[92]

The government also asked Americans to collect scrap of various kinds for recycling so that precious raw materials could be used for the war effort. Throughout the war, campaigns were conducted for collecting scrap paper, rubber, metal (especially aluminum), and kitchen fats, as well as planting "victory gardens" and buying more than $156 billion in war bonds and stamps.[93] During the National Defense Aluminum Collection campaign held in July 1941 the Boy Scouts actually conducted the collection, and in January 1942 they began collecting scrap paper as well. During January their efforts brought them $13.40 for club activities.[94] And by the middle of July 1945, the Lions Club reported that the previous year's activities had included collecting thirty tons of scrap paper.[95]

In describing a scrap rubber drive that ended in July 1942, the *Franklin News-Post* noted that "little tots are trudging to the service stations with one or two tires. Others are bringing in hot water bottles, baby rattles, rubber teething rings, rubber tooth brushes, rubber balls, pieces of rubber hose, gum shoes, soles from sneakers, etc. And the remains of one or two girdles were seen in a collection at a local service station." The response to the scrap rubber campaign proved so great that the campaign was extended to 10 July as by 3 July more than forty-five tons had already been collected.[96]

The Rocky Mount Lions Club, in keeping with the war spirit, chose the slogan "Scrap to Slap the Japs" for its scrap metal drive in 1942. The scrap was sold to wholesale dealers in Roanoke and the money used to buy glasses for underprivileged children and for other club projects. One member stated, "There are possibly enough old plow points on Franklin county farms to build a battleship," so all the farmers were encouraged to contribute.[97] By 2 October sixty tons of scrap had been collected in three local communities[98] and included toy trains and engines, children's discarded wagons, hot water tanks, iron beds and springs, lawn mowers, pumps, bird cages, tricycles, and household utensils.[99]

Among many other activities that started in December 1941 to support the war effort was the sale of defense stamps and bonds.[100] From April 1943 until July 1945, Franklin County participated in the second through the seventh war loan drives. One of the more interesting war loan drives was the third that began in September 1943. As part of that drive, Charles J. Davis, county chairman, held an auction ("a monster celebration") at the courthouse on 25 September that featured "a genuine German saber and sheath, captured from a Nazi officer" in the Tunisian invasion. The sale also included a number of items given locally: for example, antiques and farm products, "which will be of value to War Bond purchasers"; a Stetson hat or ten dollars in merchandise; a ton of coal; a haircut, shave, and massage; fifty pounds of leaf tobacco; a five-year subscription to the *Franklin News-Post* as well as a similar subscription to the *Franklin Gazette*; and 100 pounds of Gambill's Best Flour. In addition, according to the local paper, "H. Lester LaPrade ha[d] prepared an excellent Hitler dummy which w[ould] be nailed in his coffin as a feature of the exercises," so that every time bonds totaling $5,000 were sold Master Sergeant Thomas Tench, of Kentucky, who was home on leave, drove a nail in the coffin. "[Judge H. D.] Dillard [m.c.] kept the crowd, which jammed the court house yard, in a spirit of merriment throughout the sale and added to the occasion by his personal anecdotes and clever manner of the 'Hitler' dummy nailed in his coffin." The auction raised more than $150,000.[101]

Because Franklin was located 250 miles from the coast between two trunk line railroads and two industrial cities and not far from the gunpowder plant at Radford, the mission of the local defense force was to protect the area from incendiary bombs and resulting fires. With the formation of the Franklin County Aircraft Warning Service, the county was divided into strategic observation districts for spotting enemy planes.[102] By 15 June 1941, twenty-four warning posts had been established.[103] Sixteen men or women staffed each station and were available for twenty-four-hour service without pay, which was considered to be a patriotic duty. On so-called "demonstrator days" U.S. planes were flown over for practice.[104] Although Franklin was located on a projected direct enemy flight path because of the Radford gunpowder plant, Dublin ordnance plant, and Roanoke railroad facilities, it was an inactive area for airplane spotting because enemy planes should have been detected long before they reached Franklin.[105] Nevertheless, county citizens did their part as Franklin had been designated an enemy target area.[106]

By the end of May 1941, the state nutrition committee for national defense had selected two local representatives to promote good nutrition in Franklin. Each community in the county had a nutrition committee that gave talks at the PTA, women's clubs, and civic organizations. The committees also examined the school lunch program and helped farm families plant vegetable gardens and raise chickens, cows, and pigs. Residents were asked to contribute garden seeds and lend plows, pressure cookers, and jars.[107] Evidently these efforts were not long-lasting as in September 1944 a public meeting was held at the courthouse to start a countywide nutrition campaign to teach the citizens how to eat properly.

Thereafter twice-yearly meetings were held for educational purposes so that no one else would miss out on entering service because of poor nutrition. The *Franklin News-Post* described this as the first meeting of its kind in the county.[108]

In November 1944 the black unit of the county nutrition committee held its first meeting at the County Training School.[109] Several months earlier, on 3 May 1944, local (Rocky Mount) merchants had begun closing their businesses at 1:00 P.M. on Wednesday afternoons to work in their Victory gardens during the summer.[110]

In November 1942 the county board of supervisors agreed to put up a marker on the courthouse lawn as an honor roll of men in World War II and in May 1943 a contract was let for the honor roll.[111] Seven months later some of the county's churches followed suit by putting up their own plaques to honor the men in service. By that time, the Methodist church in Rocky Mount had already entered thirty-six names on its plaque.[112] A "monster patriotic celebration" was held to unveil the county's honor roll on 5 July. More than seven thousand people attended and 1,453 names eventually appeared on the plaque. The day chosen was court day so that rural citizens could attend the festivities. A Bedford band of about one hundred members ("a well known musical organization") provided the music.[113]

A shelter for servicemen and -women was dedicated on North Main Street near the Methodist church in September 1944; a sign on the shelter read "Stop—Pick Up a Service Man." Members of the American Legion had arranged to construct the shelter for service personnel who had to hitch rides home or back to camp. Everyone driving out of Rocky Mount was asked to stop by the shelter and " 'pick up' any man or woman in uniform who [was] seeking transportation to or from his [or her] military camp."[114]

Although the disruption of the war in Europe was a personal reality to relatives and friends in many other parts of the country, this was not ordinarily the case in Franklin County. In November 1943, however, those disruptions came home to local merchant Isadore Davidman when he received a radiogram from his brother. Davidman's brother was well and living in the Soviet Union; he had not been heard from since before the war broke out when he and the rest of Davidman's family had been living in Romania. Davidman's radiogram did not tell him how his brother had arrived in the Soviet Union, however, or where his father, another brother, and other relatives were.[115]

One of the most unusual occurrences in the Franklin area during World War II was the introduction of German prisoners of war into the former Civilian Conservation Corps camp at Sandy Level near the Franklin line in neighboring Pittsylvania County. After the fall of North Africa in May 1943, thousands of German and Italian prisoners of war were brought to the United States. In Virginia, Camps Lee and Pickett were chosen in August to be the first military installations to house POWs, with nine other primary sites added later. By April 1944 there were 2,256 Germans and 952 Italians in the state. When the POWs proved to be amenable to civilian labor, they were sent to branch camps from which they were assigned to assist local farmers and others in agricultural and forestry activities. The CCC camp at Sandy Level thus became a German POW branch camp of Camp Pickett in September 1944.[116]

Several hundred Franklin and area county farmers applied for POWs to help with more than three thousand acres of pulpwood timberland.[117] By the end of August 1944 County Agent E. W. Carson had received applications for 150 POWs to pick apples and another 250 to cut timber and pulpwood.[118] In order to receive POW assistance the farmers had to prove that they had no other source of manpower for the harvesting.[119] At the same time, the first group arrived—48 POWs who had been captured in the Sicilian campaign.[120] By the first of September, the new arrivals had prepared the camp for the influx of the other POWs and had erected a barbed-wire fence and guard towers. Eventually about 250 German prisoners were housed at the Sandy Level CCC camp.

From 31 August 1944 until 16 October 1945, when the Sandy Level camp was "deactivated," the German POWs worked in harvesting, food processing, pulp-wood cutting, and other farm work. For instance, fifty Germans were employed full-time by the Soil Conservation Service at Pigg River, near Sandy Level.[121] As an example of the savings gained from POW labor, the camp report for 31 December 1944 showed that for the last two weeks of that month if the labor had been performed by civilians it would have cost the government about $2,500, but the POWs cost less than $500. At the same time contractors were billed about $4,200 and the POWs were paid $2,300, so that the government had received a total value from POW labor of almost $3,900.[122]

News of the D-Day landings reached Franklin County early on 6 June 1944, "from the German radio in Berlin shortly after midnight stating that the invasion had started." Immediately, scores of telephones rang and by midmorning "the county was alive with speculation and hope."[123] By 5:45 A.M., church bells began to ring, factory whistles to blow, and at Rocky Mount Methodist Church (among others), the organist "at the console, pealed out the invasion news in both sacred and patriotic music . . . and for an hour and more the mellow tones of sacred hymns rent the early morning air." At eight o'clock that night services were held in most of Franklin's churches and attended by many in the county, especially "the rural folk who represent[ed] a large proportion of the 1,955 Franklin county men" in service.[124]

By 23 June 1944 the county had received the first word of casualties from D-Day. At that time Staff Sergeant Alfred L. Arrington, son of Mr. and Mrs. H. Morton Arrington, was reported missing in action, but by 11 August 1944 his status had been updated to killed in action. Sergeant Arrington had been overseas nineteen months before his death and had seen action in the Tunisian and Sicilian campaigns as well as on the Italian mainland as a tank commander.[125] Another Franklin County soldier who died during the Normandy invasion was Benjamin H. Plybon, son of Mr. and Mrs. T. R. Plybon, who was also killed in action on 6 June 1944; he had been in service two years.[126] Staff Sergeant Roy H. Dempsey, son of Mrs. J. P. Dempsey, of Martinsville, was wounded during the invasion and awarded the Purple Heart. His brother, Staff Sergeant W. W. ("Stump") Dempsey, who was in the air force, had won the Air Medal with four oak-leaf clusters and three campaign stars. Sergeant Winton Walker, son of Mr. and Mrs. P. C. Walker, of Rocky Mount, was also wounded by a shrapnel burst with the invasion troops at Normandy.[127]

Several families received letters from their husbands or sons who had partici-pated in the D-Day landings. In July Mrs. Curtis Ramsey heard from her husband that he had taken part in the invasion as a member of the navy: "he and the men on his landing craft made the beach with little difficulty." Known as Stumpy, Ramsey was a fireman, first class, on LCT 554, one of the landing craft shown in *Life* magazine as being among the first to land on the beach.[128]

Mr. and Mrs. J. A. Clingenpeel, of Callaway, had also received word from their son Private First Class Raymond Clingenpeel, who was with the 29th Division, the first to land in France, "that he arrived there safely on D-day. He says it was plenty hot for them but they came through OK and had whipped everything they had met and they hope to be able to continue the good work. He writes that he had some exciting experiences and hopes that he never has to go through another day like D-day. He also stated that he had read in the papers that his division had been highly praised for its successful exploits which he knows from personal experience his division deserves."[129] Staff Sergeant Millard ("Dusty") Sloan, Jr., the nineteen-year-old son of Mr. and Mrs. Millard Sloan, of Ferrum, was also with the 29th Division in France, and had seen action since D-Day. Of his experiences he said that he and the "swell group of boys" with him "have the Hellions on the run and intend to keep them that way."[130]

About two months after the Normandy landings, a new invasion in Europe took place on 15 August, with some Franklin County men involved. But the only one the *News-Post* knew of was Fireman First Class Stumpy Ramsey, USN, who had recently been transferred with his crew and LCI (Landing Craft Infantry) from England and Italy. After taking part in the Normandy invasion, Ramsey was next heard from in Italy when he was about to participate in the 15 August invasion, which hit southern France and opened up a beachhead from Nice to Marseilles, with the Germans greatly overwhelmed.[131]

By August then, it had become apparent that the war in Europe was entering its final stages and as a result the Rocky Mount Town Council became worried about too much celebrating when the victory over Germany occurred. Thus with council's concurrence and at the request of the official board of the Rocky Mount Baptist Church, Mayor J. Bradie Allman asked the State ABC Board to order local

Frank M. Wray, killed in post–D-Day com- bat. (Service Record Book of Men and Wom- en of Rocky Mount, Va., and Community [N.p.: V.F.W. Post No. 6002, n.d.].)

ABC stores in Rocky Mount and across the state to close for two days as soon as the European hostilities ceased.[132] Worries about too much exuberance involving alcoholic beverages reemerged in February 1945 when the Rocky Mount Town Council decided after much discussion to ask the ABC Board to declare the first Monday of each month (court day) in Franklin a holiday so the ABC stores would close. On 1 January there had been no arrests for public drunkenness at court day, but in February there were ten arrests and the number could have been four or five times higher "if we had taken all who really should have been locked up."[133]

By September 1944 the state and local governments began to plan strategies to help servicemen and -women reenter civilian life after the war. The local Citizens' Post-War Employment Committee was formed in the middle of the month, with Mayor J. Bradie Allman as chairman. A group from several county industries met with the Virginia State Planning Board to discuss employing returning service personnel.[134]

As the war in Europe approached its close, the county undertook a campaign from 9 until 21 April 1945 to collect used clothing for war-torn countries, a part of the United Nations Relief and Rehabilitation Administration. R. W. Wilkins served as general chairman, with the Lions clubs, Woman's Club, Parent-Teachers Association, Boy and Girl Scouts, public schools, and churches as sponsors. Everyone was asked to give five pounds per person of everyday clothes for infants, women, and girls especially. The national goal was 150 million pounds.[135] In late May it was reported that Franklin had contributed more than 3,000 pounds of old clothing for European refugees. All of the clothes were in good condition, some excellent.[136]

The *News-Post* on 27 April offered a $25 war bond as a reward for the first Franklin County man into Berlin, and asked the families to notify the paper as soon as they knew. Criteria to determine the winner included the minute, hour, and day the soldier entered Berlin. Three judges would select the winner for Berlin and later for Tokyo.[137]

President Franklin D. Roosevelt died of a stroke while at Warm Springs, Georgia, on 12 April 1945. A Franklin County serviceman, Private First Class Marvin G. Wray, USMC, son of Mr. and Mrs. J. O. Wray, of Rocky Mount, formed part of the honor guard at Warm Springs for the late president. Wray had graduated from Rocky Mount High School in June 1941, and spent twenty months in the South Pacific before being wounded on Saipan and receiving the Purple Heart and other commendations.[138]

On 5 May 1945 German resistance ceased in Italy and on 7 May Germany unconditionally surrendered to the Allies at Rheims. The *News-Post* cheered the news of Italy's collapse in the 4 May edition, saying "there's rejoicing in many a Franklin county home this week" as there were "hundreds of Franklin county boys . . . with the American forces in Italy, and the cessation of hostilities there means that the fighting is over so far as they are concerned."[139] On Wednesday, 9 May many of Franklin's citizens celebrated the end of the war in Europe by attending services in their churches. "There were tears of joy, there were tears of grief, and there were those who just bubbled over when the first news of the unconditional surrender of Germany unleashed a torrent of pentup emotions within them which had been building up since the day our boys first answered the call to arms. The war is over in Europe." Despite the happiness of the moment, however, everyone realized that the war was only half won and consequently "local industries reported there were few men absent from their jobs on V-E Day, with little interruption in normal production."[140]

With victory in Europe the War Production Board lifted its ban on electrical use for advertising, window and sign lighting, and other similar applications. According to the Appalachian Electric Power Company there had never been a shortage of electricity in the Franklin area. On 9 May the ban on racing and nightclubs was also lifted, but tires and gasoline were still rationed.[141] By the end of May, the Appalachian Electric Power Company began planning to run more electrical lines into rural areas throughout its territory now that materials had become available again to do the work. The company would string 4,288 miles of line to serve 18,260 farm and rural customers in twenty counties in its operating area including Franklin. The company was then operating in twenty-nine counties with 4,004 miles of line to 24,016 farm and rural customers.[142]

About a week after V-E Day, Private First Class Guilford L. Hodges, of Penhook, became the first soldier demobilized as he had achieved enough points to be discharged. On Tuesday, 15 May, he reported to the local draft board for reassignment to civilian duties. Hodges had enlisted in the army on 5 November 1941 and arrived overseas on 11 May 1942; he fought in the Rome-Arno campaign, the battle for Tunisia, the Naples-Foggia campaign, on the Anzio beachhead, at Monte Casino, in the North African campaign, and at the Casserine Pass. During his service Hodges had received two Bronze Stars, the Good Conduct Medal, Distinguished Unit Badge, European-African-Middle Eastern Campaign medals, and American Defense Medal. On 21 March, he had rotated home to Fort Meade, Maryland, from Italy. With the end of the war in Europe, a demobilization plan was set up and as Hodges had ninety-one points, he qualified as the first county man to be discharged.[143]

At the same time, Franklin County men being held prisoner in German POW camps began to be released and started for home. Among them was Lieutenant

William N. Shearer, Jr., prisoner of war in a German camp. (Service Record Book of Men and Women of Rocky Mount, Va., and Community [N.p.: V.F.W. Post No. 6002, n.d.].)

William N. Shearer, Jr., a bombardier with the Eighth Air Force, and a German prisoner since 21 November when he was shot down over Merseburg, Germany, during a bomber raid on the oil refineries there. Shearer had entered the service in February 1943 and been reported as a POW on 8 January 1945. He was imprisoned in Stalag Luft III at Sagan in Lower Silesia, Poland.[144] While Shearer was still in Europe his wife, Ruth Preston Shearer, on 22 May, received his Air Medal and two oak-leaf clusters, "for meritorious achievement while participating in sustained bomber combat operations over Germany and German-occupied countries. The courage, coolness and skill displayed by this officer upon these occasions reflect great credit upon himself and the armed forces of the United States." Shearer was the son of William N. Shearer; his brother, Private First Class John Shearer, was with the 6th Marines on Okinawa.[145]

Two other Franklin County soldiers reported liberated in late May were Private First Class Claude A. Hodges, son of Mrs. Laura A. Hodges, who had been serving with the 99th Infantry Division of the First Army when he was captured in the Battle of the Bulge on 18 December 1944; and Private Lee LaPrade, son of Gus T. LaPrade, of Rocky Mount, who had been taken prisoner at the battle for Brest. By early June the latter two men were "well and happy again and gaining back their normal weight after a forced prison diet chiefly of thin barley soup and black bread." Hodges had weighed 100 pounds when he was released on 29 April and gained 63 pounds during the next month.[146]

Recalling his experiences as a POW, Hodges remembered being marched after capture for about twelve hours without a rest, "passing through German villages where the people lined the streets and made all kinds of fun of us." They finally reached a railroad and were packed sixty into a boxcar without room even to sit down, so that "we had to sleep standing up and leaning on each other." They were on the train for three days; "it was on Christmas day that we were first allowed off the train, and what a Christmas it was with nothing to eat or drink. En route on the train, we had less than a loaf of black bread per man and very little water." For the first two months he spent his time in bed at the POW camp because he and the others received only twelve lumps of coal a day in their barracks, which were not enough to keep warm. Breakfast consisted of tea and lunch of a cup of weak barley soup or sugar beet soup. For supper there was a loaf of black bread for every six men with "a small piece of meat once a week." In mid-February Hodges was sent to Schweinfurt as part of a labor gang to dig ditches. The city had been completely leveled by Allied bombing raids. Upon evacuation of the city, Hodges was marched ahead of the advancing Allies until 29 April when "the German guards had laid down their guns, the first American jeep hove into sight and he was a free man again."[147]

Like Claude Hodges, Lee LaPrade stated the food was not good in the POW camp, and the prisoners spent much of their time planning menus for when they came home. They dreamed of all the good things they had eaten while in the United States before the war and then awoke to disappointment. LaPrade's story of his rescue was as exciting as Hodges's. LaPrade had been surrounded and captured first by the Germans and then by the Russians, and had been a POW in a German camp for about eight months. " 'It was on the Siegfried line last September that we found ourselves surrounded and were taken prisoner,' he said. 'There were about 60 of us who fell into nazi hands at that time. We were taken to a barracks which was formerly an old residence, and all of us housed in one large room.' " LaPrade received the "real thrill" of his imprisonment when the Russians advanced to join with the Americans coming from the west.

> You can imagine how we felt with Russians surrounding us on the north and south and another bunch of them making a spearhead toward the American lines, especially since our barracks was in the line of the spearhead. There was considerable confusion when the Russians finally reached us because they didn't seem able to tell the difference between the Americans and the Germans. It took a lot of explaining through one of our bunch who could speak a little Russian before we made the Reds understand that we were American prisoners. We were under heavy German guard until the Russian advance came up to us and then the German guards threw their rifles into a pond of water. That was the signal we had been waiting for. Some of us beat it down the road and the others went another way, all making for the American line which the Russians told us was only about 18 to 20 miles away. We finally made it, and here we are.[148]

Several other Franklin County men returned or were en route home in mid-June after being released from German POW camps. Private First Class Townes T. Dunahoo, son of Mr. and Mrs. N. J. Dunahoo, of Boones Mill, had been a POW in Germany from September 1944 to 29 April 1945, when he, too, was liberated. He had been overseas with the infantry since July 1944.[149] In addition, the following had been freed: Private Billy C. Altice, son of Mrs. Helen B. Altice, Route 4, Rocky Mount; Private Alfred C. Divers, son of William J. Divers, Route 1, Penhook; Staff Sergeant Andrew B. Mullins, son of Mrs. Lillie A. Mullins, Route 1, Sydnorsville[150]; and Corporal Elwood Rice Law, son of Mrs. Julia Law. By 15 June, Law was home on furlough after being released from a hospital in France where he had been taken after gaining his freedom. He had been reported missing in action on 18 December 1944 and in March 1945 as a prisoner. Captured after a battle in the Luxembourg area, Law was held a prisoner at Stalag IV-B in Mühlberg, Germany. He had entered the service in November 1942 and arrived overseas in July 1944. When released, Law weighed 135 pounds but gained 40 more pounds soon thereafter.[151]

The war continued in the Far East, and in mid-June it was announced that two county boys had been reported killed in action on Okinawa. Both were the second members of their families to die in service. Sergeant Howard H. LaPrade, son of Mr. and Mrs. A. O. LaPrade, and nephew of H. Lester LaPrade, of Rocky Mount, succumbed on Okinawa on 6 May. His brother Staff Sergeant Cecil C. LaPrade had perished in an airplane accident in California on 2 February 1945. Private First Class Jasper Hodges, son of Mr. and Mrs. Garfield Hodges, of Rocky Mount, died on Okinawa on 4 May, two days before Howard LaPrade. Hodges's brother Private First Class Sydney Hodges had been killed in an accident in training camp in Georgia in March 1943.[152]

At the end of June 1945, Private Willard J. Underwood, of Callaway, the first Franklin County man drafted through the local selective service office, obtained his discharge, "after a thrilling experience that carried him through training camp, across the submarine-infested Atlantic, through Africa, Sicily and Italy and back home." He had received the EAME Campaign medal with three combat stars and six overseas bars for three years in European service. He was the son of Mrs. Elizabeth Webb, of Route 2, Callaway.[153]

Douglas MacArthur had promised "I shall return" when he left the Philippines on 11 March 1942 as the Japanese continued their sweep through Southeast Asia and the South Pacific. Before the Allies could stop them, the Japanese had taken most of the area except for Australia. The Battles of the Coral Sea (7–8 May 1942), Midway (4 June 1942), and Guadalcanal (7 August–15 November 1942) were fought before the Allies could take the initiative from the Japanese and begin to realize MacArthur's promise to recover the Philippines. The strategy in the Pacific consisted of leapfrogging Japanese-held islands until the home islands of Japan could be taken. By October 1944, the Allies had begun the campaign for the Philippine islands with the battle for Leyte Gulf (20–25 October 1944). In February 1945, enough of the Philippines had been recovered that the Allies could start to recapture the islands that immediately protected Japan. The battle for Iwo Jima began on 19 February 1945 and ended 14 March with heavy Allied losses. The next step was Okinawa starting on 1 April where the Japanese relied largely on kamikaze attacks to prevent Allied victory, and there Allied losses were also great. The kamikazes, however, operated to no avail, and by late June the island was conquered.[154] Because Japan clearly intended to fight to the last man, President Harry S. Truman made the decision to drop the atomic bomb on Hiroshima on 6 August. "The bomb wiped out the Second Japanese Army to a man, razed four square miles of the city, and killed 60,175 people, including the soldiers. Around noon 9 August, a few hours after Russia declared war on Japan, the second atomic bomb exploded over Nagasaki, killing 36,000 more." On 14 August, Emperor Hirohito overrode his chief military advisors and surrendered.[155]

On 17 August 1945, the *News-Post* announced that "all the pent-up enthusiasm of four days of waiting for the Jap answer to our surrender terms was loosed in a mighty flood of joyous celebration Tuesday evening [14 August]. The largest radio audience in the country's history heard the President's historic announcement that the war was over."[156]

When the county received the news at 7 P.M., on Tuesday, 14 August, "tears mingled with shrieks of joy as thought turned immediately to those boys of ours . . . who would now be spared the horrors of further war. The war is over. . . . Japan has surrendered. . . . Pearl Harbor is avenged."[157]

> The town siren was the first to blast forth in tumultuous glee. It was a different note, too—not of danger, but of joy. Soon joined the factory whistles and the court house bell and the bell on the colored Baptist church, all blending in the symphony of joy that peace has returned—that the war is over.[158]

People from all over the county rushed into Rocky Mount to join in the celebration, and while many of the younger citizens "in their cars toured the streets time and time again all through the night," many others went to their churches "to offer prayers of thanksgiving that their sons were to be spared further war weariness." President Truman declared Wednesday a national holiday for government employees and Governor Colgate Darden did the same for state workers. Yet "with it all . . . with all the excitement and jubilation and riotous merrymaking . . . police state[d] that there was not a single accident reported to mar the occasion." And for those who had worried about the citizenry's becoming too enthusiastic about the news, the *News-Post* reassured its readers that "the sale of beer was stopped as soon as the victory news was received and Mayor Allman reports that there was not a single arrest during the celebration Tuesday night. The ABC store was closed Wednesday." The flag that flew from the Episcopal church in Rocky Mount, it was noted, was the same one flown when the county's young men paraded in 1917 en route to the First World War, again when armistice was signed in November 1918, during "patriotic celebrations during the past quarter century," and finally to commemorate the end of the Second World War.[159]

A week later it was announced that as of that date 55 of 2,309 Franklin County servicemen and -women had been killed during the war: 2.4 percent of the total. Seventeen had died in the Pacific, four of those in the invasion and capture of Okinawa; others had lost their lives in Africa, Italy, at Normandy, and in the drive to the "heart of the German empire," along with those who died accidental deaths. The number 2,309 was slightly less than 10 percent of Franklin's 1940 population. Of that entire group thirteen were women, who served in the WACs, WAVEs, SPARs, and nursing corps. And as of 24 August, 243 Franklin men had been honorably discharged from service.[160] Franklin County men and women had served all over the world, the men "in practically every invasion and major engagement in the European war":

> they ha[d] felt the bite of the sub-zero weather of Iceland, the hot life-sapping temperatures of the tropical jungles. They ha[d] fought on the snow-capped mountains of Italy, through the sands of Africa. They ha[d] had a part in the invasions at Casablanca, at Anzio, on the Normandy beaches of France, and ha[d] followed the Stars and Stripes across the hedgerows of France, through Holland, through Belgium, right to the heart of the Nazi kingdom.
>
> On the other side of the globe they . . . carr[ied] on their heroic work [to] bring the Jap to his death as a people and a nation.
>
> In the skies over every section of the world, under the water in submarine warfare, on the sea, and on the land, boys from Franklin county ha[d] upheld the glory and the traditions of our country in a manner which makes us all proud of them.[161]

TWENTY-ONE

Franklin County Rediscovered

For most of its history Franklin County mirrored the nation and the state of Virginia; it was overwhelmingly rural with some scattered hamlets and villages. Since the end of World War II, however, while America became increasingly urbanized, Franklin County retained much of its rural character. In recent years its small towns and rolling countryside have attracted the attention of nonresidents who view its way of life with some nostalgia. Some of the newcomers are refugees from urban centers, others are retired, while still others want to commute to jobs in urban areas and spend their evenings and weekends in a quieter, slower-paced environment.

A few of the newcomers are businesses and industries. They offer jobs and a better standard of living to Franklin County residents and otherwise improve the local economy. They also attract still more taxpayers to the county. The new residents and new businesses make increasing demands on the services that the county and the utility companies provide.

Ironically, as new dwellings and facilities are constructed to meet the demand, the very qualities that have attracted so many to the county are threatened. Twisting, tree-shaded country roads are widened, straightened, and trimmed of trees. Farms are replaced by housing developments and shopping centers. Old houses significant to the county's history are abandoned in favor of new brick ranchers. Slowly but surely the historic fabric of the county is nibbled away. Such artificial assemblages as the Blue Ridge Farm Museum at Ferrum, although vastly better than allowing significant buildings to be destroyed, are only substitutes for the real thing that still survives in a few areas of the county.

Just as the county's residents and built environment have changed over time, so too have its institutions. When Franklin County was created in 1786 its government consisted of the sheriff and his deputies, the county surveyor, the clerk of court, the commonwealth's attorney, and the justices of the peace. In addition, commissioners of the revenue appointed by the justices for each tax district in the county collected the real estate and personal property taxes. Thus

449

the court controlled the county's executive, legislative, and judicial functions. In 1869 the commonwealth ratified a new constitution that changed county government throughout the state. A single county judge took over judicial matters, and the county board of supervisors now undertook administrative and legislative duties. The new constitution also added town, city, and county treasurers to the governmental structure. Under the Virginia Constitution of 1869 the General Assembly elected each county's judge. Hugh Nelson served as Franklin's first judge under the new system, followed by Thomas H. Bernard, George D. Peters, and John P. Lee (who served from 1899 until 1904 when the Constitution of 1902 took effect and the county and circuit courts were consolidated).[1]

Franklin County began the twentieth century served by the county judge, court clerk, commonwealth's attorney, sheriff, treasurer, surveyor, coroner, superintendents of the poor and of schools, four commissioners of the revenue, and ten supervisors, overseers of the poor, constables, and justices of the peace representing the ten magisterial districts: Rocky Mount, Snow Creek, Union Hall, Gills Creek, Bonbrook, Little Creek, Maggodee, Blackwater, Long Branch, and Brown Hill. As the century progressed the governmental life of the county grew much faster than in previous centuries and many new officers and functions were added. The county health department was established by 1909 and is "supervised, staffed and operated by the State Department of Health."[2] By 1924, Franklin had its first Electoral Board. The juvenile court judge first appeared in the 1926–1927 secretary of the commonwealth report. By 1930 a county farm agent and by 1938 a home demonstration agent appeared on the roster for the first time, both chosen by the board of supervisors from a list recommended by the Agricultural Extension Service at what is now Virginia Polytechnic Institute and State University.[3]

In the same year that the county hired its first home demonstration agent, it also hired its first superintendent of public welfare (Marjorie D. Tibbs) who replaced the superintendent of the poor. The overseers of the poor ceased to be listed in 1938. J. Bradie Allman became the county's first trial justice in 1934. That judgeship ceased to function in 1955 and was replaced by a circuit court judge. In 1973 the Virginia court system experienced a complete revision so that corporation, hustings, law and chancery, chancery, and law and equity courts were consolidated into the circuit court system, which was reduced from forty to thirty judicial circuits. Moreover, the state's numerous trial courts with limited jurisdiction such as police, county, municipal, and juvenile and domestic relations courts were combined into a new district court system with two courts per district: the general district and juvenile and domestic relations courts in thirty-two districts. Finally, the phasing out of the position of justice of the peace began on 1 January 1974 and the duties of that officer were taken over by magistrates appointed by the chief circuit judge.[4] Thus Franklin County is part of the Twenty-Second Judicial Circuit (which also includes Pittsylvania County and the city of Danville) as well as being in the Twenty-Second General District.

Other changes in the county's government have taken place since the 1950s: the commissioner of accounts first appeared in the 1950–1951 report, the parks and recreation director in 1969, and the chairman of the planning commission in 1969 as well. In 1959 Franklin's ten magisterial districts were reduced to seven:

Blackwater, Gills Creek, Boone, Blue Ridge, Rocky Mount, Snow Creek, and Union Hall, which are still in existence.

Virginia's voters ratified its most recent constitution in November 1970 and the Constitution of 1971 took effect on 1 July 1971.[5] Thereafter, Franklin County saw a substantial growth in county government with the creation of the following positions: county administrator, assessor of real estate, building inspector, electrical inspector, finance director, fire chief, inspections director, director of planning, personnel director, probation officer, purchasing agent, and registrar, all of whom appeared for the first time in the 1974–1975 secretary of the commonwealth report. By that same year two other positions were renamed: the superintendent of public welfare became the public welfare director and what had been the health officer became the public health officer. All of these officers are still fulfilling their responsibilities for the county.

When World War I ended, American citizens believed that they had just completed the "war to end all wars." Within twenty-one years, however, World War II began and once again United States soldiers had to fight on foreign soil. But the way the Second World War ended—on the edge of confrontation with the Soviet Union—did not allow anyone to conclude that war had become a thing of the past. Within five years, Americans once again fought on foreign soil, this time to contain the spread of communism in Asia.

On 25 June 1950 Communist North Korean troops crossed the 38th parallel between their country and South Korea carrying Soviet-made weapons. Within a week the United Nations Security Council had adopted a resolution calling for armed intervention in Korea, and a week later President Harry S. Truman sent U.S. ground troops to South Korea. For the first of three years, U.S. troops including about 150,000 Virginians fought an active war and then engaged in a two-year stalemate until an armistice was signed on 27 July 1953. With the signing of that armistice South Korea was again divided from North Korea approximately along the same 38th parallel as when the war had begun. Virginia had sustained 849 battle deaths, 5 of them Franklin County men: Emmett L. Love and James W. Lawrence were killed in July 1950, one of the six months during the entire conflict with the greatest number of Virginia casualties. James M. Bailey died in February 1951 and Jimmie L. Watkins in May 1951, and Everett Holland was killed in August 1952. The U.S. Department of Defense reported in 1985 that 148,000 living Virginians were veterans of Korea, some of them still living in Franklin County.[6]

Like Korea, the Vietnam War was considered a police action instead of a declared war. Once again the United States entered into an Asian land war to halt the spread of communism and once again the outcome was a stalemate. This time, however, the United States had engaged in what became the most unpopular war in its history. By 1965 President Lyndon B. Johnson had enlarged America's involvement from what had begun as a small military advisory role to full-scale "war" and by 1968 about 541,000 U.S. troops were stationed in Vietnam, the peak year of the war. Finally, on 27 January 1973 the United States signed an agreement with representatives of all sides in the war that provided for the withdrawal of the remaining U.S. troops in Vietnam. During the conflict 57,000 Americans died, among them seven Franklin County men: from the U.S. Army, Michael D. Cannaday on 1 January 1967, Roland A. Cutchins on 26 March 1967,

James Eddy Turner on 4 July 1967, Sherman Alvin Furrow, Jr., on 8 October 1968, Mills Beale III on 11 May 1969, and Joseph C. Spence, Jr., on 24 December 1970; and from the U.S. Marines, Richard Wayne Perdue on 5 April 1969.[7] Many more, of course, were wounded.

Until 1952 Franklin County residents who needed hospitalization had to go to Roanoke or Martinsville. But on 3 May 1952 Dr. Mack Stanholtz, state health commissioner, gave the principal address at the dedication of the Franklin Memorial Hospital in Rocky Mount, and the new facility opened its doors three days later. Beginning with a forty-bed capacity, the hospital has grown to sixty-two beds. During the 1977–1985 period the hospital experienced further growth with the addition of a number of new services and departments including the Social Services Department (1978), a full-time pharmacist (1978), physical therapy (1979), telemetry units (1980), quality assurance (1981), ultrasound (1983), the Home Health Department (1984), ambulatory surgery (1984), and stress testing (1985). The Franklin County Health Center occupies a portion of the hospital and provides a well-baby clinic, family planning, Medicaid screening, and physical therapy. There are also eight medical clinics throughout Rocky Mount and the county, as well as two nursing and two adult homes. The Franklin County Health Department supplies medically related services to the county's residents, along with nine dentists, one orthodontist, one podiatrist, and seventeen physicians and surgeons.[8]

Franklin County's public library also is located in Rocky Mount. For years it was housed in a small, brick, Colonial Revival–style building on Court Street behind the courthouse lot on the site of the old clerk's office. The building opened in 1941; it was constructed as the county's first public library through the generosity of a former Charlotte County delegate, Ambassador David K. E. Bruce. In 1954 the library systems of Franklin and Patrick counties merged to form a regional library system; it operated a bookmobile for the two counties. The two systems became independent once again in 1975.[9]

The county constructed a new public library building near the old one in 1986. About triple the size of the former structure, the new library can hold between seventy-five and eighty thousand volumes. Among the services and programs provided in the new building are interlibrary loan, photocopying, outreach to nursing homes, and reading programs for children. Recently the library established the Gertrude C. Mann Room to house the local history and genealogy collection assembled by the late Franklin County historian. County residents may also use the eighty thousand volumes in the Stanley Library at Ferrum College.[10]

Franklin County enjoys a good supply of surface water from its rivers and major creeks: the Roanoke, Pigg, Blackwater, and Smith rivers, and Gills, Maggodee, Chestnut, Snow, and Story creeks. Although public water authorities supply Rocky Mount, Ferrum, and Boones Mill, the latter two communities depend on wells (and for Boones Mill also on springs) for their public water supplies. By 1986 a new water treatment plant had been built on the Blackwater River to provide water for Rocky Mount, used at the rate of about 835,000 gallons a day. Rocky Mount and Ferrum both have sewage treatments plants, and Boones Mill expects to obtain one as well.[11]

The Appalachian Power Company provides the county with electricity and is one of the largest electric utilities in the state. The county also "has two major hydroelectric impoundments for the production of electric power—Smith Mountain and Philpott Reservoirs." Electrical service first came to the county in the early 1900s when a group of local businessmen formed the Rocky Mount Power Company. In 1926 the Appalachian Power Company of Roanoke bought out Rocky Mount Power and extended electrical service to other areas of the county. Boones Mill, for instance, obtained electricity in 1929. World War II slowed the spread of electrical service throughout the county, but in the postwar period such service spread rapidly. Appalachian Power is perhaps best known for its development of Smith Mountain Lake in the 1960s.[12] The northern portion of the county as well as Rocky Mount receive natural gas service from the Roanoke Gas Company, while the southern portion of the county is served by the Southwestern Virginia Gas Company, of Martinsville.[13]

Telephone service began in Franklin County in 1900 with the organization of the Franklin Telephone Company on 7 March. At that time only about thirty Rocky Mount residents had telephones, but within four years the service was extended to Boones Mill and Callaway. At the same time a line was run to Roanoke through an agreement with the Virginia and Tennessee Telephone Company. It was not too long before Taylors Store, Wirtz, Union Hall, Redwood, Glade Hill, and Sontag received telephones as well. By 1912 the Mutual Telephone Companies operated at Retreat, Boones Mill, Old Glade Hill, Scruggs, and Ferrum, among others. Burgie Lee Fisher took over management of the Franklin Telephone Company in 1904 and in the early 1920s built an exchange at Stuart in Patrick County that connected Franklin's phone service to Patrick. From this beginning, Fisher bought the Franklin Telephone Company, reorganized it as the Fisher Telephone Company, later merging the Fisher and Stuart companies into the Lee Telephone Company by 1930. In 1930 Fisher added the Martinsville telephone company to his holdings. Fisher's company pioneered tandem toll-dialing (no longer relying on calling another operator to dial any telephone in the company's exchanges) for long-distance telephoning in 1943. In 1965 Lee Telephone Company joined the Central Telephone System (Centel). As of 1986, there were 12,825 telephone subscribers to Centel in Franklin County.[14]

Although still primarily rural, Franklin County has experienced a gradual decline in the number of farms in operation. Between 1964 and 1974, for example, the farm totals dropped from 1,860 to 1,274, while the proportion of the county's land devoted to farming declined from 56.3 percent to 43.5 percent. During the same period, however, the total value of farm products sold more than doubled from $8,884,481 to $18,481,000.[15] Farming, then, has continued to be a vital part of the county's economy.

In 1986, the bicentennial edition of the *Franklin News-Post* included a summary of the county's agriculture industry after two hundred years. From a county primarily raising tobacco, the predominant farm activity has become dairying along with the raising of beef cattle, and its attendant hay, corn silage, and corn crops. The 1987 agricultural census tells the story. The total sales for Franklin's agricultural products was $31,893,000. Of that sum, livestock, poultry, and their products furnished $26,362,000. Hay, silage, and field seeds produced an additional $148,000, with $121,000 for grains (including corn, wheat, soybeans, and oats). Fruits, nuts, and berries supplied $1,325,000 and nursery and greenhouse crops a further $175,000. Finally, Franklin had 376 farms of 111,380 acres, with an average of 296 acres per farm and an average of $85,000 in agricultural products per farm.[16] As the *News-Post* concluded, "These small farms constitute the county's most important industry."[17]

Jesse S. Amos farm, Sontag: a typical tobacco farm in transition to diversified agriculture and dairying, with tobacco buildings on top of hill and dairy and other buildings in middle distance. Mid-1950s photo. (J. Francis Amos, Rocky Mount, Va.)

In the years since World War II, Franklin County's businesses and industries have employed a greater proportion of the population than was the case in the prewar years. By 1986, in fact, "most of those in the job market [were] employed in industrial, business and professional jobs." The county boasted approximately thirty industries. Several of them date from the early twentieth century including the Blue Ridge Talc Company, which was begun in Henry in 1920. The company manufactures caulks, paint, and coatings, and employs about seventy people. Another longstanding industry is the Weaver Mirror Company, started by Robert Weaver in 1932, and still owned by his family. The company was the first, in fact, to move into the new Rocky Mount–Franklin County Industrial Park in 1985 and employs about fifty persons. A third prewar industry still operating in the county is MW Manufacturers (original Rocky Mount Manufacturing Company). Begun in 1939 with 225 employees, the company produces wooden doors and windows and has a work force of around 600.[18]

Other early industries have changed ownership over the years and are now part of nationally known companies. One of them is the Lane Company, the county's largest employer (of more than 700 people), which in 1957 bought out the Bald Knob Furniture Company (founded in Franklin in 1903 with a work force of 65 by 1910). With several plants throughout the South, Lane is known for its bedroom and dining furniture and especially for its cedar chests. The other is J. P. Stevens, Inc., which purchased the Angle Silk Mills, Inc., in 1959. The silk mill had been chartered in 1929 and as part of J. P. Stevens produces various types of cloth with a staff of about 163 workers.

Several other industries related to the textile trade that operate in Franklin are Burlington Industries, Inc., begun in the county in 1969, which employs 95 people and produces waterbed sheets; Virginia Apparel Corporation, started in 1971 to produce women's clothing with a work force of more than 200 people (a second plant operated in Ferrum from 1972 until 1982), along with a plant in Blackstone; and Chalaine, Inc., where about 40 people sew wearing apparel at a plant in Boones Mill that opened in 1973. In September 1990, Virginia Apparel, "a supplier of clothing to mail-order merchant L. L. Bean," opened a new plant in Rocky Mount that is nearly twice the size of its previous Rocky Mount location.[19] Another clothing manufacturer located in the county is Bassett-Walker, Inc., which opened a Ferrum division in 1982 employing about 150 people. The company produces knitted outerwear and has grown to least 275 employees. Established in Rocky Mount in 1951, Bristol Manufacturing Company, Inc., engages about 240 workers to sew nurses' uniforms. And one of the county's youngest industries is Doyle Enterprises, Inc., located in the Truevine Elementary School with a work force of 96 employees sewing sportswear. In 1990 the company opened several new plants, in Pittsylvania County at Callands and Gretna, and in West Virginia.[20]

Lumber-related industries that operate in the county include the Guyer-Roberts Manufacturing Company, started in 1946 in Rocky Mount, which employs 74 people and produces wooden frames and furniture parts. The Terry F. Cundiff Lumber Company began in 1947 and provides work for 15 persons. Boones Mill was home to Cooper Wood Products, Inc., started in 1952 by George Cooper and now located near Grassy Hill, which employs about 275 people and makes wooden frames and doors. Begun as a one-man operation in 1956, Leo Scott's Cabinets has grown to a staff of 53 people who produce custom cabinets for sale to housing manufacturers and individuals in the Franklin County area. Since 1970 Custom Woodwork Company near Ferrum has employed 14 persons in the manufacture of prehung doors and windows. Erath Veneer Corporation of Virginia has provided work for about 100 local residents since 1965, manufacturing face veneer for its local, national, and foreign markets. The former Franklin Tie and Wood, which opened in 1956 and is now known as Commodities Services, Inc., employs 10 people to produce railway crossties and block and ship lumber. Lee's Wood Products began in Rocky Mount in 1974 and engages 15 workers to make mirror and picture frames. Rocky Top Wood Preservers Corporation, also in Rocky Mount, began in 1977 with 4 employees and has experienced yearly growth. It manufactures pressure-treated lumber for retailers.[21]

Two county industries produce modular homes: Marley-Continental Homes, Inc., started in Boones Mill in 1955, now employs about 280 people; and Mod-U-Kraf Homes, Inc., in Rocky Mount, begun in 1971, which engages about 150 persons to build prefabricated housing units for residential and commercial purposes as well as townhouse, condominium, and motel units. Martin Processing, Inc., and its 150 Franklin County employees have made and dyed processed carpet yarn since 1972. In 1990 the operation changed its name to Ronile. Mine Systems, Inc., opened its steel fabrication plant near Rocky Mount in 1980; and Burroughs Corporation has produced business forms at its local site since 1976 with a labor force of about 160 employees. The Franklin Body Works, Inc., manufactures truck body products. And Franklin's most recent industrial acquisition is Datacard. At the end of World War II, the *Franklin News-Post* interviewed a number of local manufacturers who anticipated a bright future in the coming years. Their vision has been realized.

In 1976 the West Piedmont Planning District Commission in cooperation with the Franklin County Planning Commission released a comprehensive land-use plan for the county that included a discussion of the major transportation networks. The principal and only United States highway in the county is Route 220, a north-south route that connects Franklin with Martinsville and North Carolina on the south and Roanoke on the north. There are three principal state highways as well, Routes 40, 116, and 122. Virginia Route 40 is the dominant state route in the county and passes in an east-west direction. From Rocky Mount, Route 40 connects on the east with Glade Hill, Union Hall, and Smith Mountain Lake, and on the west with Ferrum, Endicott, and Philpott Reservoir. State Routes 116 and 122 are located in the northeast section of Franklin County and give access to Roanoke and Bedford counties respectively. With U.S. Route 220, these three state highways provide 93.84 miles of primary road to the county. There are also 993.96 miles of secondary roads traversing Franklin, although there are fewer secondary roads in the western and southeastern areas of the county. Altogether then, Franklin County has 1,115.14 miles of roads, primary and secondary.[22]

Since 1880 the county has been served by railroad lines (the Franklin and Pittsylvania Railroad completed in 1880 and abandoned in 1932 and the Roanoke and Southern Branch of the Norfolk and Western Railroad since 1892). Sometime before 1976 passenger service ceased to be available by railroad in the county, but freight service was provided to Ferrum, Boones Mill, and Rocky Mount by the N&W on its route from Winston-Salem, North Carolina, to Roanoke. Ten years later, the N&W had become the Norfolk Southern Corporation (by combining N&W with the Southern Railway) serving the county with bulk and mixed freight service.

In addition, in 1976 four bus lines served the county: Greyhound and Tri-State Bus lines offered passenger and freight service, Greyhound between Roanoke and Winston-Salem and Tri-State each way between Rocky Mount and Martinsville as well as Rocky Mount and Roanoke. The other two lines (Houston Bus Lines and H&W [Hodges and Wray]) carried industrial workers to and from their factories, primarily from Rocky Mount to Martinsville and Henry County. By 1986, Intercity Bus Lines provided the county with out-of-town and out-of-state passenger and freight service.

Franklin County has no major long-distance trucking firms located within the county's borders, but it is served by fourteen interstate carriers as well as a few that provided intrastate service. United Parcel Service provides express service to the county. In addition, the county's industrial, commercial, and agricultural needs are partly met by special hauling equipment that is "available in the county to handle such items as petroleum products, refrigerated foodstuffs, steel products, and machinery." Some of the industries and commercial houses provide their own trucking facilities. There are also some small operators and independent owners who have trucks on hand for hire to meet the county's hauling requirements.

Finally, several airports serve the county's air travel needs although none is located in the county itself. Roanoke Municipal Airport, Woodrum Field, is found ten miles from Franklin County and in 1976 Eastern and Piedmont Airlines provided service there. The Blue Ridge Airport, about thirty miles south of Rocky Mount in Henry County, since 1966 has offered charter service and flight instruction. Smith Mountain Airport is located at Moneta in Bedford County and also provides charter service. Two other airports serve the county, although they are located at greater distances: Danville Municipal Airport, which offers commercial air service, and the Greensboro–High Point Regional Airport, near Greensboro, North Carolina, seventy miles south of Rocky Mount. For those willing to drive 125 miles, the Raleigh-Durham, North Carolina, Airport provides commercial passenger flights. There are several helicopter ports in nearby Roanoke.

Until the 1960s public transportation was racially segregated, as were the schools. The teachers' salary issue of 1940–1941 was but one of many inequities in black education in need of correction, however, and it required the United States Supreme Court, through its 1954 decision in the case of *Brown* v. *Board of Education of Topeka*, to order the end of the separate and unequal division of the school system. In Virginia, as throughout the South, the white establishment responded with the policy called "Massive Resistance" to racial desegregation; eventually, however, the inevitable was accepted and the public schools were opened to all citizens. In Franklin County the new order was effected slowly with but little of the overt violence that occurred elsewhere.

In 1986 the public school system taught 6,330 students. The county had eleven elementary schools, a middle school, a high school, and a special education center. Three private schools operated in the county, and one institution of higher education—Ferrum College.

By the end of World War II Ferrum Training School–Junior College was poised on the edge of financial collapse. Its small size and aging facilities made it uneconomical to operate. Over the next ten years the school struggled to survive, until Dr. C. Ralph Arthur, its seventh president, took office in 1954. He quickly decided that the school's salvation lay in expansion. Over the course of his administration as president, Arthur led successful campaigns to enlarge the school's endowment, negotiated loans for new construction, saw to completion the building of virtually an entire new campus, initiated a program of inter-collegiate athletics, and more than tripled the student enrollment. Perhaps most important for the students, in 1960 the Southern Association of Colleges and Secondary Schools accredited Ferrum Junior College; this meant that a Ferrum student could transfer his credits to any college or university that would admit him. In 1976 the association accredited Ferrum as a four-year college.[23] The college had been racially integrated in 1965 with the admission of black day students.[24]

In 1973 the college expanded its vision beyond traditional curricula when it established the Institute of Mountain Lore to "include programs focused on the history, culture, arts and crafts, music, and economy of Franklin County and the Blue Ridge Mountains of Southwest Virginia."[25] Within a few years the institute, which was renamed the Blue Ridge Institute, had under the direction of J. Roderick Moore, a nationally recognized expert on folk art, assembled sizable collections of musical recordings, artifacts, and furniture of the region. Today its programs have expanded substantially. The institute established a Blue Ridge

Heritage Archive that contains oral histories, photographs, student papers, and manuscripts concerning mountain life. It also constructed the Blue Ridge Farm Museum, consisting of two farmsteads (of 1800 and 1900), using threatened structures that were disassembled and moved to a site across Route 40 from the college. Costumed living-history interpreters operate the museum. As of 1988 the institute had produced a series of recordings containing authentic regional music. Each October it sponsors the Blue Ridge Folklife Festival, at which craftsmen, musicians, and quilters demonstrate their talents.[26] Only authentic crafts, music, and food are allowed, and more than twenty thousand visitors attend the festival each year.

Blue Ridge Institute Farm Museum and Ferrum College: early 19th-century Prillaman barn and Bottoms House (foreground); *Vaughn Chapel and Carillon* (center background). (Blue Ridge Institute, Ferrum, Va.)

Besides the festival, two other attractions draw visitors as well as new residents to Franklin County every year: Philpott Lake and Smith Mountain Lake. The Army Corps of Engineers created Philpott Lake on the Smith River in southwestern Franklin County between 1948 and 1953 for flood control. Turbines and generators also provide electricity. The 2,880-acre lake is roughly three-quarters of a mile wide and fourteen miles long; it has around a hundred miles of shoreline that is shared by Franklin, Patrick, and Henry counties. About seven thousand federally owned acres of land surround the lake and are used for agriculture and wildlife conservation. Along the shore are marinas, campgrounds, and picnic tables.[27]

Smith Mountain Lake was constructed on the Staunton River between 1960 and 1966 to produce electrical power. The dam is 816 feet long and 227 feet high, creating a 40-mile-long, 20,600-acre lake. More than five hundred miles of shoreline are shared by Franklin, Bedford, and Pittsylvania counties. Because the property around the lake is privately owned, the area has experienced considerable residential and commercial development. Rising property values have encouraged many farmers to sell their land. The farms have been replaced for the most part by residential developments consisting of primary homes occupied by commuters to Roanoke and retirees as well as second homes owned by prosperous nonresidents.[28]

Some traditional activities other than farming seem to have survived the pressures of modern life, however. Franklin County's special brand of lawlessness—moonshining—has continued to thrive despite the efforts of revenue agents to stamp it out. Large stills occasionally are discovered; the entrance to one of the most famous recent stills was disguised as a family cemetery with cinder blocks painted white and the roadway to the still masked by dead trees. But increasingly too a new breed of moonshiner has taken over the centuries-old business, one who also deals in drugs as well. This type of illicit distiller has proved much more dangerous than his predecessors and more likely to shoot his "way out of a jam." V. K. ("Kenny") Stoneman who spent fourteen years as a state Alcoholic Beverage Control Commission agent-in-charge in Franklin County concluded that "you can make a lot more money a lot easier [dealing drugs]—but if you're caught, you'll spend a lot more time in jail."[29]

The moonshining life was not always that way. In his first years as Franklin County special agent-in-charge, Stoneman learned that his initial impression was wrong that moonshiners were dangerous criminals who would break any and all laws of the state. "In fact, in some cases, I soon developed compassion for some of the old-timers. In most cases, aside from their moonshining or illicit whiskey dealing, they were honest, law-abiding, accommodating people who were respected in the community." During the time he spent as Franklin's agent, Stoneman met perhaps hundreds of "moonshiners, bootleggers, and transporters." Indeed, early in his career, he received a sharp lesson in driving when he discovered that the " 'wheelmen' in their huge Chevys with souped-up engines . . . were so good they could hurtle down a backwoods dirt road at 100 MPH with their lights off at midnight, loaded to the gills with moonshine, and never spill a drop." One such driver taunted Stoneman at least once a month even if he were not hauling moonshine. "He'd come flying by and I'd go after him. I never caught him. Their cars were faster than ours, and that guy was a helluva driver."[30]

Despite the vast amount of moonshine whiskey produced during the 1926–1935 period as revealed in the famous moonshine conspiracy trial, the largest illegal distillery found in the county to date was destroyed on 18 December 1972 when federal Alcohol, Tobacco, and Firearm and state ABC agents raided the operation, located about a half mile off of Route 778 in the so-called "Republican Church" section of the county about four miles southwest of Ferrum. Agents found twenty-four 718-gallon submarine stills worth thousands of dollars with a product worth hundreds of thousands of dollars. Twenty-two of the stills had been "mashed in" and held 15,796 gallons of mash. The new appearance of the stills, however, led to the conclusion that the business had not been underway for long. As a cozy touch, the operators (who escaped capture by running into the nearby woods) had placed a mailbox on one of the posts supporting the shed that housed many of the stills. The writer, Morris Stephenson, who reported the raid noted, however, that the mailbox "contained no mail."[31]

What had previously been considered the county's largest operation ever destroyed was raided the previous February, upon discovery of twenty 718-gallon submarine stills. State ABC agents had to drive through a large concrete culvert over which N&W railroad tracks lay to reach the distillery. The operation was capable of producing 1,436 gallons of moonshine a week, which would account for a $17,323 weekly tax loss to the state (at $12 per gallon). This time the agents arrested three people, seized two vehicles, and destroyed 10,000 gallons of mash and 260 gallons of illicit whiskey.[32]

A week later, the *Franklin News-Post* printed an editorial calling for a grand jury investigation of the moonshine business in the county. "Everytime we run a story and pictures of a moonshine operation being raided we are accused of giving the county a bad name," the writer complained. Thus the *News-Post* published the ABC Commission's 30 June 1971 report to show "loud and clear as to just who is responsible for moonshining in Franklin County and who is giving Franklin County a bad name." Of the 277 stills destroyed in Virginia during that fiscal year, 119 were in Franklin. The nearest "competitor" was Buchanan with 20. The editorialist concluded that until the people of Franklin County demanded something stronger than "merely slapp[ing the moonshiners] on the wrist and call[ing] them naughty boys, . . . the moonshine business will flourish in Franklin County."[33]

When Special Agent-in-Charge Kenny Stoneman later analyzed modern moonshining in Franklin he noted that during the twenty-five-year period from 1959–1960 to 1984–1985, of 124 stills destroyed statewide in 1959–1960, 55 were in Franklin; of 294 destroyed in 1968–1979, 63 were in Franklin; of 177 destroyed statewide in 1980–1981, 78 were in Franklin; and the following year of 158 statewide, 74 were in Franklin; the number had dropped by 1984–1985 to 26 for Franklin. But despite that drop in stills destroyed, Stoneman concluded that "as long as the sun rises over Smith Mountain Lake and sets over Philpott Lake to the west, there will be liquor made in Franklin County."[34]

Echoing the days of the moonshine conspiracy trial, in 1988 the producers of illicit spirits in the county found themselves short of a once-abundant ingredient—sugar—after 16 million pounds of it had been sold in a three-year period. On 31 August law enforcement officers raided a Rocky Mount sugar broker who allegedly had supplied moonshiners with such massive quantities. The resulting sugar shortage was temporary but keenly felt. As one officer said, "It breaks my heart. They probably don't have enough sugar for their coffee."[35]

In January 1992 the reputed owner of the largest still ever destroyed in Franklin County pleaded guilty to five counts of bribery of a state ABC agent and received a ten-year prison sentence. As secretly recorded conversations revealed, the man bragged that "he owned the largest moonshine still ever discovered in Franklin County—a 24-pot operation that is pictured on T-shirts [and caps] sold at local convenience stores." Despite his claim of having made $1,000 a day from that operation before the revenuers cut it up, "moonshine no longer has the hold on Franklin County that it once had during Prohibition, when—the saying went— the moon rolled over the mountains in quart jars." Perhaps fewer than a dozen operators "still make enough for shipment to big cities along the Eastern Seaboard."[36]

Blockading, or transporting illegal liquor in specially equipped cars, is said by some to be the inspiration for stock car racing. Reportedly, "some of the best NASCAR drivers in the history of that organization got their starts running 'shine through the backwoods of Franklin County and western Virginia."[37] The sport of stock car racing has long been popular in Franklin County, whatever its origins. The first speedway in Franklin did not open, however, until April 1967 when Callaway Speedway, built by Wilton Agee and Donald Guilliams, ran its initial races on a dirt track. Seating five hundred people, the one-quarter-mile racetrack proved a success in its first year. Two years later, Agee opened Franklin County

Speedway on Route 641 east of Callaway, a three-eighths-mile track with seating for a thousand fans. Shortly thereafter, problems with the dirt track caused Agee to have it paved and it became known as "the fastest 3/8-mile track in the world." Agee recalled that the largest crowd to witness a race at the FCS was one in the early 1970s—the 5,012 fans who saw Ray Hendrick, of Richmond, compete with local driver Max Berrier, who had been almost unbeatable before that event, and defeat him in every race. Although Berrier had the faster car, some new problem caused the automobile to fail him before the end of every race with Hendrick.[38]

Stock car at race in Roanoke, Charlie Williamson driving. 1950 photo. (Blue Ridge Institute, Ferrum, Va.)

Only one driver has lost his life racing in Franklin, Grayson Moye, of Roanoke County, who sustained severe head injuries during practice on 23 September 1973 and died three weeks later on 12 October without ever regaining consciousness. Richie Evans, another competitor in Franklin, who died at Martinsville in October 1985, set perhaps the fastest time recorded at the Franklin County Speedway, when he was clocked at 13.39 seconds, or 101.39 miles per hour.

The FCS changed hands twice more by the end of the 1970s. Agee sold the track in 1975 to Charles ("Squeek") McGuire, former race driver, who in turn sold it to Donald F. ("Whitey") Taylor, Roanoke businessman, in 1978. Taylor garnered probably his greatest headlines with the track in 1980 when Willie Nelson was scheduled to appear at a two-day "Great Southeastern Music Festival" on 9–10 August. Expecting an estimated gate of fifty-thousand spectators, Taylor found his plans dashed by the Franklin County Board of Supervisors and the county sheriff, W. Q. Overton. Shortly before the event was to take place, Overton announced that he would arrest Nelson if he drank on stage, Nelson's customary practice. Nelson promptly canceled the show. Only a few hundred people attended the festival so Taylor sued Nelson for $12 million, but eventually the suit lapsed. Taylor recovered from the Nelson episode, however, by adding other features to his race program to increase attendance such as wet T-shirt, "red neck," and "ugly" contests, and professional wrestling. One of his major successes came in 1984 when "Grand National arch-rivals" Darrell Waltrip and Bobby Allison competed against each other and Franklin's drivers on 21 July before a crowd estimated at 14,000. As the county approached its bicentennial, stock car racing continued to attract fans at both the Franklin County Speedway and the Log Cabin Raceway that opened in 1981 in the southwestern part of the county near Henry.

Despite the failure of Willie Nelson to appear in the county in 1980, music has always played an important role in the life of Franklin County, and over the years the county has produced a number of well-known musicians, especially practitioners of "mountain music." According to one writer, "It is generally accepted that the musical traditions of the English, Scotch-Irish, German[s] and the Africans fused to become what we are familiar with as mountain music." In the twentieth century two of the most famous Franklin County mountain musicians were county native Posey Rorer and North Carolina native Charlie Poole. Rorer and Poole met in West Virginia where Rorer was working in the coal mines and together they returned to Franklin where they formed the North Carolina Ramblers and made a little moonshine liquor. Poole played the banjo, using an unusual three-finger style necessitated by an old baseball injury to his hand, a style that has since been imitated by many other country musicians. Rorer's instrument was the fiddle, and Norman Woodlief, of Spray, North Carolina, strummed the guitar.

The trio worked at dances in barns, homes, and other locales, fiddlers' conventions, picnics, and on street corners in Franklin, as well as in West Virginia, North Carolina, Ohio, Tennessee, and other states. Because Poole liked to "ramble" more than to accept steady work he gained as much of a reputation for drinking and having a good time as he did for making music. One of his more popular songs was supposed to have been written while he was in jail, "Hungry Hash House." Two other of his hits reflect his favorite lifestyle, "He Rambled" and "Ramblin' Blues." His rambling ways caused the breakup of his first marriage but a second marriage to Posey Rorer's sister Lou Emma was more successful.

Poole and his Ramblers cut their first record in New York on the Columbia label in 1925. The 1926 *County News* supplement reported that "at the conclusion of the last engagement in New York, the company presented Mr. Poole with one of the handsomest banjos that could be obtained in the city." Two of their early hits included "Don't Let Your Deal Go Down Blues" and "Can I Sleep in Your Barn Tonight, Mister." The former, also known as "The Deal," was their greatest seller "and is still a popular tune among old time country musicians." Reportedly Poole wrote the song while he was in Franklin County. With a second record released within weeks of the first, the group became full-time traveling musicians and began performing in states all around the area. Their new record came out more than a year later with Roy Harvey, of West Virginia, as guitarist. In 1928 Lonnie Austin, of North Carolina, joined the group as fiddler since Rorer had moved to Spray, North Carolina, to live. Poole died in 1931, within a year of recording his last song, "Just Keep A-Waiting 'til the Good Times Come." Rorer performed on sixteen records that the Ramblers made at Columbia Records and wrote a song as well, "Budded Roses." Supposedly he was inspired by "a beautiful rose bush" at the home of Charlie Foster whose daughter Addie he was courting at the time and later married.[39]

Two other musicians who were well known in the county in the 1920s and 1930s were Howard Maxey and James Walter ("Peg") Hatcher. Their Ferrum String Band consistently won prizes at the fiddlers' conventions held during that period. Maxey on fiddle and Hatcher on banjo (later taking up the fiddle) were joined by Morton Pinkard on banjo, Jim Mullins and Raymond Sloan on guitar, and Archie Ross on mandolin. In 1928 at the fiddlers' convention at Ferrum Training

School, for instance, Howard Maxey won first prize for playing "Western Union" and at another convention Will Ross (Archie's father) playing clawhammer banjo and Peg Hatcher on fiddle won for duet combination for "Soward Mountain." Hatcher recalled that early in his career he played all night for dances called the "husk KO" and many times played "Shout Lu" by himself all night. Later, his band "was in great demand throughout the area."[40]

String bands played an important role in the black community as well, and one of the last county musicians to play in that style is John Lawson Tyree, of Sontag. In 1917, Rocky Mount boasted a black symphony orchestra, which on 25 January provided music for "one of the most enjoyable social functions of the season."[41] Another music style popular especially in the black community was the blues played by local bluesmen such as John Tinsley and Archie Edwards and particularly by Lewis ("Rabbit") Muse. Muse was born in the Tank Hill area of Franklin in 1908 and began performing at the age of twelve in minstrel shows for the Lions clubs in Rocky Mount and Boones Mill. He moved on to fairs, medicine shows, and eventually television. Muse played the ukulele, flute, and jazz horn in his act, which also included all phases of dance, comedy, and song. When interviewed in 1976 about his career, Muse said he planned to "continue to dance, play and sing, and that he will work a little if called upon. Mostly he plan[ned] to follow his hobbies of hunting and fishing."[42] Muse died in 1982.

White string bands gained in popularity in the 1970s and 1980s, and several of them concentrated on old tunes and songs rather than playing contemporary songs in an old-fashioned style. Such groups include the Dryhill Draggers, the Original Orchard Grass Old-Time String Band, and Pedro Cooper and the Pumpkin Vines (Cooper is a one-handed banjo player). Among the other modern country bands are the Blue Ridge Cardinals and Lost and Found.

Many Franklin County residents display their musical talents in a religious, rather than a secular, context. Gospel music is heard in and out of church—two of the better-known present-day gospel groups are the Star Gospel Singers and the

Big Brothers Quartet (left) *and Ladies Stringband from Ferrum vicinity* (below). (Blue Ridge Institute, Ferrum, Va.)

Starlight Gospel Singers, both heard on local radio shows for more than twenty-five years. And some congregations, particularly those of the Brethren and Primitive Baptists, are known for their *a cappella* singing (unaccompanied by instruments).

Besides traditional music, present-day Franklin County offers many of the modern amenities of more developed counties but still maintains its largely rural setting; it offers a sense of continuity as well as change. That spirit was rediscovered in 1986 when the county celebrated the bicentennial of its founding.[43]

On 23 May 1984 the Franklin County Bicentennial Commission held its organizational meeting. Among its officers were Dr. J. Francis Amos, chairman; Mrs. Mary Hopkins, vice-chairman; Mrs. Virginia Crook, secretary; and Mr. Rick Huff, treasurer (Mr. Huff resigned in May 1985 and Mr. Mike Meeks took his place). During the course of the next year and a half the commission met frequently to plan the bicentennial celebration and raise the funds necessary to carry the plans into effect.

"Gentlemen Justices" (Franklin County Board of Supervisors) and guests. Seated, left to right: *Blue Ridge District Supervisor Thurman E. Scott, Jr.; Boone District Supervisor Homer Murray; Rocky Mount District Supervisor Gus Forry; Union Hall District Supervisor Miles Holland; Gills Creek District Supervisor John Booth; Snow Creek District Supervisor Noell Parcell.* Standing, left to right: *Rev. McKinley Hamilton; Rev. Clarence E. Byerly; T. Keister Greer; Blackwater District Supervisor Billie Robertson, chairman of the Board of Supervisors; Allen O. Woody, Jr., mayor of Rocky Mount; Franklin County General District Court Judge W. N. ("Bill") Alexander II; Fifth District Congressman W. C. ("Dan") Daniel; Senator Virgil H. Goode, Jr.; Assistant County Administrator John Lester; Franklin County Administrator Richard E. Huff II; Delegate Willard R. Finney; Dr. J. Francis Amos, chairman of the Franklin County Bicentennial Commission. 1986 photo. (Bicentennial Reflections* [N.p.: Franklin County Bicentennial Commission, 1986], 9. Reprinted with permission.)

A committee chaired by Mrs. Jeanne Bernard coordinated a publicity campaign to develop a bicentennial logo and theme or motto. An attractive logo containing three red stripes and the theme "Progressing with Confidence, Remembering with Pride" was selected to appear on telephone books and bumper stickers.

The bicentennial year began on 1 January 1986 with a reenactment of the first county court meeting at The Farm, the home of Dr. and Mrs. J. Francis Amos, site of the first county court meeting in 1786. The Franklin County Board of Supervisors convened as the "gentlemen justices" of 1786 and wore colonial garb. The proceedings were broadcast on radio and television; the supervisors agreed to wear colonial costume at their regular meetings throughout the remainder of the year.

A wide variety of activities took place during the bicentennial year to remind residents of their past. The activities included a tour of many of the historic houses and sites described in this book, such as the Carolina Road, The Farm, the Washington Iron Works furnace, the site of Dickinson's store, the Booker T. Washington Birthplace National Monument, the site of Germantown, the Phoebe Needles Conference Center, Algoma, and Ferrum College. A memorial service was held at the old Tanyard Cemetery to honor Franklin County's war dead and its early settlers; among those buried in the cemetery is Robert Hill, the pioneer whose life is discussed in Chapter Two. A bicentennial photograph collection project resulted in the discovery and preservation of many of the pictures that are used to illustrate this book. A number of the photographs that were copied during the course of the project were published in *Franklin County Life and Culture: A Pictorial Record* (1986).

A once-familiar institution of the nineteenth century—court day—came to life once again on 26 April 1986, complete with horse traders, string bands, merrymakers, and a mock court. Other festival-type events included dances and balls, the Franklin County High School Band Bicentennial Spring Concert, the Blue Ridge Draft Horse and Mule Show, the Boones Mill Apple Festival, two long-distance foot races (the Great Country Five Miler and the White Lightning Run), and the Bicentennial July 4th Celebration.

The Punkin Vine railroad line carried passengers once more on a special excursion train that sold all its seats well in advance of the trip. Making local stops at Boones Mill, Rocky Mount, Ferrum, and Henry, the train included older county residents who shared their memories of the original Punkin Vine with their children and grandchildren. Many county residents took part in a special bicentennial drama, *Faith of Our Fathers*, commemorating the founding of the county and written by Rex Stephenson, of Ferrum College. A time capsule containing assorted Franklin County memorabilia, including a 1986 gold coin and messages from attendees to their future descendants, was buried in front of the courthouse. A publication, *Bicentennial Reflections*, contained more than two dozen articles on the history of the county. Among other activities, a bicentennial parade—"the greatest parade ever staged in Franklin County"— was highlighted by an original Conestoga wagon later given to the Blue Ridge Institute, portrayals of early Franklin County life, an 1887 fire truck that had rescued Civil War general Jubal A. Early in 1890, and many other vehicles and floats. The featured speaker, Jon McBride, astronaut of the space shuttle *Challenger*, returned to his ancestral home and addressed about three thousand

Franklin County middle and high school students. He recalled that his father had driven horse-drawn buggies in Franklin and had lived to see his son travel in space.

All of the bicentennial year's activities proved to be so successful that a thirty-thousand-dollar surplus was realized at the end of the year. With that sum, the Franklin County Bicentennial Commission was able to endow a Heritage Day speaker for the Franklin County High School, as well as the Gertrude C. Mann Room at the Franklin County Public Library in Rocky Mount to enlarge the library's collection of county historical and genealogical materials. Other moneys were used for acquisitions of a local history nature at the Blue Ridge Institute, and three state historical highway markers were erected: at Boones Mill to mark the Carolina Road crossing the Blue Ridge at Maggotty Gap, on Route 116 to commemorate the birthplace of General Jubal A. Early, and on Main Street in Rocky Mount at the site of the Washington Iron Works.

The bicentennial celebration was a success because it encouraged Franklin County residents to participate, not merely observe. The *Roanoke Times and World-News*, reviewing all the activities that took place during the year, declared that "seldom has a Western Virginia county examined its past as thoroughly as the people of Franklin have done in their 200th anniversary year."

Franklin County, as it exists today, is the product of more than two hundred years of experience and slow evolution as a predominantly rural community. Its history, architecture, and tempo of life, as well as the values of its inhabitants, reflect that evolution. The pace of change, however, has quickened in recent years, in Franklin County as in the rest of the country. How to control inevitable change is one of the greatest challenges its inhabitants face. As Franklin County prepares to enter the twenty-first century, its citizens seek to be informed of their past—as the bicentennial celebration proved—in part so that they may weigh the demands of population growth, commercial and residential development, recreation, and the expansion of government services against what they may lose of their traditional, rural heritage. Perhaps, with a greater understanding of their county's history, they will find and maintain a satisfactory balance.

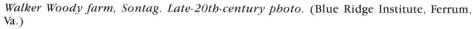

Walker Woody farm, Sontag. Late-20th-century photo. (Blue Ridge Institute, Ferrum, Va.)

NOTES

Short Titles and Symbols

Duke   Manuscript Department, William R. Perkins Library, Duke University, Durham, N.C.

FCPL   Franklin County Public Library, Rocky Mount, Va.

NARA   National Archives and Records Administration, Washington, D.C.

UNC   Southern Historical Collection, Library of the University of North Carolina at Chapel Hill.

UVA   Special Collections Department, University of Virginia Library, Charlottesville.

VDHR   Virginia Department of Historic Resources, Richmond.

VHS   Virginia Historical Society, Richmond.

VMHB   *Virginia Magazine of History and Biography.*

VSLA   Archives Branch, Virginia State Library and Archives, Richmond.

WPA   Works Progress Administration Historical Inventory, General Library Division, Virginia State Library and Archives, Richmond.

. . .

Chapter One: Prehistory and European Exploration

[1] Emily J. Salmon, ed., *A Hornbook of Virginia History,* 3d ed. (Richmond: Virginia State Library, 1983), 3–5.

[2] Keith Frye, *Roadside Geology of Virginia* (Missoula, Mont.: Mountain Press Publishing Company, 1986), 163.

[3] Richard V. Dietrich, *Geology and Virginia* (Charlottesville: University Press of Virginia, 1970), 162.

[4] Frye, *Roadside Geology,* 19.

[5] William M. McGill, *Outline of the Mineral Resources of Virginia,* Bulletin 47, Educational Series No. 3 (Richmond: Division of Purchase and Printing, 1936), 28, 44, 50, 55, 62; William M. Fontaine, "Notes on the Geology and Mineral Resources of the Floyd, Va., Plateau," *Virginias* 4 (1883): 167, 178–180; field notebook, George W. Boyd, pp. 84–85, Geological Survey of Virginia, 1836–1841, VSLA.

[6] In this instance we have given the traditional names and limits of the Staunton and Roanoke rivers. Typically in this work, however, we have used as our authority Thomas H. Biggs, *Geographic and Cultural Names in Virginia* (Charlottesville: Virginia Division of Mineral Resources, 1974). This book lists place-names, water features, land forms, and

467

religious institutions as they appear on recent topographic maps prepared by the United States Geological Survey. The names and their spellings are those agreed upon by various state and federal bureaucracies; they do not necessarily agree with traditional or local names and spellings. "Officially," for example, the Staunton River does not exist in Southside Virginia; the river is the Roanoke from the Blue Ridge to the ocean. As irritating as such official, homogenized names may be to historians, they are in fact the names and spellings one is likely to encounter on road signs, bridges, and highway maps. As a compromise, therefore, we have used the modern, official names of features in the text but included their historical variants whenever possible.

[7]Fontaine, "Geology and Mineral Resources of the Floyd, Va., Plateau," 180.

[8]Dietrich, *Geology and Virginia*, 56–57.

[9]Seth J. Diamond and Robert H. Giles, Jr., "A Vegetational History of Virginia's Ridge and Valley Province," *Quarterly Bulletin, Archeological Society of Virginia* 42 (1987): 177.

[10]The following discussion of Native American history in Virginia is taken from Mary Ellen N. Hodges, *A Brief Relation of Virginia Prehistory* (Richmond: Department of Conservation and Historic Resources, 1981).

[11]Diamond and Giles, "Vegetational History," 182.

[12]Hodges, *Virginia Prehistory*, 8.

[13]John R. Swanton, *The Indians of the Southeastern United States* (Washington, D.C.: Smithsonian Institution Press, 1979), 152, 164.

[14]Keith T. Egloff, Joey T. Moldenhauer, and David E. Rotenizer, "The Otter Creek Site (44FR31): A Late Woodland Hamlet Along the Blue Ridge Escarpment," *Quarterly Bulletin, Archeological Society of Virginia* 42 (1987): 1.

[15]Howard A. MacCord, Sr., "The Meador Site, Franklin County, Virginia," *Quarterly Bulletin, Archeological Society of Virginia* 25 (1971): 206.

[16]Richard P. Gravely, Jr., "Indians in Franklin County, Virginia," *Bicentennial Reflections* (n.p.: Franklin County Bicentennial Commission, 1986), 10.

[17]J. Francis Amos, "The Patterson Site, Franklin County, Va.," *Quarterly Bulletin, Archeological Society of Virginia* 21 (1967): 81–82.

[18]Howard A. MacCord, Sr., "The Brubaker Site, Franklin County, Virginia," *Quarterly Bulletin, Archeological Society of Virginia* 24 (1970): 232.

[19]Egloff, Moldenhauer, and Rotenizer, "Otter Creek," 6; a report on this site (44FR11) by L. C. Carter has been published. *See* "Bone Bottom," *Quarterly Bulletin, Archeological Society of Virginia* 3 (1948): n.p.

[20]Egloff, Moldenhauer, and Rotenizer, "Otter Creek," 6.

[21]Ibid.

[22]William Buttram patented land at the "Indian Town" in 1742. This evidence suggests that the village may have been abandoned not long before, if the remains of the impermanent village structures still were visible.

[23]Egloff, Moldenhauer, and Rotenizer, "Otter Creek," 13.

[24]Ibid.,

[25]Ibid., 7.

[26]Ibid., 13.

[27]Ibid.

[28]Gravely, "Indians," 13.

[29]Clarence Walworth Alvord and Lee Bidgood, *The First Explorations of the Trans-Allegheny Region by the Virginians, 1650–1674* (Cleveland: The Arthur H. Clark Co., 1912), 184.

[30]Alan Vance Briceland, *Westward from Virginia: The Exploration of the Virginia-Carolina Frontier, 1650–1710* (Charlottesville: University Press of Virginia, 1987), 13.

[31]Ibid., 197.

[32]Alvord and Bidgood, *First Explorations*, 186.

[33]Ibid.

[34]Briceland, *Westward*, 138.

[35]Alvord and Bidgood, *First Explorations*, 185.

[36]Briceland, *Westward*, 140.

[37]Ibid., 143–145.

[38]Alvord and Bidgood, *First Explorations*, 193.

[39]Ibid.

Chapter Two: Southside Frontier

[1]William Byrd, "History of the Dividing Line betwixt Virginia and North Carolina Run in the Year of Our Lord 1728," in *The Prose Works of William Byrd of Westover*, ed. Louis B. Wright (Cambridge, Mass.: The Belknap Press of Harvard University Press, 1966), 250–302; idem, "A Journey to the Land of Eden Anno 1733," ibid., 389.

[2]Joseph Ewan and Nesta Ewan, *John Banister and His Natural History of Virginia, 1678–1692* (Urbana: University of Illinois Press, 1970), 354.

[3]Marian D. Chiarito, *Entry Record Book, 1737–1770 (Land Entries in the Present Virginia Counties of Halifax, Pittsylvania, Henry, Franklin, and Patrick)* (N.p.: Marian D. Chiarito, 1984).

[4]Michael L. Nicholls, "Origins of the Virginia Southside, 1703–1753: A Social and Economic Study" (Ph.D. diss., College of William and Mary, 1972), 14.

[5]Ewan and Ewan, *John Banister*, 384–385.

[6]George T. Hunt, *The Wars of the Iroquois: A Study in Intertribal Trade Relations* (Madison: University of Wisconsin Press, 1960; reprint, 1967), 3.

[7]Maud Carter Clement, *The History of Pittsylvania County, Virginia* (Lynchburg, Va.: J. P. Bell Co., 1929; Baltimore: Regional Publishing Co., 1981), 84.

[8]Hunt, *Iroquois*, 4.

[9]Byrd, *Prose Works*, 257–258.

[10]Jack H. Wilson, Jr., "A Study of the Late Prehistoric, Protohistoric, and Historic Indians of the Carolina and Virginia Piedmont: Structure, Process, and Ecology" (Ph.D. diss., University of North Carolina, 1983), 185.

[11]John R. Swanton, *The Indians of the Southeastern United States* (Washington, D.C.: Smithsonian Institution Press, 1979), 179, 201; Wilson, "Indians of the Carolina and Virginia Piedmont," 197.

[12]T. Keister Greer, "Genesis of a Virginia Frontier: The Origins of Franklin County, Virginia, 1740–1785" (Senior honors thesis, University of Virginia, 1946), 20–23.

[13]Richard R. Beeman, *The Evolution of the Southern Backcountry: A Case Study of Lunenburg County, Virginia, 1746–1832* (Philadelphia: University of Pennsylvania Press, 1984), 25–26; Greer, "Genesis of a Virginia Frontier," 54.

[14]Nicholls, "Virginia Southside," 63–64.

[15]Clement, *Pittsylvania County*, 89.

[16]Ibid., 89–91.

[17]Chiarito, *Entry Record Book, 1737–1770*, 45, 72–73.

[18]Greer, "Genesis of a Virginia Frontier," 31.

[19]Chiarito, *Entry Record Book, 1737–1770*, 4.

[20]Ibid.

[21]Ibid., 9.

[22]Greer, "Genesis of a Virginia Frontier," 32.

[23]Land Office, Patents No. 27, 1748–1749, Reel 25, pp. 298–300, VSLA.

[24]Chiarito, *Entry Record Book, 1737–1770*, 15.

[25]Land Office, Patents No. 27, 1748–1749, pp. 426–427, VSLA.

[26]Chiarito, *Entry Record Book, 1737–1770*, 44.

[27]Landon C. Bell, *Sunlight on the Southside: Lists of Tithes, Lunenburg County, Virginia, 1748–1783* (Philadelphia: George S. Ferguson Co., 1931; Baltimore: Genealogical Publishing Co., 1974), 79, 93; map of tax districts opposite p. 58.

[28]Ibid., 85, 96; map of tax districts opposite p. 58.

[29]Land Office, Patents No. 31, 1751–1756, Reel 29, p. 711; Patents E, 1775–1776, 1780–1781, Reel 46, p. 176, VSLA. The second Robert Hodges likely was another man with the same name.

[30]Chiarito, *Entry Record Book, 1737–1770*, 71.

[31]Nicholls, "Virginia Southside," 46–47.

[32]J. Francis Amos, "Early Roads in Franklin County," *Bicentennial Reflections* (N.p.: Franklin County Bicentennial Commission, 1986), 27; Jeanne Bernard, "The Franklin County Bicentennial Driving Tour," ibid., 87.

[33]Amos, "Early Roads," 27.

[34]Ibid., 27–28.

[35]Chiarito, *Entry Record Book, 1737–1770*, 42.

[36]Bell, *Sunlight on the Southside*, 83; map of tax districts opposite p. 58.

[37]William J. Hinke and Charles E. Kemper, eds., "Moravian Diaries of Travels through Virginia," *VMHB* 12 (1905): 273.

[38]Ibid., 273.

[39]Ibid., 273–274.

[40]Ibid., 275.

[41]Greer, "Genesis of a Virginia Frontier," 33–63.

[42]Ibid., 66–85.

[43]Marshall Wingfield, *Pioneer Families of Franklin County, Virginia* (Berryville, Va.: Chesapeake Book Co., 1964), 120–121.

[44]Bell, *Sunlight on the Southside*, 96.

[45]Chiarito, *Entry Record Book, 1737–1770*, 133.

[46]Henry County, Will Book 1, 1777–1799, Reel 15, p. 7, VSLA, lists sons Swinfield and Thomas and daughters Ruth, Mary, Johanah, and Hannah.

[47]Greer, "Genesis of a Virginia Frontier," 23.

[48]Wingfield, *Pioneer Families*, 121.

[49]Clement, *Pittsylvania County*, 66.

[50]Ibid., 88.

[51]Greer, "Genesis of a Virginia Frontier," 25.

[52]Howard A. MacCord, Sr., "The Brubaker Site, Franklin County, Virginia," *Quarterly Bulletin, Archeological Society of Virginia* 24 (1970): 227, 233.

[53]John F. D. Smith, a Scottish traveler, quoted in Lela C. Adams et al., *Henry County: A Proud Look Back* (Bassett, Va.: First National Bank of Bassett, 1975), 12.

[54]Ibid., 14.

[55]Clement, *Pittsylvania County*, 82–83.

[56]Ibid., 83–84.

[57]Petition, Robert Pusey to House of Burgesses, 3 June 1775, quoted in Greer, "Genesis of a Virginia Frontier," 24.

[58]Patricia G. Johnson, *The New River Early Settlement* (Pulaski, Va.: Edmonds Printing, 1983), 168.

[59]Greer, "Genesis of a Virginia Frontier," 28.

[60]Clerk's Office, Henry County Courthouse, Martinsville, Va.

[61]Franklin County, Will Book No. 1, 1786–1812, Reel 18, p. 67, VSLA.

[62]Architectural Survey File 33–81, VDHR.

[63]Ibid., 33–80.

[64]Ibid., 33–340.

[65]Ibid., 33–30.

⁶⁶Chiarito, *Entry Record Book, 1737–1770*, 180.

⁶⁷Ibid., 243.

⁶⁸Clement, *Pittsylvania County*, 105.

⁶⁹Ibid., 52–54.

⁷⁰Hinke and Kemper, "Moravian Diaries," 274.

⁷¹Clement, *Pittsylvania County*, 118, quoted from the Camden Parish Vestry Book.

⁷²Robert G. Gardner, "Virginia Baptist Statistics, 1699–1790," *Virginia Baptist Register* 21 (1982): 1020–1038.

⁷³Henry County, Will Book 1, p. 13. Hill's is the oldest marked grave in Franklin County and is located in Old Tanyard Cemetery in Rocky Mount; the date on his tombstone—18 Aug. 1778—is in error, however. His will, which is recorded on p. 7 of Will Book 1, was written on 31 July 1777 and probated on 16 Mar. 1778, after he died. Assuming that the day and month recorded on the tombstone are correct, his death must have occurred on 18 Aug. 1777, not 1778.

⁷⁴Ibid., 7.

⁷⁵It is possible that the Robert Hodges discussed here is the son of Robert Hodges the pioneer (letter, Robert L. Hodges, Richmond, Va., to J. Francis Amos, Rocky Mount, Va., 6 June 1990).

⁷⁶Charles P. Blunt IV, comp., *Complete Index and Abstract of the Henry County Order Books #1 and #2 (1777–1782)* (Richmond: Briarwood Publications, 1978), 67.

⁷⁷Ibid., 80.

Chapter Three: Revolution in the Backcountry

¹Page Smith, *John Adams*, 2 vols. (Garden City, N.Y.: Doubleday & Co., 1962), 2:1097.

²William J. Van Schreeven, Robert L. Scribner, and Brent Tarter, eds., *Revolutionary Virginia: The Road to Independence* (Charlottesville: Published for the Virginia Independence Bicentennial Commission by the University Press of Virginia, 1973–1983), 1:72–77.

³Ibid., 78–84.

⁴Ibid., 96–98.

⁵Ibid., 102.

⁶Ibid., 2:268, 300.

⁷Maud Carter Clement, *The History of Pittsylvania County, Virginia* (Lynchburg, Va.: J. P. Bell Co., 1929; Baltimore: Regional Publishing Co., 1981), 148.

⁸Ibid., 151; Auditor of Public Accounts, Revolutionary War Pension Records, Lewis Davis, VSLA; Receipt, William Bartee to Alexander Brownlee, Henry County, 22 Apr. 1779, Clerk's Office, Henry County Courthouse, Martinsville, Va.

⁹Affidavit of Jacob McNiel, Sr., Franklin County, 3 Sept. 1832, File S5745, Revolutionary War Pension Records, NARA.

¹⁰Ibid.

¹¹Warren Moorman, "John Hook, Storekeeper," *Bicentennial Reflections* (N.p.: Franklin County Bicentennial Commission, 1986), 29.

¹²John Hook Papers, 1737 (1770–1848), 1889, Duke.

¹³Van Schreeven, Scribner, and Tarter, *Revolutionary Virginia*, 3:162, 207.

¹⁴Ibid., 230.

¹⁵Ibid., 234–235.

¹⁶John Hook Papers, 1763–1806, Misc. Reel 642, Memorandum, 1776, VSLA.

¹⁷Bedford County, Order Book 6, 1774–1782, Reel 40, p. p. 116–117, VSLA.

¹⁸Juliet Fauntleroy, "John Hook as a Loyalist," *VMHB* 33 (1925): 402–403.

¹⁹Bedford County, Order Book 6, p. 290.

²⁰Ibid., 234–235, 287–289.

[21]Ibid., 296.

[22]Ibid., 298–300.

[23]Ibid., 300.

[24]Ibid., 300–303.

[25]Ibid., 305.

[26]Records of the General Assembly, Legislative Petitions, Bedford County, 21 Nov. 1780, VSLA.

[27]Henry County, Order Book 1, 1777–1778, Reel 20, pp. 3–4, VSLA.

[28]Henry County, Order Book 2, 1778–1782, Reel 20, pp. 52, 112, 114–115, 117, 136, 146, VSLA.

[29]Quoted in Lela C. Adams et al., *Henry County: A Proud Look Back* (Bassett, Va.: First National Bank of Bassett, 1975), 30.

[30]William W. Hening, *The Statutes at Large* . . . (New York: Printed for the Editor, 1809–1823), 10:225.

[31]Thomas Jefferson, *Papers of Thomas Jefferson*, edited by Julian P. Boyd et al. (Princeton: Princeton University Press, 1950–), 5:213.

[32]Ibid., 353.

[33]Albert H. Tillson, Jr., "The Localist Roots of Backcountry Loyalism: An Examination of Popular Political Culture in Virginia's New River Valley," *Journal of Southern History* 54 (1988): 401.

[34]Emory G. Evans, "Trouble in the Backcountry: Disaffection in Southwest Virginia during the American Revolution," in Ronald Hoffman, Thad W. Tate, and Peter J. Albert, eds., *An Uncivil War: The Southern Backcountry During the American Revolution* (Charlottesville: Published for the United States Capitol Historical Society by the University Press of Virginia, 1985), 194.

[35]Jefferson, *Papers*, 5:310.

[36]Auditor of Public Accounts, Revolutionary War Pension Records, VSLA.

[37]Christopher Ward, *The War of the Revolution* (New York: The Macmillan Co., 1952), 2:721–731.

[38]File R1017, Revolutionary War Pension Records, NARA; typescript in FCPL.

[39]Ward, *War of the Revolution*, 2:783–794.

[40]Affidavit of John Vest, 1818, quoted in Essie W. Smith Papers, FCPL.

[41]Virginia Revolutionary War Pension Records, Reel 2, Folder 40, VSLA.

[42]John Frederick Dorman, *Virginia Revolutionary Pension Applications* (Washington, D.C.: John Frederick Dorman, 1958–), 3:17–18.

[43]Ibid., 1:8.

[44]Ibid., 15:17.

[45]Ibid., 22:74–75.

[46]Ibid., 26:41–42.

[47]Ibid., 22:84–85.

[48]Ibid., 28:1.

[49]Affidavit of William Wade, Oct. 1818, quoted in Essie W. Smith Papers, FCPL.

[50]Dorman, *Virginia Revolutionary Pension Applications*, 24:28.

[51]Mark M. Boatner III, *Landmarks of the American Revolution* (Harrisburg, Pa.: Stackpole Books, 1973), 312–313.

[52]Affidavit of Thomas Dunn, Franklin County, 30 Nov. 1832, File S16373, Revolutionary War Pension Records, NARA.

[53]Affidavit of William Cuff, 25 May 1825, quoted in Essie W. Smith Papers, FCPL.

[54]Ibid.

[55]Affidavit, 12 Sept. 1832, on file at Franklin County Courthouse, Rocky Mount, Va.; typescript courtesy of Mrs. Virginia Greer Williams, Rocky Mount, Va.

[56]Adams et al., *Henry County: A Proud Look Back*, 19.

[57]William Wirt, *Sketches of the Life and Character of Patrick Henry*, 9th ed. (Philadelphia: Thomas, Cowperthwait and Co., 1845), 389–390.

[58]Ibid., 390–391.

[59]Franklin County, [District Court] Order Book 1, 1789–1793, Reel 35, p. 30, VSLA.

[60]Audrey K. Spence, "John Hook, Loyalist," *VMHB* 34 (1926): 149.

Chapter Four: "Called and known by the name of Franklin"

[1]Records of the General Assembly, Legislative Petitions, Bedford County, 24 May 1779 (two petitions), 27 May 1779, VSLA.

[2]Ibid., Bedford County, 24 May 1779, 23 May 1780 (two petitions), 21 Nov. 1781 (two petitions).

[3]Ibid., Henry County, 8 June 1782 (two petitions), 15 Nov. 1788 [*sic*] (two petitions).

[4]Ibid., 23 Nov. 1782.

[5]Ibid., 4 June 1783.

[6]Ibid., 27 Oct. 1785.

[7]Ibid., 24 May 1779.

[8]Ibid., 2 Nov. 1779.

[9]Ibid., 23 Nov. 1782 (one petition from each county).

[10]William W. Hening, *The Statutes at Large* . . . (New York: Printed for the Editor, 1809–1823), 12:70.

[11]Henry County, "A List of Souls, Dwelling Houses, &c. taken by Swinfield Hill Esq. for the Year 1785," Clerk's Office, Henry County Courthouse, Martinsville, Va.

[12]The floorboards in the present dining room to the left of the stair hall have been lengthened by adding short boards next to the partition that supports the stairs; this indicates that the partition has been moved, probably when the house was remodeled in 1856, to make the stair hall somewhat narrower than the flanking rooms. In the basement the view is clear from chimney to chimney, with no intervening foundation walls to indicate that the house ever had any fewer than three rooms. In other words, the house was not built on the hall-parlor plan with a third room added later.

[13]Franklin County, Order Book [1], 1786–1789, Reel 27, p. 15, VSLA.

[14]Kent Druyvesteyn, "Courthouses of Franklin County," *Virginia Cavalcade* 21 (1971): 16–17.

[15]Franklin County, Order Book [1], pp. 1–3.

[16]Ibid., 6–11.

[17]T. Keister Greer, "The First County Court," *Bicentennial Reflections* (N.p.: Franklin County Bicentennial Commission, 1986), 19; Cynthia Miller Leonard, comp., *The General Assembly of Virginia, July 30, 1619–January 11, 1978: A Bicentennial Register of Members* (Richmond: Published for the General Assembly of Virginia by the Virginia State Library, 1978), 98, 100, 104, 110, 150.

[18]Greer, "First County Court," 19; Leonard, *General Assembly*, 126.

[19]Greer, "First County Court," 19; Leonard, *General Assembly*, 164, 172.

[20]Greer, "First County Court," 19; Leonard, *General Assembly*, 191, 195, 211, 215, 219, 223, 227, 231, 243.

[21]Greer, "First County Court," 19; Leonard, *General Assembly*, 130, 134, 138, 142, 146, 154.

[22]Greer, "First County Court," 20; Leonard, *General Assembly*, 187, 195, 199.

[23]Greer, "First County Court," 20; Leonard, *General Assembly*, 157, 160.

[24]Greer, "First County Court," 19.

[25]Ibid.; the last mention of Smith (assuming it is the same John Smith) in the Franklin County Court records is in 1796.

[26]Franklin County, Order Book [1], p. 215.

[27]Henry County, Order Book No. 3, 1782–1785, Reel 20, pp. 186, VSLA.

[28]Franklin County, Order Book [1], p. 10.

[29]John Smith Papers, 1724–1923, Acc. 2027, Tracy W. McGregor Library, UVA.

[30]Franklin County, Order Book [1], p. 7.

[31]Auditor of Public Accounts, Land and Personal Property Tax Books, Franklin County, 1786, VSLA. The following information was extracted for each person listed in the tax books and entered into the data base in the SYSTAT ("The System for Statistics") program: name, number of white male tithes, number of slaves aged 12 to 16, number of slaves over 16, total number of slaves, number of cattle, number of horses, amount of personal property tax, acreage and tax on up to six tracts of land, total amount of land tax, combined total of land and personal property tax, type and amount of any other tax (such as for stud horses), and total amount of all taxes. It was assumed that any male taxpayer whose name appeared without any white male tithables noted was a nonresident of the county (generally only a landowner). To produce a list of residents only, the SYSTAT program was directed to extract those persons who met the criteria for nonresidence. The statistical analyses presented in this and other chapters was computed by the program from the list of residents.

[32]To arrive at this figure we instructed the SYSTAT program to delete from the list of resident taxpayers all those who did not own at least one tract of land. We then used the "Statistics" module of the program to compute the mean size of the first tract owned by each taxpayer; because most persons owned no more than one tract, we believe 280 acres is reasonably accurate. In addition, the first tract listed for any one taxpayer usually was the most valuable—most developed—tract. In other words, if the first tract listed was two hundred acres and the second was six hundred acres, the first usually was worth more per acre (indicating more of it was in farmland) than the second (indicating less of it was in farmland). The acreage and value of the first tract listed, then, is a better indicator of the relative wealth and income potential of the taxpayer.

[33]Only two taxpayers in this group owned more than two horses, and only five owned seven or more cattle; none owned slaves.

[34]Out of 325 resident landowners identified from the 1786 tax lists, only 12 (about 3.5 percent) owned neither horse nor cow, and 9 of them were women—probably widows who were supplied with labor, meat, and produce by their children.

[35]Franklin County, Will Book 1, 1786–1812, Reel 18, pp. 39–40, VSLA; administrator's bond taken out by his widow, Jane Akin, on 2 Mar. 1789 and recorded the same day.

[36]Ibid., 41; inventory and appraisement made 11 Sept. 1789 and recorded 5 Oct. 1789.

[37]On 3 Dec. 1787 James Akin was exempted from future payments of county and parish levies—an exemption sometimes granted the elderly or poor; Franklin County, Order Book [1], p. 187.

[38]Franklin County, Will Book 1, p. 39; inventory and appraisement taken 6 June 1789 and recorded 3 Aug. 1789.

[39]Ibid., 37; will proved 4 May 1789.

[40]Ibid., 2; recorded 5 July 1787.

[41]Ibid., 4–5; proved 3 July 1786; his children were Mary, Agg, James, Isham, David, Sally, John, Penelope, Molly, Henry, Benjamin, and Ruth.

[42]Ibid., 34–35; recorded 5 Jan. 1789.

[43]Ibid., 26–28; proved 3 Nov. 1788.

Chapter Five: Founding Fathers and County Politics

[1]Tadahisa Kuroda, "The County Court System of Virginia from the Revolution to the Civil War" (Ph.D. diss., Columbia University, 1970), 17.

[2]Bedford County, Order Book 8, 1784–1786, Reel 41, list of justices written on endpaper, VSLA.

[3]Henry County, Order Book 4, 1785–1788, Reel 20, list of justices compiled from various pages, VSLA.

[4]Henry County, Order Book 1, 1777–1778, Reel 20, p. 22 (21 Oct. 1777), VSLA.

[5]Marshall Wingfield, *An Old Virginia Court: Being a Transcript of the Records of the First Court of Franklin County, Virginia, 1786–1789* (Memphis: West Tennessee Historical Society, 1948), 223.

[6]Franklin County 1786 land and personal property tax books as analyzed by the SYSTAT program.

[7]Ibid. Dickenson ranked sixty-first in the pool of 689 taxpayers who were residents of the county.

[8]Franklin County, Will Book 1, 1786–1812, Reel 18, pp. 70–71 (will, written 26 May 1790 and probated 3 Aug. 1791), 85–87 (inventory and appraisement, recorded Feb. 1793), VSLA.

[9]Ibid., 75; recorded 2 July 1792.

[10]Records of the General Assembly, Legislative Petitions, Franklin County, 5 Nov. 1793, VSLA.

[11]Franklin County, Will Book 1, pp. 116–118 (will written 28 Dec. 1789; probated Apr. 1797).

[12]Ibid., 132 (inventory and appraisement taken 3 Feb. 1798; recorded Feb. 1798).

[13]Thomas Arthur, Franklin County, to Gov. Patrick Henry, Richmond, 20 May 1786, Office of the Governor, Letters Received, VSLA.

[14]Ibid., John Rentfro, Franklin County, to Patrick Henry, Richmond, 23 May 1786.

[15]Franklin County, Order Book [I], 1786–1789, Reel 27, p. 145, VSLA.

[16]Ibid., 152, 7 Aug. 1787.

[17]Ibid., 195.

[18]Peter Saunders, Sr., Franklin County, to Gov. Beverley Randolph, Richmond, 25 Feb. 1791, Office of the Governor, Letters Received.

[19]Franklin County Suit Papers, 1786–1865, Acc. 23707, Aug. 1791, *Robert Williams* v. *Thomas Arthur and Mark Rentfro* (security), VSLA.

[20]"Diary of Richard N. Venable 1791–92," *Tyler's Quarterly Historical and Genealogical Magazine* 2 (1920): 135.

[21]Court order of 8 Mar. 1791 enclosed in letter of Peter Saunders, Sr., Franklin County, to Gov. Beverley Randolph, Richmond, 29 Mar. 1791, Office of the Governor, Letters Received.

[22]Franklin County Suit Papers, Acc. 23707, Aug. 1791, *Daniel Brown* v. *Thomas Arthur.*

[23]Wingfield, *An Old Virginia Court*, 206.

[24]Franklin County, Order Book, 1789–1793, Reel 27, pp. 220, 227, VSLA.

[25]Legislative Petitions, Franklin County, 5 Nov. 1793, VSLA.

[26]Franklin County, Deed Book 1, 1786–1789, Reel 1, p. 14, VSLA.

[27]General Assembly, Contested Elections, Franklin County, 1791, deposition of Stephen Smith, 5 Sept. 1791, VSLA.

[28]Ibid., deposition of Guy Smith, 5 Sept. 1791.

[29]Ibid., deposition of Alexander Ferguson, 5 Sept. 1791.

[30]Ibid., statement of George Turnbull, John Dickenson, John Hook, and Samuel Hairston, commissioners for the contested election, 5 Sept. 1791.

[31]Ibid., deposition of Joshua Rentfro, 5 Sept. 1791.

[32]Ibid., deposition of Thomas Charter, 5 Sept. 1791.

[33]Ibid., deposition of James Richardson, 5 Sept. 1791.

[34]Ibid., deposition of Anthony Pate, 5 Sept. 1791.

[35]Ibid., deposition of Amos Richardson, 5 Sept. 1791.

[36]Ibid., deposition of Jacob Boon, 5 Sept. 1791.

[37]Ibid., deposition of Hugh Innes, 5 Sept. 1791.

[38]Ibid., deposition of Daniel Brown, 3 Oct. 1791.

[39]William Henry Foote, *Sketches of Virginia, Historical and Biographical*, new ed. (Richmond: John Knox Press, 1966), 177.

[40]Franklin County, Deed Book No. 4, 1800–1804, Reel 2, p. 237, VSLA; ibid., Order Book, 1800–1805, Reel 28, p. 81, ibid. (no record of Napier's incarceration in Eastern State Hospital, if it occurred, has been found).

[41]John S. Salmon, *The Washington Iron Works of Franklin County, Virginia, 1773–1850* (Richmond: Virginia State Library, 1986), 19.

[42]Trent's and Callaway, Rocky Ridge, to Dodson, Daltera, and Company, Liverpool, 16 Feb. 1770, U.S. Circuit Court, Virginia District, Ended Cases, 1811, *Trent and Callaway* v. *Dodson's Executors*, VSLA.

[43]John Hook Papers, 1737 (1770–1848), 1889, Duke.

[44]Mutual Assurance Society of Virginia, Declarations, Volume 31, Policy 46 (5 Nov. 1805), Reel 3, VSLA.

[45]Legislative Petitions, Franklin County, 14 Dec. 1803. Two identical petitions (signed by different residents) were submitted on the same date.

[46]Samuel Shepherd, *The Statutes at Large of Virginia . . .* (Richmond: Samuel Shepherd, 1835) 1:45–46.

[47]Kent Druyvesteyn, "Courthouses of Franklin County," *Virginia Cavalcade* 21 (1971): 17.

[48]Franklin County, Order Book, 1830–1835, Reel 30, p. 11, VSLA. The order book for the period between June 1828 and May 1830 is missing.

[49]Ibid., 19.

[50]Ibid., 113, 139.

[51]Ibid., 139.

[52]Ibid., 142.

[53]Ibid., 144, 208.

[54]Photograph of 1831 courthouse printed in Druyvesteyn, "Courthouses," 15.

[55]Jacob Sours, Rocky Mount, to John Dickson Sours, York Springs, Pa., 21 Apr. 1851, Sours Family Papers, Acc. 4435, UNC.

[56]Office of the Governor, Militia Commission Papers, Franklin County, petition of Robert Innes, Sept. 1808, VSLA.

[57]Ibid., statement of Joseph Hale, 8 Sept. 1808.

[58]Ibid., statement of Joseph Webb, 9 Sept. 1808.

[59]Ibid., petition of Lieutenant George Crump et al., n.d.; Innes was a member of the House of Delegates from Franklin County during the following sessions: 5 Dec. 1803–3 Feb. 1804, 5 Dec. 1807–18 Feb. 1809, 4 Dec. 1809–9 Feb. 1810, 30 Nov. 1812–23 Feb. 1813, 17–26 May 1813, 6 Dec. 1813–16 Feb. 1814, and 10 Oct. 1814–19 Jan. 1805.

[60]Ibid., petition of Robert Innes, Sept. 1808.

[61]Office of the Governor, Letters Received, Gov. John Floyd, Nov.–Dec. 1831, statement of James Callaway, Jr., n.d.

[62]Office of the Governor, Militia Commission Papers, Franklin County, 1808, petition of Lieutenant George Crump et al., n.d.

[63]Ibid.

[64]Ibid., statement of Robert Innes, Sept. 1808.

[65]Office of the Governor, Letters Received, Gov. John Floyd, Oct.–Nov. 1830.

[66]Ibid., Anthony Street to Gov. John Floyd, 1 Nov. 1830.

[67]Ibid., statement of Cassimer Cabiness, 19 Nov. 1830.

[68]Ibid., petition of Anthony Street to the governor and Council of State, n.d.

[69]Ibid., Anthony Street to Gov. John Floyd, 1 Nov. 1830.

[70]Ibid., petition of Anthony Street to the governor and Council of State, n.d.

[71]Ibid.

[72]Ibid., statement of Elisha Keen, 30 Nov. 1830.

[73]Ibid., petition of Anthony Street to the governor and Council of State, n.d.

[74]Ibid., on reverse of 1 Nov. 1830 recommendation of the Franklin County Court.

[75]Legislative Petitions, Franklin County, 17 Jan. 1831.

[76]Ibid., reverse of petition.

[77]Anthony Street to Gov. John Floyd, 10 Nov. 1831, Office of the Governor, Letters Received, Nov.–Dec. 1831.

[78]Ibid.

[79]Ibid., statement of Dr. Richard M. Taliaferro, 9 Nov. 1831.

[80]Ibid., statement of James Callaway, Jr., 8 Nov. 1831.

[81]Ibid., statement of Jubal Early, 8 Nov. 1831. The Franklin County personal property tax books list an Edmund Saunders only once, in 1811.

[82]Ibid., statement of Tarleton Brown, 9 Nov. 1831.

[83]Ibid., on reverse of 7 Nov. 1831 recommendation of Franklin County Court.

[84]Ibid., Jan.–Feb. 1832, recommendation of Franklin County Court, 6 Feb. 1832.

[85]Ibid., 1 Nov.–1 Dec. 1832, recommendation of Franklin County Court.

[86]Ibid., Nov.–Dec. 1833, recommendation of Franklin County Court.

[87]Ibid., Gov. Littleton Waller Tazewell, Nov.–Dec. 1834, recommendation of Franklin County Court.

[88]Ibid., Henry Carper to Gov. Littleton Waller Tazewell, 2 Dec. 1834.

[89]Ibid., on reverse of recommendation of Franklin County Court, 1 Dec. 1834.

[90]Ibid., Nov.–Dec. 1835, recommendation of Franklin County Court, 2 Nov. 1835.

[91]Abraham C. Shelton to Fleming Saunders, 20 May 1836, Saunders Family Papers, property of Mr. William Lee, Bleak Hill, Franklin County, Va.

[92]Office of the Governor, Letters Received, acting governor Wyndham Robertson, Aug.–Nov. 1836, recommendation of Franklin County Court.

[93]Marshall Wingfield, *Pioneer Families of Franklin County, Virginia* (Berryville, Va.: Chesapeake Book Co., 1964), 85–92; Cynthia Miller Leonard, comp., *The General Assembly of Virginia, July 30, 1619–January 11, 1978: A Bicentennial Register of Members* (Richmond: Published for the General Assembly of Virginia by the Virginia State Library, 1978), 298, 323, 329, 509, 522.

[94]From Adams's Memoirs, quoted in Leonard D. White, *The Jeffersonians: A Study in Administrative History, 1801–1829* (New York: The Macmillan Co., 1951), 47–48.

[95]*Alexandria Gazette*, 19 Feb. 1821.

[96]*Richmond Enquirer*, 22 Feb. 1821.

[97]Except for the specific quotes above, this sketch of the life of William A. Burwell is derived from the following sources: Dumas Malone, *Jefferson and His Time* (Boston: Little, Brown and Co., 1948–1981), 4:414–421, 5:35,140; *Biographical Directory of the United States Congress, 1774–1989* (Washington, D.C.: Government Printing Office, 1989), 679; Leonard, *General Assembly Register*, 235, 240, 243. There is also a tombstone for the Burwells in Greenmount Cemetery, Baltimore, Md.

[98]Franklin County, Will Book No. 2, 1812–1825, Reel 18, p. 375, VSLA.

[99]Ibid., Order Book, 1800–1805, court meetings of 6 June and 10 Nov. 1803, VSLA; ibid., 1806–1811, Reel 28, ibid., court meeting of 4 June 1810.

[100]*Biographical Directory of the United States Congress, 1774–1989*, 778; Leonard, *General Assembly Register*, 260, 266, 312, 317, 322, 327; Allen Johnson and Dumas Malone, eds., *Dictionary of American Biography* (New York: Charles Scribner's Sons, 1928–1937), 2:113–114.

[101]Daniel P. Jordan, *Political Leadership in Jefferson's Virginia* (Charlottesville: University Press of Virginia, 1983), 143.

[102]Wingfield, *Pioneer Families*, 218.

[103]Secretary of the Commonwealth, Registers of Virginia Justices and County Officers, 1793–1852, 1852–1865, Misc. Reel 458a, VSLA.

Chapter Six: Minding The Business

[1]William J. Hinke and Charles E. Kemper, eds., "Moravian Diaries of Travels through Virginia," *VMHB* 12 (1905): 277.

[2]Henry County, Will Book 1, 1779–1799, Reel 15, pp. 96–97, will of John Hickey, probated 23 Dec. 1784, VSLA.

[3]Trent's and Callaway, Rocky Ridge, to Dodson, Daltera, and Company, Liverpool, 16 Feb. 1770, U.S. Circuit Court, Virginia District, Ended Cases, 1811, *Trent and Callaway* v. *Dodson's Executors,* VSLA; ibid., lists of goods to be shipped to Trent's and Callaway from Liverpool, 16 Feb. and 15 Aug. 1770.

[4]Franklin County, Order Book [1], 1786–1789, Reel 27, pp. 122, 124, 126, VSLA.

[5]Franklin County Suit Papers, 1786–1865, Acc. 23707, Jan. 1800, *John Hook* v. *Thomas Osbourne,* VSLA.

[6]Franklin County, Will Book 2, 1812–1825, Reel 18, pp. 484–487, VSLA.

[7]Ibid., 467.

[8]Ibid.

[9]Ibid., 480, 483.

[10]Draft of letter, John Hook, [?] 1796, to [?], John Hook Papers, 1737 (1770–1848), 1889, Duke.

[11]Franklin County, Will Book 2, pp. 469–483.

[12]Virginius C. Hall, Jr., "Virginia Post Offices, 1798–1859," *VMHB* 81 (1973): 55–97.

[13]Marquis James, *The Life of Andrew Jackson* (New York: The Bobbs-Merrill Co., 1938), 49.

[14]Maud Carter Clement, *The History of Pittsylvania County, Virginia* (Lynchburg, Va.: J. P. Bell Co., 1929; Baltimore: Regional Publishing Co., 1981), 151; Auditor of Public Accounts, Revolutionary War Pension Claims, Lewis Davis, VSLA; Receipt, William Bartee to Alexander Brownlee, Henry County, 22 Apr. 1779, Clerk's Office, Henry County Courthouse, Martinsville, Va.

[15]The foregoing account of the origin and development of the Washington Iron Works is adapted from an article written by John S. Salmon and published in *Virginia Cavalcade* 35 (1986): 184–191. It is reprinted here with permission of the Virginia State Library and Archives, Richmond.

[16]John S. Salmon, *The Washington Iron Works of Franklin County, Virginia, 1773–1850* (Richmond: Virginia State Library, 1986), 36–38.

[17]Jacob Sours, Rocky Mount, to John Dickson Sours, York Springs, Pa., 21 Apr. 1851, Sours Family Papers, Acc. 4435, UNC; William Sours, Rocky Mount, to John Dickson Sours, York Springs, Pa., 5 Mar. 1851, in ibid.

[18]Peter Saunders, Jr., Rocky Mount, to Alice W. Saunders, Campbell County, 1 Sept. 1851, Irvine-Saunders-Watts Family Papers, 1745–1914, Acc. 38-33, Manuscripts Division, UVA (hereafter cited as Saunders Papers, UVA).

[19]William Sours, Rocky Mount, to John Dickson Sours, Lock Haven, Pa., 26 Aug. 1851, Sours Family Papers.

[20]William Waller Hening, *The Statutes at Large* . . . (New York: Printed for the Editor, 1809–1823), 13:585–586.

[21]Records of the General Assembly, Legislative Petitions, Franklin County, 16 Oct. 1792, VSLA.

[22]Ibid.

[23]Ibid., 14 Dec. 1803. Two identical petitions (signed by different residents) were submitted on the same date.

24Franklin County, Order Book, 1800–1805, Reel 28, passim, VSLA.

25Ibid., Order Book, 1806–1811, Reel 28, passim.

26Itinerant Peddler's Diary, 30 Oct. 1807–22 Jan. 1808, Mss5:1Un3:1, VHS. William Calhoon presented his peddler's license from the Montgomery County Court on 7 July 1806 (Franklin County, Order Book, 1806–1811, p. 44); Thomas Whitworth was issued an ordinary license on 1 June 1807 (ibid., 127).

27Auditor of Public Accounts, License Returns, 1829–1839, Franklin County, VSLA.

28Jonathan Cundiff Diary, 1820–1824, Blue Ridge Institute, Ferrum College, Ferrum, Va.

29Auditor of Public Accounts, License Returns, 1829–1839, Franklin County.

30Franklin County, Order Book, 1860–1865, Reel 33, p. 339, VSLA.

31Lorenzo Dow, *History of Cosmopolite: or the Writings of Rev. Lorenzo Dow*, 8th ed. (Cincinnati: Applegate and Co., 1855), 208.

32Ibid., vii.

33A. R. Newsome, ed., "John Brown's Journal of Travel in Western North Carolina in 1795," *North Carolina Historical Review* 11 (1934): 288; the names of John Nofsinger, Elizabeth Ferguson, Luke Standifer, and John Barksdale are derived from road orders in Franklin County, Order Book, 1793–1799, Reel 27, VSLA.

34Joseph Martin, *A New and Comprehensive Gazetteer of Virginia, and the District of Columbia* . . . (Charlottesville, Va.: Joseph Martin, 1836), 178.

35Ibid.

36Virginia Greer Williams, "Communities and Villages of Franklin County," *Bicentennial Reflections* (N.p.: Franklin County Bicentennial Commission, 1986), 36.

37Auditor of Public Accounts, Land Tax Book, 1832B, Reel 105, VSLA. The highest lot number given is fifty-six; taxes were paid on forty-three lots.

38*Lynchburg Press and Public Advertiser,* 1 Oct. 1818.

39"Head of Staunton," 12 May 1818, Lynchburg, Va., broadside in the possession of Dr. J. Francis Amos, Rocky Mount, Va.

40William Sours, Rocky Mount, to John Dickson Sours, York Springs, Pa., 5 Mar. 1851, Sours Family Papers.

41Marvin U. Neighbors, *Franklin Co., Va., Census of 1850* (Salem, Va.: Book Mart, 1975), 1–2.

42United States Census, Industry Schedules, 1850, 1860, Franklin County, Reels 232, 236, VSLA.

43Franklin County, Will Book, 1880–1883, pp. 491–492, Clerk's Office, Franklin County Courthouse, Rocky Mount, Va.

Blacksmiths listed in 1850: John Abshire, James W. Amos, Caleb Angle, Thomas Angle, Benjamin Betz, John F. Betz, Peter S. Bowles, Dabney Carter, Wiley Clingenpeel, James L. Doss, William Durham, Samuel Fisher, Jacob Frailin, William Gore, James Hiett, John Huffman, Henry Jones, Jonathan Kesler, Sparrel Lavinder, Samuel Michael, John Montgomery, Silas Perdue, William Starky, John Thurmond, Stephen Trisler, Josiah Webb, Anselm Wright, and Joseph Wright. Blacksmiths listed in 1860: John Abshire, Jubal A. Abshire, Barnabas Arthur, James M. Barber, Mathew C. Belcher, John W. Bishop, Samuel W. Bishop, Peter S. Bowls, Andrew J. Brickey, Peter Campbell, Hartwell Carter, John W. Chitwood, Wiley Clingenpeel, John T. Dudley, Sparrel Dudley, John A. Edwards, Ferguson and Hatcher, Richard Fisher, Samuel B. Fisher, Thomas Frailin, J. F. Gray, Otey Hambrick, Silas Hartwell, Benjamin Henry, Burwell Hodges, Henry S. Hodges, Isham Hodges, Creed F. Jones, Henry A. Jones, Stephen Jones, Daniel Kessler, Susannah A. Livesay (a woman), E. McGuire and Company, John Martin, John K. Mason, William J. Mead, George L. Minnix, John A. Minnix, Robert Mitchell, Ambrose B. Moore, John A. Newberry, George A. Simmons, Buford Smithers (a free black), William Starkey, John Terry, John T. Thurmon, William Turner (a free black), George W. Tyree, Giles Tyree, Anselm Wright, and James G. Wright, Jr. Wagonmakers listed in 1850: Matthew R. Allen, Peter Cockram, Cornelius

Kinsey, and James Nunery. Wheelwrights listed in 1850: Thomas Handy, Thomas Pearson, Benjamin T. Pinkard, William Pinkard, and William Stewart. "Waggoner" listed in 1860: Andrew P. Drewry. Coachmakers in 1860: J. H. Martin and William H. Startzman. Wheelwrights in 1860: William Arnold, Henry Bowsman, Isaac Custer, Edward Dangerfield, James Doss, Isaac Gillespie, Thomas Handy, R. A. Howell, James Lavinder, John Lavinder, Thornton Lavinder, George W. Kinsey, Jeremiah Meador, Stephen H. Prillaman, William H. Weaver, Lewis F. Wingfield, and Lewis Wysong. Saddlers listed in 1850: Sneed T. Adams, James D. Anderson, John Ashinghertt, Samuel G. Bright, James M. Davis, Thomas R. Hamner, Albertis Hill, and Lewis S. Howell. Saddlers in 1860: Sneed Adams, Thomas L. Booker, A. B. Hill, William H. Keeney, and master saddler Samuel G. Bright, who employed three journeymen (Peter Hill, Landern T. Jones, and Davis P. Mitchell). Shoemakers listed in 1850: Charles Ashworth, Mathias Crook, Michael Crook, William D. Gallaway, John M. Gates, Jubal T. Gates, Reuben Gear, Luke Guilliams, Robert Guilliams, Green Jones, Hambleton Kirk, Stephen McBride, William McGuire, Ozias Maxey, James W. Sawyer, and Calvin T. Smith. Shoemakers in 1860: William F. Amos, A. T. Angle, Nathaniel Crook, Eli Cundiff, Wyatt Dowdy, Lervy Downs, George Faldin, John H. Greer, Luke Guilliams, Peter Guilliams, John Guthry, Reed Holcombe, Shelton Hutts, Ambrose M. Jones, Green Jones, James Jones, James R. Kemp, Anderson Laprade, James E. Martin, Ozias Maxey, James Moore, Stephen Mullins, Nathan Peasly, Fleming Pugh, John Ray, Bosher W. Smith, Thomas Vernon, John West, William E. Wilks, and James Wilson. Tailors listed in 1850: William C. Barbour, William Davis, William Daws, James Eames, George L. Fisher, Daniel Lipford, and Jesse S. Oakes. Tailors in 1860: William E. Andrews, George L. Fisher, and Joseph Friedell; Ruth Powers (tailoress); and Frances Friedell and Jane H. Hunt (seamstresses). Cabinetmakers listed in 1850: Hiram Hale, Thomas Hutts, Robert McGuffin, George W. Suselstern, Ferdinand Winston, and John H. C. Winston. Cabinetmakers in 1860: Mathew Barton, Abram Betz, A. B. Crouch, John B. Crum, William H. Davis, Peter B. Forbes, Robert P. Forbes, B. L. Hunt, Thomas Hutts, John Janney, and George W. Thompson. Coopers listed in 1860: Joseph H. Austin, Wiley Doss, John Gusler, William Jarrell, Thomas Kingery, Obadiah Massie, Mathew Ratliff, and John Trexler.

[44]Carpenters listed in 1850: Peter Angle, Benjamin A. Bernard, Swinfield Bernard, George Bowman, Frederick Cook, Abraham Crum, Jonathan Davis, Alfred Hale, Samuel Hale, Benjamin L. Hunt, Riley Hunt, George Hutcherson, Robert Jenkins, George Lavinder, Addison A. Neal, Caleb Newman, John Oxly, James Turnbull, Jourdan Updike, Charles Weatherwood, Nathaniel Webster, and John M. Witheford. Carpenters in 1860: Giles W. Abshire, Creed H. Adams, Henry Anderson, Anderson R. Angle, J. W. Angle, Joseph A. Angle, Joseph P. Angle, Joshua H. Angle, Green Arthur, Thomas Ashworth, Henry Bailey, Nathaniel Barbour, Benjamin A. Bernard, Thomas O. Bernard, William T. H. Brown, L. C. Carter, Larkin Cassell, Jacob Colthard, Frederick Cook, William M. Crum, Jonathan Davis, Middleton Davis, Robert L. Dent, Stephen Dunning (a free black), Silas W. Eanes, Lafayette Ferguson, George W. Flora, Gabriel Foster, Jr., William Gates, Preston Gearhart, Alfred Hale, Francis Hale, Jr., Giles Hale, William Hale, Thomas M. Hawkins, Mathew Hix, G. Robert Hodges, Bennett H. Hopkins, Daniel Hurt, Frank Hutcherson, Levi Hutchinson, John Janney, Samuel Jones, Samuel Lavinder, John P. Lyon, Daniel D. Mason, Jubal Mills, A. A. Noell, Henry Orange, S. C. Overstreet, Samuel S. Parsley, Green H. Payne, Robert Payne, Samuel Payne, Michael D. Peters, Seth Richerson, Thomas Richerson, John Ridgeway, Tinsley S. Rucker, George Snyder, Jacob Snyder, Jordan Updike, James Wells, Frances M. White (a woman), Zebedee C. Whitlock, and Archibald Wilks.

[45]U.S. Census, Social Statistics, 1850, 1860, Franklin County, Va., Reels 232, 237, VSLA.

Chapter Seven: Agriculture and Transportation

[1]Anne Carter Lee, "Farming in Eighteenth-Century Franklin County," *Bicentennial Reflections* (N.p.: Franklin County Bicentennial Commission, 1986), 15.

[2]Gertrude Casler Mann, "Migration Patterns," *Bicentennial Reflections,* 34–35.

[3]Essie W. Smith Papers, FCPL.

[4]Franklin County Suit Papers, 1786–1865, Acc. 23707, 1787, *Harmon Cook* v. *Baxter Sympson.*

[5]William Mavity, Franklin County, to Col. Robert Williams, Pittsylvania County, 21 Apr. 1786, in ibid., Mar. 1789, *William Mavity* v. *Thomas Jones and William Standifer.*

[6]Ibid., May 1791, *William and Isabella Crawford* v. *Joseph Ritter.*

[7]Ibid., Mar. 1791, *John Hook* v. *Henry Loving.*

[8]Ibid., Aug. 1791, *Nicholas Alley* v. *Thomas Arthur.*

[9]Ibid., Aug. 1786, *William Hill, orphan, by Dennit Hill (guardian)* v. *Obediah Ferguson.*

[10]Ibid., Mar. 1789, *Moses Hudgins* v. *William King.*

[11]Ibid.

[12]Ibid., May 1791, *Thomas Livesay* v. *Parker Gee.*

[13]Ibid., 1786?, *Archibald Graham* v. *Reaf [Ralph] Dangger.*

[14]Ibid., Jan. 1798, Articles of agreement, John Early and William Bradley.

[15]In some parts of the South the overseers and farm managers were the younger, landless sons of farmers. Often they worked for successful farmers in order to learn the business and acquire some capital so they could purchase their own farms. Because of the lack of the necessary information in the census and tax records for Franklin County, the authors were unable to identify overseers and follow their careers to determine whether the same was true of the younger sons of the county's farmers.

[16]Fleming Saunders, Bleak Hill, Franklin County, to Alice W. Saunders, Flat Creek, Campbell County, 6 Jan. 1833, Irvine-Saunders-Watts Family Papers, 1745–1914, Acc. 38–33, Manuscripts Division, UVA (hereafter cited as Saunders Papers, UVA).

[17]Articles of agreement, 21 Dec. 1860, in ibid.

[18]James H. Roberts, Indian Valley, Floyd County, to Mr. [Fleming] Saunders, 3 Mar. 1861, in ibid.

[19]Ibid., 30 Apr. 1861.

[20]The average size was computed by dividing the sum of the acreage for the first tract listed for each landowner by the total number of landowners. The first tract listed usually was the most valuable, indicating that it was the primary farm under cultivation. Most Franklin County farmers only owned one or two tracts.

[21]All statistics having to do with Franklin County farms, crops, and livestock between 1850 and 1860 are taken from: United States Census, Agriculture Schedules, Franklin County, 1850 (Reel 230), 1860 (Reel 234), VSLA.

[22]Franklin County, Will Book 5, 1837–1845, Reel 20, p. 338, VSLA.

[23]Fleming Saunders, Bleak Hill, Franklin County, to Alice W. Saunders, Flat Creek, Campbell County, 6 Apr. 1833, Saunders Papers, UVA.

[24]Franklin County, Order Book [1], 1786–1789, Reel 27, p. 328, VSLA; ibid., 1800–1805, Reel 28, p. 297, ibid.

[25]Fleming Saunders, Rocky Mount, to Mrs. Mary Watts, Campbell County, 5 Dec. 1823, Saunders Papers, UVA.

[26]Sam Bowers Hilliard, *Atlas of Antebellum Southern Agriculture* (Baton Rouge: Louisiana State University Press, 1984), map 109, p. 76.

[27]Peter Saunders, Jr., Rocky Mount, to Fleming Saunders, n.p., 26 Mar. 1860, Saunders Papers, UVA.

[28]Donald B. Dodd and Wynelle S. Dodd, *Historical Statistics of the South, 1790–1970* (University, Ala.: University of Alabama Press, 1973), 60.

[29]Franklin County, Will Book 5, p. 361.

[30]William Sours, Rocky Mount, to John Dickson Sours, York Springs, Pa., 5 Mar. 1851, Sours Family Papers, Acc. 4435, UNC.

[31]U.S. Census, Agriculture Schedules, 1850, Franklin County, Reel 230.

[32]U.S. Census, Slave Schedules, 1850, Franklin County, Reel 223, VSLA.

[33]U.S. Census, Agriculture Schedules, 1860, Franklin County, Reel 234, VSLA.

[34]Henry Hopkins, "Agriculture in Franklin County," *Bicentennial Reflections,* 68.

[35]U.S. Census, Slave Schedules, 1860, Franklin County, Reel 226, VSLA.

[36]U.S. Census, Agriculture Schedules, 1850, Franklin County, Reel 230.

[37]U.S. Census, Slave Schedules, 1850, Franklin County, Reel 223.

[38]U.S. Census, Agriculture Schedules, 1860, Franklin County, Reel 234.

[39]U.S. Census, Slave Schedules, 1860, Franklin County, Reel 226.

[40]Fleming Saunders, Bleak Hill, Franklin County, to Alice W. Saunders, Flat Creek, Campbell County, 21 Mar. 1835, Saunders Papers, UVA.

[41]Franklin County, Order Book [1], p. 1a.

[42]Ibid., 3.

[43]Records of the General Assembly, Legislative Petitions, Franklin County, 23 Nov. 1796, VSLA.

[44]Ibid., 4 Dec. 1799.

[45]Board of Public Works, Pittsylvania, Franklin, and Botetourt Turnpike, 1838–1853, VSLA.

[46]Ibid., Richard M. Taliaferro, Rocky Mount, to William H. Brown [acting second auditor and secretary of the Board of Public Works], Richmond.

[47]J. Francis Amos, "Early Roads in Franklin County," *Bicentennial Reflections,* 28.

[48]John Wade, Franklin County, to James Brown, Jr., Second Auditor, Richmond, 16 Sept. 1850, Board of Public Works, Pittsylvania, Franklin, and Botetourt Turnpike, 1838–1853.

[49]Legislative Petitions, Franklin County, 6 Jan. 1844.

[50]Ibid., 9 Feb. 1848.

[51]Ibid., 21 Feb. 1848.

[52]Board of Public Works, Rocky Mount Turnpike Company, 1847–1859.

[53]Ibid.

[54]Ibid., Pleasant Preston, president, Lynchburg, to James Brown, Jr., second auditor, Richmond, 29 Oct. 1850.

[55]Ibid., deed, Rocky Mount Turnpike Company to Commonwealth of Virginia, 5 June 1854.

[56]Ibid., S. C. Hunt, secretary, Lynchburg, to secretary of the Board of Public Works, Richmond, 12 Feb. 1859.

[57]Peter Saunders, Jr., Bleak Hill, Franklin County, to Fleming Saunders, Flat Creek, Campbell County, 8 May 1861, Saunders Papers, UVA.

[58]Ibid., 16 Jan. 1854.

[59]Ibid., 5 Dec. 1859.

Chapter Eight: Domestic Life

[1]Alice W. Saunders, Franklin County, to Mrs. Mary Watts, [Flat Creek, Campbell County], 18 Oct. 1814, Irvine-Saunders-Watts Family Papers, 1745–1914, Acc. 38–33, Manuscript Division, UVA (hereafter cited as Saunders Papers, UVA).

[2]Ibid., 22 Oct. 1814.

[3]Ibid., 13 Jan 1815.

[4]Ibid., 25 Jan. 1815.

[5]Marshall Wingfield, *Pioneer Families of Franklin County, Virginia* (Berryville, Va.: Chesapeake Book Co., 1964), 197.

[6]Alice W. Saunders, Franklin County, to Mrs. Mary W. Morris, Flat Creek, "Near New London," Campbell County, 25 June 1821, Saunders Papers, UVA.

[7]Ibid., 9 May 1826.

[8]Ibid.

[9]Franklin County, Will Book 1, 1786–1812, Reel 18, pp. 41–42, VSLA.

[10]Fleming Saunders, Patrick Courthouse, Patrick County, to Mrs. Alice Saunders, n.p., 5 Oct. 1823, Saunders Papers, UVA.

[11]Fleming Saunders, n.p., to Master Edward C. Saunders, New London Academy, 13 Mar. 1834, in ibid.

[12]Alice W. Saunders, Franklin County, to Mrs. Mary Watts, Campbell County, 9 May 1826, in ibid.

[13]Ibid., 15 Apr. 1822.

[14]Franklin County, Order Book [1], 1786–1789, Reel 27, pp. 193–194, VSLA.

[15]Ibid., 1800–1805, Reel 28, p. 261, VSLA.

[16]Ibid., 1806–1811, Reel 28, p. 207 (4 July 1808), VSLA.

[17]Ibid., 221.

[18]Ibid., 1786–1789, pp. 217–218.

[19]Marshall Wingfield, *Marriage Bonds of Franklin County, Virginia, 1786–1858* (Baltimore: Genealogical Publishing Co., 1973), 176.

[20]Franklin County, Order Book [1], p. 213.

[21]Ibid., Order Book, 1789–1793, Reel 27, p. 35, VSLA.

[22]Ibid., 40.

[23]Ibid., 1806–1811, p. 8.

[24]Ibid., 1800–1805, p. 223.

[25]Ibid., Order Book [1], p. 257.

[26]Wingfield, *Marriage Bonds,* 105. The marriage bond was taken out on or before the date of the wedding. Since the marriage may not have taken place until a few days after the date of the bond, the text usually reads that the marriage occurred "about" a certain date rather than "on" that date.

[27]Franklin County, Order Book [1], p. 285.

[28]Wingfield, *Marriage Bonds,* 147.

[29]Franklin County, Order Book [1], p. 281.

[30]John S. Salmon, *The Washington Iron Works of Franklin County, Virginia, 1773–1850* (Richmond: Virginia State Library, 1986), 45.

[31]Franklin County, Order Book, 1800–1805, pp. 80, 82–83.

[32]Ibid., 69.

[33]Ibid., 225, 231, 254, 426, 443.

[34]Wingfield, *Marriage Bonds,* 71.

[35]Marvin U. Neighbors, *Franklin Co., Va., Census of 1850* (Salem, Va.: Book Mart, 1975), 39.

[36]Wingfield, *Marriage Bonds,* 146.

[37]Neighbors, *Census of 1850,* 113.

[38]Franklin County, Order Book, 1806–1811, p. 188 (10 Mar. 1808).

[39]Ibid., 93, 223 (5 Sept. 1808).

[40]Ibid., Deed Book 2, 1789–1793, Reel 1, p. 255, VSLA; deed dated 25 Mar. 1791 and recorded 1 Aug. 1791.

[41]Ibid., Deed Book 3, 1793–1800, Reel 3, p. 252, VSLA.

[42]Ibid., 351; deed dated 30 June 1796 and recorded July 1796.

[43]Ibid., Deed Book 4, 1800–1804, Reel 2, p. 574, VSLA; deed written 13 Dec. 1803 and recorded 2 Apr. 1804.

[44]Ibid., Deed Book 2, pp. 63–64; deed written 4 Sept. 1789 and recorded 5 Oct. 1789.

[45]Franklin County Suit Papers, 1786–1865, Acc. 23707, Nov. 1791, *Robert Johns and Elizabeth (Lyon) Johns* v. *Mary Lyon, administratrix of Elisha Lyon, deceased,* VSLA.

[46]Wingfield, *Marriage Bonds,* 100; 1 May 1786, Joseph Greer and Fannie Lyon, surety Elisha Lyons.

[47]Franklin County Suit Papers, Acc. 23707, Nov. 1791, *Joseph Spearpoint* v. *Jacob Prilliman.*

[48]Franklin County, Order Book [1], p. 5.

[49]Ibid., 1800–1805, p. 194. ——

[50]Ibid., Deed Book 2, p. 546.

[51]Ibid., Will Book 6, 1845–1849, Reel 20, pp. 348–349, VSLA; will probated 5 June 1848.

[52]Marshall Wingfield, *Franklin County, Virginia: A History* (Berryville, Va.: Chesapeake Book Co., 1964), 123.

[53]Alice W. Saunders, Franklin County, to Miss Sarah W. Saunders, Flat Creek, Campbell County, 13 July 1829, Saunders Papers, UVA.

[54]Alice W. Saunders, Franklin County, to Peter Saunders, Flat Creek, Campbell County, 18 May 1834, in ibid.

[55]Alice Watts Saunders, Franklin County, to Mrs. Mary Watts, "Near New London," 25 Dec. 1814, in ibid.

[56]Alice W. Saunders, Franklin County, to Sarah W. Saunders, n.p., 18 February 1830, in ibid.

[57]Architectural Survey File 157–21, VDHR.

[58]Ibid., 33–6. According to David A. Edwards, architectural historian with the Virginia Department of Historic Resources, the house appears of too late a construction style to have been the house in which Jubal Early was born; it looks like a house of the 1820s or 1830s. It is possible, however, that part of the house may have been built earlier and heavily remodeled and expanded later.

[59]Architectural Survey File 33–11.

[60]Auditor of Public Accounts, Land Tax Books, Franklin County, 1857–1867, VSLA. Booth apparently purchased the property from fellow justice John S. Hale in 1857 but neglected to record the deed until 1867.

[61]Architectural Survey File 33–66.

[62]Peter Saunders, Jr., Franklin County, to Mrs. Alice W. Saunders, n.p., 23 Mar. 1856, Saunders Papers, UVA. A century and a quarter later, while it was being restored in the 1970s, the house at Flat Creek was destroyed by fire.

[63]Architectural Survey File 33–2.

[64]Jonathan Cundiff Diary, 1820–1824, Blue Ridge Institute, Ferrum College, Ferrum, Va.

[65]Alice W. Saunders, Mount Retreat, Franklin County, to Mrs. Mary W. Morris, Flat Creek, Campbell County, 26 Sept. 1814, Saunders Papers, UVA.

[66]Thomas Goode, *The Invalid's Guide to the Virginia Hot Springs* (Richmond: P. D. Bernard, 1846), 51.

[67]Ibid., 28–29.

[68]Peter Saunders, Jr., Sweet Springs, Monroe County, to Alice W. Saunders, n.p., 24 Aug. 1856, Saunders Papers, UVA.

[69]Jonathan Cundiff Diary, 1820–1824.

[70]Auditor of Public Accounts, License Returns, 1829–1839, Franklin County, VSLA.

Chapter Nine: The Women's Sphere

[1]Alice W. Saunders, Mount Retreat, Franklin County, to Mrs. Mary W. Morris, Flat Creek, "Near New London," Campbell County, 26 Sept. 1814, Irvine-Saunders-Watts Family Papers, 1745–1914, Acc. 38–33, Manuscripts Division, UVA (hereafter cited as Saunders Papers, UVA).

[2]Ibid., 18 Oct. 1814.

[3]Ibid., 18 Feb. 1817.

[4]Judith Hale, Gills Creek, Franklin County, to Sarah W. Saunders, Lynchburg, 2 Feb. 1830, in ibid.; Architectural Survey File 33–2 (Bleak Hill).

[5]Franklin County, Order Book [1], 1786–1789, Reel 27, p. 67, VSLA.

[6]Ibid., 107.

[7]Franklin County Suit Papers, 1786 –1865, Acc. 23707, May 1787, *Rachel Jones* v. *Mary Webb,* VSLA.

[8]Franklin County, Will Book 1, 1786–1812, Reel 18, pp. 4–5, VSLA.

[9]Ibid., 2; inventory and appraisal taken 29 Sept. 1786 and recorded 5 Feb. 1787.

[10]Auditor of Public Accounts, Land Tax Books, Franklin County, 1786, VSLA.

[11]Franklin County, Order Book [1], p. 217; court meeting of 8 Apr. 1788.

[12]Ibid., 225–226.

[13]Ibid., Order Book, 1789–1793, Reel 27, p. 50, VSLA; court meeting of 2 Mar. 1790.

[14]Franklin County Suit Papers, Acc. 23707, Aug. 1791, *John Hook* v. *Penelope Guthrey.*

[15]Ibid., Nov. 1791, *Henry Guthrey (Penelope Guthrey, exor)* v. *John Hook.*

[16]Franklin County, Order Book [1], pp. 114–115.

[17]Ibid., 126, 155.

[18]Ibid., 128.

[19]Franklin County Suit Papers, Acc. 23707, Aug. 1790?, *John Brammer* v. *William Griffith;* ibid., Mar. 1791, *John Brammer* v. *William and Susannah Griffith and Thomas and Mary Jones.*

[20]Franklin County, Order Book [1], p. 285.

[21]Ibid., Order Book, 1806–1811, Reel 28, p. 63, VSLA.

[22]Ibid., Order Book, 1789–1793, p. 38.

[23]Ibid., 1806–1811, p. 209.

[24]Ibid., 1800–1805, Reel 28, p. 5, VSLA.

[25]Ibid., District Court, Order Book 3, 1797–1802, Reel 35, pp. 196, 198, VSLA.

[26]Ibid., Deed Book 5, 1804–1811, Reel 3, p. 639, VSLA.

[27]Franklin County Suit Papers, Acc. 23707, Apr. 1800, *Rebecca Quigley, Spinster* v. *Jackson Griffin (Griffith);* Marshall Wingfield, *Marriage Bonds of Franklin County, Virginia, 1786–1858* (Baltimore: Genealogical Publishing Co., 1973), 101, 143.

[28]Franklin County, Deed Book 2, 1789–1793, Reel 1, pp. 405–406, VSLA; deed written and recorded 6 Aug. 1792.

[29]Wingfield, *Marriage Bonds,* 210.

[30]Franklin County, Deed Book 3, 1793–1800, Reel 2, p. 14, VSLA.

[31]Fleming Saunders, Franklin County, to Alice W. Saunders, Flat Creek, Campbell County, 13 Jan. 1833, Saunders Papers, UVA.

[32]Franklin County, Deed Book 2, pp. 213–214.

[33]Ibid., Order Book, 1800–1805, p. 96.

[34]Records of the General Assembly, Legislative Petitions, Franklin County, 18 Dec. 1807 and 10 Dec. 1810, VSLA.

[35]Wingfield, *Marriage Bonds,* 40, 205; the bond for the marriage to Boon was dated 27 June 1817 and the one for Sigmon was dated 5 Apr. 1819.

[36]Ibid., 157; date of bond 30 Apr. 1833.

[37]Franklin County, Will Book 5, 1837–1845, Reel 20, pp. 181–185 (will probated 6 July 1840), VSLA.

[38]Legislative Petitions, Franklin County, 3 Dec. 1845.

[39]Ibid., 16 Dec. 1842.

[40]Ibid., affidavit of John Cook, 29 Nov. 1842.

[41]Ibid., affidavit of Isham Belcher, 26 Oct. 1842.

[42]Marshall Wingfield, *Pioneer Families of Franklin County, Virginia* (Berryville, Va.: Chesapeake Book Co., 1964), 217. The book, which was compiled before 1936, gave the genealogy of the Tate family, including Edmund Tate and his descendants, but omitted his daughter Mildred C. Tate.

[43]Judith Hale, Gills Creek, Franklin County, to Sarah Watts Saunders, Flat Creek, Campbell County, 9 May 1830, Saunders Papers, UVA.

[44]Legislative Petitions, Franklin County, 11 Feb. 1833.

[45]Ibid., affidavit of Thomas Hale, 2 Feb. 1833.

[46]Ibid., affidavits of Elizabeth and Robert H. Colhoun, 2 Feb. 1833.

[47]Ibid., affidavit of Mrs. Harriet Hale, 2 Feb. 1833.

[48]Ibid., affidavit of Burwell C. Keatts, 2 Feb. 1833.

[49]Ibid., affidavit of Michael D. Holland, 2 Feb. 1833.

[50]Ibid., affidavit of Burwell C. Keatts, 2 Feb. 1833.

[51]Ibid., affidavit of John S. Hale, 2 Feb. 1833.

[52]Ibid., affidavit of James C. Tate, 11 Feb. 1833.

[53]Ibid., James C. Tate, Rocky Mount, to Samuel Hale and Wiley P. Woods, Richmond, 12 Feb. 1833.

[54]*Acts Passed at a General Assembly of the Commonwealth of Virginia . . . [1832–1833]* (Richmond: Thomas Ritchie, 1833), 197.

[55]Gertrude C. Mann Collection, XCII, pp. 3, 819, FCPL.

[56]Wingfield, *Marriage Bonds,* 82.

[57]Franklin County, Will Book 4, 1829–1837, Reel 19, pp. 516–517, VSLA; inventory and appraisal taken 16 Nov. 1837 and recorded 2 Sept. 1839.

[58]Ibid., 49.

[59]Franklin County, Will Book 6, 1845–1849, Reel 20, pp. 406–407, VSLA.

[60]Franklin County, Order Book [1], p. 195.

[61]Franklin County, Will Book 1, pp. 14–15; will probated 1 Oct. 1787.

[62]Legislative Petitions, Franklin County, 5 Nov. 1793.

[63]Franklin County, Order Book [1], p. 298.

[64]Ibid., 30–31; inventory recorded 1 Dec. 1788.

[65]Ibid., Will Book 1, p. 35; recorded 4 May 1789.

[66]Wingfield, *Marriage Bonds,* 236.

[67]Franklin County, Will Book 1, p. 54.

[68]Ibid., 56 (inventory and appraisal, recorded 6 Dec. 1790).

[69]Ibid., 119.

[70]Ibid., 136 (inventory and appraisal recorded Dec. 1798).

[71]Ibid., Will Book 3, 1825–1833, Reel 19, p. 516, VSLA; Will Book 4, pp. 114–115, 288–289.

[72]Ibid., Will Book 6, pp. 346–348; will probated 5 June 1848.

[73]Ibid., Deed Book 3, p. 572; deed recorded 4 May 1798.

[74]Ibid., Deed Book 4, 1800–1804, Reel 2, pp. 441–442, VSLA; deed recorded 4 Apr. 1803.

[75]Record of Appointment of Postmasters, 1832–Sept. 30, 1971, Roll 132, Virginia, Fluvanna-Jefferson Counties, Volume 10, ca. 1832–44, Volume 23, ca. 1857–67, Records of the Post Office Department, Record Group 28, NARA.

[76]Franklin County Suit Papers, Acc. 23707, Mar. 1787, *Milly Thomas* v. *John Livesay;* Franklin County, Order Book [1], p. 107.

[77]Ibid., Oct. 1790, *Benjamin Skinner Duvall* v. *Susannah Barton.*

Chapter Ten: Churches and Schools

[1]Katherine L. Brown, *Hills of the Lord: Background of the Episcopal Church in Southwestern Virginia, 1738–1938* (Roanoke: The Diocese of Southwestern Virginia, 1979), 140–141.

[2]William Meade, *Old Churches, Ministers and Families of Virginia* (Philadelphia: J. B. Lippincott Co., 1857), 2:17.

[3]United States Census, Social Statistics, Franklin County, 1850, Reel 232, VSLA; ibid., 1860, Reel 237.

[4]Roger E. Sappington, *The Brethren in Virginia: The History of the Church of the Brethren in Virginia* (Harrisonburg, Va.: The Committee for Brethren History in Virginia, 1973), 20, 28–29.

[5]*The Brethren Encyclopedia* (Philadelphia: The Brethren Encyclopedia, Inc., 1983–1984), 2:838.

[6]Franklin County, Deed Book 3, 1793–1800, Reel 2, p. 138, VSLA; ibid., Order Book, 1800–1805, Reel 28, p. 225.

[7]*Brethren Encyclopedia,* 2:1191.

[8]Sappington, *Brethren in Virginia,* 46.

[9]Thomas Bailey Greer, Franklin County, to Jubal A. Early [Richmond], 25 Apr. 1861, in "Civil War Letters from Franklin County Residents, 1861–1864," FCPL.

[10]C. Dirck Keyser, "The Virginia Separate Baptists and Arminianism, 1760–1787," *Virginia Baptist Register* 23 (1984): 1110.

[11]Robert G. Gardner, "Virginia Baptist Statistics, 1699–1790," ibid. 21 (1982): 1020–1038.

[12]Thomas Jefferson, *Notes on the State of Virginia,* ed. William Peden (Chapel Hill: University of North Carolina Press, 1955), 159.

[13]Ibid., 224.

[14]Records of the General Assembly, Legislative Petitions, Franklin County, 27 Oct. 1785, VSLA.

[15]Warren Thomas Smith, "Eighteenth Century Encounters: Methodist-Moravian," *Methodist History* 24 (1986): 141–156.

[16]Franklin County, Deed Book 2, 1789–1793, Reel 1, pp. 67, 161, 178, VSLA; (Henry Merrett) Franklin County, Order Book, 1789–1793, Reel 27, p. 154.

[17]Lorenzo Dow, *History of Cosmopolite: or the Writings of Rev. Lorenzo Dow,* 8th ed. (Cincinnati: Applegate and Co., 1855), 187, 191.

[18]Franklin County, Order Book, 1800–1805, Reel 28, p. 155, VSLA.

[19]Ibid., p. 174.

[20]Ibid., Deed Book No. 1, 1786–1789, Reel 1, p. 14, VSLA.

[21]Legislative Petitions, Franklin County, 14 Dec. 1799.

[22]Ibid., 16 Dec. 1813.

[23]Ibid., 7 Dec. 1826.

[24]Reuben E. Alley, *A History of Baptists in Virginia* (Richmond: Virginia Baptist General Board, 1974), 203.

[25]Jeremiah Bell Jeter, *The Recollections of a Long Life* (Richmond: The Religious Herald Co., 1891), 65–66.

[26]Legislative Petitions, Franklin County, 10 Dec. 1844.

[27]Ibid., 13 Dec. 1844.

[28]Fleming Saunders, "Mount Hymettus," Franklin County, to Alice W. Saunders, Flat Creek, Campbell County, 29 Aug. 1832, Irvine-Saunders-Watts Family Papers, 1745–1914, Acc. 38–33, Manuscripts Division, UVA (hereafter cited as Saunders Papers, UVA).

[29]Jeter, *Recollections,* 98–99.

[30]Ibid., 99.

[31]Ibid.

[32]Fleming Saunders, Bleak Hill, Franklin County, to Alice W. Saunders, Flat Creek, Campbell County, 2 Dec. 1832, Saunders Papers, UVA.

[33]Legislative Petitions, Franklin County, 15 Jan. 1848.

[34]Ibid.

[35]William W. Sweet, *Methodism in American History* (New York: The Methodist Book Concern, 1933), 244–253.

[36]Alley, *Baptists in Virginia,* 218–219.

[37]Marshall Wingfield, *Franklin County, Virginia: A History* (Berryville, Va.: Chesapeake Book Co., 1964), 101–105, 113–117.

[38]William Henry Foote, *Sketches of Virginia, Historical and Biographical*, new ed. (Richmond: John Knox Press, 1966), 208.

[39]Wingfield, *Franklin County*, 108; *Brethren Encyclopedia*, 1:248, 385.

[40]Wingfield, *Franklin County*, 116.

[41]Jacob Sours, Rocky Mount, to John Dickson Sours, York Springs, Pa., 21 Apr. 1851, Sours Family Papers, Acc. 4435, UNC.

[42]Marian D. Chiarito, *Entry Record Book, 1737–1770 (Land Entries in the Present Virginia Counties of Halifax, Pittsylvania, Henry, Franklin, and Patrick)* (N.p.: Marian D. Chiarito, 1984), 180.

[43]Franklin County Suit Papers, 1786–1865, Acc. 23707, May 1790, *Robert Jones* v. *Zachary Warren*, VSLA.

[44]Ibid., June 1791, *Samuel King* v. *David Beheler*.

[45]Ibid., Sept. 1794, *Samuel Webb* v. *Jacob Sally*.

[46]Ibid., Sept. 1799, *Daniel French* v. *John McMillian*.

[47]Franklin County, Order Book, 1800–1805, p. 188.

[48]Alice Watts Saunders, Bleak Hill, Franklin County, to Mrs. Mary Watts, Flat Creek, Campbell County, 8 Nov. 1825, Saunders Papers, UVA.

[49]Ibid., 12 Apr. 1829.

[50]Ibid., 21 June 1829.

[51]Alfred J. Morrison, *The Beginnings of Public Education in Virginia, 1776–1860* (Richmond: Superintendent of Public Printing, 1917), 11–12, 53–54.

[52]Franklin County, Deed Book 13, 1830–1833, Reel 7, pp. 10, 563–564, VSLA.

[53]Legislative Petitions, Franklin County, 4 Feb. 1843.

[54]t. S. S. Davis, New London, Bedford County, to Fleming Saunders, Bleak Hill, Franklin County, 18 Jan. 1836, enclosing account, Saunders Papers, UVA.

[55]Fleming Saunders, Bleak Hill, Franklin County, to Edward Saunders, New London Academy, Bedford County, 20 Mar. 1836, in ibid.

[56]Legislative Petitions, Franklin County, 6 Dec. 1826.

[57]U.S. Census, Social Statistics, Franklin County, 1850, Reel 232, ibid., 1860, Reel 237.

[58]Jefferson, *Notes on the State of Virginia*, 147.

Chapter Eleven: Social Problems

[1]Franklin County, Order Book, 1800–1805, Reel 28, p. 58, VSLA.

[2]Ibid., 174.

[3]Ibid., 341.

[4]Franklin County Suit Papers, 1786–1865, Acc. 23707, May 1792, *Samuel Davis* v. *Samuel Patteson*, VSLA.

[5]Ibid., Aug. 1795, *Arthur Edwards* v. *Burwell Rives*.

[6]Ibid., Aug. 1800, *Ashford Napier* v. *John Kindley*.

[7]Ibid., 3 Aug. 1798, affidavit of William Dickenson.

[8]Franklin County, Deed Book No. 5, 1804–1811, Reel 3, p. 32, VSLA.

[9]Jeremiah Bell Jeter, *The Recollections of a Long Life* (Richmond: The Religious Herald Co., 1891), 33.

[10]Mary S. Watts, Salem, Botetourt County, to Sarah Watts Saunders, Lynchburg, 24 Apr. 1830, Irvine-Saunders-Watts Family Papers, 1745–1914, Acc. 38–33, Manuscripts Division, UVA (hereafter cited as Saunders Papers, UVA).

[11]Records of the General Assembly, Legislative Petitions, Franklin County, 18 Jan. 1854, VSLA.

[12]Franklin County Suit Papers, 1786, Acc. 25144, Nov. 1786, *Thomas Miller, Jr.* v. *George Griffith*.

[13]Marian D. Chiarito, Entry *Record Book, 1737–1770 (Land Entries in the Present*

Virginia Counties of Halifax, Pittsylvania, Henry, Franklin, and Patrick) (N.p.: Marian D. Chiarito, 1984), 243; Maud Carter Clement, *The History of Pittsylvania County, Virginia* (Lynchburg, Va.: J. P. Bell Co., 1929; Baltimore: Regional Publishing Co., 1981), 105.

[14]Board of Public Works, Pittsylvania, Franklin, and Botetourt Turnpike, 1838–1853, Field Notes (1838), VSLA.

[15]*American Turf Register and Sporting Magazine* 5 (1834): 437–438.

[16]Franklin County, Order Book [1], 1786–1789, Reel 27, p. 5, VSLA.

[17]Ibid., 174.

[18]Ibid., 223.

[19]William Henry Foote, *Sketches of Virginia, Historical and Biographical,* new ed. (Richmond: John Knox Press, 1966), 177.

[20]Franklin County, Order Book [1], 1786–1789, Reel 27, p. 146.

[21]Ibid., 228.

[22]Ibid., 229, 233.

[23]Ibid., 104.

[24]Ibid., 105.

[25]Ibid., 1800–1805, p. 106.

[26]Ibid., 116.

[27]Ibid., 200.

[28]Ibid., 1806–1811, Reel 28, p. 123, VSLA.

[29]Ibid., 1800–1805, p. 72, 3 Aug. 1801.

[30]Legislative Petitions, Franklin County, 2 Jan. 1845.

[31]Ibid., 19 Jan. 1856.

[32]Franklin County, Order Book [1], p. 145.

[33]Ibid., Order Book, 1789–1793, Reel 27, p. 75, VSLA.

[34]Peter Saunders, Sr., Franklin County, to Gov. Beverley Randolph, Richmond, 25 Feb. 1791, Office of the Governor, Letters Received, VSLA.

[35]Franklin County, Order Book, 1800–1805, p. 310.

[36]Ibid., 1789–1793, p. 252.

[37]Legislative Petitions, Franklin County, 2 Feb. 1835.

[38]Franklin County, Order Book, 1806–1811, pp. 110, 113.

[39]Ibid., 126; Franklin County, District Court, Order Book 5, 1804–1809, Reel 36, p. 198, VSLA.

[40]Franklin County, Order Book [1], p. 57.

[41]Ibid., 8.

[42]Ibid., 49.

[43]Ibid., 189.

[44]Ibid., 194.

[45]Ibid., 1800–1805, p. 206.

[46]Ibid., 1806–1811, p. 83.

[47]Ibid., District Court Order Book 5, pp. 157, 164.

[48]Office of the Governor, Letters Received, Box 194, Governor James Barbour, Pardons, 1812–1813.

[49]The story is repeated in Frank Triplett, *The History, Romance, and Philosophy of Great American Crimes and Criminals* (Saint Louis: N. D. Thompson and Co., 1884); Marshall Wingfield, *An Old Virginia Court: Being a Transcript of the Records of the First Court of Franklin County, Virginia, 1786–1789* (Memphis: West Tennessee Historical Society, 1948), 185–187; and Howard Newlon, Jr., Nathaniel Mason Pawlett, et al., *Backsights* (Richmond: Virginia Department of Highways and Transportation, 1985), 53–54.

[50]*The Life and Adventures of Joseph T. Hare, the Bold Robber and Highwayman, With 16 Elegant and Spirited Engravings* (New York: H. Long and Brother, 1847), 67–69.

[51]Wingfield, *An Old Virginia Court,* 185; *Life . . . of Joseph T. Hare,* 69–71.

[52]A search of the pardon papers in the Office of the Governor, Letters Received, series for the years 1812–1815 failed to verify Hare's claim of a pardon.

[53]Franklin County Order Book [1], pp. 246–248.

[54]Ibid., 1789–1793, pp. 107–108.

[55]Ibid., 1800–1805, p. 311.

[56]Ibid., 396–397.

[57]Ibid., 1806–1811, p. 66.

[58]Ibid., 1786–1789, p. 321; ibid., 1789–1793, p. 22.

[59]Franklin County Suit Papers, Acc. 23707, May 1789, *Thomas Jones* v. *Thomas Prunty.*

[60]Ibid., Aug. 1789, *Edward Willson* v. *John England.*

[61]Ibid., Mar. 1796, *Prunty* v. *O'Neal.*

[62]Franklin County Suit Papers, 1786, Acc. 25144, Nov. 1786, *Samuel Dillion* v. *Blankenships.*

[63]Franklin County, Order Book, 1789–1793, p. 9.

[64]Franklin County Suit Papers, Acc. 23707, Aug. 1790?, *John Brammer* v. *William Griffith.*

[65]Franklin County, Order Book, 1800–1805, p. 227.

[66]Ibid., 33.

[67]Ibid., Deed Book 5, 1804–1811, pp. 561–562.

[68]The general outline of this incident is from Langhorne Jones, "Witcher-Clement Case," *Bicentennial Reflections* (N.p.: Franklin County Bicentennial Commission, 1986), 45–46. *See also* Melanie M. Burnette, "A Scandal That Won't Die," *Roanoker* 10 (Oct. 1983): 32–33, 40–43, 48–50.

[69]Coroner's inquest report quoted in Essie W. Smith Papers, "The Witcher-Clement Murder Trial," FCPL.

[70]Franklin County, Order Book, 1855–1860, Reel 32, pp. 520–524, VSLA.

[71]Peter Saunders, Jr., Rocky Mount, to Alice W. Saunders, Flat Creek, Campbell County, 14 Mar. 1860, Saunders Papers, UVA.

[72]Franklin County, Order Book, 1855–1860, Reel 32, p. 524, VSLA.

[73]Peter Saunders, Jr., Bleak Hill, Franklin County, to Fleming Saunders, n.p., 26 Mar. 1860, Saunders Papers, UVA.

[74]Franklin County, Order Book, 1800–1805, p. 191.

[75]Legislative Petitions, Franklin County, 5 Dec. 1811.

[76]Ibid., 10 Oct. 1857.

[77]Ibid., 29 Jan. 1845.

[78]Franklin County, Order Book, 1855–1860, pp. 277–278.

[79]United States Census, Social Statistics, 1850, Franklin County, Reel 232, VSLA; ibid., 1860, Reel 237.

[80]Auditor of Public Accounts, Overseers of the Poor, Reports, 1829, Franklin County, VSLA.

[81]Franklin County, Order Book, 1830–1835, Reel 30, pp. 286, 316, VSLA.

[82]Ibid., 316.

[83]Ibid., Deed Book 14, 1833–1836, Reel 7, pp. 6–7, VSLA.

[84]Ibid., Order Book, 1830–1835, p. 338 (court meeting of 7 Aug. 1833).

[85]U.S. Census, List of Inhabitants, Franklin County, 1850, Reel 56; Auditor of Public Accounts, Overseers of the Poor, Reports, 1829, Franklin County.

Chapter Twelve: Life at the Bottom: Slaves and Free Blacks

[1]Franklin County Suit Papers, 1786–1865, Acc. 23707, Nov. 1794, *David Morgan* v. *William Lee,* affidavit of James Stone, n.d., VSLA.

[2]Ibid., affidavit of Elizabeth Ray, 6 Aug. 1794.

[3]Ibid., deposition of William Wade, 21 June 1794.

[4]Ibid., Nov. 1794, complaint of David Morgan against William Lee, 6 May 1794.

[5]Ibid., deposition of Thomas Prunty, 4 Nov. 1794.

[6]Ibid., deposition of James Stone, n.d.

[7]Ibid., deposition of George Mabry, Sr., 29 Nov. 1794.

[8]Ibid., answer of William Lee to complaint of David Morgan, 28 July 1794.

[9]Charles L. Perdue, Jr., Thomas E. Barden, and Robert K. Phillips, eds., *Weevils in the Wheat: Interviews with Virginia Ex-Slaves* (Charlottesville: University Press of Virginia, 1976), 264–265 (interview with Martha Showvely). The interviewer, a black named William T. Lee, was attempting to replicate Mrs. Showvely's dialect.

[10]Franklin County Suit Papers, Acc. 23707, Nov. 1790, *John Hook* v. *Henry Loving.*

[11]Perdue, Barden, and Phillips, *Weevils in the Wheat,* 82–83 (interview with Baily Cunningham, prior to 14 Mar. 1938).

[12]Alice W. Saunders, Franklin County, to Mrs. Mary Watts, "Near New London," Campbell County, 25 Dec. 1814, Irvine-Saunders-Watts Family Papers, 1745–1914, Acc. 38–33, Manuscripts Division, UVA (hereafter cited as Saunders Papers, UVA).

[13]Henry Dillard, Call Book, 1861, in possession of Dr. J. Francis Amos, Rocky Mount, Va.

[14]Auditor of Public Accounts, Personal Property Tax Books, Franklin County, 1786, 1800, VSLA.

[15]*Heads of Families at the First Census of the United States Taken in the Year 1790* (Baltimore: Genealogical Publishing Co., 1966), 9; Francis A. Walker, dir., *The Statistics of the Population of the United States . . . Compiled from the Original Returns of the Ninth Census (June 1, 1870)* (Washington, D.C.: Government Printing Office, 1872), 1:68–69.

[16]Auditor of Public Accounts, Personal Property Tax Books, Franklin County, 1861.

[17]Franklin County Suit Papers, Acc. 23707, Mar. 1787, *Milly Thomas* v. *John Livesay.*

[18]Ibid., Mar. 1800, *Thomas Pinckard* v. *William Ryan and Thomas Sherwood.*

[19]Fleming Saunders, Franklin County, to Mrs. Alice W. Saunders, New London, Campbell County, 6 Jan. 1833, Saunders Papers, UVA.

[20]Ibid., agreement dated 23 Jan. 1862.

[21]Franklin County Suit Papers, Acc. 23707, 1786, *William Walton* v. *Isaac Rentfro,* mortgage dated 19 July 1785.

[22]Ibid., Aug. 1787, *Joseph Martin (assignee of Thomas Hutchings)* v. *James Parbury.*

[23]Franklin County, Order Book, 1800–1805, Reel 28, p. 201, VSLA.

[24]Peter Saunders, Jr., Bleak Hill, Franklin County, to Fleming Saunders, n.p., 28 July 1859, Saunders Papers, UVA.

[25]William S. Morris, Lynchburg, to Fleming Saunders, Abingdon, 3 Sept. 1848, in ibid.

[26]Alice W. Saunders, Franklin County, to Mrs. Mary Watts, "Near New London," Campbell County, 25 Dec. 1814, in ibid.

[27]James H. Roberts, Indian Valley, Floyd County, to Fleming Saunders, Jr., n.p., 30 Apr. 1861, in ibid.

[28]Ibid., 9 May 1861.

[29]Alice W. Saunders, Franklin County, to Mrs. Mary Watts, [Flat Creek], Campbell County, 25 Jan. 1817, in ibid.

[30]Fleming Saunders, Franklin County, to Mrs. Alice W. Saunders, New London, Campbell County, 21 Mar. 1835, in ibid.

[31]Franklin County, Order Book, 1800–1805, pp. 80–81.

[32]Ibid., 1789–1793, Reel 27, pp. 107–108, VSLA.

[33]Auditor of Public Accounts, Condemned Blacks Executed or Transported, 1824, VSLA.

[34]Fleming Saunders, Franklin County, to Mrs. Alice W. Saunders, Flat Creek, Campbell County, 6 Apr. 1833, Saunders Papers, UVA.

[35]Ibid., 9 Apr. 1833.

[36]Peter Saunders, Jr., Bleak Hill, Franklin County, to Fleming Saunders, [Flat Creek, Campbell County], 26 Mar. 1860, in ibid.

[37]Auditor of Public Accounts, Condemned Blacks Executed or Transported, 1795.

[38]Ibid., 1817.

[39]Ibid., 1830.

[40]Franklin County, Suit Papers, Acc. 23707, Nov. 1790–Mar. 1791, *John Hook* v. *Henry Loving*.

[41]Louis R. Harlan, *Booker T. Washington: The Making of a Black Leader, 1856–1901* (New York: Oxford University Press, 1972), 18.

[42]Perdue, Barden, and Phillips, *Weevils in the Wheat,* 80–83 (Cunningham), 264–265 (Showvely), 343–345 (Zeigler).

[43]Stacy Gibbons Moore, " 'Established and Well Cultivated': Afro-American Foodways in Early Virginia," *Virginia Cavalcade* 39 (1989): 70–83.

[44]Perdue, Barden, and Phillips, *Weevils in the Wheat,* 81.

[45]Booker T. Washington, *Up From Slavery: An Autobiography* (Garden City, N.Y.: Doubleday and Co., 1963), 6–7.

[46]Perdue, Barden, and Phillips, *Weevils in the Wheat,* 81.

[47]Ibid., 82.

[48]Washington, *Up From Slavery,* 8–9.

[49]Perdue, Barden, and Phillips, *Weevils in the Wheat,* 82.

[50]Washington, *Up From Slavery,* 1–4.

[51]Joseph Mayo, *A Guide to Magistrates . . . Adapted to the New Code of Virginia* (Richmond: Colin, Baptist and Nowlan, 1850), 443.

[52]A. R. Newsome, ed., "John Brown's Journal of Travel in Western North Carolina in 1795," *North Carolina Historical Review* 11 (1934): 288.

[53]Perdue, Barden, and Phillips, *Weevils in the Wheat,* 82.

[54]Ibid., 265.

[55]Washington, *Up From Slavery,* 4.

[56]Perdue, Barden, and Phillips, *Weevils in the Wheat,* 82.

[57]Ibid., 80, 82.

[58]Franklin County, Will Book 1, 1786–1812, Reel 18, pp. 242–243, VSLA.

[59]Ibid., Order Book, 1800–1805, p. [453], 1 Oct. 1804.

[60]Mayo, *A Guide to Magistrates,* 437.

[61]Census takers used the letter *M* to indicate "mulatto" and *B* to indicate "black"; no letter *W* was used for a white person. Jane Smithers, for instance, is listed in both the 1850 and 1860 censuses of Franklin County. In 1850 she is described as "mulatto," but in 1860 that indicator was dropped, suggesting that the census taker regarded her as white. Occasionally the same thing occurred in the personal property tax records when FN, the usual abbreviation for "Free Negro," eventually vanished from beside a taxpayer's name.

[62]Franklin County, Will Book 2, 1812–1825, Reel 18, p. 375, VSLA.

[63]Glenna Donelle Hawkins, "Free Black Persons of Color in Franklin County, Virginia, 1786–1865" (Master's thesis, Virginia Polytechnic Institute and State University, 1976), 22.

[64]Franklin County, Order Book, 1850–1855, Reel 32, court meeting of 4 Jan. 1853 (no page numbers in order book); ibid., 1855–1860, Reel 32, p. 134, VSLA.

[65]Ibid., Deed Book 21, 1849–1851, Reel 11, pp. 265–266, VSLA.

[66]Ibid., 423.

[67]Ibid., Will Book 8, 1852–1854, Reel 21, pp. 135–137, VSLA; inventory and appraisal of estate of Henry T. Callaway made 13 Aug. 1853 and recorded 5 Dec. 1853.

[68]Ibid., 23–24.

[69]Ibid., Order Book, 1800–1805, p. 367.

[70]Ibid., 1806–1811, p. 17.

[71]Ibid., 1800–1805, p. 234.

[72]Ibid., Will Book 1, pp. 203–204.

[73]Ibid., Order Book, 1806–1811, Reel 28, p. 152, VSLA.

[74]Walker, *The Statistics of the Population of the United States . . . (June 1, 1870)*, 1:68–69.

[75]Frank Lincoln Mather, ed., *Who's Who of the Colored Race* (Chicago: F. L. Mather, 1915), 222; Congressman Powell's father, Adam Clayton Powell, Sr., was born in Franklin County on 5 May 1865; in 1908 he became the pastor of the Abyssinian Baptist Church in New York.

[76]Franklin County, Will Book 4, 1829–1837, Reel 19, p. 402, VSLA; will dated 5 Mar. 1834 and proved 6 Aug. 1838.

[77]Ibid., Order Book, 1800–1805, pp. 357, 417 (court meetings of 7 Jan. and 5 Aug. 1805).

[78]Ibid., Will Book 3, 1825–1833, Reel 19, p. 506, VSLA; will written 30 May 1831 and probated 7 June 1831.

[79]Ibid.

[80]Hawkins, "Free Black Persons of Color in Franklin County," 91–94 (Appendix 7); 40 (Table 8).

Chapter Thirteen: Civil War

[1]George H. Reese, ed., *Proceedings of the Virginia State Convention of 1861* (Richmond: Virginia State Library, 1965), 4:58–59.

[2]Ibid., 59.

[3]Ibid., 3:359.

[4]United States Office of the Adjutant General, Virginia Case Files for U.S. Pardons, 1865–1867, Acc. 31057, Reel 13, VSLA.

[5]Reese, *Proceedings*, 1:427–433, 437–438, 486–488; 3:725–729.

[6]Ibid., 3:729.

[7]Greer to Early, [Richmond], in "Civil War Letters from Franklin County Residents, 1861–1864," FCPL.

[8]The outlines of Early's career are described in Terry R. Moss, "General Jubal A. Early," *Bicentennial Reflections* (N.p.: Franklin County Bicentennial Commission, 1986), 41–42.

[9]Patricia L. Faust, ed., *Historical Times Illustrated Encyclopedia of the Civil War* (New York: Harper and Row, 1986), 23, 233.

[10]Information gathered from will books, deed books, and maps in the Clerk's Office, Franklin County Courthouse, Rocky Mount, Va., by Virginia Greer Williams.

[11]Auditor of Public Accounts, Condemned Blacks Executed or Transported, 1860, VSLA.

[12]John S. Wise, *The End of an Era*, ed. Curtis C. Davis (New York: Thomas Yoseloff, 1965), 227–228.

[13]Jubal A. Early, *Autobiographical Sketch and Narrative of the War Between the States*, ed. Gary Gallagher (Wilmington, N.C.: Broadfoot Publishing Co., 1989), i–v.

[14]Early, *Autobiographical Sketch*, xv–xvii.

[15]Jubal A. Early, *A Memoir of the Last Year of the War for Independence, in the Confederate States of America*, 2d ed. (Lynchburg, Va.: Charles W. Button, 1867), 129.

[16]*Lynchburg Virginian*, 22 May 1865.

[17]Early, *Memoir*, 139–140.

[18]Typescript of story supposedly related by Early, in possession of Dr. J. Francis Amos, Rocky Mount, Va.

[19]Mattie Brown to "Lizzie," in "Civil War Letters from Franklin County Residents, 1861–1864," FCPL.

[20]James H. Roberts, Indian Valley, Floyd County, to Capt. Fleming Saunders, Jr., n.p., 30 Apr. 1861, Irvine-Saunders-Watts Family Papers, 1745–1914, Acc. 38-33, Manuscripts Division, UVA (hereafter cited as Saunders Papers, UVA).

[21]Articles of Agreement, 24 June 1861, in ibid.

[22]The histories of the organization and activities of the 42d, 57th, and 24th regiments are taken respectively from John Chapla, *42nd Virginia Infantry* (Lynchburg, Va.: H. E. Howard, Inc., 1983); Charles W. Sublett, *57th Regiment Virginia Infantry* (Lynchburg, Va.: H. E. Howard, Inc., 1985); and Ralph W. Gunn, *24th Regiment Virginia Infantry* (Lynchburg, Va.: H. E. Howard, Inc., 1987). The history of the 37th Battalion Virginia Cavalry is taken from J. L. Scott, *36th and 37th Battalions Virginia Cavalry* (Lynchburg, Va.: H. E. Howard, Inc., 1986), 49–104.

[23]Henry Hopkins, "The War," in *Bicentennial Reflections,* 47–49; Lee A. Wallace, Jr., *A Guide to Virginia Military Organizations, 1861–1865,* 2d ed. (Lynchburg, Va.: H. E. Howard Co., 1986), 51–52.

[24]Hopkins, "The War," 47; Wallace, *Guide,* 41.

[25]Hopkins, "The War," 48–49.

[26]Booth, Loudoun County, to "Sister," [Franklin County], in "Civil War Letters from Franklin County Residents, 1861–1864," FCPL.

[27]Young to "Sister," in ibid.

[28]Finney to mother, in ibid.

[29]*The War of the Rebellion: A Compilation of the Official Records of the Union and Confederate Armies. Prepared Under the Direction of the Secretary of War by Robert N. Scott* (Washington, D.C.: Government Printing Office, 1880–1901), ser. 1, 11:488; 12:550; 19:41.

[30]Ibid., 19:219, 712.

[31]Ibid., 21:544; 25:253, 794; Faust, *Encyclopedia of the Civil War,* 126, 431.

[32]*Official Records,* 27:291, 335, 345, 713, 1064.

[33]Kathleen R. Georg and John W. Busey, *Nothing But Glory: Pickett's Division at Gettysburg* (Hightstown, N.J.: Longstreet House, 1987), 494–495.

[34]Faust, *Encyclopedia of the Civil War,* 517.

[35]Young brothers to "Sister," in "Civil War Letters from Franklin County Residents, 1861–1864," FCPL.

[36]Richards to "Mother, Sister and Friends," [Franklin County], 19 Apr. 1862, and to Harriet Richards (wife), [Franklin County], 7 June 1862, Richards Papers, photocopies of typescripts in possession of Dr. J. Francis Amos, Rocky Mount, Va.

[37]Finney to mother, in "Civil War Letters from Franklin County Residents, 1861–1864," FCPL.

[38]Richards, "Camp near Guinea's Station," to Harriet Richards (wife), [Franklin County], 11 Jan. 1863, Richards Papers, photocopies of typescripts in possession of Dr. J. Francis Amos, Rocky Mount, Va.

[39]Copy of transcript of diary of George H. T. Greer; original diary in possession of Miles W. Greer, Harrington Park, N.J.

[40]Wise, *End of an Era,* 225, 229–230.

[41]Heros von Borcke, *Memoirs of the Confederate War for Independence* (New York: Peter Smith, 1938), 2:316.

[42]Ibid., *Colonel Heros von Borcke's Journal, 26 April–8 October 1862,* ed. Stuart Wright (Winston-Salem, N.C.: Palaemon Press, 1981), 11–12.

[43]Greer diary.

[44]Ibid.

[45]Finney, near Chester Station, to "Cousin Wesly & Martha," [Franklin County], in "Civil War Letters from Franklin County Residents, 1861–1864," FCPL.

[46]Mat W., [Story Creek, Franklin County, Va.], to Miss Elvira Phillips, n.p., 19 Sept. 1863,

Edith Sigmon Collection, photocopy of typescript in possession of Dr. J. Francis Amos, Rocky Mount, Va.

[47]*Lynchburg Virginian*, 14 Sept. 1863.

[48]Chapla, *42nd Virginia Infantry*, 124.

[49]*Lynchburg Virginian*, 16 Sept. 1863.

[50]Ibid., 24 Sept. 1863.

[51]Ibid., 29 Sept. 1863.

[52]Mollie, Indian Valley [Floyd County], Va., to "Cousin Ell," n.p., 28 Sept. 1864, Edith Sigmon Collection, photocopy of typescript in possession of Dr. J. Francis Amos, Rocky Mount, Va.

[53]Chapla, *42nd Virginia Infantry*, 39–40, 76.

[54]Finney, near Chester Station, to "Cousin Wesly & Martha," [Franklin County], in "Civil War Letters from Franklin County Residents, 1861–1864," FCPL.

[55]Sublett, *57th Virginia Infantry*, 68.

[56]Gunn, *24th Virginia Infantry*, 79.

[57]Turner to mother and father, in "Civil War Letters from Franklin County Residents, 1861–1864," FCPL.

[58]Stone to "Sue," in ibid.

[59]Linus H. Bernard, Martha Bernard, E. T. Ingrum, and Matilda Ingrum, [Floyd County], to "Mr. and Mrs. Bernard," [Franklin County], n.d. [1861], in Bernard Family Papers, photocopies in possession of Dr. J. Francis Amos, Rocky Mount, Va.

[60]Franklin County, Order Book, 1860–1865, Reel 33, p. 117, VSLA.

[61]Ibid., 114–115.

[62]Ibid., 115.

[63]Ibid., 120–121.

[64]H[enry] Dillard, Rocky Mount, to C. Y. Thomas, n.p., 25 Jan. 1862, Richard P. Gravely, Jr., Papers, Acc. 28996, VSLA.

[65]Auditor of Public Accounts, Licenses, 1863, Franklin County, VSLA.

[66]*Journal of the Senate of the Commonwealth of Virginia* (Richmond: James E. Goode, 1864), 32.

[67]Franklin County, Order Book, 1860–1865, p. 182.

[68]Ibid., 189.

[69]Armistead F. Ramsey, *Memoirs of Armistead Fuller Ramsey, 1856–1937* (N.p.: n.p., 1949), 18–19.

[70]Franklin County, Order Book, 1860–1865, p. 239.

[71]Ibid., 429–455.

[72]Ibid., 466.

[73]Ibid., 198a.

[74]Ibid., 252.

[75]Ibid., 242.

[76]Ibid., 243–245.

[77]Ibid., 242.

[78]Receipt, J. W. Patterson, agent for Peter Saunders, Sr., n.p., to C. Y. Thomas, n.p., 25 Dec. 1864, Richard P. Gravely, Jr., Papers.

[79]Franklin County, Order Book, 1861–1865, pp. 492–493.

[80]Ibid., 185.

[81]Ibid., 277–278.

[82]Ibid., 307–308.

[83]Ibid., 333–334.

[84]Ibid., 375.

[85]Ibid., 459.

[86]Ibid., 428, 459.

[87]Ibid., 396.

[88]Ibid., 460.

[89]Ibid., 486.

[90]Wise, *End of an Era*, 219.

[91]Ibid., 222–223.

[92]Ibid., 223–224.

[93]Roger E. Sappington, *The Brethren in Virginia: The History of the Church of the Brethren in Virginia* (Harrisonburg, Va.: Park View Press, 1973), 64–80; Auditor of Public Accounts, Military Service Exemption Fines, Franklin County, 1863.

[94]Sappington, *Brethren in Virginia*, 81–84.

[95]David E. Johnston, *Four Years a Soldier* (Princeton, W.Va.: n.p., 1887), 281.

[96]Booker T. Washington, *Up From Slavery: An Autobiography* (Garden City, N.Y.: Doubleday and Co., 1963), 14–15.

[97]Ibid., 14–16.

[98]Franklin County, Order Book, 1860–1865, pp. 497–498.

[99]Ibid., 498.

[100]Charles H. Kirk, *History of the Fifteenth Pennsylvania Volunteer Cavalry* (Philadelphia: n.p., 1906), 498.

[101]Ibid., 500.

[102]Related in a memoir by Miss Maggie Holland, a niece of Asa Holland, n.d., n.p., typescript in possession of Dr. J. Francis Amos, Rocky Mount, Va.

[103]Ibid.; perhaps the second horse was unreconstructed.

Chapter Fourteen: Reconstruction, Freedmen, and the New Social Order

[1]Arthur M. Schlesinger, ed., *The Almanac of American History* (New York: G. P. Putnam's Sons, 1983), 294.

[2]Ibid., 304–306.

[3]William T. Alderson, "The Influence of Military Rule and the Freedmen's Bureau on Reconstruction in Virginia, 1867–1870" (Ph.D. diss., Vanderbilt University, 1952), 28–31a. Franklin was part of the nine-county district number 7; Schlesinger, *Almanac of American History*, 293.

[4]Bureau of Refugees, Freedmen, and Abandoned Lands, Records of the Assistant Commissioner for the State of Virginia, 1865–1869, Acc. 30080 (hereafter cited as BRFAL), Records Relating to Court Cases Involving Freedmen: Narrative Reports of Criminal Cases Involving Freedmen, Mar. 1866–Feb. 1867, Reel 59, Report of W. F. DeKnight, 30 Sept. 1866, NARA.

[5]Letter of M. F. ("Fannie") Burroughs, Halesford, Franklin County, Va., 6 July 1865, in the Booker T. Washington Files, FCPL.

[6]Letter of George W. Booker, Richmond, 20 Apr. 1867, to C. Y. Thomas, Henry County, Richard P. Gravely, Jr., Papers, Acc. 28996, VSLA.

[7]*Lynchburg Virginian*, 24 July 1865, quoted in John Preston McConnell, *Negroes and Their Treatment in Virginia from 1865 to 1867* (Pulaski, Va.: B. D. Smith & Brothers, [1918]), 33–34.

[8]Asa Holland Papers, Acc. 902, Manuscripts Division, UVA.

[9]Ibid., letters of William E. Duncan, Sandy River, to Asa Holland, Halesford, 10 and 17 Nov., and 23 Dec. 1865.

[10]Ibid., letters of William E. Duncan to his wife, Sallie E. Duncan, 18 Aug. 1867, and to Captain Craft, 30 Oct. 1867.

[11]Peter Saunders, Jr., Bleak Hill, Franklin County, to Mrs. Alice Watts Saunders, Flat Creek, Campbell County, 26 May, 6 Sept., and 9 Nov. 1866, Irvine-Saunders-Watts Family

Papers, 1745–1914, Acc. 38–33, Manuscripts Division, UVA (hereafter cited as Saunders Papers, UVA).

[12]Lynda Joyce Morgan, "Emancipation in the Virginia Tobacco Belt, 1850–1870" (Ph.D. diss., University of Virginia, 1986), 168–170.

[13]Virginia Census Schedules, List of Inhabitants, Franklin County, 1850, 1860, 1870, Reels 559, 1346, and 1647; Virginia Agriculture Census, 1870, Schedule 3, Franklin County, Roll 240; Auditor of Public Accounts, Land Tax Books, Franklin County, 1870, VSLA.

[14]BRFAL, Reports of Operations and Conditions in Virginia: Monthly Narrative Reports of Operations and Conditions, July–Oct. 1866, Report of 30 Sept. 1866, Reel 45, NARA.

[15]Ibid.

[16]Ibid., Records Relating to Court Cases Involving Freedmen, Narrative Reports of Criminal Cases Involving Freedmen, Mar. 1866–Feb. 1867, Reel 59, p. 0197, 30 Apr. 1866.

[17]Ibid., pp. 0227–0228, 31 May 1866.

[18]Ibid., Monthly Narrative Reports of Operations and Conditions in Virginia, 30 Sept. 1866, p. 0548; Records Relating to Court Cases, 30 Sept. 1866, pp. 0723–0725. Interestingly enough, local tradition states that Taliaferro himself fathered five children by a black woman named Smithers who lived on Grassy Hill.

[19]Ibid., Report of 30 Sept. 1866, Reel 45. DeKnight remarked that "the amalgamation here, between the two races must be far greater than even it is in the North."

[20]Ibid., Report of 31 October 1866, Mistreatment of Freedmen, Reel 58.

[21]BRFAL, Report of 30 Sept. 1866, Reel 45; the 1870 Virginia Census index lists a Daniel Perdue, age 44, living in the Bonbrook District: Bradley W. Steuart, ed. *Virginia 1870 Census Index*, vol. 3, L–R (Bountiful, Utah: Precision Indexing, 1989), 2602.

[22]BRFAL, Report of 31 Oct. 1866, Reel 45.

[23]Ibid., This and the following paragraph come from Reports for 31 Jan. 1866 (Reel 44) and 31 July, 1 and 30 Sept. 1866 (Reel 45).

[24]Ibid., Report for 30 Sept. 1866, Reel 45.

[25]Ibid.

[26]The indexes to the 1850, 1860, and 1870 Virginia censuses reveal two Harkriders in Roanoke County in 1850, two in Pittsylvania County, and one in Bedford County in 1860, and a Miss Lucinda Harkrider in Roanoke in 1870 (who was a domestic servant). No Harkriders appear for Franklin County in any of these indexes.

[27]BRFAL, Report of 28 Feb. 1867, Reel 46.

[28]Ibid., Report of 28 Feb. 1867.

[29]Ibid., Report of 31 Mar. 1867.

[30]Elizabeth Dabney Saunders, Bleak Hill, Franklin County, to Fleming Saunders, n.p., 23 Mar. 1867, Saunders Papers, UVA.

[31]BRFAL, Reports of 30 Apr. and 31 May 1867, Reel 47.

[32]Ibid., Report of 30 June 1867.

[33]Ibid., Report of 31 July 1867.

[34]Alderson, "The Influence of Military Rule," 166–168 (quotation) Circular Letter, 28 May 1867, in BRFAL; *Richmond Enquirer*, 1 June 1867, p. 2, c. 1: the *Enquirer* noted that "General Brown, of the Freedmen's Bureau for this State, has entered the political canvass. Under the convenient report that somebody is going to keep the negroes of the State from registering,—which nobody ever thought of doing,—he instructs all his subordinates to urge upon them both to register and to vote, and such Bureau officers as may omit a single freedman in his attentions is to be dealt with for a direliction."

[35]BRFAL, Report of 30 June 1867, Reel 47.

[36]Ibid., Report of 31 July 1867.

[37]Eric Foner, *Reconstruction: America's Unfinished Revolution, 1863–1877* (New York: Harper & Row, Publishers, 1988), 282.

[38] *Great Republic*, 23 Aug. 1867, p. 769. H. J. Brown may have been Henry J. Brown, of Philadelphia, Pennsylvania, a member of the Pennsylvania State Equal Rights' League in 1865, the H. J. Brown who helped to write an "Address of the Colored Men's Border State Convention to the People of the United States, Baltimore, August 5–6, 1868," or Dr. H. J. Brown, of Maryland, who served as a delegate to the National Convention of the Colored Men of America in 1869, a member of that convention's Committee on Permanent Organization, and an advocate of admitting women as delegates to that convention, saying "he wanted [the other male delegates] to know that this was a progressive age, and that women would yet have a vote": Philip S. Foner and George E. Walker, eds., *Proceedings of the Black National and State Conventions, 1865–1900* (Philadelphia: Temple University Press, 1986), 1:158, 322–324, 351, 353. The editors have indexed all three as Henry J. Brown.

[39] Also known as Captain Peter Saunders, he was the son of Samuel Saunders and had become ironmaster of the Washington Iron Works in 1846. After serving in the Convention of 1861, Saunders was elected to the state Senate for the term beginning in 1863 and served until Apr. 1867: John S. Salmon, *The Washington Iron Works of Franklin County, Virginia, 1773–1850* (Richmond: Virginia State Library, 1986), 65; Cynthia Miller Leonard, *The General Assembly of Virginia, July 20, 1619–January 11, 1978: A Bicentennial Register of Members* (Richmond: Virginia State Library, 1978), 475, 487, 503; T. Keister Greer, "The Convention of 1861," *Franklin County Times*, 15 Aug. 1968, reprinted in *Franklin News-Post*, 1 Jan. 1986, Special Bicentennial Edition, Section B, p. 25.

[40] Peter Saunders, Jr., was the son of Fleming Saunders, graduated from Washington College in 1843, practiced law, was a Franklin County justice of the peace, and served in the Virginia House of Delegates 1861–1863 and 1883–1887. When he died in Aug. 1904, he was described as the "sage of Bleak Hill": Salmon, *Washington Iron Works*, 65; Leonard, *General Assembly Register*, 479, 538, 541; Marshall Wingfield, *Pioneer Families of Franklin County, Virginia* (Berryville, Va.: Chesapeake Book Co., 1964), 198; *Richmond Times-Dispatch*, 16 Aug. 1904, p. 5, c. 2; Franklin County Order Book, 1860–1865, Reel 33, pp. 542–544, VSLA. During the winter of 1860–1861, Saunders suffered a severe illness and did not participate in secession activities, which he claimed to oppose: U.S. Office of the Adjutant General, Virginia Case Files for U.S. Pardons, 1865–1867, Acc. 31057, Reel 13, VSLA.

[41] BRFAL, Report of 31 Aug. 1867, Reel 47.

[42] Foner, *Reconstruction*, 283.

[43] Susie Lee Owens, "The Union League of America: Political Activities in Tennessee, the Carolinas, and Virginia, 1867–1870," (Ph.D. diss., New York University, 1943), 7–8.

[44] *Great Republic*, 23 Aug. 1867, p. 769.

[45] BRFAL, Report of 31 Aug. 1867, Reel 47.

[46] Ibid.

[47] Ibid., Report of 30 Sept. 1867. Hale had been born in Richmond but came to Franklin County as a young man (he was listed as a twenty-year-old student living in the home of Samuel Hale, Bonbrook district, in the 1860 census: Virginia Census Schedules, List of Inhabitants, 1860, Franklin County, Reel 1346, p. 309). The first mayor of Rocky Mount, when he died in 1933 he was the last surviving member of General Jubal A. Early's staff: *Roanoke Times*, 9 Sept. 1933, p. 2, c. 4; Marshall Wingfield, *Franklin County, Virginia: A History* (Berryville, Va.: Chesapeake Book Co., 1964), 25. In 1926, the supplement to the *County News* stated that at that time Hale was the oldest resident of the county, the next oldest being ten years younger, and that Hale had come to Franklin from Richmond in 1867: J. H. Claiborne, comp. and ed., "Franklin County, Virginia: Historical and Industrial—Past, Present and Future," *County News*, supplement ([Rocky Mount, Va.], 1926), 29.

[48]BRFAL, Report of 30 Sept. 1867, Reel 47.

[49]The convention met in Richmond from 3 Dec. 1867 to 16 Apr. 1868, and included seventy-three radicals of whom twenty-four were black Virginians and thirty-three were white men of northern or foreign birth. Thirty-two others were members of the newly formed Conservative party, mostly young Confederate veterans without prewar political experience. Under the leadership of New Yorker John C. Underwood, who served as president, the convention created the Virginia Constitution of 1869 that provided for universal manhood suffrage, abolished viva voce voting, and established a system of state-supported public schools: Emily J. Salmon, ed., *A Hornbook of Virginia History*, 3d ed. (Richmond: Virginia State Library, 1983), 42.

[50]BRFAL, Report of 31 Oct. 1867, Reel 48; other candidates were G. W. Finney, "a Repudiationist" who received 325 white and 15 black votes for a 340 total; Mordecai Cook, a "conservative," 243 white and 1 black vote; Daniel Blevins, "a loyal, poor man, of no capacity" with 31 white and 95 black votes for 126; Daniel Flora, "a loyal, 'Conservative' Candidate," with 109 white and 4 black votes for 113; the Reverend G. L. Stone, "an unprincipled 'Red String' Candidate," who got 8 votes, 7 white and 1 black; Fountain Boules, "not a candidate, principles unknown," who received 1 white vote; Peter Saunders, "a republican—not a candidate," with 1 white vote; B. H. Hutcherson "unknown—not a candidate," with 1 white vote; W. T. Scott, "a loyal, poor man—not a candidate," 1 white vote; and John R. Martin, "a Rebel Preacher—not a Candidate," who also secured 1 white vote.

[51]Ibid.

[52]Ibid., Report of 30 Nov. 1867.

[53]Ibid., Report of 31 Dec. 1867.

[54]Ibid., Report of 31 Jan. 1868.

[55]Ibid.

[56]Ibid.

[57]Ibid., Report of 29 Feb. 1868.

[58]Ibid., Report of 31 Mar. 1868.

[59]Ibid.

[60]Ibid., Report of 31 Dec. 1867.

[61]Ibid., Reports of 29 Feb. and 31 Mar. 1868. From Apr. through June, Egbert simply reported that what he had had to say in his Mar. 1868 report was still true. Thereafter, there are no further reports from Franklin from July through Dec. 1868, when this series ends.

[62]Ibid., Mar.–Dec. 1868, Reels 48–49,; Salmon, *Hornbook of Virginia History*, 42–43.

[63]Ninth United States Census, Virginia, Agriculture, 1870, Schedule 3, Franklin County, Roll 240, Rocky Mount Township, taken by Thomas B. Claiborne, assistant marshal, 8 17 Aug. 1870, p. 1, line 24, VSLA; Virginia Census Schedules, List of Inhabitants, Franklin County, 1870, Film 524, Roll 1647, Rocky Mount, taken 29 Aug. 1870, Household 53, John P. DeHaven.

[64]Francis A. Walker, dir., *The Statistics of the Population of the United States . . . Compiled from the Original Returns of the Ninth Census (June 1, 1870)* (Washington, D.C.: Government Printing Office, 1872), 1:68–69.

[65]Foner, *Reconstruction*, 85.

[66]Ibid.; Virginia Census Schedules, List of Inhabitants, 1870, Franklin County, Roll 1647.

[67]Ninth U.S. Census, Virginia, Agriculture, 1870, Schedule 3, Franklin County, Roll 240; there were a total of 1,394 farmers listed in this schedule and of that number 36 of them can be identified as blacks.

[68]Ibid.; Virginia Census Schedules, List of Inhabitants, Franklin County, 1870, Roll 1647.

Chapter Fifteen: Rocky Mount Comes of Age

[1]*Bedford Sentinel*, 23 Feb. 1872, p. 2, c. 4.

[2]*Acts and Joint Resolutions Passed by the General Assembly of the State of Virginia, at Its Session of 1871–'72* (Richmond: Superintendent of Public Printing, 1872), 429–430.

[3]Clare White, *Roanoke: 1740–1982* (Roanoke, Va.: Roanoke Valley Historical Society, 1982), 59–63.

[4]The history of the Franklin and Pittsylvania Railroad is recounted in Dorothy Cundiff and A. D. Ramsey, "Old Franklin & Pittsylvania Railroad is Loving Memory for Many," *Bicentennial Reflections* (N.p.: Franklin County Bicentennial Commission, 1986), 58–60.

[5]E. F. Pat Striplin, *The Norfolk and Western: A History* (Roanoke, Va.: Norfolk and Western Railway Co., 1981), 101.

[6]*Roanoke Daily Times*, 22 Feb. 1890, p. 1, c. 5.

[7]Quoted in ibid., 27 Feb. 1890, p. 4, c. 5.

[8]Ibid., 15 June 1890, p. 1, c. 8.

[9]Ibid., 17 Aug. 1890, p. 1, c. 4; ibid., 25 Sept. 1890, p. 4, c. 3; ibid., 25 Oct. 1890, p. 4, c. 3.

[10]"Recollections of the 'Punkin Vine,'" *Norfolk and Western Magazine* 35 (Feb. 1957): 99.

[11]*Acts and Joint Resolutions Passed by the General Assembly of the State of Virginia at its Session of 1872–'73* (Richmond: Superintendent of Public Printing, 1873), 65–66.

[12]Ibid., 57; Minutes and Ordinances of the Town of Rocky Mount, 1872–1882, VSLA. The first five pages of the minute book are missing, but on pages 6 through 29 Scott signed the minutes at the end of each meeting between 2 Aug. 1873 and 15 Aug. 1874 as "president." Between 12 Sept. 1874 and 10 July 1876 (pp. 28–57) he signed as "mayor."

[13]Minutes and Ordinances of the Town of Rocky Mount, 1872–1882.

[14]Ibid., 70, 111, 126, 151–152, 160, 205.

[15]Ibid., 7, 16, 18.

[16]Typescript of newspaper article, "Wooden Structure over Pigg River to be Razed," 24 Nov. 1939, n.p., in possession of Dr. J. Francis Amos, Rocky Mount, Va.

[17]Minutes and Ordinances of the Town of Rocky Mount, 1872–1882, pp. 11–12.

[18]Ibid., 199.

[19]Typescript of memoir of Braxton Bragg Tyree, 28 Nov. 1964 and 5 May 1965, p. 6, photocopy of typescript in possession of Dr. J. Francis Amos, Rocky Mount, Va.

[20]Minutes and Ordinances of the Town of Rocky Mount, 1872–1882, pp. 25–26.

[21]Ibid., 19–20.

[22]*Acts and Joint Resolutions Passed by the General Assembly . . . 1871–'72,* pp. 94–95; *Acts of the General Assembly of Virginia* (Richmond: Public Printer, 1850), 130; J. H. Chataigne, comp., *Chataigne's Virginia Business Directory and Gazetteer, 1880–81* (Richmond: Baughman Brothers, 1880), 216; *Franklin Times-Democrat*, 29 Sept. 1899, 2 Oct. 1903, and 1 July 1904; *Franklin Chronicle*, 12 Nov. 1908.

[23]Minutes and Ordinances of the Town of Rocky Mount, 1872–1882, pp. 15–17.

[24]Ibid., 16.

[25]Nelson M. Blake, *William Mahone of Virginia: Soldier and Political Insurgent* (Richmond: Garrett and Massie, 1935), 185 (map).

[26]Ibid., 249 (map).

[27]*Richmond Dispatch*, 2 Nov. 1889, p. 4, c. 2.

[28]*Richmond Planet*, 30 Aug. 1890, quoted in Samuel N. Pincus, "The Virginia Supreme Court, Blacks, and the Law, 1870–1902" (Ph.D. diss., University of Virginia, 1978), 317.

[29]*Richmond Dispatch*, 3 Nov. 1889, p. 5, c. 3.

[30]Ibid.; George W. Hansbrough, *Reports of Cases Decided in the Supreme Court of Appeals of Virginia* (Richmond: Superintendent of Public Printing, 1890), 86:936.

[31]*Daily Virginian*, 23 Aug. 1890, p. 1, c. 2.

[32]*Richmond Dispatch*, 23 Aug. 1890, p. 2, c. 4.

[33]Hansbrough, *Reports* (1890–1891), 87:218.

[34]Ibid., 218.

[35]Ibid., 219–220.

[36]Ibid., 219.

[37]Ibid.

[38]*Richmond Planet*, 20 Dec. 1890, p. 2, c. 4.

[39]Hansbrough, *Reports* (1892–1893), 89:381–382.

[40]*Journal of the House of Delegates of the State of Virginia, for the Session of 1891–'92* (Richmond: Superintendent of Public Printing, 1891), 19; *Journal of the Senate of the Commonwealth of Virginia Begun and Held at the Capitol in the City of Richmond on Wednesday, December 4, 1895* (Richmond: Superintendent of Public Printing, 1895), 15.

[41]Blake, *William Mahone*, 227.

[42]E. Griffith Dodson, *Speakers and Clerks of the Virginia House of Delegates, 1776–1955* (Richmond: 1956), 111; *Cases Decided in the Supreme Court of Appeals of Virginia* (Richmond: Division of Purchase and Printing, 1931), 155:v–xi; *Proceedings of the Thirty-Third Annual Meeting of the Virginia State Bar Association of Virginia* (N.p.: n.p., 1922), 82–85.

[43]Abstracted from several unidentified newspaper articles published between 1935 and 1946, in possession of Dr. J. Francis Amos, Rocky Mount, Va.

[44]*Richmond News Leader*, 24 July 1945, p. 1, c. 2.

Chapter Sixteen: Business and Industry

[1]*Elliott & Nye's Virginia Directory, and Business Register for 1852. Number One* (Richmond: Elliott & Nye, Printers, 1852), 31–32. Information throughout this chapter from Virginia business directories 1871–1917 come from the following sources: *Virginia State Business Directory, 1871–72* (Richmond: Benjamin Bates, Bookseller and Publisher, 1871), passim; Chataigne and Gillis, comps., *Virginia Business Directory and Gazetteer*, and *Richmond City Directory: 1877–78* (Richmond: J. W. Randolph & English, 1877), 474–475; J. H. Chataigne, comp., *Chataigne's Virginia Business Directory and Gazetteer, 1880–81* (Richmond: Baughman Brothers, 1880), 216–217; Chataigne, *Chataigne's Virginia Gazetteer and Classified Business Directory, 1884–'5* (Richmond, 1884), 252–255; Chataigne, *1890–91* (Richmond: J. H. Chataigne, Publisher, 1890), 437–445; Chataigne, *1893–94* (Richmond: J. H. Chataigne, Compiler and Publisher, 1893), 499–508; *Virginia State Gazetteer and Business Directory, 1897–'98*, vol. 7 (Richmond: J. L. Hill Printing Company, 1896), 451–460; *Virginia Business Directory and Gazetteer, 1906*, vol. 8 (Richmond: Hill Directory Company, Publishers, 1906), 455–462; ibid., *1911*, vol. 9 (Richmond: Hill Directory Company, Publishers, 1911), 396–401; ibid., *1917*, vol. 10 (Richmond: Hill Directory Company, Inc., Publishers, 1917), 385–390.

[2]*Franklin News-Post*, 17 Sept. 1943, p. 5, cc. 5–6, Brooks and Company also sold dry goods, notions, shoes, and school supplies; ibid., 1 Jan. 1986, Special Bicentennial Section, "Franklin County: The First 200 Years," Section D, pp. 10, 19.

[3]Gloria Woods and Mary Hopkins, "Yesterday in the Black Community," *Bicentennial Reflections* (N.p.: Franklin County Bicentennial Commission, 1986), 79; Franklin County Historical Society, comp., *Cemetery Records of Franklin County* (Baltimore: Gateway Press, Inc., 1986), 177, 402; *News-Post*, 10 Jan. 1957, p. 1, c. 2; 7 Nov. 1974, p. 3, c. 1.

[4]J. H. Waid's accounts and receipts, in possession of Dr. J. Francis Amos, Rocky Mount, Va.; typescript of memoir of Braxton Bragg Tyree, dated 5 May 1965, in possession of Dr.

Amos, Rocky Mount. *See also Franklin County, 1785–1978, Yesterday & Today* ([Rocky Mount, Va.: *Franklin County Times*, 1978]), 70, for a photograph of the tannery, which Creed Bernard later sold to the father of Tip Hudson.

[5]Typescript of memoir of Braxton Bragg Tyree, dated 28 Nov. 1964, in possession of Dr. J. Francis Amos, Rocky Mount.

[6]"Robert Lee Kent—Merchant," *Franklin County 1977, Yesterday & Today* (Rocky Mount, Va.: *Franklin County Times*, 1977), [20–21].

[7]Ibid.; *News-Post,* 29 Apr. 1968, p. 1, c. 4. *See also Franklin County, 1977, Yesterday & Today*, [53], for photographs of Kent's tomato cannery.

[8]Virginia Census Schedules, Industry, 1870, Franklin County, Reel 243, VSLA.

[9]*Franklin Chronicle*, 3 Feb. 1927.

[10]Virginia Census Schedules, Industry, 1880, Franklin County, Reel 259, VSLA.

[11]*Elliott & Nye's Virginia Directory, and Business Register for 1852*, 31–32; *Virginia State Business Directory, 1871–72*, passim.

[12]Lester J. Cappon, *Virginia Newspapers, 1821–1935: A Bibliography with Historical Introduction and Notes, Guide to Virginia Historical Materials, Part I* (New York: D. Appleton-Century Co., Inc., 1936), 199; J. H. Claiborne, comp. and ed., "Franklin County, Virginia: Historical and Industrial—Past, Present and Future," *County News*, supplement ([Rocky Mount, Va.], 1926), 7.

[13]Essie Wade Smith, "History of Franklin County, Virginia—Unpublished Manuscript and Notes," (Franklin County Bicentennial Commission, 1977), Chap. 21, n.p. Information about Franklin's newspapers also comes from the Virginia business directories and Kermit W. Salyer, "Newspapers in Franklin County," *Bicentennial Reflections*, 74–75; *see also* Marshall Wingfield, *Franklin County, Virginia: A History* (Berryville, Va.: Chesapeake Book Co., 1964), 75–76.

[14]*Franklin Chronicle*, 13 Apr. 1916.

[15]For a fuller discussion of Franklin County newspapers, *see* Salyer, "Newspapers in Franklin County," *Bicentennial Reflections*, 74–75.

[16]United States Census, Virginia, 1870, Henry County, Horse Pasture Township, Reel 161 a, b, p. 43, VSLA; Toney Ross was twelve years old when this census was taken in Oct. 1870; Auditor of Public Accounts, Land Tax Books, Franklin County, 1901, Blackwater District, VSLA. The house was enlarged in 1932 to nine rooms with two long porches and painted dove gray, in the style of many area houses. It burned in Jan. 1987, and, although the old barn has collapsed, the corncrib and granary building constructed of oak by Toney Ross still stands: from reminiscences of Toney Ross's son Harry Willie Ross and daughter-in-law Viola Ross, ca. 1990, in possession of Mrs. Mary G. Hopkins, Rocky Mount, Va.

[17]Reminiscences of Toney Ross's son Harry Willie Ross and daughter-in-law Viola Ross, Franklin County, ca. 1990, and accounts of Toney Ross, scattered dates, 1904–1912.

[18]*Franklin Chronicle*, 12 Nov. 1908.

[19]Ibid., 13 Apr. 1916.

[20]*Franklin County News*, 14 Apr. 1927.

[21]Claiborne, "Franklin County," 35.

[22]*Franklin Times-Democrat*, 29 Sept. 1899.

[23]J. H. Waid's accounts and receipts, in possession of Dr. J. Francis Amos, Rocky Mount, Va.

[24]Sketch of Ferrum written by Pedro T. Slone, Jan. 1955, in possession of Dr. J. Francis Amos, Rocky Mount, Va.

[25]"Ferrum Started in 1889," *News-Post*, 1 Jan. 1986, Special Bicentennial Section, Section E, p. 7; Henry Hopkins, "Industry in Franklin County, 1900–1940," *Bicentennial Reflections*, 64, 65.

[26]Franklin County Historical Society, *Cemetery Records of Franklin County, Virginia*, 180; Marshall Wingfield, *Marriage Bonds of Franklin County, Virginia, 1786–1858*

(Memphis: West Tennessee Historical Society, [1939]; Baltimore: Genealogical Publishing Co., Inc., 1973), 23; Essie W. Smith, "Nathaniel Peter Angle," 1941, Biographical Files, Virginia Writers' Project Papers, VSLA.

[27]Angle served as president of the People's National Bank and the Bankers' Trust Company and bought the Franklin and Pittsylvania Railroad Company (known locally as the "Fast and Perfect"): Essie W. Smith, "Nathaniel Peter Angle"; Dorothy R. Cundiff and A. D. Ramsey, "Old Franklin & Pittsylvania Railroad is Loving Memory for Many," *Bicentennial Reflections*, 60; Hopkins, "Industry in Franklin County 1900–1940," ibid., 63–65; Kermit W. Salyer, "Newspapers in Franklin County," ibid., 74–75; Wingfield, *Franklin County*, 46.

[28]Interview with Dr. J. Francis Amos, Rocky Mount, Va., 5 Aug. 1990. Angle was buried on Christmas Day 1936: "Members of both races in this community put aside Christmas festivities today to pay a final tribute to Nathaniel P. Angle, long one of Franklin county's chief manufacturers, business men and civic leaders." Hundreds filed past the body as it lay in state at Rocky Mount Methodist Episcopal Church, while a silent vigil was kept by Angle's personal servant, fifty-five-year-old Dan Sheffey. "During the funeral, Sheffey sat in the front pew closet to the casket," the only person on that row. Angle's family sat in the rows behind him. "Sheffey, with head bowed, walked next to the body as it was borne from the church after the services": *Roanoke Times*, 26 Dec. 1936, p. 2, c. 1.

[29]May M. and Earl C. Frost, *Garst, Sherfey, Graybill Genealogies and Peffley, Peffly, Pefley Supplement* (Los Angeles: May M. and Earl C. Frost, 1940), 319.

[30]*News-Post*, 3 Jan. 1941, p. 1, cc. 4–5; *History of Virginia* (Chicago and New York: The American Historical Society, 1924), 6:548–549; Frost and Frost, *Garst, Sherfey, Graybill Genealogies*, 321.

[31]*Virginia Business Directories*; Virginia Census Schedules, Industry, 1870, Franklin County; *News-Post*, 1 Jan. 1986, Special Bicentennial Section, Section E, p. 3; *Franklin County, 1785–1976, Yesterday & Today* (Franklin County: 5th Annual Fiddler's Convention, 1976), 167. For a list of mills in Franklin County throughout its history and a discussion of milling, *see* Wingfield, *Franklin County*, 62–64. On p. 62 Wingfield lists fifty-one mills that existed in Franklin at one time or another from Altick's Mill on Chestnut to Zeigler's Mill on Pigg River.

[32]Elizabeth Dabney Coleman, "The Night Ride That Made Roanoke," *Virginia Cavalcade* 4 (Summer 1954): 9–13.

[33]*Franklin Chronicle*, 25 Jan. 1917.

[34]*Franklin County News*, 14 Apr. 1927.

[35]*Franklin Chronicle*, 3 Feb. 1927.

[36]*News-Post*, 17 Apr. 1942, p. 1, c. 7; typescript history of industry in Franklin County, Ed. T. Robertson, 12 July 1976, entry 2, "Bald Knob Furniture Company," in the possession of Dr. J. Francis Amos, Rocky Mount, Va.

[37]*News-Post*, 24 Dec. 1943, p. 1, c. 7.

[38]Hopkins, "Industry in Franklin County, 1900–1940," *Bicentennial Reflections*, 63–64; Essie W. Smith, "Industries of Rocky Mount, Franklin County, Virginia—1940," ibid., 66.

[39]Hopkins, "Industry in Franklin County, 1900–1940," 64, 65; *News-Post*, 1 Jan. 1986, Special Bicentennial Section, Section E, p. 22.

[40]"Iron Ore Items," *Virginias* 1 (1880): 53, 93, 96, 116, 140; in 1882 the *Franklin Gazette* published the information that Major Mason and the Virginia Midland Railway Company, who held a lease on the Franklin iron mines near Rocky Mount, were expected to build a furnace there since "the ores are fairly good, and well worth smelting there, but will not pay for transportation in the rough to Pennsylvania or other distant markets," "Iron Ore Items," ibid. 3 (1882): 125; this news was repeated in the *Advance* with the addition that the Franklin and Pittsylvania narrow-gauge road might be widened to conform with

the Virginia Midland Railway, ibid., pp. 130, 137; Professor William M. Fontaine, "Notes on the Geology and Mineral Resources of the Floyd, Va., Plateau," ibid. 4 (1883): 167–168; "Virginia Minerals for the New Orleans Exposition," ibid. 5 (1884): 196; magnetite from the "Franklin" mine owned by John Hale was included among the Virginia ores and minerals that Major Jedediah Hotchkiss, the *Virginias* editor and assistant U.S. commissioner for Virginia to the New Orleans Exposition, had been collecting to exhibit at the exposition. By 1879 a railroad station had been built at what was called Franklin Junction; the name was changed to Gretna in 1916: Raus McDill Hanson, *Virginia Place Names: Derivation, Historical Uses* (Verona, Va.: McClure Press, 1969), 159.

[41]Hopkins, "Industry in Franklin County, 1900–1940," *Bicentennial Reflections*, 63. Presumably Hopkins got his information from the 1900 census.

[42]Claiborne, "Franklin County," 40.

[43]Hotchkiss, "Virginia Minerals for the New Orleans Exposition," *Virginias* 5 (1884): 196. Hotchkiss described Smithers's quarry as being located one mile northwest of Rocky Mount and a half mile from the railway to the iron mines.

[44]"Flagstone Quarry Near Rocky Mount," essay by Essie W. Smith, ca. 1940s, in Essie W. Smith Papers, FCPL.; Hopkins, "Industry in Franklin County, 1900–1940," *Bicentennial Reflections*, 64; Franklin County Historical Society, *Cemetery Records of Franklin County*, 414; (flagstone used for Trinity Episcopal Church) interview with Dr. J. Francis Amos, Rocky Mount, Va., 5 Aug. 1990.

[45]Fontaine, "Notes on the Geology and Mineral Resources," *Virginias* 4 (1883): 167.

[46]Unidentified newspaper, 11 Mar. 1938, in possession of Dr. J. Francis Amos, Rocky Mount, Va.

[47]Fontaine, "Notes on the Geology and Mineral Resources," *Virginias* 4 (1883): 179.

[48]Claiborne, "Franklin County," 13. A short discussion of the soapstone deposits in Franklin County is found in Fontaine, "Notes on the Geology and Mineral Resources," *Virginias* 4 (1883): 178–179.

[49]Hopkins, "Industry in Franklin County, 1900–1940," *Bicentennial Reflections*, 64; Claiborne, "Franklin County," 27; Wingfield, *Franklin County*, 79; Chestnut Mica Company was first listed in the 1917 Virginia business directory. A somewhat different account of mica mining at Chestnut Mountain is found in William Randall Brown, *Mica and Feldspar Deposits of Virginia* (Charlottesville: Virginia Division of Mineral Resources, 1962), 152, which states that the Chestnut Mountain Mica Company functioned from just before World War I, and at one point operated a sheeting house at Chestnut Mountain and a sheeting house and manufacturing plant at Rocky Mount, until about 1920 when J. T. Mullaney organized the Clinchfield Mica Corporation that ran the company until around 1924. The Central Mica Corporation of Rocky Mount carried on operation from 1924 until 1929, when the main properties were leased by H. C. Fields, of Martinsville, who continued the business until 1934. In the latter year the U.S. Mica Manufacturing Company built a modern "separatory plant" and undertook activities on the south side of Route 619 until 1944. On the north side of Route 619 mining was continued until at least 1943 by a subsidiary of Asheville Mica Company, of North Carolina, and into 1945 by Rocky Mount's Nelson Mica Company. A short discussion of the mica deposits at Snow Creek is found in Fontaine, "Notes on the Geology and Mineral Resources," *Virginias* 4 (1883): 179.

[50]*News-Post*, 6 Feb. 1942, p. 1, c. 1.

[51]*Franklin County Life & Culture: A Pictorial Record* (N.p.: Blue Ridge Institute of Ferrum College, 1986), 30; Hopkins, "Industry in Franklin County, 1900–1940," *Bicentennial Reflections*, 64; "Once Upon a Time, A Man Had a Dream," *Franklin County, 1977, Yesterday & Today*, [92]; *Franklin County, 1785–1980* (Rocky Mount, Va.: *Franklin County Times*, 1980), 6, shows an artist's conception of the Rocky Mount Lithia–Magnesia Springs. A discussion of the Coca-Cola operation in the 1920s can be found in ibid., [100].

[52]C. R. Perry, "Early Beginnings: The Community of Callaway," *News-Post*, 1 Jan. 1986, Special Bicentennial Section, Section E, p. 18; Wingfield, *Franklin County*, 79–80.

[53]Ibid. James A. Martin added a sawmill to his business ventures by 1890 but it was not listed in 1906, its last listing being 1897. In 1917, Mrs. J. A. Martin was listed as running a boardinghouse at Callaway. The woolen mill building was finally torn down in 1947.

[54]M. Parell was a tobacco manufacturer in 1890 as well and had a tobacco warehouse at Shady Grove in 1893 and 1897. In 1890 F. Cook at Shady Grove was also a tobacco manufacturer and had a tobacco warehouse there in 1893 and 1897.

[55]"Ferrum Started in 1889," *News-Post*, 1 Jan. 1986, Special Bicentennial Section, Section E, pp. 7–9. *See also* Frank Hurt, "History of Village of Ferrum," *Franklin County's Third Annual Fiddler's Convention Souvenir Book* (Rocky Mount, Va.: *Franklin County Times*, 1974), [8].

[56]Hopkins, "Industry in Franklin County, 1900–1940," *Bicentennial Reflections*, 63; "Aunt Ollies Restaurant and Boarding House," *Franklin County, 1785–1978, Yesterday & Today*, 87; interview with the Franklin County Bicentennial Commission book committee, Rocky Mount, Va., 5 Aug. 1990. According to committee members, Ollie Hopkins had been born a Warren and during the 1920s or 1930s Depot Street where her restaurant was located (near the Midway Cleaners) was renamed Warren Street in her honor.

[57]*Franklin Times-Democrat*, 2 Oct. 1903; *Walsh's Roanoke, Virginia, City Directory* (Charleston, S.C.: The Walsh Directory Co., Inc., 1908), 265, and ibid., 1910, p. 316; *Roanoke Times*, 2 Aug. 1936, p. 12, ran an ad for Horne's, dealer in millinery, lingerie, and hosiery, at 410 S. Jefferson Street.

[58]*Franklin Chronicle*, 12 Nov. 1908.

[59]Wingfield, *Franklin County*, 228.

[60]Record of Appointment of Postmasters, 1832–Sept. 30, 1971, Roll 132, Virginia, Fluvanna-Jefferson Counties, Volume 10, ca. 1832–44, Volume 23, ca. 1857–67, Records of the Post Office Department, Record Group 28, NARA.

[61]Auditor of Public Accounts, Licenses Other Than Liquor, July 1912, Franklin County, District 2, VSLA. *See also Franklin County, Virginia, 1786–1986, 200 Years, Yesterday and Today* ([Rocky Mount, Va.]: n.p., 1987), 21, for photographs of Wiley A. Byrd and his wife, Elizabeth Margaret Hudson Byrd.

[62]Kendrick's obituary appeared in the *Roanoke Times*, 3 Aug. 1936, p. 1, c. 7; Hopkins, "Industry in Franklin County, 1900–1940," *Bicentennial Reflections*, 63, 64. One of the major stockholders in the Blue Ridge Chemical Corporation was Taylor Hodges, owner of a general store at Penhook, who served sixteen years as supervisor of highways (1910–1926): *Franklin County, 1785–1978, Yesterday & Today*, 139; *Sixteenth Annual Report of the State Corporation Commission* . . . (Richmond: Davis Bottom, Superintendent of Public Printing, 1919), 328. Nathaniel P. Angle was listed as president of J. Kyle Montague Medicine Company, which had a capital investment of $100,000.

[63]Claiborne, "Franklin County," 42; the Black Prince Overall Company, Inc., was chartered on 15 Dec. 1920, charter no. 21107, with a maximum capital stock of $100,000, *Eighteenth Annual Report of the State Corporation Commission* (Richmond: Davis Bottom, Superintendent of Public Printing, 1921), 343.

[64]*Roanoke Times*, 13 Jan. 1927, p. 1, c. 8; p. 4, cc. 3–4; ibid., 14 Jan. 1927, p. 1, c. 6.

[65]*Franklin County, 1785–1976, Yesterday & Today*, 144.

[66]Reprinted from the 27 Jan. 1927 *Roanoke Times* in the *Franklin Chronicle*, 3 Feb. 1927, p. 1, c. 4.

[67]Ibid.

[68]*Roanoke Times*, 13 Jan. 1927, p. 4, c. 4.

[69]Ibid., 13 Jan. 1927, p. 1, c. 8; p. 4, cc. 3–4; *News-Post*, 1 Jan. 1986, Special Bicentennial Section, Section D, pp. 42–43.

[70]*Roanoke Times*, 16 Jan. 1927, p. 1, c. 5.

[71]Ibid., 18 Jan. 1927, p. 2, c. 8; Hopkins, "Industry in Franklin County, 1900–1940," *Bicentennial Reflections*, 63.

[72]Hopkins, "Industry in Franklin County, 1900–1940," 64.

[73]*Roanoke Times*, 8 Feb. 1937, p. 1, c. 8; and 9 Feb. 1937, p. 2, c. 3.

[74]*News-Post*, 25 Oct. 1940, p. 1, c. 1; p. 5, c. 2.

[75]Ibid., 4 July 1941, p. 1, c. 6.

[76]Ibid., 10 Apr. 1942, p. 1, c. 5.

[77]Ibid., 7 Mar. 1941, p. 1, c. 6.

[78]Ibid., 30 June 1944, p. 1, c. 6.

[79]Ibid., 14 Sept. 1945, Tobacco Market section, n.p.

[80]Ibid., 27 Apr. 1945, p. 1, c. 8; ibid., 29 June 1945, p. 1, c. 3.

[81]Ibid., 4 Jan. 1946, p. 1, c. 8; *Forty-Fourth Annual Report of the State Corporation Commission . . .* (Richmond: Department of Purchases and Printing, 1947), 540.

[82]The source for this and the following paragraph is the *News-Post*, 4 Jan. 1946, p. 1, c. 8.

[83]Ibid., 1 Jan. 1986, Special Bicentennial Section, Section E, p. 22.

[84]This and the next two paragraphs are from ibid, 4 Jan. 1946, p. 1, c. 8.

Chapter Seventeen: Agriculture and Farm Life

[1]Marshall Wingfield, *Franklin County, Virginia: A History* (Berryville, Va.: Chesapeake Book Co., 1964), 27.

[2]Eighth United States Census, Virginia, Schedule 4, Productions of Agriculture for the Year Ending June 1, 1860, Franklin County, Roll 236. The figures for Franklin's agricultural production for 1860 were 2,643,434 pounds of tobacco, 367,587 bushels of Indian corn, 226,804 bushels of oats, 124,396 bushels of wheat, 5,789 bushels of rye, and 2,798 tons of hay.

[3]U.S. Department of Commerce, Bureau of the Census, *Thirteenth Census of the United States Taken in the Year 1910, Volume VII, Agriculture, 1909 and 1910, Reports by States with Statistics for Counties* (Washington, D.C.: Government Printing Office, 1913), 812–813. Franklin's agricultural output was now 5,441,321 pounds of tobacco, 604,365 bushels of corn, 51,505 bushels of wheat, along with 161,348 bushels of oats, 5,490 bushels of rye, and 9,440 tons of hay.

[4]Ibid., *U.S. Census of Agriculture: 1959, Final Report, Vol. 1, Part 24, Counties, Virginia* (Washington, D.C., Government Printing Office, 1959), 268–269; ibid., *1974 Census of Agriculture, Virginia, State and County Data* (Washington, D.C., Government Printing Office, July 1977), Table 26, Virginia, 11–49; ibid., *1987 Census of Agriculture, Volume 1, Geographic Area Series, Part 46, Virginia, State and County Data* (Washington, D.C.: Government Printing Office, July 1989), 444. By 1959, Franklin's production of tobacco had dropped to 3,926,184 pounds, but that figure had increased to 4,175,824 in 1974. Total tobacco production had decreased to 3,453,388 pounds in 1982 and 2,473,829 in 1987 and the number of farms growing tobacco had declined from 283 in 1982 on 1,604 acres to 190 in 1987 on 1,123 acres.

[5]Wingfield, *Franklin County*, 49.

[6]Ibid.

[7]Ibid., 49–50.

[8]Ibid., 51–52.

[9]Ibid., 52.

[10]Ibid.

[11]Ibid., 53–54.

[12]Ibid., 54–55, 56–57.

[13]Ibid., 57.

[14]Ibid., 57–58.

[15]Ibid., 58–59.

[16]Ibid., 30.

[17]Ibid.

[18]Ibid., 31–32.

[19]Typescript of memoir of Braxton Bragg Tyree, dated 5 May 1965, in possession of Dr. J. Francis Amos, Rocky Mount, Va. Tyree was ninety-four at the time his memoir was recorded; he died in 1972: Franklin County Historical Society, comp., *Cemetery Records of Franklin County* (Baltimore, Md.: Gateway Press, Inc., 1986), 129.

[20]Pedro Thomas Slone, "The Way of Life in Turner's Creek Valley Sixty Years Ago," an unpublished typescript, Feb. 1943, in possession of Dr. J. Francis Amos, Rocky Mount, Va.

[21]Wingfield, *Franklin County*, 14; transcript of a memoir by Braxton Bragg Tyree, 28 Nov. 1964, in possession of Dr. J. Francis Amos, Rocky Mount, Va.

[22]J. H. Waid's accounts and receipts, in possession of Dr. J. Francis Amos, Rocky Mount, Va.; U.S. Census Bureau, Population Schedule, 1920, Franklin County, Virginia, Rocky Mount, Enumeration District 38, household 251; Auditor of Public Accounts, Franklin County, 1918–1919, "Table of Tracts of Land, Standing Timber Trees and Buildings," VSLA.

[23]J. H. Waid's accounts.

[24]Joseph Clarke Robert, *The Tobacco Kingdom: Plantation, Market, and Factory in Virginia and North Carolina, 1800–1860* (Durham, N.C.: Duke University Press, 1938), 175 n. 29.

[25]U.S. Census, Industry Schedule, 1860, Franklin County, Va., Reel 236, VSLA; Henry Hopkins, "Agriculture in Franklin County," *Bicentennial Reflections* (N.p.: Franklin County Bicentennial Commission, 1986), 68.

[26]J. G. Claiborne, comp. and ed., "Franklin County, Virginia, Historical and Industrial— Past, Present and Future," *County News*, supplement ([Rocky Mount, Va.], 1926), 24; Wingfield, *Franklin County*, 80–81; the 1884–1885 Virginia business directory listed six tobacco manufacturers in Franklin, one at Dickinson's, one at Helm's, three at Rocky Mount, and one at Waidsboro: J. H. Chataigne, comp., *Chataigne's Virginia Gazetteer and Classified Business Directory, 1884–'5* (Richmond: J. H. Chataigne, 1884), 255.

[27]Nannie May Tilley, *The Bright-Tobacco Industry, 1860–1929* (Chapel Hill: University of North Carolina Press, 1948), 685–689, citing Oscar Hammerstein, "U.S. Tobacco Journal Directory, 1881–82."

[28]Wingfield, *Franklin County*, 81; Claiborne, "Franklin County," 24; *1989 Rocky Mount, Virginia, City Directory* (Richmond: R. L. Polk & Co., [1989]), section 3, p. 29. In 1860, for example, John S. Hale had a $54,500 capital investment in his tobacco factory, employed fifty-eight workers, and produced 220,000 pounds of tobacco worth $54,000. His raw materials included 282,524 pounds of leaf tobacco, 2,500 feet of box plank, 1,600 pounds of nails, 10,000 pounds of licorice, and 30 gallons of olive oil: Robert, *Tobacco Kingdom*, 255.

[29]Hopkins, "Agriculture in Franklin County," *Bicentennial Reflections*, 68; Wingfield, *Franklin County*, 80–81.

[30]*Virginia State Gazetteer and Business Directory, 1897–'98* (Richmond: J. L. Hill Printing Company, 1897), 459.

[31]*Chataigne's Virginia Gazetteer, 1884–'5*, 255; *Virginia Business Directory and Gazetteer, 1917* (Richmond: Hill Directory Company, Inc., 1917), 390; Hopkins, "Agriculture in Franklin County," *Bicentennial Reflections*, 68; *Rocky Mount, Virginia, City Directory* (1960) lists both the Franklin and Farmers warehouses, but neither was listed in the 1963 city directory.

[32]Claiborne, "Franklin County," 6.

[33]U.S. Department of Commerce, Bureau of the Census, *Fourteenth Census of the United States Taken in the Year 1920, Volume VI, Part 2, Agriculture* (Washington, D.C.: Government Printing Office, 1922), 176–177.

[34]Claiborne, "Franklin County," 6.

[35]A week after the market opened Rocky Mount's tobacco sales had set a high for all the markets reporting in the "Old Belt." Some of the bright leaf tobacco had brought $43 per hundred pounds; by the second week of the season all grades were selling at four cents to twenty cents better at midweek than in the previous season. The high average was $33.83, both for the "Old Belt" and for the previous twenty-five years. In addition, more than twice the amount sold per day previously was being sold in the 1941 market and the floor was being cleared every day; a new high of $44 came on 2 Oct., rising to $45 by 10 Oct., and to $61 for a pile of wrappers by 17 Oct.: *Franklin News-Post*, 19 Sept., p. 1, c. 8; ibid., 26 Sept., p. 1, c. 8; ibid., 3 Oct., p. 1, c. 8; ibid., 10 Oct., p. 1, c. 4; ibid., 17 Oct., p. 4, cc. 6–7; and ibid., 7 Nov. 1941, p. 1, c. 8.

[36]The tobacco market opened on 22 Sept. 1942 with an average of $41.16 per hundred pounds. The opening day figures, in fact, were 182,860 pounds at $74,972.60, once again the biggest single-day receipts in twenty-five years. As in 1941, all the tobacco was being cleared on each sale day: ibid., 18 Sept. 1942, p. 1, c. 8; ibid., 25 Sept. 1942, p. 1, c. 8.

[37]Ibid., 9 Oct. 1942, p. 1, c. 2. On 9 Oct. it was reported that the leaf market had hit a high of $50 per hundred pounds sold by John Walker, of Dickinson. The average was running $41 to $42.86, with some sellers getting as much as $46 to $49.

[38]The average on the tobacco market for Franklin for 1942 was $40.51 per hundred, $1.35 more than the nearest market, Martinsville. Danville had the highest average with $42.68. Total sales in the Old Belt were 90,829,797 pounds at $38,070,680 or an average of $41.91: ibid., 15 Jan. 1943, p. 1, c. 1.

[39]Ibid., 11 June 1943, p. 1, c. 6.

[40]Ibid., 10 Sept. 1943, p. 1, c. 7.

[41]Ibid., 17 Sept. 1943, p. 1, c. 8, by that date about a dozen farmers had already done so.

[42]Ibid., 24 Sept. 1943, p. 1, c. 2. The following week tobacco averaged $41.92 per hundred pounds with $50 being the high of the week, ibid., 1 Oct. 1943, p. 1, c. 4; and the next week, the average price of tobacco was $43.13, ibid., 8 Oct. 1943, p. 1, c. 2.

[43]Ibid., 15 Oct. 1943, p. 1, c. 3, according to the U.S. Department of Agriculture. For the other markets Danville's average was $41.42; Martinsville, $40.74; South Boston, $39.83; Brookneal, $38.80; Petersburg, $38.72; Lawrenceville, $37.43; Clarksville, $37.30; South Hill, $36.70; Kenbridge, $35.38; and Chase City, $35.37. Rocky Mount received $1.60 more this year than the last highest average ($41.86).

[44]Ibid., 15 Oct. 1943, p. 1, c. 4. The writer noted that 20 percent would increase the tobacco yield more "than has been seen in many years."

[45]Ibid., 12 Nov. 1943, p. 1, c. 3, prices were back to the usual high level that week: $42.02 average, with better grades bringing $45 to $50, and common grades the "best of the season as a whole"; ibid., 11 Feb. 1944, p. 1, cc. 6–7, the figures for the year's activity came from the Virginia Cooperative Crop Reporting Service. At Rocky Mount 1,935,800 pounds were sold, an increase of 322,350 over 1942, and $42.06 per hundred was an increase of $1.55 per hundred over the 1942 average. For the state the figures were Danville, $42.81; Rocky Mount, $42.06; Petersburg, $41.02; South Boston, $40.81; Brookneal, $40.23; Martinsville, $40.20; Lawrenceville, $39.94; Clarksville, $39.83; South Hill, $39.61; Chase City, $38.08; Kenbridge, $37.10. Rocky Mount had the smallest volume of resales, 63,676 pounds, of any flue-cured market in the state, with the highest average resale price of $38.65 per hundred pounds.

[46]Ibid., 30 June 1944, p. 1, c. 4, Rocky Mount's tobacco market was expected to open on 18 Sept.; it was also expected that the local crop would exceed 2 million pounds for 1944; both warehouses—Franklin and Farmers—were to be used; ibid., 28 July 1944, p. 1, c. 8, the OPA had set a ceiling of 39 cents for untied and 43 1/2 cents for tied tobacco, but the producers were asking for 41 and 45 1/2 cents respectively; ibid., 4 Aug. 1944, p. 1, c. 4, the OPA was still holding the ceiling price of tobacco for Rocky Mount at 43 1/2 cents; everyone now expecting 3 million pounds to be sold there; ibid., 8 Sept. 1944, p. 1, c. 7.

[47]Ibid., 29 Sept. 1944, p. 1, c. 8.

[48]Ibid., 17 Nov. 1944, p. 1, c. 6.

[49]Again Rocky Mount led Martinsville where the average sales had been $40.90 per hundred pounds. At Danville the average was $43.98. According to reports by Virginia's flue-cured warehousemen to the state commissioner of agriculture, total producers' sales for the season were 124,612,338 pounds with a total value of $54,029,440, and an average of $43.36 per hundred pounds. This was 22,835,675 pounds (22 percent) more than the 1943 sales (101,776,663 pounds) and also greater than any other year on record except 1939 when the total was 129,957,301 pounds. Finally, the average price for 1944 was the highest since 1919, and the increase in value over 1943 of $12,045,538 (29 percent) was the largest on record: ibid., 9 Mar. 1945, p. 1, c. 2.

[50]U.S. Department of Commerce, Bureau of the Census, *United States Census of Agriculture: 1945, Volume I, Part 15, Virginia and West Virginia, Statistics for Counties* (Washington, D.C.: Government Printing Office, 1946), 74; Hopkins, "Agriculture in Franklin," *Bicentennial Reflections*, 68; U.S. Department of Commerce, Bureau of the Census, *1987 Census of Agriculture, Volume 1, Geographic Area Series, Part 46, Virginia, State and County Data* (Washington, D.C.: Government Printing Office, July 1989), 379.

[51]Eighth Census, 1860, Virginia Agriculture, Franklin County, Roll 236; Bureau of the Census, *United States Census of Agriculture: 1945, Volume I, Part 15, Virginia and West Virginia*, 94–95; Hopkins, "Agriculture in Franklin," *Bicentennial Reflections*, 68; Wingfield, *Franklin County*, 77.

[52]Claiborne, "Franklin County," 11; Wingfield, *Franklin County*, 77–78; Samuel S. Guerrant's obituary, *News-Post*, 1 Nov. 1940, p. 1, c. 2; p. 5, c. 2.

[53]Samuel S. Guerrant's obituary, *Roanoke Times*, 29 Oct. 1940, p. 2, c. 4; Guerrant's obituary notice in *Virginia Fruit* 28 (December 1940): 8.

[54]Claiborne, "Franklin County," 43.

[55]Wingfield, *Franklin County*, 78. At his death in Oct. 1940, Guerrant owned 3,825 acres and was the largest individual taxpayer in the county; he had spent years "perfecting apple strains that have become nationally known": *Roanoke Times*, 29 Oct. 1940; *News-Post*, 1 Nov. 1940.

[56]*Franklin County, Virginia, Yesterday and Today*, 13th ed. (Rocky Mount, Va.: Franklin County Retail Merchants Association, 1984), 31.

[57]Hopkins, "Agriculture in Franklin County," *Bicentennial Reflections*, 68; *News-Post*, 16 Sept. 1976, p. 1, cc. 7–8.

[58]T. W. Rickard, "Boones Mill Noted for Apples," *News-Post*, 1 Jan. 1986, Special Bicentennial Section, Section E, pp. 5–6.

[59]In 1909, Franklin had a total of 251,265 orchard trees (apple, peach, pear, plum, and cherry) and harvested 164,653 bushels of fruits. Of that total, 187,258 of the trees were apple, with a harvest of 157,307 bushels. In 1920, the agricultural census divided the trees by number of nonbearing and bearing, so that Franklin had a total of 83,119 nonbearing and 212,645 bearing trees for a total of 295,764 trees, a 15 percent increase. For apples the total number of trees (bearing and nonbearing) in 1920 was 220,952, again a 15 percent increase. The increase in yield, however, was 42 percent, now 273,228 bushels: Bureau of the Census, *Thirteenth Census of the United States Taken in the Year 1910, Volume VII, Agriculture, 1909 and 1910*, 812 813; ibid., *Fourteenth Census of the United States Taken in the Year 1920, Volume VI, Part 2, Agriculture*, 176–177.

[60]In 1940 there were 153,899 trees of all types, with a harvest of 262,866 bushels. Five years later county apple growers harvested 286,816 bushels, but with only 145,949 trees of all kinds. Thus in twenty-five years there had been only a 13,588-bushel increase in the apple harvest: Bureau of the Census, *United States Census of Agriculture: 1945, Volume I, Part 15, Virginia and West Virginia*, 94–95.

[61]Bureau of the Census, *U.S. Census of Agriculture, 1954, Volume 1, Counties and State Economic Areas, Part 15, Virginia and West Virginia* (Washington, D.C.: U.S. Department of Commerce, 1956), 174; *U.S. Census of Agriculture: 1959, Final Report, Vol. 1, Part 24, Counties, Virginia*, 276–277.

[62]*1987 Census of Agriculture*, 466–467.

[63]*Chataigne's Virginia Gazetteer, 1884–'5*, p. 252; this statement was made in every business directory thereafter: 1890–1891, 1893–1894, 1897–1898, 1906, 1911, and 1917. The 1890–1891 business directory first listed cattle dealers in Franklin (thirty-two located throughout the county); by 1911 the category had become "live stock dealers" and that year the county had thirteen of them. The number had declined to nine in 1917.

[64]Eighth Census, 1860, Virginia Agriculture, Franklin County, Roll 234; Bureau of the Census, *Thirteenth Census of the United States Taken in the Year 1910, Volume VII, Agriculture, 1909 and 1910*, 802.

[65]Hopkins, "Agriculture in Franklin County," *Bicentennial Reflections*, 68–69.

[66]Claiborne, "Franklin County," 16.

[67]Hopkins, "Agriculture in Franklin County," *Bicentennial Reflections*, 69; *News-Post*, 23 Dec. 1940, p. 1, c. 8; *Virginia Business Directory* (1917), 387, lists six dairies in Franklin: L. M. Bussey's, S. A. Bussey's, and B. T. Flora's at Boones Mill, along with J. J. Mullins's at Waidsboro, W. D. [*sic?*] Saunders's at Ferrum, and Charles Renick's at Callaway.

[68]*News-Post*, 7 Feb. 1941, p. 1, c. 8.

[69]It was expected that as much as $150,000 would be paid to farmers in the first year for their milk. County Extension Agent E. W. Carson, the Rocky Mount Lions Club, and the business and professional men of the county had worked hard to bring the milk-receiving station to Rocky Mount and, the *News-Post's* editor noted, "deserve the utmost credit for their successful efforts." He encouraged everyone to help "mak[e] this new farm-products industry the biggest thing that has ever happened in Franklin county. It has wonderful potential opportunities for everyone. Hard work and energetic effort will make the year 1941 an epoch in the lives of the farmers of Franklin county, thanks to Bossie, the cow": ibid., 11 Apr. 1941, p. 1, c. 7; p. 6, c. 1.

[70]Ibid., 9 May 1941, p. 1, c. 8; ibid., 27 June 1941; ibid., 4 July 1941; ibid., 29 Nov. 1941; ibid., 16 Jan 1942, p. 1, c. 5, by that date almost all the necessary equipment was in place, but some small valves were delaying the opening. Even though the milk company had a high priority rating, the army and navy had such a demand for refrigeration equipment that receiving the valves was taking time. The Franklin County Farm Defense Board had taken a hand in the process, however, and hoped that action would result soon. R. T. Hopkins stated that "the farmers of Franklin county are no more anxious to get the Rocky Mount plant in operation than we are. We are badly in need of milk": ibid., 27 Feb. 1942, p. 1, cc. 7–8.

[71]Ibid., 6 Mar. 1942, p. 1, c. 4.

[72]By mid-June 1942 the plant was receiving milk at the rate of more than fifteen hundred gallons a day and expecting to reach two thousand gallons per day soon. Much demand existed for powdered milk so that the current price of $2.20 was far greater than the price usually paid at that time of year. The U.S. Agriculture Department wanted the powdered milk for the Lend-Lease program to Great Britain and Russia. Since powdered milk took up only one-fourth the amount of space that evaporated milk did, it better met shipping restrictions. But the price support would remain in effect for evaporated milk until the switch over to powdered could be made: ibid., 12 June 1942, p. 1, c. 1; by early July Franklin farmers were up to more than 2,000 gallons a day and eight routes with more to go into effect soon. They had taken in about 101,000 pounds in Mar., 164,000 in Apr., 300,000 in May, and more than 400,000 in June. Franklin's farmers had received more than $2,000 apiece in June for their milk. Since the quality was good, only a few cans of milk had been refused for being sour. Franklin milk was taken to Christiansburg to be converted to powdered milk and other processed items: ibid., 3 July 1942, p. 1, c. 1.

[73]Ibid., 15 Jan. 1943, p. 1, c. 4. Two months later, the *News-Post* reported that Franklin's

dairies were making record production. According to R. H. Hopkins at a Friday night meeting, "Milk production in Franklin county is maintaining a higher average for this time of the year than any other county in this area, and it would be difficult for our Christiansburg plant to operate efficiently without the daily supplies from the farms of Franklin county." Hopkins thought "that Franklin county was making a record in dairy improvement and milk production that would be far reaching in the economic life of the county within a few years": ibid., 12 Mar. 1943, p. 1, c. 8.

[74]Ibid., 28 May 1943, p. 1, c. 4,; ibid., 30 July 1943, p. 1, c. 8; ibid., 3 Dec. 1943, p. 1, c. 2, the local plant could pay for Grade C, Grade A, and cream.

[75]The milk-receiving plant indeed showed that it could provide competition to other farming pursuits when the local plant manager, J. Carl Bussey, released the figure early in 1944 that a total of $264,459.94 for 1943 had been paid to the 600 farmers for their milk, 1,038,800 gallons. In 1942, the total number of gallons received from the plant's opening in Mar. to the end of the year was about 451,000 gallons: ibid., 4 Feb. 1944, p. 1, c. 2; milk production continued its steady increase; receipts for Mar. and Apr. 1944 were 80 percent more than for the same months in 1943: ibid., 5 May 1944, p. 1, c. 3; by the end of June 1944 more than 600 farmers in Franklin and the surrounding area were sending in about 6,000 gallons of milk per day, at $1,500 per day or about $500,000 per year and peak production had not yet been reached. In May the farmers received 58 percent more than the previous May: ibid., 30 June 1944, p. 1, c. 8. By May 1945, the milk-receiving plant had seen dramatic growth with the receipt of more than 45,000 gallons of milk per day, a 67 percent increase over May 1944. More than 700 farmers were receiving about 45,000 per month: ibid., 4 May 1945, p. 1, c. 6.

[76]Bureau of the Census, *United States Census of Agriculture: 1945, Volume I, Part 15, Virginia and West Virginia*, 116.

[77]Ibid., *1987 Census of Agriculture, Volume 1, Geographic Area Series, Part 46, Virginia, State and County Data*, 379.

[78]*News-Post*, 1 Jan. 1986, Special Bicentennial Edition, Section D, p. 5. For a description of the typical Virginia farmer in 1990, *see* the *Richmond News Leader*, Business Section, 26 Nov. 1990.

Chapter Eighteen: Religion and Education

[1]Roger E. Sappington, *The Brethren in Virginia: The History of the Church of the Brethren in Virginia* (Harrisonburg, Va.: The Committee for Brethren History in Virginia, 1973), 120; Architectural Survey Files, 33–39, VDHR.

[2]Sappington, *Brethren in Virginia*, 195.

[3]Ibid., 121.

[4]Marshall Wingfield, *Franklin County, Virginia: A History* (Berryville, Va.: Chesapeake Book Co., 1964), 100–105.

[5]Katharine L. Brown, *Hills of the Lord: Background of the Episcopal Church in Southwestern Virginia, 1738–1938* (Roanoke: Diocese of Southwestern Virginia, 1979), 62, 99.

[6]Wingfield, *Franklin County*, 113–117.

[7]Ibid., 117–120; Architectural Survey Files, 33–192.

[8]Wingfield, *Franklin County*, 108–112.

[9]Ibid., 109.

[10]*Franklin News-Post*, 14 Feb. 1941, p. 1, c. 5.

[11]Wingfield, *Franklin County*, 89; Jeanne Bernard, "The Franklin County Bicentennial Driving Tour," *Bicentennial Reflections* (N.p.: Franklin County Bicentennial Commission, 1986), 87; Brown, *Hills of the Lord*, 99.

[12]Wingfield, *Franklin County*, 89; Brown, *Hills of the Lord*, 99–100.

[13]J. G. Claiborne, comp. and ed., "Franklin County, Virginia, Historical and Industrial— Past, Present and Future," *County News*, supplement ([Rocky Mount, Va.], 1926), 15; Architectural Survey File, 33–232.

[14]*News-Post*, 1 Jan. 1986, Special Bicentennial Section, "Franklin County: The First 200 Years," Section C, p. 3; Frank B. Hurt, *A History of Ferrum College* (Roanoke: Stone Printing Co., 1977), 21.

[15]Frank B. Hurt, "Reflections on the Origin of Ferrum College," *Bicentennial Reflections*, 61; *Franklin Chronicle*, 29 July 1915, "Ferrum on the Boom," p. 1.

[16]Claiborne, "Franklin County," 7.

[17]*The Answer is Ferrum, 1989–90 Catalog, Ferrum College* (Ferrum, Va.: Ferrum College, 1988), introduction.

[18]*Virginia School Report, 1871. First Annual Report of the Superintendent of Public Instruction, for the Year Ending August 31, 1871* (Richmond: Superintendent of Public Printing, 1871), 149.

[19]Betty Mansfield, "That Fateful Class: Black Teachers of Virginia's Freedmen, 1861–1882" (Ph.D. diss., The Catholic University of America, 1980), 318–319.

[20]*Virginia School Report, 1871*, 201.

[21]Department of Education, State Board of Education, Minutes, 1870–1873, pp. 41–42, VSLA.

[22]Harold W. Ramsey, "Franklin County Public Schools," *Bicentennial Reflections*, 55.

[23]Saunders Family Papers, Mss1Sa878a, evaluation of Duncan as candidate for reappointment as superintendent, n.d. [1886], VHS.

[24]*Bedford Democrat*, 4 Sept. 1857, p. 2, c. 7.

[25]The school is being reconstructed on the property of the Dudley School as a community project to provide a hands-on historical and educational experience. The building will serve as a museum for county youth.

[26]Saunders Family Papers, Mss1Sa878a, petition for the reappointment of William E. Duncan as superintendent, n.d. [1886], VHS.

[27]Ibid., John S. Hale, Rocky Mount, to [Delegate Peter Saunders, Jr.?], 22 Jan. 1886.

[28]Ibid.

[29]Department of Education, Superintendent of Public Instruction, Annual Reports of Division Superintendents of Schools, Franklin County, 1888, VSLA.

[30]Ibid.

[31]State Board of Education, Minutes, 1870–1873, p. 130.

[32]Ibid., 92–125.

[33]Ibid., 83–84.

[34]Annual Reports of Superintendents, 1888.

[35]Teacher's certificate, 4 Oct. 1888, Wade-Muse Family Papers, ca. 1880–ca. 1920, in possession of Dr. J. Francis Amos, Rocky Mount, Va.

[36]Ibid., Article of Agreement, 29 Oct. 1888, and Monthly Report, Apr. 1889.

[37]J. H. Chataigne, comp., *Chataigne's Virginia Gazetteer and Classified Business Directory, 1884–'5* (Richmond: J. H. Chataigne, 1884), 255; *Virginia State Gazetteer and Business Directory, 1890–'91, 1893–'94, 1897–'98* (Richmond: J. L. Hill Printing Company, 1890, 1893, 1897), 444, 507, 459.

[38]Broadside, [1891?], Mountain View Normal School, Asa Holland Papers, Acc. 902, Manuscripts Division, UVA.

[39]Ibid.

[40]Claiborne, "Franklin County," 5.

[41]Ibid., 25.

[42]*News-Post*, 11 Feb. 1944, p. 1, c. 8; ibid, 21 Apr. 1944, p. 1, c. 3; ibid., 20 July 1945, p. 1, c. 7; ibid., 1 Jan. 1986, Special Bicentennial Section, "Franklin County: The First 200 Years," Section C, pp. 15–16.

[43]Annual Reports of Superintendents, Franklin County, 1888.

[44]Ibid.

[45]Ibid.

[46]Gloria Woods and Mary Hopkins, "Black Schools," *Bicentennial Reflections*, 57; Claiborne, "Franklin County," 24.

[47]William A. Link, *A Hard Country and a Lonely Place: Schooling, Society, and Reform in Rural Virginia, 1870–1920* (Chapel Hill: University of North Carolina Press, 1986), 177–179.

[48]*News-Post*, 17 Jan. 1941, p. 1, c. 6; p. 8, c. 3.

[49]Ibid., 4 Aug. 1944, p. 1, cc. 2–3.

[50]Ibid., 8 Sept. 1944, p. 1, c. 8; ibid., 22 Sept. 1944, p. 1, cc. 6–7.

Chapter Nineteen: Prohibition and Bootlegging in Franklin County

[1]The first portion of this chapter has been previously published in *Virginia Cavalcade* as "Thicker'in Huckleberries: Franklin County, 1900–1930" 41 (1992): 132–143, and is used with permission of the Virginia State Library and Archives, Richmond; Edward D. C. Campbell, Jr., "Of Vines and Wines: The Culture of the Grape in Virginia" *Virginia Cavalcade* 39 (1990): 106–108.

[2]Jess Carr, *The Second Oldest Profession: An Informal History of Moonshining in America* (Englewood Cliffs, N.J.: Prentice-Hall, Inc., 1972), 12, taken from Philip Alexander Bruce, *Economic History of Virginia in the Seventeenth Century* (New York: The Macmillan Co., 1907), 2:216.

[3]Carr, *Second Oldest Profession*, 13; "The Virginia General Assembly of 1641. A List of Members and Some of the Acts," *VMHB* 9 (1901–1902): 58; William Waller Hening, *The Statutes at Large* . . . (New York: Printed for the Editor, 1809–1823), 1:226, 319.

[4]Carr, *Second Oldest Profession*, 13.

[5]Tun Yuan Hu, *The Liquor Tax in the United States, 1791–1947: A History of the Internal Revenue Taxes Imposed on Distilled Spirits by the Federal Government* (New York: Columbia University Graduate School of Business, 1950), 13.

[6]Arthur M. Schlesinger, Jr., ed., *The Almanac of American History* (New York: G. P. Putnam's Sons, 1983), 159.

[7]Hu, *Liquor Tax*, 19–20.

[8]Schlesinger, *Almanac*, 161, 165.

[9]Carr, *Second Oldest Profession*, 21–22.

[10]Franklin County, Order Book, 1806–1811, Reel 28, p. 316, court of 6 Nov. 1809, VSLA.

[11]Robert A. Hohner, "Prohibition and Virginia Politics, 1901–1916" (Ph.D. diss., University of Virginia, 1965), 4–5; Joseph Martin, *A New and Comprehensive Gazetteer of Virginia, and the District of Columbia* . . . (Charlottesville: Joseph Martin, 1836), 178.

[12]Hunter Dickenson Farish, *The Circuit Rider Dismounts: A Social History of Southern Methodist, 1865–1900* (Richmond: The Dietz Press, 1938), 307, quoted in Hohner, "Prohibition and Virginia Politics," 8.

[13]Ibid., 8–11.

[14]Ibid., 5–7.

[15]Ibid., 42–49, 55–64.

[16]Ibid., 120–126, 150–151, 167–168, 193.

[17]Ibid., 181.

[18]Auditor of Public Accounts, Liquor License Returns, 1885–1916, July 1906, July 1910, Franklin County, for R. F. Rakes, barkeeper, VSLA.

[19]*Franklin Chronicle*, 12 Nov. 1908.

[20]Ibid.

[21]*Virginia Business Directory and Gazetteer, 1911*, vol. 9 (Richmond: Hill Directory Company, Publishers, 1911), 396–401; ibid., *1917*, vol. 10 (Richmond: Hill Directory Company, Inc., Publishers, 1917), 385–390.

[22] *Roanoke Evening News*, 5 Dec. 1904, p. 1, cc. 3–5; p. 4, c. 5.

[23] Ibid., 5 Dec. 1904, p. 4, c. 5.

[24] Notes taken on "The Revenue: Federal Authority in the Southern Mountains, 1876–1900," a paper presented by Wilbur R. Miller, State University of New York, Stony Brook, at the Southern Historical Association annual meeting, 11 Nov. 1988.

[25] Joseph Earl Dabney, *Mountain Spirits: A Chronicle of "Corn Whiskey" from "King James' Ulster Plantation" to "America's Appalachians" and the "Moonshine Life"* (New York: Charles Scribner's Sons, 1974), xv.

[26] *Roanoke Evening News*, 29 Jan. 1904, p. 6, c. 4.

[27] Ibid., 2 Feb. 1904, p. 2, c. 3.

[28] Ibid., 7 Dec. 1903, p. 8, c. 3.

[29] Ibid., 10 Feb. 1904, p. 4, c. 3.

[30] Ibid., 11 Feb. 1904, p. 1, c. 4. With regard to Jeff Nowlin's case, his attorneys argued a demurrer on both charges. Nothing further has been found about Nowlin's prosecution.

[31] Ibid., 21 Sept. 1905, p. 1, cc. 1–2.

[32] Ibid., 1 Feb. 1904, pp. 1, cc. 5–6, and 2, c. 3.

[33] Ibid., 16 Mar. 1904, p. 3, c. 3.

[34] Ibid., 23 Apr. 1904, p. 1, cc. 3–5; ibid., 6 Aug. 1904, p. 3, c. 4.

[35] *Franklin Times-Democrat*, 1 July 1904, p. 4, c. 5.

[36] *Roanoke Evening News*, 4 May 1904, p. 1, c. 3.

[37] Ibid., 6 Aug. 1904, p. 3, c. 4.

[38] Gee had recently made a big raid in southwestern Virginia and in four years had "cut out" 194 illegal stills: ibid., 6 Aug. 1904, p. 1, c. 4; ibid., 8 Aug. 1904, p. 1, c. 7.

[39] *Roanoke Times*, 17 Aug. 1904, p. 6, c. 2.

[40] *Roanoke Evening News*, 24 Oct. 1904, p. 1, c. 3.

[41] Ibid., 1 Nov. 1904, p. 1, c. 6.

[42] Ibid., 2 Nov. 1904, p. 3, c. 3.

[43] Ibid., 3 Dec. 1904, p. 1, c. 3. The newspaper account gave both Gorman and Norman as Via's first name.

[44] Ibid., 21 Dec. 1904, p. 1, c. 5.

[45] Ibid., 5 Jan. 1905, p. 1, c. 2.

[46] Ibid., 18 Jan. 1905, p. 1, c. 6.

[47] Ibid., 20 Jan. 1905, p. 1, c. 1.

[48] Ibid., 3 Feb. 1905, p. 1, c. 3.

[49] Ibid., 27 July 1905, p. 3, c. 3; transcript of the trial record, 24–25 Aug. 1905, copied by Dr. J. Francis Amos at the Franklin County Courthouse, Rocky Mount, Va.

[50] *Roanoke Evening News*, 27 July 1905, p. 3, c. 3; ibid., 28 July 1905, p. 1, c. 4; ibid., 29 July 1905, p. 1 c, 4; ibid., 31 July 1905, p. 1, cc. 1–4; trial transcript, testimony of Joseph Belcher and Sparrell Callaway.

[51] *Roanoke Evening News*, 29 July 1905, p. 1, c. 4; ibid., 31 July 1905, p. 1, cc. 1–4; trial transcript, testimony of W. D. Haynes.

[52] Trial transcript, testimony of Cephas Poindexter.

[53] Trial transcript; *Roanoke Evening News*, 25 Aug. 1905, p. 1, c. 1; ibid., 26 Aug. 1905, p. 1, c. 1; ibid., 24 Nov. 1905, p. 1, cc. 4–5.

[54] V. K. Stoneman, "Franklin County Moonshine," *Bicentennial Reflections* (N.p.: Franklin County Bicentennial Commission, 1986), 70.

[55] *Annual Reports of the Commissioner of Prohibition to the Governor and General Assembly of Virginia* (Richmond: Davis Bottom, Superintendent of Public Printing, 1922–1927; Division of Purchase and Printing, 1929–1933).

[56] *Roanoke Times*, 25 June 1935, p. 1, c. 1. A fictionalized account of the conspiracy can be found in Jess Carr, *The Moonshiners* (Nashville: Aurora Publishers, Inc., 1977).

[57] Ibid., 27 Apr. 1935, p. 11, c. 8.

⁵⁸Nationwide prohibition had no chance of success in the United States of that time and probably under no circumstances could it ever succeed. As the Wickersham Commission found, "Few things are more easily made than alcohol" (National Commission on Law Observance and Enforcement, *Report on the Enforcement of the Prohibition Laws of the United States* [also known as the Wickersham Report], [71 Cong., 3 Sess. H.D. 722, Summary, p. 33). Because federal prohibition agents were not covered by civil service and thus their salaries compared unfavorably with those of garbage collectors and because "they were expected to work long hours and put their lives in danger from the attacks of armed bootleggers," it came as no surprise that approximately 9 percent of these agents succumbed to the bribes of bootlegging rings making more than a million dollars per month: Andrew Sinclair, *Prohibition: The Era of Excess* (Boston: Little, Brown and Co., 1962), 182–184.

⁵⁹*Roanoke Times*, 24 Apr. 1935, p. 4, c. 7.

⁶⁰Ibid., 29 June 1935, p. 16, cc. 2–5. The other twenty-three defendants entered pleas of "not guilty." They were Deputy Sheriff Henry T. Abshire, of Boones Mill; former state prohibition officer Edgar A. Beckett, of Callaway; Jack Bess, of Roanoke; Tom Cooper, of Callaway; Leonard Davis, of Martinsville; Earl Easter, of Roanoke; Charles Guilliams, of Roanoke; C. P. ("Cap") Griffith, of Ferrum; Walter ("Peg") Hatcher, of Ferrum; Willard R. Hodges, of Glade Hill; Posey Jones, of Henry; Commonwealth's Attorney Charles Carter Lee, of Rocky Mount; Deputy Sheriff Howard L. Maxey, of Ferrum; Clifford Martin, of Rocky Mount; former member of the Virginia House of Delegates David A. Nicholson, of Ferrum; his son Wilson Nicholson, of Roanoke; T. Roosevelt Smith, of Ferrum; Claude Shively, of Ferrum; J. O. Shively, of Rocky Mount; John H. and Walter Turner, of Henry; Deputy Sheriff Will Wray, of Henry; and former federal prohibition agent Samuel O. White, of Roanoke. In addition, fifty-five people were named as unindicted coconspirators: Muscose Barker; Clayton Bernard; A. J. Bondurant; B. H. Bondurant; J. F. Bondurant; Harry Bryant; Luther Burnett; Ernest Daniels; T. Frank Davis; George Dixon; Harry Dixon; Forest Dodson; Tony Ferguson; Herbert Foster; Quill Foster; Virgil Foster; Lee Guilliams; Thomas Guilliams; Alphonso Hodges; George S. Hodges; J. P. Hodges, Sr., former sheriff, deceased; Joseph P. Hodges, Jr.; Kent Hodges; Ursel Hurt; Dewey Jones; Roy Jones; Coleman Lawrence; Ikey Levine; Willie Mason; Leo C. (alias Gummy Coleman) Mays; Dewey Merriman; Melvin Nicholson; Elmer ("Boss") Peters; Lewis Radford; Charles L. Rakes, former deputy sheriff, deceased; Thomas Jefferson ("Jeff") Richards, deceased former deputy sheriff; Lewis Melvin Scott; Mrs. Willie Carter Sharpe; Ed Sigmon; Norman Sigmon; Pete (J. D.) Sigmon; Esley (E. W.) Sledd; Ellis Sloane; Rodney St. Clair; Will Stanley; Russell Steele; Cecil Steineke; Rufus Underwood; Posey Webb; William McKinley Webb; Walter Willis; Allen Wimmer; Esley Wimmer; Owen Wimmer; and Harvey Worley. Furthermore, sixty-eight overt acts were enumerated that the grand jury alleged had been "committed in furtherance of the conspiracy." A month later, at a federal district court on 4 March 1935, all of the defendants pleaded not guilty and the trial was set for 22 April. At that time, four of the accused changed their pleas to guilty and seven others along with the corporation pleaded nolo contendere ("I do not choose to contest," thus abiding by the verdict of the jury). Those who pleaded guilty were former sheriff D. Wilson Hodges, of Rocky Mount; Leonard L. Fralin and H. J. ("Jake") Wright, of Union Hall; and Thomas C. Cundiff, of Penhook, then serving three years in the state penitentiary for malicious assault. The Ferrum Mercantile Company, Inc., its four partners: Grover L. Martin, Guy W. Nolen, C. Buford Nolen, and Herman Shively, along with Robert P. DeHart, of Shooting Creek, country store owner; Nick Prillaman, of Prillaman's Switch; and Charles C. Greer, former deputy sheriff, of Rocky Mount, all pleaded nolo contendere: ibid., 23 Apr. 1935, p. 1, c. 8.

⁶¹In April 1927, Sheriff Hodges had a short announcement printed in the local newspaper to the effect that complaints he had received lately "as to the activities of certain officers of Franklin County, the complaining parties thinking that such officers are

my deputies," actually applied to "such officers [who] were not in fact my deputies, and . . . I had nothing to do either with their appointment, and am in no way responsible for their actions." Hodges listed his deputies and their areas of responsibility: J. W. Montrief, Rocky Mount and Snow Creek Districts; T. M. Hodges, Sydnorsville; C. W. Wray, Brown Hill District; L. R. Davidson, Union Hall District; J. H. Robertson, Gills Creek District; O. C. Kesler, Bonbrook District; H. T. Abshire, Boones Mill; J. O. Abshire, Dillons Mill; C. L. Rakes, Endicott; and L. A. Smith, Ferrum: *Franklin County News*, 14 Apr. 1927.

[62]Ironically, when Hodges announced his candidacy for sheriff in Apr. 1927, he noted that "during my fifteen years incumbency in this office, no breath of suspicion, or charge of want of fidelity has ever been so much as rumored. I have upheld the laws of the state of Virginia in accordance with my oath of office, and I promise to continue to do so in the future, without fear or favor if re-elected": ibid.

[63]*Roanoke Times*, 24 Apr. 1935, p. 4, c. 6.

[64]Ibid. Former deputy sheriff Charles Greer, who gave up his nolo contendere plea to take the stand, supported much of Bridges's testimony regarding the events surrounding the division of the county. But he also aided the defense concerning Carter Lee by stating that he had never known of Lee's receiving any of the protection money or of failing to turn in fines to the clerk of court. Greer did not know how much he personally received in protection money but stated that "if anybody walked up and give me anything I took it": ibid., 24 Apr. 1935, p. 1, c. 8.

[65]Ibid., 25 Apr. 1935, p. 13, c. 6.

[66]Ibid., 2 July 1935, p. 9, c. 5.

[67]Ibid., 14 Oct. 1934, p. 1, c. 8.

[68]Ibid., 27 Apr. 1935; 27 May 1937, p. 1, c. 1.

[69]Ibid., 28 May 1935, p. 1, c. 1.

[70]Ibid., 26 Apr. 1935, p. 10, c. 5.

[71]Ibid., 27 Apr. 1935, p. 1, c. 1.

[72]Ibid., 24 May 1935, p. 1, c. 1. After three years in the federal women's reformatory at Alderson, West Virginia, Sharpe fled to Saint Louis, Missouri, in Nov. 1934, after having been subpoenaed by the grand jury at Harrisonburg and having received the warning of defense attorney Samuel R. Price that she was a coconspirator and might be indicted.

[73]Ibid., 24 May 1935, p. 1, c. 1; p. 9, c. 6.

[74]*Liberty*, Nov. 1935, p. 13; Kim Townsend, *Sherwood Anderson* (Boston: Houghton Mifflin Company, 1987), 299.

[75]*Roanoke Times*, 7 May 1935, p.1, cc. 4–5, the figures were 70,448 pounds of a single brand of yeast; 33,839,109 pounds of sugar; 13,307,477 pounds of cornmeal; 2,408,308 pounds of rye meal; 1,018,420 pounds of malt; 30,366 pounds of hops; and miscellaneous feed products amounting to 15,267,071 pounds. In addition there were 115,004 pounds of copper; 205 carloads of containers at 516,176 pounds, and 1,263 single five-gallon cans, with an average of 3,000 cans to the carload for a total of about 700,263 five-gallons cans transported to Franklin in that period.

[76]Ibid., 26 June 1935, p. 10, c. 1.

[77]Ibid. Four of Hodges's deputies testified to this effect: Bridges's testimony is found in the account of 24 Apr., Fralin's in that of 3 May, Wright's in 4 May, and Greer's in 28 May 1935.

[78]Ibid., 27 June 1935, pp. 1, 9.

[79]Ibid., 19 June 1935, p. 1, cc. 4–5; p. 4, cc. 4–5.

[80]Ibid., 18 June 1935, p. 1, c. 2.

[81]Ibid., 14 June 1935, p. 13, c. 3.

[82]Ibid., 18 June 1935, p. 4, c. 5.

[83]State Senator George W. Layman, of New Castle, quoted in ibid., 14 June 1935.

[84]Ibid., 28 June 1935, p, 15, c. 4. The client was Tom Cooper, of Callaway, one of the small-time operators.

[85]Ibid., 29 June 1935, p. 4, c. 7.

[86]Ibid., 29 June 1935, p. 1, c. 1.

[87]Ibid., 30 June 1935, p. 16, cc. 2–3.

[88]It took the jury a little more than two days to reach its verdict, bringing it in at 4:07 P.M., only forty minutes after reporting to the judge that the members were in disagreement: ibid., 2 July 1935, p. 1, cc. 6–8.

[89]Ibid., p. 1, c. 8. The others found guilty were Walter Hatcher, alias Peg Hatcher, of near Ferrum; T. Roosevelt Smith, of near Ferrum; Willard R. Hodges, Glade Hill; John H. Turner, Henry; Walter Turner, Henry; Claude Shively, Ferrum; J. O. Shively, Rocky Mount; Jack Bess, Roanoke; Tom Cooper, Callaway; Leonard Davis, Martinsville; Earl Easter, Roanoke; C. Wilson Nicholson, Ferrum; Charles Guilliams, Roanoke; Posey Jones, Henry; Clifford Martin, Rocky Mount; and C. P. Griffith, alias Cap Griffith, Ferrum.

[90]Ibid., p. 9, c. 5.

[91]When Judge Paul passed sentence on the defendants found guilty, he imposed prison and jail sentences totaling eighteen years and eight months and fines of $39,500 for those being jailed. He also imposed $15,000 in fines against the corporation and six individuals who pleaded nolo contendere, bringing the total fines to $54,500. Those receiving sentences and fines were: Edgar A. Beckett, of Callaway, two years in the state penitentiary and a fine of $5,000 (the maximum sentence for conspiracy was two years and a fine of $10,000); former deputy sheriff Henry T. Abshire, eighteen months and a fine of $3,000. Receiving fines of $3,000 apiece and sentences of fifteen months: Walter ("Peg") Hatcher, Willard R. Hodges, Clifford Martin, J. O. Shively, T. Roosevelt Smith, John Turner, and Walter Turner. Sentences of fifteen months and fines of $2,000: Samuel O. White (former federal prohibition agent) and Jack Bess. Sentences of nine months and a $1,000 fine each were handed down to Earl Easter, Leonard Davis, and Charles Guilliams, as well as to former House of Delegates member David A. Nicholson ("but in consideration of his physical condition the sentence was suspended and Nicholson was placed on probation": *Richmond Times-Dispatch*, 10 July 1935, p. 1, c. 5; in addition, his fine was reduced to $500 if he paid it within three months, since Nicholson was a huge man weighing about 320 pounds and prison might aggravate a serious illness: *Roanoke Times*, 10 July 1935, p. 3, c. 6). Claude Shively received six months and a $1,000 fine (Judge Paul suspended Shively's six months' sentence as he had already served time in West Virginia for activities that were covered in this trial), Wilson Nicholson and Posey Jones six months and a $750 fine, and Tom Cooper and C. P. ("Cap") Griffith four months each. Those who pleaded nolo contendere were given fines as follows: Nick Prillaman, of Prillaman's Switch, $4,500; Robert P. DeHart, of Shooting Creek, $3,500; and Herman Shively, $2,500. The Ferrum Mercantile Company, Inc., $3,000, and its officers: Grover L. Martin, C. Buford Nolen, and Guy W. Nolen, $500 apiece. For those who pleaded guilty at the beginning of the trial, sentences of three years' probation as follows: D. Wilson Hodges, former sheriff of Franklin County; Charles C. Greer (who changed his plea from nolo contendere to take the stand), former deputy sheriff; Leonard L. Fralin and H. J. ("Jake") Wright, both of Union Hall; and Thomas C. Cundiff, of Penhook, then serving three years in the state penitentiary for malicious assault: ibid., 10 July 1935, p. 1, c. 8.

[92]*Richmond Times-Dispatch*, 3 July 1935, p. 10, cc. 2–3.

[93]Marshall Wingfield, *An Old Virginia Court* (Memphis, Tenn.: West Tennessee Historical Society, 1948), 202–203; *Roanoke Times*, 4 Apr. 1936, p. 1, c. 1; p. 16, c. 2. Beckett and White entered pleas of not guilty. Fifteen of the others entered pleas of nolo contendere. Of that group all but one had been found guilty at the conspiracy trial. Only Thomas L. Foster had not been mentioned in the indictments at the previous trial. Finally, the twenty-fourth person indicted for jury tampering, S. Claude Slusher, committed suicide before the new trial began in May 1936.

[94]*Norfolk Virginian-Pilot*, 1 Apr. 1936, p. 1, c. 4; p. 7, cc. 1–2; *Roanoke Times*, 1 Apr. 1936, p. 1, c. 1; p. 16, c. 4. The defendants were charged with violation of title 18, section 242, U.S. Code.

[95]*Norfolk Virginian-Pilot*, 2 Apr. 1936, p. 6, c. 2.

[96]*Roanoke Times*, 19 May 1936, p. 1, c. 1.

[97]*Roanoke World-News*, 22 May 1936, p. 1, c. 8.

[98]Ibid., 23 May 1936, p. 1, c. 8; p. 10, cc. 1–2; *Roanoke Times*, 24 May 1936, p. 1, c. 8; p. 4, cc. 4–5. Judge Paul handed down sentences for nine of the twenty-two defendants found guilty, or pleading guilty or nolo contendere. He placed the other thirteen on probation. Thus Hugh Rakes (who had pleaded guilty) received perhaps the most severe penalty, two years in the federal penitentiary at Atlanta and a $1,000 fine. He joined his cousin Amos Rakes and Edgar T. Marshall in Atlanta, along with Thomas L. Foster (eighteen months, no fine), Edd Rakes (Hugh's brother, who got a year and a day), and Claude Shively (the same year and a day). The other three, including Claude's brother A. Herman Shively, drew sentences in jail—nine months for Herman and for M. Clifford Martin (to run concurrently with the remainder of his sentence from the liquor conspiracy trial), and six months for Charles J. Guilliams. Everyone else was put on three years' probation: Henry T. Abshire, Edgar A. Beckett, Jack Bess, Leonard Davis, Earl Easter, J. Walter ("Peg") Hatcher, Willard R. Hodges, C. Wilson Nicholson, T. Roosevelt Smith, John H. Turner, Walter Turner, Samuel O. White, and C. Will Wray.

[99]Ibid., 23 May 1936, p. 1, c. 8. But the *Roanoke Times* of 24 May 1936 noted that Paul also told the defendants that he would leave decisions about parole to the parole board: p. 4, c. 5. Of those placed on probation, however, three had already served their sentences and one (C. Will Wray) had been acquitted in the liquor conspiracy trial: *World-News*, p. 10, c. 1.

[100]This and the following two paragraphs are cited from the *Roanoke Times*, 24 May 1936, p. 6, c. 1.

[101]*Roanoke World-News*, 25 May 1936, p. 6, cc. 1–2. The *World-News* reviewed the history of moonshine in Franklin County, noted that the land in some sections of the county was so poor that "the temptation to turn a corn crop into ready money seems to have been irresistible," and concluded that indeed "in some families, the processes of distillation have been known for generations."

[102]*Roanoke Times*, 18 July 1936, p. 1, c. 8; p. 4, c. 2.

[103]Ibid., p. 6, c. 1.

[104]Ibid., 22 Sept. 1936, p. 5, c. 2; ibid., 18–31 July 1936.

[105]Ibid., 22 Sept. 1936, p. 1, c. 8; p. 5, c. 2; ibid., 26 Feb. 1934, p. 8, c. 3.

[106]Ibid., 24 Sept. 1936, p. 1, c. 3; ibid., 25 Sept. 1936, p. 1, cc. 2–3; p. 15, cc. 5–6; ibid., 31 July 1936, p. 14, c. 2.

[107]Ibid., 22 Sept. 1936, p. 5, cc. 2–3; ibid., 27 Sept. 1936, p. 1, c. 8.

[108]Ibid., 8 Dec., p. 1, c. 1; ibid., 9 Dec. p. 1, c. 6; ibid., 16 Dec., p. 4, c. 7; ibid., 18 Dec. 1936, p. 1, c. 8.

[109]Ibid., 19 Dec. 1936, p. 6, c. 1.

[110]Ibid., 27 Feb. 1937, p. 6, c. 1.

[111]Ibid., 14 Apr. 1937, p. 2, c. 2.

[112]Ibid., 18–23, 25–27 May 1937.

[113]Ibid., 27 May 1937, p. 6, c. 1.

[114]Work Projects Administration, Virginia Writers Project Life Histories, Essie W. Smith, "Confessions of a Bootlegger," May 31, 1939, Box 178, VSLA. Originally organized in May 1935 as the Works Progress Administration, after 1 July 1939 it became the Work Projects Administration. In addition, at the same time, the Virginia Writers' Project became the Virginia Writers' Program.

[115]Ibid.

Chapter Twenty: The World Wars

[1]Arthur M. Schlesinger, Jr., ed., *The Almanac of American History* (New York: G. P. Putnam's Sons, 1983), 425–432; Samuel Eliot Morison, *The Oxford History of the American People* (New York: Oxford University Press, 1965), 848–860.

[2]J. H. Claiborne, comp. and ed., "Franklin County, Virginia: Historical and Industrial—Past, Present and Future," *County News,* supplement ([Rocky Mount, Va.], 1926), 17.

[3]Mrs. W. C. Menefee, "Franklin County in War Time: A Community History," in *Virginia Communities in War Time*, ed. Arthur Kyle Davis, Publications of the Virginia War History Commission, vol. 6 (Richmond, Va.: The Executive Committee, 1926), xi, 165.

[4]The choir included the Misses Mary Dillard and Mary Robertson, along with Mesdames H. N. Dillard, H. D. Dillard, B. S. Robertson, G. C. Greer, L. N. Price, and J. C. Shearer: ibid., 165.

[5]Ibid., 165–166.

[6]Others who died during the war were Cabell Allman, Jack Altice, Jack Ames, Charles Blankenship, Jim Bowles, Harold Brodie, Lloyd Davis, Ben W. Foster, Herbert Hale, Penn Holland, Harvey Leonard Holland, Clarence Lumsden, Raymond Mason, Agie Mitchell, Roy Mitchell, L. S. Nolen, Graddfield Pasley, Grover Pasley, Seth Prillaman, Richard Roberts, John Stanley, two members of the Underwood family, George Patrick Washburne, Parker Thompson Willard, Richard Wright, and Crockett Wright: ibid., 167.

[7]Arthur Kyle Davis, ed., *Virginians of Distinguished Service of the World War*, Publications of the Virginia War History Commission, vol. 1 (Richmond, Va.: The Executive Committee, 1923), (quotation on 125), xxii–xxiii, 125–126; Claiborne, "Franklin County," 26.

[8]*Baltimore Evening Sun*, 18 Nov. 1919; Schlesinger, *Almanac of American History*, 435.

[9]*Baltimore Evening Sun*, 18 Nov. 1919.

[10]*Franklin County News*, Apr. 1933; copies in possession of Dr. J. Francis Amos, Rocky Mount, Va.

[11]This and the following two paragraphs were taken from Claiborne, "Franklin County," 26; Davis, *Virginians of Distinguished Service* 1:xxii–xxiii, 81, 125–126; and Davis, *Virginia Military Organizations in the World War, With Supplement of Distinguished Service*, Publications of the Virginia War History Commission, vol. 5 (Richmond, Va.: The Executive Committee, 1927), 452, 454.

[12]Morison, *Oxford History of the American People*, 874–875.

[13]Menefee, "Franklin County in War Time," 168–169; *Franklin Chronicle*, 26 Sept. 1918.

[14]Other women who served as captains in the drives were Mesdames W. L. Hopkins, C. A. Johnson, George Mattox, R. L. McNeil, and E. W. Saunders. Members of the women's teams included Mesdames N. P. Angle, W. A. Belcher, Herbert Fields, G. C. Greer, G. P. Holland, L. M. Menefee, H. D. Menefee, J. L. Perdue, and E. Y. Poole, along with the Misses Ruby Adams, Mamie Davis, Mary Dillard, Gladys Greer, Flora Greer, Ann Joplin, Elizabeth Mitchell, Frances Shearer, Myrtle Shoaf, and Mary Nelson Strayer: ibid., 26; *Franklin Chronicle*, 26 Sept. 1918, p. 1, c. 7.

[15]Menefee, "Franklin County in War Time," 168.

[16]Morison, *Oxford History of the American People*, 873–874.

[17]Other speakers were the Reverends B. T. Candler, W. T. Roberts, and E. Y. Poole; state Senator Beverly A. Davis, Sr.; the Honorable H. D. Dillard; attorney H. N. Dillard; Dr. B. M. Beckham; W. R. Davis, cashier of the First National Bank of Rocky Mount; C. J. Davis, cashier of the People's National Bank of Rocky Mount; and B. L. Fisher, manager of the Franklin County Telephone Company: Menefee, "Franklin County in War Time," 168; Claiborne, "Franklin County," 21.

[18]Menefee, "Franklin County in War Time," 169.

[19]Serving as officers were Judge Saunders as chairman, the Reverend B. T. Candler as vice-chairman, Mrs. W. C. Menefee, as secretary, and A. W. Robbins, former editor of the *Franklin Chronicle*, as treasurer: ibid., 168–170.

[20]Ibid., 170.

[21]First Mrs. N. B. Hutcherson and later Mrs. Z. Bernard served as director of knitting units for the Franklin County chapter. In addition, Mrs. T. W. Carper acted as director for comfort kits, and Mrs. D. C. Grubb as director of hospital garments and supplies: ibid., 170, 171.

[22]Other rural residents singled out for mention were Dr. W. P. Reese, Mr. and Mrs. F. A. Turner, Mr. and Mrs. Harris Ferguson, Mr. and Mrs. G. M. Law, Mr. and Mrs. W. F. Mills, Miss Hattie Reese, Mrs. George Helms, Miss Mieme Dudley "and many, many others": ibid., 171.

[23]This and the next two paragraphs are from ibid. Mrs. C. A. Johnson chaired the drive for used clothing and Miss Ann Joplin led the canteen contributions for the canteen headquarters in Roanoke.

[24]The members were E. G. Adams, Buford B. Angle, Lewis W. Angle, Louis W. Bowles, A. Newton Carroll, Beverly A. Davis, Jr., Gordon G. Fralin, E. T. Frith, Charles C. Greer, Edwin Greer, Walter M. Greer, Leonard A. Hodges, Clack Dickinson Hopkins, Walter Lee Hopkins, William Benjamin Hopkins, G. B. Kesler, Oscar T. Kittenger, Rufus E. McGhee, Richard Y. Melton, L. Morton Menefee, D. H. Mills, Harry E. Mills, C. A. Montgomery, J. E. Montgomery, James N. Montgomery, Jr., Bryant M. Morris, Charles N. Parcell, Word Day Peake, Edward W. Saunders, Jr., Dalton D. Webb, Posey Lee Webb, Allen O. Woody, and P. A. Young. The first officers were Walter L. Hopkins, commander; James N. Montgomery, Jr., senior vice-commander; A. Newton Carroll, junior vice-commander; Allen O. Woody, quartermaster; Walter M. Greer, adjutant; Clack D. Hopkins, sergeant-at-arms; and Charles N. Parcell, chaplain: Essie W. Smith, "Franklin County in the World War," Essie W. Smith Papers, FCPL; Marshall Wingfield, *Franklin County, Virginia: A History* (Berryville, Va.: Chesapeake Book Co., 1964), 136–137.

[25]The other officers were Mrs. H. W. Peake, second vice-president; Mrs. A. B. Garrett, secretary; and Miss Mabel Montgomery, treasurer. The auxiliary's charter members were Mrs. B. L. Angle, Mrs. Minnie S. Bennett, Mrs. Raymond Davis, Mrs. J. A. Dinwiddie, Miss Mary Dinwiddie, Mrs. Thomas Dudley, Mrs. A. B. Garrett, Mrs. C. S. Greer, Miss Flora Greer, Mrs. Walter L. Hopkins, Miss Ann Joplin, Miss Josie Menefee, Miss Mabel Montgomery, Mrs. H. W. Peak, Mrs. W. T. Roberts, Mrs. B. S. Robertson, Mrs. W. D. Rucker, Mrs. Edward Watts Saunders, Miss Sarah Saunders, Mrs. C. J. Shoaf, and Miss Loline Shoaf: Wingfield, *Franklin County*, 137.

[26]Menefee, "Franklin County in War Time," 173–174.

[27]Morison, *Oxford History of the American People*, 889–890.

[28]Schlesinger, *Almanac of American History*, 482; *Franklin News-Post*, 1 Nov. 1940, p. 1, c. 8.

[29]*News-Post*, 1 Nov. 1940, p. 1, cc. 7–8. By that date seventeen young men from the county had already volunteered for either land or sea service. For the account of one Franklin County man's experience in the U.S. Navy, *see* Elizabeth Nash Dillard, *Coming Hither—Going Hence: A Memoir of Herbert Nash Dillard, 1913–1976* (Verona, Va.: McClure Printing Co., Inc.), 11–14.

[30]Ibid., 8 Nov. 1940, p. 1, c. 1.

[31]Ibid., 22 Nov. 1940, p. 1, c. 7.

[32]Ibid., 29 Nov. 1940, p. 1, c. 8.

[33]Ibid., 18 Apr. 1941, p. 1, c. 3.

[34]The totals for the county ranged from 23 in Providence to 598 in Rocky Mount: ibid., 1 May 1942, p. 1, c. 8.

[35]Ibid., 31 July 1942, p. 1, c. 5.

[36]Ibid., 15 Jan. 1943, p. 6, c. 1.

[37]Ibid., 11 Sept. 1942, p. 4, c. 2.

[38]Ibid., 29 Jan. 1943, p. 8, c. 3.

[39]Ibid., 18 Apr. 1941, p. 1, c. 7; p. 10, c. 5.

[40]Ibid., p. 1, c. 7.

[41]Ibid., p. 1, c. 1.

[42]Ibid., 5 June 1942, p. 1, c. 2.

[43]Ibid., 24 July 1942, p. 1, c. 1.

[44]Wray Peters in the infantry at New Bern, N.C.; William Keith Peters with the 8th Training Battalion in Wheeler, Ga.; and Berlin E. Peters, who left for induction on 25 Mar. 1942: ibid., 13 Mar. 1942, p. 1, c. 3.

[45]James D., age twenty-two, in Europe; William J., age twenty, doing coast artillery duty at Fort Story, Va.; and Garland L., nineteen, in Honolulu; their sister Mary was a junior at Rocky Mount High School: ibid., 24 Apr. 1942, p. 7, c. 1.

[46]Private J. G. Marshall, Jr. (army), Corporal Edgar W. Marshall (army), Sergeant G. Harrison Marshall (Marines), Corporal Kay Marshall (Marines), Sergeant J. Samuel Marshall (army), and son-in-law, Dr. E. C. Jamison (Army Air Force): ibid., 26 Mar. 1943, p. 1.

[47]Ibid., 14 May 1943, p. 8, c. 4.

[48]The father, O. L. Holland, CSF, USN, formerly of Wirtz, then in California assigned to shore duty; and sons, Duvery Holland, pharmacist mate third class, Harold W. Holland, motor machinist's mate third class, and Odur L. Holland, Jr., seaman second class: ibid., 15 Dec. 1944, "Men in Service," p. 8, c. 3.

[49]Richard had been killed on 11 Oct. 1918, his brother Crockett was killed ten days later on 21 Oct., and their brother Moody died of wounds received in Germany on 10 Oct. 1944: ibid., 26 Jan. 1945, p. 1, cc. 3–5, with photos of the three brothers. Their mother was 73 at this time and had seven sons and three daughters living. She was residing with her son Hobert W. Wright, of Rt. 4, Rocky Mount.

[50]Technician Fifth Grade Mose C. Adams had been in service two years and was then in the hospital in New Guinea; Private First Class Fred A. Adams, also in service two years, was an instructor at Fort McClellan, Ala.; Private Silvus C. Adams, was in training at Fort Bragg, N.C.; Private First Class Edward Wilson Adams was in service with the Marines in the Philippines; Private First Class Raymond Adams, in service three years, was somewhere in the Pacific; Private Brady L. Adams, in service two years, was with the army in France; and a sixth son Esmond E. Adams, deceased, had served fourteen months in World War I: ibid., 9 Mar. 1945, p. 1, cc. 6–7, photo of Mrs. Mose A. Adams, of Rocky Mount, and her six sons who were doing [or had done] all they could for the war effort.

[51]Ibid., 17 Oct. 1941, p. 1, c. 4.

[52]Ibid., 24 Oct. 1941, p. 6, c. 1.

[53]*Dictionary of Naval Fighting Ships* (Washington, D.C.: Government Printing Office, 1968), 3:441.

[54]*News-Post*, 11 Sept. 1942, p. 1, c. 3.

[55]He was the son of J. A. Boone and brother of Harry V. Boone, of Rocky Mount. His wife, Petronella Boone, lived in California: ibid., 16 Oct. 1942, p. 1, cc. 1–2.

[56]*Dictionary of American Naval Fighting Ships* (1970), 5:416–417.

[57]*News-Post*, 11 May 1945, p. [15], cc. 1–2; W. Edwin Hemphill, ed., *Gold Star Honor Roll of Virginians in the Second World War* (Charlottesville: Virginia World War II History Commission, 1947), 80–81; *Service Record Book of Men and Women of Rocky Mount, Va., and Community* (N.p.: V.F.W. Post No. 6002, n.d.).

[58]Ibid., 19 June 1942, p. 1, c. 8. Dr. Julian B. Doss, of Penhook, had been commissioned a lieutenant in the army several months earlier and had arrived in Kanai, Hawaii, on 15 Mar. 1942 for "foreign service": ibid., 13 Mar. 1942, p. 1, c. 2; ibid., 3 Apr. 1942, p. 1, c. 5.

[59]Dr. Sam Rucker, of Moneta, had already left for service, followed on 10 Sept. 1942 by his brother, Dr. J. H. Rucker, who became a lieutenant in the dental corps (at Fort Knox).

He had served Rocky Mount for eight years. A sister was in England as a nurse in the armed forces. Those doctors still at home hoped their patients would come for office visits before 7:00 P.M. at night and not ask for home visits unless absolutely necessary. There would be no more doctors moving into the area to replace those who had been drafted: ibid., 19 June 1942, p. 1, c. 8; ibid., 4 Sept. 1942, p. 1, c. 4.

[60]Dr. E. C. Jamison, a general practitioner who had served fourteen years in the county, entered the U.S. Army Medical Corps as did Dr. Harry Lee, a county native practicing in Roanoke and "acknowledged [as] one of the leading surgeons of the State": ibid., 14 Aug. 1942, p. 1, c. 7.

[61]Dr. A. K. Taylor, of Bent Mountain, replaced Dr. C. L. Dillon, who had died: ibid., 4 Sept. 1942, p. 1, c. 2.

[62]Ibid., 11 Aug. 1944, p. 1, c. 5.

[63]Ibid., 26 June 1942, p. 1, c. 6. At the time Goode was living at Henry with his seventy-six-year-old mother.

[64]Ibid., 31 Mar. 1944, p. 1, c. 7.

[65]Goode divided the money as follows: to the Franklin County branch of the American Red Cross, $100, to be used in the county "as the local chapter deems wise"; American Legion, Franklin Post No. 6, $150 "for a plaque to be hung in the legion rooms commemorating the valor of Franklin county men" and the "remainder of fund to be used as legion deems best"; Tuberculosis Association, $50, for sanitarium beds for county patients; infantile paralysis, $25; Virginia Cancer Foundation, $25; United Service Organizations, $10; Rocky Mount Lions Club, $25; Boones Mill Lions Club, $25; West Franklin Men's Club, Ferrum, $25; Callaway Ruritan Club, $25; Rocky Mount Woman's Club, $25; $10 apiece to the Boy Scout troops of Rocky Mount, Boones Mill, Ferrum, Burnt Chimney, and the black troop in Rocky Mount, and $10 for the Girl Scout troop in Rocky Mount; and $100 for the school superintendent, Harold W. Ramsey, "for American flags for the county schools where suitable flags are not now in use. This applies to all one-room schools as well as the larger schools": ibid., 5 May 1944, p. 1, c. 8.

[66]Ibid., 13 Nov. 1942, p. 1, c. 3.

[67]Ibid., p. 1, c. 4.

[68]Ibid., 15 Jan. 1943, p. 1, c. 5.

[69]Ibid., 1 Oct. 1943, p. 1, c. 7.

[70]Ibid., 24 Aug. 1945, p. 1. c. 3.

[71]Ibid., 19 Dec. 1941, p. 1, cc. 7–8; ibid., 26 Dec. 1941, p. 1, c. 8. The volunteers were needed for the following: air raid wardens, auxiliary police, auxiliary firemen, bomb squad fire watcher, medical aid, rescue squad, motor corps, decontamination corps, messenger, demolition and clearance, road repair, nurse's aide, home nursing, nutrition, emergency, food and housing, first aid, recreation, radio operator, blood donor, aircraft spotter, telephone operator, clerk, stenographer, orderly, and forum speaker.

[72]Ibid., 26 Dec. 1941, p. 1, c. 8.

[73]Ibid., 16 Jan. 1942, p. 1, c. 4.

[74]Ibid., 13 Mar. 1942, p. 1, c. 6; ibid., 1 May 1942, p. 1, c. 7; ibid., 26 Feb. 1943, p. 1, c. 8. During the week of 1 May 1942 the largest class then training in first aid received their certificates; of 102 taking the course, 51 were certified. And by Feb. 1943 six communities had established home nursing classes, including Snow Creek, Callaway, Sontag, Lanahan, Redwood, and Neadmore–Tank Hill.

[75]Ibid., 27 Mar. 1942, p. 1, c. 7.

[76]Ibid., 29 May 1942, p. 1, c. 2.

[77]Ibid., 12 June 1942, p. 1, c. 5.

[78]Ibid., 25 Oct. 1940, p. 1, c. 1.

[79]Ibid., 10 Apr. 1942, p. 1, c. 5.

[80]Ibid., 17 Apr. 1942, p. 1, c. 7.

[81]Ibid., 22 Aug. 1941, p. 1, c. 1; ibid., 31 Oct. 1941, p. 1, c. 4.

[82]Ibid., 15 May 1942, p. 1, c. 1; ibid., 22 May 1942, p. 1, c. 1.

[83]Ibid., 22 May 1942, p. 1, c. 5; ibid., 3 July 1942, p. 1, c. 8.

[84]Ibid., 26 June 1942, p. 1, c. 8.

[85]Ibid., 24 July 1942, p. 1, c. 2; ibid., 31 July 1942, p. 1, c. 7.

[86]Ibid., 8 Aug. 1941, p. 1, c. 3.

[87]Ibid., 19 Dec. 1941, p. 1, c. 2.

[88]Ibid., 26 Nov. 1943, p. 1, c. 8.

[89]Ibid., 19 Dec. 1941, p. 1, cc. 5, 7–8.

[90]Ibid., 9 Mar. 1945, p. 1, c. 3.

[91]Ibid., 16 Mar. 1945, p. 1, c. 2.

[92]Ibid., 21 Jan. 1944, p. 8, cc. 3–4.

[93]Schlesinger, *Almanac of American History*, 495.

[94]*News-Post*, 8 Aug. 1941, p. 1, cc. 7–8; ibid., 15 Aug. 1941, p. 6, c. 4; ibid., 2 Jan., p. 1, c. 1; ibid., 23 Jan. 1941, p. 1, c. 3; ibid., 29 May 1942, p. 1, c. 8.

[95]Ibid., 13 July 1945, p. 1, c. 4.

[96]Ibid., 3 July 1942, p. 1, c. 5.

[97]Ibid., 10 Apr. 1942, p. 1, c. 6.

[98]Ibid., 2 Oct. 1942, p. 1, c. 4.

[99]Ibid., 9 Oct. 1942, p. 1, c. 4.

[100]Ibid., 19 Dec. 1941, p. 1, cc. 5, 7–8.

[101]Ibid., 27 Aug. 1943, p. 1, c. 2: "Back the Attack with War Bonds" was the slogan for the Third War Loan Drive; ibid., 3 Sept. 1943, p. 1, c. 8; ibid., 10 Sept 1943, p. 1, c. 8; ibid., 17 Sept 1943, p. 1, c. 7; ibid., 24 Sept. 1943, p. 1, cc. 4–5; ibid., 1 Oct. 1943, p. 1, c. 8; ibid., 8 Oct. 1943, p. 1, cc. 3–5, 8; ibid., 15 Oct. 1943, p. 1, cc. 6–7; ibid., 22 Oct. 1943, p. 1, c. 2.

[102]Ibid., 30 May 1941, p. 1, c. 8.

[103]Ibid., 13 June 1941, p. 1, cc. 7–8; 20 June 1941, p. 1, c. 1.

[104]Ibid., 6 June 1941, p. 1, cc. 7–8.

[105]Ibid., 20 Mar. 1942, p. 1, cc. 3–4.

[106]Ibid., 15 May 1942, p. 1, c. 5.

[107]Ibid., 23 May 1941, p. 2, c. 1.

[108]Ibid., 22 Sept. 1944, p. 1, c. 5.

[109]Ibid., 17 Nov. 1944, p. 1, c. 4.

[110]Ibid., 5 May 1944, p. 1, c. 5.

[111]Ibid., 20 Nov. 1942, p. 1, c. 5; ibid., 21 May 1943, p. 1, c. 7.

[112]Ibid., 11 Dec. 1942, p. 1, cc. 6–7.

[113]Ibid., 4 June 1943, p. 1, c. 8; ibid., 9 July 1943, p. 1, c. 8.

[114]Ibid., 15 Sept. 1944, p. 1, c. 2.

[115]Ibid., 26 Nov. 1943, p. 1, cc. 4–5.

[116]By mid-1945 there were eleven base POW camps in Virginia and sixteen branch camps (for a total of twenty-seven). Camp Pickett, a base camp, had six branch camps, four of which housed German naval personnel, including Sandy Level: John Hammond Moore, "Hitler's Wehrmacht in Virginia, 1943–1946," *VMHB* 85 (1977): 260–265.

[117]Ibid., 261.

[118]*News-Post*, 25 Aug. 1944, p. 1, c. 2; those farmers who needed POWs had to make their requests a week to ten days in advance and transport the prisoners back and forth to work; the farmers received reimbursement of one cent per mile per man per day, but not more than fifty cents a day per man. The prisoners worked in groups of ten, and the army furnished the necessary guards and the noonday meal, which was carried to them from the branch camp: ibid., 1 Sept. 1944, p. 1, c. 1.

[119]Moore, "Hitler's Wehrmacht," 260.

[120]*News-Post*, 8 Sept. 1944, p. 1, c. 6.

[121]Ibid., 4 Aug. 1944, p. 1, c. 8.

[122]U.S. Provost Marshal General, Enemy POW Information Bureau, Reporting Branch, Subject File, 1942–1946, Camps Inactivated—Third Service Command, Box 2491, NARA.

[123]*News-Post*, 9 June 1944, p. 1, cc. 7–8.

[124]Ibid., 9 June 1944, p. 1, cc. 7–8.

[125]Arrington had entered the service in 1939 and had been in England since Jan. 1944; before the war he had worked at the Rocky Mount Coca-Cola bottling plant: ibid., 23 June 1944, p. 1, cc. 6–7; ibid., 11 Aug. 1944, p. 8, cc. 1–3. For a list of Franklin's servicemen killed in action *see* Hemphill, *Gold Star Honor Roll*, 79–81.

[126]*News-Post*, 18 Aug. 1944, p. 8, "Men in Service," c. 1.

[127]Ibid., 4 Aug. 1944, p. 8, c. 2.

[128]Ibid., 7 July 1944, p. 1, c. 2.

[129]Ibid., 28 July 1944, p. 8, c. 4. The Clingenpeels had four sons and two sons-in-law, three of whom had received honorable discharges; one son (Herman) had been wounded while in foreign service.

[130]Ibid., 11 Aug. 1944, p. 8, cc. 2–3. Later that month, the editor of the *News-Post* received a 100-franc note from Master Sergeant Thomas A. Tench, then serving with the invasion forces in France, to pay for his subscription. The editor asked that Tench let him know what the note was worth in U.S. currency, but nevertheless he was renewing the subscription for a year and framing the note for the office "as a real souvenir from the invasion coast": ibid., 25 Aug. 1944, p. 8, c. 2.

[131]Ibid., 18 Aug. 1944, p. 1, cc. 6–7.

[132]Ibid., p. 1, c. 8. In Sept. the State ABC Board decided to close the ABC stores as soon as word was received that victory in Europe had been declared unless word came after closing on a Saturday night, in which case the ABC stores would reopen on Monday morning as usual: ibid., 8 Sept. 1944, p. 1, c. 2. ABC stores would stay closed that day, if word received before 6 P.M., and reopen the next morning. If word received before 6 P.M. Saturday stores would close to reopen Monday morning, but if they were notified between 6 P.M. Saturday and 6 P.M. Sunday there would be no store closing. If word received after midnight during the week, ABC stores would not open that day.

[133]Ibid., 16 Feb. 1945, p. 1, c. 2.

[134]Ibid., 22 Sept. 1944, p. 1, c. 8.

[135]Ibid., 30 Mar. 1945, p. 1, c. 3.

[136]Ibid., 25 May 1945, p. 7, c. 2.

[137]Ibid., 27 Apr. 1945, p. 1, c. 2. Whether or not the newspaper paid up has not been discovered.

[138]Ibid., 27 Apr. 1945, p. 1, c. 5.

[139]Ibid., 4 May 1945, p. 1, cc. 6–7.

[140]Ibid., 11 May 1945, p. 1, c. 8.

[141]Ibid., p. 1, c. 1.

[142]Ibid., 25 May 1945, p. 1, c. 6.

[143]Ibid., 18 May 1945, p. 1, c. 3; Hodges was twenty-eight years old when he was discharged; he was the son of Mr. and Mrs. J. W. Hodges, of Penhook.

[144]For the story of life at Stalag Luft III, *see* Arthur A. Durand, *Stalag Luft III: The Secret Story* (Baton Rouge: Louisiana State University Press, 1988), and especially Chapter 16, "Evacuation," for the experiences of the prisoners after they were forcibly removed from Sagan on 17 Jan. 1945. Stalag Luft III was the POW camp from which "the Great Escape" took place in Mar. 1944. It resulted in the execution of fifty POWs when the Germans broke the rules of the Geneva Convention and retaliated: Paul Brickhill, *The Great Escape* (New York: W. W. Norton & Company, Inc., 1950); Aidan Crawley, *Escape From Germany* (New York: Dorset Press, 1985), 229–266.

[145]*News-Post*, 25 May 1945, p. 1, cc. 2–3.

[146]Ibid., with photo of Shearer; ibid., 8 June 1945, p. 1, c. 3; p. 7, c. 3.

[147] Ibid., 8 June 1945, p. 1, c. 3; p. 7, c. 3.

[148] Ibid., 15 June 1945, p. 1, c. 7; p. 8, c. 6.

[149] Ibid., p. 1, c. 6.

[150] Ibid., p. 8, c. 4.

[151] Ibid., 22 June 1945, p. 8, c. 4. Law was on a sixty-day furlough at the time, after which he was to report to Camp Pickett.

[152] Ibid., 15 June 1945, p. 1, c. 4.

[153] Ibid., 29 June 1945, p. 1, c. 7.

[154] Morison, *Oxford History of the American People*, 1003, 1010–1017, 1024–1027, 1033–1036, 1041–1043.

[155] Ibid., 1043–1045.

[156] *News-Post*, 17 Aug. 1945, p. 1, cc. 4–5, 7–8; p. 6, c. 5.

[157] Ibid., p. 1, c. 7; ibid., 24 Aug. 1945, p. 8, c. 3; Admiral Nimitz released a list of Pacific fleet ships that participated in the finishing off of Japan to conclude the war, covering the period 10 July through the surrender. Franklin County men were on the following: USS *Belleau Wood*, Lt. Donald Kelsey, Rocky Mount; *Bataan*, James H. Morris, son of Mr. and Mrs. Frank Morris, Rocky Mount; *Oakland*, Calvin E. Brown; and *Norman Scott*, W. Day Peake, soundman first class, son of Mr. and Mrs. W. D. Peake, Rocky Mount.

[158] Ibid., 17 Aug. 1945, p. 1, c. 7.

[159] Ibid., p. 1, cc. 4–5, 7–8; p. 6, c. 5.

[160] SPARS ("Semper Paratus") were members of the U.S. Coast Guard Women's Auxiliary: ibid., 24 Aug. 1945, p. 1, c. 3. There were still no numbers for those wounded, but none of the wounded had been discharged; instead they were in hospitals and camps awaiting final recovery.

[161] Ibid., 11 May 1945, p. 1, c. 2; p. 6, c. 7.

Chapter Twenty-One: Franklin County Rediscovered

[1] William Edwin Hemphill, Marvin Wilson Schlegel, and Sadie Ethel Engelberg, *Cavalier Commonwealth*, 2d ed. (New York: McGraw-Hill Book Co., Inc., 1963), 544; Marshall Wingfield, *Franklin County, Virginia: A History* (Berryville, Va.: Chesapeake Book Co., 1964), 139.

[2] George W. Jennings, *Virginia's Government: The Structure and Functions of the State and Local Governments of the Commonwealth of Virginia*, ed. John R. Broadway, Jr., and Martha D. Marks (Richmond: Virginia State Chamber of Commerce, 1982), 55.

[3] This and the following three paragraphs are taken from the reports of the secretary of the commonwealth for the years 1905, 1909, 1924–1925, 1926–1927, 1931–1932, 1932–1933, 1934–1935, 1937–1938, 1939–1939, 1942–1943, 1949–1950, 1950–1951, 1954–1955, 1955–1956, 1959–1960, 1965–1966, 1969–1970, 1974–1975, 1975–1976, and 1985–1986.

[4] Edward B. McConnell and Arne Schoeller, *Commonwealth of Virginia: Court Organization Profile* (Denver, Colo.: National Center for State Courts, 1978), 1.

[5] Emily J. Salmon, ed., *A Hornbook of Virginia History*, 3d ed. (Richmond: Virginia State Library, 1983), 70.

[6] Arthur M. Schlesinger, Jr., ed., *The Almanac of American History* (New York: G. P. Putnam's Sons, 1983), 522, 524–525; Donald C. Harrison, *Distant Patrol: Virginia and the Korean War* ([Richmond]: Virginia Korean–Vietnam War History Council, Department of Historic Resources, 1989), 5–11, 93; "List of Casualties Incurred by U.S. Military Personnel in Connection with the Conflict in Korea by Home State of Record: Virginia" (Washington, D.C.: n.p., [197?]).

[7] Schlesinger, *Almanac of American History*, 572; "List of Casualties Incurred by U.S. Military Personnel in Connection with the Conflict in Viet-Nam by Home State of Record: Virginia" (Washington, D.C.: n.p., [197?]), 1648, 1655, 1659, 1673.

[8]"Hospital Started as a Dream," *Franklin News-Post*, 1 Jan. 1986, Special Bicentennial Section, Section C, pp. 21–23; Marshall L. Flora, "Franklin County Today—1986," *Bicentennial Reflections* (N.p.: Franklin County Bicentennial Commission, 1986), 84; West Piedmont Planning District Commission, "Comprehensive Land Use Plan, 1975–1985" (Martinsville, Va.: West Piedmont Planning District Commission, 1976), 80–81; *Centel Telephone Directory for Rocky Mount . . . , December 1989*, yellow pages 27–28, 33, 52, 73–78.

[9]Diane R. Jennings and Hannah McLay, *Franklin County, Virginia: The Community and Its Public Library* (Rocky Mount, Va.: n.p., 1978), 42.

[10]Flora, "Franklin County Today—1986," *Bicentennial Reflections*, 84.

[11]"Comprehensive Land Use Plan, 1975–1985," 99–106.

[12]"Electricity Given Push in 1926," *News-Post*, 1 Jan. 1986, Special Bicentennial Section, Section E, p. 2 (for electricity in Boones Mill), 14.

[13]"Comprehensive Land Use Plan, 1975–1985," 109; Flora, "Franklin County Today—1986," *Bicentennial Reflections*, 85. Flora states that the county receives no natural gas, but that the Roanoke Gas Company holds an option to provide that service when feasible. The 1989 phone book lists dealers in bulk and cylinder gas but no gas companies.

[14]"Burgie Lee Fisher: A Success Story," *News-Post*, 1 Jan. 1986, Special Bicentennial Section, Section E, pp. 15–16; "Phone Subscribers: From 30 to 12,825," ibid., pp. 15–16; J. H. Claiborne, "Franklin County, Virginia: Historical and Industrial—Past, Present and Future," *County News*, supplement ([Rocky Mount, Va.]), 1926, 21.

[15]Jennings and McLay, *Franklin County . . . Public Library*, 32.

[16]United States Department of Commerce, Bureau of the Census, *1987 Census of Agriculture, Volume 1, Geographic Area Series, Part 46, Virginia, State and County Data* (Washington, D.C.: Government Printing Office, July 1989), 379.

[17]*News-Post*, 1 Jan. 1986, Special Bicentennial Section, Section D, p. 5.

[18]This and the following paragraph are based on Linda Willis's "The Job Market Much Improved," ibid., Section E, pp. 22–23.

[19]*Richmond News Leader*, Business Section, 24 Sept. 1990, p. B–25.

[20]Willis, "The Job Market Much Improved," *News-Post*, 1 Jan. 1986, Special Bicentennial Section, Section E, pp. 22–23.

[21]This and the following paragraph are from ibid.

[22]This and the following three paragraphs are based on "Franklin County Comprehensive Land Use Plan, 1975–1985," pp. 65–70, and "Export Markets Accessible," *News-Post*, 1 Jan. 1986, Special Bicentennial Section, Section E, p. 13. The figures for the primary and secondary roads come from Table SC–6, "Interstate, Primary, Secondary, Frontage and Urban Road Mileage as of December 31, 1984," in William P. Overman Associates, P. C., *Virginia Counties and Cities Data Book, 1986* (Virginia Beach: William C. Overman Associates, P. C., 1986), 2:234.

[23]Frank B. Hurt, *A History of Ferrum College* (Roanoke: Stone Printing Co., 1977), 107–117; Hurt, "Reflections on the Origin of Ferrum College," *Bicentennial Reflections*, 61–62.

[24]Hurt, *Ferrum College*, 136.

[25]Ibid., 198.

[26]*Ferrum College Catalog, 1987–88* (Ferrum, Va.: Ferrum College, 1986), 14.

[27]Eric H. Ferguson, "The Land Between The Lakes—Philpott and Smith Mountain Lakes," *Bicentennial Reflections*, 82–83.

[28]Ibid., 83.

[29]T. W. Rickard, "Moonshining: A Way of Life," *News-Post*, 1 Jan. 1986, Special Bicentennial Section, Section E, p. 25.

[30]Ibid., p. 24; V. K. Stoneman, "Franklin County Moonshine," *Bicentennial Reflections*, 72.

[31]*News-Post*, 21 Dec. 1972, pp. 1, 12.

[32]Ibid., 14 Feb. 1972, pp. 1, 2.

[33]Ibid., 17 Feb. 1972, p. 1, c. 1.

[34]Stoneman, "Franklin County Moonshine," *Bicentennial Reflections*, 72.

[35]*Richmond News Leader*, 14 Oct. 1988.

[36]*Roanoke Times and World-News*, 13 Jan. 1992, p. 1, cc. 1–5; p. 2, cc. 3–5; Richmond *News Leader*, 14 Jan. 1992. The largest still in the area to date (breaking Franklin's 1972 record) was discovered in Pittsylvania County not far from Penhook in Jan. 1993: *Roanoke Times and World-News*, 8 Jan. 1993, pp. A1 (bottom) and A8, cc. 1–2.

[37]Rickard, "Moonshining: A Way of Life," *News-Post*, 1 Jan. 1986, Special Bicentennial Section, Section E, p. 24.

[38]This and the following two paragraphs are based on a description of stock car racing in Franklin partly provided by Wilton Agee to Morris Stephenson in the *News-Post*, 1 Jan. 1986, Special Bicentennial Section, Section D, pp. 34–39.

[39]"Franklin County: The First 200 Years," ibid., pp. 36–41; Claiborne, "Franklin County," 7: the writer believed that Poole and Rorer were "geniuses, and some day they will, in all probability, become world famed."

[40]*Franklin County, 1785–1976, Yesterday & Today* (Franklin County, Va.: Published for the 5th Annual Fiddler's Convention, July 1976), 36–37, 120.

[41]*Franklin Chronicle*, 25 Jan. 1917.

[42]Kip Lornell and Vaughn Webb, "Franklin's Traditional Music," *Bicentennial Reflections*, 73; *Franklin County, 1785–1976*, 66.

[43]The following account of the activities held during the bicentennial year is taken from the *Report of the Franklin County Bicentennial Commission, Inc.* (1987).

INDEX

552   INDEX

inflation, 373; tobacco
sales, 369–371;
volunteerism, 434, 435,
437, 438, 442
Worley, Harvey, 515
Wortz, J. W., 349
Wray, Ben, 257; C. Will, 407,
414, 415, 515–516, 518;
Daniel, 216; Mr. and Mrs.
J. O., 442; John, 249; Mrs.
John, 249; Marvin G., 442
Wray and Boon, 122
Wren, John, 327, 330
Wright, Anselm, 479–480;
Crockett, 519, 521;

George, 66; H. J., 408,
515, 517; H. S., 212;
Hobert W., 521; James,
215–216; James G., Jr.,
479; Joseph, 479; Martha,
304; Moody, 521; Richard,
519, 521; Robert, 185,
353; William, Jr., 113
Wright family, 126, 432
W. S. Smithers's Paint Shop,
356
Wysong, Lewis, 480
Wythe Co., Va., 55, 86, 226
Wytheville, Va., 52, 261, 403

Yale and Dunley, 116

Yellow Tavern, Va., battle of,
274
Yorktown, Va., siege of, 52,
54–56, 58–59
Young, F. Ross, 386; George
O., 278; James, 216;
Joseph, 211; Juriah, 242;
P. A., 520; Mrs. S. M., 352;
Sallie A., 353; William D.,
267, 278, 281
Young's Store, 105, 353

Zeigler, Allie, 352; John K.,
336; Martha, 243; Michael,
122
Zeigler and Angle, 336

*Franklin County, Virginia, 1786–1986:
A Bicentennial History* was set in Garamond
by the Delmar Company, of Charlotte, North Carolina,
and printed on 60-lb. Gladfelter,
an acid-free permanent/durable paper,
by the Delmar Company, of Charlotte, North Carolina

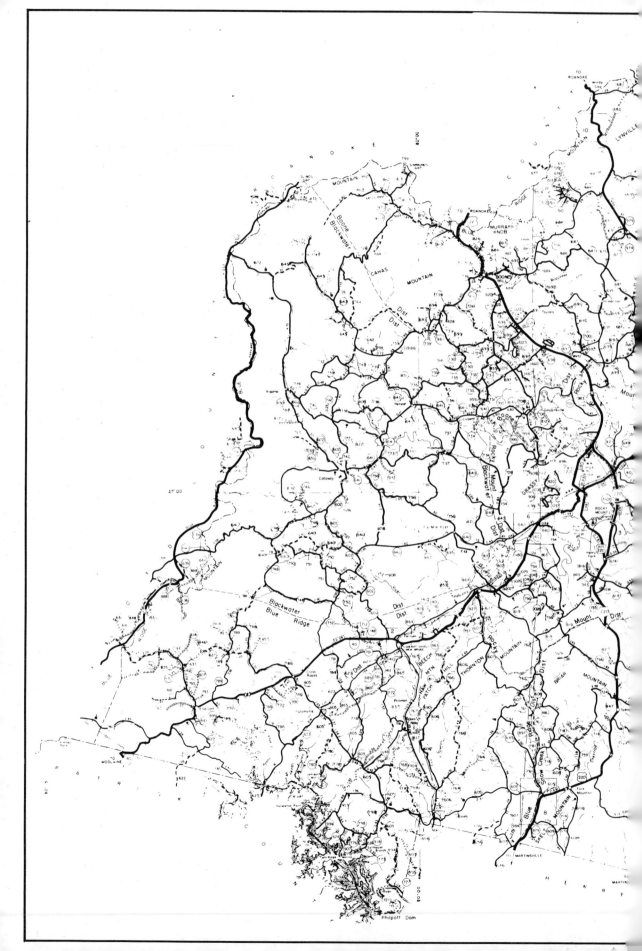